STUDIES IN INDIAN AND TIBETAN BUDDHISM

MIND SEEING MIND

Mahāmudrā and the Geluk Tradition of Tibetan Buddhism

Roger R. Jackson

Wisdom

Wisdom Publications, Inc.
199 Elm Street
Somerville, MA 02144 USA
wisdomexperience.org

Library of Congress Cataloging-in-Publication Data
Names: Jackson, Roger R. (Roger Reid), 1950– author.
Title: Mind seeing mind: mahamudra and the Geluk tradition of Tibetan Buddhism / Roger R. Jackson.
Description: Somerville, MA: Wisdom Publications, Inc., [2019] | Series: Studies in Indian and Tibetan Buddhism | Includes bibliographical references and index. |
Identifiers: LCCN 2018060736 (print) | LCCN 2019018333 (ebook) | ISBN 9781614296010 (ebook) | ISBN 9781614295778 (hardcover: alk. paper)
Subjects: LCSH: Mahamudra (Tantric rite) | Dge-lugs-pa (Sect) | Buddhism—China—Tibet Autonomous Region—History.
Classification: LCC BQ8921.M35 (ebook) | LCC BQ8921.M35 J33 2019 (print) | DDC 294.3/420423—dc23
LC record available at https://lccn.loc.gov/2018060736

ISBN 978-1-61429-577-8 ebook ISBN 978-1-61429-601-0

23 22 21
5 4 3 2

Cover image "Tsongkhapa as a Mahasiddha" is courtesy of the Rubin Museum of Art.
Cover design by Tim Holtz. Interior design by Gopa&Ted2. Typeset by Kristin Goble.
Set in Diacritical Garamond Pro 10.5/13.

Printed on acid-free paper and meets the guidelines for permanence and durability of the Production Guidelines for Book Longevity of the Council on Library Resources.

Printed in the United States of America.

Ed elli a me: "Questa montagna è tale,
che sempre al cominciar di sotto è grave;
e quant' om più va sù, en men fa male.
Però, quand' ella te parrà soave
tanto, che sù andar ti fia leggero
com' a seconda giù andar per nave,
allor sarai ad fin d'esto sentiero;
quivi di riposar l'affanno aspetta.
Più non rispondo, e quest so per vero."

And he to me: "This mountain is such
that beginning from below is always hard;
and the higher you go, the less the affliction.
So, when it seems to you so gentle
that going up is as easy for you
as going downstream in a boat,
then you'll reach the end of this path,
where rest from your troubles awaits.
More I cannot say, but this I know is true."

Dante, *Purgatorio* 4.88–96

འདི་ལ་གང་ཡང་མ་གྲུབ་སྟེ།།
ཅིར་སྣང་རང་བཞིན་མེད་པར་ཤེས།།
སྣང་བ་རང་གྲོལ་ཆོས་ཀྱི་དབྱིངས།།
རྟོགས་པ་རང་གྲོལ་ཡེ་ཤེས་ཆེ།།
གཉིས་མེད་མཉམ་པ་ཆོས་ཀྱི་སྐུ།།
ཆུ་བོ་ཆེན་པོ་རྒྱུན་འབབ་ལྟར།།
གང་ལྟར་གནས་ཀྱང་དོན་དང་ལྡན།།
འདི་ནི་རྟག་ཏུ་སངས་རྒྱས་ཉིད།།
འཁོར་བ་ཡུལ་མེད་བདེ་བ་ཆེ།།

Know that nothing is established here,
so appearances have no essence.
Appearances free themselves into the realm of truth;
understanding frees itself into great awareness.
The nondual self-same Dharma body
is like a great river's downward current:
whatever there is is beneficial.
This is eternal buddhahood,
great bliss beyond saṃsāra's realm.

Nāropa, *Verses Summarizing Mahāmudrā*
(ཕྱག་ཆེན་ཚིགས་བསྡུས)

To the memory of my parents, Margaret Reid Jackson (1918–2008) and Robert Edward Jackson (1925–2010), both of whom lovingly supported me in countless ways in life and now have opened the final seal and seen face to face what I can limn only through a dusky glass.

Publisher's Acknowledgment

The publisher gratefully acknowledges the generous help of the Hershey Family Foundation in sponsoring the production of this book.

Contents

Preface xv

Permissions xxiii

Technical Note xxv

Introduction 1

A Summary of the Book (10)

Part 1. The Background to Geluk Mahāmudrā

1. Mahāmudrā in India: Hindus and Buddhists, Sūtras and Tantras 17
   Seals and Great Seals in Hindu Traditions (18)
   Seals and Great Seals in Sūtra-Based Buddhism (23)
   Tantric Buddhism (25)
   Mahāmudrā in the "Lower" Buddhist Tantras (30)
   Mahāmudrā in the Mahāyoga and Yoginī Tantras (34)
2. Mahāmudrā in India: The Mahāsiddhas 41
   The Seven Attainment Texts (42)
   Saraha: The Essential Trilogy and Beyond (44)
   Śavaripa and Virūpa (48)
   Tilopa and Nāropa (51)
   Maitrīpa and the Practice of Nonmentation (56)
   A Perfection Vehicle Mahāmudrā? (61)
3. Mahāmudrā in Some Tibetan Renaissance Schools 65
   Transmitting Mahāmudrā to Tibet (65)
   Atiśa and the Kadam (68)
   Shiché and Chö (73)

Shangpa Kagyü (76)
Sakya (78)
Nyingma (79)

4. Mahāmudrā in Early Marpa Kagyü 83
Marpa and Milarepa (83)
Rechungpa and Gampopa (87)
Gampopa's Successors (92)
Shang Rinpoché and the Tsalpa Kagyü (93)
Phakmo Drupa Kagyü and Drigung Kagyü (95)
Drukpa Kagyü (98)
Early Karma Kagyü (101)

5. Mahāmudrā in Later Marpa Kagyü 105
Sakya Paṇḍita's Critique of Kagyü Mahāmudrā (105)
The Third Karmapa, Rangjung Dorjé (107)
Great Madhyamaka, Shentong, and the Jonang Tradition (109)
The Fourteenth and Fifteenth Centuries (111)
Sixteenth-Century Scholasticism (117)
Karma Trinlepa and Pawo Tsuklak Trengwa (117)
The Eighth Karmapa and Dakpo Tashi Namgyal (119)
Pema Karpo (122)
The Ninth Karmapa (124)
The State of Kagyü Discourse in 1600 (126)
The Kagyü-Geluk Conflict (128)

PART 2. EARLY GELUK MAHĀMUDRĀ

6. Tsongkhapa, the Geluk, and Mahāmudrā 133
Tsongkhapa's Life and Works (134)
Tsongkhapa's Secret Teachings (143)
From Tsongkhapa to Paṇchen Chögyen, and Back Again (147)
Tsongkhapa and Mahāmudrā: A Closer Look (149)
Mahāmudrā in Tsongkhapa's Tantric Writings (150)

Tsongkhapa's Views of His Contemporaries' Meditation Practices (153)
Did Tsongkhapa Teach His Own Mahāmudrā System? (159)

7. From Tsongkhapa to Paṇchen Chögyen: Khedrup Jé and the Main Line of the Hearing Transmission 165
Khedrup Jé (166)
Tokden Jampal Gyatso (170)
Baso Chökyi Gyaltsen (171)
Chökyi Dorjé (172)
The Great Ensapa (174)
Khedrup Sangyé Yeshé (176)

8. From Tsongkhapa to Paṇchen Chögyen: Masters Outside the Main Line of the Hearing Transmission 179
Gendun Drup, the First Dalai Lama (179)
Khedrup Norsang Gyatso (181)
Gendun Gyatso, the Second Dalai Lama (184)
Paṇchen Sönam Drakpa (187)
Sönam Gyatso, the Third Dalai Lama (193)
Khöntön Paljor Lhundrup (195)

9. Paṇchen Chögyen in Focus 199
Paṇchen Chögyen's Life and Works (199)
Highway of the Conquerors (202)
Lamp So Bright (206)
Mahāmudrā Lineage Prayer (215)
Like a Treasure Inventory (216)
Offering to the Guru (218)
Paṇchen Chögyen's Spiritual Songs (226)
Why Mahāmudrā? (235)

PART 3. LATER GELUK MAHĀMUDRĀ

10. Paṇchen Chögyen's Successors 241
The Fifth Dalai Lama (243)
Shar Kalden Gyatso (245)

Jamyang Shepa (252)
Kalsang Gyatso, The Seventh Dalai Lama (254)

11. Yeshé Gyaltsen 257
Works Focused Mainly on Mahāmudrā (259)
Works Focused Mainly on the Madhyamaka View (270)
Works Focused Mainly on Guru Yoga (272)
Final Remarks (278)

12. Four Later Commentators 279
Gugé Losang Tenzin (279)
Gungthang Könchok Tenpei Drönmé (281)
Ngulchu Dharmabhadra (284)
Keutsang Losang Jamyang Mönlam (286)

13. Later Lamas from Amdo and Kham 291
Changkya Rölpai Dorjé (291)
Thuken Losang Chökyi Nyima (295)
Shabkar Tsokdruk Rangdröl (298)
Gyalrong Geshé Tsultrim Nyima (302)
Akhu Sherab Gyatso (304)
Choné Lama Lodrö Gyatso (306)
Losang Dongak Chökyi Gyatso (309)

14. The Twentieth Century and Beyond 313
Phabongkha Rinpoché (315)
Geshé Rabten (319)
Geshé Acharya Thubten Loden (321)
Gelek Rinpoché (323)
Geshé Kelsang Gyatso (327)
The Fourteenth Dalai Lama (331)
A Note on Recent Tibetan Editions (337)

PART 4. PERSPECTIVES ON GELUK MAHĀMUDRĀ

15. Three Issues in Geluk Mahāmudrā 341
The Name of the Tradition (341)

Geluk and Kagyü Mahāmudrā Compared (346)
The Place of Mahāmudrā in Geluk Life (358)

16. Archer Among the Yellow Hats: Geluk Uses of Saraha 363
Tsongkhapa and Saraha (364)
Khedrup Norsang Gyatso and Saraha (367)
Paṇchen Chögyen and Saraha (369)
Khöntön Paljor Lhundrup and Saraha (373)
Jamyang Shepa and Saraha (375)
Final Remarks (378)

17. The Big Picture: Sixteen Questions 381
1. Is There Scriptural Warrant for Mahāmudrā? (382)
2. To Which Dharma Wheel Does Mahāmudrā Belong? (384)
3. Is There Mahāmudrā outside the Tantras? (386)
4. Is Sudden Realization Possible? (389)
5. Can a Single Realization Suffice? (391)
6. Are We All Already Buddhas? (393)
7. What Sort of Negation Is Emptiness? (396)
8. Of What Is Buddha Mind Empty? (399)
9. What Is Serenity and What Is Insight? (402)
10. Is There a Place for Reason in Mahāmudrā? (405)
11. Is There a Place for Devotion in Mahāmudrā? (409)
12. Does Mahāmudrā Transcend Ritual? (412)
13. Is There Room for Ethics in Mahāmudrā? (415)
14. Is Mahāmudrā Expressible? (419)
15. Is All Mahāmudrā Realization the Same? (423)
16. What Is Mind? (427)

PART 5. TRANSLATIONS

1. Synopsis of the Spiritual Practice Taught by the Exalted Mañjughoṣa 435
Tsongkhapa Losang Drakpa

2. Bright Lamp of the Excellent Path: An Excerpt 439
Kachen Yeshé Gyaltsen

3. Mahāmudrā Lineage Prayer 457

4. Highway of the Conquerors 469
Paṇchen Losang Chökyi Gyaltsen

5. Lamp So Bright 481
Paṇchen Losang Chökyi Gyaltsen

6. The Hundred Deities of Tuṣita 539
Dulnakpa Palden Sangpo

7. The Bright Lamp of Mahāmudrā 543
Khedrup Norsang Gyatso

8. Offering to the Guru 567
Paṇchen Losang Chökyi Gyaltsen

9. The Crystal Mirror of Tenet Systems: Excerpts 597
Thuken Losang Chökyi Nyima

10. Poetic Expressions 611
Paṇchen Losang Chökyi Gyaltsen

Appendix A: The Geluk Mahāmudrā Uncommon Proximate Lineage 643

Appendix B: The Geluk Mahāmudrā Uncommon Distant Lineage 645

Appendix C: Keutsang Jamyang Mönlam's Outline of *Highway of the Conquerors* 647

Bibliography 651

Index 689

About the Author 717

Preface

WHEREVER YOU ARE reading this, pause for a moment and ask: Who or what is doing the reading? Who or what is doing the comprehending? One obvious answer to both questions is "the mind." We usually think of the mind as intending this or that object, like the words on this page or the daydream we drift to when the words can't keep our interest. Now, though, step back from your mind's usual preoccupations, take a few slow, deep breaths, and settle into the clear awareness that is mind itself. If thoughts appear, let them subside to their source, and relax again into awareness without content. When you have stabilized that calm, clear awareness, ask yourself what the true nature of this calm, clear awareness is. Where is it found? Is it in your body-mind as a whole? Particular parts of your body-mind? Your brain? A certain part of your brain? Your neurons? Your senses? The rise and fall of thoughts? The interrelation of thoughts? Thoughts at rest? Completely outside your body-mind? No matter where you look for the mind, you never arrive at an absolute point at which you can say, "Ah, that's it!" Not finding the mind may at first seem frustrating or even frightening, but when you understand that that's just the way it is, you can rest in that not-finding, in the clear, empty, aware state that is your natural mind, mind as it really is. Resting in the natural mind, you feel joyous, and so fulfilling is that joy that it spontaneously overflows the boundaries of your "self" and into concern for others, so that, brimming with wisdom and compassion, you return to the world—in the old Zen expression—with gift-bestowing hands.

What you've just gone through is a basic exercise in *mahāmudrā* meditation, a first step to opening the "great seal" (*mahā-mudrā*) of the natural mind. In the West, this is often all mahāmudrā is imagined to be, but in its traditional Asian settings, it is not just an isolated contemplation but a bodily practice, a religious practice, and a social practice as well. Indeed, mahāmudrā rarely occurs outside the context of the very particular—and for Westerners, quite challenging—ritual and meditative technique known as *guru yoga*, in which one worships one's guru, absorbs blessings from them, and ultimately comes to identify with their mind, seen as inseparable from that of the buddhas, hence luminous, blissful, and empty.

In the popular imagination, mahāmudrā is associated almost exclusively with the Kagyü schools of Tibetan Buddhism, where it is a core wisdom teaching about the nature of mind and how to realize that nature through meditation so as to attain the awakened state of buddhahood. Partly because of its focus on such meditation practices as mahāmudrā and the tantric six Dharmas of Nāropa, and partly because of the reputations enjoyed by such yogīs as Milarepa, Gampopa, Jikten Sumgön, Rangjung Dorjé, and Jamgön Kongtrul, the Kagyü is often characterized as the Tibetan contemplative school par excellence. It sometimes comes as a surprise, then, to learn that there is a living tradition of mahāmudrā theory and practice in the Geluk tradition, which usually is depicted as the most scholastic and conservative of Tibetan orders. Many of the common characterizations of Tibetan schools, of course, are little more than caricatures, and it is as foolish to think that Gelukpas are uninterested in meditation as to assume that Kagyüpas are indifferent to scholarship. Certainly, the association of mahāmudrā with the Kagyü is not misplaced, for the concept does lie at the heart of Kagyü religious discourse. Nevertheless, mahāmudrā has been a vital term for Gelukpas for nearly four centuries, where it has been taught as part of a secret hearing transmission (*snyan brgyud*) known either as the Geden Oral Transmission (*dge ldan bka' brgyud*, after an alternative name for the Geluk), the Ensa Hearing Transmission (*dben sa snyan brgyud*, after a hermitage in west-central Tibet where several masters of the lineage resided), or—as is now most common—the Ganden Hearing Transmission (*dga' ldan snyan brgyud*, after the first Geluk monastery). Attributed to the tradition's founder, Tsongkhapa Losang Drakpa (1357–1419), Geluk mahāmudrā initially was publicized by the First Paṇchen Lama, Losang Chökyi Gyaltsen (or Paṇchen Chögyen, 1570–1662). It was further developed a century later by Kachen Yeshé Gyaltsen (1713–93), then revived in the twentieth century by Phabongkha Rinpoché Dechen Nyingpo (1878–1941). Since then it has continued to be an important Geluk practice tradition. Mahāmudrā may not be as central to the worldview and experience of Gelukpas as of Kagyüpas, but it forms an important strand within the overall fabric of Geluk tradition—more so than it does in the other two great Tibetan Buddhist orders, the Nyingma and Sakya. And however central or marginal mahāmudrā may be for the Geluk, the topic has generated a significant literature within the order. Some of it predated Paṇchen Chögyen's seminal contributions, but most of it came in his wake.

Scholarship on Geluk mahāmudrā in Western languages has been relatively sparse. In 1966, Herbert Guenther brought out *Tibetan Buddhism without Mystification* (revised and published in 1976 as *Tibetan Treasures on the Middle Way*), which includes a number of texts by Yeshé Gyaltsen that are at least tangentially related to Geluk mahāmudrā. In 1975, the Library of Tibetan Works and Archives in Dharamsala published a translation of Paṇchen Chögyen's root text on mahāmudrā, with commentary by Geshé Ngawang Dhargyey, under the title *The Great Seal of Voidness: The Root Text for the Ge-lug/Ka-gyu Tradition of Mahāmudrā*. In 1995, Janice Dean Willis brought out *Enlightened Beings: Life Stories from the Ganden Oral Tradition*, which includes considerable discussion of the Ganden Hearing Transmission, a translation of Yeshé Gyaltsen's long biographies of the main early lineage-holders, and a translation of the Geluk mahāmudrā lineage prayer. In 1997, the Fourteenth Dalai Lama and Alexander Berzin published *The Gelug/Kagyü Tradition of Mahāmudrā*, which includes a lengthy introduction by Berzin, a fresh translation of Paṇchen Chögyen's root verses, and the Dalai Lama's detailed and scholarly commentary on both the root verses and Paṇchen Chögyen's autocommentary.

In 2001, I contributed an article entitled "The dGe ldan-bKa' brgyud Tradition of Mahāmudrā: How Much dGe ldan? How Much bKa' brgyud?" to a volume honoring Jeffrey Hopkins. In his 2005 book on meditation, *Gom*, Gelek Rinpoche devoted a chapter to mahāmudrā, which includes a verse-by-verse commentary on all of Paṇchen Chögyen's root verses except those devoted to insight. In 2005, Victoria Sujata brought out *Tibetan Songs of Realization: Echoes from a Seventeenth-Century Scholar and Siddha in Amdo*, a study of the spiritual songs of an important eastern Tibetan Geluk mahāmudrā practitioner, Kalden Gyatso (1607–77). In 2009, Geshe Acharya Thubten Loden published *Great Treasury of Mahamudra*, a massive, traditional presentation of sūtra- and tantra-based Geluk mahāmudrā practice that actually says little about the distinctive form of mahāmudrā introduced by Paṇchen Chögyen or the special transmission of which is it said to be part. The same year, I published a journal article entitled "Archer Among the Yellow Hats: Some Geluk Uses of Saraha." In 2011, the Fourteenth Dalai Lama and José Cabezón published *Meditation on the Nature of Mind*, a translation and analysis of a meditation manual by a contemporary of Paṇchen Chögyen with strong ties to the Geluk, Khöntön Paljor Lhundrup (1561–1637), which is influenced by the discourse of Kagyü mahāmudrā and the Nyingma great perfection (*rdzogs chen*) but shows no real connection to the Geluk approach to mahāmudrā or the Ganden Hearing Transmission. In 2015, I published a journal article entitled "Did Tsongkhapa Teach Mahāmudrā?" In 2017, B. Alan Wallace brought out a translation of texts related to the Lerab Lingpa lineage of the great perfection, which includes three texts touching on mahāmudrā by the early-twentieth-century Geluk scholar from Amdo Losang Dongak Chökyi Gyatso (1903–57).

In late 2018, two books based on mahāmudrā discourses were published: Lama Thubten Yeshe's *Mahamudra: How to Discover Our True Nature* and Zasep Tulku Rinpoche's *Gelug Mahamudra: Eloquent Speech of Manjushri*; unfortunately, both appeared too late for more than cursory consideration in this volume. Victoria Sujata's translation of Kalden Gyatso's spiritual songs (*Journey to Distant Groves*) should appear in 2019, and Ven. Tenzin Gaché's translation of Chöden Rinpoche's commentary on the First Paṇchen's root verses (*Mastering Meditation*) is scheduled for publication in 2020; neither has been available to me. Apart from passing references in writings devoted to other topics, and several works that focus primarily on Geluk tantric mahāmudrā or on the important Ganden Hearing Transmission–based tantric liturgy by Paṇchen Chögyen known as *Offering to the Guru*, that is the extent of the important Western-language work on the topic as of late 2018.

What no one has attempted before is a work on Geluk mahāmudrā that, at once, analyzes it in the context of previous Indian and Tibetan discourse on mahāmudrā; investigates its history, doctrines, and practices from a critical scholarly standpoint; and provides translations of multiple Tibetan works crucial to the tradition. That is what I undertake here.

This book, as Bob Dylan might put it, has been a slow train coming. I first became interested in mahāmudrā in the early 1970s, during my undergraduate days at Wesleyan University, when I read the Kagyü-inflected works of W.Y. Evans-Wentz, John Blofeld, and Lama Anagarika Govinda. To me, the great seal sounded like a rather more exotic version of Zen, which at the time I took to be a mystical, paradoxical way of seeing and being that was nothing less than the acme of human spiritual inquiry. When, after college, I eventually began to study Buddhism seriously, it turned out to be the Tibetan variety and not the Japanese, and of Tibetan schools not the experience-focused Kagyü but the academic and clerical Geluk. After studies at Kopan Monastery near Kathmandu and the Library of Tibetan Works and Archives in Dharmasala, I moved to Madison, Wisconsin, to study with Geshé Lhundub Sopa. In my academic studies at the University of Wisconsin and my personal study at what is now known as Deer Park Monastery, my orientation was primarily philosophical; indeed, I focused on the work of Dharmakīrti, one of the knottiest of the great Indian thinkers. The personal and intellectual appeal of a direct, nonconceptual approach to truth remained strong, however, and I wrote a number of graduate papers on the Indian Buddhist tantric poet-saints, the great Chinese-Indian debate on the role of reason in spiritual life held at the Tibetan court in the eighth century, and various aspects of the Kagyü tradition, including mahāmudrā.

Out of grad school and teaching at various colleges and universities, I turned my research attention in the late 1980s to the Geluk mahāmudrā tradition—on which at that point almost no scholarship had appeared. My original plan was to offer a few translations of important texts from the tradition, preceded by a brief introduction, and be done with it. While researching the introduction, however, I fell down a scholarly rabbit hole: the attempt to make sense of Geluk mahāmudrā forced me to read seriously in the literature of Kagyü mahāmudrā. Understanding Kagyü mahāmudrā turned out to require some understanding of the Indian texts and contexts in which discourse on the great seal had first arisen, including the works of Saraha and other tantric *mahāsiddhas*, or great adepts (sometimes simply referred to as *siddhas* for short). Just as the project began to mushroom far beyond my initial conception, however, it was relegated to the proverbial back burner by a series of collaborative editorial projects that occupied most of the next two decades: collections of essays on Tibetan literary genres and "Buddhist theology," a translation of Thuken Chökyi Nyima's *Crystal Mirror of Philosophical Systems*, and a collection of scholarly essays on mahāmudrā and Kagyü traditions. It was only with the completion of the last-mentioned volume, in 2011, that I felt able to return to the book on Geluk mahāmudrā that had been simmering so long. In many ways, this postponement was a good thing, for in the three decades since I started the project, I have learned an immense amount about mahāmudrā, whether through receiving teachings from lamas in various Tibetan traditions, reading and rereading Indian and Tibetan texts, digging into a range of modern scholarly writings, or conversing (in person or by email) with Tibetan- and Western-trained scholars. I don't know if this project ever could be fully cooked—in the manifold senses of the Indian word *pakkā*—but I feel that I've done what I could, and so I humbly offer it up in the hope that it may be of benefit or interest to a few readers, here or there, who wish to join me in the luminous darkness of the rabbit hole that is study of the great seal.

I am grateful to many, many people for help along the way.

Among the Tibetan teachers whose discourses have directly or indirectly deepened my understanding of mahāmudrā are such Gelukpa lamas as H. H. the Dalai Lama, Geshe Lhundup Sopa, Lama Thubten Yeshe, Thubten Zopa Rinpoché, Ven. Lobsang Namgyal, Lochö Rinpoché, Yangsi Rinpoché, Geshe Losang Tenzin Ngari, and Ganden Tri Rinpoché Losang Tenzin; such Kagyüpa lamas as the previous Kalu Rinpoché, Chögyam Trungpa Rinpoche,

Khenpo Karthar Rinpoché, Khenpo Könchog Gyaltsen, Drigung Chetsang Rinpoché, Mingyur Rinpoché, Khenpo Tenpa Gyaltsen, Khenpo Kunga Gyaltsen, Khandro Rinpoché, and Khenpo Kunga Trinlé; such Nyingmapa lamas as Khenpo Sherab Sangpo, Tsoknyi Rinpoché, and Chökyi Nyima Rinpoché; and such Sakyapa lamas as H. H. Sakya Trichen and H. E. Jetsun Chimé Luding Rinpoché. To all of them, I am most grateful—as I am to a singular Sri Lankan Theravāda meditation master with whom I had several fruitful exchanges on mahāmudrā in 1993, the late and still-lamented Godwin Samararatne.

Scholarly friends who have aided my understanding and provided encouragement along the way are far too numerous to acknowledge fully, but I would like to specially mention Lara Braitstein, José Cabezón, Thupten Jinpa, Matthew Kapstein, Donald Lopez, Klaus-Dieter Mathes, John Newman, and Jan Willis for their learned interest and support at many points during the project—and in the cases of José and John, all the way through.

I would also like to acknowledge the encouragement and help I received from Yael Bentor, James Blumenthal, Michael Broido, Donna Brown, Ven. George Churinoff, Cortland Dahl, John Davenport, Ronald Davidson, Martina Draszczyk, John Dunne, Artemus Engle, David Fiordalis, Jim Fisher, Ven. Tenzin Gaché, Ruth Gamble, Alexander Gardner, Holly Gayley, David Germano, Laura Gibson, Luís Gómez, Janet Gyatso, Paul Hackett, Sarah Harding, David Higgins, John Holt, Jeffrey Hopkins, David Jackson, Ven. Ani Jampa, Edwin Kelley, Casey Kemp, Yaroslav Komarovski, Ulrich Timme Kragh, Lewis Lancaster, Tomoko Makidono, John Makransky, Dan Martin, Sara McClintock, Eric Mortensen, Tenzin Namgyal, Beth Newman, Troy Omafray, Richard Payne, Andrew Quintman, David and Nancy Reigle, Jim Rheingans, Geshe Ngawang Samten, Kurtis Schaeffer, Alexander Schiller, Michael Sheehy, Shen Weirong, Jan-Ulrich Sobisch, Julia Stenzel, Michael Sweet, John Thiel, Robert Thurman, Tenzin Trinley (Sharpa Tulku), Alan Wallace, Christian Wedemeyer, Tom Yarnall, Dan Smyer Yu, and Leonard Zwilling.

I also have benefited greatly from the fruits of several visionary projects that have made much of the Indian and Tibetan Buddhist literary heritage available in digital form, most notably the Asian Classics Input Project, the Buddhist Digital Resource Center, and the Buddhist Canons Research Database.

My many colleagues over the course of three decades in the Religion Department at Carleton College consistently expressed a lively interest in my work. I would mention especially Bardwell Smith, Richard Crouter, Ian Barbour, Anne Patrick, Louis Newman, Mike Ashcraft, Mark Unno, Shahzad Bashir, Michael McNally, Lori Pearson, Will Elison, Asuka Sango, Noah Salomon, Kristin Bloomer, Shana Sippy, Sonja Anderson, and Matt Robertson. I am particularly grateful to the members of a 2012–13 Humanities Center seminar I directed, on "Dimensions of Mind"—Ken Abrams, Kristin Bloomer, Lauren Feiler, Trish Ferrett, and Tun Myint—for their inquiries into my work from angles I could scarcely imagine, and to Cathy Yandell and Susannah Ottaway for their support of the seminar. Carleton College, on more than one occasion, generously provided me with financial support so I could pursue this research, through several internal term-release grants and, at the end, funds to help defray indexing expenses.

Toward the end of the drawn-out process of putting this book together, I enjoyed several strokes of especially good fortune, which helped push it toward completion. In the fall of 2013, I offered a seminar on mahāmudrā at McGill University in Montreal. I am grateful to Lara Braitstein for inviting me to teach there and to the students in the seminar—especially Julia Stenzel—for their hard work and probing questions. In the spring of 2014, I was able to give two lectures on mahāmudrā at Rangjung Yeshe Institute in Boudhnath, Nepal. I thank Chökyi Nyima Rinpoche for inviting me to visit, and the faculty, students, and staff of RYI for their hospitality, curiosity, and enthusiasm. During the summer of 2015, I was able to attend four weeks of teachings on Paṇchen Chögyen's mahāmudrā texts, and the commentary on them by Keutsang Jamyang Mönlam, which were given in Madison by the then Jangtsé Chöjé Rinpoché—now Ganden Tripa—Losang Tenzin, who kindly took the time to answer a number of my questions on the texts and their practice. In early 2016, I presented my work over the course of a weekend at Sravasti Abbey, in Newport, Washington; I thank Thubten Chodron and the nuns for their kind invitation, their hospitality, and their spirited questioning of my historical and doctrinal perspective. Around the same time, Alan Wallace used my draft translation of Paṇchen Chögyen's autocommentary in a course he taught in Tuscany and was kind enough to provide detailed suggestions for improvement, from which my rendition has benefited greatly. In 2018, my long-time friend and colleague José Cabezón carefully read sections 1–4 of the draft manuscript and made many useful comments and suggestions. He also arranged for his graduate students at the University of California at Santa Barbara to read those sections and invited me to UCSB to discuss with them the issues it raised. I greatly appreciated their questions and observations as well. Lastly, between 2016 and 2019, I was able to present aspects of my analysis and translations to students and community members at Maitripa College in Portland, Oregon. I am grateful to Namdrol Miranda Adams, Leigh Miller, and Tiffany Patrella as well as Sunitha Bhaskaran, Daryl Dunigan, Linda Brown, and Amanda Russell for their help in making my stays in Portland so productive and enjoyable, to the members of my 2016

Tibtean translation class for their sharp and constructive comments on my draft translation of Paṇchen Chögyen's autocommentary, to the students in the Mahāmudrā course I helped teach in early 2019 for their thought-provoking questions and their garuḍa-like eye for typos, and above all to Yangsi Rinpoche for his deep interest in and encouragement of my project over the course of more than a decade, and for the confidence he has displayed in asking me to speak and teach about Mahāmudrā at Maitripa over the past several years. I deeply admire Rinpoche's curiosity and open-mindedness—not to mention his erudition—and have learned immensely from our wide-ranging conversations.

At Wisdom Publications, I was most fortunate to have as my editor, David Kittelstrom, who was my student at Carleton College three decades ago, and who has more than amply repaid any debt he feels he owes me, through his careful, sympathetic, and knowledgeable reading and his incomparable skill at reshaping academic writing so that it comes across smoothly in English without sacrificing the precision required of serious scholarship. I would also like to thank Ben Gleason and Laura Cunningham at Wisdom for help in the production of the book and Ian MacCormack for preparing the index.

Finally, I am beholden to many friends who, though not academically trained Buddhism scholars, have been no less encouraging of my work and no less probing in their questions to me than those inside the academy. Here I would single out Paul Arllen, Mike Atkins, John Barbour, Frank Barone, Ann Chavez, John Costello, Morgan Groves, Cathy Kennedy, David Monroe, Kelly O'Neill, Sue Solomon, Ken Tobacman, and Peter Wilson. No project this long in the works can come to pass without the interest and encouragement—not to mention tolerance—of one's family, so I reserve my last and deepest thanks to my son Ian Jackson, my brother Blair Jackson, the other members of our far-flung Jackson-Percy-Beakley-McMahon-Sawyer-Steinert clan—and above all, to my beloved co-conspirator and muse in this life, both on and off the cushion, Pam Percy.

Sarva mangalam!

Roger R. Jackson
Northfield, Minnesota
May 28, 2019

Permissions

PORTIONS OF A number of the chapters here have appeared elsewhere and are published with permission:

Portions of the introduction and chapters 1–5 appeared in "Mahāmudrā in India and Tibet," in *Oxford Research Encyclopedia of Religion* (Online: http://religion.oxfordre.com/view/10.1093/acrefore/9780199340378.001.0001/acrefore-9780199340378-e-184, accessed August 2016).

Portions of chapter 6 appeared as "Did Tsong kha pa Teach Mahāmudrā?," *Zentralasiatische Studien* 44 (2015): 79–97.

Portions of chapters 10 and 11 appear in "Assimilating the Great Seal: The Dge lugs pa–ization of the *Dge ldan bka' brgyud* Tradition of Mahāmudrā," in *Mahāmudrā in India and Tibet*, edited by Roger R. Jackson and Klaus-Dieter Mathes, 210–27 (Leiden: Brill, 2019).

The first two segments of chapter 15 appeared in an earlier form in "The dGe ldan bka' brgyud Tradition of Mahāmudrā: How Much dGe ldan? How Much bKa' brgyud?" in *Changing Minds: Contributions to the Study of Buddhism and Tibet In Honor of Jeffrey Hopkins*, edited by Guy Newland, 155–92 (Ithaca: Snow Lion Publications, 2001).

Most of the material in chapter 16 appeared as "Archer Among the Yellow Hats: The Uses of Saraha in Geluk Tradition," *Indian International Journal of Buddhist Studies*, 10 (2009): 103–31.

Most of the questions in chapter 17 appeared in seminal form in "Mahāmudrā: Natural Mind in Indian and Tibetan Buddhism" *Religion Compass* 5/7 (2011): 286–99.

Technical Note

TIBETAN NAMES AND terms are rendered in phonetics; the transliterated Tibetan spelling may be found under the appropriate entry in the index. In general, I try to provide phonetic spellings for Tibetan names that approximate their Lhasa-dialect pronunciation. Two notable exceptions, however, are Paṇchen, which is usually pronounced *penchen*, and Dalai, which when uttered by a Tibetan (it is a Mongolian word) is more like *talei*. Paṇchen and Dalai are so well known in those spellings that I render them thus throughout the book. Similarly, because the phonetic spellings of many modern teachers' Tibetan names have become standardized in English, I will usually spell them following that standard rather than my own conventions.

Sanskrit text titles are generally translated into English, with the Sanskrit equivalent noted parenthetically after the first occurrence. The Sanskrit title also may be found under the appropriate entry in the index.

Tibetan text titles are generally translated into English, with the Tibetan title *not* noted parenthetically after the first occurrence. The Tibetan title may be found under the appropriate entry in the index.

Full information on original Indic texts referred to in the footnotes is found in the bibliography under "Indic Sources." Texts for which an author is known are indicated in the following format: Xx*YY* (e.g., Sd*BA* for Śāntideva's *Bodhicaryāvatāra*). Authorless texts—mostly sūtras and tantras—are indicated in the following format: *XXX* (e.g., *SRS* for the *Samādhirāja Sūtra*).

Full information on original Tibetan texts referred to in the footnotes is found in the bibliography under "Tibetan Sources." Texts for which an author is known are indicated in the following format: Xx*YYYY* (e.g., Bz*YSGM* for Paṇchen Chögyen's *Phyag chen yang gsal sgron me*). Authorless texts—mostly edited volumes—are indicated in the following format: *XXXX* (e.g., *NGCS* for *Dpal dge ldan pa'i lugs kyi lam rim dang snyan brgyud kyi chos skor*).

With regard to translations (especially of verse) that are cited in parts 1–4, I have in many cases slightly amended existing translations—whether my own or others'—for the sake of stylistic and terminological consistency. Such instances are noted by "translation adapted" appearing in parentheses. I ask that readers forgive me this mild breach of scholarly protocol.

Along similar lines, in my own translations in part 5 (and elsewhere) I have generally eliminated the brackets that indicate content not explicitly stated in the original text yet obvious from context, in the hope that this will make the translations more readable. Scholars may, of course, consult the original text to see what liberties I have taken and judge my amendments accordingly.

In the footnotes to the translations, quotations whose source I have not been able to locate are indicated by SNL.

Finally, on the matter of gendered pronouns, in passages of my own I have tried to allow for equality or neutrality wherever possible, by utilizing either "he or she" or "they" and their variants. In my translations, however, I have generally left in place the pronouns employed by their authors, who were, overwhelmingly, operating within an androcentric cultural and linguistic system. Readers should appreciate, however, that when a generic person or practitioner is referred to by an author as a "yogī" or simply as "he," an implicit "[or yoginī]" or "[or she]" may be supplied.

Introduction

Mahāmudrā—Sanskrit for "great seal," "great symbol," or "great gesture"—is one of the most vital and variable terms in Indian and Tibetan Buddhism. It refers to, among other things, a symbolic hand gesture in tantric ritual, a consort employed for sexual yoga practices, an experience of gnostic bliss, the view of emptiness as the nature of all persons and phenomena, a meditative system in which mind contemplates its own empty and luminous nature, or the culmination of the spiritual path in buddhahood. In all its contexts, mahāmudrā reveals much about the ways in which Buddhists conceive of the nature, activity, and potential of that most ubiquitous yet elusive of subjects: the mind. Those conceptions raise in turn a range of questions endemic not just to Buddhism but to all religious traditions—indeed to any cultural tradition concerned with exploring the philosophical, psychological, aesthetic, corporeal, social, and ethical implications of trying to understand—and alter—consciousness in the interest of human flourishing and meaning-making. In both India and Tibet, mahāmudrā was celebrated in song by mystics, analyzed in detail by scholastics, and debated vigorously by philosophers. Indeed, it was (and continues to be) the pretext for some of the most evocative poetry, profound metaphysical speculation, creative meditative experimentation, and acute philosophical debate ever produced in the Indian and Tibetan Buddhist worlds. To study mahāmudrā is to understand a crucial notion in Indian and Tibetan religious culture and a key source of Buddhist views on reality, life, and the mind.

Mahāmudrā is of particular importance in Indian tantric (or Mantra Vehicle) Buddhism (ca. 600–1200 CE) and the Tibetan Buddhist "Renaissance" (after ca. 1000 CE). In early Indian Buddhist tantras, the term referred primarily to a particular ritual hand gesture, a mode of reciting mantras, or the visualization of oneself as a deity. As tantric discourse in India became more esoteric, mahāmudrā acquired further significance, most often denoting one of a set of "seals" to tantric meditation and ritual, a female consort employed in sexual yoga practices, and the connate[1] blissful gnosis—equivalent to buddhahood—revealed by such practices. Finally, in late Indian Buddhism it became a single term—bridging the sūtras and tantras—that evokes Buddhist ultimacy in all its aspects: the emptiness that is the true nature of all persons and phenomena; the buddha nature, or capacity for awakening (*buddhadhātu, tathāgatagarbha*), inherent in all beings; the mind's natural freedom from delusion and duality; any mode of meditation that reveals the mind's intrinsic nature;[2] a free and spontaneous way of living and acting in the world; and the awakened state at the culmination of the Buddhist path. In India, mahāmudrā is associated above all with the texts and practices of such yoginī (or mother) tantra systems as Cakrasaṃvara, Hevajra, Vajrayoginī, and Kālacakra, and with such great and charismatic tantric mahāsiddhas as Saraha, Śavaripa, Virūpa, Tilopa, Nāropa, and Maitrīpa.

In Tibet, mahāmudrā (*phyag rgya chen po*) bore all these meanings and became a central topic of philosophical and meditative discourse in the vari-

1. The Sanskrit term *sahaja* has most often been translated as "innate" or—reflecting the Tibetan *lhan cig skyes pa*—"coemergent." These are reasonable, but the little-used English word *connate* captures perfectly the original term's sense that things are born or arise (*ja*) together or simultaneously (*saha*). On *sahaja*, see, e.g., Kvaerne 1975; Davidson 2002b.

2. The Sanskrit term *svabhāva* (Tib. *rang bzhin*) is one of the most important in the Buddhist lexicon. It has been translated variously as "essence," "own-being," "self-existence," "inherent existence," or "intrinsic nature." Generally, it refers to the intrinsic, inherent, or essential nature of something, by virtue of which it is what it is. In the Abhidharma of the Sarvāstivādins, it is that characteristic of a phenomenon (a *dharma*) without which it could not be distinguished from other phenomena and through which the phenomenon's existence is vouchsafed. In the Perfection of Wisdom sūtras and the works of Nāgārjuna and other early Mādhyamikas, it is *svabhāva* that is the chief target of philosophical criticism: it is rejected on the grounds that it is explicitly or implicitly conceived as a permanent, unitary, independent "real," whereas under analysis it turns out that *nothing* exists in that way, because all phenomena are dependently arisen, in that they are produced by causes and conditions, made up of parts, and/or merely nominal designations imputed by thought. In that sense, their real nature is emptiness (*śūnyatā*), a term that appears nihilistic but is quite the opposite, since it is precisely the fact that phenomena lack ultimate or intrinsic existence—that they are *not* permanent, partless, or independent—that assures their conventional validity. If things existed intrinsically, they could not change, yet it is evident that the world in which we live consists of impermanent, dependently arisen phenomena. Since dependent arising and emptiness are synonymous, the reality of things can be vouchsafed only by their emptiness. In Indian and Tibetan sources, *svabhāva/rang bzhin* is used to describe both the conventional (or phenomenal) and ultimate natures of things. For example, fire may be described conventionally as being of the *nature* of heat or as ultimately empty of any intrinsic, essential *nature*. Sometimes an author intends the conventional usage, sometimes the ultimate, and sometimes their usage may be ambiguous. Here, where the conventional status of something seems intended, I will generally translate *svabhāva/rang bzhin* as "nature," and where the ultimate status seems intended, I will translate it as "intrinsic nature," all the while recognizing that the two are not always or easily distinguishable.

ous traditions that are traced to the great eleventh-century translator Marpa Chökyi Lodrö and go under the name Marpa Kagyü. For the Marpa Kagyü, *mahāmudrā* denotes the true nature of reality and the mind, a set of contemplations in which the "natural mind" is realized, a relaxed and spontaneous way of being in the world, and the attainment of the awakened state of a buddha. From the very inception of the Marpa Kagyü in the eleventh century, virtually every important master of the lineage has written on mahāmudrā. Most of these masters worked in multiple genres—as a baseline, virtually all of them composed songs and ritual texts—but they are usually best known for one or two works, or kinds of work:

- Marpa (1012–97) for his transmission of Indic tantric practice traditions and his translations of important Indic texts
- Milarepa (1040–1123) for his ascetic lifestyle and his inspiring and instructive spiritual songs
- Gampopa (1079–1153) for his account of the stages of the Perfection Vehicle path and his analytical treatises on various types of mahāmudrā, including one that does not require tantric empowerment
- Drigung Jikten Sumgön (1143–1217) for his epigrams on the Single Intention behind all the Buddha's teachings and his teaching of a five-fold, gradual system of mahāmudrā
- Shang Rinpoché (1123–93) for his exposition of a radical, instantaneous approach to mahāmudrā
- Götsangpa Gönpo Dorjé (1189–1258) for his systematization of mahāmudrā theory and practice
- The Third Karmapa Rangjung Dorjé (1284–1339) for his popular mahāmudrā prayer and his discussions of mahāmudrā in relation to Indian Buddhist philosophy
- Gö Lotsāwa Shönu Pal (1392–1481) and Pawo Tsuklak Trengwa (1504–66) for their historical chronicles, which prominently feature the Marpa Kagyü and mahāmudrā lineages
- Tsangnyön Heruka (1452–1507) for his biographies and song collections related to Marpa and Milarepa
- The Seventh Karmapa Chödrak Gyatso (1454–1506) for his great anthology of Indian mahāmudrā texts
- The Eighth Karmapa Mikyö Dorjé (1507–54) for his anthology of Kagyü poems and his Madhyamaka (or middle way) commentaries
- Pema Karpo (1527–92) for his philosophical treatises, his practice manuals, his history of Buddhism, his autobiography, and his grand overview of mahāmudrā lineages and practices

- Dakpo Tashi Namgyal (1512–87) and the Ninth Karmapa Wangchuk Dorjé (1556–1603) for their great compendia of mahāmudrā practices
- Karma Chakmé (1613–78) for his texts on "mountain Dharma" and his synthesis of mahāmudrā and the great perfection
- Situ Paṇchen Chökyi Jungné (1700–1774) for his autobiography, retreat manual, and mahāmudrā commentaries
- Jamgön Kongtrul Lodrö Thayé (1813–99) for his encyclopedic overviews and anthologies
- Chögyam Trungpa (1939–87) for his revealed mahāmudrā treasure text (*terma*) and his modernizing interpretations of the practice

To paraphrase an early Buddhist sūtra, just as the ocean has everywhere the taste of salt, so the Kagyü has everywhere the taste of mahāmudrā.

Because mahāmudrā was a crucial term in late Indian Buddhism, it made its way into all the major Tibetan traditions, so there has been discussion of it not just among the Kagyü but also in the Kadam, Shiché, Shangpa Kagyü, Sakya, Nyingma, Jonang, and Geluk schools. Apart from the Shangpa and Marpa Kagyü, it is the Geluk tradition of Tsongkhapa and the Dalai and Paṇchen Lamas that has placed the most emphasis on mahāmudrā. According to later sources, Tsongkhapa (1357–1419) received from his divine teacher, the wisdom buddha Mañjughoṣa (or Mañjuśrī), a special oral tradition (*bka' srol*) or hearing transmission (*snyan brgyud*) that included a mahāmudrā meditation practice, which Tsongkhapa then taught in full solely to his student the contemplative and visionary Tokden Jampal Gyatso (1356–1428). The tradition was handed down secretly from one master to another until, in the sixteenth century, it reached Losang Chökyi Gyaltsen (1570–1662), a scholar at Tashi Lhunpo Monastery in Tsang who would gain renown as the First (or Fourth)[3] Paṇchen Lama and chief tutor of both the fourth and fifth Dalai Lamas. Paṇchen Chögyen (as he is known for short) published a set of verses describing the Geluk mahāmudrā practice and a prose commentary on his own verses; it is from these two texts—*Highway of the Conquerors* (*Rgyal ba'i*

3. Paṇchen Chögyen was the First Paṇchen Lama to be so recognized and usually is numbered accordingly, but tradition actually regards him as the fourth, preceded in the lineage by Khedrup Jé Gelek Palsang (1385–1438), Sönam Choklang (1438–1505), and Ensapa Losang Döndrup (1505–68). It is in this system of enumeration that the current (disputed) Paṇchen Lama is the eleventh. I will generally refer to Losang Chökyi Gyaltsen as Paṇchen Chögyen (a common Tibetan abbreviation of his name), and when I indicate his place in the succession of Paṇchen Lamas, I will designate him as the First Paṇchen.

gzhung lam) and *Lamp So Bright* (*Yang gsal sgron me*),[4] respectively—that most subsequent Geluk mahāmudrā literature stems.

In those foundational texts, the Paṇchen—who shows considerable familiarity with the writings of both Indian tantric mahāsiddhas like Saraha and the early masters of the Tibetan Kagyü—divides mahāmudrā into sūtra mahāmudrā and mantra mahāmudrā. The latter, which is discussed only briefly, is found within the completion-stage practices of unexcelled yoga tantras (*yoganiruttaratantra*), with *mahāmudrā* itself described as the gnosis of connate great bliss that arises after the vital winds (*prāṇa*; *rlung*) have been made to enter, abide, and dissolve within the central channel of the subtle body. Sūtra mahāmudrā, to which Paṇchen Chögyen devotes most of his attention, is practiced within the context of guru yoga and involves serenity meditation on the conventional nature of the mind, as clear and aware, followed by insight meditation on the ultimate nature of the mind, as empty of intrinsic existence, and a postmeditative recognition of all phenomena as illusion-like. The Paṇchen also wrote a number of poetic, biographical, and ritual texts that conveyed various elements of the mahāmudrā teaching.

The hearing lineage continued after Paṇchen Chögyen's death, and out in the open now, the mahāmudrā aspect became increasingly widespread, both in the central Tibetan provinces of Ü and Tsang and in the northeastern region of Amdo. By the late eighteenth century, through the efforts of Kachen Yeshé Gyaltsen (1713–93) and others, commentaries on Paṇchen Chögyen's texts and accounts of the practice were appearing regularly. A key factor in the expansion of the tradition was Yeshé Gyaltsen's explicit linkage of mahāmudrā meditation with an important ritual text composed by the First Paṇchen, *Offering to the Guru* (*Bla ma mchod pa*). The mahāmudrā tradition, though popular in Amdo throughout the nineteenth century, waned somewhat in central Tibet, but it was revived there by the influential early twentieth-century lama Phabongkha Rinpoché Dechen Nyingpo (1878–1941). Today, it is frequently taught to both Tibetan and non-Tibetan audiences by Gelukpa lamas—including, on numerous occasions, the Fourteenth Dalai Lama.

To understand how this came to pass, it is necessary to set the Geluk appropriation of mahāmudrā within the context of the discourse and history of mahāmudrā as a whole. That discourse and history begin not in Tibet but in India, and because the adoption of mahāmudrā by the Geluk comes relatively late in the history of Tibetan Buddhism, any attempt to understand the place

4. These are Bz*GBZL* and Bz*YSGM*, respectively. Alternative renderings of these titles, adopted by a number of translators, include *The Main Path of the Victors* and *The Re-Illuminating Lamp*, respectively.

of Geluk mahāmudrā within Buddhist tradition requires a preliminary survey of the development of mahāmudrā more broadly, both in India and Tibet.

To talk about either the discourse or the history of mahāmudrā is no simple matter, however. The discursive difficulty is starkly indicated in a statement by one of the most prominent members of the Kagyü mahāmudrā lineage, the Indian mahāsiddha Tilopa:

> The real can't be shown by the guru's words,
> so the disciple cannot comprehend.
> The fruit of the connate tastes ambrosial;
> who teaches the real to whom?[5]

This appeal to ineffability would seem to stymie any attempt to study mahāmudrā right at the start, on the grounds that it is, essentially, trans-linguistic and incommunicable. Its ineffability, in turn, is rooted at least in part in the fact that both the object and the subject of mahāmudrā realization are *nothing*—or, perhaps more properly, no *thing* to which we may assign ontological, epistemological, or axiological status. Subject, object, and realization are, in a word, empty. Indeed, true mahāmudrā is beyond either subject or object, and to the degree that our language depends on dualistic distinctions, the great seal is beyond any meaningful predication, and anything said about it is a lie. In this sense, discourse about mahāmudrā is similar to other forms of Buddhist negative rhetoric, from atomistic analyses of no-self (*anattā*) in the Pāli canon to the repetitive rhetorics of emptiness (*śūnyatā*) in the Perfection of Wisdom sūtras—and similar, too, to the apophatic discourse of mystics in many traditions, who insist that ultimate reality cannot be conceived, let alone described, by language or any other human construct.

As is well known, however, the mystic's insistence on the ineffability of the subject, object, or experience of ultimate reality is mired in paradox, for the very denial of communicability is itself a form of communication. By the same token, the Perfection of Wisdom sūtras may attempt to negate all philosophical assertions, but that negation tells us something about the ultimate, even if only provisionally, and positive language inevitably finds its way into the sūtras' discourse, as well. The *Heart Sūtra*, for instance, may negate every Abhidharma category within its compass, but in the end it affirms that there is awakening and a path that leads to it—even if that path is a sort of *via negativa*. In the passage cited above, Tilopa not only tells us something about mahāmudrā by describing it as indescribable but actually slips in a positive

5. Tp*DK* 131 (translation adapted).

claim about the nature of mahāmudrā (or, in this case, its synonym, "the connate," *sahaja*), saying that it "tastes ambrosial." Thus, like so many mystics, he asserts something about reality by his very denials, and like mystics, too, he mixes his negative rhetoric with metaphors and images that actually are intended to convey something positive about what it is like to know the ultimate. In the case of mahāmudrā discourse in particular, for every negation there seems to be an equal and opposite affirmation: the insistence on the emptiness of subject, object, or cognitive act is often followed by an assertion that "mind itself"—despite, or perhaps because of, its emptiness—is luminous and undefiled, the true nature of reality. This is clear in another pair of verses by Tilopa. In the first, he asks rhetorically:

> If you think, "this is the self," "this is the cosmos,"
> how will you waken to mind that's naturally stainless?[6]

To counter the negative rhetoric of the first verse, he follows immediately with this:

> I am the cosmos, I am the Buddha, I am the unadorned,
> I am nonmentation—I've broken existence![7]

In other words, the negation of our ordinary, deluded conceptions of self, mind, and world is not a negation pure and simple but clears the way for an appreciation of the natural purity possessed by all of these. Hence, in the proper context, positive imagery is just as appropriate an indicator of the real as negative imagery; indeed, each requires the other, if we are to take seriously the fundamental Buddhist axiom that the truth transcends the extremes of "is" and "is not."

Furthermore, and again mirroring a paradox in the study of mysticism, Indian and Tibetan writers concerned with mahāmudrā have produced an immense literature on this supposedly empty and ineffable topic. Scholars, whether traditional insiders or modern outsiders, have plenty of material on which to draw if they wish to analyze the nature and history of the great seal. In the face of this, however, the insider may point out that the written record of mahāmudrā, whether Indic or Tibetan, is only a husk and that the kernel of mahāmudrā practice and understanding always and only is to be found in the pith instructions (*man ngag*) transmitted orally since time immemorial

6. Tp*DK* 115.

7. Tp*DK* 115 (translation adapted).

from guru to disciple. This may well be so, and anyone who writes about mahāmudrā must acknowledge this argument respectfully—just as they must acknowledge that, at the highest level, mahāmudrā cannot be understood or described in finite terms, and that the historical record as it can be discerned with the tools of modern scholarship is not the only way to understand the human past, let alone bring meaning to it. That point conceded, however, the writer may turn with a relatively clear conscience to the vast corpus of texts that bear directly or indirectly on mahāmudrā.

Doing so, however, engenders new problems. For one thing, it is hard to know precisely how to delimit a mahāmudrā corpus, especially on the Indian side. For all the Indic texts that mention *mahāmudrā*—the term is peppered throughout tantras, mahāsiddha songs, and treatises from the eighth century on—there are precious few that actually make it their explicit and primary subject. Very late in the history of Indian Buddhism, figures like Maitrīpa's disciple Vajrapāṇi (b. 1017) began to group together different sets of texts that supposedly pertained to mahāmudrā, including the Seven Attainment Texts written by various mahāsiddhas and tantric commentators, three *Dohā Treasuries* attributed to Saraha, twenty-five texts on nonmentation (*amanasikāra*, also translated as "no mental engagement") associated with Maitrīpa, and a number of other collections, mostly drawn from the writings of Saraha and Maitrīpa.[8] Tibetan scholars, including the compilers of the canon of Indian treatises known as the Tengyur (*bstan 'gyur*), adopted these groupings, and when the Seventh Karmapa Chödrak Gyatso produced his great anthology of Indian mahāmudrā texts, he included not only the core collections just mentioned but virtually every poetic work (and many prose writings, as well) attributed to any Indian siddha of any importance, thereby vastly expanding the corpus of mahāmudrā literature. What's more, to the degree that mahāmudrā had come, by the late period of Buddhism in India, to be associated with almost any Buddhist idea pertaining to ultimate reality, a vast number of sūtras, tantras, and treatises—including the Perfection of Wisdom sūtras, the Hevajra and other highly esoteric tantras, works on buddha nature, and the writings of Nāgārjuna—came to form a sort of outer, or supplementary, mahāmudrā corpus, to the point where it is only a slight exaggeration to say that there was little in Indian Buddhist literature that did *not* seem to pertain to the great seal.[9] Beyond "canonical" mahāmudrā literature, of course, a scholar interested in mahāmudrā has available additional texts, some Indian but most Tibetan, that directly or indirectly bear on the topic: histori-

8. See, e.g., Roerich 1976, 864–66.

9. For a further discussion of these issues, see R. Jackson 2008.

cal chronicles, biographies and autobiographies, philosophical and polemical texts, commentaries, lineage lists, letters, poems, and so forth.

The wealth—indeed, embarrassment—of available research materials begs a further question, however: what historiographical approach should a researcher adopt? Should one take an *emic* approach and treat mahāmudrā as a timeless, unchanging teaching of the buddhas, or should one employ an *etic* stance, in which it is seen as a contested and complex term that evolved relatively late in the history of Indian Buddhism? From the standpoint of those Indian and Tibetan traditions that first identified mahāmudrā as a term whose history was worth relating, discourse on the topic can be traced back to the Buddha himself. After all, if the Buddha was (in one form or another) truly the source of the vast array of sūtras and tantras attributed to him by Mahāyāna tradition, and those texts contain both explicit and implicit references to mahāmudrā, then mahāmudrā discourse can be traced back to the time of the Buddha. If mahāmudrā discourse did not appear again until a thousand years after the Buddha's passing, it is not because it was invented then but because it took centuries for the karmic circumstances to be such that the teachings long transmitted in secret could finally be revealed. Furthermore, because "the Buddha" is not limited to the emanation body (*nirmāṇakāya*) that manifested in the sixth/fifth century BCE, fresh revelations are possible in later times, so whether a seminal mahāmudrā master like Saraha was part of an unbroken lineage that stretched back a millennium or more, or whether he received instruction from forms of the Buddha appearing to him contemporaneously as the female wisdom beings known as *ḍākinīs* really is of little consequence: one way or another mahāmudrā can be traced to the Buddha. Indeed, if not traceable to the Buddha, it would lose its legitimacy and fall to the level of mere human invention. If there are gaps in the literary record, whether in early or more recent times, this is because mahāmudrā, as noted above, is essentially an *oral* teaching, transmitted from master to disciple. And if there are contradictions in the written teachings, either they are only apparent—to be adjudicated by the guru's instruction—or they are the result of inevitable shortcomings involved in the process of literary production and reproduction.

Certainly, scholars who wish to trace the development of mahāmudrā through modern critical methods find themselves beset with problems. The Indic material is notoriously difficult to date, either absolutely or relatively, and in all too many cases we lack the Indic-language originals and hence must rely on Tibetan (or, occasionally, Chinese) translations to get a sense of how the text must once have looked. Authorship is nearly as difficult to establish as dating: texts sometimes are credited to more than one author; one author may bear multiple names; and in any case, many of the authors are simply unfindable as historical actors. Much of what we think we know about the teachers and texts of mahāmudrā in India is found in Tibetan writings, and although on the surface problems of dating and authorship seem less serious in Tibet than in India, the Tibetan material is less helpful to the historian than might be imagined. Most crucially, because the identification of the great seal as a central teaching of Indian Buddhism is mainly a function of religious and social developments from the eleventh century on in *Tibet*, much of the literature that identifies key Indian mahāmudrā texts and reports on the lives and teachings of the masters of mahāmudrā in India was produced many centuries after the fact, shaped by intellectual, literary, sectarian, and even political concerns unique to one or another Tibetan teacher or institution far more than by what we would call critical historical method. Furthermore, many Tibetan texts purported to be of great antiquity appear to have been composed considerably later, so the history of Tibetan mahāmudrā is not much easier to construct than the Indian. Even if we do regard the Tibetan material as trustworthy, we find so many contradictions between one text and another that those texts' value in determining any definite chronology or narrative—any history in our contemporary sense of the term—is dubious at best.

This does not mean that a history of mahāmudrā cannot be written. It does mean that the sources available for such a history are in most cases compromised, so that any narrative we produce is subject to a great many qualifications and must be regarded as tentative at best.

A Summary of the Book

The book is divided into five major parts.

Part 1, "The Background to Geluk Mahāmudrā" (chapters 1–5), provides context for the Geluk mahāmudrā tradition by surveying the development of the discourse, practice, and problematics of mahāmudrā in India and Tibet. The first two chapters (1–2) trace the origins and development of the concept of mahāmudrā in India, from its first appearance in the Buddhist tantras, through its employment by the mahāsiddhas, to its eventual integration with concepts and practices familiar from sūtra-based literature. In these chapters, we see mahāmudrā take on an ever-expanding set of referents, including a tantric hand gesture, the clear visualization of oneself as a buddha deity, one of a set of four "seals" (*mudrā*) to tantric meditation, a sexual consort, the bliss-emptiness gnosis generated by subtle-body yogas, and a term synonymous with emptiness, buddha nature, dharmakāya, and other Mahāyāna Buddhist "ultimates"—such that by the end of the Buddhist period in India, it had become one of the most significant items in the Indian Buddhist lexicon, associated with both tantras and sūtras, and articulated in the languages of both nondual paradox and esoteric praxis. Chapters 3–5 trace the pre-Geluk history of mahāmudrā in Tibet, beginning with its introduction to the plateau in the eleventh century, and turning then to its place in a number of important lineages that developed during the so-called Tibetan Renaissance that followed: Kadam, Shiché/Chö, Shangpa Kagyü, Sakya, and Nyingma (chapter 3). The final two chapters of part 1 (4–5) concentrate on the powerful and long-lasting tradition in which mahāmudrā has been most central, the Marpa Kagyü, with particular attention to the ways in which both earlier and later Kagyü masters balanced considerations of esoteric or nondual rhetoric, sūtra- or tantra-based practices, and gradual or sudden approaches to awakening.

Part 2, "Early Geluk Mahāmudrā" (chapters 6–9), provides an overview of the lives and mahāmudrā-oriented works of Geluk masters from Tsongkhapa through Paṇchen Chögyen—that is, from the late fourteenth century to the mid-seventeenth century. Chapter 6 sets the context for a discussion of Geluk mahāmudrā by surveying the life and work of Tsongkhapa and examining his life and writings in an attempt to understand how he used the term *mahāmudrā,* how he felt about Kagyü traditions and their mahāmudrā practices, and whether a distinctive great seal teaching of his own is discernible in his works. The next two chapters (7–8) concentrate on the period between Tsongkhapa and Paṇchen Chögyen in considerable detail, focusing on the lives and writings of masters both inside and outside the Ganden Hearing Transmission, with an eye to their familiarity with mahāmudrā. These masters include many of the most important figures in the formation of the Geluk tradition, among them the earliest Dalai Lamas. Chapter 9 explores in some detail the life and writings of Paṇchen Chögyen. It traces the contours of Paṇchen Chögyen's career and summarizes the texts he composed that have come to form the heart of the Geluk mahāmudrā tradition: his *Highway of the Conquerors* and his *Lamp So Bright* commentary; the mahāmudrā lineage prayer, whose earliest version Paṇchen Chögyen composed; his brief biographies of the mahāmudrā lineage masters, *Like a Treasure Inventory*; his mahāmudrā-related tantric liturgy, *Offering to the Guru*; and selected spiritual songs relevant to mahāmudrā that are scattered throughout his writings. The chapter concludes with a consideration of the broader question as to why Paṇchen Chögyen chose to focus on mahāmudrā as, and when, he did.

Part 3, "Later Geluk Mahāmudrā" (chapters 10–14), provides an overview of the lives and mahāmudrā-oriented works of Geluk masters from Paṇchen Chögyen's disciples through the Fourteenth Dalai Lama—that is, from the mid-seventeenth century to the early twenty-first century. Chapter 10 discusses the attitudes toward and writings about mahāmudrā generated by two direct disciples of Paṇchen Chögyen—the Fifth Dalai Lama and Shar Kalden Gyatso—and by other Geluk masters of the late seventeenth and early eighteenth centuries. Chapter 11 is devoted to Kachen Yeshé Gyaltsen (1713–93), who wrote more works on mahāmudrā than any other Geluk master, and probably did more than anyone besides the First Paṇchen to shape the way the tradition's history and practices are understood today. The next two chapters examine, respectively, four masters of the eighteenth and nineteenth centuries who commented directly on Paṇchen Chögyen's root verses and autocommentary (chapter 12), and the work of a number of other later contributors to the tradition from eastern Tibet, especially the northeast region of Amdo (chapter 13). Chapter 14, "The Twentieth Century and Beyond," discuses a number of more recent contributors, including Phabongkha Rinpoché and the major Gelukpa figure of the late twentieth and early twenty-first century, the Fourteenth Dalai Lama Tenzin Gyatso.

Part 4, "Perspectives on Geluk Mahāmudrā" (chapters 15–17), examines a number of questions and problems that arise from a study of Geluk mahāmudrā. Chapter 15 analyzes three major issues in the Geluk great seal tradition: (1) whether the name given the tradition by Paṇchen Chögyen shows he intended it to be a synthesis of Geluk and Kagyü or solely Geluk, (2) how the Geluk mahāmudrā tradition compares to selected mahāmudrā traditions among the Kagyü with respect to Paṇchen Chögyen's textual citations, way of distinguishing sūtra from mantra mahāmudrā, ordering of serenity and insight, and accounts of serenity and insight meditation, and (3) what the actual place is of mahāmudrā is in Geluk ritual, meditative, and institutional life. Chapter 16 examines a variety of different ways in which Geluk authors have treated the seminal Indian mahāmudrā adept Saraha. Finally, chapter 17 considers sixteen key questions of theory and practice explicitly or implicitly posed by Tibetan discourse on mahāmudrā and relates them to broader questions in Buddhist studies and, beyond that, religious studies in general and the study of mysticism in particular.

Part 5 presents translations, from the Tibetan, of ten major texts that express different aspects of, and perspectives on, mahāmudrā in the Geluk tradition:

(1) *Synopsis of the Spiritual Practice Taught by the Exalted Mañjughoṣa* is a translation of Tsongkhapa's transcription and analysis of a set of verses imparted to him in a vision by Mañjughoṣa that summarize the entire path to enlightenment, including advice on meditation and the view that resonates strongly with that of the mahāmudrā traditions.

(2) An excerpt from *Bright Lamp of the Excellent Path* is a translation of a brief history of Geluk mahāmudrā found in Yeshé Gyaltsen's great discourse

on Paṇchen Chögyen's basic great seal text. It illustrates the role of sacred narrative in the tradition.

(3) The *Mahāmudrā Lineage Prayer* is a translation of the prayer to the great seal masters of the Ganden Hearing Transmission composed by Paṇchen Chögyen and updated by Kachen Yeshé Gyaltsen in the eighteenth century, Phabongkha Rinpoché in the nineteenth or early twentieth century, an unidentified lama or lamas and Trijang Rinpoché in the late twentieth century, and Thubten Zopa Rinpoché in the early twenty-first century.

(4) *Highway of the Conquerors* is a translation of Paṇchen Chögyen's root verses on how to practice mahāmudrā according to the Geden Oral Transmission. Although he touches on tantric practice, his major focus is on mahāmudrā meditation according to the sūtra, or Perfection Vehicle, tradition.

(5) *Lamp So Bright* is a translation of Paṇchen Chögyen's detailed prose commentary on *Highway of the Conquerors.*

(6) *The Hundred Deities of Tuṣita* is a translation of a brief but influential fifteenth-century recitation and meditation text by Dulnakpa Palden Sangpo that is often used as a jumping-off point for mahāmudrā meditation along the lines of the sūtra tradition.

(7) *The Bright Lamp of Mahāmudrā* is a translation of the earliest-known text on mahāmudrā by a Gelukpa, a fifteenth-century analysis, focused on Mantra Vehicle mahāmudrā, by Khedrup Norsang Gyatso, tutor to the Second Dalai Lama.

(8) *Offering to the Guru* is a translation of perhaps the most popular of all Geluk ritual texts, which has its origins in the same Ganden Hearing Transmission, includes teachings on mahāmudrā, and may provide a context for mahāmudrā meditation.

(9) Excerpts from *The Crystal Mirror of Tenet Systems* are translations of a discussion of various philosophical problems posed by mahāmudrā in its Tibetan setting, drawn from the "Kagyü" chapter of the great history of Asian religions by Thuken Losang Chökyi Nyima.

(10) *Poetic Expressions* comprises translations of twenty-two of the songs of spiritual experience (*mgur*) composed by Paṇchen Chögyen drawn from either his autobiography or a collection of songs inspired by the life and example of Milarepa.

Five of the texts presented here (nos. 3, 4, 6, 8, and 9) have previously been translated elsewhere; the other five (nos. 1, 2, 5, 7, and 10) have not. The purpose of bringing them together in this volume is to demonstrate how mahāmudrā is a concept that may be woven through the entire fabric of religious life: in textual analysis, prayer, sacred narrative, ritual performance, meditative practice, aesthetic expression, and philosophical disputation.

The volume concludes with three appendixes. Appendixes A and B provide charts of the proximate and distant lineages of Geluk mahāmudrā masters. Appendix C provides one of the most detailed and interesting of all commentarial outlines of *Highway of the Conquerors*, that of Keutsang Jamyang Mönlam.

Part 1
The Background to Geluk Mahāmudrā

1. Mahāmudrā in India: Hindus and Buddhists, Sūtras and Tantras

OVER THE CENTURIES, the Sanskrit term *mudrā*—usually derived from the verbal root *mud*, meaning "to enjoy"[10]—came to convey a wide range of meanings, but the most basic seem to involve sealing, stamping, or signifying. Drawing on such sources as the *Mahābhārata*, *kāvya* literature, the Purāṇas, and the *Rājataraṃgiṇī* (roughly dateable to the early centuries of the common era), Monier-Williams defines it as:

> a seal or any instrument used for sealing or stamping, a seal-ring, signet-ring . . . , any ring . . . ; type for printing or instrument for lithographing . . . ; the stamp or impression made by a seal &c; any stamp or print or mark or impression; . . . an image, sign, badge, token . . . ; authorization, a pass, passport . . . ; shutting, closing . . . ; a lock, stopper, bung . . . ; a mystery.[11]

Although a derivative meaning, the best-known referent of *mudrā*—perhaps stretching back as far as the Vedic period—is as a symbolic gesture or hand position displayed in ritual, dramatic, and artistic settings. In a dramatic context, such as that of dance, it expresses a character's intentions or actions. In an artistic medium such as sculpture or painting, it identifies a human or divine figure and particular actions or attitudes associated with that figure. In a religious setting, the mudrā effects, confirms, or "seals" various aspects of yogic and/or ritual performance.[12] The term *mudrā* is used widely—and in a variety

10. In spite of the ingenious etymological suggestions of Indian pandits (see, e.g., Gupta et al. 1979, 116, and Dyczkowski 1992a, 78) this derivation is far from obvious, and I believe that serious attention ought to be paid to the theory of Fritz Hommel, that "*mudrā* . . . is derived from the Babylonian (*musarū*, 'writing,' 'seal') through Old Persian, which changed *z* into *d* (*musarū* > *muzrā* > *mudrā*)" (paraphrased by Eliade 1970, 405).

11. Monier-Williams 1974, 822.

12. See, e.g., Gonda 1972, 29, and Gray 2011, 425–26.

of different senses—in Indic religious traditions, including many forms of Hinduism and Buddhism, as well as Jainism. Some mudrās, considered especially important or "great," are referred to as *mahāmudrā*.

Seals and Great Seals in Hindu Traditions

In Hindu traditions, *mudrā* carries all of the meanings just mentioned and more. It is a particularly significant term in the Hindu tantric culture that flourished from the mid-first millennium CE onward, frequently intersecting with similar Buddhist and Jain cultures. For our purposes here, I would define *tantra* as "an esoteric tradition of thought and practice, rooted in South Asia, that requires empowerment by a qualified master and has as its aim the exercise of power over divinities to the point where one identifies one's own body, speech, and mind with one or more of those divinities and, in the end, transforms onself into one of those divinities." Visualizations, maṇḍalas or yantras, mudrās, mantras, and the manipulation of both external forces and energies found within a "subtle body" are part of most (but not all) tantric traditions, while sexual, scatological, morbid, and/or wrathful imagery, as well as transgressive behavior, occurs in some (but not all) tantric traditions. The presence of one or more of the above-listed elements in a tradition does not assure that it is "tantric" (for those elements are the common currency of many South Asian traditions), nor do all of the elements have to be present to assure that a tradition *is* tantric. Indeed, the efforts of traditional and modern scholars notwithstanding, there is no "essential" defining characteristic of tantra, merely a set of interlocking features like those listed above. In Hindu traditions generally regarded as tantric, four major usages of the term *mudrā* can be identified.

The first is its best known sense: as one of a multitude of hand gestures (or, secondarily, body positions), demonstrated by deities and employed in ritual by humans to effect certain ends. A clear account of the tantric sense of this is provided by Douglas Brooks:

> By showing the *mudrā*, the Tantric creates a physical manifestation and visual display of divine form; not only do *mudrās* give "shape" to the divine in a ritual context, they also provide a conceptual link to the qualities or attributes of divinity that are made part of the Tantric's personality. As the Tantric adept shows the *mudrā* in the course of contemplative worship (*upāsana*), he or she acquires the power associated with that particular aspect of divinity. The adept is said to achieve the level of realization with which the

> *mudrā* is associated. The *mudrā* literally "seals" the relationship between the adept and the deity invoked in the form of the *mudrā*.[13]

The second tantric usage of *mudrā* is as a type of fermented grain, cereal, or kidney bean employed in tantric rituals as one of the "five m's" (*pañcamakāra*) spurned by brahmans and used especially by tāntrikas of the "heroic" (*vīra*) type: liquor (*madya*), fish (*matsya*), meat (*māṃsa*), grain, cereal, or beans (*mudrā*), and copulation (*maithuna*). The *Mahānirvāṇa Tantra* specifies that this mudrā is of three kinds: superior, middling, and inferior: "The excellent and pleasing kind is that made from Shāli rice, white as a moon beam, or from barley or wheat, and which has been fried in clarified butter. The middling variety is made from fried paddy. Other kinds of fried grain are inferior."[14] In some sources, this type of mudrā is considered originally or primarily to have been fermented, hence to have intoxicating qualities;[15] in others, it consists of any savory treat.

The third tantric meaning of *mudrā*, found especially in Śākta systems that developed in Bengal and elsewhere, is as a synonym for *śakti*, in the specific sense of "the consort of a male adept, or the female counterpart of a male divinity."[16]

A fourth Hindu tantric usage of *mudrā* is as the clear, blissful awakened state of consciousness—that of Śiva—attained by the adept of Kashmir Śaivism, a tradition that arose around the same time as some of the later Buddhist tantric systems. Thus, the *Śiva Sūtra* (2:5) states, "When the knowledge connately inherent in one's own nature arises, [that is] Śiva's state—[the gesture of] the one who wanders in the sky of consciousness."[17] The commentator, Bhāskara, explains:

13. Brooks 1990, 59. Cf., e.g., Avalon 1972, xciv–xcv, Eliade 1970, 405–7, Gupta et al. 1979, 115–17, and Dyczkowski 1992a, 77–79. In his pioneering study of the topic, Saunders traces the phenomenon of the hand gesture back to, e.g., the Vedas and *Nāṭyaśāstra* but does not comment on the origins of the particular term *mudrā* (1960, 10–16).

14. Avalon 1972, 104.

15. See, e.g., Bharati 1970, 242ff.

16. Gray 2011, 426. Gray is drawing on the pioneering work of Gonda (1972). See also Gupta et al. 1972, 117.

17. Dyczkowski 1992a, xiv and 76. It is worth noting that the term *mudrā* does not actually appear in the original Sanskrit, which simply reads: *vidyāsamuttāne svabhāvike khecarī śivāvasthā*; a literal translation would be: "When intrinsic knowledge arises, that is skywalking, the state of Śiva." The *khecarī* is taken by virtually all commentators to refer to *khecarīmudrā*, the gesture or seal of skywalking, which is one of the most important of all tantric mudrās and has several different senses. As a physical gesture, it involves either (a) "turning the tongue backwards into

> Pure Knowledge is said to be the light of one's own nature (*svāloka*) which dawns when [the yogī] emerges from the higher stages of contemplation .... [At the same time] it is the uncreated and connate (*sahaja*) power ..., inherent in one's own nature. As it is such, the vitality of *Mudrā* expands within it. It is Śiva's state, called [the gesture of] "the one who wanders in the Sky of Consciousness" because it is risen ... in the sky of Śiva and because [it is the power of awareness] which moves ... in the expanse ... of the firmament of one's own consciousness. It is the dawn of realisation [in which the yogī perceives] his identity with [Śiva], the object of [his] meditation. And so, [this gesture] that possesses the contemplative absorption ... which penetrates into one's own nature, is Śiva's state.[18]

The addition to the term *mudrā* of the adjectival prefix *mahā*, or "great" (or a synonym), is relatively rare in Hindu contexts, but a number of instances, and several different usages, can be found. The most common sense of *mahāmudrā*, it would seem, is as a particular body position (*āsana*), especially important in the yoga traditions of Śākta tantrism. *Mahāmudrā* is described by Ajit Mookherjee as an *āsana* "in which the practitioner sits with the left heel pressed against the perineum (yoni-place) and the right leg stretched out, while holding the right foot with both hands."[19] It is one of a number of *śakticālanā* (energy-moving) mudrās[20] that "are combined with postures, breath-techniques and mantras to awaken Kuṇḍalinī."[21] According to Arthur Avalon, once the position has been assumed,

the throat, blocking the orifice of the nasal passages so that the nectar flowing down from the Sahāsrāra after the rise of Kuṇḍalinī is arrested" (Mookerjee 1983, 105; cf. Muller-Ortega 1989, 37–38, and Singh 1991, 73), or (b) turning the tongue back inside the cranium and directing the gaze between the eyebrows (Singh 1991, 73 and 76). As a meditation, it involves fixing the mind at the navel, then drawing it upward into the head, where it identifies with three *śaktis* (Singh 1991, 73). Finally, it may be taken as attainment itself, "that state in which the *yogī* remains in Śiva consciousness all the while, in which his consciousness moves in all beings" (Singh 1991, 73; cf. Muller-Ortega 1989, 190, and Dyczkowski 1987, 130–31); a term with similar connotations to this last usage is *jñānamudrā*, an "internal spiritual union" that is to be distinguished from *kriyāmudrā*, or actual ritual sexual intercourse (Abhinavagupta 1989, 209; cf. Avalon 1972, 79n4, where *jñānamudrā* is explained).

18. Dyczkowski 1992a, 77–78. Bracketed interpolations are in the original. "Connate" for *sahaja* here was changed from "innate" to conform to the terminology of the present volume.

19. Mookerjee 1983, 105.

20. The others are *vajroli, aśvinī, sahajoli, khecarī,* and *yoni.*

21. Mookerjee 1983, 32.

> Jālaṃdhara-Bandha[22] is then done. When Kuṇḍalinī is awakened, the Prāṇa [energy] enters the Suṣumnā [central channel], and Iḍā and Piṅgala [the left and right channels], now that Prāṇa has left them, become lifeless. Expiration should be done slowly, and the Mudrā should be practiced an equal number of times on the left and right sides of the body. This Mudrā, like other Haṭha-yoga Mudrās, is said to ward off death and disease.[23]

Swami Muktananda adds that, through *mahāmudrā*,

> all the *nadis* are activated and physical inertia dispelled. It aids the retention of semen. The body becomes calm and glowing, the digestive fire gets stronger, the senses become easier to control, and the process of aging is slowed down. When practiced constantly, it eradicates diseases such as tuberculosis, leprosy, piles, hernia, dyspepsia, and spleen trouble.[24]

In this sense, then, *mahāmudrā* is an important technique for dissolving vital winds into the central channel of the subtle body, a crucial step on nearly any tantric practitioner's path to liberation.

In Hindu tantra, *mahāmudrā* or one of its cognates may also refer to:

1. The "great vulva" (*mahāyoni*) found at the *śāktapīṭha* of Kāmākṣyā, in the Himalayas[25]
2. The supreme goddess of a tantric system, who is invoked so as to possess the disciple[26]
3. A consort for sexual yoga practice[27]

22. "Jālaṃdhara-Bandha is done by deep inspiration and then contraction of the thoracic region . . . , the chin being firmly held against the root of the neck at a distance of about four fingers . . . from the heart. This is said to bind the sixteen Ādharas, or vital centres, and the nectar . . . which flows from the cavity above the palate, and is also used to cause the breath to become Laya [dissolved] in the Suṣumnā. If the thoracic and perineal regions are simultaneously contracted, and Prāṇa is forced downward and Apāna upward, the Vāyu [wind] enters the Suṣumnā" (Avalon 1974, 210–11).

23. Avalon 1974, 208; see also plate XVI, facing page 489.

24. Muktananda 1978, 102.

25. Bhattacharya 2000, 284.

26. Gray 2011, 444.

27. Gray 2011, 426.

4. The "great seal" (*mahāmudrā*) that in some Kashmir Śaiva emanation schemes (e.g., that of Kṣemarāja) seals off, or blocks, the supreme experience of *śāṃbhavamudrā*, in which "the supernal 'nectar' of the paramount bliss of one's own nature flows uninterrupted 'from the ocean of consciousness,' which is the conscious nature consisting of the harmonious unity (*sāmarasya*) of Light and Bliss"[28]
5. The "supreme gesture" (*paramamudrā*) that in other Kashmir Śaiva systems (e.g., that of Utpaladeva's *Īśvarapratyabhijñā*) is the secret, internal experience of the perfected yogī "established on the plane of Bliss relishing the objects of sense that appear before him . . . the perfect and unobstructed expansion of the Awakened"[29]
6. The "great gesture" (*mahatīmudrā*) that in still other Kashmir Śaiva authors (e.g., Maheśvarānanda) is the subsumption of physical gestures to the process of yogic reflection (*rāva*) and "the intuition (*parāmarśa*) of one's own nature [that] is the supreme worship"[30]

In brief, we see that both *mudrā* and *mahāmudrā* (or its cognates) came to have a wide range of meanings in Hindu—and especially Hindu tantric—traditions, from such relatively "concrete" (though still symbolic and transformative) referents as a kind of grain, a hand gesture, a bodily posture, a goddess, or a consort for sexual yoga to rather more abstract associations with advanced states of awareness involving luminosity, bliss, and an understanding of the true nature of self, consciousness, and reality. Many of these usages are shared by Hindu and Buddhist traditions alike. Of those mentioned, Buddhists will come to speak of *mudrā/mahāmudrā* in terms of (a) hand gestures that seal one's identification with a deity, (b) goddesses and human female consorts, and (c) the nature of reality and/or a blissful and luminous awareness that is the true nature of mind. Buddhists less often use the terms to refer to forbidden grains or specific bodily postures. Although the very earliest usages of *mudrā* probably are Hindu (or proto-Hindu), the provenance of *mahāmudrā* is very much in doubt—there being no certainty that the earliest Hindu usages of then term predate its first appearances in Buddhist texts. In any case, it is within Buddhism that discourse on mahāmudrā became most prominent, and—with these Hindu echoes still in mind—it is to Buddhist discussions of seals and great seals that we now turn.

28. Dyczkowski 1992b, 61–62.

29. Dyczkowski 1987, 95.

30. Dviveda 1992, 129.

Seals and Great Seals in Sūtra-Based Buddhism

There is general agreement among traditional Tibetan scholars, as well as modern researchers, that although Foundational[31] and Mahāyāna Buddhist literature are replete with references to *mudrā*, the term *mahāmudrā* does not appear in the Buddhist sūtras and is, rather, a product of the tantras. In Pāli Buddhist literature (ca. 300 BCE–400 CE), *muddā* is used primarily to mean either a seal as a physical implement, such as a royal seal (*rājamuddā*), a method of calculation using the fingers, or signs that may be communicated manually, as sign language (*hatthamuddā*).[32] In nontantric Sanskrit Buddhist literature (especially of the early centuries CE), it may refer to finger calculation, a coin, or an unspecified high number,[33] as well as the hand gesture employed by a buddha, bodhisattva, or deity, but its primary usage, again, seems to be as a seal, albeit sometimes in a less than concrete sense. The literature of the Great Vehicle, the Mahāyāna, uses the term *mudrā* in a number a creative ways, some of which prefigure meanings that *mahāmudrā* will come to have later on. Thus, the *Questions of Sāgaramati Sūtra* (*Sāgaramatiparipṛcchāsūtra*) describes all phenomena—dharmas[34]—as being "marked by the seal of intrinsic freedom . . . the seal of sameness."[35] The *Questions of Gaganagañja Sūtra* (*Gaganagañjaparipṛchhāsūtra*) gives a list of ten seals, those of (1) the tathāgata, (2) nonarising, (3) emptiness, (4) signlessness, (5) wishlessness, (6) uncompoundedness, (7) nonattachment, (8) suchness, (9) the utmost limit, and

31. I use this term in preference to the pejorative Hīnayāna, the restrictive Śrāvakayāna, or such alternative English terms as Early Buddhism, Nikāya Buddhism, or Mainstream Buddhism—each of which, I feel, poses nearly as many problems as it solves. It is worth noting that the Mahāyāna Buddhist traditions of East and Inner Asia preserve many of the Foundational works in their canons.

32. Rhys Davids and Stede 1994, 538.

33. Edgerton 1972, 2:435.

34. *Dharma/dharmas* is a difficult term. Here, I will retain the Sanskrit term (now an English term) where it refers to the Buddha's or some other master's teaching, or simply to the truth. Where it refers, however, to the constituent categories into which reality may be analyzed (e.g., the five aggregates, the six senses and their objects, minds and mental events, nonassociated compositional factors, various types of cessation, etc.), I will generally translate it as "phenomena," though sometimes—especially in poetic contexts—I render it as "things," in the sense of objects "that one need not, cannot, or does not wish to give a specific name to" (https://en.oxforddictionaries.com/definition/thing); one could, of course, give them names if one so chose.

35. *SPS* 120a.

(10) space.[36] A famous (and sometimes misquoted) passage in the *King of Concentrations Sūtra* (*Samādhirājasūtra*) asserts, "the concentration called 'the proclamation of the essential sameness (*samatā*) of all phenomena' . . . is the seal of all phenomena (*mudrā sarvadharmāṇām*)."[37] Other sūtras mention the "seal of emptiness," the "seal of awareness," or the "seal of realities."[38] In other contexts Buddhist scholars developed a list of four "seals" of the Buddhist teaching: all contaminated entities are unsatisfactory, all compounded phenomena are impermanent, all phenomena are empty, and nirvāṇa is peace. The third and fourth seals clearly are consonant with the "ultimate" seals mentioned in the sūtras and implicitly indicate some of the referents to which the term *mahāmudrā* eventually would be applied.

Quite apart from ultimate-level usages of *mudrā* in sūtra literature, many Tibetan authors regarded the entire sūtra-based tradition—both the Foundational Vehicle and the Great Vehicle or Perfection Vehicle (*pāramitāyāna*)—as replete with ideas that later would be intrinsic to conceptions of mahāmudrā. To the degree that, eventually, *mahāmudrā* came to connote understanding of and meditation upon the empty, luminous, nondual nature of mind, virtually any sūtra-tradition passage that refers to lack of self, voidness, or simply the nature of mind may be read as "about" mahāmudrā. Thus, mahāmudrā may be seen in anything from Foundational Buddhist passages asserting that we neither are nor possess a permanent self, to the discourse on emptiness in the Perfection of Wisdom sūtras and the treatises of Nāgārjuna and other Mādhyamikas; from the *Dhammapada*'s opening statement that "phenomena are preceded by mind, they are founded on mind, they are composed of mind,"[39] to the Yogācāra school's claim that "all the three worlds are mind-only";[40] from the *Aṅguttara Nikāya*'s oft-echoed claim that mind by nature is luminous and its defilements merely incidental,[41] to Mahāyāna texts on buddha nature that describe permanence, purity, bliss, and selfhood intrin-

36. *GPS* 363b–364a.

37. *SRS*s 4–6. The passage sometimes is read by Tibetan authors as containing the term *mahāmudrā*, but it is present in neither the Sanskrit nor the Tibetan versions of the sūtra available to me. Cf. below, note 1501.

38. For some references, see Dakpo Tashi Namgyal 1986, 97–98.

39. *DHP* vv. 1–2, pp. 1–2.

40. *BAS ga*:145b; see also Vasubandhu's famous assertion, at the outset of his *Twenty Verses* (*Viṃśatikā*), to the effect that "[All] this is indeed only consciousness because of the appearance in it of nonexistent objects"; Vb*SK* verse 1, p. 122; trans. Tola and Dragonetti 2004, 134.

41. *AN* 1.52; trans., e.g., Bodhi 2012, 97.

sic to awareness at its deepest level;[42] from accounts in the early sūtras of such "formless" contemplative states as infinite space, infinite consciousness, nothing whatsoever, and neither perception nor nonperception, to descriptions in Mahāyāna sūtras and treatises of the practice of nonduality in view, meditation, and action.

Tantric Buddhism

However much an implicit discussion of mahāmudrā may be read *ex post facto* into the literature of Foundational and Mahāyāna Buddhism, it is only in the texts of that branch of the Mahāyāna variously called the Secret Mantra Vehicle (*guhyamantrayāna*), the Mantra Way (*mantranaya*), or the Vajra Vehicle (*vajrayāna*), that the term *mahāmudrā* actually appears. The tantric tradition, whose articulation in India dates roughly to the last half of the first millennium CE, is set off from other forms of Buddhism by its intense focus on a combination of ritual and gnostic practices that are intended to swiftly transform a practitioner into a fully awakened buddha by "taking the goal as path": becoming buddha by first *seeing* oneself as buddha and identifying oneself with buddha in every thought, word, and deed, then *being* buddha through transforming one's ordinary psychophysical being into the body and mind of an awakened being. One achieves this above all through the mediating figure of the tantric guru, who gives one access to, and instruction on, (a) a particular lineage of teachings traced back to the Buddha, or *a* buddha, and (b) a range of buddha deities, the practice of whose rituals and meditations become the vehicle for one's own awakening. The ritual context in which the guru—in exchange for pledges of secrecy and loyalty—grants the qualified disciple access to the buddha deity is a formal consecration, initiation, or empowerment (*abhiṣeka*) that enables him or her to practice the contemplative ritual (*sādhana*) of the particular buddha deity that is the focus of the rite, such as Avalokiteśvara, Tārā, or Hevajra.

It is important to stress that tantric empowerment only is conferred upon *qualified* disciples. A "qualified" disciple is, in principle, one who already has internalized the basic ideas and values of Foundational and Mahāyāna Buddhism. Like Foundational Buddhist aspirants to arhatship, they must:

- Acknowledge that the mind is a primary and potent force in the cosmos, and that its training is central to the spiritual path

42. See, e.g., *SSS* 445b; translated at Wayman and Wayman 1974, 102; cf. *RGV* verses 1 and 37–38.

- Recognize the essential cosmological distinction between the repeated, unsatisfactory series of rebirths that is saṃsāra and the undecaying bliss of nirvāṇa, and key their practice to the four noble truths:
  - There is *suffering*, whether through birth, sickness, aging, dying, separation from the pleasant, encounter with the unpleasant, or not getting what one wants.
  - There are *causes* for suffering, often condensed to the three poisons—ignorance, desire, and anger—of which ignorance is usually regarded as the most basic.
  - There is a *cessation* of suffering, nirvāṇa, which may be experienced in the world or attained utterly beyond it.
  - There is a *path* to the cessation of suffering, which may be divided in a number of ways, including into the three trainings in morality, concentration, and wisdom.
- Aspire to eliminate defilements (such as the three poisons) and unskillful actions (*karma*), so as to eliminate the saṃsāric suffering that results from these
- Assiduously practice morality, concentration, and wisdom in pursuit of liberation from saṃsāra
- Attain the transformative realization that no person anywhere possesses a permanent, partless, independent self

And, like Mahāyāna bodhisattvas, they must:

- Acknowledge the fundamental purity and power of the mind as enshrined in the concept of buddha nature, the notion that all beings have the capacity to become buddhas
- Aspire to full buddhahood, a state in which one not only transcends defilement and suffering but possesses three (or four) "bodies":
  - A Dharma body (*dharmakāya*) that involves direct, simultaneous, and nonconceptual apprehension of ultimate reality (*dharmatā*) *and* complete omniscience, along with limitless compassion and knowledge of the skillful means (*upāyakauśalya*) through which one might help suffering beings
  - An enjoyment body (*saṃbhogakāya*), a glorified, subtle form through which one may give Mahāyāna teachings to high-level bodhisattvas in a pure realm until saṃsāra ends (if, in fact, it ever ends)
  - An emanation body (*nirmāṇakāya*), which may appear in various guises (including that of the historical Śākyamuni Buddha) in order to assist and enlighten ordinary beings

  - A nature body (*svabhāvikakāya*), which may be regarded as the unity of the three other bodies or, in certain cases, simply as the empty aspect of the Dharma body
- Develop and express confidence in the Buddha and his Dharma, in part through such virtuous activities as going on pilgrimage, circumambulating holy objects, reciting and copying sūtras, and practicing the sevenfold worship rite or seven-limbed pūjā (*saptāṅgapūjā*), consisting of prostration, offering, confession, rejoicing in the virtues of awakened and ordinary beings, entreating the buddhas not to disappear into nirvāṇa, requesting them to turn the wheel of Dharma, and dedication of merit
- Pursue the path to buddhahood not only for the sake of one's own awakening but for the awakening of all sentient beings (*bodhicitta*), making it the basis for mastering the perfections (*pāramitā*) of generosity, morality, patience, effort, concentration, and wisdom, and ascending through the various paths and levels of the bodhisattva
- Develop a range of skillful techniques for compassionately teaching and helping others (*upāyakauśalya*)
- Attain the transformative realization of emptiness (*śūnyatā*), whether understood (as in the Madhyamaka school) as the lack of intrinsic existence that is the ultimate nature of all persons and phenomena, or (as in some Yogācāra traditions) as external objects' lack of difference from the mind that perceives them, or (as in other Yogācāra and buddha-nature traditions) as the mind's essential purity and luminosity, which is empty of any defilements but implicitly contains all the qualities of Buddhahood

In any case, the sādhana practice that follows upon empowerment generally entails the dissolution of the world and one's ordinary appearance into emptiness, after which the world is reconstituted as a divine abode, or maṇḍala, with oneself as a buddha deity at the center of that maṇḍala. In many traditions, the three basic stages of generating oneself as a deity—reduction of one's ordinary appearance to emptiness, generation of a "seed" syllable/sound from emptiness, and generation of the deity's luminous form from the seed syllable—are said, respectively, to purify the three "existential events" (death, intermediate existence, and rebirth) and to prefigure the attainment of the Dharma body, enjoyment body, and emanation body of a buddha. After one's self-generation as the deity, the maṇḍala is populated by a range of other deities that represent the enlightened transformation of various aspects of one's psychophysical being: aggregates, physical elements, senses, body parts, bodily functions, and so forth. Situated at the center of the maṇḍala, one utters the mantra of oneself as the central deity, then those of the surrounding deities, in the process sending out purifying and illuminating light-rays to all sentient beings, who are visualized as being cleansed and awakened, then as absorbing into oneself. As part of sādhana practice, one develops "divine pride" in one's identity as a buddha deity and tries in all circumstances to imagine one's surroundings as a maṇḍala or pure land, see other beings as deities, hear and speak all sounds as mantras, and think all thoughts as a buddha would—to the degree that a buddha "thinks" at all. In some tantric systems, especially earlier ones, mastery of the sādhana, with its range of contemplative and ritual procedures, may lead to buddhahood.

In the later, more esoteric, tantric systems, sādhana, called the "generation stage" (*utpattikrama*), is merely preliminary to a "completion" or "perfection" stage (*saṃpannkrama*) that involves manipulation and transformation of various physical and mental elements within a subtle body (*sukṣmaśarīra*) or diamond body (*vajrakāya*) consisting of channels, vital winds, and drops (*nāḍī-prāṇa-bindu*), and the wheel-like channel intersections known as *cakras*. The empowerment that is the basis for practice at these more advanced levels is typically fourfold, involving:

1. The *vase* (*kalaśa*) empowerment, in which the disciple is purified by contact with various consecrated substances, among them a vase of sanctified water. This purifies the disciple's body and their rebirth process, enables them to practice the generation stage, and sows the seeds for their attainment of the emanation body of a buddha.
2. The *secret* (*guhya*) empowerment, in which the guru enters into sexual union either with their own consort or with the disciple's consort and offers the disciple a taste of the resulting sexual fluids, which induce an experience of great bliss. This purifies the disciple's speech and their intermediate-state process, enables them to reach the illusory-body phase of the completion stage, and sows the seeds for their attainment of the enjoyment body of a buddha.
3. The *wisdom-gnosis* (*prajñajñāna*) empowerment, in which the disciple enters into sexual union with his own or the guru's consort and experiences four levels of progressively greater joy, which culminate in a state of great bliss that is connate (*sahaja*) with wisdom realizing the nature of reality. This purifies the disciple's mind and their death process, enables them to reach the luminosity phase of the completion stage, and sows the seeds for their attainment of the Dharma body of a buddha.
4. The *fourth* (*turiya*) or *word* (*śabda*) empowerment, in which the guru offers the disciple instruction on the nature of reality and/or

> the mind, which induces in the disciple a profound realization of that reality. This purifies the disciple's body, speech, and mind all at once, enables them to attain the union phase of the completion stage, and sows the seeds for their attainment of the nature body or, alternatively, the great-bliss body (*mahāsukhakāya*) of a buddha.[43]

In these highly esoteric traditions, such basic forces as sexual desire, anger, and even death itself may be harnessed toward spiritual ends, and the literature related to the traditions is replete with transgressive rhetoric and descriptions of countercultural performance or conduct (*caryā*), which may include inhabiting charnel grounds, consorting with low-caste women, wearing bone ornaments, behaving as if mad, and singing and dancing at tantric ritual feasts (*gaṇacakra*). There has been much debate among modern scholars as to whether such practices are a sign of Buddhism's degeneracy in its late phases in India, an indication that the tantras are motivated by religious and social protest, or, in fact, a carefully controlled phase of tantric practice that does little to undermine orthodoxy.[44] Completion-stage yogas include practices—some of them requiring a sexual consort—aimed at producing such experiences as inner heat (*caṇḍalī*), the four joys (*caturānanda*), luminosity (*prabhāsvara*),[45] the illusory body (*māyādeha*), and the gnosis of inseparable bliss and emptiness. These practices eventually were codified under such titles as the five stages of Guhyasamāja, the six Dharmas of Nāropa, or the six yogas of Kālacakra.[46] All of them require the practitioner to direct the vital winds from the "outer" channels of the subtle body to the central channel (*avadhūti*)—where one moves the winds up and down through the cakras, manipulating the various drops that are found there, producing experiences of supernal joy and

43. For discussion of these empowerments, see, e.g., Snellgrove 1987, 1:213–77, Lessing and Wayman 1978, 309–37, Panchen Sonam Dragpa 2006, 77–84, and Williams and Tribe 2000, 231–35. At some point, possibly in India and certainly in Tibet, enactments of the sexual elements in these ceremonies became for the most part imaginative rather than embodied.

44. See, e.g., R. Jackson 1996, Davidson 2002a, chaps. 5–7, and Wedemeyer 2013.

45. The Sanskrit *prabhāsvara* is best translated as "luminosity" or "radiant light." The Tibetan *'od gsal* can be, and often is, translated as "clear light," but here I will generally maintain the translation that is closest to the sense of the Sanskrit term.

46. According to Tibetan tradition (which differs slightly from the Indian on the nomenclature), the five stages of Guhyasamāja are isolated speech, isolated mind, illusory body, luminosity (or clear light), and union. The six Dharmas of Nāropa are usually identified as inner heat, illusory body, dream yoga, luminosity, intermediate state, and transfer of consciousness. The six yogas of Kālacakra are individual withdrawal, absorption, breath control, retention, recollection, and concentration.

realizations of emptiness, and, in the end, purifying the subtlest basis of one's mental and physical being (located at the heart cakra) and transforming them into, respectively, the Dharma body and form body (or bodies) of a buddha, thereby completing the tantric path. It should be noted that in later Indic and in Tibetan tantric traditions, the mind's blissful realization of its own natural luminosity and/or emptiness during the completion stage often came to be synonymous with mahāmudrā, as was the state of buddhahood that ensued from completion-stage practices.

Mahāmudrā in the "Lower" Buddhist Tantras

It is difficult to know precisely where and when the term *mahāmudrā* first appeared, because the historiographical problems endemic to the study of Indian Buddhism in general pertain to the tantric traditions as well. Any relative chronology, let alone firm dating, of tantric literature still is quite tentative.[47] What little solidity it has comes through piecemeal evidence provided by, for instance, linguistic analysis, quotation of one text by another, stray historical references, the existence of an early Tibetan translation in the caves at Dunhuang, or the date of a Chinese translation where there is one (most of the later tantric material, unfortunately, was not translated into Chinese). One reasonable—if far from foolproof—approach to a chronology of Indian Buddhist tantra assumes that it may *roughly* correspond to the different types of tantric systems that eventually were identified by a few Indian scholars and later by many Tibetan ones. These systems, which seem to show "development" from more external, ritualized, and purificatory practices to those that are increasingly internal, gnostic, and transformational, have been arranged in various ways; one useful sequence, frequently discussed by modern scholars, involves the classes of tantra known as action (*kriyā*), performance (*caryā*), yoga, mahāyoga, and yoginī.[48] Generally speaking, the first three classes contain "early" tantras, composed before the end of the eighth century, while the last two contain "later" tantras, mostly dating from the eighth through eleventh centuries. In outlining the history of mahāmudrā in India, I will—with due acknowledgment of their artificiality and arbitrariness—employ these five categories and two phases.

47. See, e.g., Nakamura 1987, chap. 6, Williams and Tribe 2000, chap. 7, Davidson 2002a, chap. 4, Harper and Brown 2002, Samuel 2008, chap. 9, and Gray 2016.

48. The last two roughly correspond to the unexcelled-yoga-tantra categories of "father" and "mother" tantras recognized by such Tibetan New Translation (*gsar ma*) traditions as the Kagyü, Sakya, and Geluk.

Most of the texts classified as action and performance tantras have as their focus the service of and identification with one or another buddha, bodhisattva, or deity, primarily of peaceful disposition.[49] Action and performance tantras contain copious references to and descriptions of mudrās as hand gestures, but they rarely, if ever, mention mahāmudrā. Perhaps the earliest tantra in which the term occurs is the massive *Root Tantra of Mañjuśrī* (*Mañjuśrīmūlakalpa*), often classed as an action tantra.[50] There, the great seal refers principally to a "five-peaked" (*pañcasikhā*) ritual hand-position, that of Mañjuśrī himself, which signifies the attainment of all mundane and ultimate aims.[51] In chapter 36, eight mahāmudrās are listed:

1. The mahāmudrā of the Dharma wheel of the Blessed One
2. The mudrā of the buddhas' conquest of all obstructors
3. The mahāmudrā called the buddhas' non-arousing of all defilements
4. The mudrā of the great compassion of all the buddhas
5. The mahāmudrā called "raising the spear against all views"
6. The mahāmudrā called "the attainment of all spells"
7. The mahāmudrā called "the pacifier of all disasters"
8. The mahāmudrā called "fortunate"[52]

Chapters 43–46 of the *Root Tantra*[53] are explicitly devoted to mahāmudrā, which is not only taken there as the five-peaked mudrā but, more abstractly, associated with various ultimate notions, such as no-self, emptiness, and the gnosis of the buddha, and described as "the highest Dharma, undeclining, the highest step" (43:22).[54] In a subsequent but still relatively early tantra, *Chanting the Names of Mañjuśrī* (*Mañjuśrīnāmasaṅgīti*), variously classed as a performance tantra, yoga tantra, or mahāyoga tantra,[55] mahāmudrā is identified as one of six great buddha families (3:2), that associated with the tathāgata Amoghasiddhi, master of the all-accomplishing wisdom, who is described

49. See, e.g., Tsongkhapa 1977 and Tsongkhapa 1981.

50. For a brief discussion of mahāmudra in the *Root Tantra of Mañjuśrī*, see Wallis 2002, 238–39n49, and Hartzell 2012, 139–40. It is likely that the text was composed over the course of many decades, if not centuries, and that different strands of tantric thought and practice have been woven into it.

51. *MMK* 17, line 32; cf. Wallis 2002, 189 and 238–39n49.

52. See, e.g., *MMK* 303, lines 8–16.

53. *MMK* 369–401; cf. Hartzell 2012, 139–40.

54. *MMK* 370.

55. Davidson (1981, 2) argues that its strongest affinity is with the latter. See also Tribe 2016.

elsewhere as "avoiding all imagination; whose incessant realm is without constructive thought; the unchanging supreme Dharma realm (*dharmadhātu*)" (6:15).[56] We see, then, that even in some of the earliest Buddhist tantras, *mahāmudrā* bears multiple significations. It may be a hand gesture or a buddha family, but it also evokes the true nature of reality and the supreme attainment at the end of the path—though its bearing on questions of ultimate reality and knowledge is less obvious in these texts than it will be later on.

In the yoga tantras[57]—which form the core of the esoteric Buddhist traditions of East Asia but also were influential in the early period of Buddhism in Tibet—mahāmudrā takes on further associations. It still may be regarded simply as a symbolic hand gesture (such as the "vajra fist"), and in the root tantra of the class, the *Compendium of the Realities of All the Tathāgatas* (*Sarvatathāgatatattvasaṃgraha*), it is used, perhaps for the first time, to refer to goddesses and female consorts.[58] The major contribution of the yoga tantras to mahāmudrā discourse, however, lies first in its tendency to define the term primarily in terms of the clear visualization of oneself as a buddha deity and second in its inclusion of the term into a scheme of four mudrās—the great seal (*mahāmudrā*), pledge seal (*samayamudrā*), Dharma seal (*dharmamudrā*), and action seal (*karmamudrā*)—each of which involves particular hand gestures and mantras, and each of which is associated with a particular (a) buddha family, (b) tathāgata, (c) maṇḍala, (d) basis of purification, (e) defilement to be purified, and (f) buddha gnosis. In the *Compendium of the Realities of All the Tathāgatas*, the seals are arrayed as follows:

1. The great seal is primarily the process and product of visualizing a buddha deity, or oneself in the form of a buddha deity; it is associated with (a) the tathāgata family, (b) Vairocana, (c) the "great" maṇḍala, (d) the body, (e) the defilement of desire, and (f) the mirror-like gnosis.
2. The pledge seal involves visualizing the deity through certain meaningful symbols (such as a sword or lotus); it is associated with (a) the vajra family, (b) Akṣobhya, (c) the "retention" maṇḍala, (d) the mind, (e) the defilement of anger, and (f) the gnosis of equality.
3. The Dharma seal involves visualizing the maṇḍala deities within their symbols on their respective thrones; it is associated with (a) the

56. *MNS* 65, 78.

57. For a Tibetan summary of the principles and practices of the yoga tantras, see, e.g., Tsongkhapa 2005b.

58. Gray 2011, 451–52.

lotus family, (b) Amitābha, (c) the "doctrine" maṇḍala, (d) speech, (e) the defilement of wrong view, and (f) the discriminating gnosis.

4. The action seal involves seeing the peripheral deities in the maṇḍala as offering goddesses; it is associated with (a) the jewel and action families, (b) correspondingly, Ratnasambhava and Amoghasiddhi, (c) the "action" maṇḍala, (d) activities, (e) the defilement of miserliness, and (f) the all-accomplishing gnosis.[59]

As Jacob Dalton notes, a key point emerging from the *Compendium*'s four-mudrā scheme is that there, because of its association with the Buddha's mind, the pledge seal is the most important of the set, while the great seal, associated with the Buddha's body, is less vital—an order of priority that will be reversed in later tantric theory, where mahāmudrā comes to be associated with ultimate reality and the ultimate attainment, buddha mind.[60]

Other yoga tantras, such as the *Vajra Peak* (*Vajraśekhara*), *Conquest of the Three Worlds* (*Trailokyavijaya*), and the *Purification of All the Lower Realms* (*Sarvadurgatipariśodhana*), lay out the scheme in slightly different ways, but in each case, *mahāmudrā* denotes the clear visualization of the bodily form of a maṇḍala deity, usually accompanied by a hand gesture and mantras.[61] The *Conquest of the Three Worlds* adds, "Like a high edict with the king's seal that should not be broken and is difficult to contradict, the symbolic form of a great spirit is *mudrā*. . . . This feature of all *mudrā* arises through the yoga of the mental image of the vajra of body, speech, and mind. . . . Ultimate reality is *mudrā*."[62]

While certain texts within the earlier tantric systems—the action, performance, and yoga tantras—already demonstrate a complex notion of mahāmudrā, such that it may refer to a hand gesture, a buddha family, a goddess, the visualization of a deity, one of a set of four interrelated seals, or the ultimate attainment at the culmination of the path, it is probably fair to say that the predominant usages of the term in these early texts were related to the employment of hand gestures and the clear visualization of deities, which were believed to help effect one's ultimate transformation into a buddha.

59. Tsongkhapa 2005b, 31–32; on the *Compendium*, see also Kwon 2002.

60. See Dalton 2019.

61. For the *Vajra Peak*, see Giebel 2001, 11 and 84–97; for the *Purification*, see Skorupski 1983, 22–25. See also Saunders 1960, 36, and Gray 2011, 427–34.

62. Gray 2011, 431–32.

Mahāmudrā in the Mahāyoga and Yoginī Tantras

The mahāyoga tantras, most of which were likely composed between the late seventh and mid-ninth centuries, are the first set of tantras to focus strongly on practices using sexual desire, anger, and other "negative" forces. Together with the still later yoginī tantras, they form the most esoteric—and for Tibetans, the "highest"—corpus of Indian Buddhist tantras, which are distinguished by their elaborate visualizations and maṇḍala rituals (what came to be known as the generation stage) and their intricate meditations within the subtle body (what came to be known as the completion stage). As noted above, these practices are typically preceded by a set of four empowerments. The vase empowerment empowers the disciple to practice the generation stage, and the secret, wisdom-gnosis, and fourth (or word) empowerments empower them to practice various aspects of the completion stage. In the secret empowerment, the disciple experienced great bliss by ingesting the sexual secretions produced by the guru's intercourse with the consort, while in the wisdom-gnosis empowerment great bliss was induced in the disciple through their own intercourse with the consort. The fourth empowerment, by contrast, involves transmission of transcendental awareness through an understanding of emptiness. In Nyingma schemes, the mahāyoga and yoginī tantras correspond, respectively, to the "inner" tantras of mahāyoga and anuyoga, beyond which lies the highest teaching, atiyoga. In the New Translation schemes, they roughly correspond, respectively, to the father (or method) and mother (or wisdom, or yoginī) tantras of the unexcelled yoga tantra, the culmination of a fourfold classification that begins with action, performance, and yoga tantras. The mahāyoga and yoginī tantras both show evidence of Śaiva influences, though they bend the originally Hindu images, myths, and symbols very much to Buddhist purposes.

In the mahāyoga tantras, we see clear signs that mahāmudrā's web of signification is shifting from the realm of hand gestures and visualized deities to themes at once more transgressive and more transcendental. Although in the *Net of Illusion* (*Māyājāla*) collection, mahāmudrā once again primarily signifies the clear visualization of oneself as a buddha/deity, a number of other mahāyoga tantras pick up on the sexual themes that had appeared spottily, or not at all, in the action, performance, and yoga tantras. For instance, the *Mantra Ritual Section of the Supreme Primordial One* (*Śrīparamādyamantrakalpakhaṇḍa*) refers to mudrās as goddesses/consorts to be evoked by ritual practices,[63] and mahāmudrā as an epithet for the consort

63. Gray 2011, 453.

of the central deity of the tantra's maṇḍala, Paramādya[64]—but also as ultimate reality itself, which must be contemplated before the creation of the tantra's maṇḍala.[65] Similarly, a mahāyoga tantra closely related to the *Net of Illusion*, the *Secret Essence* (*Guhyagarbha*)—which is highly important in the Nyingma tradition—also associates mahāmudrā with a sexual consort and suggests as well that it may be equated, in a "gnostic" sense, with the highest realization and attainment of the tantric path.[66] The most influential mahāyoga tantra, the *Guhyasamāja* (*Secret Assembly*)—which actually specifies (17.46) that those who desire awakening should *not* perform mudrās with the hands[67]—refers to *mahāmudrā* as a consort (*mudrā*) for the practice of sexual yoga and as the realization ensuing from that practice (10.21); a contemplation-recitation that leads to attainment of the vajra body, speech, and mind of the tathāgatas (11.1–3); or the essence of the vows of the tathāgatas, meditation on which assures buddhahood (17.45).[68] Although it does not refer directly to mahāmudrā, the second chapter of the *Guhyasamāja* is devoted to a discussion of the awakening mind (*bodhicitta*), which is, like mahāmudrā, taken to be the "essence" of the vajra body, speech, and mind of the tathāgatas (2.1). This awakening mind is described as beyond meditation; pure in essence; space-like; free from thought or its objects; the way to awakening in which there is no awakening; beyond the aggregates, sense fields, and elements; identical with the lack of self in phenomena; eternally unarisen; and in the nature of emptiness (2.3–4).[69] Though it is implicit and somewhat tentative, the *Guhyasamāja*'s linkage between mahāmudrā and ultimate realization presages the even greater significance that the term will assume in the yoginī tantras.

The yoginī tantras, the last major class of tantras to emerge in India (starting around the ninth century), aim to produce a blissful, nondual gnosis through (a) worship of and identification with female (and male) deities in their maṇḍalas (the generation stage), (b) meditations centered in the channels and cakras of the subtle body (the completion stage), and (c) the practice of sexual yoga and other unconventional types of behavior (*caryā*, or tantric performance). It is in the yoginī tantras that *mahāmudrā* becomes a term of central ritual, philosophical, and soteriological importance. In the systems based

64. Gray 2011, 457.

65. Gray 2011, 460–61.

66. See, e.g., Dalton 2019.

67. *GST* 388, trans. 130.

68. *GST* 240, trans. 58; 242, trans. 59; 388, trans. 130.

69. *GST* 190–92, trans. 34–36.

on such tantras as the *Cakrasaṃvara* (*Pledge Wheel*), *Hevajra*, and *Kālacakra* (*Wheel of Time*), it still may be seen as one of three or four mudrās that "seal" tantric experiences, but it now usually is the most important in the sequence, the great seal that betokens a full understanding of the nature of reality. At the same time, *mahāmudrā* in the yoginī tantras increasingly is treated on its own, referring sometimes to a goddess to be invoked, sometimes to a consort in sexual yoga, sometimes to the gnostic great bliss ensuing from that practice, and sometimes to the ultimate reality, emptiness—experience of which is inseparable from great bliss.[70]

The yoginī tantra generally regarded as the earliest, the *Union of All the Buddhas* (*Sarvabuddhasamāyoga*), does not refer to mahāmudrā but clearly associates the term *mudrā* with consorts and the goddesses they symbolize, asserting that "Through this mudrā, the yogī / goes, comes, and flies as he pleases." Further, and a bit more abstractly,

> Women . . . are the supreme treasure,
> enjoying everything, of the substance of space.
> Through uniting yourself to the insubstantial,
> you become equal to space
> and always will accomplish
> the supreme bliss of the ḍākinīs' magic.[71]

In the *Cakrasaṃvara Tantra*, *mahāmudrā* is mentioned in the context of the "most accomplished great seal" (*adhisiddhā mahāmudrā*)—that is, a sexual consort—who is deserving of worship.[72]

In the *Hevajra Tantra*, it is a synonym for emptiness (1:10.20), a consort for sexual yoga (2:8.1–5), the bliss arising from sexual yoga (2:4.50), an empowerment that produces great bliss (2:2.31), and the "eternal state" that is the goal of tantric practice (1:8.43), the final achievement of the mind of connate and inseparable bliss and emptiness (2:8.5).[73]

70. For a detailed analysis of the yoginī tantras that focuses on mahāmudrā as consort, see Gray 2011.

71. *SBS* 282a; cf. trans. Gray 2011, 471.

72. Gray 2007, 306. Chapter 40 of the tantra (327–28) is called "The Procedures of Subjugating the Five Social Classes, and Mahāmudrā." Its actual content, however, is focused solely on the former topic; it contains no material suggesting any of the commonly known meanings of *mahāmudrā*.

73. *HVT* 1:2.36, trans. 1:116; 1:2.88–90, trans. 1:105; 1:2.68, trans. 1:91; 1:2.48, trans. 1:77; 1:2.90, trans. 1:116, respectively.

In the *Buddha Skull Tantra* (*Buddhakapālatantra*), *mahāmudrā* refers primarily to a consort for sexual yoga practice[74] but also may denote the culmination of the tantric path, buddhahood, which is in part conferred by the consort.[75] The combination of the two is neatly summarized in a verse that reads:

> By that very caressing and thrusting,
> one will also see the great seal;
> those who meditate thusly
> will accomplish it right here, no doubt![76]

Finally, in the *Kālacakra Tantra*, mahāmudrā is the inexpressible, unchanging bliss transcending other mudrās (1.12), as well as the empty-form buddha-aspect in which one awakens (1.15) and the final attainment (*siddhi*) that is the gnosis of buddhahood (1.41).[77] The notion of a fruitional "attainment of mahāmudrā" (*mahāmudrāsiddhi*) would become prevalent in later Indian tantric discourse and carry over to Tibetan Buddhism as well. David Gray well summarizes the complexity of mahāmudrā in the yoginī tantras when he writes, "*mahāmudrā* ultimately becomes the *mudrā* qua consort qua symbol; it is the realization of ultimate reality, or *buddhajñāna*, as symbolized by the goddess Prajñāpāramitā, who in turn is reflected in . . . various other goddesses, and ultimately in the woman who serves as a consort."[78]

The mahāyoga and yoginī tantras spawned an immense commentarial literature, including "explanatory tantras" (*vyākhyātantra*), in which the Buddha purportedly clarifies the obscurities of the root tantras (*mūlatantra*). Composed later than the root tantras, these texts often reflected an era in which mahāmudrā had gained greater currency, and so they tended to focus on the term even more strongly. In the widely read Cakrasaṃvara-based *Arising of the Pledge Tantra* (*Saṃvarodayatantra*), for instance, *mahāmudrā* is "the clear and perfect awakening to great bliss" (3:16).[79] In a Hevajra-related tantra called the *Drop of Mahāmudrā* (*Mahāmudrātilaka*), *mahāmudrā* is the "supreme state of bliss . . . sublime mystery, indefinable, inexhaustible, and

74. *BKT* 9a, 40a, 41a, 41b.

75. *BKT* 33a, 40a, 41a, 42a.

76. *BKT* 41a. See also Davidson 2002a, 250–52.

77. Newman 1987, pp. 224, 225, and 231, respectively.

78. Gray 2011, 462.

79. *SOT* 171, trans. 246.

unborn . . . formless . . . indeterminable, unaffected by concepts . . . unstained lucidity . . . a steady illumination of the sublime expanse . . . free from the space-time dimension . . . not subject to birth and death."[80] The *Drop of Mahāmudrā* goes on to specify that

> One who does not know mahāmudrā,
> even if a buddha, is not a yogī.
> . . . .
> When you understand mahāmudrā perfectly,
> you become the glorious Vajrasattva.[81]

The *Drop of Mahāmudrā* also is credited by some Tibetan authors with a classic etymological definition of the term, the first of many to follow: "*mu* is the gnosis of emptiness, *drā* is freedom from saṃsāric dharmas, *mahā* is their union."[82] Mahāmudrā also is prominent in a number of tantras spun off from the *Guhyasamāja* tradition. For instance, the *Vajra Garland* (*Vajramālā*) describes it as "great bliss that possesses one great flavor . . . a vast space . . . the awareness of the Tathāgata . . . a state without discrimination . . . the realm of indivisible mind . . . free from dualistic movements . . . like space that is unclouded."[83]

The commentarial traditions surrounding the mahāyoga and yoginī tantras also maintained and developed the multiple-seal scheme that originated in the yoga tantras. Now, though, mahāmudrā typically was regarded as the most important in the sequence. In some traditions related to the Cakrasaṃvara system, mahāmudrā is the third of the four seals, the "awakening mind of great bliss" (*mahāsukhabodhicitta*) that succeeds the action seal (physical consort) and Dharma seal (visualized consort), and paves the way for the manifestation of divine images, the pledge seal.[84] In the literature surrounding the *Hevajra Tantra*, it often is seen as the fourth in the sequence of seals:

1. The action seal represents, among many other equivalents, the goddess

80. *MMT* 471a–b; cf. trans. Dakpo Tashi Namgyal 1986, 103.

81. *MMT* 471b–472a; cf. trans. Dakpo Tashi Namgyal 1986, 96–97.

82. Dakpo Tashi Namgyal 1986, 93. Although Tashi Namgyal attributes this passage to the *Drop of Mahāmudrā*, an online search has not turned it up in *MMT*. It is, however, found in Tilopa's *Dharma of the Bodiless Ḍākinī* (Tp*VD* 84b), which is translated in Duff 2005, 1–8.

83. *VMT* 64b–65a; trans. Dakpo Tashi Namgyal 1986, 102.

84. Wayman 1987, 251–52.

Locanā, the experience of joy in the subtle body, and attainment of the emanation body of a buddha.
2. The pledge seal represents the goddess Māmakī, the experience of perfect joy in the subtle body, and attainment of the Dharma body of a buddha.
3. The Dharma seal represents the goddess Pāṇḍaravāsinī, the experience of the joy of cessation in the subtle body, and attainment of the enjoyment body of a buddha.
4. Mahāmudrā represents the goddess Tārā, the experience of the connate joy in the subtle body, and attainment of the great-bliss body of a buddha.[85]

Like that of many later tantric traditions, the *Kālacakra* literature often refers to a three-seal scheme consisting of the action seal, which is a physical consort in sexual yoga practices, the gnosis seal (*jñānamudrā*), which is a visualized consort, and succeeding and transcending these two, mahāmudrā, which is supreme, immutable bliss.[86] Puṇḍarīka's Kālacakra commentary, the *Stainless Light* (*Vimalaprabhā*), further specifies that mahāmudrā entails "emptiness devoid of differentiated representations and provided with all excellent aspects, the accomplishment of omniscience, devoid of differentiated representations."[87] A Guhyasamāja explanatory tantra, the *Matrix of Gnosis* (*Jñānagarbha*), goes so far as to subsume four tantric seals under mahāmudrā: the action seal (a physical consort), the pledge seal (tantric vows), the gnosis seal (a visualized consort), and the Dharma seal (the nature of phenomena).[88]

In short, *mahāmudrā* was a term and concept that was employed with increasing frequency and sophistication by both Hindus and Buddhists in India, especially during and after the second half of the first millennium. It was more significant in Buddhism than Hinduism, and within Buddhism, its origins clearly lay in the tantras and their commentarial literature, where its denotation evolved from a ritual hand gesture signifying the visualization of oneself as a buddha, to a goddess or consort employed in tantric subtle-body practice, to a signifier of ultimate reality and the ultimate attainment, buddhahood itself. By the time the yoginī tantras—the last major class of Buddhist tantric

85. Snellgrove 1987, 248–49.

86. This is credited by Tashi Namgyal to the *Kālacakra Root Tantra*; Dakpo Tashi Namgyal 1986, 99.

87. Lesco 2009, 75.

88. *JGT* 475b; trans. Dakpo Tashi Namgyal 1986, 96.

literature—were composed, *mahāmudrā* was a term to conjure with, but it was the charismatic great adepts, the mahāsiddhas, who embodied, sang out, and wrote about the tantric approach to the world, that would bring it near the center of late Indian Buddhism. It is to them that we now turn.

2. Mahāmudrā in India: The Mahāsiddhas

THE MAJOR EXPONENTS of the mahāyoga and yoginī tantras were the charismatic, wonder-working, and often quasi-legendary Buddhist mahāsiddhas, who were often said by later scholars to number eighty-four. In treatise and song these figures distilled essential themes from the mahāyoga and yoginī tantras, criticizing social mores while celebrating the bliss and freedom found in yogic contemplation and an unconventional way of life. They lived in cremation grounds or retreated to the mountains, often consorted with low-caste women, and generally acted out a religious performance or mode of conduct (*caryā*) that appeared to turn brahmanical—and Buddhist—values upside down.[89] In traditional accounts of their lives, their often transgressive practices inevitably culminate in the "attainment of mahāmudrā" (*mahāmudrāsiddhi*), which is equivalent to buddhahood. In their works, mahāmudrā has many more meanings as well, and takes on great importance, whether as an explicit topic of discourse or through discussion of related terms, such as the connate purity of our primordial mind (*sahaja* or *nijacitta*) or the practice of nonmentation (or inattention, or mental nonengagement, *amanasikāra*), a type of formless, concept-free meditation.[90] As a result, many of the mahāsiddhas' writings were incorporated into anthologies of mahāmudrā texts compiled centuries later by Indian or Tibetan scholars. The three most widely recognized collections are known as the Seven Attainment Texts, the Essential Trilogy, and the Twenty-Five Works on Nonmentation; our discussion of the contributions of the mahāsiddhas will be keyed—though not limited—to these three.

89. On the mahāsiddhas, see, e.g., Abhayadatta 1979, Tāranātha 1983, Linrothe 2006, and Lopez 2019. As noted already, the degree to which they truly were transgressive rebels has been debated; for contrasting views on the matter, see, e.g., Davidson 2002a, chaps. 5–7, and Wedemeyer 2013.

90. See, e.g., Higgins 2006 and Mathes 2015.

The Seven Attainment Texts

The Seven Attainment Texts,[91] most of which probably date from the eighth through tenth centuries, are by mahāsiddhas who base themselves closely on one or another system of mahāyoga or yoginī tantra (especially the Guhyasamāja, Cakrasaṃvara, or Hevajra) and presuppose familarity with those systems on the part of their readers. They emphasize practice over theory but do occasionally discuss philosophical matters. It is in that context that they are likeliest to mention mahāmudrā—yet of the authors of the Attainment Texts, only Padmavajra and Indrabhūti mention the term with any frequency. In the *Secret Attainment* (*Guhyasiddhi*), Padmavajra refers to mahāmudrā as that which is cultivated when one has abandoned practice with either a physical consort or imagined consort and has "abandoned multiple concepts"; "the perfection of all ornaments, pacification into supreme formlessness, lucid, faultless, stainless"; and realization of the unproduced, selfless nature of mind.[92] In the *Attainment of Gnosis* (*Jñānasiddhi*), Indrabhūti describes mahāmudrā as "pervasive and without characteristics, like the sky . . . the ultimate, the unsurpassed vajra gnosis, the all-good . . . the Dharma body, the mirror-like gnosis," the "abandonment of all conceptuality" by which all the buddhas and siddhas achieved awakening in a single life.[93] Terms synonymous with *mahāmudrā* emphasized in other Attainment Texts include the connate (*sahaja*), described by Ḍombī Heruka in the *Attainment of the Connate* (*Sahajasiddhi*) as final perfection, beyond ritual and expression, the essential thatness (*tattva*) pervading the triple world, by identification with which the yogī attains great bliss.[94] In the *Attainment of the Nondual* (*Advayasiddhi*), Lakṣmīṅkarā (one of the few important female mahāsiddhas) does not mention mahāmudrā per se, but she does describe the nondual as the signless and baseless nonabiding nirvāṇa that pervades all beings, which is achieved not through astronomical calculation, ritual observance, or tantric meditation but solely through the recognition that all entities are selfless, unproduced, and stainless, whereby one attains the nondual gnosis of buddhahood.[95]

91. The listing of these texts is not always consistent. See, e.g., Krug 2019 and R. Jackson 2008, 160–62.

92. Pv*GSs* 3.34, p. 23; Pv*GSs* 4.15, p. 29; Pv*GSs* 4.40–41, p. 32. See also Davidson 2002a, 255–57.

93. Ib*JS* 1.44–47, p. 97; Ib*JS* 1.56–57, p. 97.

94. Dh*SS* 1.1–2, p. 185, trans. Shendge 1967, 145; DSS 2.1 and 2:14–15, pp. 188 and 189, trans. Shendge 1967, 146–47.

95. Lk*AS* 30, p. 163, trans. Mishra 1993, 35; AS 2, 11, 23, pp. 161, 162, 163, trans. Mishra

Apart from the Seven Attainment Texts, many other tantric commentaries and treatises touch on mahāmudrā, including:

- Commentaries on *Chanting the Names of Mañjuśrī* by Narendrakīrti and Ḍombi Heruka[96]
- Nāgārjuna's *Five Stages* (*Pañcakrama*), an exposition of the subtle-body practices of the Guhyasamāja tradition[97]
- Āryadeva's *Lamp that Integrates the Performance* (*Caryāmelapradīpa*), a detailed explanation of the "gradual path" of the Guhyasamāja[98]
- Commentaries on the *Cakrasaṃvara Tantra* by Bhavabhaṭṭa, Vīryavajra, and Kambala[99]
- Kṛṣṇācārya's *Jewel Garland of Yoga* (*Yogaratnāvalī*), a word-by-word explanation of the *Hevajra Tantra*[100]
- Puṇḍarīka's *Stainless Light* (*Vimalaprabhā*), a massive commentary on the *Kālacakra Tantra*[101]
- Nāropa's *Commentary on the "Teaching on Empowerment"* (*Sekoddeśaṭīkā*), also related to the *Kālacakra* but drawing on multiple mahāyoga and yoginī tantra sources[102]

In most of these, *mahāmudrā* has the same sense of ontological and soteriological ultimacy as in the Seven Attainment Texts and frequently is "read in" to passages in the root tantras in which it is not explicitly mentioned. But it also frequently refers to a female consort, and occasionally describes a meditation, the Perfection of Wisdom, nondiscursive awareness, vibrationless pleasure, or the word empowerment.

1993, 31, 32, 34.

96. *MNS* 65, 78, and 101.

97. Ng*PK* 3.41, p. 37; 4.32, p. 46; 5.28, p. 53; Thurman 1995, 256 and 260.

98. Wedemeyer 2007, pp. 290, 295, 298, 308, and 326.

99. Gray 2007, pp. 168n25, 172n2, 251n4, 275n20, 283n8, and 325n1.

100. Farrow and Menon 1992, pp. 5, 19, 23, 95, 101, 129, 138, 141, 154, 159–62, 173, 186, 218–20, 224–25, and 271–72.

101. Newman 1987, pp. 224, 225, 246, 247, 261, 263, 264, 281, 282, 283, 287–88, 367, 373, 383, 410–11, and 418.

102. Nr*ST*; for mahāmudrā references in the Italian translation, see Gnoli and Orofino 1994, pp. 167, 184, 186, 200, 204, 223, 224, 236, 238, 259, 313–14, 324–25, 327, 351, and 356–57.

Saraha: The Essential Trilogy and Beyond

The Essential Trilogy comprises three poetic works attributed to the mahāsiddha Saraha,[103] who probably lived in east India late in the first millennium. In legend, he is said to have learned arrow-making from a yoginī with whom he consorted; his name literally means "fletcher." Author of a commentary on the *Buddha Skull Tantra*[104] and clearly conversant with the yoginī tantras in general, Saraha is regarded by most Tibetan traditions as the earliest and greatest Indian exponent of mahāmudrā. He is reputed to have been the guru of the great philosopher (and tantric mahāsiddha) Nāgārjuna and of the mountain-hermit Śavaripa, both of whom would come to figure importantly in Tibetan mahāmudrā lineages.[105]

The works of the Essential Trilogy—the *Dohā Treasury Song* (*Dohākoṣagīti*), *Dohā Treasury Instruction Song* (*Dohākośopadeśagīti*), and *Performance Song Dohā Treasury* (*Dohākoṣanāmacaryāgīti*)—are commonly referred to as, respectively, the *People*, *Queen*, and *King Dohā Treasuries*. Tibetan tradition tells us that Saraha sang each of these collections of aphoristic couplets (*dohākoṣa*) for a particular segment of the populace in a kingdom he was visiting. Various versions of the *People Dohās* in the medieval Indian language of Apabhraṃśa have been discovered, but the *Queen* and *King Dohās* are known only from their Tibetan translations. Although they are considered foundational texts for Tibetan mahāmudrā practice lineages, Saraha's *Treasuries* seldom use the term; indeed, *mahāmudrā* is explicitly mentioned only in the *Queen Dohā*, which refers to it as the abiding state of natural nonduality, the sameness of saṃsāra and nirvāṇa, a consort for sexual yoga practice, and the goal of the tantric path.[106] The *King Dohā* emphasizes the fundamental purity of mind rather than mahāmudrā, but it does mention the four seals and implicitly equates mahāmudrā with the unborn, empty nature of all phenomena, insisting that "all the worlds in their diver-

103. On Saraha, see especially Schaeffer 2005a and Braitstein 2014, 1–37.

104. Saraha's commentary mostly follows the patterns of *BKT*, but he does offer this rather broader reading of a passage where mahāmudrā is described as a consort: "When the tathāgatas apply a seal through the nature of great emptiness, that is the great seal" (Sa*BK* 146b). See also Davidson 2002a, 250–51.

105. If, as Tibetans do, we regard the philosopher Nāgārjuna (usually dated to the second century CE) as identical to the tantric Nāgārjuna (late first millennium), the dating of Saraha becomes quite problematic. Like most recent scholars, I assume that the two are distinct and that the Nāgārjuna whom Saraha taught is the late-first-millennium tantric author.

106. Sa*QD* 28b, 29a, 31a, 31b, 33b, verses 1, 40, 46, 80; trans. R. Jackson 2011, pp. 174, 178, 179, and 184, respectively.

sity have this very nature."[107] The *People Dohās*, the best known, most studied, and most often quoted of the three, focuses not on mahāmudrā but on cognate concepts, such as the connate, the yoginī, great bliss, thatness, the natural mind, the stainless nature, and mind itself—all of which are equated to buddhahood, and all of which are described in terms familiar to us from discussions of mahāmudrā elsewhere in tantric literature. One of the most frequently cited verses from the *People Dohās* summarizes his attitude well:

> The single seed of everything is mind,
> where existence and nirvāṇa both arise.
> Bow down to it; like a magic jewel,
> it grants the things you wish.[108]

Though the Essential Trilogy is Saraha's best-known work, he discusses mahāmudrā in far greater detail in other texts, especially in a trilogy of vajra songs (*vajragīti*) consisting of the *Body Treasury* (*Kāyakoṣa*), *Speech Treasury* (*Vākkoṣa*), and *Mind Treasury* (*Cittakoṣa*). In the *Body Treasury*, for instance, mahāmudrā is described as "unchangeable great bliss,"[109] "experienced like ocean and space,"[110] "the sameness of all phenomena,"[111] "the nature of fruition,"[112] "from nothing other than oneself,"[113] "the highest union . . . single taste in the unborn nature,"[114] "instantaneous full awakening,"[115] "reflexive awareness,"[116] and "the mind itself."[117] As he sings,

> Hey! In the great seal are present body, speech, and mind. . . .
> It is the unsurpassed secret vehicle, the essence of all.
> The essentials of path and fruition are distilled there,
> the authentic highest Mahāyāna and the distinctness of the vehicles.

107. Sa*KD* 28a, 28b, verses 27, 33; trans. Thrangu 2006, 92 and 105, respectively.

108. Sa*PDa* 73.

109. Sa*KK* verse 7, p. 170, trans. 126.

110. Sa*KK* verse 20, p. 173, trans. 129.

111. Sa*KK* verse 33, p. 176, trans. 132.

112. Sa*KK* verse 35, p. 176, trans. 132.

113. Sa*KK* verse 56, p. 180, trans. 136.

114. Sa*KK* verse 62, p. 181, trans. 137.

115. Sa*KK* verse 71, p. 183, trans. 139.

116. Sa*KK* verse 83, p. 185, trans. 141.

117. Sa*KK* verse 96, p. 188, trans. 144.

> The characteristics by which one ascertains mahāmudrā are:
> recollection and nonrecollection are unarisen and nondual.
> Why would it not remain like space, beyond the intellect?[118]

In the *Speech Treasury*, he sings:

> Mahāmudrā is manifest presence:
> if you reject it, you will never meet it,
> while if you hear of mahāmudrā just for an instant,
> then, whether you're subjected to blame or not,
> just by that teaching, just by remaining single-pointed, you'll get it;
> anyone who contemplates the connate meaning,
> unwavering in pure recollection, will get it.[119]

Later in the same text, he makes an important point about the dependence of the mahāmudrā yogī on a guru:

> Hey! Whoever possesses mahāmudrā, the supreme qualities,
> has the basis of all yogic attainments because of delighting the guru.
> Not abandoning the precious guru, the qualities arise.[120]

In the *Mind Treasury*, he identifies mahāmudrā as:

> . . . the lamp of connate gnosis,
> the meaning of the union of means and wisdom,
> unarisen, empty, luminous, impartial,
> a special gnosis, suchness,
> nondual, uninterrupted bliss,
> self-arisen, nonconceptual, the uprooting of all propensities.[121]

The vajra songs explicitly equate mahāmudrā with a full range of Mahāyāna and Vajrayāna Buddhist terms for ultimacy while also relating it to various categorical sets, such as the four joys experienced through subtle-body yogas (joy, supreme joy, joy of cessation, and connate joy), the four stages of meditation on

118. Sa*KK* verses 35–36, pp. 176–77, trans. 155–56 (translation adapted).

119. Sa*VK* verses 24–25, p. 198; cf. trans. 132–33.

120. Sa*VK* verse 48, pp. 202–3; trans. 160 (translation adapted).

121. Sa*CK* verses 6–7, p. 205, trans. 162.

emptiness (recollection, nonrecollection, nonarising, and beyond mind), and the four bodies of a buddha (the Dharma, enjoyment, emanation, and great-bliss bodies)—with mahāmudrā in each case equivalent to the fourth and highest of the set. Finally, in another text attributed to him, the *Dohā Song on View, Meditation, Conduct, and Result* (*Dṛṣṭibhāvanācaryāphaladohāgīti*), Saraha introduces the four practice-stages mentioned in the title—view, meditation, conduct, and result—all of which are required for the attainment of "the mahāmudrā of transcendent union," here described as:

> . . . clear and nonconceptual like the sky,
> so it pervades and expands as great compassion,
> appearing yet essenceless, like a moon in water,
> clear, beyond designation, without circumference or center,
> unclothed, stainless, beyond hope or fear,
> ineffable, like the dream of a mute.[122]

Much of Saraha's radically nondual rhetoric about mahāmudrā suggests that it transcends both the sūtra-based and tantric vehicles of Buddhism, but it cannot, in fact, really be understood outside the esoteric context of tantric discourse and practice—especially that of the yoginī tantras. In that respect, it is important to note that Saraha affirms again and again that the realization of the ultimate—whether termed mahāmudrā, mind itself, the connate, or thatness—cannot simply be "produced" through this or that technique. Rather, realization arises when one relinquishes control. In terms of meditation, relinquishment involves relaxing into the open, luminous, blissful nature of mind. Yet meditative relinquishment—indeed any genuine approach to mahāmudrā—requires a prior and even deeper relinquishment, whereby one places all one's confidence in the guru. If one cannot trust the guru, all one's exertions will come to naught, but when, as Saraha puts it, "the guru's words but enter your heart, it's as if you've been handed assurance."[123] This will be an important theme in much of the mahāmudrā discourse to follow, whether among later Indian mahāsiddhas or the various Tibetan masters who gave the term cultural prominence.

Seminal though he was, Saraha was far from the only master to compose songs to express his understanding of mahāmudrā. Indeed, the Tibetan canon is replete with translations of dohās, vajra songs, and performance songs by scores, if not hundreds, of different tantric mahāsiddhas, both male

122. Sa*DD* 3a–3b.

123. Sa*PDa* 63.

and female. Those most important for mahāmudrā lineages in Tibet include Śavaripa, Virūpa, and, most especially, Tilopa and Nāropa.

Śavaripa and Virūpa

Śavaripa (or Śabara, ninth century?),[124] sometimes said to be a disciple of Saraha or Nāgārjuna, was a mountain-dwelling yogī particularly adept in the tantras of Mahākāla and Vajrayoginī. He is credited with a number of Apabhraṃśa performance songs in which he describes himself as a madman and a drunkard, the bliss-besotted lover of a mountain girl known variously as Lady No-Self or the Empty Lady (*nairāmaṇi*).[125] He also is credited with at least two poetic works explicitly or implicitly related to mahāmudrā, the *View of Emptiness* (*Śūnyatādṛṣṭi*)[126] and the *Dohā Treasury of Mahāmudrā Instruction* (*Dohākoṣamahāmudropadeśa*). The former, written in the style of a performance song, plays on the traditional imagery of emptiness as female, to which the mind is often the male counterpart. Thus he begins:

> The pinnacle of mind, which is reality,
> is said to be the seed in the sky realm;
> embraced around the neck by Lady No-Self,
> I abide in the state of wakefulness.[127]

And the song ends:

> "Reject!" "Avoid!" These confuse the self.
> Embracing the Empty Lady,
> I, Śavari, dwell in great bliss.[128]

The *Dohā Treasury of Mahāmudrā Instruction*, which is often attributed to Saraha rather than Śavaripa,[129] begins with homage to the "greatly

124. See Davidson 2002a, 227–33.

125. See Davidson 2002a, 227, and Kvaerne 1977, 181–88 and 262–68.

126. Sv*SD*; see alternative Tibetan edition in Davidson 2002a, 394n217, and trans. 229.

127. Sv*SD* 40a; cf. trans. Davidson 2002a, 229.

128. Sv*SD* 40a–b; cf. trans. Davidson 2002a, 229.

129. It is attributed to Saraha in, e.g., the Derge Tengyur and the *DZG*, while it is credited to Mahāśabara Saraha in the Peking Tengyur and to Śabari (i.e., Śavaripa) in Jamgön Kongtrul's *Gdams ngag mdzod* (Lt*DNDZ*, vol. 5, contents: 1).

blissful connate gnosis body."[130] It goes on to sing of mahāmudrā as primordial nonmind, that which is attained when the mind—even in its wavering—is understood by mind itself through a process of nonmentation. For:

> Where mind is nonexistent, by whom could phenomena be conceived?
> When you seek mind and the appearance of phenomena,
> neither they nor the seeker can be found.
> Nonexistent throughout the three times, neither arising nor ceasing,
> that which does not change into anything else,
> it has great bliss as its nature.
> Therefore all appearances are the Dharma body.
> All sentient beings are buddhahood.
> All karmic formations are primordially the Dharma realm.
> All concepts are like horns of a rabbit.[131]

Thus he advises:

> Not holding breath or restraining your mind,
> rest in effortless awareness like a little child.
> When a thought arises, just see its nature;
> do not conceive of water and waves as different.
> In the mahāmudrā of nonmentation (*amanasikāra*),
> there is not even an atom on which to meditate.
> Not being separate from nonmeditation is supreme meditation.
> The flavor of the nondual connate great bliss
> has one taste, like water poured into water.[132]

The ethical consequences are:

> Like a crazy man without calculation,
> like a little child, one should act without acting.
> The mind arises from the mud of saṃsāric existence like a lotus.
> There are no faults to defile it.[133]

130. Sv*MU* 122a; cf. trans. Thaye 1990, 80.

131. Sv*MU* 122b; cf. trans. Thaye 1990, 81.

132. Sv*MU* 123b; cf. trans. Thaye 1990, 84.

133. Sv*MU* 123b; cf. trans. Thaye 1990, 85.

At the same time:

> With the spontaneous action of realization,
> when we meet foolish beings,
> tears readily well up from the force of unbearable compassion;
> having exchanged self for others, we accomplish their benefit.[134]

Śavaripa is said to have appeared in visions to a later mahāsiddha, Maitrīpa, and to have helped provide the basis for the latter's account of mahāmudrā as nonmentation, discussed below.

Virūpa (tenth century?) is a figure of great importance for the Sakya traditions of Tibet. In legend, he is one of the most colorful of the mahāsiddhas, famous above all for his love of drink and for performance songs that celebrate it. In the incident that provides the basis for his usual iconographic representation, he is said to have drunk so much at a tavern that the owner made him promise to drink only until sundown—at which point he raised his hand, pointed to the sun, and stopped it in the sky. As always with such material, it is difficult to know whether the song is to be taken literally, figuratively, or on multiple levels.[135] The *Vajra Verses* (*Vajrapāda*) attributed to him by Sakyapas are regarded as the root text of the path and fruit (*lam 'bras*) meditation system that is central to Sakya contemplative life. In the *Vajra Verses*, Virūpa discusses the "three appearances" that arise for afflicted beings, yogīs, and buddhas, respectively: impure appearance, experiential appearance, and pure appearance. Through practice rooted in the four unexcelled-yoga-tantra empowerments, "the obstructions to great bliss cease and awakening is clear.... Mahāmudrā... is omniscience by way of the four... empowerments."[136] In his own *Treasury of Dohās* (*Dohākoṣa*), Virūpa describes mahāmudrā as:

> The great seal of saṃsāric existence and peace,
> essentially pure like the sky;
> without a real nature that could be shown,
> it is cut off from the ways of verbal designation.
> It's naturally unelaborated,[137] its essence free from every dependent
> dharma.

134. Sv*MU* 124a; cf. trans. Thaye 1990, 85.

135. See Davidson 2002a, 258.

136. Stearns 2006, 13 (translation adapted).

137. The Tibetan term *spros pa* (Skt. *prapañca*) refers to discursiveness or conceptual activity; here, I translate it either as "mental elaboration" or simply "elaboration." Often, as in this

> It lacks investigation or analysis, and is free from any exemplary sign. . . .
> Connate from the beginning, not to be sought elsewhere,
> mind itself, empty of names and unelaborated, is mahāmudrā.[138]

Furthermore:

> If you're free from paying any attention, you're stainless without a doubt;
> when you're purified of mind and mental objects, reality nakedly appears.
> But if you haven't realized primordial mahāmudrā,
> then, ever driven by dualistic grasping, you hanker after everything. . . .
> If you don't abide on the unerring meaning, you'll wander and circle throughout saṃsāric existence.[139]

In short, *mahāmudrā* is the "great word," a synonym for "emptiness of any basis of designation," understanding of which makes one fit to be called a buddha.[140]

Virūpa's two great disciples, Ḍombī Heruka and Kṛṣṇācārya (also known by his Apabhraṃśa name, Kāṇha), both were important mahāsiddhas in their own right. The former, as we saw, is the author of *Attainment of the Connate* as well as numerous performance songs; the latter, as also noted, wrote an important commentary on the *Hevajra Tantra,* as well as some of the most famous of all performance songs, in which he sings of his passion for a woman from the untouchable *ḍombī* caste.[141]

Tilopa and Nāropa

Tilopa, or Tillipāda, (928?–1009), is regarded as the fountainhead of the Marpa Kagyü traditions of Tibet. He received four great oral practice transmissions from a range of human teachers and ḍākinīs, as well as the tantric buddha Vajradhara. His main disciple was Nāropa, to whom—after subjecting

context, it is used in the negative (*spros bral*) to refer to freedom from elaboration, or simplicity, which is a yogic ideal in mahāmudrā traditions.

138. Vr*DK* 134a.

139. Vr*DK* 134b–135a.

140. Vr*DK* 135b.

141. See Kvaerne 1977, pp. 100–104, 109–31, 150–58, 231–34, and 238–41.

him to extraordinary trials[142]—he transmitted twelve major practices, drawn from a range of mahāyoga and yoginī traditions:

1. The preliminary practices known as the ordinary wish-fulfilling gem
2. Equal taste
3. Commitment
4. Inner heat
5. Illusory body
6. Dream yoga
7. Luminosity
8. Transfer of consciousness
9. Resurrection
10. Incorruptible bliss
11. Mahāmudrā
12. Intermediate-state yoga[143]

At least one text attributed to Tilopa, *Instruction on the Six Dharmas* (*Ṣaddharmopadeśa*), reduces these twelve practices to a set of six: (1) inner heat, (2) illusory body, (3) dream yoga, (4) luminosity, (5) intermediate state, and (6) transfer of consciousness.[144] The first four—drawn from the Cakrasaṃvara or Hevajra system (no. 1) and the Guhyasamāja system (2–4)—are crucial for the attainment of awakening on the completion stage of unexcelled yoga tantra; the last two are special instructions—drawn primarily from the *Four Seats* (*Catuṣpīṭha Tantra*)[145]—for exploiting the death process for spiritual purposes.

Tilopa is credited with several works related exclusively to mahāmudrā, including a *Dohā Treasury* (*Dohākoṣa*) in which he instructs: "Quick! Kill the thought that is not rooted in mind; this is mahāmudrā, stainless in the triple world,"[146] and the *Inconceivable Mahāmudrā* (*Acintyamahāmudrā*), where he sings:

> I bow down to the unborn, unceasing
> reality-luminosity, which is the path of mahāmudrā,

142. See Guenther 1963, 37–85.

143. See Guenther 1963, 130–249.

144. Tp*SO*; trans. Mullin 1997, 25–29.

145. On this tantra, see Szántó 2012 and Szántó 2015.

146. Tp*DK* 140 (translation adapted).

inexpressible by speech, unidentifiable,
nonmentation, profound, peaceful, uncompounded.[147]

Tilopa's best-known poetic work is the *Instruction on Mahāmudrā* (*Mahāmudropadeśa*), better known as the *Mahāmudrā Song of Mother Ganges* (*Mahāmudrāgaṅgāmā*), in which he instructs Nāropa, as follows:

Just as in space, nothing supports anything,
so in mahāmudrā, there is no objective support.
Rest relaxed in the uncontrived, natural state;
if you loosen your bonds, you'll doubtless be free.
Just as when you look into space, seeing is stopped,
so when you look at mind with mind,
the mass of conceptions stops, and you obtain unexcelled awakening.[148]

In the same work, Tilopa provides a famous set of similes for the progress of the mind as one masters mahāmudrā: at the beginning, inundated by thoughts, it is like a cascading waterfall; in the middle, as one begins to gain some control, it is like a flowing mountain stream; at the end, when one is completely accomplished, it is like a vast ocean, in which the appearance of waves on the surface does not affect the still and limpid depths.[149]

Nāropa, or Naḍapāda, (956?–1040) was a great scholar and abbot who, tradition tells us, abandoned the monastery in midlife to seek tantric teachings from Tilopa. From Tilopa he received the twelve great teachings mentioned above, as well as the aforementioned sixfold list, which—justly or not—came to be known as the six Dharmas of Nāropa: (1) inner heat, (2) illusory body, (3) dream yoga, (4) luminosity, (5) the intermediate state, and (6) transfer of consciousness.[150] The list of six Dharmas was far from stable: the order might change, and other yogas, such as resurrection or the action seal, might be included while others were subsumed under a different yoga or dropped entirely.[151] Indeed, the one text attributed to Nāropa that touches on these practices, *Vajra Verses of the Hearing Transmission* (*Karṇatantravajragāthā*), actually lists ten yogas, those of:

147. Tp*AM* 145b.

148. Tp*GM* 243b; cf. trans. Brunnhölzl 2007, 97.

149. Tp*GM* 243b–244a; cf. trans. Brunnhölzl 2007, 100.

150. Of the many sources on these practices, see especially Guenther 1963, Mullin 1996, Mullin 1997, Kragh 2011, Kragh 2015, 345–95, and Roberts 2011, 333–72.

151. See the discussion and translation in Mullin 1996, 29–33.

1. The generation stage
2. Inner heat
3. Illusory body
4. Dream yoga
5. Luminosity
6. Transfer of consciousness
7. Resurrection
8. The action seal
9. Cultivating the view
10. The intermediate state[152]

Whatever the arrangement, however, the six Dharmas of Nāropa eventually came to be regarded by the Kagyü as constituting the "path of means" (*upāyamārga*, *thabs lam*), the esoteric or tantric form of mahāmudrā. Although not connected to the six Dharmas, Nāropa's Kālacakra-related *Commentary on the "Teaching on Empowerment"* is a rich source of tantric discourse on mahāmudrā, where, in line with usages in the yoginī tantras, it is referred to as a goddess, a consort, the culmination of the path, and as "the essential result . . . [whose] characteristic is gnosis of original immutable bliss."[153]

Nāropa also taught what Kagyü traditions came to call the "path of liberation" (*vimuktimārga*, *thar lam*), mahāmudrā as a nondual-wisdom instruction on the empty and luminous nature of mind and a nonconceptual meditation for realizing that nature. Thus, in the section on the yoga of the view in his *Vajra Verses of the Hearing Transmission* (*Karṇatantravajragāthā*), he instructs the disciple to "keep the three doors unmoving . . . view the characteristics of mind without seeing . . . settle [the mind] in its own place, unfabricated and objectless," and thereby "illuminate mahāmudrā gnosis."[154] Through this:

> The two obstructions are self-purified; you are free from the extremes of object and subject.
> The perceiving mind, and all phenomena of saṃsāra and nirvāṇa, disappear.
> The measure of knowledge is self-perfected with the full extent of virtues,

152. Nr*KG*; see Mullin 1997, 33–41.

153. Nr*ST* 56; cf. trans. Gnoli and Orofino 1994, 314. For further references, see note 102 above.

154. Nr*KG* 303b; cf. trans. Mullin 1997, 38.

and you become a self-born buddha, transcending thought or
expression.[155]

As the outcome of the path, buddhahood, mahāmudrā is to be understood as follows:

Mind itself, unborn and empty, is the Dharma body;
whatever appears as unceasing, luminous clarity is the emanation body;
the union of nonabiding and great bliss is the perfect enjoyment body.[156]

In short, the term *mahāmudrā* is glossed thusly:

Mu is recognizing nondual gnosis;
drā is untying the knots of saṃsāra;
mahā is the self-liberated Dharma body,
born from the lamp of union and nothing else.[157]

Nāropa writes in his *Verses on Mahāmudrā* (*Mahāmudrāsaṅgamita*), sometimes attributed to Maitrīpa,[158] that mahāmudrā

. . . is not an intrinsic nature that can be shown . . .
but when anyone realizes it as it is,
all that appears and exists is mahāmudrā; . . .
settling genuinely into the uncontrived nature . . .
settling without seeking—is meditation.[159]

In his *Summary of the View* (*Adhisidhisamā*), he sings of "unelaborated self-awareness," which is synonymous with mahāmudrā and:

. . . itself is actually saṃsāra,
itself is also nirvāṇa,
itself is also the great middle way,
itself is also what is to be seen,

155. Nr*KG* 304a; cf. trans. Mullin 1997, 39.

156. Nr*KG* 304a; cf. trans. Mullin 1997, 39.

157. Nr*KG* 304a; cf. trans. Mullin 1997, 39.

158. This is the attribution in *DZG* 24a, but most other sources credit it to Nāropa.

159. Nr*MS* 22b; cf. trans. Thrangu 1997, 98.

itself is also what is to be contemplated,
itself is also what is to be gained,
itself is also the valid truth.[160]

Kagyü tradition tells us that Nāropa was the teacher of the Tibetan founder of the Kagyü, the translator Marpa Chökyi Lodrö (1012–97), although the traditional claim has been questioned by some modern scholars.[161]

Maitrīpa and the Practice of Nonmentation

The Twenty-Five Works on Nonmentation[162] are attributed to Maitrīpa (986?–1063),[163] a mahāsiddha also known as Advayavajra or Advaya Avadhūtipa. According to Tibetan historians, he studied with Nāropa, received teachings from Śavaripa in visionary encounters, debated with the Yogācāra scholar Ratnākaraśānti, and was the main mahāmudrā guru of the Indian scholar Vajrapāṇi and the Tibetan translator Marpa, each of whom was instrumental in transmitting mahāmudrā traditions to Tibet during the eleventh century. Maitrīpa also is said to have had a complex connection to Atiśa Dīpaṃkara Śrījñāna (982–1054)—later the inspirer of the Kadam tradition of Tibet—who studied mahāmudrā texts with him but also may have had him expelled from Vikramaśīla Monastery for his involvement with transgressive tantric practices.[164]

In his intellectual and spiritual life, Maitrīpa is said to have focused on the *King of Concentrations Sūtra* as an important early source for understanding mahāmudrā and to have rediscovered—and linked to mahāmudrā—*Distinguishing the Precious Lineage* (*Ratnagotravibhāga*), also known as the *Sublime Continuum* (*Uttaratantra*), a poetic treatise on buddha nature supposedly transmitted to the fourth- or fifth-century Mahāyāna master Asaṅga by the future Buddha, Maitreya.[165] The Twenty-Five Works on

160. Nr*AS* 24b; cf. trans. Thrangu 1997, 14.

161. See, e.g., Davidson 2005, 143–48.

162. As with the Seven Attainment Texts, the listing of these texts is not always consistent. See, e.g., R. Jackson 2008, 163–66, and more recently, Mathes 2015, 1–22.

163. On Maitrīpa, see, e.g., Tāranātha 1983, 11–13, Tatz 1987, Brunnhölzl 2007, 125–31, and Mathes 2015, 23–40.

164. See Roerich 1976, 843–44, Tāranātha 1983, 11, Shizuka 2015, and Apple 2019a, 22.

165. On the link between the *King of Concentrations* and mahāmudrā, see, e.g., Thrangu 1994, 11–135, and Thomas 2019. On the *Sublime Continuum* and mahāmudrā, see, e.g., Brunnhölzl 2014, 151–282. The full title of the treatise is *Distinguishing the Precious Lineage:*

Nonmentation, most of which are available in Sanskrit,[166] is an anthology of treatises, some in verse, some in prose, and some in a mixture, that deal with a variety of topics in Mahāyāna and Vajrayāna thought and practice. They rarely mention mahāmudrā, while only a few discuss nonmentation in detail, and the text often regarded as most seminal, the *Ten Verses on Thatness* (*Tattvadaśaka*), mentions neither—yet whether taken individually or as a whole, the texts in the anthology are still regarded by Tibetans as foundational for understanding both concepts.

In the texts that do mention mahāmudrā, it is referred to in a variety of ways already familiar to us. The *Way to Condense the Empowerments* (*Saṃkṣiptasekaprakriyā*) describes it as the final result of tantric empowerment.[167] The *Twenty Verses on Thatness* (*Tattvaviṃśaka*) refers to a "yogī who sees reality and is intent on mahāmudrā," and who, furthermore, "is himself mahāmudrā, is himself the Dharma, enjoyment, and emanation bodies, is himself everything."[168] The *Instruction on Empowerment* (*Sekanirdeśa*) asserts that mahāmudrā is obtainable "from scripture, self-awareness, and the teaching of a true guru."[169] It is described there as "not abiding anywhere . . . stainless self-awareness that is bereft of the arising of multiplicity."[170] In the end, Maitrīpa asserts,

> The one who neither abides in the realm of the antidote nor is attached to reality
> nor desires the fruit: that is the one who knows mahāmudrā.[171]

The *Holy Pith Instruction on Settling Thought without Dispersion or Concentration* announces that:

The Mahāyāna Treatise on the Sublime Continuum (*Ratnagotravibhāga-mahāyānottaratantra-śāstra*), on the basis of which scholars often will refer to it as the *Ratnagotravibhāga*. Tibetans, however, refer to it as the *Gyü Lama* (*Rgyud bla ma*), a straightforward translation of *Uttaratantra*, that may be rendered in English as either "Sublime Continuum" or "Later Transmission."

166. The most reliable edition is in Mathes 2015, 319–542, but see also Shastri 1927.

167. Mt*SP* 128b. This text is not included among those edited and translated in Mathes 2015 or edited in Shastri 1927.

168. Mt*TV* 460 (verse 11), 462 (verse 18); cf. trans. 189, 190.

169. Mt*SN* 385 (verse 27); cf. trans. 107. See also Isaacson and Sferra 2014.

170. Mt*SN* 386 (verse 29); cf. trans. 107.

171. Mt*SN* 388 (verse 36); cf. trans. 109.

Through the taste of emptiness,
even meditation becomes realization;
because of this, through wisdom meditation,
everything is mahāmudrā.

Even something discordant [with reality]
is mahāmudrā.
In this naturally relaxed, unthinking state,
as soon as dualistic details arise,
they dissolve back to whence they came.[172]

As we might expect, Maitrīpa mentions mahāmudrā with some frequency in the *Succession of the Four Seals* (*Caturmudrānvaya*),[173] where it is listed as the third in the sequence of four seals: it is preceded by the action seal (a physical consort) and Dharma seal (wisdom and compassion connate), and followed by the pledge seal (the manifestations of enlightened mind). In itself, the great seal is described as follows:

> It is without intrinsic nature, free from the obstructions to knowledge and so on. It is immaculate, like the center of the stainless sky of autumn. It is the basis of the possession of infinite excellences. It is the single self-nature of saṃsāric existence and nirvāṇa. It is the body of objectless great compassion. It is the single form of great bliss. . . .[174]

The poetic portion of the section goes on to pay homage to the mahāmudrā yogī, "whose thought is thoughtless and whose mind is unabiding, / who is unremembering, without mentation, objectless."[175] Also, as sometimes is the case in tantric commentarial literature—especially but not solely in the context of Hevajra—*mahāmudrā* is the name of an empowerment (*abhiṣeka*), in this case equivalent to the third of the four unexcelled-yoga-tantra empowerments,

172. Mt*MD* 507–8 (verses 5–6); cf. trans. 270. As Mathes notes (2015, 21) the text is not included in Indian recensions of the Twenty-Five Works but is accepted as part of the collection by the Seventh Karmapa.

173. Alternatively ascribed to Nāgārjuna, under the title *Ascertaining the Four Seals* (*Caturmudrāniścaya*; Dergé no. 2225).

174. Mt*CA* 398; cf. trans. 123–24. Cf. also Brunnhölzl 2007, 132, and Kvaerne 1975, 119.

175. Mt*CA* 399; cf. trans. 124. Cf. also Brunnhölzl 2007, 133, and Kvaerne 1975, 119

that of wisdom-gnosis, in which, typically, the initiate joins in sexual union with his or her consort, inducing thereby an experience of great bliss.[176]

Texts among the Twenty-Five Works that do *not* mention mahāmudrā—such as the *Illumination of Great Bliss* (*Mahāsukhaprakāśa*), *Six Verses on the Connate* (*Sahajaṣaṭaka*), *Upholding Nonmentation* (*Amanasikārādhāra*), *Six Verses on Madhyamaka* (*Madhyamakaṣaṭaka*), the *Jewel Garland of Thatness* (*Tattvaratnāvalī*), and, not least, the *Ten Verses on Thatness*—nevertheless are regarded as dealing with topics related to the great seal and are revered by Tibetans as key parts of Indian mahāmudrā literature.[177] One particular contribution of Maitrīpa to Indian philosophical discourse, which would have important repercussions in Tibet, was his division of Madhyamaka into the Madhyamaka of Nonabiding (*apratiṣṭhāna*) and the Madhyamaka of Illusion-Like Nonduality (*māyopamādvaya*) subschools. As the name suggests, the Illusion-Like Nonduality school focused on the way in which all phenomena are the same in being like an illusion, while the Madhyamaka of Nonabiding, which would be the viewpoint adopted by many thinkers in the Marpa Kagyü tradition in Tibet, was said to eschew any ultimate description of phenomena or reality at all, thereby clearing space for the experiential apprehension of the empty luminosity that is the nature of mind. At the hands of Maitrīpa's commentators, such as Rāmapāla and Vajrapāṇi, this Madhyamaka of Nonabiding was explicitly identified with mahāmudrā, as well as with nonmentation and the concept of buddha nature articulated in the *Sublime Continuum*.[178]

It is in a long (188-verse) poetic text usually classed outside the Twenty-Five Works (and unavailable in Sanskrit), the *Golden Garland of Mahāmudrā* (*Mahāmudrākanakamālā*), that Maitrīpa explicitly discusses mahāmudrā in the greatest detail. At the outset of each of the text's three chapters, he lists a number of mahāmudrā masters, including Nāgārjuna, Śavaripa, Saraha, Śāntideva, Virūpa, Tilopa, Ḍombī Heruka, and curiously, two names of the purported author himself: Avadhūtipa and Maitrīpa.[179] In the poem's first

176. Mt*CA* 402; trans. 126. In other contexts, the fourth, or word, empowerment may be designated as the "mahāmudrā empowerment," as occasionally in the works of Abhayākaragupta and Vītakarma.

177. For editions of these and other texts, see Mathes 2015; for translations, see Brunnhölzl 2007, Duff 2010, and Mathes 2015.

178. See, e.g., Mathes 2015, 77–94.

179. Mt*MK* 512 (verse 1.8; trans. 274–75), 519 (2.1; trans. 283), and 526 (3.1; trans. 292). The inclusion of Maitrīpa's own name makes one wonder whether (a) portions of the text were composed after the author's death or (b) the *Golden Garland* is simply a "gray text," written by an Indian or Tibetan in the Tibetan language and attributed to an Indian master.

mention of mahāmudrā, Maitrīpa explicitly links it to the doctrine for which he is best known, saying:

> Meditation and nonmeditation are within the range of conceptual mind;
> the unwavering ground free from the thought even of nonmeditation
> is nonmentation, the mahāmudrā path.
> Kye ho! It is free from activity, unarisen, beyond mind.[180]

Along similar lines, Maitrīpa affirms:

> The path of mahāmudrā is realization of the meaning
> of mind itself, the bliss-emptiness Dharma realm;
> in it, there is no object, subject, or act of meditation,
> no thought of anything at all.[181]

Furthermore:

> Mahāmudrā is spontaneously present within you;
> settle into the condition of nonmentation, noncognition, and
> inactivity.
> It isn't nihilism because you yourself can experience it in direct
> experience;
> it isn't eternalism because it's union without attachment.[182]

These three verses convey well the flavor of Maitrīpa's approach to mahāmudrā in the *Golden Garland*. He also describes it as a path on which emptiness and compassion are inseparable; the nonduality through which one's own primordial buddhahood is realized; and the great seal of nonmentation that eliminates even the subtlest propensity to defilement from those on the path to awakening.[183]

180. Mt*MK* 512 (verse 1.5); cf. trans. 274.

181. Mt*MK* 516 (verse 1.29); cf. trans. 279.

182. Mt*MK* 517 (verse 1.39); cf. trans. 281.

183. Mt*MK* 525 (verse II:38; trans. 290); 526 (III:3; trans. 292); 541 (III:93; trans. 310).

A Perfection Vehicle Mahāmudrā?

It is clear from reading Maitrīpa that, to a greater degree than perhaps any other mahāsiddha, he moves comfortably in the worlds of both Perfection and Mantra Vehicle discourse, and equates *mahāmudrā* as readily with concepts found in Madhyamaka, Yogācāra, and buddha nature literature as with tantric empowerments, maṇḍalas, or subtle-body practices. This should not surprise us, especially when we remember that Maitrīpa, like many of the mahāsiddhas, spent at least part of his life at a great monastic university—in his case, Vikramaśīla. We know that in the last centuries of the first millennium, such institutions as Vikramaśīla, Nālandā, and Odantapuri offered a curriculum that combined the study of Perfection Vehicle texts and practices with that of Mantra Vehicle texts and practices. Thus, regardless of whether the particular sūtras, treatises, or commentaries studied in the monasteries explicitly linked terms from one vehicle with those in another, many students, simply by dint of their regular exposure to both vehicles, must have established connections in their own theory and practice—and sometimes articulated those connections. Since mahāmudrā—a term of tantric origin—was increasingly important in Maitrīpa's time, it is entirely possible that he sought to align the great seal with ideas and practices of nontantric origin.[184] In the end, Maitrīpa's own writings leave it open to question whether he saw mahāmudrā as (a) a doctrine and practice inseparable from the tantras, (b) a tantra-based doctrine and practice that also is found independently in the sūtra tradition, or (c) a doctrine and practice that both combines and transcends the Perfection and Mantra Vehicles.

Maitrīpa's disciple Sahajavajra certainly seems to have allowed for the second or third possibilities. In his *Commentary on the "Ten Verses on Thatness"* (*Tattvadaśakaṭīkā*), he describes his master's purpose as providing "condensed pith instructions on the perfection of wisdom that accord with the mantra system."[185] Sahajavajra goes on to quote a number of important Mahāyāna figures, such as Nāgārjuna and Maitreya, and sūtras, including the *King of Concentrations* and the *Descent to Laṅkā* (*Laṅkāvatāra*), in support of the idea that the realization attained by those intent on mahāmudrā is described in Perfection Vehicle literature, and that even if the methods of the Perfection Vehicle cannot result in mahāmudrā without the blessing and instruction of a guru, those who receive such instructions "have utter certainty about the suchness of the single taste of emptiness; they are like villagers who grab a

184. On this issue, see especially Mathes 2006, Mathes 2007, and Isaacson and Sferra 2014.

185. Sh*TT* 161a; cf. trans. Brunnhölzl 2007, 142; see also Mathes 2008, 37–40.

snake and play with the snake but are not bitten by it."[186] As with Maitrīpa himself, it is not clear whether Sahajavajra is describing a mahāmudrā that is strictly Mantra Vehicle, strictly Perfection Vehicle, or a great seal that combines and transcends both approaches,[187] but at the very least he establishes a consonance between the tantric realization of mahāmudrā and the sūtra tradition's realization of emptiness.

Sahajavajra, in turn, was echoing suggestions to the same effect made in a handful of earlier texts.[188] Thus, in his *Entrance into Thatness* (*Tattvāvatāra*), Jñānakīrti observes that ordinary beings who strive to complete the Mahāyāna perfections and practice serenity and insight meditation may realize nondual mahāmudrā.[189] As he puts it in a well-known verse:

> The union of method and wisdom:
> just that meditation is the highest yoga;
> the victors call it the meditation
> of the mahāmudrā union.[190]

Elsewhere in the text, Jñānakīrti explicitly or implicitly equates mahāmudrā with the "nonseeing of all phenomena" mentioned in the Perfection of Wisdom sūtras[191] and describes the unelaborated meditative stage of "resting in nonappearance" mentioned in the *Descent to Laṅkā Sūtra* (10.256–57) as the true meaning of Mahāyāna, for which mahāmudrā is a synonym.[192] He further insists that perfection-vehicle practitioners who can master these techniques are, in fact, practicing mahāmudrā, which is simply another name for Mother Prajñāpāramitā.[193] Along similar lines, another late text, an anonymous commentary on the *Kālacakra Tantra* called *The Lotus Holder* (*Padminī*), says, "mahāmudrā is she who gives birth to all tathāgatas appearing in the past, future, and present, that is, Prajñāpāramitā. Since she seals bliss through the nonabiding nirvāṇa . . . . she is the seal. Since she is superior to the action seal and gnosis seal and free from the latent tendencies of cyclic existence,

186. Sh*TT* 175a; cf. trans. Mathes 2015, 237–38, and Brunnhölzl 2007, 183.

187. Mathes (2015, 238–40) seems to prefer the third.

188. On these, see especially Brunnhölzl 2007, 134–36.

189. Jk*TA* 40a; cf. Brunnhölzl 2007, 135.

190. Jk*TA* 43a; cf. Mathes 2008, 36, and Brunnhölzl 2007, 135.

191. Jk*TA* 64b, 65a; cf. Brunnhölzl 2007, 135.

192. Jk*TA* 64b; cf. Mathes 2008, 36 and 433n165, and Brunnhölzl 2007, 135–36.

193. Jk*TA* 42a; cf. Mathes 2008, 36, and Brunnhölzl 2007, 135.

she is great."[194] Finally, in a tantric commentary related to the Cakrasaṃvara tradition entitled *Illuminating the Significance of the Yoginī's Pure Conduct* (*Yoginīsaṃcaryānibandhapadārthaprakāśa*), in the course of glossing certain terms from the root tantra, Maitrīpa's near-contemporary, Vīryavajra, asserts,

> "Mahāyāna" is nonconceptual gnosis. . . . The "seal" is the Dharma realm (*dharmadhātu*). The nonduality of the Dharma realm and the gnosis being is the Dharma body (*dharmakāya*). . . . The Dharma body is taught as mahāmudrā. Mahāmudrā is the Dharma realm. "All yogas" implies serenity and insight. Among objects of serenity and insight, there is no object superior to mahāmudrā.[195]

None of this assures us that either Maitrīpa or others of his era actually conceived of a Perfection Vehicle system of mahāmudrā. Even less, of course, does it specify precisely what it might *mean* to equate mahāmudrā with the perfection of wisdom. After all, virtually all Mahāyānists accept the Perfection of Wisdom sūtras as authoritative and foundational, and many different—and at times contrasting—ideas have been drawn from them, from Nāgārjuna's Madhyamaka notion of emptiness, to Maitreya and Asaṅga's Yogācāra ideas of the three natures or mind-only, to the concept of the natural purity and luminosity of the mind, which is central to buddha-nature literature.

For instance, if we grant for the sake of argument that emptiness is the central philosophical teaching of the Perfection Vehicle, in what sense is "emptiness" meant? When the sūtras assert that "everything from form through omniscience" is empty, are form and omniscience, or buddha mind, empty in precisely the same way, or might they be empty in different ways? Many Mādhyamikas, especially those who came to be known as Prāsaṅgikas, assert that, indeed, all phenomena are empty in exactly the same way, and that their emptiness is a "mere," or nonaffirming, negation—that is, a negation in which nothing positive is implied by the negation. Other thinkers, especially those partial to Yogācāra and buddha-nature discourse (and this may include self-proclaimed Mādhyamikas like Maitrīpa), will insist that while form and other conventional phenomena may be empty in the sense of a nonaffirming negation, buddha mind itself is empty in a different sense, as an affirming negation. It is empty of anything saṃsāric, but emptiness implies the presence of all buddha qualities, such that buddha mind is empty of everything *other* than its own natural purity, luminosity, and omniscience. Still other

194. Brunnhölzl 2007, 136.

195. VvYS 144b.

interpreters, even more deeply shaped by Yogācāra, go so far as to suggest that everything in the cosmos is empty primarily in the sense that it is simply an emanation, or reflex, or activity of an inconceivable, perfect, blissful gnosis, which is the fundamental reality, and itself empty in the sense of containing infinite potential. This, too, is an affirming negation.

This is just within the context of the Perfection Vehicle; when we consider that all these ideas shaped the philosophical discourse of the Mantra Vehicle, which in turn—at least in later Indic Buddhism—influenced the way in which Perfection Vehicle concepts, like emptiness, were conceived and discussed, then the picture gets still more complicated. Indeed, it is from the matrix of these complex interactions that mahāmudrā originated and expanded as a topic of Mahāyāna discourse. In Tibet, as we will see, the whole question of the legitimacy of a Perfection Vehicle tradition of mahāmudrā became a major topic of debate, and the works of Maitrīpa and his disciples would loom large in those debates.

These issues notwithstanding, it is clear that, as the meaning of *mahāmudrā* rippled outward from a symbolic hand gesture, to the visualization of a deity, to a female consort, to ultimate reality, it became an increasingly significant term in Indic Buddhism. And precisely to the degree that it came to signify the ultimate reality, realization, and attainment (whatever that might mean), it was with increasing frequency read back into earlier sūtra-based or tantra-based texts in which it never or rarely occurred. For instance, Maitrīpa's commentary on Saraha's Essential Trilogy, Munidatta's commentary on the multi-author *Treasury of Performance Songs* (*Caryāgītikoṣa*), and (as we have just seen) Sahajavajra's commentary on Maitrīpa's *Ten Verses on Thatness* all find references to mahāmudrā "hidden" in the verses on which they comment.[196] And, as we also have seen, many tantric commentators of the ninth to eleventh centuries—like Narendrakīrti, Nāgārjuna, Āryadeva, Bhavabhaṭṭa, Kṛṣṇācārya, Vīryvajra, Puṇḍarīka, and Nāropa—discovered mahāmudrā "between the lines" of the fundamental tantras that shaped later Indian Buddhism. Tibetan authors would read mahāmudrā into a range of Indian texts with even greater zeal, but the interpretive tendency to do so had clearly been established by the Indians themselves even before the dawn of the Tibetan Renaissance.

196. See, respectively, Guenther 1993, Kvaerne 1977, and Brunnhölzl 2008.

3. Mahāmudrā in Some Tibetan Renaissance Schools

ALTHOUGH SOME MEANINGS of *mahāmudrā*—those of the "lower" and mahāyoga tantras—undoubtedly would have been familiar to educated Tibetans during the imperial period, or the "earlier spread of the Dharma" (seventh–ninth centuries), it was during the so-called Tibetan Renaissance, the "later spread of the Dharma" (tenth–fourteenth centuries),[197] that it became a central topic of religious discourse on the plateau. Indeed, it can be argued that singling out mahāmudrā as a focus of study and practice is really a Tibetan idea. Certainly, much of what we know about Indian mahāmudrā and its practitioners we owe to Tibetan sources, and mahāmudrā took on an importance for at least some Tibetan traditions that surpassed anything seen in India. Yet Tibetans did not simply imagine that mahāmudrā was important in Indian Buddhism. When, after nearly two centuries of limited contact, Tibetans in the eleventh century resumed visiting India to collect texts and receive teachings, and Indians resumed traveling to Tibet carrying texts and teachings, mahāmudrā was a far more central part of what was transmitted than it had been during the imperial period—largely due to the prominence of the yoginī tantras and the literature they spawned, especially the works of the mahāsiddhas.[198]

Transmitting Mahāmudrā to Tibet

Unlike in the early period of Buddhism's spread in Tibet, the notions of mahāmudrā imported to the plateau starting in the eleventh century showed

197. See Davidson 2005 and Roerich 1976.

198. A search of the AIBS online database of the Kangyur and Tengyur (April 1, 2017) reveals around 8,200 instances of the term *mahāmudrā* (as either *phyag rgya chen po*, *phyag rgya che*, or *phyag chen*) scattered among around 700 texts. By comparison, the term *śūnyatā* (as either *stong pa nyid* or *stong nyid*) is found 65,597 times scattered among approximately 1,500 texts, and *sahaja* (as either *lhan cig skes* or *lhan skyes*) is found 2,816 times scattered among around 700 texts.

the full range of the term's development in India. Thus, among other things, *mahāmudrā* could denote:

1. A hand gesture signifying clear visualization of a deity
2. One of a series of "seals" (with or without hand gestures) that confirm tantric ritual procedures
3. A buddha family
4. A consort employed in sexual yoga practices
5. A tantric empowerment
6. The great bliss and luminous gnosis that result from subtle-body practices
7. A meditation technique in which mind contemplates its own nature
8. A way of living in the world freely and spontaneously
9. The omniscient buddhahood that is the final outcome of the tantric path

As part of a growing web of Buddhist soteriological terms, *mahāmudrā* came to be synonymous with such ideas as emptiness, the middle, sameness, the connate, the natural mind, luminosity, the single taste, nonduality, nonmentation, buddha nature, nonabiding nirvāṇa, and a buddha's Dharma body—to name just a few.

Amid these abundant denotations and connotations, we find two major conceptions of mahāmudrā. What we might call *esoteric mahāmudrā* focuses on the generation of a nonconceptual, blissful gnosis of reality—the natural mind—through subtle-body practices described in the literature of the mahāyoga and yoginī tantras; it corresponds roughly to what Kagyü traditions would refer to as the "path of means." By contrast, what we might call *nondual mahāmudrā* focuses on attaining a direct and unmediated experience of the natural mind through a sudden transcendence of thought, image, and effort, as described in the songs and treatises of the mahāsiddhas; it corresponds to the Kagyü "path of liberation."[199] Although these two approaches to mahāmudrā are distinguishable, they are not mutually exclusive, since the mahāyoga and yoginī tantras contain numerous passages that suggest the unadorned views and practices of nondual mahāmudrā, while the mahāsiddhas who expound nondual mahāmudrā usually do so within a context profoundly shaped by the

199. Along similar lines, the Fourth Shamarpa Chödrak Yeshé (1453–1524) distinguishes between an esoteric "mahāmudrā of the connate gnosis of bliss and emptiness" (*bde stong lhan skyes ye shes phyag chen*) and the nondual "mahāmudrā of awareness and emptiness" (*rig stong phyag chen*), which is synonymous with nonmentation. See Draszczyk 2019.

esoteric practices of the "higher" tantras. Nor should esoteric and nondual mahāmudrā be conflated with the oft-used Tibetan categories of *perfection* and *mantra mahāmudrā*, since the distinction between those two often presupposes non-overlapping styles of practice, while both esoteric and nondual mahāmudrā—their differing emphases notwithstanding—are deeply steeped in both the sūtras and tantras.

Broadly speaking, reflection on mahāmudrā in renaissance Tibet was stimulated by the gradual translation of the late Indian tantric literature—especially the yoginī tantras and the writings of the mahāsiddhas—in which the term had gained such importance. At the same time, a number of Indian and Tibetan masters involved in the revival of Buddhism in Tibet focused prominently on mahāmudrā texts and teachings, helping the term to stand out from the welter of concepts that were being newly transmitted across the Himalayas. In most cases, these masters—who interacted frequently with one another—came to be regarded as at or near the origin of various practice lineages that developed in Tibet, and at least some of these practice lineages became sufficiently institutionalized that they developed into identifiable "orders" or "schools"—some of which have survived to the present day. Traditions that arose in eleventh-century Tibet based primarily on the new tantric texts and translations that began to appear then are generally designated as New Translation schools. These include the Marpa Kagyü, Kadam, Shiché, Chö, Shangpa Kagyü, Sakya, Jonang, and Geluk. (The last two schools arose two to three centuries later.) The one tradition that situates its origins in the imperial period, and often follows the tantric texts and translations available then, is designated as the Old Translation school, the Nyingma. As we will see, all of these traditions incorporated notions of mahāmudrā into their discourse to one degree or another.

Just as the mahāsiddha Maitrīpa stands near the culmination of mahāmudrā discourse in India, so he is in some ways the fountainhead of many, if not all, Tibetan traditions that focus on the term. He never visited Tibet, but several of his Indian disciples and grand-disciples did, and a number of Tibetan masters traveled to India to retrieve teachings from him. In terms of the long-term development of mahāmudrā discourse in Tibet, Maitrīpa's most important disciple by far was the founder of the Marpa Kagyü tradition, Marpa Chökyi Lodrö (1012–97), to whom we will return shortly. The most significant figure in the actual transmission of mahāmudrā texts and teachings to Tibet during the eleventh century was Maitrīpa's disciple Vajrapāṇi (b. 1017),[200] who is less renowned for his writings than for twice visiting Tibet, transmitting and

200. See, e.g., Roerich 1976, 843 and 857–59, and Schaeffer 2005a, 62–63.

cotranslating a number of important mahāmudrā text cycles, and instructing a variety of South Asian and Tibetan students. Among his important Tibetan disciples were Drok José, Nakpo Sherdé, and Maban Chöbar, who all were instrumental in spreading mahāmudrā texts and practices in Tibet. Vajrapāṇi's most significant South Asian disciple was Balpo Asu, a Nepalese brahman (known to Tibetans as Kyemé Dechen) who took a special interest in Saraha's works.[201] Asu traveled to Tibet and there became a teacher of Rechungpa, an important figure in Kagyü lineages, and of Ngaripa, who helped reconcile differences between the approaches of Vajrapāṇi and Asu and whose granddisciple, Parphuwa Lodrö Sengé, wrote voluminously and influentially on Saraha's songs. Another figure important in the transmission of Saraha's songs to Tibet was Kor Nirūpa (1062–1102), a disciple of both Maitrīpa's student Karopa and (perhaps) the great translator Vairocanarakṣita, who was himself an important and widely traveled scholar.[202] As crucial as all these men were in the development of mahāmudrā discourse in Tibet—they provided many of the textual foundations on which later traditions built—few of them were assigned a significant place in the lineages that carried mahāmudrā ideas and practices down through the centuries. Quite apart from Marpa, though, three other figures purported to be disciples of Maitrīpa and thus deeply learned in mahāmudrā did come to be regarded as founding figures of lineages that left their long-term mark on Tibetan Buddhism: Atiśa, Phadampa Sangyé, and Nigumā.

Atiśa and the Kadam

Atiśa, also known as Dīpaṃkara Śrījñāna (982–1054),[203] was a Bengali paṇḍita renowned as one of the "reformers" of Buddhist thought and practice during the Tibetan Renaissance. A master of the sūtra and tantra traditions, he placed special emphasis on living a morally pure life dedicated to the development of love, compassion, and the awakening mind and, in his *Lamp on the Path to Awakening* (*Bodhipathapradīpa*) and its autocommentary, articulated an all-inclusive, gradual training that became a model for the "stages of the path" (*lam rim*) literature that would be adopted by every major Tibetan order. He was invited to Gugé in western Tibet in 1042 and eventually made his way to the Lhasa area, where he spent the remainder of his life, teaching,

201. See Guenther 1969 for a translation of his commentary on Saraha's *King Dohā Treasury*.

202. On these persons and events, see Roerich 1976, chapter 11, and Schaeffer 2005a, 62–67.

203. See, e.g., Chattopadhyaya 1967, Roerich 1976, 241–63, Snellgrove 1987, vol. 2, Gyaltsen 1990, 145–86, Davidson 2005, chaps. 3–4, Apple 2019a, and Apple 2019b.

writing, translating, and attracting a coterie of disciples who inaugurated the Kadam lineage. The Kadampa *geshés* (*dge bshes*), or spiritual friends, were for many centuries famed for their ascetic rigor, their extensive writings on mind training (*blo sbyong*), and their role in promulgating important Indian philosophical traditions in Tibet, especially those of two seventh-century thinkers, the logician Dharmakīrti and the Mādhyamika Candrakīrti. Though the Kadam order lacked the institutional power and persistence of other orders and faded by the fourteenth century, it was "resurrected" around 1400 in the form of the Geluk order, whose founder, Tsongkhapa, self-consciously modeled himself on the Kadam geshés in general and on Atiśa in particular.

Atiśa's precise connection to Maitrīpa and mahāmudrā is ambiguous. The great fifteenth-century Tibetan historian Gö Lotsāwa asserts that Atiśa studied the *Sublime Continuum*, Saraha's songs, and other mahāmudrā-related texts with Maitrīpa and eventually became one of the first promulgators of mahāmudrā teachings in Tibet. At the same time, the sixteenth-century historian Tāranātha claims that Atiśa was responsible for Maitrīpa's expulsion from Vikramaśīla Monastery on the grounds of immorality.[204] Gö does go on to relate how Atiśa's foremost Tibetan disciple, Dromtönpa (1000–64), urged his master not to teach Saraha's songs in Tibet, lest their antinomian rhetoric be misunderstood and taken literally—as had happened before in Tibet with tantric teachings. Gö also reports that Atiśa's disciple Potowa (1027–1105) expressed reservations about the Kagyüpas' use of the *King of Concentrations Sūtra* in conjunction with mahāmudrā practice.[205] It is true that Atiśa and his successors placed somewhat less emphasis on tantric teachings, including mahāmudrā, than did many other Indians and Tibetans of the eleventh century; as a later commentator noted, the Kadampas "did not recite the secret mantra in the marketplace."[206] Nevertheless, Atiśa was well schooled in the tantras. Not only did he situate tantric practices at the culmination of the gradual path he espoused, but he is credited with a number of "minor" texts that address tantra in general and mahāmudrā in particular.

For instance, in the section on the completion stage in his Cakrasaṃvara-tradition treatise *Discerning the Higher Realization* (*Abhisamayavibhaṅga*),

204. Roerich 1976, 843–44, Tāranātha 1983, 11, Shizuki 2015, and Apple 2019a, 22. Of course, these two facts need not be contradictory. In his recent study of Atiśa's mahāmudrā teachings, James Apple (2017, 27) concludes that Atiśa did not study mahāmudrā with Maitrīpa, though he does not deny that they may have been acquainted.

205. Roerich 1976, 844 and 452. For a discussion of Kagyü uses of the *King of Concentrations*, see Thomas 2019.

206. Tk*SGML* 74; trans. Thuken 2009, 113.

Atiśa discusses "the ultimate, the uncompounded . . . the object of nonreferential wisdom, which is . . . the nondual mahāmudrā union." Later, he adds, "not abiding anywhere, not abiding in the two extremes—that is the mahāmudrā union. . . . Abiding in the glow of luminosity . . . the yogī who abides in the mind of mahāmudrā union does not display nirvāṇa."[207] Another Cakrasaṃvara-based text, the *Great Exposition of View and Meditation* (*Lta sgom chen mo*) includes an extended discussion of the view entertained by a perfect mind (*yang dag pa'i yid kyis lta ba*), which is the connate, luminous mind, whose "clarity is like a lamp, whose transparency is like calm water, and whose purity is like the center of pure space. . . . It is unutterable, inconceivable, inexpressible, unproduced, the character of the essence of space, the character to be known by oneself, and an object of superior gnosis."[208] It is, in short, mahāmudrā.[209] In his *Diamond Song [Sung] at the Diamond Seat* (*Vajrāsanavajragīti*), Atiśa, in the words of James Apple, "play[s] upon literal erotic sentiment and metaphoric gnostic realization, which induce the practitioner to achieve the nondual unity of clear light and uncontaminated virtuous qualities, resulting in the great seal."[210] Atiśa's root verses[211] do not mention mahāmudrā, but his commentary to the poem specifies that "Lady No-Self, a lovely young woman, possesses the uncontaminated virtues of experiencing luminosity and the connate. Thus, through quickly accomplishing the union of the two, one attains the fruitional mahāmudrā."[212]

Although less renowned than his *Lamp on the Path to Awakening*, Atiśa's *Stages of the Path to Awakening* (*Byang chub lam gyi rim pa*) includes instructions on insight meditation that, as Apple notes, "significantly differ from the analytical thought utilizing reasoning found in the *Lamp on the Path*," in that they "focus on pointing out the connate nature of one's own mind, a nature equivalent to the Dharma body (*dharmakāya*)."[213] For instance, Atiśa writes:

> Mind itself, spontaneously established from the beginning, cannot be accomplished by the many, who search for signs of it. When one

207. At*AV* 200b; cf. Apple 2017, 4.

208. At*TG* 634; trans. Apple 2017, 9.

209. At*TG* 635.

210. Apple 2017, 15.

211. At*VG*.

212. At*VV* 210a; cf. Apple 2017, 15.

213. Apple 2017, 22 (translation adapted). Mahāmudrā is mentioned just three times in Atiśa's autocommentary to *Lamp on the Path*, in each case in the sense of the great-seal accomplishment at the end of the path; see At*BP* 250a, 289a, 290a; trans. Sherburne 1983, pp. 45, 173, and 175.

> meditates without a view and is free of activity, the result, not to be sought elsewhere, is established from the beginning. Whether it's taught through the conditions provided by a guru or not, whether a yogī meditates or not, whether the wise realize it or not, unconditioned mind itself is free from causes and conditions.[214]

Although the term *mahāmudrā* is not specifically applied to this practice, it is very much in line with earlier Indian, and Tibetan, contexts in which the term is used. A final mahāmudrā-oriented text by Atiśa is his *Special Instructions on the Connate Union* (*Lhan cig skyes byor gyi gdam ngag*), also known as the *Mahāmudrā Given by Atiśa to Gönpawa* (*Jo bo rjes dgon pa ba la gnang ba'i phyag chen*). As the title indicates, Atiśa supposedly taught the practice to his disciple Gönpawa Wangchuk Gyaltsen (1016–82); it was, according to Apple, orally transmitted among early Kadampas and eventually written down by Kagyü monks.[215] As in the *Stages of the Path*, Atiśa focuses on realization of the primordial connate mind, which is equivalent to a buddha's Dharma body, instructing practitioners to rest unswervingly in the nonconceptual, nondual nature of mind and leading them to realization through four yogas: single-pointedness, nonelaboration, single taste, and nonmeditation.[216] When one has traversed the four paths and attained realization, one's eventual death becomes an easy matter: one's mind and vital winds absorb into the central channel and "ascend to the place where gnosis connate with reality (*dharmatā*) naturally abides. In this way, when a person already acquainted with this through the power of meditation recognizes it upon meeting it, and when the natural luminosity and the luminosity of meditation meet, one gains the accomplishment of mahāmudrā."[217]

Although these texts did not achieve the fame or influence of Atiśa's teachings on the stages of the path or on mind training, his mahāmudrā-related writings were preserved and eventually incorporated into the Tengyur, and there seems little doubt that he transmitted them, whether orally or in written form, to certain disciples. The sixteenth-century Kagyü scholar Dakpo Tashi Namgyal, for instance, asserts that Atiśa passed on instructions on how to meditate on the "quintessence of reality," i.e., mahāmudrā (received not from Maitrīpa

214. At*BK* 55; cf. trans. Apple 2017, 20.

215. Apple 2017, 23.

216. As Apple notes (2017, 26), although these four yogas bear the same names as the four yogas discussed in Kagyü mahāmudrā literature, their definitions differ somewhat.

217. At*LC* 878; cf. Apple 2017, 34, trans. 31.

but his contemporary, Ḍombī Heruka), to Naljorpa and Gönpawa,[218] suggesting that a tradition of mahāmudrā practice persisted among small circles of Kadampas, out of the public eye. Evidence for this possibility is furnished by the fact that a twelfth-century scholar, the aforementioned Parphuwa Lodrö Sengé (a student of both Kadam and Kagyü masters), wrote commentaries on a number of Saraha's songs and promulgated their study.[219] Further evidence may be gleaned between the lines of some of the wisdom teachings found in various Kadam mind-training texts and the *Book of Kadam*,[220] as well as in the gnomic *Oral Teaching of the Precious Father Chegom*, composed by Chegom Sherab Dorjé (b. 1130?), a master of both Kadam and Kagyü traditions[221] who does not mention mahāmudrā explicitly but employs discourse deeply resonant with that of mahāmudrā traditions, advising, for instance:

> Knowing saṃsāric worldly appearances to be mind,
> realizing mind itself to be empty,
> not grasping at your realizations as superior—
> that is completion of the view.
>
> Imbibing the nectar of the unwavering,
> settling within the uncontrived,
> not grasping at a fixed object of meditation—
> that is the completion of meditation.
>
> Taking unpleasant conditions onto the path,
> cutting desire for pleasant things,
> not arguing about what's to be done and shunned—
> that is the completion of conduct. . . .
>
> Purifying basic awareness,
> keeping the Dharma body as your natural place,
> doing good for others, though they lack self—
> that is completion of the result.[222]

218. Kn*PCOZ* 132a; trans. Dakpo Tashi Namgyal 1986, 143.

219. Schaeffer 2005a, 74–75.

220. See Jinpa 2006 and Jinpa 2008.

221. For information and further bibliographic resources related to Chegompa, see Martin 2008.

222. Lc*CGZN* 52. I am grateful to José Cabezón for bringing this text to my attention.

Chegompa also composed a work on various aspects of twelfth-century Tibetan thought and practice, the *Jewel Mound of Pith Instructions* (*Man ngag rin chen spungs pa*), that addresses mahāmudrā more explicitly. Chegompa touches on issues important to mahāmudrā discourse, such as the relation between sūtra and mantra systems and sudden and gradual approaches to awakening.[223] Furthermore, he specifically expounds a mahāmudrā practice tradition primarily linked to Gampopa, the connate union (*lhan cig skyes sbyor*), in which the scrutiny of delusions leads to their "self-liberation," and eventually to full buddhahood.[224] Thus his credentials as a Kadampa cognizant of, and willing to teach, mahāmudrā seem quite solid.

It has recently been suggested that, despite traditional Kagyü claims that their mahāmudrā tradition is rooted primarily in the teachings of Nāropa, Maitrīpa, Marpa, and Milarepa, the immensely influential versions of mahāmudrā promulgated in the twelfth century by Gampopa actually owe a great deal to Atiśa and the Kadampas, whose doctrines Gampopa learned in his youth.[225] This is perhaps debatable, but it does seem fair to say that mahāmudrā figured much more prominently in the writings of Atiśa and the lives of the Kadampas than generally is believed, and that the concept of mahāmudrā found in the tradition includes instances both of esoteric mahāmudrā and nondual mahāmudrā.

Shiché and Chö

Phadampa Sangyé (d. 1117)[226] was a peripatetic master from South India. He is traditionally said to have studied at the feet of fifty-four mahāsiddhas, both male and female, who comprise a veritable who's who of Indian Buddhist masters, including the likes of Nāgārjuna, Asaṅga, Dharmakīrti, Śāntideva, Padmasambhava, and Lakṣmīṅkarā. His instructors in mahāmudrā are said to have included Saraha, Śavaripa, and Maitrīpa. There obviously are some chronological problems posed by Phadampa's discipleship with masters spanning nearly a thousand years, but even if some of the guru-disciple connections seem unlikely (or are best explained as visionary encounters), his acquaintance

223. Kapstein 2000, 77. Kapstein mentions that, according to an informant, Chegom's works still are studied in some Gelukpa circles. Given his strong connection to the Kadam, this is not surprising. I have never, though, seen or heard it suggested that his works influenced the development of Geluk mahāmudrā.

224. Bentor 1997, Martin 2008. As noted above, "connate union" was used earlier, by Atiśa.

225. Apple 2017, 1–3.

226. See, e.g., Roerich 1976, 902–26, and Molk 2008.

with Maitrīpa is plausible, as their lifespans almost certainly overlapped. Phadampa traveled and studied in every part of the subcontinent and visited Tibet five times, spending twelve years in China between his fourth and fifth Tibetan sojourns. His travels in Tibet took him all over the country, where he taught a multitude of disciples and helped transmit perfection, mantra, and mahāmudrā ideas and practices through his own teachings and seventeen anthologies of songs by Indian mahāsiddhas that he compiled. A number of traditions insist that he met the great yogī Milarepa, with whom he exchanged teachings and songs, including a famous and quite amusing poetic dialogue about the yogic "madness" they shared.[227] He is most closely associated with Dingri, in the Himalayan region, where he spent his final years, sang a famous song of advice to the inhabitants, and instructed a wide range of students in his signature meditation practice, pacification (*zhi byed*).[228] Pacification, or Shiché, derives its name from a line in the *Heart Sūtra* (*Prajñāpāramitāhṛdaya*) that associates the perfection of wisdom—that is, insight into emptiness—with the "pacification of all suffering."[229]

The practice of pacification—also referred to as the Mahāmudrā of Symbols (*brda'i phyag chen*) or the Stainless Drop of Mahāmudrā (*phyag chen dri med thig le*)—involves common and uncommon teachings, which correspond roughly to nondual and esoteric mahāmudrā, respectively. The common approach, which the Geluk scholar Thuken Chökyi Nyima describes as "the activation of the stages of the path of the perfection of wisdom, a little-known special instruction for putting into practice the entire meaning of the three Perfection of Wisdom sūtras,"[230] involves direct, nonconceptual realization of the mind's true nature. In some contexts, Phadampa transmits the teaching through symbolic actions (e.g., binding up his mouth with a sling to show that reality is ineffable) or gnomic utterances (e.g., "Stay naked!" that is, maintain awareness).[231] Elsewhere, he defines *mahāmudrā* as "being free of mental activity," which is synonymous with "a mind free of bias . . . one's own pure mind . . . what is beyond speech or expression . . . spontaneous connate awareness."[232] This nondual mahāmudrā approach is complemented by

227. See Chang 1989, 2:606–14, Kunga and Cutillo 1995, 85–89, and Tsangnyön Heruka 2016, 629–36.

228. See Roerich 1976, 867–71, Schaeffer 2005a, 88–96, and Molk 2008, 27–174.

229. *PHS* 112–13, trans. 113.

230. Tk*SGML* 119–20, trans. Thuken 2009, 163.

231. Molk 2008, 179 and 189.

232. Molk 2008, 289.

the uncommon approach, which understands mahāmudrā in far more esoteric terms, derived from the "path of means" teachings of such mahāsiddhas as Saraha, Virūpa, and Nāropa.

Probably the most famous mahāmudrā tradition originating from Phadampa was Chö, the practice of severance (or "cutting off," *gcod*). More fully, it was the "severance mahāmudrā whose objective is the severing of demons," which, tradition tells us, was popularized in Tibet beginning with his great Tibetan female disciple (or grand-disciple), Machik Lapdrön (1055–1143).[233] Like pacification, severance is traced to the Perfection of Wisdom literature, in this case to passages that speak of a bodhisattva's severance of four *māras*, or demons—aggregates, defilements, the lord of death, and the desirous young devas—through the awakening mind, understanding of emptiness, keeping one's word, and being blessed by the buddhas. Also like pacification, severance has both nondual and esoteric strands to it. Its nondual side, in which the meanings of the four mudrās and the perfection of wisdom are "combined inseparably into one"[234] is expressed in a variety of verses attributed to Machik, where she speaks of mahāmudrā in now-familiar terms:

> Primordially connate, like space
> it does nothing, depends on nothing.
> In just the same way, the mind itself
> possesses no support, possesses no object:
> let it rest in its natural realm, without fabrication.
> When the bonds are loosed,
> you will be free, no doubt.[235]

Esoteric severance mahāmudrā includes teachings on both maṇḍala and subtle-body practices and on the idiosyncratically Chö-lineage technique of offering up one's body to visualized demons in order to sever grasping at self. At one point, Machik divides tantric mahāmudrā into phenomena mahāmudrā (realizing emptiness), action mahāmudrā (experiencing bliss

233. On Machik, see, e.g., Roerich 1976, 983–84, Edou 1996, and Harding 2003. In a paper presented at the thirteenth seminar of the International Association of Tibetan Studies, Sarah Harding (2013) has questioned whether we really can be certain that Machik taught severance, though tradition certainly insists upon it.

234. Harding 2003, 88. Cf. Thuken 2009, 166, "The essence of the Chö instruction is the practice of the perfection of wisdom that is in conformity with mantra."

235. Edou 1996, 165. The last two lines are taken from Saraha, who sometimes is said to be the originator of the severance tradition (Gyatso 1985, 324).

through a consort), pledge mahāmudrā (maintaining secrecy), bliss-emptiness mahāmudrā (an experience of bliss induced by realizing emptiness), and clarity-emptiness mahāmudrā (the experience of all things as illusion-like).[236] According to the nineteenth-century scholar Jamgön Kongtrul, nondual mahāmudrā practices establish the mind in its own empty nature, while the various esoteric practices connected with visualization, subtle-body yogas, and self-sacrifice enable one to attain the culmination of tantric practice: the attainment of mahāmudrā, which is synonymous with the great middle way (*mahāmadhyamaka*) and the great perfection (*mahāsaṅdhi, rdzogs chen*).[237]

Although Shiché and Chö are both important practice lineages, the wandering yogic lifestyle favored by most of its practitioners militated against the lineages becoming institutionalized into orders centered in major temples or monasteries. Despite this, Shiché and Chö—especially the latter—were incorporated into a range of traditions that did institutionalize, and they have been preserved, along with their distinctive perspectives on mahāmudrā, down to the present day in all four major orders of Tibetan Buddhism: Nyingma, Kagyü, Sakya, and Geluk.

Shangpa Kagyü

Another important yogic lineage stemming at least in part from Maitrīpa is the Shangpa Kagyü,[238] which is distinguished from the Marpa Kagyü in terms of its Indian and Tibetan sources. Rather than Nāropa and Marpa, it is traced to Nāropa's consort (or sister), Nigumā, and the Tibetan master Khyungpo Naljor—though Maitrīpa appears as a mahāmudrā teacher common to both. According to Tibetan historians, Khyungpo Naljor (d. 1135)[239] was a practitioner of both Bön and Nyingma in his youth, and as an adult traveled to Nepal and India in search of further teachings, eventually studying under one hundred fifty masters. Of these, the most significant were Puṇyākaragupta, better known as Dorjé Denpa; Maitrīpa; Rāhulagupta; and (in visionary form) the female siddha-ḍākinīs Nigumā and Sukhasiddhī. The most influential of all was Nigumā, from whom he received—along with many other tantric teachings—the five golden Dharmas that form the "tree" of Shangpa practice: (1) the "root," the six Dharmas, which are the same as those of Nāropa (inner

236. Harding 2003, 114.

237. Edou 1996, 46.

238. See, e.g., Thuken 2009, 118–20.

239. See, e.g., Roerich 1976, 732ff., Sopa et al 2009, 118–19, and Jamgön Kongtrul 2003, 61–83.

heat, illusory body, dream yoga, luminosity, transfer of consciousness, and intermediate state), (2) the "trunk," the amulet box (*ga'u ma*) mahāmudrā, (3) the "branches," the three integrations (in which all sights, sounds, and thoughts are understood as guru, deity, and illusion and become the three buddha bodies), (4) the "flowers," the meditative ritual of white and red forms of Khecarī, or Vajrayoginī, and (5) the "fruit," the attainment of the immortal mind and the infallible body of buddhahood.[240]

The amulet box mahāmudrā, elements of which Khyungpo received from both Maitrīpa and Nigumā, was so named by Khyungpo because he carried the instructions in an amulet box he wore around his neck. Because an amulet box usually is divided into two interlocking sections, the term also came to connote the way in which, in mahāmudrā practice, one conjoins method and wisdom, clarity and emptiness, or bliss and emptiness. Fundamentally, the practice of the amulet box mahāmudrā involves (from Nigumā) the "natural settling" of body, speech, and mind in serenity and insight, (from Maitrīpa) releasing faults through gaining certainty about the true nature of mind, and (from Sukhasiddhī) recognizing that one's ordinary mind is the three bodies of a buddha.[241] The root texts for the practice are two teachings attributed to Nigumā but written down by Khyungpo, the *Vajra Lines of the Amulet Mahāmudrā* and *Naturally Free Mahāmudrā*, which contain such familiar notions as "the natural resting of mind" and being "without mentation, free of all hopes and fears," such that "one's mind without distraction is the Dharma body," in which "by knowing that in suchness of mind, even when engaging in the five sense desirables, one does not move out of the nature of things."[242] The language of these poems has the feel of the nondual mahāmudrā of the mahāsiddhas, but it is important to note that—like so many mahāmudrā transmissions early in the Tibetan Renaissance—the amulet box mahāmudrā is deeply embedded within the context of esoteric tantric practice.

Khyungpo Naljor made numerous trips to South Asia and, once settled in Tibet, attracted many disciples and founded numerous monasteries in the Shang region, west of Lhasa, where he transmitted the teachings he had received. In the long term, the Shangpa Kagyü did not develop into a fully independent order. Rather, like the Shiché and Chö lineages, it was adopted into other traditions. It has been preserved more or less intact within the Marpa Kagyü, in which it has continued as a distinct lineage until the present

240. Harding 2010, 30–33.

241. Harding 2010, 32.

242. Harding 2010, pp. 145, 147, and 151 (translation adapted).

day. It also has been preserved within the Jonang tradition in the northeastern region of Amdo.

Sakya

Two other traditions that may be traced to the eleventh century, the Sakya and the Nyingma, are less obviously connected to Maitrīpa than the Marpa Kagyü, Kadam, Shiché, Chö, and Shangpa Kagyü, yet mahāmudrā entered the discourse of each.

The Sakya, named after the site in Tsang where the tradition's main monastery was founded in 1073, has from its inception been connected with the Khön family, an important clan in west-central Tibet. Its patriarch, Khön Könchok Gyalpo (1034–1102), rejected the Nyingma affiliation (if not all the Nyingma practices) of his ancestors and turned to the study of the yoginī and other later tantras under the translator Drokmi Lotsāwa (d. 1064), who himself had studied in India with Virūpa's disciple Ḍombī Heruka and in Tibet with the Indian paṇḍita Gayādhara. Over the course of two hundred years, such descendants of Könchok Gyalpo as Sachen Kunga Nyingpo (1092–1158), Drakpa Gyaltsen (1147–1216), and Kunga Gyaltsen, better known as Sakya Paṇḍita, or Sapaṇ (1182–1251), would shape the Sakya into an order that combined deep study of tantric traditions (especially the Hevajra and the Vajrakīlaya systems) with extraordinary philosophical and literary attainment, and would become for a time, under the sponsorship of the Mongol Yuan dynasty of China (1271–1368), a major political force in Inner Asia. After the collapse of the Yuan, the Sakya became marginalized politically but continued their strong traditions of scholarship and practice, which are maintained to the present day.

The central practice tradition for the Sakya is the path and fruit (*lam 'bras*), an integrated system of sūtra- and tantra-based discourses and rituals that is said to have been transmitted to Drokmi by Gayādhara, who in turn traced it back through several generations of teachers to Virūpa, and based it primarily on the *Hevajra Tantra*. As we have seen, both the *Hevajra* and Virūpa use *mahāmudrā* in a number of different senses, and Sakya tradition is as broadly conversant with the yoginī tantras and the works of the great Indian siddhas as any other New Translation school. In addition, Gayādhara is said by one Tibetan source to have studied with Maitrīpa and by several others to have actually impersonated him in Tibet.[243] Nevertheless, as path and fruit discourse developed, the usages of *mahāmudrā* became relatively restricted: for the most part, follow-

243. Stearns 2001, 51, and Davidson 2005, 178.

ing on a statement in Virūpa's *Vajra Verses*, it was used to refer to the result of an advanced tantric path that begins with empowerment: the omniscient buddhahood known as the *mahāmudrā attainment*. It also was used occasionally to denote the view attained as the result of empowerment or a tantric practice, but in most cases the referents presuppose tantric empowerment.[244] This relatively narrow, purely esoteric Sakya definition of mahāmudrā stood in marked contrast to the expansive ways in which the term was used in a number of other New Translation schools, especially the Marpa Kagyü, and as we will see below, this contrast would serve as the basis for a major debate on mahāmudrā between Sakyapas and Kagyüpas beginning in the thirteenth century.

It is worth adding that, despite the Sakyapas' rather restricted usage of the term *mahāmudrā*, many of the meditations and other practices associated with the path and fruit tradition, under such names as the Inseparability of Saṃsāra and Nirvāna (*'khor 'das dbyer med*) or the Three Appearances (*snang gsum*), bear a striking resemblance to those that, in other traditions, go under the name of mahāmudrā. Perfection Vehicle path and fruit meditations include such practices as severing the apprehension of true existence or nonexistence (on the basis of Nāgārjuna's teachings) or severing the mistaken appearances of object and subject (on the basis of Maitreya's teachings). Mantra Vehicle meditations include seeking, then recognizing or identifying, the nature of mind, after which one gains the threefold understanding that appearances are mind, mind is illusory, and illusions are intrinsically nonexistent. The Mantra Vehicle also includes various practices and realizations that involve the conjunction of the awareness of emptiness with experiences of clarity, bliss, and nonduality.[245] To use traditional categories, the view, meditation, conduct, and fruit associated with any of these could be—and were—taken as referents of *mahāmudrā* in a range of Indian and Tibetan settings, but the Sakyapas persisted for the most part in maintaining their quite specific, tantrically inflected sense of the term.

Nyingma

Nyingma traditions[246] find their sources of authority not in the texts and teachers of the Tibetan Renaissance but, rather, in those of Tibet's imperial period. They emphasize such commonly accepted texts as the *Guhyasamāja* and *Vajrakīlaya* tantras and the eighteen *Māyājāla* tantras; and such idiosyncratically Nyingma

244. Stearns 2006, 577 and 42–43.

245. See, e.g., Thuken 2009, 186–95.

246. See especially Dudjom 1991.

sources as the *Secret Essence Tantra*, the *Tantra of the All-Creating Sovereign* (*Kulayarāja Tantra*), and the *Sūtra That Gathers Intentions* (*Mdo dgongs pa 'dus pa*). They honor such late-first-millennium Indian teachers as Garab Dorjé, Śrī Siṃha, Mañjuśrīkīrti, Vimalamitra, Vairocana, and—above all—Padmasambhava. Padmasambhava, a charismatic mahāsiddha from Oḍḍiyāna, generally believed to have been located in northwest India, is widely credited by Tibetans with helping establish Buddhism in their land in the late eighth century, but he is an elusive figure, one whose purported activities and very existence have sometimes been doubted. Yet, as new texts and teachers flooded into Tibet in the eleventh century, followers of the older traditions began to shape their own sectarian identity, based in large part on their evocation of Padmasambhava. They saw "Guru Rinpoché" not just as a long-ago siddha and royal preceptor but as a buddha in his own right who continued to manifest in visionary encounters and miraculous deeds, and whose secret teachings were uncovered as "treasures" (*gter ma*) hidden in the earth, or a pillar, or the revealer's own mind.

The teaching tradition that became definitive of the Nyingma was the great perfection (or completeness, *rdzogs chen*), a radical, nondual system of thought and practice traceable to texts and teachers from the imperial period. It did not receive strong articulation, however, until early in the Tibetan Renaissance and only was expounded in full at the time of the great Longchen Rabjampa (1308–63).[247] According to David Germano, the great perfection may have originated in the Himalayas in the eighth or ninth centuries as "an aestheticized and streamlined" style of tantric meditation,[248] deeply beholden to the Indian mahāyoga tantras but also influenced by Chinese Chan and native Tibetan conceptions.[249] In time, it came to be regarded as the acme of the Buddha's teaching, transcending even the esoteric completion- or perfection-stage (*rdzogs rim*) subtle-body practices of advanced tantras—hence the appellation "great perfection" (*rdzogs chen*). It was eventually analyzed into three progressively advanced classes of texts and practices: mind, expanse,

247. Among the many works on the great perfection, see especially Karmay 1988, Tulku Thondup 1989, and van Schaik 2004.

248. Germano 1994, 215.

249. Germano 1994, 211. It is not impossible, either, that the great perfection developed in conversation with Kashmir Śaiva circles: there are certain doctrinal resonances between the two traditions (e.g., in their emphasis on nonduality, the primacy of consciousness, and a penchant for gnostic cosmogony), and they seem to have arisen in roughly the same geographical area—the western Himalayas—and at roughly the same time, the eighth through tenth centuries.

and esoteric instruction.[250] At the highest level, its practice is divided into phases in which the yogī first relaxes into the pure, open space of primordial gnosis (*khreg chod*, "breakthrough") and then thinks, speaks, and acts freely, spontaneously, and creatively within that realm (*thod rgal*, "transcendence"). Although its terminology is specialized, rooted as it is in texts and teachings developed long before the Tibetan Renaissance, the great perfection's blend of esoteric and nondual styles of discourse is reminiscent of that of mahāmudrā. As Germano notes, the great perfection probably originated "among Himalayan yogic circles belonging to a similar Buddhist milieu as that which generated other such traditions, reflected in Dohā literature and mahāmudrā."[251] At the same time, though, as Thuken Losang Chökyi Nyima (1737–1802) observes, the great perfection "is a lot like mahāmudrā, but . . . there are great differences in meaning between the two, because mahāmudrā practitioners place their emphasis on the object, while great-perfection practitioners establish the subject, mind itself, as awareness that is empty and primordially pure."[252]

Nyingma terminology is distinctive and draws on a vocabulary developed before mahāmudrā became a major term in Indian Buddhism. As a result, there is not much discussion of mahāmudrā in early Nyingma literature, although it does, of course, turn up in some of the tantras that are accepted in common by the Old and New Translation schools, such as the *Māyājāla* and *Guhyasamāja*; occasionally, too, it appears in idiosyncratically Nyingma tantras, such as the *Secret Essence*.[253] At the dawn of the Tibetan Renaissance (or perhaps earlier), Nyingmapas developed their own sixfold scheme for classifying Buddhist tantras as action, performance (or method, *upa*), yoga, mahāyoga, anuyoga, and atiyoga, which initially included only Old Translation tantras but later incorporated New Translation tantras—mainly the yoginī tantras—as well. Thus, in fully developed schemes like that of Longchenpa, mahāmudrā gained a small but significant foothold in Nyingma discourse. In yoga tantras,

250. Germano 1994, 215.

251. Germano 1994, 215.

252. Thuken 2009, 87; cf. Germano 1994, 324. Most Kagyü scholars would observe that Thuken's characterization of mahāmudrā as object-oriented might fit with the Geluk approach to the great seal, but that the Kagyü approach to it is in fact subject-oriented, hence closer to the approach to meditation identified by Thuken with the great perfection. That Kagyüpas are subject-oriented and Gelukpas object-oriented is in fact the view of Thuken's Gelukpa predecessor, Paṇchen Sönam Drakpa; see below, page 192.

253. See Dalton 2019.

it refers to physical gestures,[254] in mahāyoga, to the clear visualization of oneself as a deity during a sādhana ritual, and in anuyoga, to the luminous and blissful realization of emptiness effected by subtle-body practices.[255] Nyingmapas also occasionally used mahāmudrā in the sense of the supreme attainment at the end of the path,[256] but in the literature of atiyoga, the highest level of tantra, it is the great perfection that usually receives this distinction.

From the early Tibetan Renaissance on, there was considerable interchange between proponents of the New and Old translations, and they influenced one another in significant ways. With respect to the specific connections between mahāmudrā and the great perfection, Nyingmapa masters granted mahāmudrā practices an increasingly prestigious place in their tradition and sometimes drew on New Translation tantras and the writings of such figures as Saraha, but they never permitted mahāmudrā to displace the great perfection at the summit of the spiritual pyramid. At the same time, masters of the New Translation schools, especially in the Marpa Kagyü, drew occasionally on Nyingma classifications, terminology, or practice, and in some rare but notable cases implicitly or explicitly attempted to forge a synthesis between mahāmudrā and the great perfection.[257]

254. Tulku Thondup 1989, 20.

255. See Tulku Thondup 1989, 13.

256. Tulku Thondup 1989, 365, and Germano 1994, 306.

257. Particularly prominent in this endeavor are Karmapa Rangjung Dorjé (1283–1339) and Karma Chakmé (1613–78). With the rise of the "nonsectarian" (*ris med*) movement in eastern Tibet in the nineteenth century, attempts at synthesis accelerated, and today many Kagyüpa masters are conversant with the great perfection, and many Nyingmapas know a considerable amount about mahāmudrā. It should be noted that Nyingmapas and Kagyüpas sometimes engaged in polemics against one another, debating which "great"—the great perfection or the great seal—was greater. On this last point, see, e.g., below, pages 245 and 609.

4. Mahāmudrā in Early Marpa Kagyü

MAHĀMUDRĀ WAS, TO a greater or lesser degree, an important concept in all the schools described in chapter 3. For the Marpa Kagyü lineage, though, it was essential.[258] Indeed, mahāmudrā is as crucial a term to the identity of the Marpa Kagyü as mind training to the Kadam, severance to the Shiché, the path and fruit tradition to the Sakya, or the great perfection to the Nyingma. Through the influence of Kagyü writers, it would eventually receive renewed attention in schools that already had a place for the term, and find a place in later schools, such as the Geluk—where the masters responsible for articulating the Ganden Hearing Transmission clearly were familiar with Marpa Kagyü treatments of mahāmudrā. In this chapter and the next, we will briefly review the contributions to mahāmudrā discourse made by a number of important Marpa Kagyü teachers.

Marpa and Milarepa

Marpa Chökyi Lodrö (1012–97)[259] was a wealthy farmer from south-central Tibet who studied translation with Drokmi Lotsāwa, then traveled multiple times to India and Nepal to collect texts and teachings. There, tradition tells us, he encountered Nāropa,[260] from whom he received such esoteric teachings as the six Dharmas, and Maitrīpa, with whom he studied a number of tantras as well as mahāmudrā. Thanks to Maitrīpa, Marpa says, he "realized unborn reality . . . saw the primordial nature, reality free from elaboration . . . and met the three mother buddha bodies face to face."[261] Marpa

258. See, e.g., Roerich 1976, 399–725 and 839–66, Chang 1986, Dakpo Tashi Namgyal 1986, D. Jackson 1994, Brown 2006, Roberts 2011, Roberts 2014, Kragh 2015, and Higgins and Draszczyk 2016.

259. See, e.g., Roerich 1976, 399–427, Nālandā Translation Committee 1982, Gyaltsen 1990, 97–122, Davidson 2005, 140–48, Tsangnyön Heruka 2010, and Ducher 2017.

260. Or perhaps disciples of Nāropa; see Davidson 2005, 140–48.

261. Th*MPNT* 134; cf. Nālandā Translation Committee 1982, 144–45.

EARLY MARPA KAGYÜ

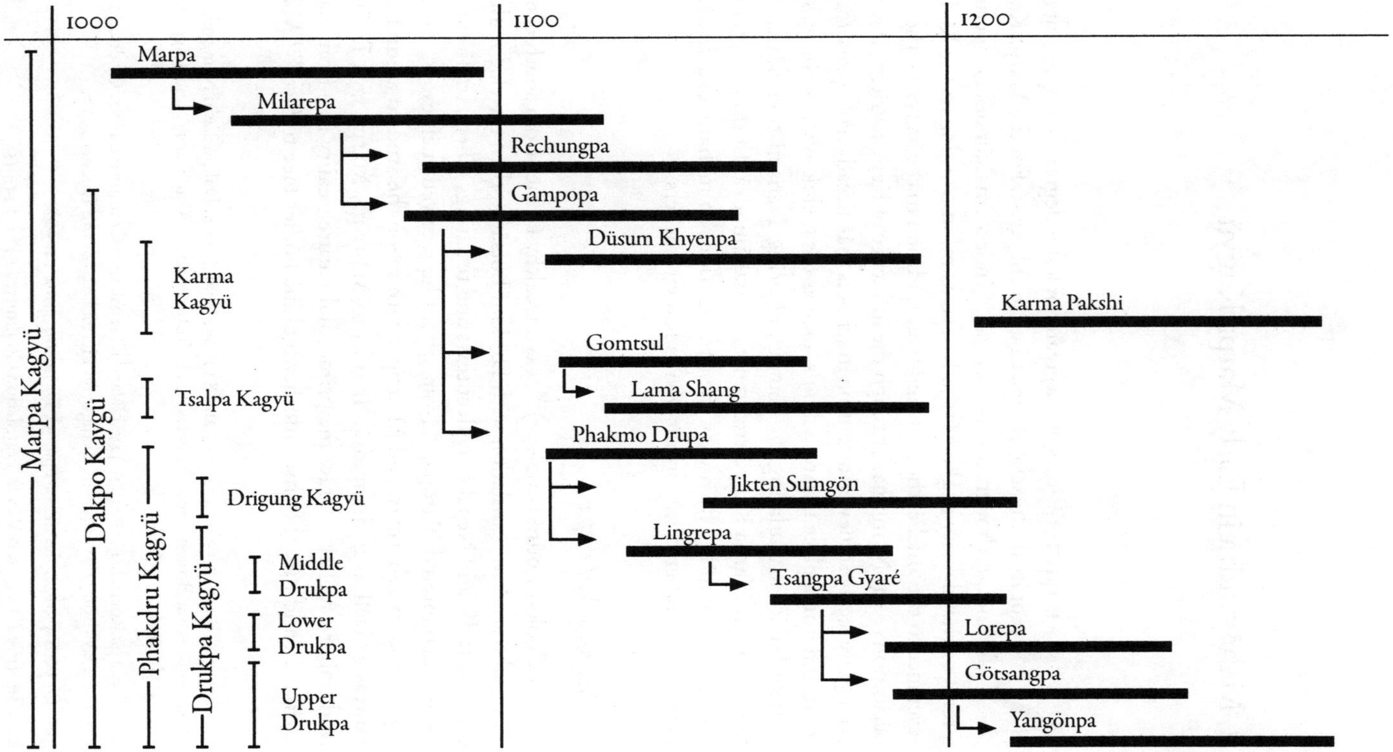

also reported dream and visionary encounters with Saraha, which further cemented his understanding. Established in Tibet as a translator and teacher, Marpa attracted a large number of disciples, to whom he transmitted the various mahāyoga and yoginī tantra traditions he had received in India and Nepal, and to whom—if tradition be believed—he taught a method for composing and singing dohās and vajra songs in Tibetan. In the songs attributed to him, Marpa usually speaks of mahāmudrā in nondual style, for instance as that in which "all the various outer and inner schools are realized and unified . . . unobstructed self-luminous insight . . . spontaneous wisdom . . . with nothing to add or subtract, self-liberation, connate great bliss, free from hope or fear."[262] He also associates mahāmudrā with esoteric practices, describing it as the one doorway that assures success in transfer of consciousness[263] and linking it with the luminosity contemplation that is one of the six Dharmas of Nāropa.[264] In a "meditation song of mahāmudrā," he instructs a disciple to practice sexual yoga and—when fixed in bliss-emptiness concentration—to "rest your mind free from thought. . . . This is the unperverted natural state . . . don't corrupt it with a mist of conceptualizations."[265] Although Marpa asserts that a practitioner must master both the path of means—that is, the six Dharmas of Nāropa—*and* the "unborn mahāmudrā," in which all things are seen to be without foundation,[266] and argues that the "insight-emptiness" realized through the sūtras and the "bliss-emptiness" realized through the tantras are not different,[267] there is no evidence that he divided mahāmudrā into nondual and esoteric (let alone sūtra and tantra) approaches. What is clear is that he brought back with him to Tibet a rich and complex sense of the possibilities of the term.

Marpa's most celebrated disciple was the reformed black magician and peripatetic poet-yogī, Milarepa Shepai Dorjé (1040–1123),[268] whose life and songs have been a source of inspiration for all Tibetans, regardless of sect. After severe trials, Mila received most of the core Kagyü teachings from Marpa and would, in turn, pass them on to his two major disciples, Rechungpa and Gampopa.

262. Th*MPNT* 30; trans. Nālandā Translation Committee 1982, 29–30.

263. Th*MPNT* 93; trans. Nālandā Translation Committee 1982, 96.

264. Th*MPNT* 114; trans. Nālandā Translation Committee 1982, 121.

265. Th*MPNT* 179–80; trans. Nālandā Translation Committee 1982, 192–93.

266. Th*MPNT* 156, 158; trans. Nālandā Translation Committee 1982, 167, 170.

267. Th*MPNT* 41; trans. Nālandā Translation Committee 1982, 41.

268. See, e.g., Roerich 1976, 427–36, Gyaltsen 1990, 123–44, Tsangnyön Heruka 2010, and Quintman 2014.

Mila's songs are suffused with references to mahāmudrā. Like Marpa, he most often refers to the great seal in its nondual sense, describing it to a disciple as "the natural state . . . clear, radiant, ample and relaxed, without hope or fear . . . free from virtue or sin, without plans or expectations, neither saṃsāra nor nirvāṇa, . . . beyond thought, beyond concepts—unmistakable!"[269] Describing his own practice, he remarks:

> Illumined in the luminous realm, saṃsāra and nirvāṇa
> are held in place by hand
> and imprinted with the great seal.[270]

Along similar lines, in responding to a challenge from some logicians, he sings:

> When I meditate on mahāmudrā,
> I rest effortlessly in the state of actuality;
> I rest relaxedly within nondistraction;
> I rest luminously within emptiness;
> I rest consciously within bliss;
> I rest naturally within nonthought;
> I rest evenly within multiplicity.
>
> In mind itself resting thus,
> multiple insights arise unceasingly;
> self-illumined, I accomplish deeds without effort;
> my mind not aspiring for the fruit, I'm oh so blissful;
> free from dualistic grasping at hope or fear, I'm oh so joyous;
> when delusions arise as gnosis, I'm oh so happy.[271]

Milarepa also frequently uses *mahāmudrā* in a more esoteric sense. Like Marpa, he associates it with the experience, within the subtle body, of luminosity (again, one of the six Dharmas of Nāropa),[272] and in a song describing the inner-heat practice (another of the six Dharmas), he sees

269. Kunga and Cutillo 1986, 183. As Andrew Quintman (2014) and others have noted, because of Milarepa's cultural importance, his name has been affixed to many songs that may actually be later compositions. In the current context, I will not attempt to separate out "genuine" Mila songs from the "spurious" ones, simply accepting them all as part of a "Mila tradition."

270. Th*MLNT* 176; cf. trans. Lhalungpa 1977, 166–67, and Tsangnyön Heruka 2010, 194.

271. Th*MLGB* 418–19; cf. trans. Chang 1989, 2:378, and Tsangnyön Heruka 2016, 398–99.

272. Kunga and Cutillo 1995, 91.

mahāmudrā as a result of success in that tantric procedure: "When you've obtained keen skill in objectives, then bliss-warmth of inner heat burns in your body. . . . Come to the undistracted realm of birthless mahāmudrā."[273] Crucially, Mila asserts in a number of songs that mahāmudrā is an achievement that presupposes the four standard higher tantric empowerments and practice of the path of means. Specifically, mahāmudrā is the practice and realization ensuing from the fourth, or word, empowerment, and he asks rhetorically, "Without empowerment, how can it be done?"[274] In the end, it would seem that for Milarepa the relationship between nondual and esoteric senses of mahāmudrā is quite complex. Although, like other masters of his time, Mila often seems to use mahāmudrā in a straighforwardly nondual sense—as the empty and luminous nature of all things, the direct experience of the natural mind, a carefree and spontaneous way of living, and the attainment of the three buddha bodies—the historian Gö Lotsāwa is probably right to assert that "the venerable Mila did not teach the path of means and mahāmudrā separately."[275]

Rechungpa and Gampopa

One of Mila's two great disciples, Rechungpa Dorjé Drak (1083–1161),[276] studied with Kadampa masters early in life and traveled to India and Nepal, where he received mahāmudrā teachings from Vajrapāṇi's Nepalese disciple Balpo Asu and yoginī tantra instructions from Tipupa and other South Asian masters.[277] Like those of Marpa, the mahāmudrā teachings received by Rechungpa were an important vehicle for introducing into Tibetan Buddhism the various traditions related to the songs of Saraha and other Indian mahāsiddhas. The yoginī tantra teachings are preserved in a highly esoteric hearing transmission related to Cakrasaṃvara, which some consider the basis of the Rechung Kagyü, a branch of Marpa Kagyü that is distinct from the Dakpo tradition that flows from Gampopa.[278] Rechungpa eventually went to study with Milarepa, from whom he received countless instructions,

273. Kunga and Cutillo 1995, 165.

274. Kunga and Cutillo 1995, 85.

275. Roerich 1976, 459 (translation adapted).

276. On Rechungpa, see especially Roberts 2007.

277. Roberts 2007, 158–61.

278. Sernesi 2011. The Rechung Nyengyü eventually was brought under the aegis of the Dakpo, primarily through the efforts of masters of the Drukpa subschool. Some of its teachings also are preserved in the Surmang (*zur mang*) tradition, an offshoot of the Karma Kagyü.

including teachings on mahāmudrā said to be superior even to those of Asu. Rechungpa also studied the great perfection with Nyingma masters and was among the first Tibetans to suggest that the great perfection and mahāmudrā are essentially the same, for in each, "one's own mind's appearances are the 'light' or 'adornments' or 'great display' of the Dharma body."[279]

Milarepa's other great disciple, Gampopa Sönam Rinchen (1079–1153)[280]—also called Dakpo Lharjé, "the doctor from Dakpo," after his original profession—trained as a monk in the Kadam order after the death, in an epidemic, of his young wife and children. He went on to study with Mila, learning a whole range of practices from him, none more crucial than mahāmudrā. After Mila's death, he established a retreat center at Gampo, southeast of Lhasa, where he began the process of organizing the Kagyü into a religious order, distinguished by its combination of institutional monasticism, Kadam gradualism, esoteric tantric practice, and nondual mahāmudrā meditation. It was Gampopa who brought mahāmudrā firmly to the center of the Kagyü worldview and set the terms for most subsequent discourse about the term, relating it to a wide range of Buddhist categories, such as perfection and mantra; buddha nature; the two truths; emptiness; sudden and gradual paths; the triad of ground, path, and fruit; the quartet of view, meditation, conduct, and fruit; ordinary and awakened mind; philosophical and meditative approaches to awakening; serenity and insight meditation; and the three bodies of a buddha—to name just a few.[281] Because he described mahāmudrā in so many ways and in such familiar terms, we might paraphrase Alfred North Whitehead's comment about Plato and suggest that all Kagyü reflection on mahāmudrā is really but a series of footnotes to Gampopa.

Gampopa offered numerous definitions of *mahāmudrā*, one of the most intriguing of which is found in his *Mahāmudrā Instructions on the Lightning Strike:*

> *Mahāmudrā* is emptiness. Emptiness is twofold: artificial emptiness and natural emptiness. Through the latter, awakening occurs; through artificial emptiness it does not. . . . Natural emptiness is not some cavern; it is not some open expanse; it cannot be indicated by any analogy; it cannot be reduced to any objective meaning.

279. Roberts 2007, 133.

280. For biographical material on Gampopa, see, e.g., Roerich 1976, 451–63, Stewart 1995, Gampopa 1998, 305–32, Gyatrul 2004, 18–93, and Kragh 2015, 82–153.

281. See, e.g., Roerich 1976, 451–63, D. Jackson 1994, 9–52, Kragh 1998, and Kragh 2015, 30–79 and 396–482.

> Thus it cannot be expressed by any words. All speech being false, mahāmudrā does not entail a view. If it entailed a view, it would have directions and divisions. So, when one severs the continuum of mind, one settles into freshness, naturalness, and relaxation.[282]

Elsewhere, he remarks that mahāmudrā is "one's intrinsic experience of the nature of things . . . one's intrinsic experience of the connate . . . one's intrinsic experience of the primordial . . . the intrinsic nature of one's mind."[283] The nature of one's own mind, in turn, is both existent and non-existent: it is non-existent because "it cannot truly be identified, not even a hundredth of a tip of a hair's worth"; it is existent because, nevertheless, "it truly can be experienced and it truly can be realized."[284] Thus, "the nature of mind cannot be identifed as clarity and emptiness, yet it definitely appears as an unbroken stream of clarity and emptiness."[285] Expressing his realization, Gampopa sings:

> This naturally clear and empty intrinsic awareness—
> now I understand: it's the Dharma body.
> This pure, limitless intrinsic mind—
> now I understand: it is the fruit![286]

Finally, like a number of his predecessors, Gampopa also offers an etymological definition of *mahāmudrā*, explicating its Tibetan equivalent as follows:

> *Phyag* is the intuitive understanding that all that appears and is possible, saṃsāra and nirvāṇa, does not go beyond the realm of the ultimate, which is unoriginated. *Rgya* means that all that appears as something and can become something does not go beyond that which alone is genuine. *Chen po* means that this happens because of the intuitive understanding that the ultimate is free in itself.[287]

Gampopa emphasized a number of distinctive mahāmudrā practices. These included sudden methods, such as the lightning strike (*thog 'bab*),

282. Gp*PCTB* 141–42.

283. Cited Kn*PCOZ* 252a; cf. trans. Dakpo Tashi Namgyal 1986, 309–10.

284. Cited Kn*PCOZ* 252a; cf. trans. Dakpo Tashi Namgyal 1986, 310.

285. Cited Kn*PCOZ* 252a; cf. trans. Dakpo Tashi Namgyal 1986, 310.

286. Cited Kn*PCOZ* 299a; cf. trans. Dakpo Tashi Namgyal 1986, 297.

287. Cited in Guenther 1963, 235.

in which one settles unerringly on the nature of mind as "bliss, clarity and nonconceptuality—without artifice, free from seeking or attainment";[288] the connate union (*lhan cig skyes sbyor*), where "mind, concepts, and Dharma body are connate from the beginning and then are united through [a guru's] instructions";[289] and the white panacea (*dkar po chig thub*), the single (*chig*) spiritual "remedy"—seeing the nature of mind—that, by itself, is able (*thub*) to cure spiritual ills and effect awakening.[290] He also taught more gradual techniques, such as the fivefold mahāmudrā (*lnga ldan*)—generation of awakening mind, deity yoga, guru yoga, mahāmudrā, and dedication of merit[291]—and the four yogas (*rnal 'byor bzhi*) that would serve as a key organizing principle for subsequent Kagyü discussions of the path of mahāmudrā: the yoga of *single-pointedness* (*rtse gcig*), which is "a lucid, unceasing, momentary awareness"; the yoga of *nonelaboration* (*spros bral*), "understanding the essential state of that awareness as nonarising [emptiness], which transcends conceptual modes of reality and unreality"; the yoga of *single taste* (*ro gcig*), which is "understanding diverse appearances as being one from the standpoint of their intrinsic nature"; and the yoga of *nonmeditation* (*sgom med*), "an unceasing realization of the union of appearance and its intrinsic emptiness."[292] At times, too, Gampopa equated mahāmudrā with "ordinary mind" (*tha mal gyi shes pa*), identifying concepts with the Dharma body[293] and insisting that, "what is designated as 'ordinary mind' is your own cognition. Undisturbed by any aspected phenomena, unmuddied by any mundane consciousness and unclouded by dullness, depression, or thought, it settles within itself. If you recognize it,

288. Gp*PCTB* 137.

289. Cited Pk*PCGZ* 120. In later times, connate union became a more gradual practice, as for instance in the accounts of it by Rangjung Dorjé and Pema Karpo (Roberts 2011, 153–68 and 135–52, respectively). For a brief historical reflection, see Gyatrul 2004, 61n161.

290. See, e.g., D. Jackson 1994, 13 and n26.

291. See Duff 2008b.

292. Cited Kn*PCOZ* 335b–336a; trans. Dakpo Tashi Namgyal 1986, 358–59. For a detailed discussion, see Schiller 2014, pp. 76–97, 104–22, 216–33, and 714–19. As noted earlier, the four yogas may have originated in Tibet with Atiśa and hence predated Gampopa by a half century or more. Fourfold meditation sequences are commonplace in Buddhism, from the four noble truths and four absorptions of Foundational Buddhism, to similarly numbered lists found in Mahāyāna sources as disparate as the *Descent to Laṅkā Sūtra*, Maitreya's *Disitinguishing Phenomena from Reality* (*Dharmadharmatāvibhaṅga*), the *Guhyasamāja Tantra*, the *Stages of Meditation* of Kamalaśīla, and the writings of Ratnākaraśānti. For discussion of and references to Mahāyāna material, see Bentor 2000.

293. Cited Kn*PCOZ* 219b; cf. trans. Dakpo Tashi Namgyal 1986, 232.

it is the gnosis of intrinsic awareness; if you fail to realize it, it is coemergent ignorance."[294]

Like Marpa and Milarepa before him, Gampopa recognized mahāmudrā's connection to the esoteric traditions of the tantras, but he was most renowned for introducing—and perhaps even favoring—a Perfection Vehicle mahāmudrā practice, which could be found in such Mahāyāna texts as the Perfection of Wisdom sūtras, with their discourse on emptiness; the *King of Concentrations Sūtra*, with its discussion of the "sameness" that is the "seal of all phenomena"; the *Sublime Continuum*, with its emphasis on the natural purity of mind, or buddha nature;[295] and perhaps the writings of Maitrīpa and his circle.[296] In Gampopa's Perfection Vehicle mahāmudrā, a disciple need not receive tantric empowerment in order to attain awakening; hearing the guru's experiential introduction to the nature of mind through a "pointing-out instruction" (*ngo sprod*)[297] will suffice. In the words of Ulrich Kragh, "by relying first on the teacher's blessing and thereafter on uncontrived meditation, where one rests directly in an experience of the nature of mind, one can practice the highest level of the [Unexcelled Yoga] Tantras . . . without having to rely on the usual tantric techniques."[298] Still, over the range of his writings, Gampopa may be read as holding as many as four different views of the place of mahāmudrā: one in which it is primarily or exclusively a Perfection Vehicle teaching, one in which it is a Mantra Vehicle teaching, one in which it is a teaching inclusive of both Perfection and Mantra Vehicle practices, and one in which it is a third, exclusive, way, transcending and/or extracting the key insights and practices from both Perfection and Mantra—what later Kagyü scholars would call "essence mahāmudrā." It is hard to say whether Gampopa was truly ambivalent about the place of mahāmudrā in Buddhist tradition, or whether the various approaches he articulated can be reconciled—by claiming, for instance, that mahāmudrā as a "third" path is simply a way of integrating Perfection and Mantra on the level of the ultimate realization. We would be wise to bear in mind Michael Broido's observations to the effect that (1) Gampopa, for all his integrative genius, probably was not attempting to produce an airtight system like those beloved by later Tibetan scholastics but, rather, analyzing topics as

294. Cited Kn*PCOZ* 233a–b; cf. trans. Dakpo Tashi Namgyal 1986, 245.

295. See, e.g., Gampopa 1998, 233–56.

296. On this question, see, e.g., Mathes 2006 and Mathes 2007.

297. As a verb, *ngo sprod* means to indicate, identify, point out, introduce, or recognize. I will typically translate it as "recognize," but I will refer to the teachings passed on from guru to disciple as "pointing-out instructions."

298. Kragh 1998, 79.

the situation warranted;[299] and (2) just as in later Indian Buddhist literature, so in that of Tibet, especially of the Kagyü, it is nearly impossible any longer to separate the Perfection Vehicle (especially Madhyamaka philosophy) from the Mantra Vehicle, so thoroughly intertwined have they become.[300]

What is certain is that with the writings and teachings of Gampopa, mahāmudrā truly moved to the heart of the Kagyü tradition and to a place of great prominence in philosophical and meditative discourse in Tibet; it is certain as well that the complexity of Gampopa's writings about the nature and place of mahāmudrā within Buddhist teaching led to a considerable range of views on the topic among later members of the Dakpo tradition as well as among those outside it.

Gampopa's Successors

Gampopa's major students and their many disciples were responsible for founding monasteries that became the seats of the various orders and suborders that now go under the name Dakpo Kagyü. In the most common listing, there are four major orders—the Tsalpa, Phakdru, Karma, and Barom—and eight suborders, all stemming from the Phakdru: the Drigung, Drukpa, Taklung, Trophu, Martsang, Yalpa, Shuksep, and Yasang. With Gampopa as a common source, all the Dakpo Kagyü orders and suborders placed mahāmudrā at the center of their theoretical and practical concerns. Each, however, differed from the others in emphasis and interpretation, so that certain schools became renowned for specializing in one or another of the many approaches to mahāmudrā offered by Gampopa and other early Tibetan Renaissance figures. For instance, the Tsalpa was famed for its promulgation of the radical white-panacea mahāmudrā teaching; the Phakdru and Drigung for their teachings on the Single Intention (*dgongs gcig*) and the graduated fivefold mahāmudrā; the Drukpa for its emphasis on the connate union and the equal taste (*ro snyoms*) and its embrace of the Rechung Hearing Transmission; the Taklung for its emphasis on discipline and its fusion of Perfection and Mantra approaches to the path; the Trophu for its focus on the nine-meaning mahāmudrā (*don dgu phyag chen*) and the severance teachings of Phadampa Sangyé and Machik Lapdrön; the Karma for its incorporation of the teachings of Saraha and other Indian mahāsiddhas, its brilliant scholastic tradition, and its openness to the great perfection; and the Barom for its emphasis on the esoteric practice of mahāmudrā entailed by the six Dharmas of Nāropa, as

299. Broido 1985a, 13–14.

300. Broido 1985a, 7–12 and 43.

distilled into the teaching on mixture and transference (*bsre 'pho*). Over the course of time, each of these schools produced saints and scholars alike and contributed to the development of mahāmudrā discourse in Tibet. The most prominent were the Tsalpa, Phakdru, Drigung, Drukpa, and Karma.

Shang Rinpoché and the Tsalpa Kagyü

The Tsalpa Kagyü[301] was a relatively short-lived order, but the striking political and intellectual profile of its founder and greatest luminary, Yudrak Tsöndrü Drakpa, usually known as Lama Shang or Shang Rinpoché (1123–93),[302] made it a force to contend with in the twelfth and thirteenth centuries in Central Tibet (Ü). Lama Shang was highly controversial as a public figure, but his poetic masterpiece, the *Ultimate Supreme Path of Mahāmudrā*, is undeniably one of the greatest works in the Marpa Kagyü canon, a brilliant, systematic exposition of mahāmudrā from a multitude of perspectives. In the very first chapter, Shang defines *mahāmudrā* as the "pervading mind" inseparable from appearances, emptiness, or bliss. Its nature is emptiness, its characteristic is clarity, and its essence is the indivisibility of all apparent dualities. It is "inexhaustible, imperishable, indestructible... pure as crystal, untarnished by stains."[303] Elsewhere, mahāmudrā is identified with "the definitive meaning," "nonmentation," "buddhahood," "conceptualization liberating itself," and "complete enlightenement."[304]

Shang goes on to identify three classes of mahāmudrā practitioners: the gradual, the nonconsecutive, and the sudden. The gradual and sudden approaches—which correspond roughly to the esoteric and nondual approaches described above—are discussed in considerable detail. Typically, the gradualist will ascend in stages through the three main vehicles of Buddhism, the self-regarding "Hīnayāna," the altruistic Mahāyāna, and the esoteric Vajrayāna, progressing from lay practitioner, to monastic, to bodhisattva, to fully initiated tantric practitioner.[305] Once initiated into tantra, the gradualist will practice virtue, observe vows and pledges, perform ritual service to lama and deity, and slowly develop inner and outer freedom, arriving finally at the practice of the

301. See, e.g., Thuken 2009, 128.

302. See Martin 1992, D. Jackson 1994, and Yamamoto 2012. Shang visited Gampo but never met Gampopa, studying instead with his nephew and successor, Gompa Tsultrim Nyingpo, or Gomtsul (1116–69), on whom see Roerich 1976, 464–69.

303. Roberts 2011, 87–88.

304. Roberts 2011, pp. 88, 105, 113, 123, and 125, respectively.

305. Roberts 2011, 93–96.

four yogas. The final yoga, that of nonmeditation, is itself "the attainment of mahāmudrā,"[306] or buddhahood.

Nonmeditation also is indicative of the sudden, or subitist, approach to religious life, which Shang considers superior. The subitist "should please the guru . . . receive empowerment and blessing, and uplifted by awakening mind, together with practice of the deity . . . meditate from the very beginning on the definitive meaning, mahāmudrā. . . . The desire for numerous complexities obscures the naturally present wisdom. There is no need for a precise plan of action in the practice of mahāmudrā."[307] In meditation, therefore, one should simply relax, for "this mind that is obscured by thoughts, when left as it is, unmodified, will clarify as the Dharma body. . . . Whether thoughts appear or not, do not purposefully meditate, but rest naturally."[308] Indeed, whatever one does, "it's essential that it be done with the natural mind."[309] For Shang, the subitist approach eliminates all negativity with a single blow, such that "in the instant you realize your own mind, all good qualities, without exception, are suddenly completed without having to accomplish them."[310]

This all-at-once quality of the sudden path leads Shang to equate it with a term used by Gampopa: the *white panacea*, the single, powerful medicinal substance that cures all ills with one application. Although Shang cautions that a gradual path is required for those who still cling to self,[311] the predominance of what scholar Bernard Faure calls the "rhetoric of immediacy"[312] in his text would make it a target for those—most notably the great Sakya Paṇḍita—who felt that his account of mahāmudrā gave short shrift to conventional virtues and to the term's tantric provenance. Shang does not discuss the nonconsecutive practitioner in much detail, merely indicating that such a person proceeds neither sequentially nor immediately to awakening, moving, rather, in fits and starts.[313]

306. Roberts 2011, 113.

307. Roberts 2011, 96.

308. Roberts 2011, 96–97.

309. Roberts 2011, 101.

310. Roberts 2011, 126.

311. Roberts 2011, 129.

312. See Faure 1994.

313. Roberts 2011, 106.

Phakmo Drupa Kagyü and Drigung Kagyü

The Phakmo Drupa (or Phakdru) and Drigung Kagyü[314] were closely related orders that—while administered from different main monasteries, Densa Thil and Drigung, respectively—shared many of the same teachers and teachings. The Phakdru was a major political power in Central Tibet from the mid-fourteenth to the early seventeenth century, after which it receded into the background, while the Drigung was less concerned with mundane matters. Also unlike the Phakdru, it has thrived down to the present day. Their founders, Phakmo Drupa and Drigung Jikten Sumgön, respectively, made influential contributions to mahāmudrā theory and practice that resonated throughout the subsequent literature of the Marpa Kagyü and found their way into Geluk conceptions of mahāmudrā as well.

Phakmo Drupa Dorjé Gyalpo (1110–70)[315] traveled from his native Kham in eastern Tibet to study with Gampopa. He realized mahāmudrā under Gampopa's guidance, then went on to found Densa Thil Monastery in his native region and to gather an illustrious circle of disciples. He transmitted to them a wide range of Perfection and Mantra traditions he had learned from various masters, including teachings on logic, philosophy, and the tantric path of means. Unlike Shang Rinpoché, Phakmo Drupa generally favored a more gradual and synthetic approach to Buddhist practice. He strongly recommended mastery of the three precept traditions of Buddhism—monastic (and lay) vows, bodhisattva vows, and tantric vows—and taught a meditative progression that begins with Foundational Buddhist perspectives and then moves into those of the Perfection and Mantra Vehicles of the Mahāyāna. He spoke and wrote in detail about the mahāmudrā practices he had studied with Gampopa, most notably the fivefold mahāmudrā enumerated above and fleshed out below. He defines *mahāmudrā* as nonduality whose nature is "unobstructed clarity and comprehension," whose essence is "freedom from arising, cessation, or elaboration," and whose characteristic is "appearing as the multiplicity of saṃsāra and nirvāṇa."[316] It is synonymous with the connate union, a practice in which "the three—mind, concepts, and Dharma body—are connate from the beginning" and are to be united in the mind,[317] "like a brahman spins yarn,

314. See, e.g., Thuken 2009, 126–28 and 129–30.

315. See Roerich 1976, 552–69, Gyaltsen 1990, 205–19, and Schiller 2014.

316. Cited in Kn*PCOZ* 203b; cf. trans. Dakpo Tashi Namgyal 1986, 214.

317. Cited in Kn*PCOZ* 213a; cf. trans. Dakpo Tashi Namgyal 1986, 224.

relaxed in a fresh, uncontrived state."[318] Like Gampopa, Phakmo Drupa divided the path of mahāmudrā meditation into the four yogas, but he was among the first to subdivide each of the four into lower, middling, and greater levels, thereby providing a considerably more detailed description of the processes involved, and the realizations required, on each level.[319] He also contributed an extended, original analysis of the way in which ordinary thoughts, experiences, and defilements are to be understood as empty and "carried on the path" (*lam du 'khyer*), likening the ease with which this occurs to (a) the meeting and recognition of old friends, (b) the melting of snow on a heated rock, (c) the spread of a forest fire, and (d) the experience of bliss, clarity, and emptiness in which "even a pinprick induces bliss."[320]

The founder of the Drigung suborder, Jikten Sumgön Rinchen Pal, or Jikten Gönpo (1143–1217),[321] went to study with Phakmo Drupa while in his twenties and heard from him teachings on both the path of means and mahāmudrā. In much of his discourse on mahāmudrā, Jikten Sumgön followed the style of his predecessors—for instance, in defining *mahāmudrā* as "just this self-awareness"[322] and insisting that "enhancement of mahāmudrā is assured by respect for the holy master."[323] His distinctiveness lies in his articulation of two major approaches to Buddhist thought and practice: the single intention (*dgongs gcig*) and the fivefold mahāmudrā.

The single intention[324] consists of a series of 150 principles, each of which underscores the profound unity lying beneath the apparent diversity of Buddhist doctrines and practices, and shows that categories like the two vehicles, the two truths, the three sets of vows, or the gradual and subitist paths are deceptive. It is easy to see how a critic could conclude—as Sakya Paṇḍita later would—that the single intention undermines relative truth and gradual practices in favor of a radically absolutist fusion of all Buddhist categories, but Jikten Sumgön seems less intent on fusing Buddhist teachings than showing their common denominators—above all, the emptiness that is the nature of all phenomena. His acceptance of convention is evident from

318. Cited in Kn*PCOZ* 263a–b; cf. trans. Dakpo Tashi Namgyal 1986, 278.

319. Kn*PCOZ* 346b–347b; trans. Dakpo Tashi Namgyal 1986, 373–74.

320. Cited in Kn*PCOZ* 268a–b; trans. Dakpo Tashi Namgyal 1986, 283–84.

321. See Roerich 1976, 596–601, Gyaltsen 1986b, and Gyaltsen 1990, 220–69.

322. Cited in Kn*PCOZ* 206b; cf. trans. Dakpo Tashi Namgyal 1986, 218.

323. Cited in Kn*PCOZ* 299b; cf. trans. Dakpo Tashi Namgyal 1986, 283–84.

324. Js*GCTB*; although generally attributed to Jikten Sumgön, it was committed to writing and expanded upon by his disciple Sherab Jungné (1187–1241).

numerous passages about karma and defilements, or the results of meditation, or the locus of the Buddha, and his gradualism is evident from his assertions that "all paths are traversed via the ten bodhisattva levels" and "all paths are entered gradually."[325] And, conversant though he was with the nondual perspective of mahāmudrā, he makes it clear in his discussion of the term that it does not entail an abrogation of morality. Indeed, although mahāmudrā is separate from an ethics of acceptance or rejection, "conduct that is separate from acceptance or rejection is itself precious morality"; although mahāmudrā and morality may apppear to be contradictory, "mahāmudrā and precious morality are one"; and although mahāmudrā transcends good qualities and faults, "mahāmudrā is the very selfhood of good qualities."[326]

The tendency toward synthesis evident in the single-intention teaching is even more clear in Jikten Sumgön's articulation of the fivefold mahāmudrā first taught by Gampopa. The classic formulation of the fivefold is found in a realization song Jikten Sumgön is said to have sung to Phakmo Drupa when he mastered the practice. There, he says that:

1. Generation of the awakening mind is like racing a stallion around the track of love and compassion, thereby eliciting cheers from gods and humans.
2. Visualizing oneself as a deity is like knowing that one is a king or queen, thereby attracting "clouds of ḍākinīs."
3. Guru devotion is like letting the sun shine on the "snow mountain of the guru's four bodies," thereby bringing forth the river of blessings.
4. Mahāmudrā is like clearing "the cloud mass of deluded conceptions" from "the sky of nonconceptual mind, the Dharma body," thereby allowing the "planets and stars of the two knowledges" to shine.
5. Dedication of merit is like polishing the wishing jewel of the two collections (merit and gnosis), thereby assuring that "the fruits you need and desire" will arise.[327]

Although only one of them is designated *mahāmudrā*, for Jikten Sumgön all five practices are mahāmudrā, since the meaning of the term, if not the term itself, can be found in all Buddhist traditions.

Indeed, in another song, he applies each of the well-known four tantric seals to *every* type of practitioner, with mahāmudrā as the fourth and highest

325. Js*GCTB* 360; cf. Roberts 2011, 375.

326. Js*GCTB* 373; cf. Roberts 2011, 386 (also 6, 11–14).

327. See, e.g., Gyaltsen 1986b, 56–57, and below, page 498.

in each case. Thus, for a Foundational Buddhist śrāvaka, mahāmudrā is "the nirvāṇa without aggregates remaining," for a Mahāyāna bodhisattva, it is "the equal taste of emptiness and compassion," for a practitioner of esoteric secret mantra (the path of means), it is "the manifestation of connate gnosis," and for one on the nondual path of liberation, it is "spontaneity."[328] This reflects about as inclusive a notion of mahāmudrā as could possibly be developed, but innovative as it appears, we must remember that Gampopa already had charted such a direction by "joining the two streams of Kadam and mahāmudrā" as well as by teaching nondual mahāmudrā meditation to those who were not equipped to practice the esoteric variety. We must remember, too, that as soon as mahāmudrā comes to be equated with emptiness and its realization, where emptiness is said to be the nature of all things and its realization essential on all Buddhist paths, it requires only a small conceptual adjustment to argue that mahāmudrā is associated with all possible Buddhist practices.

Drukpa Kagyü

The Drukpa Kagyü[329] was famed initially for its preponderance of charismatic, wandering yogīs in the style of Milarepa, and in later times for its "crazy" poet-saints and its brilliant scholars, creative writers, and publishers. A southern ("lower") branch of the Drukpa became the main religious power in Bhutan early in the seventeenth century, and remains so to this day; the northern ("upper") branch continues in parts of Tibet and in Ladakh. The early masters of the Drukpa were renowned for their yogic prowess but also contributed to the refinement of Kagyü scholasticism, including discourse on mahāmudrā. The sect's charismatic founder, Lingrepa Pema Dorjé (1128–88),[330] a lapsed monk who gained realization of mahāmudrā under the tulelage of Phakmo Drupa, left a number of ritual and meditational texts and a collection of spiritual songs impressive enough that some dubbed him the Saraha of Tibet. Here is just one example of his verse:

> If you do not rest in mind just as it is,
> no other remedy will make things right.
> So all my doubts about whether it's like this or not
> have vanished into thin air.[331]

328. Cited at Bz*YSGM* 101, translated below, page 488–89.

329. See, e.g., Thuken 2009, 130–32, and Abboud et al. 2017.

330. See Roerich 1976, 659–64, Miller 2005, 381–89, and Abboud et al. 2017, 23–26.

331. Miller 2005, 401 (translation adapted).

He also was—with his contemporary, Lama Shang—among the first Kagyü masters to align the four yogas of mahāmudrā with the exoteric soteriology of the Mahāyāna five paths and ten bodhisattva levels, equating single-pointedness with the path of preparation, nonelaboration with the path of seeing, one taste with the tenth bodhisattava level, and nonmeditation with the path of completion, or no-more learning.[332] Lingrepa's great disciple, Tsangpa Gyaré Yeshé Dorjé (1161–1211),[333] helped to institutionalize and systematize the Drukpa. He founded the suborder's main monastery, Ralung, in 1180; he discovered treasure texts belonging to the Rechung Hearing Transmission, including the *Six About Equal Taste*; and he articulated teachings on mahāmudrā with both poetic expressiveness and scholastic precision. Thus he asks his listeners:

> Hey! hey! Do you know what Dharma body is?
> It's letting mind relax just as it is.
> Discursive thought is free, just as it is—
> getting your mind around it is impossible![334]

At the same time, Tsangpa Gyaré discusses the four yogas in some detail, specifying the various realizations, visions, and powers inherent in each; the criteria for determining whether one's realization of each stage is perfect or imperfect; the interrelations among the various yogas; and the connection of the yogas with the traditional levels and paths of the bodhisattva.[335] The tradition, centered at Ralung, that follows upon Tsangpa Gyaré is referred to as the Middle Druk.

Tsangpa Gyaré's two main disciples were Lorepa Wangchuk Tsöndrü (1187–1250),[336] founder of the Lower Druk, and Götsangpa Gönpo Dorjé (1189–1253),[337] who initiated the Upper Druk. Lorepa overcame fierce resistance from his family in order to become a monk, and once ordained by Tsangpa Gyaré became renowned for observing thirteen vows of austerity and for mastering inner-heat meditation to the point where, like Milarepa and his disciples, he never wore more than a simple cotton garment. He was both a generous

332. Cited in Wangchuk Dorjé 2001, 244.

333. See Roerich 1976, 664–70, Miller 2005, 389–96, and Abboud et al. 2017, 27–28.

334. Miller 2005, 401 (translation adapted).

335. Cited in Kn*PCOZ* 343b–344a, 363b, 368a, and 372b, respectively; trans. Dakpo Tashi Namgyal 1986, 369–70, 392, 398, and 403–4, respectively.

336. See Roerich 1976, 672–76.

337. See Roerich 1976, 680–86.

dispenser of gifts and a stern monastic disciplinarian. Later in life, he founded various hermitages and attracted a large number of disciples, whom he instructed on mahāmudrā and initiated into various tantras. Centuries later, his Lower Druk tradition took root in Bhutan, where, as noted, it remains the most influential single religious order.

Götsangpa was an actor in his youth, but after studying with Tsangpa Gyaré, he became a peripatetic yogī, alternating between strict retreat and wandering throughout the western Himalayas and northern India. Like Tsangpa Gyaré, he approached mahāmudrā as both a poet and a scholar. As a scholar, for instance, he carefully lined up the four yogas of mahāmudrā with various Mahāyāna path schemes,[338] and he showed the difficulty of separating serenity from insight in the practice of mahāmudrā by insisting that "the ultimate object of the analytical school of Buddhist savants and the school of fixed attentiveness of the mendicant yogīs is one and the same. The latter is regarded as the more rapid path."[339] He also argued for the legitimacy of Gampopa's nontantric version of mahāmudrā, tracing it back through Maitrīpa, to Śavaripa, to Saraha, and ultimately to Buddha Śākyamuni.[340] Götsangpa's disciple, Yangönpa Gyaltsen Pal (1213–58),[341] was a contemplative prodigy who, at age six, exclaimed to one of his teachers, "The Buddha's blessing entered into me. My theory is free from affirmation. My meditation is free from objects. My actions are free from assertions and objections. My goal is free from hope and anxiety."[342] His expositions of mahāmudrā were even more detailed than those of his Drukpa predecessors. Among other topics, he discussed the connection between "nondual awareness" and "naked ordinary mind," which he regarded as equivalent to each other and to mahāmudrā; the meditative flaws ensuing from attachment to the experiences of clarity, nonduality, and bliss; the various sensations, perceptions, and realizations involved in the four yogas;[343] and perhaps most distinctively, the relation between "mahāmudrā in the mode of actuality" (*gnas lugs phyag chen*) and "mahāmudrā in the mode of error" (*'khrul lugs phyag chen*).[344]

338. See, e.g., Kn*PCOZ* 373a, trans. Dakpo Tashi Namgyal 1986, 404, and Wangchuk Dorjé 2001, 232–40.

339. Cited in Kn*PCOZ* 63b; trans. Dakpo Tashi Namgyal 1986, 71.

340. Mathes 2008, 163–64.

341. See Roerich 1976, 688–91.

342. Roerich 1976, 689–90.

343. Cited in Kn*PCOZ* 234a, 287, and 344a–b, respectively; trans. Dakpo Tashi Namgyal 1986, 245–46, 305, and 370–71, respectively.

344. See Higgins 2015 and Higgins and Draszczyk 2016, 367–76.

Early Karma Kagyü

The Karma (or, more fully, Karma Kamtsang) Kagyü[345] would, in time, become the most powerful of the Kagyü orders, famed for its instigation of the tulku system of religious succession, its development of the influential Black Hat (*zhwa nag*) and Red Hat (*zhwa dmar*) lineages, and the way in which many of its greatest masters combined spiritual dedication, poetic brilliance, scholarly acumen, and political skill.

Its founder was Gampopa's great disciple, Düsum Khyenpa (1110–93),[346] who was born in Kham and was trained by his father in Nyingma practices from an early age. He received novice ordination at sixteen from a Kadampa master and began studying the yoginī tantras and doing retreats. According to some (though not all) sources, around this time he received a crown woven from the hair of ten thousand ḍākinīs, which became emblematic of the incarnation lineage—the first in Tibet—of which he was later identified as the first member, the Black Hat Karmapa. At nineteen, he traveled to Central Tibet, where he received full ordination and continued his Kadam studies, adding philosophical topics to his repertoire. He also studied the path and fruit tradition of the Sakya and Phadampa Sangyé's pacification practice. In 1140, now thirty, he went to study with Gampopa, who, we must recall, was an ordained Kadampa monk before he met Milarepa. At Gampopa's insistence, Düsum Khyenpa spent a great deal of time in retreat, moving from one cave or hut to another, but checking in regularly with Gampopa on the progress of his meditations. The conversations between the two were written down and are among the most interesting documents of early Kagyü literature, showing as they do the ways in which masters and disciples might actually converse.[347]

In time, Düsum Khyenpa received from Gampopa and several of his students (especially Gomtsul) a full range of Marpa Kagyü transmissions, including the six Dharmas of Nāropa and such mahāmudrā practices as the connate union and the white panacea. He began to attract students of his own but continued to enter retreat whenever possible. In the course of his contemplative life, he had a large number of unusual experiences, which included memories of his past lives and dreams and visions of deities and departed masters who imparted to him teachings or important information; he also was reputed to project himself into the dreams and visions of his disciples. After

345. See, e.g., Richardson 1998, Thuken 2009, 122–26, and Kunsang et al. 2012.

346. See Roerich 1976, 473–80, Duff 2008a, Gardner 2009b, Choesphel and Martin 2012, and Kunsang et al. 2012, 27–44.

347. See, e.g., Choephel and Martin 2012, 229–56.

Gampopa's death in 1153, Düsum Khyenpa returned for two decades to Kham, where he founded several monasteries and accumulated considerable wealth. Later in life, he returned to Central Tibet, where he distributed largesse to monasteries in the region, brokered a truce between the sometimes-belligerent Shang Rinpoché and various political factions in the Lhasa area, and in 1189 founded the monastery west of Lhasa that would become the seat of the Black Hat Karmapas, Tsurphu.

Düsum Khyenpa's two-volume collected works consists primarily of texts dealing with unexcelled-yoga-tantra practices, but in addition to his dialogues with Gampopa and some reports of his unusual experiences, he did leave behind a few songs, short treatises, or pieces of advice, some of which touch on mahāmudrā. For instance, when asked how, given all the contact he has had with impure beings, he has managed to stay undefiled, he replies, "When a yogī's mind does not perceive in terms of dualities and he has realized that all phenomena in their vast array have the same taste, he then abides without interruption in the natural state. For such a yogī . . . contamination [does not] exist."[348] In a song of advice to the people of Mon, he sings of how

> the yogī free of reference roams, keeping himself to mountain retreats
> where there is no one else to please. . . .
> If you meditate, then let mind be.
> If it gets scattered, then let mind go.[349]

In another song, he expresses the freedom he feels as a result of "grasping the mind essence and realizing that saṃsāra has no nature, nirvāṇa is not somewhere else, Buddha is in one's own mind, thoughts have the nature of the Dharma body, the two truths are inseparably the same, and knowing one frees all"; as a result of this, "the Dharma nature, let alone, has become clear."[350] In short, the meditator must "rest in the state of awareness itself and recognize the mind's nature from within awareness itself."[351] For all the subitist rhetoric found in these and other passages, a contextual reading of Düsum Khyenpa's works makes it clear that he expects of his disciples, as he expects of himself, a commitment to the fundamental Buddhist values of renunciation of worldly concerns, practice of ethical conduct, generation of the awakening mind, and

348. Choephel and Martin 2012, 49.

349. Choephel and Martin 2012, 211.

350. Choephel and Martin 2012, 208–9.

351. Choephel and Martin 2012, 147 (translation adapted).

appreciation of the philosophical view that is the basis of realizing the empty nature of mind and phenomena. Indeed, he mocks those who take the subitist rhetoric of mahāmudrā masters so literally that they think they don't need to act ethically or meditate at all. Such people, Düsum Khyenpa suggests, will continue to circle in saṃsāra, for only when "we go through complete and thorough spiritual training . . . will experience and realization come."[352]

Düsum Khyenpa passed on the teachings he had received—and mastered—to his main disciple, Drogön Sangyé Rechen (1148–1218).[353] Sangyé Rechen, in turn, transmitted the teachings to his chief pupil, Pomdrakpa Sönam Dorjé (1170–1249).[354] Pomdrakpa's most important student was Chökyi Lama, eventually known as Karma Pakshi (1204–83),[355] who became perhaps the first recognized reincarnate lama in Tibet when Pomdrakpa acknowledged him as an incarnation of Düsum Khyenpa on the basis of predictions supposedly made by the latter before his death. Chökyi Lama traveled widely, visiting China and the Mongol court of Möngke Khan and his eventual successor, Kubilai Khan. Möngke gave Chökyi Lama the Mongol title Karma Master—Karma Pakshi—and, according to sources at odds with those cited above, initiated the Black Hat Karmapa lineage by presenting him with the emblematic black crown supposedly woven from the hair of ḍākinīs. In time, Karma Pakshi came to be known as the Second Black Hat Karmapa, and his incarnation predecessor Düsum Khyenpa as the First.

Karma Pakshi is said to have written voluminously, but only a few of his works remain. The best known is a two-volume work called the *Limitless Ocean Cycle*, a survey of the nine vehicles of the Nyingma tradition. Karma Pakshi had studied with two Nyingma masters at Kathok Monastery in eastern Tibet. He makes it clear in his writings that he considers himself "one who is blessed by the lineage of Nāropa," but he also asserts that mahāmudrā differs from the apex of Nyingma practice, the great perfection, only in name, for each brings us face to face with "the essential abiding nature of the actuality of mind."[356] In this, Karma Pakshi anticipates the receptivity to Nyingma ideas and practices that will be evident in a number of Karma Kagyü masters of later times, including his next incarnation, to whom we will turn shortly.

352. Choephel and Martin 2012, 139.

353. See Roerich 1976, 480–83.

354. See Roerich 1976, 483–85.

355. See Roerich 1976, 485–88; Sorenson 2011.

356. Kapstein 2000, 105 and 103.

5. Mahāmudrā in Later Marpa Kagyü

When Karma Pakshi arrived at the Mongol court in the mid-1250s, he was not the first Tibetan lama to reside there. A decade earlier, Sakya Paṇḍita Kunga Gyaltsen, or Sapaṇ (1182–1251),[357] having been summoned by Möngke's predecessor, Godan Khan, had arrived at the court with his nephew Phakpa Lodrö Gyaltsen (1235–80)[358] and established there a strong Sakya presence. That would eventually blossom into an alliance, whereby the Sakyapas provided the Mongol-dominated Yuan dynasty of China with spiritual support and counsel, and the Mongols placed Tibet under the aegis of Sakya—though such control as the Sakyapas exercised in Tibet was in general exceedingly light. Though his last years were devoted to diplomacy, Sapaṇ is best known by Tibetans for his towering intellect, brilliant philosophical treatises, and dazzling sense of aesthetics. He composed a philosophical history of Buddhism, helped introduce to Tibet both the philosophy of Dharmakīrti and Indian poetic theory, wrote a widely beloved collection of aphorisms, and organized, as no Tibetan before him had, a categorical scheme that accounted for all possible types of knowledge, both "mundane" and Buddhist.[359] More to the point, Sapaṇ was perhaps the first Tibetan intellectual to criticize certain mahāmudrā ideas and practices articulated by the Kagyü, throwing down a gauntlet that nearly every subsequent serious scholar of mahāmudrā felt obliged to pick up.[360]

Sakya Paṇḍita's Critique of Kagyü Mahāmudrā

Sapaṇ's critique of Kagyü mahāmudrā—which is focused especially but not exclusively on the white-panacea doctrine of Gampopa and Shang Rinpoché

357. See, e.g., D. Jackson, 1987, 1:15–37, and Stearns 2001, 159–69.

358. See, e.g., Roerich 1876, 311–12 and 234–37, and Shakabpa 1984, 64–70.

359. See, e.g., van der Kuijp 1983, D. Jackson 1987, Gold 2007, and Davenport 2000.

360. On Kagyü responses to Sapaṇ, see, especially, Draszczyk 2016.

and the single-intention teaching of the Drigung—is found in a number of works,[361] perhaps no more sharply than in his *Answers to the Questions of the Kadampa Namkha Bum*, where he writes, simply:

> The doctrinal tradition of mahāmudrā according to the Drigungpa and the Taklungpa does not agree with any of the tantric systems. I think it is not a genuine path. But do not repeat this to others![362]

Sapaṇ's objections to Kagyü mahāmudrā discourse are stated most systematically in his *Clear Ascertainment of the Three Vows*, a long, versified text that discusses the precepts intended, respectively, for seekers of individual liberation, bodhisattvas, and practitioners of tantra. Sapaṇ's criticisms fall into two main types: historical and doctrinal. His historical argument centers on the claim that the white panacea has no real precedent in India and is instead a Tibetan adaptation of the sudden-awakening position argued at the Tibetan court by the Chinese Chan Buddhist monk Heshang Moheyan during the so-called Samyé debate in the late eighth century.[363] According to Sapaṇ, this position, which he equates with the great perfection, was simply renamed *mahāmudrā* early in the Tibetan Renaissance, so as to diguise its non-Indian origins.[364] Doctrinally, as David Jackson notes, Sapaṇ is attacking three basic ideas: (1) that a single practice—even meditation on emptiness—could alone suffice for liberation, (2) that the gnosis of mahāmudrā could arise through solely nonconceptual meditation, and (3) that mahāmudrā ever could be taught outside of the Mantra Vehicle.[365] The first two ideas are at least intimated in many mahāmudrā songs and treatises, especially those that focus on nonconceptual meditation and a sudden approach to awakening, including Lama Shang's writings on the white panacea and Drigung Jikten Gönpo's on the single intention. Sapaṇ counters these ideas by arguing that the Indian Buddhist tradition makes it clear that *multiple* practices (e.g., wisdom *and* method) are required for buddhahood and that meditation, in order to be effective, must include *both* nonconceptual *and* conceptual techniques. The third idea, as we have seen, is traceable to Gampopa, who is

361. See, e.g., R. Jackson 1982, D. Jackson 1994, and Sakya Pandita 2002. For a magisterial overview of the issues involved in this and other Tibetan debates, see Seyfort Ruegg 1989.

362. Sp*KDZL* 244a. Cited in Dudjom 1991, 929.

363. His name in Tibetan is *Hwa shang ma ha ya na*. For the best study to date of Chan influences on early Tibetan Buddhism, see van Schaik 2015.

364. Sakya Pandita 2002, 118–19.

365. D. Jackson 1994, 72.

widely credited with promulgating an approach to mahāmudrā that bypassed tantric empowerment. Sapaṇ counters this idea by arguing that mahāmudrā in the Indian context always and only is tantric; indeed, the term specifically refers to the gnosis that ensues from receiving the four unexcelled-yoga-tantra empowerments and practicing the generation- and completion-stage techniques authorized by those empowerments.[366] In short, in Sapaṇ's view the form of mahāmudrā promulgated in his time was both historically and doctrinally illegitimate.

As noted above, later Kagyü scholars (and a number from other traditions) were not shy about refuting Sapaṇ's criticisms, arguing that he had ignored Indian precedents for the rhetoric of immediacy used by Tibetan mahāmudrā commentators, overlooked evidence that mahāmudrā was used in India in nontantric contexts, and wrenched Tibetan nondual mahāmudrā discourse out of its broader context as part of a carefully constructed path system that was perfectly consonant with Mahāyāna theory and practice.[367] The effect of Sapaṇ's critique must not be overstated, though: it did virtually nothing to stifle the creativity of later Marpa Kagyüpas as they continued to develop their mahāmudrā traditions, building on the foundation laid by Gampopa and other great Tibetan Renaissance figures, and expanding into new areas of inquiry, new ways of systematizing theory and practice, and new genres of literary expression, including histories, textual commentaries, philosophical treatises, anthologies, and polemics.

The Third Karmapa, Rangjung Dorjé

The first important later Marpa Kagyü contributor to mahāmudrā discourse was the Third Karmapa, Rangjung Dorjé (1284–1339).[368] Born in eastern Tibet to a Nyingma father who also was well versed in Chö traditions, he drew early notice from Orgyenpa Rinchen Pal (1230–1309), a student of both the Second Karmapa and the Drukpa master Götsangpa. Recognized by Orgyenpa as the reincarnation of Karma Pakshi, Rangjung Dorjé went on to live a life typical of a charismatic lama, traveling widely, studying Buddhist literature,

366. See Sakya Pandita 2002, pp. 112, 117–19, 124, and 154.

367. For Kagyü responses, see, e.g., Kn*PCOZ* 93b–99a, trans. Dakpo Tashi Namgyal 1986, 105–9 (Tashi Namgyal); Broido 1987; Higgins and Draszczyk 2016, 2:179–94 (Pema Karpo). For a critical response from Shākya Chokden (1428–1507), a "renegade" Sakyapa quite partial to Kagyü mahāmudrā, see Higgins and Draszczyk 2016, 2:10–85. For a Geluk critique, see Tk*SGML* 109; trans. Thuken 2009, 150, and in part 5, section 9 below.

368. See, e.g., Roerich 1976, 488–93, Gardner 2011, Gamble 2013, and Gamble 2018.

undertaking retreats, gaining realizations, having visions, writing texts in a variety of genres, engaging in diplomacy, and promoting religious and public works projects. Although he spent time near the Karma Kagyü seat at Tsurphu, he lived a peripatetic life, journeying throughout Tibet and beyond. He traveled through China and resided both at the Yuan court in Beijing and in the Mongol capital, Xanadu, where he died. Rangjung Dorjé's writings include several important philosophical treatises, the most renowned of which are the *Profound Inner Meaning*, *Distinguishing Cognition from Gnosis*, and *Recognizing the Tathāgata Essence*.[369] In these and other philosophical writings, the Karmapa synthesized Madhyamaka, Yogācāra, buddha nature, and tantric discourse from India to produce an original and influential account of Buddhist thought and practice, the hallmark of which is a sharp distinction between mere cognition and true gnosis—the primordially pure awareness that all beings possess and must realize if they are to become buddhas.

As heir to a number of different Kagyü lineages, Rangjung Dorjé was well versed in mahāmudrā traditions. He composed a multitude of songs of realization, a commentary on the three dohā collections of Saraha, two expositions of Tilopa's *Ganges Mahāmudrā*, a discussion of the six Dharmas of Nāropa, a practice manual for the connate union, and the *Prayer of the Mahāmudrā of Definitive Meaning*. The last two are especially important.

The *Instructions for the Mahāmudrā Connate Union*[370] elaborates a model for mahāmudrā instruction—attributed to Gampopa—that would be adopted by many subsequent Kagyü authors. The text begins by leading an initiated disciple through a series of preliminaries, such as developing compassion and devotion, praying to the guru visualized at the crown of one's head, absorbing the guru's blessings, and dedicating merit. Next, serenity meditation is developed, first on the basis of sense objects, then on the basis of whatever mind states arise, and finally on a space-like awareness of clarity and nonconceptuality. Insight is induced by investigation of the nature of the serene mind—which is, whatever its object, understood to be clarity and nonconceptuality, unelaborated self-knowing, the inseparability of appearance and emptiness. Rangjung Dorjé goes on to discuss the three basic experiences that accompany mahāmudrā meditation—bliss, clarity/luminosity, and nonconceptuality—and the ways in which, depending on how we understand them, they either

369. The *Zab mo nang don*, *Rnam shes ye shes 'byed pa*, and *Snying po bstan pa*. For analysis and translation of *Recognizing the Tathāgata Essence*, see Schaeffer 1995; for analysis and translation of all three texts, see Brunnhölzl 2009.

370. *Phyag rgya chen po lhan cig skyes sbyor gyi khrid yid*. See Roberts 2011, 153–68, and Roberts 2014, 125–46.

enhance or diminish our realization. He concludes by noting that the connate union should be practiced in concert with the six Dharmas of Nāropa, hence bringing together the nondual and esoteric approaches to mahāmudrā.

The *Prayer of the Mahāmudrā of Definitive Meaning*[371] is probably the best known of Rangjung Dorjé's texts, having been adopted into Kagyü liturgy and discussed at length by masters of the tradition in both earlier and modern times.[372] In a mere twenty-five verses, the Karmapa provides a poetic epitome of the attitudes, realizations, and actions proper to a mahāmudrā practitioner. Framing his prayer with an opening appeal to the gurus, deities, buddhas, and bodhisattvas and a closing dedication of merit, he focuses on the view and meditative practice of mahāmudrā, which involve various perceptions and processes—including serenity and insight, as well as the development of both renunciation and compassion—but may be summarized as the blissful, clear, nonconceptual realization that "all phenomena are manifestations of the mind and the mind is without mind, empty of an essence of mind."[373] Or, even more basically: "The nature of beings is always buddhahood."[374] In his song, Rangjung Dorjé invokes such familiar schemes as basis-path-fruit and view-meditation-conduct-fruit; he uses terms from the Madhyamaka, Yogācāra, and buddha nature schools of Indian philosophy; and he declares that the freedom from mental activity characteristic of the ultimate realization is the great seal (*phyag rgya che*) and its freedom from extremes *is* the great middle way (*dbu ma chen po*), which is synonymous with the all-inclusive great perfection (*rdzogs chen*).[375]

Great Madhyamaka, Shentong, and the Jonang Tradition

This last remark—which more or less establishes equivalency among mahāmudrā, the great middle way, and the great perfection—indicates that, like his predecessor, the Third Karmapa had a considerable appreciation for traditions outside his own. Certainly, his reference to the great perfection indicates a familiarity with the Nyingma tradition (whose perspective, after all, was probably the first to which he was exposed) that is borne out elsewhere by his deliberate use of the great-perfection terms *essence* (*ngo bo*), *nature* (*rang*

371. *Nges don phyag rgya chen po'i smon lam*. See, e.g., Chang 1986, 31–36, Nydahl 1991 (which includes the Tibetan text), and Roberts 2011, 169–74.

372. See, e.g., Dorjé 1995, Roberts 2011, 175–288, and Tai Situ 2001.

373. Roberts 2011, 170.

374. Roberts 2011, 172.

375. Roberts 2011, 172.

bzhin), and *responsive capacity* (*thugs rje*) in an account of the fundamental nature of mind.[376] The reference to the great middle way, or *mahāmadhyamaka*, is a bit less clear, since most Tibetan philosophers affirm the superiority of the Indian Madhyamaka school, but the term did come frequently to refer to a notion of Madhyamaka that draws not just on overtly Mādhyamika thinkers like Nāgārjuna and Candrakīrti but also on Yogācāras like Maitreya and Asaṅga, buddha nature texts like the *Sublime Continuum*, and tantric literature, and implies an interpretation of emptiness that transcends the common Tibetan division into Svātantrika and Prāsaṅgika subschools. One feature of this interpretation is the notion that the emptiness predicated of the primordial buddha mind possessed by all beings may be quite different from the emptiness of mundane phenomena and persons. Phenomena and persons are said to be empty because they are devoid of permanence, unity, independence, or intrinsic existence; whereas buddha mind is empty because it is devoid of saṃsāric qualities extrinsic to awakening but is at the same time replete with the qualities of awakening that are implicit in buddha nature.

This distinction was most sharply articulated by a master whom Rangjung Dorjé may have known personally, Dölpopa Sherab Gyaltsen (1292–1361), founder of the controversial Jonang school. In his *Mountain Doctrine*,[377] Dölpopa describes the two positions as intrinsic emptiness, *rangtong* (*rang stong*), and extrinsic emptiness, *shentong* (*gzhan stong*), respectively, and clearly favors the latter (which, incidentally, he equates with both Madhyamaka and mahāmudrā, as well as the philosophical position of the *Kālacakra Tantra*). After Dölpopa, shentong became a popular position in Tibetan thought, but it meant many things to many people.[378] Its adherents—all Jonangpas, many Kagyüpas and Nyingmapas, at least one Sakyapa (Shākya Chokden), and likely not a single Gelukpa—often disagreed over whether extrinsic emptiness was a philosophical position or simply a metaphorical way of conveying the experience of realization. They also disputed whether the "awareness" (*rig pa*) or "mind itself" (*sems nyid*) synonymous with buddha mind truly was permanent, unitary, and independent—a claim by Dölpopa that, in the eyes of his critics, brought him perilously close to the eternalist view of Hindu schools[379]—or was, at least in some provisional sense, expressed in the momentary fluctuations of mere "mind" (*sems*) or "cognition" (*rnam shes*). Rangjung

376. Mathes 2008, 64.

377. *Ri chos nges don rgya mtsho*. See Döl-bo-ba 2006.

378. For a discussion of the contrasting views of Dölpopa, Shākya Chokden, and Tāranātha, see Mathes 2004; see also Tāranātha 2007.

379. For an argument to this effect, see Thuken 2009, 202–4.

Dorjé never used the term *shentong* and almost certainly cannot be regarded as a Shentongpa in Dölpopa's sense of the term,[380] but his creative and nuanced interpretation of a range of Indian wisdom traditions came in later times to be associated with the shentong view, which found a secure place within the Kagyü as a plausible way to understand the philosophical keys to both Madhyamaka and mahāmudrā. This was particularly the case with his assertion that emptiness, when applied to supreme gnosis or buddha mind, is an affirming negation rather than a nonaffirming negation, in the spirit of the term "emptiness endowed with all aspects" (*sarvākāvaropetaśūnyatā*). In other words, emptiness in this context is *not* a negation pure and simple but a negation that clears the way for the expression of the awakened qualities intrinsic to all beings.[381]

The Fourteenth and Fifteenth Centuries

The century and a half after Rangjung Dorjé's passing in 1339 saw the fortunes of the Marpa Kagyü generally improve. Nominal Sakyapa hegemony over Tibet ended with the consolidation of power there in the 1350s by Jangchup Gyaltsen of Phakmodru (1303–73), whose triumph ushered in an era of relative peace and prosperity, allowing religious and cultural life to develop—at least for a time—unshadowed by the prospect of war. Though shorn of political power, the Sakyapa retained their institutional and intellectual prestige; the Nyingma, spurred by the brilliant innovations of Longchen Rabjampa (1308–63), found clearer articulation and greater self-confidence than they had for many years; and the "neo-Kadam" order eventually known as the Geluk (or the Gandenpa) was founded near Lhasa by Tsongkhapa Losang Drakpa (1357–1419). Certainly, the most widespread and well-organized Marpa Kagyü suborders—the Karma, Drigung, and Drukpa—flourished, gaining institutional strength and continuing to develop scholarly and meditative traditions, including those surrounding mahāmudrā, that had been established during the Tibetan Renaissance.

Among the notable masters of this period were several lamas with loose—but by no means exclusive—ties to the Kagyü. Rangjung Dorjé's younger contemporary, Butön Rinchen Drup (1290–1364), was one of the great figures in Tibetan intellectual history, responsible for bringing to completion the Kagyur and Tengyur of the New Translation schools that, in one or another recension,

380. See Schaeffer 1995, 25–36, Mathes 2008, 75–84, Brunnhölzl 2009, 95–109, and Burchardi 2011, 318–23.

381. See Mathes 2008, 51–75.

are still in use today. Although he was affiliated with the Trophu suborder of the Kagyü, he is often remembered as a Kadampa, a Sakyapa, or even as the founder of his own school, the Buluk.[382] A later master important in very different ways was the "crazy" siddha, master of longevity, builder of stūpas and iron bridges, and inventor of the Tibetan opera Thangtong Gyalpo (1361?–1485). Although often associated with the Shangpa Kagyü, he is probably best regarded as a truly trans-sectarian figure.[383] By the same token, the brilliantly original "Golden Paṇḍita," Shākya Chokden (1428–1507), was by training and primary affiliation a Sakyapa, but—the polemics of Sakya Paṇḍita notwithstanding—he evinced great sympathy for Kagyü forms of mahāmudrā, which he saw as the pinnacle of Buddhist theory and praxis, synonymous with buddha nature and other key Mahāyāna philosophical and soteriological terms.[384] He also made important contributions to the development of Buddhist philosophy in Tibet, especially through his unique way of dividing Madhyamaka into two distinct yet ultimately complementary subschools: the analytical and apophatic Niḥsvabhāvavāda (roughly equivalent to what others called Prāsaṅgika, based on the writings of Nāgārjuna, Candrakīrti, et al.) and the experiential and cataphatic Ālikākāravāda (which he saw as the true purport of such Yogācāra thinkers as Maitreya and Asaṅga).[385] Though capable of being sharply polemical—he criticized with equal glee both the Geluk and Jonang positions on emptiness, and was reviled within his own tradition for questioning some of Sapaṇ's positions—Shākya Chokden actually was an early proponent of the ultimate unity of the superficially differing approaches to life, thought, and the practice of the path proposed by the various Tibetan Buddhist orders—which helped to foreshadow (if not greatly influence) ecumenical trends within those orders in the centuries to come.[386]

The same period also produced four remarkable figures whose affiliation was clearly Kagyü, each of whom illustrates a distinctive aspect of Kagyü culture, and each of whom helped in their own way to advance understanding of mahāmudrā: Gö Lotsāwa Shönu Pal, Tsangnyön Heruka, the Seventh Karmapa Chödrak Gyatso, and the Fourth Shamarpa Chödrak Yeshé.

Gö Lotsāwa (1392–1481) was one of Tibet's greatest historians and a learned

382. *Bu lugs*. For more on Butön, see, especially, Seyfort Ruegg 1960.

383. On his life and teachings, see, especially, Stearns 2007.

384. For his perspective on mahāmudrā, see Higgins and Draszczyk 2016, 1:44–147 and 2:10–85.

385. On his contributions to philosophy, see, e.g., Komarovski 2011.

386. On this, see Komarovski 2015.

and subtle commentator on Indian philosophical texts.[387] Primarily a student of Kagyü traditions, he also received transmissions from Nyingmapa teachers and, personally, from Tsongkhapa. His *Blue Annals*, completed in 1478, is one of the longest and most influential of all Tibetan historical works.[388] Arranged according to one or another type of practice lineage, it provides an exhaustive, hagiography-centered account of the development of Buddhism in Tibet from the eighth until the fifteenth century. By far the longest chapter in the book—accounting for nearly a third of its total—is that on the Marpa Kagyü, and unsurprisingly, many of the narratives included there prominently feature mahāmudrā, whether as a system of philosophy, a meditation practice, or a realization required for the attainment of liberation. Gö also devotes a separate, shorter chapter to the transmission of mahāmudrā lineages to Tibet, with a special focus on the different lines stemming from Maitrīpa's disciple Vajrapāṇi.[389] There he describes mahāmudrā as "the doctrine that seals all the meditative and religious practices, from the Prātimokṣa, which is the foundation of the Buddha's doctrine, to the Guhyasamāja," a salvific understanding of the nature of reality that can be grasped "only through the blessing of a holy teacher."[390] Among many other works, Gö also wrote a masterful commentary on the *Sublime Continuum*, the buddha-nature text said by Tibetans to have been transmitted in the fifth century by the future Buddha Maitreya and rediscovered in the eleventh by the mahāsiddha Maitrīpa, who taught it as a mahāmudrā text. Gö follows this approach, reading the *Sublime Continuum*—along with other texts on buddha nature and the natural purity of mind found in the Buddha's third turning of the wheel of Dharma[391]—as a key source for a sūtra-based practice of mahāmudrā.[392]

Utterly different on the surface from the scholarly Gö was Tsangnyön

387. On his life, see Mathes 2008, 131–47.

388. See Roerich 1976 for the sole complete English translation.

389. Roerich 1976, 839–66.

390. Roerich 1976, 839–41.

391. As described in the *Unraveling the Intention* (*Saṃdhinirmocana*) *Sūtra*, the first two turnings promote, respectively, the Hīnayāna view, which reduces persons and things to their dharmic constituents but is prone to being read as implying eternalism, and the Perfection of Wisdom/Madhyamaka view, which asserts the emptiness of phenomena but is prone to being read as implying nihilism. The third turning, associated most closely with Yogācāra, finds a middle way by distinguishing those entities that do not exist (imputations) from those that do exist (dependent phenomena and absolute nature). In Tibet, the third turning often came to be associated with the Buddha's promulgation of buddha nature and his teaching of the tantras.

392. Mathes 2008, esp. 34–45, 204–311, and 367–410.

Heruka (1452–1507),[393] one of a number of self-professed "madmen" (*smyon pa*) who shook up the Kagyü establishment in the fifteenth and sixteenth centuries.[394] A western Tibetan whose early teachers were primarily Sakyapas and Gelukpas, Tsangnyön in his twenties adopted the eccentric lifestyle and sometimes antinomian behavior of a wandering yogī—very much in the style of the tantric mahāsiddhas of India and the early masters of the Kagyü, especially Milarepa. Whether or not, as Gene Smith suggests, he and other *nyönpas* were seeking to re-invest the Kagyü with some of its original "fervor . . . and incandescent spirituality,"[395] he certainly attracted notice, disciples, and no small amount of patronage. That patronage enabled him to compose and, notably, to publish some of the enduring masterworks of Kagyü—indeed, of Tibetan—literature.[396] Drawing skillfully from an array of written and oral sources that had been circulating for centuries, Tsangnyön wrote the *Life of Milarepa*, the *Life of Marpa the Translator*, and the *Hundred Thousand Songs of Milarepa*,[397] each of which has become a classic of Tibetan tradition, and each of which is a rich source of information on Kagyü approaches to mahāmudrā as they developed over a number of centuries. Tsangnyön also produced a collection of Marpa's songs and did much to revive the Rechung Hearing Transmission, which had been submerged by the waves of success enjoyed by traditions derived from Mila's other great disciple, Gampopa.[398] After Tsangnyön revived it, the hearing transmission was adopted into the Drukpa subschool, which maintains it to this day. Overall, despite his countercultural performances, which undoubtedly discomfited some corrupt and complacent Kagyü clerics, in most respects Tsangnyön was, as Stefan Larsson argues, "quite orthodox"[399] and is as crucial to our appreciation of the literature of the early Kagyü as Gö is to our understanding of its religious and institutional history.

A third key late fifteenth-century figure was the Seventh Karmapa, Chödrak Gyatso (1454–1506). Born in Kham, he was reputed to have declared to his mother when only five months old, "there is nothing in the world but emptiness," and he was identified as the Karmapa tulku at the unusually early

393. See, especially, Larsson 2012.

394. On this phenomenon, see DiValerio 2015.

395. Smith 2001, 60.

396. On his publishing activities and range of literary activity, see Schaeffer 2011.

397. For translations, see, respectively, Nālandā Translation Committee 1982, Tsangnyön Heruka 2010, Chang 1989, and Tsongnyön Heruka 2016.

398. See Smith, 2001, 61, and Sernesi 2011.

399. Larsson 2011, 449.

age of nine months. He went on to live a life devoted, in varying degrees, to scholarship, meditation, diplomacy, animal protection, and public works. He is credited with founding the great "college" (*shes grwa*) at the main Karmapa monastery, Tsurphu, hence with establishing the basis for Kagyü educational practices that have persisted to this day. Among the nearly twenty works attributed to him, the two most important are the *Ocean of Texts on Reasoning* and the *Indian Mahāmudrā Texts*. The *Ocean of Texts on Reasoning* (*Tshad ma rigs gzhung rgya mtsho*) is the definitive Kagyü discussion of the tradition of Indian Buddhist logic, to which it gives a particular spin by tracing how the conventional processes of valid cognition may lead to a supramundane form of apperception or self-awareness (*rang rig*) that is a luminous awareness empty of duality. This awareness is explicitly taken to exemplify the idea of extrinsic emptiness, or shentong, not in the radical sense proposed by Dölpopa but in a "rationally structured, logically argued, moderate form"[400] that typifies Kagyü approaches to the concept. *Indian Mahāmudrā Texts* is a voluminous anthology of Tibetan translations of over two hundred Indian works explicitly or implicitly related to mahāmudrā.[401] The Seventh Karmapa's collection—the most extensive ever assembled in Tibet (or anywhere, for that matter)—is drawn mostly from the Tengyur, though it does include a single tantra from the Kangyur , the *Royal Tantra on the Unpolluted* (*Anāvilatantrarāja*),[402] and a handful of extra-canonical sources. Most of the texts are by one or another of the mahāsiddhas of late Indian Buddhist tantrism (Saraha, Tilopa, Maitrīpa, et al.), but the songs, treatises, or commentaries included seem to focus less on esoteric procedures than on concepts, practices, and realizations consonant with what we have been calling *nondual mahāmudrā*, where the great seal is understood primarily in terms of the natural purity of mind, buddha nature, or emptiness.

The Fourth Shamar ("Red Hat") hierarch, Chödrak Yeshé (1453–1524), took his ordination from the Seventh Karmapa and went on to study with Gö Lotsāwa and various other Kagyü masters. Like many a great lama, he played a number of roles over the course of his life, including teacher, scholar, preceptor, monastery founder, and—for a period of eleven years (1495–1506)—effectively the spiritual and temporal ruler of Tibet, in his role as regent for the young Phakdru heir. Among the students he attracted were two figures we will examine below, Karma Trinlepa and Pawo Tsuklak Trengwa. He

400. Burchardi 2011, 340.

401. In its most recent print edition (Cg*PCGZ*), it covers six book-format volumes. For a discussion, see Mathes 2011.

402. See R. Jackson 2010.

left behind hundreds of written works; most are tantric in orientation, but several, as well, touch on important themes in mahāmudrā theory and practice. The *Hidden Meaning of Luminosity* (*'Od gsal gyi sbas don*),[403] for instance, is framed as a commentary on the six Dharmas of Nāropa and does include discussions of the place of luminosity in that arrangement of completion-stage practices, with suitable quotations from key tantric texts, but Chödrak Yeshé is equally concerned to link the experience of luminosity to various "Sūtra Vehicle" texts, especially the *Sublime Continuum*, with its brilliant exposition of a resplendent buddha nature that is empty of any defilement and replete with all the qualities of buddhahood. Both the luminosity found in the six Dharmas and the buddha nature of the *Sublime Continuum* and other treatises are, in turn, synonymous with mahāmudrā. A second key mahāmudrā text by Chödrak Yeshé is the *Sixty Verses on Mahāmudrā* (*Phyag chen drug bcu pa*),[404] a wide-ranging treatment of the Kagyü great seal, in which he divides Madhyamaka into (a) Niḥsvabhāvavāda Madhyamaka (the Middle Way of the No-Self Position), which is roughly equivalent to Prāsaṅgika and associated with the second turning of the Dharma wheel, and (b) following Maitrīpa, Yuganaddhāpratiṣṭhāna Madhyamaka (the Middle Way of Unity and Nonabiding), which is based on such third-turning texts as the treatises of Maitreya and Asaṅga—especially those that explicate buddha nature. He explicitly identifies mahāmudrā with the Madhyamaka of Unity and Nonabiding and goes on to assert its superiority to the No-Self Position approach, whether in terms of the more definitive nature of the turning of the Dharma wheel with which it is associated, or in terms of the greater subtlety of its concept of negation. According to the Shamar, the emptiness of the mind is not a simple, nonaffirming negation, in which, for instance, the mind's emptiness is its lack of intrinsic existence pure and simple, but rather an affirming negation, in which defilements and their traces are absent from the mind but buddha qualities are implicitly present. The practical implication of this is that, with the guru's guidance, the disciple must simply identify with the mind's natural luminosity, which is identical to both buddha nature and the Dharma body. Finally, as would many Kagyü texts in the centuries to come, the *Sixty Verses* also engages in polemics, criticizing (though not by name) the Gelukpas and Jonangpas for various philosophical transgressions and defending Gampopa's notion of a Perfection Vehicle mahāmudrā against the attacks of Sakya Paṇḍita.

403. See Draszczyk 2015.

404. See Draszczyk 2019.

Sixteenth-Century Scholasticism

The sixteenth century was marked by increasing conflict between the Kagyüpas (especially the politically powerful Karmapas) and the ascendant Gelukpas, who had captured from the Kagyüpas the loyalty of the influential Phakmodru nobility—but it also witnessed an unparalleled flowering of Kagyü scholasticism in general and systematic Kagyü thought about mahāmudrā in particular. Indeed, for all the importance of the great early masters of the Kagyü and for all the influence exerted on the tradition by later scholars such as Karma Chakmé (1613–78), Situ Paṇchen Chökyi Jungné (1700–74), and Jamgön Kongtrul Lodrö Thayé (1813–99), it is above all the great intellectuals of the sixteenth century who gave a classic form to Kagyü discourse about mahāmudrā, and it is their works above all that still shape discussion of the topic today. For the most part, they drew on the terminology, categories, and sayings of the early Kagyü masters, describing the path to awakening in terms of the familiar division into sudden and gradual approaches (with a "nonconsecutive" style sometimes between them), but focusing primarily on the gradual way intended for beginners. The gradual path of mahāmudrā was understood in terms of such equally traditional categories as ground, path, and fruit; view, meditation, conduct, and fruit; serenity and insight; and the four yogas.[405] The sixteenth-century masters' contribution to the tradition lay above all in their ability to clearly and thoroughly systematize earlier teachings so that their historical depth, philosophical complexity, and practical force could be fully grasped. They form the immediate Kagyü backdrop to the first public articulation of Geluk mahāmudrā, so while we cannot discuss them or their works in detail, we will briefly summarize the contributions of the most notable among them.

Karma Trinlepa and Pawo Tsuklak Trengwa

Karma Trinlepa Choklé Namgyal (1456–1539)[406] was a scholar-siddha, combining serious scholarship with assiduous yogic practice, and was the first in a distinguished line of tulkus. He studied with two great Kagyüpa figures mentioned already—the Seventh Karmapa and the Fourth Shamarpa—and with the unorthodox Sakyapa Shākya Chokden, from whom he learned the path and fruit tradition. He himself was the teacher of several distinguished

405. For a synthetic treatment of a number of important sixteenth-century mahāmudrā sources, see Brown 2006.

406. See, e.g., Rheingans 2004; Higgins and Draszczyk 2016, 1:148–224 and 2:86–103.

scholars, most notably the great historian Pawo Tsuklak Trengwa (1504–1566). His best-known works include:

- A detailed commentary on Rangjung Dorjé's *Profound Inner Meaning* in which he argues that the Third Karmapa was, indeed, a Shentongpa, though of a different, less absolutist stripe than Dölpopa[407]
- A commentary on the Essential Trilogy—the *King*, *Queen*, and *People* dohā treasuries attributed to Saraha—which, among other things, highlights the degree to which mahāmudrā, taken as the nature of mind and reality, is a central theme in the mahāsiddha's songs[408]
- A question-and-answer (*dris lan*) text[409] in which he argues that intrinsic and extrinsic emptiness are noncontradictory because, "when correctly understood, self-emptiness is not a nonaffirming negation and because other-emptiness, natural luminosity, or the inseparability of the dharma realm and awareness does not attribute true existence to the ultimate"[410]
- A number of spiritual songs, in which he sings, for instance, of how "clarity is the manifestation of mind and emptiness is the essence of mind; their unity is the nature of mind, so mind as such is mahāmudrā"[411]

As Higgins and Draszczyk note of him, he was "a prototypical scholar-yogin, who endeavored to make a living experience of his scholastic learning, with the conviction that only the transformation of the individual through spiritual praxis will lead to genuine wisdom beyond partiality."[412] Furthermore, his Apratiṣṭhāna Madhyamaka insistence on the unity of saṃsāra and nirvāṇa, appearance and emptiness, and rangtong and shentong "set him apart from many scholars in the incendiary polemical atmosphere of the fifteenth and sixteenth centuries"[413] and pointed the way to the inclusivist approach that would be a hallmark of the Rimé (*ris med*), or nonsectarian, scholars of nineteenth-century eastern Tibet.

Karma Trinlepa's disciple, the Second Pawo Tulku Tsuklak Trengwa (who also studied with the Fourth Shamarpa), was an important hierarch who later

407. Mathes 2008, 55.

408. See Guenther 1969 and Guenther 1993.

409. Higgins and Draszczyk 2016, 2:87–94

410. Higgins and Draszczyk 2016, 2:87.

411. Higgins and Draszczyk 2016, 2:101 (translation adapted).

412. Higgins and Draszczyk 2016, 1:223.

413. Higgins and Draszczyk 2016, 1:223.

in life played a key role in administering the Karma Kagyü. He wrote at least two works on the fivefold mahāmudrā system of the Drigung Kagyü. The ninth chapter of his lengthy commentary on Śāntideva's *Engaging in Bodhisattva Conduct* (*Bodhicaryāvatāra*) remains one of the key texts for Kagyü interpretations of Madhyamaka.[414] He is best known, though, for his *Feast for Scholars*, a massive, detailed, and methodologically sophisticated history of Buddhism in India and Tibet, with some additional discussion of Mongolia and China.[415] Most of the text is taken up with Tibetan Buddhism—with useful material on both the imperial and renaissance periods, and interesting treatments of the Kadam and the Drigung Kagyü—but by far the largest chapter is an extensive account of the Karma Kagyü. To the degree that mahāmudrā is central to Karma Kagyü theory and practice, Tsuklak Trengwa's history is an important source for understanding—and justifying—the way the great seal was transmitted within a tradition that has stressed it continuously for over eight hundred years.

The Eighth Karmapa and Dakpo Tashi Namgyal

The Eighth Karmapa, Mikyö Dorjé (1507–54),[416] was a Khampa who rose to become one of the great philosophers in Kagyü history. A prolific scholar and a spirited polemicist, he composed dozens of works on a wide variety of topics, ranging from guru yoga, to mahāmudrā, to tantric ritual, to the classics of Indian Buddhism. He was the first compiler of the great anthology of Kagyü religious poetry, the *Ocean of Kagyü Songs*, to which he contributed his own spiritual songs and reflections, prompted by dreams and visions.[417] He composed a four-session guru-yoga liturgy that still is used by many Kagyüpas.[418] He also wrote a number of short works on mahāmudrā—mostly supplication and question-and-answer texts—that explore the complex relation between sūtra and tantra elements in theorizing and practicing the great seal and place a particular emphasis on the identity between Dharma body and the ordinary mind. This identity is communicated through humor, paradox, and a rhetoric of immediacy—and seeing it is thoroughly dependent upon the grace of

414. See Brunnhölzl 2004, 599–790. For a translation of the Tibetan version of the text, see Shantideva 2006.

415. See Martin 1997, 88–89.

416. See, e.g., Nālandā Translation Committee 1980, 310–13, Rheingans 2008, Higgins and Draszczyk 2016, 2:226–341 and 2:104–55, and Mathes 2019.

417. See Nālandā Translation Committee 1980, 16–26.

418. See, e.g., Karthar 2013.

the guru.[419] He also wrote a short but influential treatise on the philosophical foundations of mahāmudrā, *A Trove Containing Myriad Treasures of Profound Mahāmudrā*, which devotes special attention to the fruitional great seal, namely buddhahood, arguing for a concept of the Dharma body that involves active cognition and volition.[420] Finally, Mikyö Dorjé wrote influential treatises on the key Indian sources for the study of the Perfection of Wisdom, Vinaya, Abhidharma, and Madhyamaka. Of special importance is his commentary on Candrakīrti's *Entry to the Middle Way* (*Madhyamakāvatāra*), the *Chariot of the Dakpo Kagyü Siddhas*, which is a long, erudite, and sophisticated treatment of a variety of different topics related to Madhyamaka philosophy.[421] It includes detailed critiques of the perspectives on emptiness and the two truths propounded by Tsongkhapa and other earlier thinkers[422] and seeks to align the Madhyamaka philosophical view with mahāmudrā as a tradition of meditation and realization, identifying a major line of Kagyü Madhyamaka transmission that focuses on nondual mahāmudrā precepts taught by, among others, Saraha, Nāgārjuna, Śavaripa, and Maitrīpa in India, and Marpa, Milarepa, Gampopa, and Jikten Sumgön in Tibet.[423] Mikyö Dorjé's view of emptiness, incidentally, evolved over his lifetime: in earlier works he seems to favor a version of shentong consonant with that of Rangjung Dorjé, while in the *Chariot*, a later work, he upholds a version of rangtong, though one that is quite distinct from that of the Geluk.

The Eighth Karmapa's younger contemporary, Dakpo Tashi Namgyal (1512–87),[424] is renowned for the clarity of his exposition of Kagyü approaches to both tantra and mahāmudrā. He composed a number of texts on the Hevajra tantra, a detailed manual for practice of the six Dharmas of Nāropa, and an encyclopedic account of the stages of the tantric path according to the Kagyü, *Light Rays from the Jewel of the Excellent Teaching*.[425] He is best known, however, for his works on mahāmudrā, including a number of short guide-

419. Rheingans 2011.

420. *Zab mo phyag chen gyi mdzod sna tshogs 'dus pa'i gter.* For excerpts, see Higgins and Draszczyk 2016, 2:122–43.

421. *Dwags brgyud grub pa'i shing rta.* For an abridged translation of chapter 6, on wisdom, see Goldfield et al. 2005.

422. See, e.g., Williams 1983, Broido 1985b, Brunnhölzl 2004, 553–97, and Seyfort Ruegg 2010, 345–46.

423. See Seyfort Ruegg 2010, 323–56, and Brunnhölzl 2004, 47–68.

424. See, e.g., Kapstein 1990, and Dakpo Tashi Namgyal 2019, lxv–lxxviii.

425. *Rdo rje'i theg pa'i spyi don mdor bsdus pa legs bshad nor bu'i 'od zer.* Translated at Roberts 2011, 401–620. In this text, which shows the influence of Tsongkhapa's *Great Exposition on*

books[426] and his massive *Moonbeams of Mahāmudrā*, which remains a vital source of textual citations and meditation instructions to this day.[427] *Moonbeams of Mahāmudrā* presents a graded path of mahāmudrā practices that begins with "common" techniques for attaining serenity and insight, then moves on to the "uncommon" techniques of mahāmudrā, in the following sequence:

- The preliminary rituals related to refuge, offering the maṇḍala, purifying defilements, and aligning with the guru
- Attainment of serenity on the basis of meditation on external objects, internal objects, and, finally, the mind itself
- Attainment of insight on the basis of recognizing that all objects are products of mind and that both mind and its objects are unarisen, or empty
- A deeper exploration of the nature of mind through contemplation of the coemergence of mind, thoughts, and appearances
- Maintaining unbroken realization of ultimate reality in postmeditative everyday life
- Overcoming errors in the practice of serenity and insight
- Enhancing one's realization through an ever deeper recognition of the mind's empty nature and through transforming mundane suffering into the path
- Attaining buddhahood through the four yogas: single-pointedness, nonelaboration, single taste, and nonmeditation

In the course of his exposition, Tashi Namgyal provides copious references to Indic and Tibetan sources relevant to mahāmudrā, defends the Kagyü approach to the great seal against criticism from Sakyapas and others, and clearly locates mahāmudrā within the larger frame of the Mantra Vehicle and the Perfection Vehicle, with a special emphasis on the latter. Indeed, it is a central concern of Tashi Namgyal to establish the legitimacy of Gampopa's claim that mahāmudrā is a special teaching that at once includes and transcends both Perfection and Mantra approaches to the path.

the Stages of Mantra (*Sngags rim chen mo*), Tashi Namgyal identifies mahāmudrā with the luminosity associated with the completion states of unexcelled yoga tantra (576ff.).

426. See, e.g., Dakpo Tashi Namgyal 2001, which includes the Tibetan text.

427. Kn*PCOZ*; trans. Dakpo Tashi Namgyal 1986. For a fresh translation, issued too late for me to use here, see Dakpo Tashi Namgyal 2019.

Pema Karpo

Tashi Namgyal's most brilliant disciple, and arguably the greatest of all Kagyü scholars, was the fourth Drukchen tulku, Pema Karpo (1527–92)—dubbed "the Omniscient" by later generations. In the words of Gene Smith, Pema Karpo was "one of those rare renaissance men," a great scholar who also was "a shrewd and occasionally ruthless politician,"[428] but nevertheless possessed a countervailing hermitic streak. He almost singlehandedly systematized the teachings of the Drukpa Kagyü. Among the dozens of substantial works he left behind are a collection of searching spiritual songs,[429] tantric sādhanas and commentaries,[430] nuanced philosophical treatises,[431] a history of Buddhism in India and Tibet (at least a third of which is devoted to a history of Kagyü lineages),[432] and an autobiography that stands as an important record of political, social, and religious developments in sixteenth-century Tibet. Like other Kagyü masters of his era, he was preoccupied with mahāmudrā, which he tended to regard as a practice-tradition in which the Sūtra and Mantra Vehicles, dialectical and experiential approaches to awakening, and gradual and sudden paths are inseparable.[433] Consider, for instance, the mix of esoteric and nondual imagery in the following definition:

> Emptiness rich in the most excellent potentialities is termed *mahāmudrā* because it offers unchanging bliss in which there is complete elimination [of disturbances] and complete intrinsic awareness [of what there is].[434]

Pema Karpo dealt with mahāmudrā—as well as nonmentation and the connate—in a large number of works, including those on the esoteric mixture and transference practice (often identified with the six Dharmas of Nāropa), the four yogas (which he associated with a style of practice—the

428. Smith 2001, 81.

429. For translations, see Beyer 1974, 77–79.

430. See, e.g., Beyer 1974, 140–53.

431. See, e.g., Guenther 1977, Broido 1980, Broido 1984, Broido 1985a, Broido 1985b, and Higgins and Draszczyk 2016, 1:342–428 and 2:156–201.

432. For a summary, see Smith 2001, 80–87.

433. For a sophisticated argument to this effect, see Broido 1985a. See also Guenther 1977, 36–109.

434. Guenther 1975, 6 (modified; brackets in original); cf. Guenther 1977, 57 and 66–67.

"nonconsecutive"—that is neither sudden nor gradual),[435] the six cycles of equal taste (utilizing thoughts, defilements, gods and demons, suffering, sickness, and death on the path),[436] and the connate union, which he regarded as the quintessence of Drukpa mahāmudrā instructions.[437]

He describes the practice of the connate union in a popular manual called *Notes on Mahāmudrā,* which is structured along the lines of the four yogas.[438] After describing the posture and state of mind to be adopted for meditation, Pema Karpo lays out thirty-one distinct meditations that traverse the yogas:

- Meditations 1–18 (the yoga of single-pointedness) lead the practitioner through the stages of serenity meditation, to the point where they rest in the nature of mind itself, like a brahman weaving a thread, or a sheaf of hay after its cord has been cut, or a baby looking at a temple, or an elephant being pricked by a thorn.
- Meditations 19–24 (the yoga of nonelaboration) lead one through the stages of insight meditation, by inquiring into the nature of mind in stillness or movement; by recognizing thoughts for what they are, without acceptance or rejection; and by analyzing the mind in terms of temporal location, ontological status, and singleness or multiplicity.
- Meditations 25–27 (the yoga of single taste) deepen one's certainty as to the unity of mind and appearances through reflection on three examples of inseparability: dream and waking, water and ice, and water and waves.
- Meditation 28 (the yoga of nonmeditation) is the stage beyond all effort, where "there is nowhere else to go" but "unlocated nirvāṇa, the supreme attainment of mahāmudrā."[439]
- The concluding meditations (30–31) discuss ancillary topics, such as the details of mahāmudrā stages, paths, and experiences; how to avoid obstacles and errors in meditation; and distinctions among the various types of understanding of the nature of mind, from intellectual apprehension to direct realization.

435. For translations of two important texts on the four yogas, see Abboud et al. 2017, 73–106.

436. For a translation of one brief text on the topic, see Abboud et al. 2017, 63–72.

437. See, e.g., the translations in Abboud et al. 2017, 43–106.

438. *Phyag chen zin bris.* Fully translated in Evans-Wentz 1958, 114–54, Roberts 2011, 135–52, Roberts 2015, 103–24, and Abboud et al. 2017, 43–62; partially translated in Beyer 1974, 155–61. (Using a nineteenth-century anthology, Beyer gives a different Tibetan title—drawn from the first line of the text—but he is clearly translating the *Phyag chen zin bris.*)

439. Roberts 2011, 150; modified.

Pema Karpo's most thorough treatment of the great seal is the *Storehouse of Mahāmudrā*.[440] It details the various textual traditions of mahāmudrā that developed in India; it defines the term and relates it to such basic Buddhist categories as sūtra and mantra; it refutes mistaken opinions, most notably those of Sakya Paṇḍita with regard to the legitimacy of Kagyü mahāmudrā and those of Jonangpas and Gelukpas with regard to conventional and ultimate truth; it identifies mahāmudrā with emptiness as an affirming negation; it lays out Kagyü teachings on a number of key practices, including the connate union and the white panacea; and it establishes in detail the view, meditation, and fruit of the connate union. Key to the view is the understanding that mind and its appearances are inseparable from the Dharma body; put another way, mahāmudrā as it really is (*gnas lugs phyag chen*) does not differ essentially from mahāmudrā in its guise as error (*'khrul lugs phyag chen*).[441]

In general, as Higgins and Draszczyk note, Pema Karpo identified mahāmudrā

> as the abiding nature of mind or the unconditioned ultimate that is fully realized only when delusion stemming from the basic ignorance or nonrecognition of this reality is dispelled. A crucial point in his teachings is that the recognition of this ever-present mahāmudrā need not be sought independently of the thoughts, sensations, and feelings that manifest in ordinary mind. This is because such phenomena are differentiated manifestations of an abiding common ground—the nature of mind itself—emerging from it like waves on the surface of the ocean. To recognize these phenomena for what they truly are—expressions of mind's unborn nature—is to rediscover the single ground of their arising and ceasing.[442]

The Ninth Karmapa

A native of Kham, the Ninth Karmapa Wangchuk Dorjé (1556–1603) was the last of his line to enjoy significant temporal power. Like the Eighth Karmapa, he left behind a large collection of writings, which includes *Feast for the Fortunate*,[443] a long subcommentary on his predecessor's *Entry to the Mid-*

440. Pk*PCGZ*. For discussion, see, e.g., Guenther 1977, Broido 1985a, and Higgins and Draszczyk 2016, 1:322–428 and 2:157–79.

441. See Broido 1985a, 27–31, Higgins 2015, and Higgins and Draszczyk 2016, 1:357–98.

442. Higgins and Draszczyk 2016, 1:350; translation slightly altered.

443. *'Jug ṭīk dwags brgyud grub pa'i shing rta bde bar 'dren byed skal bzang dga' ston*. Translated

dle Way commentary; a number of shorter works on such Perfection Vehicle topics as Madhyamaka, Epistemology, and Abhidharma; and, most notably, three treatises on mahāmudrā that remain widely read classics: the short *Recognizing the Dharmakāya*, the medium-length *Mahāmudrā Eliminating the Darkness of Ignorance*, and the extensive *Ocean of Definitive Meaning*.[444] All three texts present mahāmudrā for a gradual practitioner; they follow generally similar outlines and cover much of the same material.

The *Ocean of Definitive Meaning*, the longest and most important of the three, begins with such preliminaries as aspiring for the Dharma, finding a teacher, recognizing the nature of mind in general terms, and attempting to observe mind as it is. The main practice is divided into serenity and insight meditation. In serenity meditation, one assumes the proper posture then concentrates on various external and internal objects of meditation, eventually focusing on the present mind itself and remaining fixed on that, nonconceptually, in a relaxed but alert manner, neither suppressing nor chasing the thoughts that naturally arise. In insight meditation, one first examines the mind, in movement and at rest, then "cuts the root" (*rtsa chod*) by searching the mind to see if it has an intrinsic nature. When no such nature is found, one is prepared for the four "pointing-out instructions," to the effect that appearances are mind, mind is empty, emptiness is spontaneous presence, and spontaneous presence is self-liberated. In the concluding practices, having learned to avoid various pitfalls of meditative experience and developed various skills, one traverses the four yogas of mahāmudrā—single-pointedness, nonelaboration, single taste, and nonmeditation. At the culmination of the last of these yogas, one attains buddhahood, or final mahāmudrā, from which one acts creatively and compassionately in the world for the sake of others. Alternatively, the Karmapa explains the practice in terms of ground, path, and fruit, with the ground being proper understanding of our buddha nature; the path consisting of the preliminaries, serenity and insight meditations, cutting the root, the four pointing-out instructions, and the four yogas; and the fruit being the three buddha bodies.

In the *Ocean of Definitive Meaning*, the three buddha bodies that result from mahāmudrā practice are, for the most part, conceived in classic metaphysical terms: the Dharma body is a buddha's all-pervasive, empty, omniscient awareness; the enjoyment body is the sublime form a buddha assumes for teaching

in Dewar 2008.

444. For a translation of the first (*Chos sku mdzu tshugs su ngo sprod pa*), see Wangchuk Dorjé 2009; for the second (*Phyag chen ma rig mun sel*), see Wangchuk Dorjé 1981 and Dakpo Tashi Namgyal 2019, 489–536; for the third (*Nges don rgya mtsho*), see Wangchuk Dorjé 2001.

high-level bodhisattvas; and the emanation body is a buddha's multiple magical transformations, of which the most famous is Śākyamuni Buddha. In the *Mahāmudrā Eliminating the Darkness of Ignorance*, an alternative, more "psychological" interpretation is offered, wherein the Dharma body is simply the mind's natural emptiness, the enjoyment body is simply the mind's natural clarity or luminosity, and the emanation body is simply the appearances that arise in the mind.[445] This interpretation is particularly consonant with mahāmudrā discourse, since it keeps its focus squarely on the mind—which, after all, whether ordinary or exalted, is, in the oft-quoted words of Saraha, "the single seed of everything."[446]

The State of Kagyü Mahāmudrā Discourse in 1600

By 1600, after over half a millennium of development, mahāmudrā was fixed firmly at the center of Kagyü ideology and practice. Its great masters all dealt with it as a central topic of discourse and were in general, if not universal, agreement on the following points:

- Mahāmudrā is *the* crucial term for Kagyü tradition, since it is pervasive throughout Buddhist practice, whether described in terms of Sūtra or Mantra, ground, path, and fruit, or view, meditation, conduct, and fruit.
- Mahāmudrā is synonymous with such key concepts as buddha nature, emptiness, the connate, the Dharma realm, nonmentation, luminosity, great bliss, and the Dharma body of a buddha.
- Whether implicitly or explicitly—and contrary to the views of Sakya Paṇḍita—mahāmudrā definitely is found in both the perfection (or sūtra-based) and secret mantra (or tantra-based) traditions of Indian Mahāyāna ideology and praxis.
- In terms of the view, mahāmudrā is synonymous with Madhyamaka, with the great-seal style of Madhyamaka being described variously as the Madhyamaka of Nonabiding (*apratiṣṭhāna*), the great middle way, or Prāsaṅgika Madhyamaka.
- The Indian sources of Madhyamaka typically include not just the classical treatises of Nāgārjuna and Candrakīrti but also texts sometimes associated with Yogācāra, such as the Five Maitreya Texts.
- In its esoteric mode as the path of means, mahāmudrā is equivalent to

445. See Wangchuk Dorjé 1981, 119–20 and 144–46.

446. R. Jackson 2004, 73.

the six Dharmas of Nāropa, and in its nondual mode as the path of liberation, it is simply meditation on the nature of mind.

- Mahāmudrā may be practiced suddenly or gradually (with nonconsecutive practice sometimes added as an intermediate option), but most disciples, being of inferior ability, are advised to take a gradual path.
- Mahāmudrā requires of its practitioners, whatever their spiritual level, the mastery of various preliminary practices, but most especially devotion to the guru, who at some point will identify or point out to the practitioner the nature of their mind.
- Mahāmudrā leads to an experience of realization that transcends mere conceptual thought, even though conceptuality may find its place at particular points on the mahāmudrā path.
- Mahāmudrā involves, in its standard gradual path, both serenity and insight meditation, with the former focused on an experience of the mind's fundamental luminosity and the latter intent on the analytical determination and experiential realization of the mind's emptiness—which is inseparable from luminosity.
- Though the practitioner may have to approach it gradually, true mahāmudrā serenity meditation entails settling in relaxed and spacious meditative equipoise on the mind's open and luminous nature.
- Insight meditation in mahāmudrā is based on serenity and involves searching the mind for some kind of ultimate nature—asking, for instance, whether it possesses color or shape, or how it exists in moments of stillness or movement. Finding nothing, one settles into a space-like awareness that deepens into a realization of the mind's emptiness—however that is conceived.
- The mahāmudrā path entails traversing four yogas (single-pointedness, nonelaboration, single taste, and nonmeditation), which can easily be correlated with the practice of serenity and insight and the standard categories of Mahāyāna soteriology, such as the five paths and the ten bodhisattva levels.
- Mahāmudrā meditation typically leads to experiences of clarity, bliss, and nonconceptuality, which if understood properly will advance one toward buddhahood but if misunderstood or clung to can lead one astray.
- Mahāmudrā can be understood in terms of the three (or four) buddha bodies, either in line with traditional "cosmicized" descriptions or simply in terms of the essence, nature, and manifestation of mind.

On these and other points, Kagyüpas found near unanimity. There were, though, a few issues on which they did not always agree, even among themselves—let alone when confronting the ideas and practices of other Tibetan Buddhist traditions. The most notable of these were related to such questions as the following:

- Whether it is suitable to align Kagyü practices with those of other traditions, such as the great perfection of the Nyingma, the path and fruit system of the Sakya, or the Chinese Chan tradition of Heshang Moheyan
- Whether mahāmudrā is confined to the Perfection and Mantra Vehicles, or may, as many suggested, be classified as a "third way" that both includes and transcends Perfection and Mantra
- Whether sudden or gradual (or nonsuccessive) paths are a surer way to attain awakening
- Whether philosophical analysis is an essential or dispensable part of the mahāmudrā path
- Whether traditional ethics are vital or optional for a practitioner on the mahāmudrā path or for one who has reached the end of that path
- Whether mahāmudrā realization of ultimate truth is connected, or utterly unrelated, to conventional knowledge of the saṃsāric world
- Whether the second or third turning of the Dharma wheel is the more authoritative
- Whether the mind, especially the realized mind, is empty in the sense of a nonaffirming negation—which entails a lack of intrinsic existence and implies nothing positive whatsoever (rangtong, or intrinsic emptiness)—or whether it is empty in the sense of an affirming negation—which negates the mundane and conventional but implies that "what is left" in the wake of that negation is a natural luminosity of mind or a set of buddha qualities innate to all beings (shentong, or extrinsic emptiness)

These, then, are the sorts of issues that Paṇchen Losang Chökyi Gyaltsen, with his more than passing acquaintance with Kagyü traditions, would have had in the back of his mind as he composed his seminal Geluk mahāmudrā texts in the period just before and just after 1600.

The Kagyü-Geluk Conflict

In 1604, a year after the Ninth Karmapa's death, the Fourth Dalai Lama Yönten Gyatso (1589–1617),[447] a Mongol by birth, was installed in Lhasa by a Mongol army, with the support of the Gelukpas' long-time patrons, the Phak-

447. See, e.g., Mullin 2001, 165–84.

modru nobility. This move to establish Geluk hegemony was resisted not only by the Karmapas and their own noble allies but by some anti-Mongol dissidents within the Dalai Lama's own order.[448] Yönten Gyatso was driven from Lhasa in 1605, and he died in exile twelve years later, under suspicious circumstances. The Karmapas' victory proved to be pyrrhic, however, for the next generation of Mongols, led by Gushri Khan (1582–1665), and the next Dalai Lama, the "Great Fifth" (Ngawang Losang Gyatso, 1617–82),[449] moved decisively to crush Karmapa political power throughout Tibet. After military victories in the Lhasa area, Tsang, and Kham, Gushri Khan "presented" Tibet to the Fifth Dalai Lama in 1642, ushering in a three-century period in which Geluk supremacy was largely unchallenged (especially in Ü and Tsang) and the fortunes of the Kagyüpas declined.

Whether coincidentally or not, Kagyü scholarship also declined during this era. Nevertheless, great Kagyüpa masters did regularly arise. Tselé Natsok Rangdröl (b. 1608) wrote a concise and oft-consulted manual covering the ground, path, and fruit of mahāmudrā meditation as well as a commentary on the mahāmudrā of four letters (*a ma na si*).[450] Karma Chakmé (1613–78) promoted a meditation system that self-consciously fused elements of Kagyü mahāmudrā and the Nyingma great perfection.[451] A Drukpa lineage holder, the Third Khamtrul Rinpoche Ngawang Kunga Tenzin (1680–1729), wrote a great compendium of mahāmudrā practice that centers on a detailed exposition of the four yogas, followed by a discussion of the experiential promises and pitfalls entailed by great-seal meditation.[452] Situ Paṇchen Chökyi Jungné (1700–74) mastered a wide variety of secular and religious fields (including Sanskrit, painting, and medicine), revived Kagyü monasticism and scholasticism, left an important memoir of his era,[453] and wrote an influential commentary on the Third Karmapa's *Prayer of the Mahāmudrā of Definitive Meaning*.[454] The equally great polymath Jamgön Kongtrul Lodrö Thayé (1813–99)[455] helped promote the eastern Tibetan nonsectarian (*ris med*) movement

448. Kollmar-Paulenz 2005, 60.

449. See, e.g., Shakabpa 1984, 100–124, Mullin 2001, 185–238, and Schaeffer 2005b.

450. The former is translated in Tsele Natsok Rangdröl 1989, Roberts 2011, 289–332, and Roberts 2014, 155–210. The latter is translated in Abboud et al. 2017, 107–16.

451. See, e.g., Karma Chagmé 1998.

452. See Abboud 2014, which covers only the first half of the text, the section on the four yogas.

453. See Smith, 2001, 87–96.

454. *Grub pa mchog gi zhal lung*. Translated in Dorje 1995 and in Roberts 2011, 175–288.

455. See, e.g., Smith 2001, 235–72, and Barron 2003.

that brought together Nyingma, Kagyü, and Sakya masters;[456] wrote the *Treasury of Knowledge*, an encyclopedic account of everything an educated Tibetan should know about both the mundane and transmundane;[457] and, in the *Treasury of Special Instructions* and other works, collected and edited vast numbers of texts related to various Tibetan practice traditions, including mahāmudrā.[458] These and other latter-day Kagyüpas all would influence the shape of the tradition—and of understandings of mahāmudrā—in their era and our own, but because they had little or no impact on Geluk traditions of mahāmudrā, we will not detail them here but, rather, turn at last to the history and practice of the great seal among the followers of Tsongkhapa.

456. See, e.g., Ringu 2006.

457. *Shes bya mdzod.* This has been translated in its entirety in ten volumes by various members of the Kalu Rinpoché Translation Committee (Jamgön Kongtrul 2003–12).

458. The *Gdams ngag mdzod* remains largely untranslated, but its catalogue, which is a mine of information on the sources, ideas, and practices of a range of Tibetan Buddhist traditions, is translated in Barron 2013.

Part 2
Early Geluk Mahāmudrā

6. Tsongkhapa, the Geluk, and Mahāmudrā

THE ORDER GENERALLY known as the Geluk (*dge lugs*, "the virtuous tradition") also has been referred to as the New Kadam (*bka' gdams gsar ma*) for its self-conscious continuation of the traditions of Atiśa and his followers; the Gandenpa (*dga' ldan pa*) or Galukpa (*dga' lugs pa*) for its association with its first monastery, Ganden; and the Gedenpa (*dge ldan pa*), or "the virtuous," for its emphasis on ethics as the foundation of the Buddhist path and monastic life as its vocational ideal.

In the broad course of Tibetan history, the Geluk is best known as a politically powerful, socially and religiously conservative, and highly scholastic tradition. It is famed politically for its establishment, in 1642, of a central government in Lhasa that would rule much of Tibet under the aegis of successive Dalai Lamas until the 1950s. Institutionally, the Geluk is best known for its network of highly organized monasteries, of which the most important were Ganden, Drepung, and Sera in Central Tibet, Tashi Lhunpo in Tsang, Kumbum and Labrang in Amdo, and Lithang and Chamdo Jampa Ling in Kham, as well as two tantric monasteries in Lhasa, Gyütö and Gyümé. Ethically, the Geluk is renowned for its strict adherence to the codes of conduct established for fully ordained monks, for bodhisattvas, and for initiates of the tantras. In the field of religious education, the Geluk is famed for its rigorous and scholarly geshé training program, in which candidates have to study and extensively debate five difficult Indian texts—the *Exposition of Valid Cognition* (*Pramāṇavārttika*) of Dharmakīrti, the *Ornament of Higher Realization* (*Abhisamyālaṃkāra*) of Maitreya, the *Entry to the Middle Way* (*Madhyamakāvatāra*) of Candrakīrti, the *Vinaya Sūtra* of Guṇaprabha, and the *Treasury of Higher Knowledge* (*Abhidharmakośa*) of Vasubandhu—and much else besides.[459] Philosophically, the Gelukpas are noted for their strong

459. Other Indian texts frequently studied in Geluk monasteries include the *Heart Sūtra*, Nāgārjuna's *Root Verses on the Middle Way* (*Mūlamadhyamakakārikā*), Maitreya's *Sublime Continuum* (*Uttaratantra*), Śāntideva's *Engaging in Bodhisattva Conduct* (*Bodhicaryāvatāra*), and Kamalaśīla's three *Stages of Meditation* (*Bhāvanākrama*) texts.

adherence to the Prāsaṅgika Madhyamaka viewpoint, their insistence on the harmony between emptiness and dependent arising, and their confidence that logic and epistemology can yield reliable knowledge of the conventional world. Finally, in terms of religious practice, the Geluk are famous for their cultivation of both the Perfection Vehicle and the Mantra Vehicle and their insistence that the two can be practiced through a sequence of graded meditations that lead one from initial confidence in the guru, through Foundational, Mahāyāna, and Vajrayāna Buddhist practices and realizations, to final awakening.[460]

Compared to the Tibetan orders that preceded it—especially the Nyingma, Kagyü, and Sakya, which evolved over many centuries—the Geluk coalesced relatively quickly, establishing a distinct identity and many of its permanent institutions over the course of less than two centuries.[461] That it did so is due in part to its foundation in the vibrant and strategic Lhasa area and in part to the strong support it received at its inception from the Phakmodru nobles who ruled the region. Above all, though, its rapid rise and delineation are attributable to the charismatic genius at its source, Tsongkhapa Losang Drakpa (1357–1419), usually referred to in Geluk tradition as Jé Rinpoché or Jé Lama.[462]

Tsongkhapa's Life and Works

Tsongkhapa's life is amply documented. It was detailed in numerous biographies written by his disciples, including the standard "outer" life story by his "heart son" Khedrup Jé Gelek Palsang (1385–1438), the *Entryway to Faith* (Kg*DPJN*),[463] and four treatments of his visionary life: Khedrup Jé's *Secret Life Prayer* (Kg*RPCM*), Tokden Jampal Gyatso's *Marvelous Account* (Jg*MDBT*) and his *Appendix to the Great Biography of Jetsun Tsongkhapa* (Jg*NTZD*), and Tashi Palden's *Secret Life Prayer* (Kp*NTSD*).[464] Tsongkhapa's own *Record of Teachings Received* (Ts*TKSY*) and *Condensed Stages of the Path* (Ts*LRDD*) provide additional contemporaneous documentation.

460. See, e.g., Snellgrove and Richardson 1967, chap. 7, and Thuken 2009, chaps. 10–12.

461. For a study of this process, see Ary 2015.

462. On Tsongkhapa's life, see, e.g., Thurman 1982, 3–34, Thurman 1984, 65–89, Thuken 2009, chap. 10, Zasep 2019, 27–32, and Jinpa 2019.

463. This is the main basis of the accounts of Tsongkhapa's life in Thurman 1982 and Thuken 2009. The Tibetan original, which has not been translated, is the very first entry in the first volume of Tsongkhapa's collected works.

464. The last-named is translated in Thurman 1982, 47–58. Jamyang Chöjé Tashi Palden (1379–1449), as we will see below, founded Drepung Monastery at Tsongkhapa's request.

He was born in Amdo, in northeast Tibet, in 1357, around the time that Butön was finalizing his definitive edition of the Tibetan Buddhist canon. He took layman's vows at the age of three from the Fourth Karmapa Rölpai Dorjé (1340–83) and shortly afterward began studies with the Kadampa master Döndrup Rinchen (1309–85), from whom he received novice vows at seven and with whom he began his studies of the Perfection and Mantra Vehicles, including the works of Atiśa and the practices connected to the deities that would be closest to his heart throughout his life: "Yamāntaka for the continuation of his practice, Vajrapāṇi for freedom from interruptions, Mañjuśrī for increase in wisdom and discriminating awareness, Amitāyus for long life, and the three Dharma protectors—Vaiśravaṇa, the six-armed Mahākāla, and Dharmarāja—for protection and for the availability of prerequisites while practicing."[465] Eager to further his education, Tsongkhapa left for Central Tibet around 1373, never to return to Amdo. By most accounts, his first stop in Ü was at Drigung, where he studied practices related to the awakening mind and the fivefold mahāmudrā with the abbot, Chenga Chökyi Gyalpo (1335–1407), and medicine with the great physician Könchok Khyab (dates unknown).[466] On a later visit by Tsongkhapa to Drigung, Chökyi Gyalpo would impart to him instructions on the mahāmudrā of connate union.[467] From Drigung, he moved on to the Kadam monastery of Dewachen, where he continued his medical studies and learned the Perfection of Wisdom—especially as read through the *Ornament of Higher Realization*—from various teachers.

By the time he was twenty, he had secured a reputation as a brilliant student and a formidable debater. Over the next two decades, even as he began first to teach and then to write, Tsongkhapa continued his quest for a comprehensive understanding of the entire Buddhist tradition, traveling throughout Ü and Tsang in search of experts from every Tibetan school. He studied Vinaya with the Kadampa master Kashipa Losel (dates unknown); Indian philosophical treatises with Sönam Gyaltsen (1312–75), and the Hevajra tantra with Dorjé Rinchenpa (dates unknown), both Sakyapas; Kālacakra with Jonang masters such as Choklé Namgyal (1306–86); various unexcelled yoga tantras and the six Dharmas of Nāropa with several disciples of Butön, including Khyungpo Lhepa (dates unknown); and special transmissions of Atiśa with Namkha Gyaltsen (1326–1401), a highly-respected Nyingma siddha.

In terms of mahāmudrā, apart from his study of the fivefold great seal with Chenga Chökyi Gyalpo at Drigung, he learned the amulet box mahāmudrā

465. Thurman 1982, 7 (translation adapted).

466. Kg*DPJN* 9b [19]; Thurman 1982, 7. See also Jg*NTZD* 4a [153].

467. Kg*DPJN* 40b [80]; cf. Thurman 1982, 23.

and the six Dharmas of Nigumā from a Shangpa Kagyü master from Tsang, Jakchen Jampa Pal (1310–91),[468] and the Dakpo Kagyü Dharma cycle, including the six Dharmas of Nāropa and the works of Phakmo Drupa and Drigung Jikten Sumgön, from Chenga Drakpa Jangchup (1356–86), a master at the Phakdru monastery of Densa Thil.[469] He also is known to have received teachings on—and taught—various practice cycles associated with Marpa and Milarepa.[470] From the late 1370s until the late 1390s, Tsongkhapa—all the while peripatetic—alternated between intensive study with one or another lama and offering his own teachings, sometimes in public, sometimes privately to a growing circle of close disciples. He also had visionary encounters with many deities and past masters and repeatedly underwent intensive retreat—either alone or with his students—on topics as various as the fasting practice of Avalokiteśvara, the six Dharmas of Nāropa, refuge and the Meru maṇḍala offering, the Thirty-Five Confession Buddhas, the Kālacakra tantra, and the sādhana of Yamāntaka.

Probably, Tsongkhapa's two most important spiritual mentors in his mature years were the great Sakyapa scholar Rendawa Shönu Lodrö (1349–1412)[471] and a visionary master of uncertain affiliation, Umapa Pawo Dorjé (dates unknown). Tsongkhapa first met Rendawa when he was around twenty, and his close association with him continued for over three decades. Although Rendawa was an important teacher to him—particularly when it came to the great Indian Buddhist philosophical classics—the two really were colleagues more than master and disciple, for after some time, Tsongkhapa became Rendawa's teacher, too; indeed, Rendawa is credited with composing a verse of praise to Tsongkhapa, the *Miktsema*, that still is recited throughout the Geluk

468. See Smith 2001, 55. I have not yet located a Geluk source to confirm these particulars. Tsongkhapa also apparently studied with Jakchen's disciple, Döndrup Sangpo, perhaps at Narthang; see http://tbrc.org/#!rid=P3303. According to Sarah Harding (personal communication, July 2013), Tsongkhapa sometimes is listed as a member of the Shangpa Kagyü lineage, and as such, supplicated in prayers. For contemporary evidence, see "Shangpa Kagyu."

469. Kg*DPJN* 39b–40a [38–39]; Jg*NTZD* 4b [154]. Thurman (1982, 12) mistakenly attributes this instruction to Chenga Chökyi Gyalpo of Drigung. Cf. Thuken 2009, 232.

470. Kg*DPJN* 22a [43]; Thurman 1982, 13. One later biography, by Ngari Lhatsun, tells of Tsongkhapa teaching a poem by Milarepa at É Teura Monastery in 1398 and—moved by its evocation of the tantric path of Guhyasamāja—gaining a deep appreciation for the tantra's importance, prompting him in turn to investigate the Guhyasamāja literature in detail. See Jinpa 2019. The poem taught by Tsongkhapa—which mentions mahāmudrā as the "abiding nature" (*gnas lugs*)—is a teaching on the six bardos given by Milarepa to the five Tseringma sisters. See Th*MLGB* 384; trans. Chang 1989, 1:348, and Tsangnyön Heruka 2016, 367–68.

471. See, e.g., Roloff 2009.

world.[472] The two of them often traveled and lectured in tandem, went on retreat together, and explored together with particular intensity the intricacies of Madhyamaka thought. Although their friendship remained essentially intact until Rendawa's death in 1412, a certain coolness set in during the late 1380s and early 1390s, as Tsongkhapa began to sense limitations in Rendawa's interpretation of Madhyamaka, while at the same time Rendawa expressed misgivings about Tsongkhapa's focus on tantra at the expense of sūtra-based topics.

Around the same time, Tsongkhapa met Umapa, a onetime shepherd who had been prone to visions of Mañjughoṣa since childhood and became an avid student of Dharma. According to various sources, he was a practitioner of Chö[473] and/or a disciple of Barawa Gyaltsen Palsang (1310–91), a Drukpa Kagyü master in the tradition of Yangönpa.[474] Because Mañjughoṣa is the bodhisattva of wisdom, and therefore holds the key to the interpretation of Madhyamaka, Tsongkhapa was intrigued by the mysterious visionary, and for a number of years, Umapa replaced Rendawa as his closest collaborator, spending considerable time with him in the 1390s. At first, Tsongkhapa would question Mañjughoṣa about the difficult points of Madhyamaka—for instance, about the object of negation or the relation between ultimate and conventional truth—with Umapa serving as medium. Eventually, Tsongkhapa gained visionary access to Mañjughoṣa on his own. The bodhisattva gave him advice on aspects of his life, communicated songs and prayers to him, and granted him a deeper and deeper understanding of Madhyamaka. One day in 1398, when Tsongkhapa was deeply engaged in the study of Nāgārjuna's *Root Verses on the Middle Way* (*Mūlamadhyamakakārikā*) and its commentaries, he dreamed that he was in the presence of Nāgārjuna and the Madhyamaka master's main disciples, one of whom, Buddhapālita, blessed Tsongkhapa by touching him on the head with a text. Awakening from the dream, Tsongkhapa felt sublimely blissful, and he opened Buddhapālita's commentary to a passage that specifies that the self is neither the same as nor different from

472. "Great treasure of nonreferential love, Avalokiteśvara; / lord of stainless wisdom, Mañjughoṣa; / destroyer of all the forces of Māra, Guhyapati; / crown ornament of sages of the Land of Snows, Tsongkhapa: / at the feet of Losang Drakpa I appeal." Actually, the prayer is Rendawa's slight revision of a prayer originally composed for him by Tsongkhapa. See Thurman 1982, 9, de Rossi Filibeck 1990.

473. See BDRC ID no. P3357, which associates Umapa primarily with the severance lineage and includes a number of works attributed to him. For a translation of one of these works, see Zong 2006, 193–99.

474. Kg*DPJN* 28b [56]. See also Zasep 2019, 32–33.

the aggregates.[475] At this, he experienced a direct realization of emptiness; his doubts were resolved and his understanding became lucid.

What he understood, above all, was that the key point of Prāsaṅgika Madhyamaka as taught by Nāgārjuna, Āryadeva, Buddhapālita, and Candrakīrti is the complete harmony between emptiness and dependent arising, which are, in effect, two sides of the same philosophical coin; their complementarity ensures that the Madhyamaka will neither absolutize the ultimate nor denigrate the conventional.[476] Indeed, it was Tsongkhapa's further insight that not only, as might be expected, does recognition of emptiness eliminate eternalism and recognition of dependent arising eliminate nihilism but, in fact, recognition of emptiness also eliminates nihilism and recognition of dependent arising also eliminates eternalism, for the simple reason that, for a disciple suitably advanced, the recognition of one is tantamount to recognition of the other.

This central insight entails a number of further positions:

- Ontologically, it entails that each instance of emptiness—whether of a table, a person, or buddha mind—is an "intrinsic emptiness" (rangtong), a straightforward, nonaffirming negation with no positive implications—this in stark opposition to the Jonang belief that while conventionalities may be intrinsically empty, the buddha mind exists absolutely and is empty only in the sense that it is other than, or extrinsic to, conventional and mundane phenomena (shentong).
- Epistemologically, the insight entails that it is not only legitimate but vital to employ the perceptual and inferential cognitions described by Dharmakīrti and other "logicians" as a basis for understanding both conventional and ultimate phenomena. Although conventional phenomena are intrinsically empty and illusion-like—indeed, they are mere nominal designations—they cannot simply be dismissed as unreal, and while ultimate reality is both empty and beyond rational comprehension, it cannot simply be described as "inconceivable" but must be investigated rationally.
- Soteriologically, the insight entails that in meditating on ultimate reality, one must avoid the stance of the Chinese Chan master Heshang

475. Thurman 1982, 21. The verse in question is 18.1 of Nāgārjuna's *Verses*. An alternative account (cited in Thuken 2009, 241–42) identifies the verse in question as 8.12, which asserts the complete mutual dependence of action and agent.

476. This is the perspective adopted by Nāgārjuna in chapter 24 of his *Root Verses on the Middle Way*.

Moheyan, which confuses either blissful serenity or unfocused nonconceptuality with true meditation on reality. Rather, one must distinguish clearly between serenity and insight and, in practicing insight, establish the proper object of negation—neither overestimating nor underestimating it—before undertaking a rational search for a truly existing self. The non-finding of that self, in turn, is the doorway to the direct, nonconceptual realization of emptiness that is, as so often in Buddhist systems, the prerequisite for liberation.[477]

These and other sharply articulated views have shaped philosophical doctrine among the Geluk right down to the present day. They also have drawn fire, to one degree or another, from thinkers in other traditions, including such Sakyapa luminaries as Gorampa Sönam Sengé (1429–89) and Shākya Chokden, Kagyüpa intellectuals such as the Eighth Karmapa and Pema Karpo, the great Nyingma philosopher Mipham Gyatso (1846–1912), and the renegade modern Geluk philosopher Gendun Chöphel (1903–51).[478] However much Tibetan thinkers after Tsongkhapa might have agreed or disagreed with him, though, none could ignore the positions he took—and to that degree, he set the agenda for much of the discussion of Madhyamaka in Tibet in the ensuing six hundred years.

Tsongkhapa had equally profound visions, experiences, and realizations connected to the tantras. According to Tashi Palden's *Secret Life Prayer*, he was visited constantly by mahāsiddhas (including Saraha, Tilopa, and Nāropa),[479] had visions of the major unexcelled-yoga-tantra deities and their maṇḍalas,[480] and realized for himself the deepest aspects of the completion stage. When, for instance, he received the text of the *Guhyasamāja Tantra* from Butön in a vision and touched it to his own head, he understood that the key points in Marpa's yoginī tantra–based mixture and transference doctrine have the same meaning as the special tantric instructions of Nāgārjuna

477. For discussion of Tsongkhapa's distinctive views on Madhyamaka and Buddhist philosophy more generally, see, e.g., Huntington 1983, Thurman 1984, Broido 1988, Napper 1989, Hopkins 1996, Magee 1999, Jinpa 2002, Thuken 2009, 301–310, and Sparham 2017.

478. On Gorampa, see, e.g., Cabezón and Dargyay 2007; on Shākya Chokden, see, e.g., Komarovski 2011 and Higgins and Draszczyk 2016, 1:44–147; on Pema Karpo, see, e.g., Broido 1985a, Broido 1985b, Broido 1988, and Higgins and Draszczyk 2016, 1:342–428; on the Eighth Karmapa, see, e.g., Williams 1983, Broido 1985b, and Higgins and Draszczyk 2016, 1:226–341; on Mipham, see, e.g., Pettit 1999; and on Gendun Chöphel see Lopez 2006.

479. Kp*NTSD* 3a [206]; trans. Thurman 1982, 52.

480. Kp*NTSD* 3b–4b [207–9]; trans. Thurman 1982, 53–55.

and his Guhyasamāja-based lineage.[481] Addressing Tsongkhapa, Tashi Palden describes Jé Rinpoché's tantric realizations thusly:

> Through the yoga of the nonduality
> of the illusory, empty appearances of common things and profound luminosity,
> you generated the form of a great-bliss deity
> and attained the vajra-yoga body. . . .
>
> When you recited the mantric chants [of body, speech, and mind]
> through inhalation and exhalation focused at the heart lotus,
> and the vital winds entered, abided, and dissolved [within the central channel, you experienced] the luminosity of mahāmudrā,
> and you attained the vajra-yoga speech. . . .
>
> Raising the inner heat of caṇḍalī from the navel cakra
> and melting the *haṃ* syllable at your crown down through the central channel,
> you played in the great bliss of the connate
> and attained the vajra-yoga mind.[482]

More broadly, Tsongkhapa understood that the defining characteristic of secret mantra is deity yoga, the visualization of oneself in divine form by way of a mind that cognizes emptiness. The emptiness described in the tantras—even the luminosity realized in the completion stage of unexcelled yoga tantra—is for him not objectively different from the emptiness taught by Nāgārjuna and Candrakīrti and realized through Perfection Vehicle meditations, although on the subjective side, the mind that realizes emptiness on the completion stage is the subtlest level of cognition rather than the coarser awareness employed in sūtra-based systems. Tsongkhapa also recognized that practicing the Mantra Vehicle does not in the slightest imply an abrogation of rationality or of ethics—the rhetoric of certain tantras notwithstanding. On the level of the unexcelled yoga tantras, Tsongkhapa used the Guhyasamāja tradition as the key to understanding all systems of the same class, but he wrote detailed commentaries on the Cakrasaṃvara and other traditions as well.[483]

481. Kp*NTSD* 4a–b [208–9]; cf. Thurman 1982, 53.

482. Kp*NTSD* 3b–4a [205–206]; cf. Thurman 1982, 52.

483. For treatments of Tsongkhapa's distinctive views on tantra, see, e.g., Tsongkhapa 1977, Tsongkhapa 2005a, Thuken 2009, 311–16, and Tsongkhapa 2013b.

Tsongkhapa's realization of emptiness and its significance, along with his mastery of tantric practice, were the watershed events in his life: they unleashed a torrent of activity, which continued unabated until his death, that included writing, large-scale public teaching and private instruction, public-works projects, and institution building.

Although he had composed a handful of works starting in the late 1380s—most notably a critique of the storehouse consciousness (*ālayavijñāna*) and other concepts in Yogācāra metaphysics and a Svātantrika Madhyamaka-inflected detailed commentary on the *Ornament of Higher Realization* called the *Golden Rosary*[484]—after his breakthrough he began to write in earnest. Immediately after his realization of the nature of reality, he composed a song praising the Buddha for his teaching of dependent arising, interpreted as the "positive" expression of the doctrine of emptiness.[485] On the advice of Mañjughoṣa, he then completed in 1402 the *Great Exposition of the Stages of the Path to Awakening*, a massive and deeply researched account of the entire sūtra-based path, inspired by Atiśa's *Lamp on the Path to Awakening*.[486] This was quickly followed in 1405 by an equally prodigious companion volume, the *Great Exposition of the Stages of Secret Mantra*, which is organized according to the four main tantra classes of the New Translation schools: action, performance, yoga, and unexcelled yoga tantras.[487] Together, these two texts bring virtually all Buddhist knowledge together into a single, seamless synthesis. In 1407, Tsongkhapa began work on a major commentary on Nāgārjuna's *Root Verses on the Middle Way*, the *Ocean of Reasoning*.[488] He completed it in 1409, having in the interim turned to the composition of perhaps his most brilliant philosophical treatise, the *Essence of Excellent Explanation* (*Legs bshad snying po*), a key work on Buddhist hermeneutics that asserts that the second turning of the wheel of Dharma, with its emphasis on emptiness, is definitive, and the third turning, with its emphasis on Yogācāra and buddha-nature discourse, is merely provisional and not some kind of "Great Madhyamaka." Between 1410 and 1415, he composed lengthy commentaries on the Guhyasamāja and

484. The former is the *Kun gzhi bka' 'grel*; see, e.g., Sparham 1993. The latter is the *Legs bshad gser 'phreng*; see, e.g., Makransky 1997, 289–307, and Apple 2009.

485. *Rten 'brel bstod pa.* For translations, see, e.g., Thurman 1984, 176–90, and Kilty 2001, 216–45.

486. Ts*LRCM*. For a three-volume translation, see Tsongkhapa 2000–2002.

487. *Sngags rim chen mo.* For translations of the first three sections, see Tsongkhapa 1977, Tsongkhapa 1981, and Tsongkhapa 2005b, respectively. For the generation-stage chapters of the section on unexcelled yoga tantra, see Tsongkhapa 2013a.

488. *Rigs pa'i rgya mtsho.* For a translation, see Tsongkhapa 2006.

Cakrasaṃvara tantric systems.[489] In the period just before his death, he wrote the *Middle-Length Stages of the Path* (1415) and the *Elucidation of the Intention of Madhyamaka*, a commentary on the most widely discussed Indian Madhyamaka text in Tibet, Candrakīrti's *Entry to the Middle Way*—these two contain his final thoughts on Madhyamaka philosophy.[490] In addition to these major works, he composed many short texts on path practice, songs praising various deities, question-and-answer texts on doctrinal points, and an autobiographical poem about his realizations[491]—all of which have become canonical for Gelukpas.

At the same time as he was composing the texts and transmitting the teachings that would shape Geluk tradition for the next six centuries, Tsongkhapa was becoming increasingly involved in public life in the Lhasa area. His biographers identify four particularly important activities from the period.[492] The first, in 1399, was the restoration of a great but neglected Maitreya statue at Dzingji Ling, which Tsongkhapa managed through both a fundraising campaign and religious ritual. The second, in 1403, was the summoning of a great conclave of monks from various orders for the purpose of clarifying and reinvigorating the tradition of monastic vows. The third, in 1409, was the establishment of the Mönlam Chenmo—the Great Prayer Festival—in Lhasa at the turn of the Tibetan New Year. Over the centuries, this would be a time of purification and celebration for all Tibetans and, for monks, a time for prayers, offerings, and great philosophical debates. The fourth, in 1409–10, was the founding of Ganden Monastery on a hill east of Lhasa and, in particular, furnishing the great Buddha hall there with three-dimensional maṇḍalas of the main Geluk tantric deities, Guhyasamāja, Cakrasaṃvara, and Yamāntaka.

Shortly after its founding, Tsongkhapa took up residence at Ganden and spent most of the rest of his life there. He was subsequently regarded as its first abbot, and each successive abbot—the Ganden throneholder (*dga' ldan khri pa*)—is considered the nominal head of the Geluk order. Tsongkhapa's two greatest disciples, Gyaltsab Jé Darma Rinchen (1364–1432) and Khedrup Jé, were the second and third Ganden throneholders; the current throneholder is the 104th. The two other great Geluk monasteries in the Lhasa area were also

489. On the former, the Ts*RNSG*, see, e.g., Tsongkhapa 2013b. On the latter, the *Sbas don kun gsal*, see Gray 2017 and Gray 2019.

490. For translations of significant portions of these two texts, the *Lam rim chung ba* and Ts*GPRS*, see Hopkins 2008.

491. For a selection of these texts, see, especially, Thurman 1982 and Kilty 2001.

492. On these deeds, see, e.g., Thurman 1982, 17–27, and Thuken 2009, 247–49, 263.

founded during Tsongkhapa's lifetime—Drepung by Jamyang Chöjé Tashi Palden (1397–1449) in 1416 and Sera by Jamchen Chöjé Shākya Yeshé (1355–1435) in 1419—the year of Tsongkhapa's death at age sixty-two. According to his biographers, either he attained full awakening at the moment of dying (having postponed it during his life because his monastic vows forbade the practice of sexual yoga, a *sine qua non* for buddhahood in this life) or he was reborn as a bodhisattva in Tuṣita Heaven and will attain buddhahood some time in the future.[493] Whatever the case, there is no tulku lineage traced to Tsongkhapa, though he did appear frequently in the visions of later Geluk masters. The date of his passing—the twenty-fifth day of the tenth Tibetan month (typically falling between late November and late December)—is still celebrated through the Geluk world as the Ganden Ngamchö (*dga' ldan lnga mchod*). It is marked by the burning of thousands of butter lamps, songs in praise of Tsongkhapa, and recitations of his great deeds.

Tsongkhapa's Secret Teachings

In addition to the public lecturing, writing, and public works for which he gained fame, Tsongkhapa throughout his later life engaged in private teaching activity: transmitting esoteric practices in secret to select disciples. Indeed, no less than other Tibetan schools, the Geluk recognizes a set of oral traditions (*bka' srol*), oral transmissions (*bka' brgyud*), or hearing (lit. "ear") transmissions (*snyan brgyud*). Each is said to originate with the primordial buddha Vajradhara, who communicated it (typically) to Mañjughoṣa, who in turn taught it to Tsongkhapa. All of them focus primarily on special instructions for practices that distill the quintessential teachings of the sūtras and tantras into especially rapid and effective spiritual techniques.

Tsongkhapa entrusted a number of disciples with "unique transmissions" (*chig brgyud*), given only to one disciple, that were handed down in a similar fashion through the years and sooner or later put into writing. To his teacher and disciple Rendawa Tsongkhapa gave the guru-yoga instruction found in a text called the *Uncommon Pith Instruction Offered to Rendawa*.[494] To Khedrup Jé, he transmitted a tradition—famed in part for its guru-yoga practice but best known for its special method of guiding disciples toward the proper Madhyamaka view—that came to be known as the Unique Khedrup

493. For the first account, see Thurman 1982, 62; for the second, see Thuken 2009, 263.

494. *Red mda' ba la phul ba'i man ngag thun mong ma yin pa.* It is found in vol. *na* (1–7b [5–18]) of Tsongkhapa's collected works (Zhol edition).

Jé Transmission.[495] To Khedrup Jé's younger brother, Baso Chökyi Gyaltsen, he entrusted yet another guru yoga transmission, contained in a text entitled *Guru Yoga Given as a Unique Transmission to the Dharma Lord Baso.*[496]

To his greatest tantric disciple, Sherab Sengé (1383–1445),[497] Tsongkhapa passed on three hearing transmissions focused primarily on unexcelled-yoga-tantra practice, especially that of Guhyasamāja but with reference as well to Cakrasaṃvara, Yamāntaka, and other traditions. Sherab Sengé, in turn, passed on the teachings to his disciple Dulnakpa Palden Sangpo (1402–73), who disseminated them in various parts of Ü and Tsang. The Sé tradition, which was named for the upper (*srad*) region of Tsang, where Dulnakpa founded a tantric college for the promulgation of Tsongkhapa's key tantric teachings, is most famous for a set of six great guidelines (*'khrid chen drug*), on (1) the five stages of Guhyasamāja completion-stage practice, (2–3) the Cakrasaṃvara tradition according to Lūipa and Ghaṇṭapa, (4) the four stages of Vajrabhairava/ Yamāntaka, (5) the six completion-stage yogas of Kālacakra, and (6) the six Dharmas of Nāropa. The Mé tradition, which is named after Gyümé (*rgyud smad*), the tantric monastery of lower Lhasa founded by Dulnakpa in 1433, focused on eight great guidances (*'khrid chen brgyad*): the six held in common with Sé tradition with the addition of teachings on Great Wheel Vajrapāṇi and transference of consciousness.[498] The less well known (and sometimes unmentioned) Shung (*gzhung*), or textual, transmission relates to the preservation of the traditions surrounding the study of the Guhyasamāja root tantra.[499]

Among the texts included early on in the Sé transmission is a brief guru-yoga prayer and practice called the *Hundred Deities of Tuṣita*, well known under its Tibetan name, *Ganden Lhagyama*.[500] This prayer is said to have been

495. This is found, inter alia, in texts such as the *Guru Yoga Given as a Unique Transmission to Khedrup Jé* (*Mkhas grub rjer gcig brgyud kyi tshul du gnang ba'i bla ma'i rnal 'byor*). It is found in vol. *ka* (1–3 [223–28]) of Tsongkhapa's collected works (Zhol edition). The text seems to be a later composition, as it refers to masters who appeared after Tsongkhapa's time. For a critical historical analysis of the role of Khedrup Jé in the development of Geluk tradition, see Ary 2015.

496. *Ba so chos rje la gcig brgyud kyi tshul du gnang ba'i bla ma'i rnal 'byor* (Ts*BSCG*).

497. Or, alternatively, Gendun Drup; see Chöden 2013, 2.

498. On these two, see, e.g., Thuken 2009, 285–88.

499. Oral communication from Yangsi Rinpoché, November 19, 2018. See also Dalai Lama 1988, 16 and 69, Dalai Lama and Berzin 1997, 231–32.

500. *Dga' ldan lha rgya ma* (Dl*GDHG*). On its relation to the practice of mahāmudrā, see below, pages 360–61. The ten-line version is translated below, in part 5, section 6. For a recent, detailed commentary based in turn upon the commentary by Phabongkha Rinpoché, see Chöden 2013; see also Gelek 2010.

transmitted to Tsongkhapa by Mañjughoṣa and written down by Dulnakpa. The strong focus within it on devotion to Tsongkhapa (within the broader context of the worship of Maitreya) does suggest its composition by Dulnakpa or some other later disciple. It is found in several versions. The eight-line version, which probably is the original, is essentially a form of the sevenfold worship rite directed at Tsongkhapa (and, secondarily, his two spiritual sons, Gyaltsab Jé and Khedrup Jé) as emanated from the heart of Maitreya in his abode in Tuṣita Heaven. A popular ten-line version adds at the end both the *Miktsema*, the famous prayer composed for Tsongkhapa by Rendawa, and an appeal to one's root guru, in the form of Tsongkhapa, to come and reside at one's heart chakra and grant one all yogic attainments. The *Hundred Deities* did not become a focus of serious commentary until the seventeenth century, when the First Jamyang Shepa tulku Ngawang Tsöndrü (1648–1721/22) took an interest in it. Since then it has become a major guru-yoga text among Gelukpas, used as part of a cult of Maitreya, recited in connection with tantric transference-of-consciousness practices, and often used as a preliminary to Geluk mahāmudrā meditation in the sūtra tradition.

Most significantly, tradition tells us that Tsongkhapa transmitted to his great ascetic disciple Tokden Jampal Gyatso (1356–1428)—with whom (along with seven others) he shared his longest and most intensive retreat, for four years in the 1390s—the secret teachings known variously as the Geden Oral Transmission (*dge ldan bka' brgyud*), the Ensa Hearing Transmission (*dben sa snyan brgyud*), or the Ganden Hearing Transmission (*dga' ldan syan brgyud*). Topics covered in this transmission include guru yoga; mind training; severance; a combined tantric practice of Guhyasamāja, Cakrasaṃvara, and Yamāntaka; and, most importantly for our purposes, mahāmudrā.[501] Unlike the others, this transmission was accompanied by an emanated scripture (*sprul pa'i glegs bam*), which had been presented to Tsongkhapa by Mañjughoṣa and was handed down as a unique transmission from one lineage holder to the next until it was returned to the protector deity Kālarūpa for safekeeping. There is no firm agreement as to when that return took place: depending on the source one accepts, it was either before, during, or after the time of the Paṇchen Losang Chökyi Gyaltsen (1570–1662), who was the seventh master in the line of transmission and would be the first to publicize the mahāmudrā aspect of the tradition in any detail.[502]

501. See, e.g., Willis 1995, xiv–xv, and Thuken 2009, 289–90. On the Geluk severance tradition, see Zong 2006.

502. See, e.g., Willis 1995, 161–62n114. She discusses two possible endpoints for the emanated scripture's earthly span reported by modern Gelukpas: at the time of the First Paṇchen Lama

Although each of these transmissions was distinctive and separate at the outset, we should not imagine that they were mutually exclusive, since any given master might be (and often was) the recipient of multiple sets of secret teachings. Furthermore, late in the seventeenth century, at a point where the Sé tradition was threatened with extinction, it was rescued by a trio of masters from Amdo—the Second Changkya tulku Ngawang Losang Chöden (1642–1714), the First Jamyang Shepa, and a Mongolian lama named Thangsakpa Ngödrup Gyatso (b. seventeenth century)—who combined the Sé, Mé, and Ensa transmissions into "a single river of teachings"[503]—though each tradition continued to retain a certain distinctiveness in the centuries to follow.

I have organized the foregoing discussion in terms of the transmissions Tsongkhapa passed on to individual disciples: Rendawa, Khedrup Jé, Baso Chökyi Gyaltsen, Sherab Sengé, and Tokden Jampal Gyatso. In his introduction to an anthology of Geluk hearing transmissions texts,[504] however, Thupten Jinpa employs a different organizing principle, dividing the transmissions by type, into: (1) guru-yoga practices, of which the most important textual exemplars are the *Hundred Deities of Tuṣita* and Paṇchen Chögyen's *Offering to the Guru*; (2) guidance in the Madhyamaka view, of which important written exemplars are a text attributed to Umapa Pawo Dorjé entitled *A Letter of Guidance on the View of the Equivalence of Becoming and Peace*;[505] such works by Khedrup Jé as the *Lamp Dispelling Darkness: Guidance in the View* and *Guidance in the View of the Prāsaṅgika System*;[506] and the view-oriented texts and songs of a number of later masters with whom we will concern ourselves, such as Paṇchen Chögyen, Shar Kalden Gyatso, the Fifth Dalai Lama, Jamyang Shepa, and Yeshé Gyaltsen; and (3) the pith instructions on the great seal, which are found in the mahāmudrā-related texts of Paṇchen Chögyen and the various commentaries that appeared in their wake—all of which will

in the seventeenth century or of Yeshé Gyaltsen in the eighteenth century. However, Paṇchen Chögyen himself implies in his *Like a Treasure Inventory* that its fate became uncertain at the time the hearing transmission passed from Ensapa to Sangyé Yeshé, in the mid-sixteenth century (see Bz*TKBT* 10b–11a [584–85]), a fact duly reported by Yeshé Gyaltsen in his *Bright Lamp of the Excellent Path* (Yg*LZGM* 227–28).

503. Thuken 2009, 28, and Dalai Lama and Berzin 1997, 231.

504. *NGCS* xxii–xxvii.

505. *Srid zhi mnyam nyid lta ba'i 'khrid yig*; It is found in *Sngags rdzogs dbu ma'i skor gyi dpe dkon thor bu'i rigs phyogs bsgrigs* ([Bla rung sgar: Gser ljongs bla ma rung lnga rig nang bstan slob grwa chen mo, 2005]), 416–44.

506. Respectively, these are the *Lta 'khrid mun sel sgron me*, which is found in vol. *ta* (1–26 [419–69]) of Khedrup Jé's collected works (Zhol edition), and the *Thal gyur ba'i lugs kyi lta 'krid*, which is found in vol. *a* (1–8 [91–106]) of Khedrup Jé's collected works (Zhol edition).

be treated in detail below. Jinpa also mentions a special teaching on severance practice transmitted from Mañjughoṣa to Umapa, to Tsongkhapa, and to Jampal Gyatso, from whom it descended as part of the Geden Oral Transmission.

From Tsongkhapa to Paṇchen Chögyen, and Back Again

Within a generation after Tsongkhapa's passing, spurred by his prodigious example and the support of the Phakmodru nobility, Gelukpas established major and minor monasteries throughout Ü and Tsang. There, the writings of Tsongkhapa were preserved and studied, becoming the core of a complex system of education that has persisted until the present day. At the same time, these monasteries, and the hermitages associated with them, preserved the various secret transmissions initiated by Tsongkhapa, slowly but surely committing the oral teachings to writing, though without ever sacrificing the importance of direct teacher-to-student instruction. Put together, the standard and secret teachings of Tsongkhapa, when coupled with an appreciation for monastic establishments and their organization, provide the basis for a rounded understanding of Geluk religious life, whether in the fifteenth century or in our own time.

The most important monastery outside the three Lhasa-area institutions established during Tsongkhapa's lifetime—Ganden, Drepung, and Sera—was Tashi Lhunpo, in Shigatsé, Tsang, founded in 1447 by Jé Lama's late-life disciple Gendun Drup (1391–1474), who would posthumously be recognized as the First Dalai Lama. Throughout the fifteenth and sixteenth centuries, the Geluk became increasingly well established in central and western Tibet, often at the expense of the Kagyü. During the time of Sönam Gyatso (1543–88), the Geluk forged the first in a series of critical alliances with Mongol chieftains, including Altan Khan (1507–82), who granted Sönam Gyatso the title Oceanic Guru—or Dalai Lama. He was considered to be the third in the line, following his two predecessors in the incarnation lineage, Gendun Drup and Gendun Gyatso (1475–1542). The Third Dalai Lama also helped to expand Geluk influence in Amdo and Kham, giving the order nationwide coverage. His alliances and missionary activity helped pave the way for the Fifth Dalai Lama, Ngawang Losang Gyatso (1617–82), who, as we have seen, gained control over much of Tibet in 1642 with the aid of the Mongol chieftain Gushri Khan. The Fifth Dalai Lama's most important tutor was the abbot of Tashi Lhunpo, Paṇchen Losang Chökyi Gyaltsen. Losang Chögyen also had tutored the Fourth Dalai Lama, who dubbed him Paṇchen (*paṇ chen*, "great paṇḍita"), making him (depending on the counting system employed) either the first or fourth[507] in the line of scholarly, saintly, and often politically skillful reincarnates situated at Tashi Lhunpo. The Paṇchen Lamas came to be second in importance only to the Dalai Lamas both in the Geluk order and in the history of Tibet from the seventeenth to the twentieth century.

We will have much more to say about the long, rich life and manifold works of Paṇchen Chögyen in chapter 9, but for the moment let us simply note that it was he who, sometime around 1600, composed the four basic texts of the Geluk mahāmudrā tradition:

1. The 197-line *Highway of the Conquerors: The Mahāmudrā Root-Text of the Precious Geden Oral Transmission*
2. A thirty-seven-folio prose commentary on *Highway of the Conquerors* entitled *Lamp So Bright: An Extensive Explanation of the Mahāmudrā Root-Text of the Teaching Tradition of the Precious Geden Oral Transmission*
3. The original version—later to be expanded by others—of the *Mahāmudrā Lineage Prayer*
4. The eleven-folio *Like a Treasure Inventory: A Brief Summary of the Life Stories of the Lineage Masters of the Profound Path of the Precious Geden Oral Transmission*[508]

All these texts, and others besides, will receive ample treatment shortly, but in the context of our consideration of Tsongkhapa there are two key points to note. (1) *Highway of the Conquerors* and *Lamp So Bright,* composed nearly two centuries after Tsongkhapa's passing, appear to be the first published texts to explicate a specifically Geluk approach to mahāmudrā. (2) At the same time, the two other texts—the *Mahāmudrā Lineage Prayer* and *Like a Treasure Inventory*—clearly assert that the mahāmudrā tradition the Paṇchen expounds in *Highway of the Conquerors* and *Lamp So Bright* is *not* his own invention but is in fact part of a special, restricted teaching tradition—the

507. See above, note 3.

508. (1) *Highway of the Conquerors* (Bz*GBZL*) has been translated in Dhargyey 1975, Dalai Lama and Berzin 1997, 97–102, Kachen Yeshe Gyaltsen 2014, 435–42, Yeshe 2018, 114–35, and below in part 5, section 4. (2) *Lamp So Bright* (Bz*YSGM*) is translated below in part 5, section 5; it also is paraphrased and quoted extensively in Dalai Lama and Berzin 1997, part IV. (3) The *Lineage Prayer* (Bz*PCSD*) has been translated in K. Gyatso 1982, 227–34, Willis 1995, 101–6, Kachen Yeshe Gyaltsen 2014, 445–54, Zasep 219, 13–25, and below in part 5, section 3. (4) *Like a Treasure Inventory* (Bz*TKBT*) has not so far been translated, or even much discussed, though I will summarize its contents in chapter 9.

Geden Oral Transmission (*dge ldan bka' brgyud*)—that can be traced back to Tsongkhapa. Jé Lama, in turn, is said to have derived it from instructions (and an emanated scripture) he received from Mañjughoṣa in visions he had during his retreats in southern Tibet in the 1390s; and according to the Paṇchen, Tsongkhapa in turn passed on the transmission to Tokden Jampal Gyatso, who transmitted it to Baso Chökyi Gyaltsen, who taught it to Chökyi Dorjé, who imparted it to Ensapa Losang Döndrup, who handed it over to Khedrup Sangyé Yeshé, who gave it to Paṇchen Chögyen, who wrote it down.[509] This claim about the tradition, of course, begs the vitally important "origin" question of whether Tsongkhapa did, in fact, teach the mahāmudrā tradition written down by the First Paṇchen, and it is to that question that we turn next.

Tsongkhapa and Mahāmudrā: A Closer Look

As we have seen already, in the course of his peripatetic and highly eclectic education, Tsongkhapa was exposed to Kagyü mahāmudrā-related teachings on numerous occasions in various places. To reiterate, the earliest biographies we have, those of Khedrup Jé and Tokden Jampal Gyatso, relate that at Drigung he received instruction on the fivefold mahāmudrā, the six Dharmas of Nāropa, and the connate-union mahāmudrā from Chenga Chökyi Gyalpo; at Densa Thil he received instruction on the six Dharmas of Nāropa and the works of Phakmo Drupa and Drigung Jikten Sumgön from Chenga Drakpa Jangchub; and, at Jakpa and Narthang, he received instruction on various Shangpa Kagyü practices—including the amulet box mahāmudrā and the six Dharmas of Nigumā—from the Shangpa Kagyü master Jakchen Jampa Pal and his disciple Döndrup Sangpo, respectively. He also received teachings on practice traditions connected with Marpa and Milarepa, which, in turn, he expounded publicly.[510] The Fourteenth Dalai Lama believes that, in addition, Tsongkhapa may have received certain Kagyü mahāmudrā traditions from his visionary teacher Umapa, who, according to Khedrup Jé, was a student of the Drukpa Kagyü master Barawa.[511] Khedrup Jé adds, however, that Mañjughoṣa at one point communicated to Umapa his disapproval of Barawa's interpretation of Madhyamaka[512]—although this does not mean that Umapa did not teach it to Tsongkhapa.

509. For detailed biographies of these lineage masters, see Willis 1995; for briefer accounts, see Zasep 2019, 26–40.

510. Kg*DPJN* 22a [43]; Thurman 1982, 13.

511. Dalai Lama and Berzin 1997, 230.

512. Kg*DPJN* 28b [56–57]; see also Thuken 2009, 307.

Apart from the instruction he received from Kagyüpa masters on practices related to mahāmudrā in their particular tradition, Tsongkhapa studied a wide range of Indian sūtra and tantra works that either explicitly or implicitly had come to be associated with mahāmudrā in Tibetan tradition, from the treatises of Nāgārjuna, Candrakīrti, and Maitreya to the literature surrounding such great Mantra Vehicle systems as the Guhyasamāja, Cakrasaṃvara, Hevajra, and Kālacakra, as well as special tantric transmissions credited to such mahāsiddhas as Saraha, Lūipa, Nāropa, and Kṛṣṇācārya.[513]

Mahāmudrā in Tsongkhapa's Tantric Writings

The term *mahāmudrā* turns up with some frequency in Tsongkhapa's writings. However, despite the common association of Geluk mahāmudrā with Tsongkhapa's Madhyamaka-related visions of Mañjughoṣa, Nāgārjuna, and others, there are, so far as I know, no references to mahāmudrā in any of Tsongkhapa's major Madhyamaka writings, nor in his *Record of Teachings Received* (Ts*TKSY*) does he ever refer to the mahāmudrā practice traditions he had studied with his Kagyü teachers, at least not directly. Indeed, nearly every occurrence of the term is in the context of a discussion of Indian tantric traditions. We cannot, of course, survey here all of Tsongkhapa's many tantra-related mentions of *mahāmudrā*, but will provide a few typical examples.

In his *summa* on secret mantra, the *Great Exposition of the Stages of Secret Mantra*, he mentions *mahāmudrā* nearly forty times, giving it a range of meanings commensurate with its usages in Indian Buddhist tantric literature. In his discussion of yoga tantra, he uses it to refer to a hand gesture and accompanying visualization of the divine body in yoga tantra,[514] while in his section on unexcelled yoga tantra, the uses are more diverse. In different contexts, it is the gnosis of luminosity,[515] a seven-aspected divine body,[516] a synonym for the understanding of emptiness entailed by the fourth empowerment,[517] the great bliss of the immovable perfection of wisdom,[518] the empty form described in

513. For an overview of the Tibetan "canon" of mahāmudrā, see R. Jackson 2008; on Tsongkhapa's use of Saraha, see R. Jackson 2009, 107–10, and below, chapter 16.

514. E.g., Ts*NRCM* 102b [186], 286a [573], and 339b [680]; cf. Dalai Lama et al. 2005. I would like to thank Thomas Yarnall for providing me with a searchable electronic version of the Tibetan text.

515. Ts*NRCM* 268b [538].

516. Ts*NRCM* 269a–b [539–40].

517. Ts*NRCM* 275a [551].

518. Ts*NRCM* 276a [553].

the Kālacakra tradition,[519] a mirror-like image free from any obscuration,[520] the basis for meditation on objective suchness,[521] and, of course, the final attainment on the tantric path,[522] the ultimate stage.[523]

In his major commentary on the completion-stage practices of the Guhyasamāja tradition, *A Lamp to Illuminate the Five Stages* (Ts*RNSG*),[524] Tsongkhapa discusses notions often associated with mahāmudrā, such as great bliss, luminosity, the four joys, and bliss-emptiness awareness, but the term itself appears only occasionally. In a discussion of the distinction between father and mother tantras, the "yoga of mahāmudrā" described in the *Vajra Tent* (*Vajrapañjara*) *Tantra* is identified as "the way to 'engage' in the ultimate 'reality' of emptiness."[525] Elsewhere, mahāmudrā is associated with the form of a deity visualized during generation-stage practice (a usage common in the yoga tantras)[526] or with the form of the deity created during the illusory-body phase of the completion stage.[527] Most of the references in *A Lamp to Illuminate the Five Stages*, though, simply mention mahāmudrā as the attainment (*siddhi*) that is the fruition of the tantric path.

In an important Cakrasaṃvara commentary, *Eye-Opener of the Secret View*, Tsongkhapa describes mahāmudrā as the inseparable bliss-emptiness awareness that arises from the experience of great bliss induced by bringing vital winds into the central channel.[528] In a text on the four seals based on notes taken by Gyaltsab Jé, he describes mahāmudrā as "immovable bliss,"[529] an experience of the connate brought on by moving the vital winds into the central channel,[530] and a "lightning-like" nonanalytical, luminous awareness that leads to the production of the connate.[531] In his detailed treatise on the six Dharmas of Nāropa, the *Book of Three Inspirations*, he refers to mahāmudrā

519. Ts*NRCM* 277a [555].

520. Ts*NRCM* 395a [791].

521. Ts*NRCM* 408b [817].

522. E.g., Ts*NRCM* 314b [630], 333a [667], and 431a [862].

523. Ts*NRCM* 430b [862] and 431a [863].

524. There are two English translations available: Tsongkhapa 2010 and Tsongkhapa 2013b.

525. Ts*RNSG* 6b [12]; cf. trans. Tsongkhapa 2013b, 39–40.

526. Ts*RNSG* 96a [191]; cf. trans. Tsongkhapa 2013b, 307.

527. Ts*RNSG* 163b [326], 169b [338]; cf. trans. Tsongkhapa 2013b, 504 and 522.

528. Ts*BTMB* 18a [144].

529. Ts*PZSS* 1a [770] and 4a [775].

530. Ts*PZSS* 4b–5a [776–77].

531. Ts*PZSS* 6a [779].

as the realization of the empty nature of mind as taught by Maitrīpa, Marpa, and Milarepa[532] and as the connate gnosis, or realization, produced by bringing the vital winds into the central channel and inducing the four joys.[533] Finally, in a shorter six Dharmas manual, *Taking the Practice in Hand*, he instructs the meditator to generate connate bliss, then "place the mind experiencing connate bliss in single-pointed focus on the non-intrinsic nature of the self and phenomena, and meditate in this way within the realm of inseparable bliss and emptiness."[534] On returning to everyday life, the meditator is told to "seal all objects and events that appear and occur with the seal of bliss and emptiness conjoined"—this last phrase, of course, being a frequent synonym for mahāmudrā.[535]

Along with the Sakya, the main Tibetan conduit for the tantric systems in which Tsongkhapa found mahāmudrā discourse was the Kagyü. As we have seen, biographies by his contemporaries specify that his Kagyü gurus imparted to him teachings on a range of topics, including various Indian esoteric practices and Tibetan systems of nondual mahāmudrā. Tsongkhapa's own *Record of Teachings Received* frequently lists Tilopa and Nāropa as the last Indian members of tantric (and some sūtra-based) instruction lineages he obtained, and in many cases Marpa is the next teacher named, indicating that, directly or indirectly, the transmission he received had passed through the Kagyü. This is particularly notable in the case of the Guhyasamāja lineages, which Tsongkhapa regarded as the key to understanding unexcelled yoga tantra, but he also obtained such systems as Mahāmāyā, Cakrasaṃvara, and, of course, the six Dharmas of Nāropa through lineages rooted in the Kagyü.[536] Tsongkhapa's *Record of Teachings Received*, however, is a catalogue of originally *Indian* lineages he received, so there is no corroboration in it of his biographers' claims about *Tibetan* mahāmudrā lineages transmitted to him. Indeed, apart from occasional supporting quotations from early Kagyü masters,[537] Tsongkhapa nowhere in his commonly accepted writings appears *explicitly* to discuss his opinion of the Kagyü or their systems of mahāmudrā, although we may

532. Ts*YCSD* 12a–14b [430–35]; trans. Mullin 1996, 126–31.

533. Ts*YCSD* 18b [443] and 28a [462]; trans. Mullin 1996, 139 and 158.

534. Ts*LLTD* 11a [145]; trans. Mullin 1997, 117.

535. Ts*LLTD* 11a [145]; trans. Mullin 1997, 117.

536. See, e.g., Ts*TKSY* 3a–b [237–38], 10a–12b [251–56], and 26a–29a [283–89].

537. See, e.g., Ts*YBSD* 12b–14b [431–35] and 17b–19a [441–44]; trans. Mullin 1996, 127–31 and 137–40.

assume that he generally approved of the perspectives and practices of the great early Kagyü masters whose transmissions he had inherited.

Tsongkhapa's Views of His Contemporaries' Meditation Practices

However much Tsongkhapa respected his teachers and the venerable lineages he received from them, he also felt strongly that many of his contemporaries—and these must have included some Kagyüpas—had made serious mistakes in describing view, meditation, and conduct on the Buddhist path; in fact, the stimulus for his great project of synthesizing all Buddhist thought and practice was in no small part a concern to correct these mistakes. At the same time, he generally remained quite circumspect: rather than "naming names" of those whose positions he found objectionable, he tended to characterize them more generally. Thus, those who did not share his particular interpretation of Prāsaṅgika Madhyamaka were often simply described as Realists (*dngos po smras pa*), those who absolutized buddhahood or buddha nature were referred to as Eternalists (*rtag lta ba*) or Proponents of Extrinsic Emptiness (*gzhan stong pa*), those who denigrated the conventional were called Nihilists (*chad lta ba*), and those who asserted that meditation on the ultimate required mental inactivity often were accused of reviving the discredited Chinese Heshang position. Thus, if Tsongkhapa had opinions of Kagyü mahāmudrā—especially negative ones—we would find them by reading between the lines in certain philosophical and meditative texts where he describes an unacceptable position or practice that might be identified as Kagyü. Without surveying this literature in detail, we will briefly examine passages from the serenity and insight sections of the *Great Exposition of the Stages of the Path to Awakening* and from several important question-and-answer texts on view, meditation, and practice—including *Queries from a Pure Heart*, a controversial open letter that some believe Tsongkhapa did not write but that has, in any case, often been read as directly criticizing the mahāmudrā discourse and practice of his Kagyü contemporaries.[538]

The latter portions of the *Great Stages of the Path* contain Tsongkhapa's most detailed and systematic account of serenity and insight meditation. In each case, the correct definition of the practice is contrasted with erroneous approaches. *Serenity* is defined as a clear, concentrated, nondiscursive state of mind, which is based on single-pointed placement on an object of meditation and entails an extraordinary pliancy of both mind and body.[539] Tsongkhapa

538. For an excellent analysis of some of this material, see Jinpa 1999 and Jinpa 2002, 21–36.

539. Ts*LRCM* 544 and 564; trans. Tsongkhapa 2000–2002, 3:86 and 107.

is at pains to specify that serenity meditation always intends an object, for "if you have consciousness, then you are conscious of something, so you have to accept that there is an object of consciousness in terms of which consciousness is posited."[540] Therefore, strictly speaking there cannot be any such thing as "objectless meditation."

Insight in the *Great Stages of the Path* is called "the wisdom that determines the meaning of reality"[541]—reality, in Tsongkhapa's case, being emptiness, or the lack of self of persons and phenomena. To realize emptiness, one must destroy ignorance, which is taken not merely as the absence of wisdom or insight but as a distinct, inverted view: the superimposition of a self where there is none.[542] Insight, therefore, is a matter of attaining right view rather than no view at all, and right view cannot be attained by abandoning conceptual thought but only by proper rational analysis.[543] The basis of correct rational analysis is a careful identification of the object of negation (the self of persons or phenomena), such that it is neither understated—in which case eternalism may ensue—nor overstated—such that nihilism may result.[544] Once the object has been properly identified and negated, one attains the correct view.

The key meditative practice in the *Great Stages of the Path*—key because it alone uproots defilements and leads to liberation—is the "union of serenity and insight": a nondiscursive contemplation of emptiness by a mind that has attained full single-pointed concentration on the basis of a correct rational analysis of the nature of reality.[545] Tsongkhapa goes to great lengths to specify that this meditation on emptiness does *not* involve "not thinking about anything," or "every occurrence of bliss, clarity, and nondual awareness," or "setting the mind in a nonconceptual state of suspension."[546] In short, soteriologically effective meditation on emptiness avoids the Chinese Heshang heresy. Tsongkhapa nowhere specifies that "Heshang" might be code for "contemporary Kagyüpas," but the language he associates with the Heshang approach—as pointed out earlier by Sakya Paṇḍita—is not unlike that some-

540. Ts*LRCM* 494; trans. Tsongkhapa, 2000–2002, 3:38.

541. Ts*LRCM* 564; trans. Tsongkhapa 2000–2002, 3:107.

542. Ts*LRCM* 656; trans. Tsongkhapa 2000–2002, 3:208.

543. Ts*LRCM* 704; trans. Tsongkhapa 2000–2002, 3:260.

544. Ts*LRCM* 580; trans. Tsongkhapa 2000–2002, 3:126.

545. Ts*LRCM* 798; trans. Tsongkhapa 2000–2002, 3:354.

546. Ts*LRCM* 547, 549, and 775; trans. Tsongkhapa 2000–2002, pp. 88, 89, and 332, respectively.

times found in Kagyü accounts of mahāmudrā, so it is possible that his criticisms were not solely directed at a Chinese monk six centuries dead.

If the *Great Stages of the Path* remains oblique in its criticism of contemporaneous practices, Tsongkhapa's question-and-answer texts are less so—though they are still far from explicit. The *Reply to Statements by Rendawa* criticizes those who think that "the abiding nature of things as nothing at all accords with the mind apprehending nothing at all, and advice in the sūtras and tantras to meditate on nothing at all is meditation on the abiding nature." This, says Tsongkhapa, is simply deluded.[547] In *Key Points of the Path: A Scroll Offered to Jetsun Rendawa*, Tsongkhapa outlines the Prāsaṅgika Madhyamaka view as it was explained to him by Mañjughoṣa, emphasizing that the proper view entails understanding (a) the inseparability of emptiness and dependent arising; (b) the importance of a gradual path that moves from virtuous attitudes and actions, to serenity meditation, to insight meditation; (c) the indispensability of analytical meditation on the lack of self of persons and phenomena as a prerequisite to direct insight into emptiness; and (d) the identity between the Madhyamaka view of the philosophical tradition and that of tantra. In the course of his exposition, Tsongkhapa criticizes "present-day special-instruction holders" who claim that insight may be gained through mental inactivity, arguing that such teachers misunderstand the difference between serenity and insight and overlook the crucial role of analytical meditation; therefore, they "do not describe the essence of the path."[548] Tsongkhapa also repeats verbatim the observation cited above from the *Reply to Statements by Rendawa*, to the effect that it is utterly mistaken to assert that emptiness entails meditating on nothing and that advice in the scriptures not to meditate entails mental inactivity.[549]

The *Garland of the Supremely Medicinal Nectar* recounts the answers to various questions posed to the bodhisattva Vajrapāṇi by Tsongkhapa's Nyingma/Kadam teacher Namkha Gyaltsen (or Lekyi Dorjé). (It is found in both men's collected works.) In it, Vajrapāṇi describes the great perfection as "an elevated view," but adds that an unmistaken view and real insight only can be attained by relying upon the writings of Nāgārjuna and Candrakīrti.[550] Vajrapāṇi also

547. Ts*RDSL* 44b [326].

548. Ts*SDPB* 3b–4a [676–77].

549. Ts*SDPB* 4a [677].

550. Ts*DTPB*; trans Thurman 1982, 213–30. Some Nyingmapa writers of recent times, including Getsé Mahāpaṇḍita (Dge rtse Mahāpaṇḍita, 1761–1829) and Dudjom Rinpoché (1904–87), suggest that Tsongkhapa outwardly was a Gelukpa but inwardly was a practitioner of the great perfection; see, respectively, Makidono 2018, 126–28, and Dudjom 1991, 923–25.

outlines a number of errors (*gol sa*) one may make with regard to view, meditation, and conduct. The connection among these is shown in a passage describing erroneous views, which notes that if one believes that the emptiness of things means that they don't exist, one will conceive of meditation as an unfocused vacuity of mind, and an unfocused mind will not distinguish between good and bad, leading to a collapse of proper conduct.[551] In the section on erroneous meditation, he notes that even if a lama "starkly points out the trio of essence, nature, and responsive capacity,"[552] the disciple may not understand. For if, on the basis of the lama's instructions, one is attached to mere nonconceptual inactivity, one strays into the pure abodes of the form realm.[553] Likewise, attachment to mere nonconceptual clarity leads to the lower absorptions of the form realm, attachment to mere nonconceptual bliss leads to rebirth as a desire-realm god, and attachment to mere nonconceptual emptiness leads to the formless realm.[554] Although the *Garland* is concerned primarily with a clarification of Nyingma practices, the sorts of errors it cites are similar to those identified by Kagyü masters[555] as well as those mentioned in the two texts addressed to Rendawa and in any number of Tsongkhapa's other question-and-answer texts.

The writing attributed to Tsongkhapa that comes closest to providing an explicit critique of the Kagyü and their practice of mahāmudrā is *Queries from a Pure Heart*. Apparently dating from around the late 1380s or the early 1390s, it is an open letter to the "great meditators" of Tibet that poses a series of pointed questions about their practices. Although the Kagyü never is mentioned, the term *mahāmudrā* occurs several times in the text, and the assertions Tsongkhapa questions are, in many cases, quite close to those that were common in Kagyü mahāmudrā circles. Some Tibetan scholars have doubted that Tsongkhapa really was the author of *Queries*, arguing that the style and language of the text, as well as an unusual self-description

551. Ts*DTPB* 4a [300].

552. *Ngo bo, rang bzhin*, and *thugs rje*, three aspects of buddha nature according to the great-perfection tradition.

553. The pure abodes (*śuddhāvāsa*) are the highest heavens or absorptions of the form realm. Tsongkhapa is saying that these fruits of nonconceptual meditation are detours, forestalling complete awakening.

554. Ts*DTPB* 5b [303].

555. See, e.g., Dakpo Tashi Namgyal 1986, 293–313, for a later discussion of these that liberally quotes Indian mahāsiddhas and early Kagyüpa masters on the errors (*gol sa*) to which mahāmudrā meditators may be prone.

in the colophon, raise doubts about its authorship.[556] However, most premodern Tibetan scholars—including Shākya Chokden, Pema Karpo, and Paṇchen Chögyen, who wrote a versified commentary on it (Bz*LSLZ*)—accepted Tsongkhapa's authorship, and a modern scholar who has examined the text closely, Thupten Jinpa, concludes that it is Tsongkhapa's work.[557] The Kagyü historian Pawo Tsuklak Trengwa not only accepts Tsongkhapa's authorship of *Queries* but specifies that Tsongkhapa wrote it "as a result of deep disappointment he felt at the level of ignorance among the meditators at a Kagyü retreat."[558] The Gelukpa regent and historian Desi Sangyé Gyatso (1653–1705) also accepts the text's attribution to Tsongkhapa and says that it is intended as a refutation of "the mahāmudrā of those known as the New Drukpa" (*'brug gsar*),[559] which could well be a reference to the teachings of Barawa reputedly transmitted to Tsongkhapa by Umapa. In any case, *Queries* has been taken by scholars of all stripes to be a critique of Kagyü mahāmudrā.

Tsongkhapa begins *Queries* by announcing that he will pose a series of questions aimed at exposing "errors in view, meditation, and conduct," invoking the works of Sakya Paṇḍita and also citing Nāgārjuna's warning that those who misunderstand emptiness are like fools who mishandle snakes or misuse mantras.[560] He goes on to question whether his opponents—trapped by their own negative rhetoric—are sufficiently committed to such basic elements of Buddhist conduct as taking refuge, generating the awakening mind, confessing transgressions, and contemplating the perfect human rebirth, impermanence, death, cause and effect, and the disadvantages of saṃsāra. These practices, he says, ought to be easy, but many of his contemporaries seem to find them hard.[561] In the main section of the text, he focuses on errors in view and meditation. Among the many questions he poses are these: If meditation on emptiness is simply a matter of objectless, nonprojecting, nonconceptual meditation, then how can we distinguish serenity from insight, let alone use mindfulness and alertness in placement meditation or identify the proper

556. See Jinpa 1999, 6–8, and Thuken 2009, 154.

557. Jinpa 1999, 6–7.

558. Jinpa 1999, 20n23.

559. Jinpa 1999, 20n23.

560. Ts*LSRK* 73a [343]. The passage from Nāgārjuna is *Root Verses on the Middle Way* 24.11; Ng*MK*s 274.

561. Ts*LSRK* 76b [350].

object of insight meditation?[562] If mahāmudrā meditation is simply a matter of complete mental inactivity, then how is mahāmudrā different from the teachings of Heshang, and how is it in harmony with the view and meditation taught by Nāgārjuna?[563] If statements in scripture to the effect that the best seeing is no seeing, the best meditation is no meditation, and the best conduct is no conduct are to be taken literally, then how can we make conventional distinctions at all, or *do* anything?[564] If apprehending the lack of true existence is the same as apprehending all things as untrue, then how do we avoid philosophical and ethical nihilism, or even distinguish a dog from a lion?[565]

Tsongkhapa goes on to outline a variety of conflicting contemporaneous claims about how to attain right view, many of them recognizable from Kagyü contexts. Some, he says, believe it is attained through abandoning all conceptuality, while others say it comes through multiplying conceptions. Some say that conceptuality is the basic ignorance that keeps us in saṃsāra, while others insist that it is the pristine Dharma body. Some insist that the nonprojecting, stable mind is nirvāṇa itself and that mental distraction is saṃsāra, while others say that single-pointed observation of the distracted mind is itself the Dharma body. Some describe an "emptied vision of nothingness" as the Dharma body itself, while others say that such vision only provides a glimpse of the Dharma body. Still others insist that it is a realization of extrinsic emptiness (shentong), while others connect it to the realization of intrinsic emptiness (rangtong).[566] Tsongkhapa next criticizes those who assert that the "actual mahāmudrā" resides in the first two of the six yogas of Kālacakra, *individual withdrawal* (*so sor sdud pa*, Skt. *pratyāhāra*), in which one allegedly realizes intrinsic emptiness, and *absorption* (*bsam gtan*, Skt. *dhyāna*), in which one allegedly realizes extrinsic emptiness.[567] His inquiry complete, he concludes the text by describing the proper way to ascertain and meditate on the view, which is that of Nāgārjuna and his disciples: establishing the proper sequence of study, reflection, and meditation; determining the object of negation without falling into eternalism or nihilism; performing proper analysis; arriving at a realization of emptiness; and joining serenity and insight by meditating single-pointedly on that realization. Doing this, he promises, will "send

562. Ts*LSRK* 76b–77a [352–53].

563. Ts*LSRK* 78a–80b [353–56].

564. Ts*LSRK* 80b [356].

565. Ts*LSRK* 80a–b [357–58].

566. Ts*LSRK* 82a–b [361–62]; see translation in Jinpa 1999, 15–16, and Jinpa 2002, 31–32.

567. Ts*LSRK* 83a [363].

far away any errors regarding view, meditation, and conduct—this is the deep honey of the unmistaken special instructions of the conquerors."[568]

Did Tsongkhapa Teach His Own Mahāmudrā System?

The final question to pose about Tsongkhapa's relation to mahāmudrā is the most important one. Granted that he heard instructions on mahāmudrā from his Kagyü teachers, mentioned mahāmudrā in his writings on secret mantra, and implicitly (or perhaps even explicitly) criticized Kagyü mahāmudrā ideas and practices in a number of texts on view, meditation, and conduct, *did he ever teach his own system of mahāmudrā practice?*[569]

Based solely on the written record, the answer is, essentially, no. For all their focus on Tsongkhapa's encounters with Mañjughoṣa, none of the biographies written by his direct disciples specify that he received a mahāmudrā teaching during those encounters, let alone wrote a text on the teaching.[570] Indeed, although, as we have seen, Tsongkhapa's collected writings include a number of texts in which, on the basis of his visionary experiences, he communicates special instructions to one or another disciple—Rendawa, Khedrup Jé, Baso Chökyi Gyaltsen—these are concerned with either completion-stage tantric practices, Madhyamaka, or guru yoga, not mahāmudrā, and he himself nowhere explicitly claims to have begun a mahāmudrā-centered hearing transmission of the sort described by later writers.

There is one intriguing text, found in the collection of Tsongkhapa's shorter works, that might be a candidate for a mahāmudrā text: *Synopsis of the Spiritual Practice Taught by the Exalted Mañjughoṣa*,[571] which Jé Lama wrote out while in retreat in Ölkha in the 1390s. According to later tradition,[572] it was the outcome of one of Tsongkhapa's first direct visions of Mañjughoṣa, an intense experience in which the deity appeared before him and emanated from his heart cakra a wisdom sword that pierced Tsongkhapa's own heart cakra, filling him with bliss so intense that even his nearby disciples could feel it. In gratitude, Tsongkhapa composed two verses in praise of Mañjughoṣa,

568. Ts*LSRK* 84b [366].

569. For Yeshé Gyaltsen's perspective on the question, see below, part 5, section 2.

570. As noted above, however, Tashi Palden, in his *Requests Based on the Secret Life Prayer of the Exalted Losang Drakpa*, describes Tsongkhapa's tantric realizations as involving an experience of "the luminosity of mahāmudrā." See Kp*SNSD* 3b–4a [205–6]; cf. trans. Thurman 1982, 52.

571. Ts*JBDD*, translated below in part 5, section 1.

572. See, e.g., Pb*NDSB* 313–14.

the second of which seems to be a metaphorical expression of the bliss he had experienced:

> In the city of Katara,[573]
> the flowers of the pleasure garden bloom;
> swarms of bees play there,
> drinking up the supreme nectar.

On that same occasion, Mañjughoṣa imparted to Tsongkhapa a poetic synopsis of the entire path to awakening, which includes encouragement to develop renunciation, the awakening mind, serenity meditation, and an understanding of emptiness. The latter is described in both experiential and analytic terms. Experientially, Tsongkhapa is told, "Without abiding anywhere, / contemplate mind itself as like space."[574] Later, in a more analytical mode, Mañjughoṣa instructs:

> Keep the great fire of mindfulness continuously ablaze,
> and the tinder of the six sense objects will certainly be consumed.
> All things in saṃsāra and nirvāṇa
> are boundless like space:
> they have never been nor will they ever be perceived by anyone.
> Appearing objects are like a sky flower,
> and what sugata has found the subject, the mind?
> The oneness of awareness and the Dharma realm is proven to be like a rabbit's horn.[575]

The instruction to make the mind like unlocated space, as well as the determination that both the epistemological subject and the nonconceptual self-awareness in which mind and reality are fused are, in fact, empty, is strongly reminiscent of mahāmudrā discourse, but the *Synopsis* does not mention the term.

Another text of more than passing interest in relation to mahāmudrā

573. This somewhat oblique transcribed Sanskrit term may be a corruption of *kedāra*, which refers, among other things, to a meadow. It also may refer a mountainous region containing a famous pilgrimage place in what is now Uttarakhand state of India; see Monier-Williams 1974, 309. It is unlikely, but not impossible, that Tsongkhapa was evoking this mountainous region, even though it is far to the southwest of Ölkha.

574. Ts*JBDD* 50b [298].

575. Ts*JBDD* 51a [299].

is Tsongkhapa's short poetic *Condensed Stages of the Path to Awakening* (Ts*LRDD*),[576] written at Ganden Monastery late in his life, which is often treated as a "song of experience" (*nyams mgur*) or as Jé Lama's spiritual autobiography. In twenty-five verses, Tsongkhapa outlines the entire path to Buddhahood from the perspective of the Perfection Vehicle. He begins with homage to the Buddha, Maitreya and Mañjughoṣa, Asaṅga and Nāgārjuna, Atiśa, and his own gurus (verses 1–5), then celebrates the unique effectiveness of the stages-of-the-path approach, which distills the 84,000 teachings transmitted by the Buddha in such a way that they serve as personal instruction for each disciple (verses 6–8). He begins his description of the stages of the path with the familiar foundational reflections on the importance of guru yoga, the preciousness and fragility of a human rebirth, the unsatisfactoriness of saṃsāra, and the need to seek liberation (verses 9–13). He then shifts to a Mahāyāna perspective, extolling the greatness of the awakening mind as the core and basis of the bodhisattva path, then describing in turn each of the six perfections (verses 14–23), including a description of meditation on the perfection of wisdom as entailing space-like emptiness during a practice session and illusion-like emptiness afterward. Tsongkhapa concludes the text with the summary statement that any serious practitioner must master the "three principal aspects of the path" (*lam gtso rnam gsum*): renunciation, the awakening mind, and correct view, followed by the customary dedication of merit (verses 24–25). A unique feature of the *Condensed Stages of the Path* is that each of the last seventeen exhortatory verses concludes with the refrain, "I, a yogī, have practiced thus, / and you who aspire to liberation, please do so as well." Given Tsongkhapa's characteristic modesty, this amounts to a strong claim to spiritual experience and attainment. Though the descriptions of serenity and insight as key elements of the perfections of meditation and wisdom, respectively, bear certain general similarities to elements of mahāmudrā practice found elsewhere in Tibetan tradition, the great seal is nowhere explicitly mentioned; nor in evidence is the tendency of mahāmudrā masters to focus serenity and insight meditation on the nature of mind.

In short, then, nowhere in Tsongkhapa's corpus is there a text, or even a part of a text, in which he explicitly lays out instructions on mahāmudrā practice of the sort that would be attributed to him by later Geluk tradition. The great eighteenth-century exponent of the Ganden Hearing Transmission Kachen Yeshé Gyaltsen acknowledges as much, noting that Tsongkhapa never *wrote down* his system of mahāmudrā, and citing passages from *Queries from a Pure Heart* and the *Reply to Statements by Rendawa* that seem to confirm a

576. For translations, see, e.g., Thurman 1982, 59–66, and Wangyal 1995, 173–81.

reluctance to commit such instructions to writing. In the *Reply*, Tsongkhapa refers to "uncommon instructions"—on renunciation and the awakening mind, including a direct teaching on the view that "reaches the marrow"—that should not be written about "at the present time."[577] In *Queries*, at the conclusion of his discussion of the idea that no seeing is the supreme seeing, he explains that such a teaching "is not for the uncouth, and it seems that at this point the time is not right for us to impart to those who desire it the original special instruction of the wise father guru."[578] For Yeshé Gyaltsen, the most important aspect of these passages is that they provide evidence that although Tsongkhapa did not write about mahāmudrā, he did possess such a teaching and therefore must have communicated it orally. A similar point is made in a question-and-answer text by Yeshé Gyaltsen's contemporary Changkya Rölpai Dorjé (1717–86).[579]

Along different lines, Yeshé Gyaltsen's disciple Gungthang Könchok Tenpai Drönmé (1762–1823) asserts, on the basis of information from his own guru, that Tsongkhapa had taught mahāmudrā to his disciple Gungru Gyaltsen Sangpo (1383–1450), perhaps based on teachings he had received from Umapa, who as noted, had received them in turn from the Drukpa Kagyü master Barawa.[580] It is widely reported in Geluk circles that Gungruwa taught a version of Madhyamaka in which emptiness was seen to be an affirming negation (*ma yin dgag*) rather than a nonaffirming negation (*med dgag*), and that Gungruwa's unorthodox explanation was roundly criticized by Khedrup Jé.[581] The latter, as we have seen, also reported Mañjughoṣa's displeasure with

577. Ts*RDSL* 44b [326]; cited at Yg*LZGM* 10a–b [218–19].

578. Ts*LSRK* 79b [356]; cited at Yg*LZGM* 10a [219]. The "wise father guru" is probably Mañjughoṣa.

579. Dalai Lama and Berzin 1997, 164. A considerably earlier source, Chimé Rabgyé's *Jewel Storehouse Biography: How Jé Rinpoché Possessed the Qualities of Learning, Dignity, and Excellence* (*Rje rin po che la mkhas btsun bzang gsum gyi yon tan mnga' tshul rnam thar nor bu'i bang mdzod*), which dates from around 1470, remarks in passing that Tsongkhapa refused to teach women mahāmudrā (Ary 2007, 75). The issues of sexual politics this raises quite aside, the text implies that Tsongkhapa did teach mahāmudrā to men. Of course, the text does not specify what it means by *mahāmudrā*, so we cannot be certain that the teaching to which Chimé Rapgyé refers is anything like that publicized by the First Paṇchen Lama. It could be a tantric teaching, or it could simply be a teaching on emptiness—a connotation of *mahāmudrā* often found in Geluk circles.

580. Dalai Lama and Berzin 1997, 230. The earliest reference to this possibility, so far as I know, is in the *Experiential Teaching on Mahāmudrā in the Geden Oral Transmission* (Kd*PCNK* 10a [449]), by Paṇchen Chögyen's disciple from Amdo, Shar Kalden Gyatso (1607–77); see below, page 250.

581. Thuken 2009, 278–79, and Ary 2002, 178–79.

Barawa's explanation of Madhyamaka. Despite Gungthangpa's claim, it is not clear that the teaching of Gungruwa's rejected by Khedrup Jé—of emptiness as an affirming negation—was a mahāmudrā teaching per se. And that view, even if once held by Tsongkhapa, was rejected by him later in life and became anathema within the Geluk. As Thuken rather delicately puts it, "perhaps Jé taught Gungruwa before having completed his analysis of the view."[582] As a brief aside, we should note that in his 1982 lectures on the First Paṇchen's mahāmudrā autocommentary, the Fourteenth Dalai Lama focuses considerable attention on the Barawa-Umapa-Tsongkhapa-Gungruwa succession, suggesting that it may be a key source of the First Paṇchen's mahāmudrā system. The Dalai Lama sees that system as a Kagyü-Geluk synthesis and, interestingly, regards Gungruwa's teaching more positively than does Khedrup Jé. He sees it as reflecting an atypical but genuine teaching of Tsongkhapa that—at least within the context of the luminosity manifested on the completion stage of unexcelled yoga tantra—may allow for some version of an affirming negation, some notion of extrinsic emptiness, and some elevation of teachings from the third turning of the Dharma wheel—usually described by Gelukpas as provisional (*drang don*)—to the status of definitive (*nges don*).[583] A similar view of Gungruwa's importance was asserted centuries earlier by the Nyingma master Getsé Mahāpaṇḍita (1761–1829), who writes:

> Tsongkhapa's heart son Gungru Gyaltsen Sangpo
> clearly states, [on the basis] of his precious utterances,
> how the Lord's intent is in accord with mahāmudrā and the great perfection.
> [Gungru] and others [in the Ganden Hearing Transmission]
> uniformly [asserted] that their own position, the buddha-nature doctrine,
> is in accord with the intent of mahāmudrā and the great perfection.[584]

All this notwithstanding, we may actually glean at least the seeds of the later

582. Thuken 2009, 379. Despite claims to the effect that Gungruwa held an unorthodox position on negation, scholars who have examined Gungruwa's recently published writings, including Michael Sheehy (personal communication, June 2013) and Yaroslav Komarovski (2011, 317–18n72), report finding nothing outside the Geluk norm.

583. Dalai Lama and Berzin 1997, 230–39.

584. Makidono 2018, 128; (translation adapted). I have not located the passage from Gungruwa's writings cited by Getsé Mahāpaṇḍita. The works of Gungruwa (BDRC ID no. P4340), which focus mostly on topics related to Madhyamaka and the Perfection of Wisdom, have been available only since 2007, and their study is a real desideratum.

Geluk mahāmudrā practice from passing comments made by Tsongkhapa in texts that are concerned with other topics. Certainly, his descriptions of mahāmudrā in his tantric writings—for instance in relation to the clear-light mind or the gnosis of inseparable bliss and emptiness—provide a strong basis for what would be known in the Geluk system as "mantra mahāmudrā." Furthermore, the Geluk practice of "sūtra mahāmudrā"—with its focus on undertaking serenity and insight meditation with the mind itself as the meditative object—may at least be inferred from *Queries from a Pure Heart* and the *Book of Three Inspirations*. In *Queries*, where Tsongkhapa's concern is to promulgate "Nāgārjuna's view and meditation" or "Nāgārjuna's insight," he clearly states that "the actual practice of mahāmudrā is meditation on the definitive reality, meditation on emptiness."[585] He does not specify that the mind is the object of that meditation, but given the context of his discussion, it is not unreasonable to infer that the mind is at least one possible object. The *Book of Three Inspirations* is, of course, primarily concerned with completion-stage tantric practices, but it contains a subsection on the nature of the mind that is broader in approach. There, Tsongkhapa makes it clear that (a) mind is empty of intrinsic existence in the same way as all other phenomena, (b) the realization of this fact is the same as the mahāmudrā realizations of Maitrīpa and Sahajavajra, Marpa and Milarepa, and (c) these, in turn, are in complete harmony with the Madhyamaka view of Nāgārjuna, Āryadeva, and Candrakīrti.[586]

In short, at least one of Tsongkhapa's ways of conceiving mahāmudrā is as a meditation on the nature of mind that conforms to the Prāsaṅgika Madhyamaka mode of analyzing the ontological status of *any* object, and whether one meditates in the style of the Perfection Vehicle or the Mantra Vehicle, and however coarse or subtle the cognition that performs the meditation, the nature of the mind remains the same: emptiness of intrinsic existence that is a negation, pure and simple. Thus, even though traditional and modern scholars all can agree that Tsongkhapa never committed a full account of mahāmudrā meditation to writing, the clues he has left in other texts allow us to infer—at least broadly—what such an account might have looked like, and it turns out not to differ in its essentials from the account written by the First Paṇchen Lama some two centuries after Tsongkhapa's death. This does not prove that Tsongkhapa taught mahāmudrā secretly to one or more disciples and that an unbroken transmission reached the First Paṇchen, who then wrote it down—a claim that goes beyond the textual evidence—but it does, I believe, demonstrate that claims to that effect are not implausible.

585. Ts*LSRK* 78a [353].

586. Ts*YCSD* 12a–14b [430–35]; trans. Mullin 1996, 126–31, and see also 55–58.

7. From Tsongkhapa to Paṇchen Chögyen: Khedrup Jé and the Main Line of the Hearing Transmission

As we have seen, the period between the passing of Tsongkhapa and the rise to prominence of the Fifth Dalai Lama—tutored by Losang Chökyi Gyaltsen—was one in which the Geluk order as a whole gained religious, intellectual, and institutional strength throughout Tibet. If we examine the works of major Gelukpa masters and scholars of this era—both within and outside the Ganden Hearing Transmission—we find that mahāmudrā is as marginal for most of them as it was for Tsongkhapa, and that in the three cases where Gelukpas wrote works devoted explicitly and solely to mahāmudrā, the presentation is clearly based on Kagyü models and bears little resemblance to anything Tsongkhapa had to say about the topic or to the texts on the Geden Oral Transmission of mahāmudrā published by Paṇchen Chögyen. In our search for Geluk mahāmudrā discourse in this era, we will first, in this chapter, survey the lives and writings of members of the Hearing Transmission between Tsongkhapa and Paṇchen Chögyen, beginning with Khedrup Jé—whose position with relation to the Ganden Hearing Transmission is, as we will see, somewhat ambiguous. We will continue, then, through the members of the main transmission line as enumerated by Paṇchen Chögyen and his successors: Tokden Jampal Gyatso, Baso Chökyi Gyaltsen, Chökyi Dorjé, Ensapa Losang Döndrup, and Khedrup Sangyé Yeshé; we will save our discussion of Paṇchen Chögyen himself until chapter 9. While each member of the "official" lineage is said by later tradition to have received the entirety of the transmission, with its raft of teachings on guru yoga, mahāmudrā, and other topics, and to have come into possession of the emanated scripture given to Tsongkhapa by Mañjughoṣa, we will see that, at least so far as the paper trail is concerned, there is little evidence that the specifically Geluk tradition of mahāmudrā publicized by Losang Chökyi Gyaltsen was a part of the transmission before his time. In the next chapter, we will discuss the place of mahāmudrā in the lives and works of a number of important Geluk figures outside the main transmission lineage, three of whom did write works centrally concerned with mahāmudrā.

Khedrup Jé

Khedrup Gelek Palsang, commonly known as Khedrup Jé (1385–1438),[587] was a native of Tsang who was drawn to the Geluk in its formative years, and even as a teenager established a reputation as a fierce debater, unafraid to challenge even the most famous scholars of other schools. He took full ordination with Rendawa in the Lhasa area in 1405 and was introduced to Tsongkhapa two years later. According to tradition, the two quickly established a strong rapport, and not long after they met, Tsongkhapa spent ten consecutive months imparting the full range of his teachings to Khedrup Jé, focusing on the great Indian Sūtra Vehicle classics by day and the tantras by night. Khedrup Jé also studied with senior disciples of Tsongkhapa, including the great master of logic and the Perfection of Wisdom Gyaltsab Jé. Although Gyaltsab Jé was Tsongkhapa's most important disciple at the time, the bond Khedrup Jé established with Jé Rinpoché was so close that it was he who eventually came to be regarded as Tsongkhapa's "heart son."[588] As Tsongkhapa undertook the great public works and advanced writings that would occupy much of his last decade, Khedrup Jé returned to Tsang, where he worked on behalf of his master's teaching. After Tsongkhapa's death, he remained in Tsang, founding monasteries, writing biographies, commentaries, and treatises, and regularly receiving visions of Tsongkhapa. Eventually, he was summoned to Ganden, where he became abbot upon the death of Gyaltsab Jé, who himself had been Tsongkhapa's direct successor. In all his activities, Khedrup Jé was, as José Cabezón notes, "the first major upholder and defender of the tradition after the death of his teacher, guarding the doctrine set forth by his master against the onslaught of rival theories."[589] To this day in the Geluk world, Jé Tsongkhapa, Gyaltsab Jé, and Khedrup Jé are universally referred to as the "trio of father Jé and his sons" (*rje yab sras gsum*), and commonly depicted together in temple statuary and at the center of scroll paintings of the Geluk lineage.

Although Khedrup Jé is widely credited with being the human source of an eponymous "unique transmission" of guru yoga, his relation to the Ganden

587. See Cabezón 1992, 13–19, and Ary 2015.

588. According to Ary (2015), Khedrup Jé's close bond with Tsongkhapa may have been exaggerated by later biographers. At the very least, the reader should bear in mind that what is presented here is the consensus of later tradition and not necessarily historical fact.

589. Cabezón 1992, 14.

Hearing Transmission is more ambiguous. The first author to specify a lineage for the Ensa (or Geden, or Ganden) Hearing Transmission, Paṇchen Chögyen's teacher Khedrup Sangyé Yeshé, names Khedrup Jé as Tsongkhapa's successor and as Baso Chökyi Gyaltsen's predecessor in the tradition, while his younger contemporary, the Third Dalai Lama Sönam Gyatso, reverses the order, suggesting that Khedrup Jé received the transmission from his younger brother.[590] Paṇchen Chögyen, on the other hand, excises Khedrup Jé from the list, specifying in *Like a Treasure Inventory* that "although the omniscient Khedrup possessed the scriptures and teachings of the oral transmission in a general way, only Tokden Jampal Gyatso possessed the scriptures and teachings of the oral transmission, along with the emanated scripture, in their entirety."[591] Jampal Gyatso was three decades older than Khedrup Jé, and—at least according to later accounts—he received the hearing transmission during his long group retreat with Tsongkhapa in the 1390s, when Khedrup Jé was still a boy. If, as later accounts also insist, the full transmission and the emanated scripture only were passed from one master to one disciple in each generation, then Khedrup Jé could not have received them from Tsongkhapa, because by the time he met Jé Rinpoché, they already were held by Jampal Gyatso. Whether we accept the consensus of later tradition that Khedrup Jé never possessed the full transmission or infer from the historical record that he may have "lost" his place in the lineage at the time of Paṇchen Chögyen, it is likely that Khedrup Jé was privy to many of the teachings in the transmission, including any instructions on mahāmudrā Tsongkhapa might have passed on to his close disciples.

Whatever the case, Khedrup Jé's writings deal with mahāmudrā in much the same way as Tsongkhapa's do, mentioning the term in various contexts but devoting little concerted attention to it. Thus, his *Extensive Exposition of the Arrangement of the Four Classes of Tantra* discusses mahāmudrā within the context of its appearance in the literature of the yoga and unexcelled yoga tantras. In a discussion of the "seal pledge" required as part of the empowerment of the vajra master in the two highest classes of tantras, he specifies that in yoga tantra empowerments, resorting to a great seal refers primarily to the clear visualization of oneself in the bodily form of the deity, while in unexcelled-yoga-tantra empowerments (most notably the third, or wisdom-

590. Sy*ESKG* 2b [455], and Sonam Gyatso 1982, 226–27, respectively. Ensapa's earlier guru-yoga text, *Source of All Yogic Attainments* (discussed below), gives a lineage list in which Khedrup Jé is Tsongkhapa's direct successor, but it is unclear what relation this lineage—which Ensapa does not name—bears to what will eventually be known as the Ganden Hearing Transmission.

591. Bz*TKBT* 7b–8a.

gnosis empowerment) the great seal is a physical or visualized consort—symbolic of awareness or wisdom—with whom one practices sexual yoga in order to generate an extraordinary experience of bliss.[592] In the section on the yoga tantras, Khedrup Jé lays out the system of four seals, in which mahāmudrā (sometimes listed first, sometimes last) is associated with the external or internal visualization of a deity's body. Sealed by a hand gesture, the vajra fist, this visualization allows one to transform afflictive desire and the earth-element and to understand the true nature of the deity as the nonduality of the profound and the luminous.[593] Later, in a discussion of the mother or yoginī tantras, he specifies that what distinguishes that subclass of unexcelled yoga tantras is its employment, as the "method of the perfection of wisdom," of a yoginī, or great seal, union (*rab sbyor*) with whom is tantamount to entering suchness, or reality (*de nyid du 'jug pa*). The great seal, he adds, is the gnosis of connate great bliss, the gnosis of inseparable bliss and emptiness.[594] Each of these two tantric definitions of mahāmudrā is, unsurprisingly, quite similar to those offered by Tsongkhapa in his *Great Exposition of the Stages of Secret Mantra*.

Likewise, echoing Tsongkhapa's *Great Stages of the Path*, Khedrup Jé's lengthy treatise on Madhyamaka, *A Dose of Emptiness*, offers critiques of unidentified non-Geluk views on a range of topics, some of which may be connected to approaches to mahāmudrā taken by his contemporaries. He insists, contrary to certain scholars, that the emptiness understood on the tantric path is precisely the same emptiness understood through the Perfection Vehicle, and that that understanding, whether Perfection or Mantra, is never a mere blank state but always has an object, even if that object is nonsubstantial reality.[595] It is, furthermore, always a nonaffirming negation.[596] Elsewhere, he is careful to distinguish the correct view that "all things are nonexistent" from the nihilist idea that "nothing exists," and to explain how early Yogācāra uses of the term *extrinsic emptiness* refer *not* to buddha nature that is empty of everything saṃsāric but to dependent entities' natural freedom from the substantiality that is mistakenly imputed to them.[597] Like Tsongkhapa, Khedrup Jé attacks quietist approaches to meditation on emptiness, which "posit

592. Lessing and Wayman 1978, 142–45.

593. Lessing and Wayman 1978, 228–47, especially 246–47.

594. Lessing and Wayman 1978, 262–63.

595. Cabezón 1992, 28–30

596. Cabezón 1992, 294–96 and 352–54.

597. Cabezón 1992, 32 and 49, respectively.

that no mental object should be established, that the mind should apprehend nothing."[598] This, he says, is "a den of iniquity... a kind of idiot's meditation,"[599] which is no different from the Heshang view and leads only to the formless absorptions attained by those who practice concentration uncoupled from any insight.[600] Furthermore, faith in the guru's teaching of emptiness may reduce attachment somewhat, but only if supported by logical analysis will it become a basis for a direct realization of emptiness that actually severs attachment and other defilements.[601] Finally, Khedrup Jé insists near the end of the treatise that a buddha's awareness is *not* objectless, nor does it perceive only the ultimate; it cognizes the ultimate and the conventional simultaneously—though, of course, it is not at all fooled by ordinary appearances.[602] Each of the views Khedrup Jé opposes was at one time or another held by Kagyüpa or Nyingmapa masters, but in the absence of specific identifications, we cannot be certain that they were his intended targets. Similarly, his attacks on mistaken ideas about views and meditation in two overtly polemical works, *Cleansing the Sage's Teaching* and the celebrated *Lamp Dispelling Darkness: Guidance in the View* and *Guidance in the View of the Prāsaṅgika System*, do not single out an opponent by name, but the text's close linguistic and rhetorical relation to Tsongkhapa's *Queries from a Pure Heart* point in the direction of the Kagyü in general and mahāmudrā in particular.[603]

In short, although Khedrup Jé, like Tsongkhapa before him, was often said to be a holder of the Ganden mahāmudrā tradition, he seems, like his master, to have written nothing about it and to have addressed mahāmudrā as a topic only in passing in discussions of the yoga and unexcelled yoga tantras or indirectly in discussions of Madhyamaka views and meditative practices. At the same time, while Khedrup Jé's Tsang-based incarnate successor, Sönam Choklang (1438–1505),[604] left no writings, so we cannot assess his relation to the Ganden Hearing Transmission, the next two masters in the incarnation series—first Ensapa and then Paṇchen Chögyen—were key members of the transmission. So if Khedrup Jé had little to say about mahāmudrā during his

598. Cabezón 1992, 112–13.

599. Cabezón 1992, 113.

600. Cabezón 1992, 113–14.

601. Cabezón 1992, 115.

602. Cabezón 1992, 381.

603. See Jinpa 1999, 20n13, and Cabezón 1992, 452n389.

604. On his role in monastic life in Tsang and his recognition as Khedrup Jé's successor, see Schwieger 2015, 24.

lifetime, he would have much to say about it through his second and third successors—and the incarnation lineage of which he is the source is considered, retrospectively, to be that of the Paṇchen Lamas.

Tokden Jampal Gyatso

As his dates attest, Tokden Jampal Gyatso (1356–1428)[605] was an almost exact contemporary of Tsongkhapa. He hailed from the same part of Amdo as Tsongkhapa, and like Jé Rinpoche, he developed an early interest in religion, memorizing the *King of Concentrations Sūtra* while still a child. Also like Tsongkhapa, he moved while still in his teens to Central Tibet, where he traveled from monastery to monastery, receiving teachings and empowerments. According to the later Kagyü historian Situ Paṇchen Chökyi Jungné, he was particularly drawn to Kagyü centers such as Tsurphu and Taklung, where he learned mahāmudrā, the six Dharmas of Nāropa, and severance.[606] According to Geluk sources, he heard Tsongkhapa lecture on the buddha-nature classic the *Sublime Continuum* at Dewachen when he was around twenty and became one of Jé Rinpoché's most cherished disciples. Despite his natural attraction to asceticism and retreat, at Tsongkhapa's behest he studied philosophy and the Sakya path and fruit tradition for a number of years. Eventually he was selected as one of eight attendants on Tsongkhapa's long retreat in the 1390s. He set an example for the others by his dedication to austerities. Later tradition insists that it was at this time that Tsongkhapa granted him the Ganden Hearing Transmission, including the teaching on mahāmudrā, and bestowed upon him the emanated scripture.[607] However, the earliest biography of Jampal Gyatso we possess, *Flowing River of Faith*, by his disciple Lodrö Gyaltsen (1402–72), merely describes his receiving, in their entirety, "special instructions" (*gdams ngag*), without specifying their content.[608] In any case, he developed considerable visionary powers, ability as a healer and life-prolonger, and a strong experience of the gnosis of bliss and emptiness—on which Tsongkhapa once asked *him* for advice. He also was the only disciple to witness the comings and goings of a mysterious ḍākinī who would visit Tsongkhapa at night to assist him with his practices. He spent much of his later life in hermitages, attracting a number of disciples, including Lodrö Gyaltsen and

605. Willis 1995, 33–40, Zasep 2019, 33, and below, part 5, section 2.

606. St*ZCSP* 1 and 320a [105–6]; cf. Lg*NTCG* 2a [399].

607. Willis 1995, 36, and below, part 5, section 2.

608. Lg*NTCG* 4b [404].

Baso Chökyi Gyaltsen; it was to the latter, we are told, that he entrusted the Ganden Hearing Transmission and the emanated scripture. His writings are relatively few—he is best known for his biographies of Tsongkhapa and some devotional songs—and none of them deals with mahāmudrā in a significant way, nor does he anywhere suggest that he is part of a special hearing tradition centered on the great seal. Interestingly, however, Lodrö Gyaltsen reports his insistence that various practice traditions that might appear incompatible—most notably the stages of the path and mahāmudrā—are, in fact, in harmony and result from maintaining "pure vision."[609] This may be one of the earliest expressions of the ecumenical spirit that will be evident in much of the literature of the Ganden Hearing Transmission's teaching on mahāmudrā.

Baso Chökyi Gyaltsen

Baso Chökyi Gyaltsen (1402–73)[610] was the younger brother of Tsongkhapa's great disciple, Khedrup Jé. A native of Latö, near Mount Everest, he moved to Lhasa as a youth and met Tsongkhapa before the latter's death, supposedly receiving from him the unique transmission of a guru-yoga meditation practice (Ts*BSCG*). He undertook scholastic studies with Khedrup Jé, who passed on to him other oral traditions originating with Tsongkhapa, and then was taken under the wing of Tokden Jampal Gyatso, who—tradition tells us—sometime before his own death in 1428 passed on to Baso the pith instructions of the various practices of the Ganden Hearing Transmission—guru yoga, mahāmudrā, severance, and the combined practice of Guhyasamāja, Cakrasaṃvara, and Yamāntaka—along with the emanated scripture. Like his teacher, Baso was strongly inclined to the hermitic life, and inspired in part by the example of the Indian mahāsiddha Śavaripa, spent considerable time in retreat in Tsang and southern Tibet, encountering visions, gaining realizations, and earning a reputation as a great scholar and siddha. That reputation led to his appointment, in 1464, as abbot of Ganden—a post he assumed only reluctantly after it was turned down by Gendun Drup, who insisted that he had to remain at Tashi Lhunpo, "so as to build a fortified mansion here in the midst of an enemy [i.e., Kagyü] camp."[611] He served effectively as abbot for the last decades of his life, improving the monastery in various ways and promoting the study and practice of the stages of the path as taught by Tsongkhapa

609. Lg*NTCG* 7b [410].

610. Willis 1995, 43–47, Gardner 2009a, Zasep 2019, 34, and below, part 5, section 2.

611. Willis 1995, 45.

and the generation and completion stages of the Yamāntaka and Kālacakra tantras.

He wrote relatively little, and the texts we do have—the guru-yoga practice transmitted to him by Tsongkhapa, his annotations on the *Great Stages of the Path*,[612] two works on the Madhyamaka view, and expositions of Yamāntaka and Kālacakra practices—do not deal with mahāmudrā as a separate topic. It is noteworthy, however, that one of his writings, *Great Guidance on the Madhyamaka View*,[613] specifies that the text is based upon notes taken by Khedrup Jé on Tsongkhapa's report of what Mañjughoṣa communicated to him about the true meaning of emptiness. The text provides early and important testimony as to the existence of an oral tradition derived from Tsongkhapa (and for the key role of Khedrup Jé in transmitting that tradition), but the tradition to which Baso refers is probably the unique Khedrup transmission rather than the Ganden Hearing Transmission, and in any case it is not explicitly tied to mahāmudrā.

Late in life, Baso became the teacher of the "three Dorjé brothers," three unrelated and rather mysterious great siddhas named Dorjé: Dorjé Palwa of Kham, Palden Dorjé of Tölung, and Chökyi Dorjé, whose parents were from Amdo. He instructed all three, but only to Chökyi Dorjé would he pass on the full Ganden Hearing Transmission along with the emanated scripture.

Chökyi Dorjé

Chökyi Dorjé, also known by the Sanskrit equivalent of his name, Dharmavajra (ca. 1455–ca. 1555),[614] is regarded as the emanation of an already awakened mahāsiddha, hence essentially timeless and immortal. He took birth in Central Tibet as the son of a wandering yogī and yoginī. As a child, he traveled with them on their pilgrimage rounds, eventually arriving at Ganden. There, at age eleven, he met Baso Chökyi Gyaltsen, who had been alerted by Vajrayoginī

612. Willis (1995, 179n202) believes that Baso did not write this.

613. Bs*DMTK*. I thank Laura Gibson for bringing this text to my attention and for sharing with me her draft translation of it.

614. Willis 1995, 49–55, Gardner 2015, Zasep 2019, 34, and below, part 5, section 2. Since Chökyi Dorjé is considered an immortal mahāsiddha, he is not assigned dates in the traditional literature. Gardner, however, gives his birth date as 1457, and I myself have proposed approximate conjectural dates of 1455–1555 by drawing on our knowledge of the birth and death dates of Baso and Ensapa, and from Yeshé Gyaltsen's report (in Yg*LZGM* 10b–13a [220–25]) of Chökyi Dorjé's age when Baso Chökyi Gyaltsen took him on as a student, the length of time he studied with Baso, Ensapa's age when taken on by him as a student, and the claim that he dwelled in his emanation body for a hundred years or more.

that a child would soon arrive to whom the Ganden Hearing Transmission should be entrusted. Baso ordained the child as a novice, naming him Chökyi Dorjé, and nurtured him spiritually for a number of years, leading him gradually through the stages of the sūtra and mantra paths, and finally conferring upon him the teachings of the hearing transmission, along with the emanated scripture. After receiving complete instruction in the practices of the hearing transmission, Chökyi Dorjé left Ganden and spent some time at Drepung, where he studied the Perfection of Wisdom, Madhyamaka, and the Vinaya and was granted full ordination. Moving on to Tsang, he received detailed tantric teachings from a number of important masters. He worked assiduously at all the practices he had learned, not because he had to—he was, after all, already a mahāsiddha—but so as to show others the importance of engaging with the full spectrum of religious techniques.

Eventually, he moved to isolated areas, where he spent much of his time in retreat. Tsongkhapa came to him in visions and gave him further teachings from the hearing transmission, including the special guru-yoga practice for visualizing the "three-tiered being" (*sems dpa' gsum brtsegs can*): one's own guru in the form of Tsongkhapa, at whose heart is the Buddha Śākyamuni, at whose heart, in turn, is the primordial buddha Vajradhara (often with his consort, Dharmadhātvīśvarī). This would become a common feature of Geluk guru-yoga practice. Chökyi Dorjé could have passed into the rainbow body at any point he chose, but he retained his mortal form at least until he could hand over the Ganden Hearing Transmission to its next suitable recipient, Ensapa. He did so in the mid–1520s, but if the claim that he lived a century is at all credible, then he remained in his body for at least another three decades. Although Yeshé Gyaltsen attributes to him a song in which, in typical fashion, he supplicates his guru, Baso, to reside at the crown of his head,[615] as an immortal siddha, Chökyi Dorjé left little to nothing in the way of writings,[616] hence no explicit discussion of mahāmudrā or any mahāmudrā lineage of which he might be a part. Nevertheless, in *Highway of the Conquerors* Paṇchen Chögyen describes the Geden Oral Tradition mahāmudrā practice as that of "Dharmavajra, father and son": Chökyi Dorjé and Ensapa.

615. Willis 1995, 52–53.

616. The Buddhist Digital Resource Center (ID no. P994) attributes no texts at all to him, while the Fourteenth Dalai Lama (Dalai Lama and Berzin 1997, 109) credits him with a text entitled the *Guru Yoga of the Three-Tiered Being* (*Sems dpa' gsum brtsegs can bla ma'i rnal 'byor*). I have not been able to track down this text.

The Great Ensapa

Ensapa Losang Döndrup (1505–66)[617] was a native of Tsang, a great bodhisattva whose birth, Yeshé Gyaltsen tells us, was accompanied by such extraordinary miracles that two of his future teachers—Khenpo Jelekpa and Khyabchok Palsang—were prompted to visit him not long after he entered the world, like the magi who visited the Christ child. He developed a special connection with Khyabchok Palsang, who became his root guru and helped guide him in his first steps on the path. Ordained at age eleven, Ensapa spent considerable time at Drepung, Tashi Lhunpo, and other monastic centers studying both sūtra and mantra practices under eminent masters of the day and progressing with remarkable speed, aided by visionary encounters with Mañjughoṣa and Tsongkhapa. At seventeen, he caught smallpox; while in quarantine, he was approached by Chökyi Dorjé, who knew he was destined to hold the Ganden Hearing Transmission. After a meeting at a wilderness hermitage, in which "the manner of communication between the two of them was like the pouring of water from one vessel into another,"[618] Ensapa requested the transmission in a verse, as cited by Yeshé Gyaltsen:

> In this present time, please bestow upon just me
> apprehension of the hearing transmission that is the essence of the speech
> of the guru known as Losang Drakpa,
> the supreme, prized pupil of Mañjughoṣa.[619]

Thereupon, Chökyi Dorjé conveyed to him the teachings of the hearing transmission, along with the emanated scripture.

For the next sixteen years, inspired in part by the example of Milarepa, to whom he likened himself,[620] Ensapa adopted the lifestyle of a wandering yogī, traveling from one hermitage to another and gaining miraculous powers, extraordinary linguistic abilities, and great spiritual realizations. Eventually, he returned to Drepung, took full ordination, and once more "took on the deportment and activities that were in accordance with the Dharma

617. See Willis 1995, 53–70, Adams 2008b, Zasep 2019, 35–36, and below, part 5, section 2.

618. Willis 1995, 64–65.

619. Cited at Yg*LZGM* 13a [225].

620. See Mullin 1997, 73, and below, page 450.

and Vinaya,"[621] though he continued to live mostly in retreat for another nine years. Around 1547, his disciples built a monastery for him at one of his favorite retreat places, Ensa, in Tsang, and he settled down there.

In his later years, Ensapa attracted a large number of disciples, including Sangyé Yeshé, who met Ensapa when still a boy and later would receive the Ganden Hearing Transmission from him. Ensapa taught these disciples a range of subjects, including aspects of the hearing transmission that were suitable for a more general audience, especially guru yoga.[622] He also wrote a number of texts, including a biography of Khyabchok Palsang; analyses of the Vinaya; commentaries on the stages of the sūtra path and various tantric systems; an exposition of the six Dharmas of Nāropa;[623] an important work on severance practice as understood in the Geluk; *A Teaching on the View*, which summarizes Madhyamaka as expounded by Tsongkhapa; and a guru-yoga text entitled *Source of All Yogic Attainments*. The last-named work describes a lineage—which Ensapa does not name—consisting of Vajradhara, Mañjughoṣa, Nāgārjuna, Kuntu Gé, Lālita,[624] Nāropa, Atiśa, Tsongkhapa, Khedrup Jé, Dulkarwa Lodrö Bé (1400–75), and Ensapa's own master, Chökyi Dorjé.[625] Elsewhere, Ensapa names Baso Chökyi Gyaltsen as Chökyi Dorjé's teacher but does not specify that the two are part of a particular lineage.[626] The membership of this lineage is obviously quite different from what would become the standard list, but it may suggest an early draft of such a list.

Like the guru-yoga texts, Ensapa's works on severance and Madhyamaka both bear to some degree on Geluk mahāmudrā. Severance is a practice studied by Gelukpas both outside and inside that particular hearing transmission, but it is possible that some of what Ensapa wrote about it drew on previously secret material. *A Teaching on the View*, which is a clear, if largely standard, presentation of Geluk middle way philosophy, does have an intriguing preliminary guru-yoga meditation, in which, after one's guru comes to the crown of one's head and dissolves into one, one experiences bliss and relaxes into a state of mind that involves the projection of no object whatsoever yet is quite clear and luminous.[627] This sort of language is familiar to us from mahāsiddha and

621. Willis 1995, 67.

622. The most accessible collection of Ensapa's guru-yoga liturgies is found in Es*NGSG* 1–25.

623. See Mullin 1997, 71–91.

624. I have not, so far, identified either Kuntu Gé (*kun tu dge*) or Lālita.

625. Es*LMSD* 3a [11].

626. Willis 1995, 51.

627. Es*TKNP* 2b [520]. Cf. Guenther 1976, 116–17, for a translation of this and two other

Marpa Kagyü mahāmudrā texts and anticipates some of the language that will be employed by Paṇchen Chögyen in his mahāmudrā manuals, which also are based on guru-yoga practice. In the colophon to *Highway of the Conquerors,* the Paṇchen quotes a poetic statement of Ensapa's to the effect that in setting forth the stages of the path in a particular text, he had decided not "at present" to commit to writing "the ultimate, special instruction on mahāmudrā, / which is not at present public knowledge in the Land of Snows."[628] Such an assertion clearly implies that Ensapa (perhaps like Tsongkhapa before him) knew, practiced, and even taught mahāmudrā, and could have written about it, if the circumstances had been propitious.

Khedrup Sangyé Yeshé

Unlike his two predecessors in the lineage, who spent much or all of their lives as wandering yogīs, Khedrup Sangyé Yeshé (1525–91)[629] followed a more conventional path, becoming a monk while still a boy and remaining in robes until his death. A native of Tsang, he traveled to Tashi Lhunpo when he was fifteen, thence to Tanak Monastery. There, he met his root guru, Gendun Losang, who taught him Buddhist logic and various mundane sciences. Returning to Tashi Lhunpo, he studied a range of Sūtra Vehicle texts and became a master debater. He was made head disciplinarian of Tashi Lhunpo at twenty-six. When his term was up, after further Sūtra Vehicle study, he determined to practice the Vajrayāna and traveled to Lhasa to enter the Lower Tantric College of Ganden Monastery. En route, he stopped at Ensa Monastery, where he first met Ensapa. He entreated the master to protect his practice and vowed to return at the completion of his tantric studies. He stayed at the tantric monastery for over a year then returned to Ensa to study intensively with Ensapa. Ensapa entrusted him with the Ganden Hearing Transmission—though not, perhaps, with the emanated scripture: according to Paṇchen Chögyen's *Like a Treasure Inventory*, when Sangyé Yeshé asked Ensapa for the book, he was told, "Since it is an emanated scripture, you will see it when the time is right; if the time is not right, then even if today it is not concealed, you will not see it."[630] Yeshé Gyaltsen quotes this statement in his *Bright Lamp of the Excel-*

Ensapa passages on the view cited by Yeshé Gyaltsen.

628. Bz*GBZL* 5a [89]; cf. Dalai Lama and Berzin 1997, 102. I have not been able to locate the passage in Ensapa's writings.

629. See Willis 1995, 73–82, Zasep 2019, 36–37, and below, part 5, section 2.

630. B*TKBT* 10b–11a [584–85].

lent Path, adding, "after that, it is not clearly stated that the emanated scripture is extant."[631]

After parting from Ensapa, Sangyé Yeshé served twice as abbot at Riwo Gephel Monastery, but eventually he settled at Ensa, where in his final years, he attracted a number of disciples—including his lineage successor (and Ensapa's incarnation), Losang Chökyi Gyaltsen—and wrote texts on a variety of topics, with a special emphasis on guru-yoga practices and tantric ritual procedures. In his writings, Sangyé Yeshé alludes to mahāmudrā only occasionally. Two of his spiritual songs, which focus on the experience of tantric great bliss, begin with the salutation "I bow down to mahāmudrā" but do not mention the term thereafter.[632] A question-and-answer text on completion-stage practices quotes a description of views of the nature of mind in a text on Kagyü mahāmudrā by the earlier Geluk master Khedrup Norsang Gyatso.[633] Finally, a text on training in view and meditation refers to the process of recognizing the nature of mind by way of a special pith instruction and then single-pointedly meditating on the nature thus recognized.[634] However, in his *Guru Yoga of the Ensa Oral Transmission*, Sangyé Yeshé identifies—and identifies with—a special Geluk oral lineage that is very much like the one finalized by Paṇchen Chögyen, consisting as it does of Tsongkhapa, Khedrup Jé (rather than Jampal Gyatso), Baso, Chökyi Dorjé, and Ensapa.[635] And while Sangyé Yeshé does not specify that mahāmudrā is part of this lineage, the fact that Paṇchen Chögyen mentions or quotes his guru's oral instructions on mahāmudrā several times in *Highway of the Conquerors*[636] strongly suggests that Sangyé Yeshé did, in fact, possess such a teaching—but like Ensapa and Tsongkhapa before him, he chose not to write it down.

In short, when most of Paṇchen Chögyen's predecessors in the Ganden Hearing Transmission (including Khedrup Jé) employed the term *mahāmudrā* in their writings, they usually did so in predictable tantric contexts, and when they did engage in discourse familiar from discussions of mahāmudrā in the Kagyü and elsewhere, they did so without employing the term. Such literary

631. Cited at Yg*LZGM* 13b [226]. For alternative accounts of the duration of the emanated scripture, which insist it was held by Losang Chökyi Gyaltsen, or even Yeshé Gyaltsen, see Willis 1995, 161–62n114.

632. Sy*SGDL* 3a, 3b [133, 134].

633. Sy*SGDL* 13a, [153]; for a translation of Norsang's text, see part 5, section 7, below.

634. Sy*TGNP* 2a [342].

635. Sy*ESKG* 2b [455].

636. For instance, Bz*GBZL* 5b [90], and Bz*GBZL* 4a [87] (verse 37).

evidence may provide scant basis for arguing that any of these masters possessed a Geluk system of mahāmudrā, and it is quite clear that none of them wrote it down, leaving the task to Losang Chökyi Gyaltsen. On the other hand, while the absence of any written account of Geluk mahāmudrā by a member of the hearing transmission before Paṇchen Chögyen might tempt us to conclude that the system was indeed his invention, the circumstantial evidence provided by his quotations from his two immediate predecessors, Ensapa and Sangyé Yeshé, points to the probability, though not the certainty, that the system does predate Paṇchen Chögyen, being traceable at least as far back as Ensapa, and to the possibility that it could really have been taught by Tsongkhapa himself. Again, though, the evidence is circumstantial, and the matter cannot be settled beyond a reasonable doubt.

8. From Tsongkhapa to Paṇchen Chögyen: Masters Outside the Main Line of the Hearing Transmission

THE EARLY MASTERS of the Ganden Hearing Transmission were far from the only great Gelukpa masters between Tsongkhapa and Paṇchen Chögyen. Here, we will briefly examine the works of a connected series of lamas who are in some cases better known than the teachers within the hearing transmission: the First Dalai Lama Gendun Drup, Khedrup Norsang Gyatso, the Second Dalai Lama Gendun Gyatso, Paṇchen Sönam Drakpa, the Third Dalai Lama Sönam Gyatso, and Paṇchen Chögyen's contemporary Khöntön Paljor Lhundrup. These teachers—who also interacted with members of the Ganden Hearing Transmission—form their own master-disciple chain of succession, and all sorts of Gelukpa teachings must have passed from one to the other. Unlike the members of the hearing transmission, however, they do not constitute a special lineage identified by later tradition. As we will see, mahāmudrā figures to a greater or lesser degree in the writings of all of them, and has a particular importance for Khedrup Norsang Gyatso, Paṇchen Sönam Drakpa, and Khöntön Paljor Lhundrup—though not, perhaps, in the way we might expect.

Gendun Drup, the First Dalai Lama

Just as Khedrup Jé was probably unaware that one day he would be counted as the first in a distinguished incarnation lineage, his younger contemporary, Gendun Drup (1391–1474),[637] likely had no inkling that he would eventually be regarded as the First Dalai Lama. Quite apart from his posthumous apotheosis, he enjoyed a brilliant career as one of Tsongkhapa's last great disciples and as the main promulgator of Jé Rinpoché's teachings in west-central Tibet, where he founded the monastery that would grow to be one of the most vital of all Geluk institutions, Tashi Lhunpo. He was born in 1391 to nomadic

637. On Gendun Drup's life, see, e.g., Gendun Drub 1981, 9–16, Mullin 2001, 51–86, and Shen 2005, 33–41.

farmers near Sakya, in Tsang. When he was seven, his father died, and he was sent to the great Kadam monastery at Narthang, where he studied under the abbot, Drupa Sherab, and gained a reputation as an excellent young scholar. In 1415, at age twenty-four, he traveled to Ü, where he met Tsongkhapa at Ganden. Legend tells us that at their first meeting, Jé Rinpoché cut off a patch of his robe and presented it to Gendun Drup, predicting great things for the boy. He became the last of Tsongkhapa's major disciples, and in the four years that remained of Jé Rinpoché's life, he imbibed the master's teachings as deeply as he could. After Tsongkhapa's death, Gendun Drup grew close to his lama's great tantric disciple, Sherab Sengé, with whom he traveled throughout Ü and Tsang for twelve years, spreading Geluk teachings. In 1432, he became abbot of Tanak Rikhu, a Sakya monastery in Tsang that he converted to the Geluk. He also maintained a hermitage at Jangchen Monastery, where he attracted a large number of students. In 1447, inspired by a vision and guided by ḍākinīs, he founded Tashi Lhunpo Monastery in Shigatsé, a region dominated at that time by the Sakya and Kagyü, many of whom opposed his efforts. Just as Tsongkhapa had in Lhasa, he established a great New Year's prayer festival (*mönlam*) at Tashi Lhunpo, which quickly became the main Geluk outpost in Tsang and would, more than a century after his death, become the seat of the Paṇchen Lamas.

Like so many of the greatest Tibetan lamas, Gendun Drup lived a life that combined scholarship, retreat, and large-scale public works. His collected writings are less extensive and influential than those of Tsongkhapa, Khedrup Jé, and Gyaltsab Jé, but his detailed discussions of the Vinaya are still read in Geluk monasteries to this day, as are his lucid commentary on Dharmakīrti's *Exposition of Valid Cognition* and his explanations of such vital Tibetan Buddhist topics as mind training, Madhyamaka, and the Kālacakra tantra.[638] The biographical literature about Gendun Drup points neither to any knowledge of the Ganden Hearing Transmission nor to a strong connection with mahāmudrā teachings—though if they were extant during his life, he almost certainly would have been aware of them. In his own writings—even more than in the case of Tsongkhapa or Khedrup Jé—explicit or implicit references to *mahāmudrā* are few and far between. He does discuss the term overtly in his *Notes on Kālacakra*, where (as in so many yoginī tantras) it is said to refer both to a consort in completion-stage sexual yoga practice and to the unchanging bliss that results from union with that consort. It also refers to the visualized and purified "empty form" that is the basis of the form body one will

638. Texts on the last three, and other, topics are translated in Gendun Drub 1981.

achieve with buddhahood.[639] Elsewhere, without mentioning the term specifically, Gendun Drup alludes to practices that, by his time, had come to be associated with mahāmudrā, especially among the Kagyü. In a text on mind training that is based on verses by Atiśa, he stresses the necessity of examining the nature of the unborn mind—that is, ascertaining that mind is intrinsically empty of being produced in any truly existent manner.[640] Later in the same text—and again drawing from Atiśa—he encourages us to view all confused appearances as the four buddha bodies, on the grounds that, like the buddha bodies, they are unborn, unceasing, and unabiding. "The foremost guardian of these precepts," he adds, "is meditation on emptiness."[641] As resonant with mahāmudrā discourse as these passages are, they are commonplace in Tibetan literature and cannot count as evidence that Gendun Drup was specifically invoking mahāmudrā discourse in his discussions.

Khedrup Norsang Gyatso

It was Gendun Drup's disciple, Khedrup Norsang Gyatso (1423–1513), who became the first Geluk master to devote a text entirely to mahāmudrā—though not the mahāmudrā of the Ganden Hearing Transmission. Norsang was born at Tanak Rangjung, in Tsang, in 1423.[642] A prodigy, he entered nearby Drakmar Chöding Monastery at thirteen. He moved on to Rikhu Chödé, where he studied the Tripiṭaka under the resident lama, Wangchuk Drakpa Sangpo, and with visiting Gelukpa luminaries such as Gendun Drup and Sherab Sangpo. Eventually, he went to Tashi Lhunpo to study with Gendun Drup, focusing on the Indian Buddhist classics and philosophical systems as well as the writings and oral instructions of Atiśa and Tsongkhapa. In his mid-thirties, he went to Ü, traveling the debate circuit and taking full ordination at Ganden. Shortly afterward, in 1460, he left for Ölkha, site of Tsongkhapa's great retreats some seventy years before. There, he studied the tantras under Chöjé Chökyi Drakpa, and, "without the slightest concern for this life, practicing austerities, he lived a life like that of the lord of yogins, Milarepa,"[643] traveling from hermitage to hermitage. He

639. Gendun Drub 1981, 151–52.

640. Gendun Drub 1981, 72–73.

641. Gendun Drub 1981, 77–78.

642. The summary that follows is based upon the biography of Norsang in Yeshé Gyaltsen's *Biographies of the Lineage Lamas of the Stages of the Path* (Yg*LRNT* 766–68); see also Khedrup Norsang Gyatso 2004, xv, and Cabezón 2017.

643. Yg*LRNT* 768.

lived this way for many years, meditating assiduously, gaining realizations, having visions, remembering his own and others' past lives, maintaining the practice lineage of Tsongkhapa, and eventually mastering the entirety of both the sūtra and mantra paths. Later in life, he began composing texts, focusing most of his attention on the tantric systems of Guhyasamāja and, especially, Kālacakra, though he also wrote influential works on astrology. Norsang attracted a number of disciples, including Gendun Gyatso—posthumously recognized as the Second Dalai Lama—who met him in Ölkha in 1498 and credited him with deepening his understanding of Kālacakra and Madhyamaka. Norsang died in 1513.

As noted, most of his literary output focuses on the unexcelled yoga tantras, especially the Kālacakra. His *Ornament of Stainless Light* remains one of the most influential of all Geluk Kālacakra treatises.[644] Needless to say, given the importance of the concept of the mahāmudrā of empty form in Kālacakra completion-stage practices, the *Ornament*—like any work on Kālacakra—addresses the topic in its discussion of those practices.[645] Norsang's most significant contribution to Geluk discourse on mahāmudrā, however, is the text entitled *Bright Lamp of Mahāmudrā: Proving the Kagyü and Geluk Have a Single Intention*.[646] The subtitle notwithstanding (according to Thuken Chökyi Nyima, it may be a later addition),[647] the *Bright Lamp* has relatively little to do with the Geluk tradition and does not describe a distinctively Geluk mahāmudrā practice. Rather, it is primarily an exposition of mahāmudrā as understood by the founding masters of the Kagyü. Norsang's initial homage is to the "the early Kagyüpas," and he describes his text as "a brief summary of the ways of meditating on mahāmudrā taught by those holy spiritual friends . . . the early Kagyüpas" (Nz*PCSG* 1). Nearly all of his quotations from Tibetan authors are from Kagyü masters, most often Phakmo Drupa, but also Marpa, Milarepa, and Jikten Sumgön; by contrast Tsongkhapa is only quoted a handful of times. Furthermore, the categories through which he analyzes mahāmudrā—especially sudden and gradual paths—are more common to Kagyü discourse than to Geluk. For Norsang, early Kagyü mahāmudrā is "the way of meditating on primordial mind intended in Śrī Saraha's *Dohā*" (1) and the writings of other mahāsiddhas, which reflect the

644. For a complete English translation, see Khedrup Norsang Gyatso 2004.

645. See Khedrup Norsang Gyatso 2004, e.g., chaps. 34–36.

646. Translated below in part 5, section 7. I am grateful to John Davenport for bringing this text to my attention, and for sending me a photocopy of the edition of the text kept at the Library of Tibetan Works and Archives in Dharamsala.

647. See Tk*SGML* 110–11; trans. Thuken 2009, 152.

teachings of such unexcelled-yoga-tantra traditions as the Kālacakra, Hevajra, and Guhyasamāja; he briefly discusses the approach to mahāmudrā that would be taken by a gradual practitioner but notes that mahāmudrā cannot easily be practiced by such a person. It is clear that for Norsang, tantric practice is the key to mahāmudrā. At the same time, although he relies primarily on Kagyü sources and categories, there is nothing in his account of tantric mahāmudrā that could not be expounded by a Gelukpa.

The *Bright Lamp* begins with an exposition of the primordial mind possessed by all beings, which is synonymous with the connate nature, the mind of luminosity, buddha nature, the basic Dharma body, and so on (2–4). The main part of the text describes the two ways in which the primordial mind is made manifest. First, at the time of death, it naturally and spontaneously occurs, although as Norsang notes, "the luminosity of death cannot be experienced with certainty by ordinary beings," so they continue to circle in saṃsāra (4). The second method by which primordial mind can be manifested is through an unexcelled-yoga–tantra completion-stage meditative concentration that induces the vital winds of the subtle body to enter, abide, and dissolve within the central channel of the subtle body. Practitioners of this method are divided into subitists and gradualists. Subitists, or sudden realizers, are those fortunate few who, by dint of previous practice, are able, simply by meditating single-pointedly on the empty nature of mind, immediately to draw the vital winds into the central channel, manifest the bliss-emptiness awareness of the primordial mind, and traverse the four yogas of mahāmudrā: single-pointedness, nonelaboration, single taste, and nonmeditation (4–6). Norsang identifies the subitist's meditation on the nature of mind with the white panacea and rejects Sapaṇ's criticism of Kagyü expositions of the concept, insisting that it *does* lead to the perfection of both wisdom and compassion, and to all tantric accomplishments (7–12). Gradualists, who are far more numerous, are subdivided according to their degree of experience with tantric practices. Those with no experience of the Mantra Vehicle "must first train the mind in the stages of the paths of the three types of individuals, then train in the method and wisdom of the Perfection Vehicle" (12). Those who practice tantra but have no experience of the completion stage should *not* attempt to manifest the primordial mind through serenity meditation on the nature of mind—it cannot be done. Rather they "first must train their mindstreams on the common path, then fully obtain the four empowerments. Not permitting the vows and pledges assumed at that time to deteriorate, they should grasp the generation stage and train well in the topics of the completion stage" (15). Only then will they be ready to bring the vital winds into the central channel and truly manifest the primordial mind.

By way of conclusion, Norsang asserts that the early Kagyü masters divided mahāmudrā practitioners into three types (16). The sharp-witted may be subitists, or they may be gradualists who have traversed both tantric stages in a systematic fashion. The medium-witted are still learning how to bring the vital winds into the central channel. The dull-witted, who have no experience of the completion stage, must concentrate single-pointedly on the nature of mind, then investigate whether that mind truly exists. Ascertaining that it does not truly exist, they place their minds single-pointedly on that lack of true existence, which is "meditation on emptiness as a nonaffirming negation," as taught to Norsang by his guru, Chökyi Drakpa, based on the instructions of the Kagyü master Nyernyi Rinpoché (16). It is this last style of meditation, that of the dull-witted, that most closely approximates what masters of the Ganden Hearing Transmission consider sūtra mahāmudrā. Indeed, it is the main concern of Paṇchen Chögyen's mahāmudrā root text; for Norsang, on the other hand, focused as he is on tantra, it is almost literally an afterthought.

Gendun Gyatso, the Second Dalai Lama

Khedrup Norsang Gyatso's most notable disciple was Gendun Gyatso, later recognized as the Second Dalai Lama (1475–1542).[648] He was born in Tanak, in Tsang, to a distinguished and eclectic Buddhist family. His great-grandfather, Kunga Sangpo, was a lay administrator who renounced worldly life to study with masters of the Dakpo and Shangpa Kagyü lineages, while his grandfather, Dönyö Gyaltsen, learned not only these traditions but various ideas and practices associated with the Nyingma, Sayka, and Shiché, as well. His father, Kunga Gyaltsen, was a celebrated Nyingma teacher, and his mother, Kunga Palmo, was a yoginī believed to be the incarnation of Drowai Sangmo, the consort of the early Drukpa Kagyü master Götsangpa. Both his parents were students, as well, of Gendun Drup.[649] At the time of Gendun Gyatso's birth, in 1476, the tulku system was largely undeveloped among Gelukpas, yet even while very young the boy implied strongly that he was an incarna-

648. Gendun Gyatso wrote an autobiography when in his forties (1528) and also was the subject of informative biographies by various later writers, including the Fifth Dalai Lama's regent, Desi Sangyé Gyatso, whose account is condensed in Mullin 1985, 199–211. Other useful sources on Gendun Gyatso's life include Mullin 1994, 39–117, which draws on a wide range of sources; Mullin 2001, 87–130; and Heller 2005, which draws primarily on his autobiography.

649. Indeed, Gendun Gyatso reports in his autobiography (Mullin 1994, 44) that his mother "had received many of the most profound Ganden oral transmissions directly from the First Dalai Lama." This indicates clearly that there was a sense among Gelukpas as early as the 1520s that there were special transmissions being handed down with the tradition.

tion both of the great Kadampa master Dromtönpa and of Gendun Drup. He received most of his early education from his father, who taught him a vast number of Perfection and (especially) Mantra Vehicle practices from virtually every Tibetan lineage but the Geluk, including mahāmudrā traditions from both the Dakpo and Shangpa Kagyü. At age eleven he was installed as Gendun Drup's incarnation at Tashi Lhunpo, then ordained as a novice. He began his Geluk education at Tashi Lhunpo, but—due perhaps to resentment of his incarnate status, perhaps to suspicion of his family's trans-sectarian pedigree—he found the atmosphere there increasingly uncomfortable and departed for Central Tibet while still in his late teens. He settled at Drepung, where he studied the Geluk perspective on various Perfection and Mantra Vehicle texts and practices under Jamyang Lekpai Chöjor, from whom he also received full ordination. Though he was "officially" a Gelukpa, his personal practice throughout his life included a range of techniques drawn from all the Buddhist traditions of Tibet.[650]

In 1498, he began a period of travel and retreat. He went first to Ölkha, where he met Khedrup Norsang Gyatso, and received from him intensive instruction on the Kālacakra and Guhyasamāja tantras and on Tsongkhapa's approach to Madhyamaka. These instructions led to some of the deepest realizations of his life, and he came to regard Norsang as one of his two most important teachers, along with his own father.[651] After a number of months spent traveling and practicing with Norsang, Gendun Gyatso continued his travels, going into retreat in Yarlung, visiting his father in Tsang, and, like Tsongkhapa, meditating intensively at Radreng. In 1509, he founded Chökhor Gyal Monastery near Lhamö Lhatso, a great lake southeast of Lhasa. Chökhor Gyal came to serve as a personal monastery for the Dalai Lamas, and Lhamö Lhatso, after being empowered by Gendun Gyatso, became a source of visions and prophecies, including those related to selection of subsequent Dalai Lamas. In 1512, with the earlier acrimony forgotten, he was invited back to Tashi Lhunpo as abbot, and in 1517 he was made abbot of Drepung. In his years there, he restored Geluk control of the Great Prayer Festival of Lhasa, which had been under Karmapa control for nearly two decades, and established a residence within Drepung called the Ganden Phodrang, which would serve as the main seat of the Dalai Lamas until the completion of the Potala over a century later. In 1528, while still presiding over Drepung, he became abbot of Sera as well. In his later years, he attracted many disciples, wrote voluminously, and gained both political and religious influence in many parts of

650. Mullin 1985, 210.

651. Mullin 1985, 210.

central and western Tibet. He died in 1542, with the reputation of the Geluk in general and his incarnation lineage in particular now well established.

If the First Dalai Lama's teachings and writings focused primarily, if not exclusively, on Perfection Vehicle topics, Gendun Gyatso's tilt heavily, but not exclusively, toward the tantras. He composed a number of treatises on Cakrasaṃvara and also focused, among others, on Yamāntaka,[652] Guhyasamāja, and the six Dharmas taught by Nāropa and Nigumā,[653] respectively. He also composed a ritual *Offering to the Guru* that was consulted by Paṇchen Chögyen as he composed his own great text in that genre. His nontantric writings were significant as well: they include an autobiography, a biography of his father, a commentary on Nāgārjuna's *Seventy Verses on Emptiness* (*Śūnyatāsaptatī*), an exposition of the *Book of Kadam*, a concise analysis of Indian tenet systems,[654] and a collection of spiritual songs that is among the earliest and largest produced by any Gelukpa.[655]

Given his eclectic religious background and practice, and given his tutelage under Norsang Gyatso, we might expect that Gendun Gyatso would have much to say about mahāmudrā. As with other great Geluk masters, of course, he refers to it where appropriate in his works on tantra, for instance during his discussion of the four seals in his analysis of the illusory-body practice in his summary of the six Dharmas of Nigumā.[656] We also would anticipate that mahāmudrā would be mentioned in his spiritual songs, which often are signed with such self-descriptions as "the yogī of space," "the mad beggar monk," or "melodious laughing vajra," and often invoke the triad of Nāropa, Dromtönpa, and Milarepa for inspiration. Certainly, his poems are composed in a style that sometimes suggests the ecstatic utterances of the great Kagyü spiritual poets, and he sings often of his understanding of emptiness, which in many contexts is taken to be synonymous with mahāmudrā,[657] yet the term *mahāmudrā* does not, so far as I can ascertain, occur in them.

Perhaps his most explicit discussion of the topic is found, somewhat unexpectedly, near the conclusion of his text on tenet systems, *A Raft to Cross the Ocean of Indian Buddhist Thought*. In a discussion of the paths traversed according to the various systems, he notes that the unique feature of the

652. See Mullin 1985, 73–91.

653. See Mullin 1985, 92–152.

654. See Mullin 1985, 153–82.

655. See Mullin 2001, 121–252.

656. Mullin 1985, 130–31.

657. See, e.g., Mullin 1994, pp. 136–38, 204–207, 210–12, and 223–25; Mullin 2001, 121–22.

Prāsaṅgika Madhyamaka is "the doctrine of perceiving how things are empty of a true reality status while understanding this empty nature as the true import of dependent arising,"[658] and then asks how this Prāsaṅgika view of the two truths relates to mahāmudrā, which "these days is a term . . . widely used in Tibet."[659] His answer is that "most early mahāmudrā teachers held views in accord with those of the Prāsaṅgika Mādhyamikas."[660] He does specify that *mahāmudrā* is a decidedly tantric term, describing it as "the path of subtle insight into . . . emptiness . . . an insight born together [i.e., connate, *sahaja*] with the great bliss of unexcelled-yoga-tantra practice."[661] He goes on to analyze an excerpt from a poem by Milarepa, and makes it clear that he believes the view expressed by the great yogī to be precisely that of the Prāsaṅgika Madhyamaka (as interpreted by Tsongkhapa, anyway), to the effect that on "the ultimate level of truth . . . not a single atom of the universe has true existence. . . . while on the ordinary level of truth, things appear conventionally with only a conventional validity."[662] He concludes—in an aside that might be read as political but probably is not—that he cannot decide whether contemporary mahāmudrā teachers (the vast majority, of course, Kagyüpas) are more akin to the Svātantrika or the Prāsaṅgika.[663] This opinion, to the effect that the great early Kagyüpas were Prāsaṅgikas but that their modern descendants are of less-certain affiliation—hence potentially astray from the pure view of their ancestors—is a common trope among the Gelukpas. It is implicit as far back as Tsongkhapa and becomes increasingly explicit as time goes on and mahāmudrā becomes more and more of a Geluk concern.

Paṇchen Sönam Drakpa

Among Gendun Gyatso's many disciples, none was more distinguished than Paṇchen Sönam Drakpa (1478–1554), who was a major figure in the Geluk world throughout the first half of the sixteenth century.[664] He was born in Lhokha, southeast of Lhasa, in 1478. After early training at Tsethang and

658. Mullin 1994, 180.

659. Mullin 1994, 181.

660. Mullin 1994, 181.

661. Mullin 1994, 181. Brackets mine.

662. Mullin 1994, 181.

663. Mullin 1985, 182.

664. The following biographical summary is based on Panchen Sonam Dragpa 1996, vii–ix, and Chhosphel 2010b. See also Ary 2015.

other local monasteries, he traveled to Lhasa and entered Sera at the age of sixteen. He remained there for eleven years, receiving full ordination at twenty and studying in detail, under Sera's greatest teachers, the traditions surrounding the five great Indian texts underpinning the Geluk curriculum.[665] He also studied the Mantra Vehicle at Sera and in 1505 enrolled at the tantric monastery in upper Lhasa, Gyütö, where he remained for two decades, rising to the position of master (*slob dpon*). In 1535, when he was forty-seven, the Second Dalai Lama appointed him as abbot of Loseling College at Drepung. After serving five years, he was appointed as the Fifteenth Ganden throneholder, a position he held for six years. After eight years in which he was free of administrative responsibilities and able to teach and write at leisure, he was asked in 1544 to be abbot of all of Drepung. During his four years there, he served as the first preceptor and tutor of the young Third Dalai Lama, Sönam Gyatso, and he also accepted the abbacy of Sera, a post he held for nine years, until his death in 1554.

Sönam Drakpa was unique among Gelukpa masters in having served as abbot of all three of the great Lhasa-area monasteries. He also was a prolific scholar, many of whose writings are used to this day in Geluk monastic curricula, particularly that of Loseling College within Drepung. His analyses of the five major Indian Buddhist classics still are highly regarded, and his *General Presentation of the Classes of Tantra* is considered one of the greatest latter-day Geluk analyses of the Mantra Vehicle.[666] He also wrote important works on tenet systems, the *Sublime Continuum*, and the history of the Kadam and Geluk schools. Like those of other Gelukpa scholars, his works on tantric topics make the expected references to mahāmudrā in the appropriate places—for instance in discussing the four seals of yoga tantra or the consorts or bliss-emptiness gnosis of unexcelled yoga tantra.[667] Significantly, he also wrote a major work entirely devoted to mahāmudrā entitled *Six Ornaments to Beautify the Holy Dharma of Mahāmudrā* (Sg*PCGD*). The *Six Ornaments* shows evidence of Sönam Drakpa's familiarity with Khedrup Norsang Gyatso's *Bright Lamp of Mahāmudrā*, but weighing in at fifty-two folios (a hundred pages in book format), it is far longer and more detailed than its predecessor, demonstrating Sönam Drakpa's own wide reading in a range of Indian and Tibetan sources. It does share with the *Bright Lamp* a nearly exclusive focus on Kagyü mahāmudrā; despite an occasional mention of Tsongkhapa and a couple of passing references to a "Geden Oral Transmission" (*dge ldan bka'*

665. See page 133 above.

666. For a translation, see Panchen Sonam Dragpa 1996.

667. Paṇchen Sonam Drakpa 1996, pp. 40–42, 46, and 60.

brgyud),[668] it is no more concerned to transmit a specifically Geluk version of great seal practice than its predecessor—though as we will see, Sönam Drakpa does reflect generally on the differences between Geluk and Kagyü approaches to view, meditation, conduct, and fruit in ways that at least suggest his qualms about Kagyü mahāmudrā and, implicitly, how a Geluk mahāmudrā tradition might be conceived.

As the title indicates, the *Six Ornaments* is built around a description of six approaches to the great seal: (1) the Indian scriptural sources from which the tradition derives, (2) the lives and lineages of the Indian mahāsiddhas and their Kagyüpa successors, (3) the stages-of-the-path teachings that are a necessary preliminary to great seal practice, (4) the circumstances for and actual practice of mahāmudrā meditation, (5) similarities and differences among the Tibetan schools in their Madhyamaka lineages and practices, and (6) a refutation of Sakya Paṇḍita's critique of the Kagyü mahāmudrā practices of his day. We will summarize each of these but pay the most attention to the fourth and fifth ornaments, as they are the most practically and philosophically interesting.

The first ornament, "the ornament of the scriptures and treatises from which the teaching originated" (Sg*PCGD* 434–46), is divided into a brief section on mahāmudrā-related sources in the sūtras and tantras and a longer segment on sources to be found in treatises and commentaries. The discussion of sūtra and tantra sources includes lengthy excerpts from the *Vajra Tent Tantra*, the *Descent to Laṅkā Sūtra*, and the *Perfection of Wisdom in Eight Thousand Lines*, with mentions, as well, of such third-turning scriptures as the *Matrix of the Tathāgata* (*Tathāgatagarbha*) *Sūtra* and the *Jewel Heap* collection, and such second-turning texts as the *King of Concentrations Sūtra*. The discussion of treatise and commentary sources specifies that the major tantric sources are the Seven Attainment Texts, Saraha's Essential Trilogy, and Maitrīpa's Twenty-Five Works on Nonmentation, while—on the authority of Gampopa and his Dakpo Kagyü successors—the major Perfection Vehicle source is the buddha-nature treatise the *Sublime Continuum*, which Sönam Drakpa goes on to summarize briefly.

The second ornament, "the ornament recounting the texts and special instructions of the mahāsiddhas and lamas who came in succession" (437–46), describes the various Indian transmissions of "bliss-emptiness mahāmudrā," including the completion-stage practices received by Tilopa from Vajradhara and a gnosis ḍākinī, then passed on to Nāropa, thence to Marpa; a Guhyasamāja tradition whose human transmitters include Padmavajra,

668. Sg*PCGD* 475, 510.

Anaṅgavajra, Indrabhūti, and others; and the various teachings associated with the Seven Attainment Texts, Saraha's Essential Trilogy, and Maitrīpa's Twenty-Five Works on Nonmentation. Sönam Drakpa goes on to detail the transmission of these texts and traditions to Tibet and then to concentrate on the ideas and activities of Gampopa and his successors in the various Dakpo subschools, including the Karma, Tsal, and Drigung. The explicit discussion of the Kagyü schools and subschools is one of the earliest by a Geluk author and provides information that may well have been available to Paṇchen Chögyen when he composed his mahāmudrā texts.

The third ornament, "the ornament of the way advice on the mahāmudrā path and the stages of the path to awakening are in agreement and not contradictory" (445–57), provides a set of preliminary reflections that should prepare the practitioner for the actual work of mahāmudrā meditation. These are the familiar stages-of-the-path meditations on reliance upon a spiritual friend, the spiritual opportunities entailed by a human rebirth, impermanence and death, karmic cause and effect, the disadvantages of saṃsāra, refuge in the Triple Gem, the necessity of training in the prātimokṣa vows, and training in love, compassion, and the awakening mind. As is typical throughout the text, Sönam Drakpa provides supporting quotations almost exclusively from Kagyü literature.

The fourth ornament, "the ornament of the circumstances for developing the main practice of the triad of view, meditation, and conduct" (457–507), is the longest in the text, accounting for nearly half its bulk. It is divided into six subsections. The first four of these deal briefly with the requisites for proper practice: a good location, good friends, good food and drink, and a good mental disposition. The fifth subsection, on how to maintain mahāmudrā view, meditation, and conduct, is by far the most substantial, and is itself divided and further subdivided. Broadly, and in line with many, if not all, Kagyü formulations current in Sönam Drakpa's day, it categorizes mahāmudrā as either sūtra or mantra. The section on mantra mahāmudrā (461–79) begins with a definition of the term: the tantric *great seal*, says Sönam Drakpa, is "the great seal of bliss-emptiness that is the ascertainment of suchness—which is an emptiness or emptiness-awareness that is a nonaffirming negation—by way of the connate bliss that follows upon the winds' entering, abiding, and dissolving within the central channel."[669] This is followed by an analysis of the meaning of the sudden approach to mahāmudrā; discussions of various tantric

669. Sg*PCGD* 461. It is interesting that here Sönam Drakpa defines the emptiness realized in mantra mahāmudrā as a nonaffirming negation, which is a typically Geluk perspective, but later will specify that the Kagyü perspective on emptiness entails an affirming negation.

practices that are said to bring about the full realization of the great seal, such as the six Dharmas of Nāropa; and a brief exposition of the mahāmudrā view, which is to be found in the teachings of Maitrīpa. In this regard, says Sönam Drakpa, Maitrīpa's view, while tantric in flavor, is in accord with Madhyamaka, even as described in the sūtra tradition.

The fourth-ornament subsection on sūtra mahāmudrā (479–506) is itself divided into discussions of view, meditation, and conduct. The brief exposition of the view, in turn, briefly discusses serenity (481–83) in terms of meditation on the nature of the mind as described by Kagyüpa masters then goes into considerable depth on the practice of insight (511–29). Among the topics covered in the discussion of insight are ways of applying serenity meditation to realization of the nature of mind, Kagyü practices for "seeking the mind" (*sems 'tshol*), the question of whether "not thinking" is a legitimate form of meditation, and the importance of "not finding" the mind once it has been sought. The section on insight is replete with long quotations from the likes of Milarepa, Shang Rinpoché, Chegompa, Phakmo Drupa, Jikten Sumgön, and other early masters. His analysis of the view complete, Sönam Drakpa turns to a discussion of meditation (501–5), which he analyzes in terms of the four yogas of mahāmudrā, especially as described by Shang Rinpoché, followed by a brief exhortation to engage in proper conduct (505–6). The sixth and final section of the fourth ornament discusses the dedication of merit that follows upon meditation (506–7).

The fifth ornament, "the ornament of knowing [various schools'] views on the intention of the second Dharma wheel according to the way their rationales are asserted, and knowing in particular how each [of those schools] differ" (507–17), is divided into two sections. First comes a general discussion of Madhyamaka in India and Tibet (507–14), which covers the activities of Nāgārjuna and his successors, the distinction between Svātantrika and Prāsaṅgika, various modes of Madhyamaka reasoning, and the rangtong-shentong divide over the nature of emptiness. In his discussion of the last point (509–14), Sönam Drakpa identifies the early Kadampas, the early Sakyapas, and Tsongkhapa as proponents of intrinsic emptiness, and Phadampa Sangyé, the masters of both the Dakpo and Shangpa Kagyü, and Dölpopa Sherab Gyaltsen as proponents of extrinsic emptiness.

The second section of the fifth ornament (514–17) is a brief but striking summary of the basic differences between the Geluk—here identified as "the Mādhyamikas"—and the Dakpo Kagyü with respect to view, meditation, conduct, and fruit. It is worth quoting extensively:

The two agree on the preliminary practices and practices afterward, but they differ on the main practice.

They differ on the sources for knowledge: the Mādhyamikas emphasize the second Dharma wheel, while the Kagyüpas emphasize the third Dharma wheel.

They differ on the essence of the view: the Mādhyamikas give importance to the nonaffirming negation of intrinsic emptiness, while the Kagyüpas posit the affirming negation of extrinsic emptiness.

They differ on the intentional object of meditation: the Mādhyamikas meditate mostly on emptiness of the object, while the Kagyüpas meditate mostly on emptiness of the subject.

They differ on probative reasoning: the Mādhyamikas offer proofs through reasoning based on dependence and so on, while the Kagyüpas offer proofs through reasoning based on reality.

They differ on the conditions giving rise to realization: the Mādhyamikas assert that one first sets forth arguments [conducive to] the realization of [the nature of] the logical predicate and assert that realization arises later from knowledge of [the nature of] the logical subject, while the Kagyüpas say that realization arises from the combination of the blessing of a lama with direct knowledge [of reality] and the devotion of a disciple.

They differ on how to approach the path: the Mādhyamikas approach the path through inference, while the Kagyüpas approach the path through direct perception.

They differ on how to meditate: the Mādhyamikas mostly practice investigative meditation, while the Kagyüpas mostly practice placement meditation. Although it may be explained thus, it is not the case that Kagyüpas don't practice investigative meditation or that Mādhyamikas don't teach placement meditation. Indeed, the Mādhyamikas practice placement meditation through all the stages of serenity meditation, while the Kagyüpas analyze a little when they practice seeking the mind.

They differ on how to engender the final fruit: the Mādhyamikas assert that of the two buddha bodies—the Dharma body and the form body—the wisdom realizing emptiness is the main cause only of the Dharma body, while the Kagyüpas assert that the mahāmudrā view is the main cause of both the Dharma and form bodies. . . .

Thus the view of the realization of emptiness posited by the

> Mādhyamikas and the mahāmudrā yoga posited by the Dakpo Kagyü do indeed differ on the object of meditation and how to meditate, but in the end they are similar in the way they go about destroying self-grasping and are alike in keeping the mind intent on practice while on the path to liberation.[670]

Whether this comparison between Geluk and Kagyü approaches is sufficiently nuanced is a question we cannot address here, but Paṇchen Sönam Drakpa has certainly laid out the ostensible differences between them in stark terms while acknowledging some general points of similarity. His views likely helped shape later Geluk perceptions, including those of Paṇchen Chögyen, regarding the Kagyü approach to mahāmudrā.

The sixth and final ornament, "the ornament of dispelling objections: the real way to refute [Sapaṇ's] *Clear Ascertainment of the Three Vows*" (517–30), analyzes the great Sakya master's criticisms of the Kagyü mahāmudrā practices of his era, especially the white panacea and the single intention. Though Sönam Drakpa's discussion is made up mostly of quotations from Sapaṇ and a few of the Kagyüpas Sapaṇ criticizes, he does at least briefly argue, among other things, that sūtra mahāmudrā, the practice of the four yogas, and other elements of the Kagyü great seal are not mere inventions borrowed from discredited Chinese traditions but have real antecedents in Indian Buddhism, whether in the sūtras and tantras or in the works of the mahāsiddhas.

Sönam Drakpa brings the *Six Ornaments* to a conclusion with a dedication of merit and some final verses.

Sönam Gyatso, the Third Dalai Lama

Paṇchen Sönam Drakpa's most important disciple, the dynamic and peripatetic Sönam Gyatso (1543–88),[671] was born to a distinguished family in Kyishö in Central Tibet in 1543. Even by the standards of Tibetan masters, he was a remarkable prodigy, recognized as Gendun Gyatso's incarnation at two, enthroned at Drepung and given his novice vows by Sönam Drakpa at three, and made abbot of Drepung at nine, then Sera at sixteen. After his full ordination at twenty-two, he traveled, studied, and taught extensively in Ü and Tsang. Among other institutional activities, he founded the residence at Drepung that eventually would move to the Potala and become Namgyal Col-

670. Sg*PCGD* 514–17.

671. Biographical information drawn from Mullin 2001, 131–63, Kollmar-Paulenz 2005, 52–59, and Adams 2008a.

lege, the "private monastery" of the Dalai Lamas. In 1577 he was summoned to the court of Altan Khan, who had become the most powerful Mongol ruler since the days of Kubilai Khan, and a distinct threat to Tibet. In the course of a long and perilous journey to the Mongol domain, he spread Geluk teachings in Amdo and founded Kumbum Monastery near the site of Tsongkhapa's birth. At the Khan's court, gifts and titles were exchanged: Altan was described by Sönam Gyatso as "king of truth, equal to the god Brahmā," while the Khan bestowed on his Tibetan visitor the Mongol title Wonderful Vajradhara, Good, Brilliant Commendable Ocean. Henceforth and retroactively, the Mongol word for "ocean" (a translation of the Tibetan *rgya mtsho*) would be applied to the masters in Sönam Gyatso's incarnation lineage, making them the *Dalai* Lamas (or "oceanic gurus")—though the title was used more by Mongols than Tibetans until recent times. In any case, Sönam Gyatso and Altan Khan established a "priest-patron" (*yon mchod*) relationship that led to the large-scale conversion of Mongols to Buddhism and the assurance of Mongol support to the Geluk—which would prove crucial to the order's fortunes in the century to come. After a time in Mongolia, Sönam Gyatso returned to eastern Tibet, further spreading Geluk teachings in Amdo and venturing southward to Kham, where he founded a great monastery at Lithang—one of the first significant Geluk outposts in that populous region. Though urgently requested to return to Central Tibet, he instead traveled once more to Mongolia, where he continued his missionary work and died in 1588, having, in his forty-five years, thoroughly and forever changed the religious and political landscape of Tibet.

Sönam Gyatso's nearly constant travel seems to have left him little time for writing, and his collected works are far from voluminous. Most of the texts we have are tantric in orientation, with a special emphasis on rituals related to protector deities, though he did compose an important stages-of-the-path text, the *Essence of Refined Gold*, as well as a variety of prayers, poems, and songs of praise,[672] and he left several documents related to his lengthy stays in Mongolia.[673] Although his works are, typically, replete with references to emptiness, great bliss, and the coalescence of the two, mahāmudrā does not seem to figure in his overt concerns at all—yet we are told in a later biography that even before he was fully ordained, he had received teachings on the "hearing traditions coming from Tsongkhapa" from Tölungpa Palden Dorjé, one of the three mysterious "Dorjé brothers" who had studied with Baso Chökyi Gyaltsen. After his ordination, Sönam Gyatso visited Ensa, where he met Khedrup

672. For translations of the *Essence* and a number of shorter texts, see Sonam Gyatso 1982.

673. For translations, see Sonam Gyatso 1982 and Mullin 2001, 157–75.

Sangyé Yeshé and paid homage to a statue of the great Ensapa.[674] Interestingly, in a ritual passage in his *Essence of Refined Gold,* Sönam Gyatso does list a version of a hearing-transmission lineage he had received, which differs only slightly from that of Sangyé Yeshé: Tsongkhapa, Tokden Jampal Gyatso, Khedrup Jé, Baso Chökyi Gyaltsen, Chökyi Dorjé, Ensapa, and Khedrup Sangyé Yeshé.[675] As we have seen, it is uncertain to what degree the hearing transmission at that time featured mahāmudrā, but Sönam Gyatso's involvement with the tradition further demonstrates that oral teachings stemming from Tsongkhapa—far from being fully restricted—had a place in the broader Geluk educational world as early as the sixteenth century, if not before.

Khöntön Paljor Lhundrup

The final figure in the succession of teachers and pupils we are tracing in this chapter is Khöntön Paljor Lhundrup (1561–1637), whose life is detailed in a biography written by his disciple the Fifth Dalai Lama.[676] He was born in the Central Tibetan region of É. Like Gendun Gyatso, he came from an ancient family. His father, Tsewang Norgyé, was a Nyingma lama, an expert on the *Net of Illusion (Māyājāla) Tantra,* with strong familial connections to the Sakya and a deep understanding of the Kagyü tradition as well. When Khöntönpa was ten, his parents took him to Drepung for instruction on refuge and the awakening mind from the Third Dalai Lama. It is uncertain whether Sönam Gyatso ordained him then or seven years later, but in any case, throughout his teens Khöntönpa studied primarily with his father—who imparted to him a range of Nyingma, Kagyü, Sakya, and other teachings—and to a lesser but still significant extent with the Nyingma master Nyida Sangyé. When Khöntönpa was nineteen or twenty his father died, and he enrolled in Dakpo, a Geluk college southeast of Lhasa, where he began his monastic education. Having acquired a reputation for brilliance on the basis of a short text he wrote on Madhyamaka, he moved on to Jé College at Sera Monastery, where he earned a Lingsé degree. He also studied at Tsethang, where he earned the degree of Rabjampa; Ganden, where he received full ordination in 1594; and the tantric college of Gyümé, where he studied the tantras for four years. In 1601, he was appointed master of a college at Sangphu Monastery and became a tutor to the Fourth Dalai Lama, a Mongolian boy who had just made his way to Tibet. In 1605 Khöntönpa became the fifteenth abbot of Sera Jé, a position

674. Sonam Gyatso 1982, 226–27.

675. Sonam Gyatso 1982, 199.

676. This is summarized in Dalai Lama et al. 2011, 35–48.

he held for fourteen years. In 1611 he went to Drepung to study the *Vajra Garland* (*Vajramālā*) and other tantras with Losang Chökyi Gyaltsen, who became a close friend. Retiring from the Sera Jé abbacy in 1619, he based himself for the rest of his life at the nearby hermitage of Phabongkha. He became a much sought-after teacher, his most notable student being the young Fifth Dalai Lama, to whom he transmitted a variety of Nyingma and other instructions in the mid-1630s. He died in 1637, celebrated as a great nonsectarian master and eventually recognized as belonging to incarnation lineages of both the Nyingma and Geluk.

The Fifth Dalai Lama lists some thirty-three works written by Khöntön, most of them, unfortunately, lost.[677] One composition that has survived, happily for us, is his *Wish-Fulfilling Gem of the Hearing Transmission* (Ph*NGKY*),[678] which focuses on the nature of mind, and how to realize it, in language drawn from the three great contemporaneous Tibetan discourses on the view: the great seal, great perfection, and great middle way (i.e., Geluk). The text, which probably was composed in 1609, is structured as a meditation manual. Its lengthy first section leads the practitioner through a series of contemplations, beginning with a standard list of common and uncommon preliminary practices, then proceeding to an analysis of the root basis of mind and the identification of its connate primordial nature, supported by copious citations from Indian and Tibetan texts. There follows a detailed description of the successive practices of serenity, insight, and postmeditative awareness—all with the nature of mind as the focal point. Then comes a brief discussion of mahāmudrā as ground, path, and fruit, followed by a more extended analysis of mahāmudrā view, meditation, and conduct, of the experiences entailed by the four yogas of mahāmudrā—single-pointedness, nonelaboration, single taste, and nonmeditation—and of the relation between those yogas and the five paths and ten bodhisattva levels of Mahāyāna soteriology. In the last discussion, Khöntönpa enters into his only real polemic: a response to Sakya Paṇḍita's criticism of Kagyü accounts of the four yogas. The second, and final, major section of the *Wish-Fulfilling Gem* is a brief exposition of Tsongkhapa's views on the harmonious relation between the empty, ultimate nature of things and their conventional production through dependent arising; this is followed by a typical Geluk analysis of arguments for the absence of self in either persons or phenomena.

The *Wish-Fulfilling Gem* presents itself as a nonsectarian teaching that

677. Dalai Lama et al. 2011, 141–44.

678. In Pn*KYPS*, this is mistakenly attributed to the eighth Sera abbot Nyaltön Paljor Lhundrup (1427–1514).

stresses the commonalities among mahāmudrā, the great perfection, and Great Madhyamaka. In the introductory section, Khöntönpa specifies that it is derived from teachings on "the general and pervasive view" that he had received as part of a hearing transmission "taught prior to the transmissions of the uncommon instructions of the seminal essence" (*snying thig*),[679] thereby giving it a specifically Nyingma provenance. He lists the ancient Nyingma masters first in the verses of homage, quotes Padmasambhava, Longchenpa, and Nyingma tantras several times in the course of the instructions, and specifies in the colophon that he received the teaching from his own Nyingma teacher, Nyida Sangyé.[680] Despite its Nyingma roots, however, the *Wish-Fulfilling Gem* is predominantly Kagyü in tone: its structure closely approximates that of Kagyü mahāmudrā manuals produced in the sixteenth century, the vast majority of Tibetan authors it cites are Kagyü (Shang Rinpoché and Milarepa are the most often quoted), and its terminology is generally far closer to that of mahāmudrā traditions than to those of the great perfection, containing as it does relatively little of the idiosyncratic language of the latter. Of course, by the late sixteenth century, Kagyü-Nyingma interactions had already led to occasional attempts at synthesis—particularly at the level of discourse about mahāmudrā and the great perfection—and Khöntön's early teachers, his father and Nyida Sangyé, though nominally Nyingmapas, were deeply learned in multiple traditions, including the Kagyü. Whatever their exact provenance, the meditation instructions in the *Wish-Fulfilling Gem* bear a distinctively Kagyü stamp.

The most puzzling element of Khöntön's synthesis is the ambiguous place within it of Geluk teachings. As already noted, the section expounding Tsongkhapa's views on Madhyamaka comes at the very end of the text. It seems, however, less like a culmination of all that has come before than an afterthought, perhaps even tacked on to mollify a Gelukpa audience. Tsongkhapa is presumably the teacher honored as "Guru Mañjuśrī" in the verses of homage, but no element of Geluk analysis appears overtly in the main instructions,[681] nor does any terminology or instruction related to mahāmudrā or the great perfection appear in the section on Tsongkhapa's version of Madhyamaka. This should not surprise us, for if the main instruction was received from Nyingma and/or Kagyü sources, it is unlikely that it would contain Geluk perspectives or arguments. Indeed, Khöntönpa states in his final verses that the views he

679. Dalai Lama et al. 2011, 64.

680. Dalai Lama et al. 2011, 138.

681. The Kadampa masters Atiśa and Drontönpa are cited several times each, but they were, of course, nearly as influential among the Kagyüpas as they were among the Gelukpas.

has chosen to harmonize are those of Padmasambhava and Vimalamitra, Phadampa Sangyé, and such Kagyü masters as Marpa, Milarepa, and Gampopa; Tsongkhapa receives no mention.[682] In this sense, though the *Wish-Fulfilling Gem* may place Geluk teachings in noncontradictory juxtaposition to mahāmudrā (and great perfection) views and practices, it does not really synthesize them in the way that the works of Paṇchen Chögyen do.[683]

Our survey of the succession of masters from Khedrup Jé to Khöntönpa has revealed that for many of the great figures of the Geluk during its first two centuries, mahāmudrā was a tangential topic, discussed primarily in the context of analyses of the tantras and occasionally with reference to Kagyü practices. We have seen, however, that there are one minor and three major exceptions to this generalization. The minor exception is the Second Dalai Lama, Gendun Gyatso, who investigates the philosophical view undergirding Kagyü mahāmudrā traditions, concluding that for the great early Kagyüpas, it was clearly Prāsaṅgika Madhyamaka, while for his Kagyü contemporaries, the affiliation is much less certain. The major exceptions are Khedrup Norsang Gyatso, who devoted his *Bright Lamp* to an analysis of tantric mahāmudrā practices transmitted by the early Kagyüpa masters, Paṇchen Sönam Drakpa, whose *Six Ornaments Beautifying Mahāmudrā* provides both a detailed exploration of Kagyü approaches to the great seal and some thoughtful comparisons between the Kagyü and Geluk, and Khöntön Paljor Lhundrup, whose *Wish-Fulfilling Gem* describes meditations on the nature of mind using language informed by both Nyingma and Geluk traditions but owes its structure and discourse primarily to the Kagyü. Thus, while a few of the masters discussed here produced material of real interest for a study of the place of mahāmudrā in Geluk tradition, nearly all of them treated it as a topic that was affiliated either with Indian tantric systems or with the Tibetan Kagyü. Some of what they wrote undoubtedly influenced Paṇchen Chögyen and other recipients of the Ganden Hearing Transmission, but it is largely within that transmission—and only from the time of Paṇchen Chögyen himself—that we encounter texts that describe a truly Geluk approach to mahāmudrā meditation.

682. Dalai Lama et al. 2011, 137–38.

683. Despite their relatively frequent interactions, there is no evidence to suggest either that Khöntönpa influenced Paṇchen Chögyen's approach to mahāmudrā or vice versa.

9. Paṇchen Chögyen in Focus

Paṇchen Chögyen's Life and Works

Losang Chökyi Gyaltsen lived a long and varied life, which is amply documented in his massive and informative autobiography, left unfinished at his death but completed in 1720 by his successor as Paṇchen Lama, Losang Yeshé (1663–1737).[684] The boy who would become the first to bear the title of Paṇchen Lama was born as Chögyal Palden Sangpo in the village of Drukgya, in the Tsarong region of Tsang, in either 1567 or 1570.[685] His father, Kunga Öser, was a member of the ancient Ba clan and a nephew of the Ensa Monastery abbot, Khedrup Sangyé Yeshé. At an early age, the boy was recognized by Langmikpa Chökyi Gyaltsen as the incarnation of Ensapa; Langmikpa named the boy after himself: Chökyi Gyaltsen. Until his teens, he was tutored at home by relatives, including his grandfather, his elder brother, and his great-uncle, Sangyé Yeshé, who visited every autumn and conferred upon him a variety of blessings, permissions, and empowerments. Already devout, Chökyi Gyaltsen further deepened his commitment to Buddhism at the age of seven, when he feared his life would be cut short. In 1582, aged thirteen, he was sent to Ensa Monastery to study full time with Sangyé Yeshé. He was ordained under the name Losang Chökyi Gyaltsen and began an intensive course of instruction that, over the course of five years, exposed him to a wide range of Geluk texts and practices, from basic instructions on the stages of the path to unique explanations of the generation and completions stages of Guhyasamāja tantra. His spiritual life deepened as well, and he attained the first of his many visions, this one of the goddess Sarasvatī. When he was eighteen, in 1588, he traveled to Tashi Lhunpo, where he entered Thösamling College, so as to study astrology

684. See Bz*AFPL*; Smith 2001, 119–31. For Yeshé Gyaltsen's account of his life, see Willis 1995, 85–96. See also Cabezón 1995, Gardner 2009c, Jampa 2013, 269–78, Zasep 2109, 37–38, and below, part 5, section 2.

685. See Willis 1995, 207n391.

and philosophy under Paljor Gyatso. He returned to Ensa that summer to continue his work with Sangyé Yeshé, learning from him about the works of the Drukpa Kagyü mahāmudrā master Barawa,[686] the songs of Milarepa, and the practices of the hearing transmission stemming from Tsongkhapa. Although it is nowhere specified in his autobiography or in later biographies precisely when Paṇchen Chögyen learned the Geden Oral Transmission teaching on mahāmudrā, it probably occurred during this visit to Ensa in the summer of 1588.[687]

He continued his travels back and forth between Tashi Lhunpo and Ensa until Sangyé Yeshé's death, in 1591. Shortly thereafter, he received full ordination at Tashi Lhunpo then journeyed to Ü, where he spent some time at Ganden Monastery. Having previously passed his examination in the logic and epistemology of Dharmakīrti's *Exposition of Valid Cognition*, he was further tested at Ganden on Maitreya's *Ornament of Higher Realization*, Candrakīrti's *Entry to the Middle Way*, Vasubandhu's *Treasury of Higher Knowledge*, and Guṇaprabha's *Vinaya Sūtra*. While at Ganden, he also studied tantric topics with leading lamas in the area, including Gendun Gyaltsen (1532–1607), who would go on to serve as Ganden throneholder from 1603 to 1607. Paṇchen Chögyen received a number of empowerments and teachings from Gendun Gyaltsen, including some transmitted by the Second Dalai Lama. In turn, Paṇchen Chögyen became Gendun Gyaltsen's teacher, eventually passing on to him the practices of the Geden Oral Transmission, including mahāmudrā, and composing at his request both the seminal Geluk mahāmudrā instruction text, *Highway of the Conquerors*, and its autocommentary, *Lamp So Bright*. Indeed, Gendun Gyaltsen would become Paṇchen Chögyen's first major successor in the lineage. In the 1590s, while completing his studies with various lamas, Paṇchen Chögyen became a popular teacher in his own right and sponsored the construction of new buildings at Ensa, of which he had become abbot. At some point during this decade, he was overcome by world weariness. Inspired by the examples of the mountain-dwelling hermits Śavaripa and, especially, Milarepa, he spent several months in intensive retreat, gaining visions of Tsongkhapa, who transmitted important Indian commentaries to him in his dreams. Emerging from isolation, he alternated study, teaching, and further retreats, during which, in the manner of Mila and his disciples, he sometimes wore only a light cotton cloth, while practicing the meditation on inner heat. The example of Milarepa, which also had inspired a number of his

686. As noted earlier, Barawa may have been a teacher of Umapa, who was, in turn, a teacher of Tsongkhapa.

687. See Willis 1995, 81 and 88.

predecessors in the hearing lineage, would continue to guide Paṇchen Chögyen throughout his life, and he eventually would compose a guru-yoga text dedicated to the great poet-yogī.[688]

In 1601, already in charge of Ensa and Gangchen Chöphel monasteries, Paṇchen Chögyen was appointed abbot of Tashi Lhunpo. In the decade that followed, he established a prayer-festival tradition at the monastery, sponsored the construction of numerous stūpas, and founded a tantric college. He also, like Khöntön Paljor Lhundrup, became an important tutor to the newly arrived, Mongol-born Fourth Dalai Lama, Yönten Gyatso, whom he ordained, provided with teachings and empowerments, and accompanied to the holy places of Central Tibet, helping pave the way for the foreign-born lama's acceptance by the Gelukpas, if not the Kagyüpas. In 1612, Paṇchen Chögyen visited Bhutan, where he helped convert the Lhapa clan from the Drukpa Kagyü to the Geluk tradition—the first of numerous successful missionary efforts on behalf of the Geluk. Over the next several years, at the Fourth Dalai Lama's request, he traveled regularly from Shigatsé to Lhasa to lead the Great Prayer Festival and give teachings. As noted earlier, it was the Fourth Dalai Lama who bestowed upon Paṇchen Chögyen the title "great scholar," or Paṇchen, which later would be the name of the Gelukpa tulku lineage second only in importance to that of the Dalai Lamas, with Paṇchen Chögyen, as we also know, regarded as either the first or fourth in the line.

Upon the Fourth Dalai Lama's death in 1617, Paṇchen Chögyen assumed the abbacy of both Drepung and Sera. The next decade was a tumultuous one, marked by the occupation of Lhasa by the Kagyü-aligned king of Tsang, Tsangpa repression of the Geluk, and a violent Mongol incursion in support of the Geluk. Amid all this, and in the face of innumerable hurdles, Paṇchen Chögyen used his diplomatic skills to try to maintain peace among the warring factions and succeeded in obtaining the king of Tsang's permission first to identify, and then to enthrone, the Fifth Dalai Lama, Ngawang Losang Gyatso (1617–82). Paṇchen Chögyen became the young Dalai Lama's senior tutor[689] and later served him as a diplomat, both before and after the Great Fifth gained control of all of Tibet in 1642 with the military assistance of the Qosot Mongol chieftain Gushri Khan, whose armies broke the power of the Kagyü and their allies in both Tsang and Kham. Full of age and honors, Paṇchen Chögyen died in 1762; his mummified body was sealed into an

688. This is found in Bz*MLNJ*.

689. As noted earlier, Khöntön Paljor Lhundrup was one of his major tutors in Nyingma subjects.

ornate stūpa at Tashi Lhunpo in a ceremony overseen by the Fifth Dalai Lama himself.

By traditional count, Paṇchen Chögyen left behind him 108 separate literary works. Besides his autobiography, he composed biographies; songs of praise; philosophical polemics;[690] spiritual poetry;[691] and his specialty, explanations of tantric ritual—including important discussions of the generation stage of the Guhyasamāja tantra system, the method for attaining liberation in the bardo, and the practices of the six Dharmas of Nāropa and of Cakrasaṃvara.[692] He also wrote two of the most enduring Geluk ritual and/or meditative texts, the *Offering to the Guru* and the *Path to Bliss*, and is credited as well with composing perhaps the first version of the *Six-Session Guru Yoga*, which in one form or another has been a key part of Geluk daily practice for centuries.[693] For our purposes, Paṇchen Chögyen's greatest importance lies in the fact that he focused on mahāmudrā explicitly and with an intensity never before seen in a Gelukpa. As noted in chapter 6, he composed four major texts crucial for understanding Geluk mahāmudrā: the root verses of *Highway of the Conquerors*; his own commentary on the root verses, *Lamp So Bright*; the first version of the *Mahāmudrā Lineage Prayer*; and his brief transmission-history, *Like a Treasure Inventory*. In this chapter we will summarize these four key texts and discuss as well two other sources important for an appreciation of Geluk mahāmudrā: *Offering to the Guru* and Paṇchen Chögyen's spiritual songs.

Highway of the Conquerors

Highway of the Conquerors (Bz*GBZL*) became the root text for all subsequent accounts of how to practice mahāmudrā meditation in a Geluk manner. It was written at Ganden Monastery, most likely sometime between 1591 and 1601.[694] *Highway of the Conquerors* consists of 197 lines—most containing

690. See Cabezón 1995 and Panchen Lobsang Chökyi Gyaltsen 2014.

691. A selection of these is translated in part 5, section 10, below.

692. See, respectively, Paṇchen Losang Chökyi Gyaltsen 2019, Mullin 1997, 137–53, Ngulchu Dharmabhadra and the First Panchen Lama, 2014, 115–54, and Ngulchu Dharmabhadra and the First Panchen Lama, 2010, 115–51 and 207–19.

693. The *Offering to the Guru* (Bz*LMCP*) is translated below, in part 5, section 8; see also, e.g., Dalai Lama 1988. The *Path to Bliss* is translated in, e.g., Jampa 2013. The *Six-Session Guru Yoga* is translated in, e.g., Berzin 2001.

694. I base this conjecture on the fact that (a) according to the colophon, the text was requested by two monks, Hator Sherab Sangpo and Gendun Gyaltsen, the second of whom Paṇchen

seven syllables—framed by an homage to the great seal at the beginning and a prose colophon at the end. It contains no explicit text-divisions, but its structure is reasonably clear, even without the aid of Paṇchen Chögyen's autocommentary or the commentaries of later masters of the transmission. For the sake of convenience, I divide it into forty-six verses.[695]

Paṇchen Chögyen begins with a Sanskrit homage to mahāmudrā, followed (verses 1–2) by a prefatory salutation to his guru and a promise to impart the instructions of the mahāmudrā oral tradition (*bka' srol*) of "Dharmavajra, father and son"—that is, Chökyi Dorjé and Ensapa—who possess the Geden Oral Transmission (*dge ldan bka' brgyud*). The Paṇchen's next (verse 3a) explains that his text will be divided into discussions of the preparatory background, the main practice, and follow-up reflections. He then (verses 3b–5) summarizes the preparatory practices required for the practice of mahāmudrā: taking refuge and generating the awakening mind, confessing one's transgressions through recitation of the hundred-syllable mantra of Vajrasattva, prostrating as much as possible, and repeatedly entreating the blessings of the buddhas and one's root guru, "who is inseparable from them." Paṇchen Chögyen begins his account of the actual session by specifying (verse 6) that mahāmudrā is divisible into sūtra-vehicle and mantra-vehicle approaches. Mantra mahāmudrā (verses 7–8) is described as "the great blissluminosity arising from skill in the methods of penetrating the vital points of the vajra body," which is the essence of the unexcelled yoga tantras taught by such mahāsiddhas as Saraha, Nāgārjuna, Nāropa, and Maitrīpa, and in such text collections as the Seven Attainment Texts and the Essential Trilogy. Paṇchen Chögyen states (verses 9–10) that his main focus will be on sūtra mahāmudrā, which is "a way of meditating on emptiness" taught in the Perfection of Wisdom sūtras and the works of Nāgārjuna—according to whose intention he will teach the way to recognize the mind (*sems kyi ngo sprod*). In a famous and much-quoted passage (verses 11–12), he goes on to suggest that the various Tibetan wisdom teachings—the connate union, the amulet box, the fivefold, equal taste, the four letters, pacification, severance, the great perfection, and the Madhyamaka view—are seen by a yogī who has mastered scripture, reasoning, and inner experience to come down to a single intention, or the same idea (*dgongs pa gcig*).

Chögyen met in 1591 and who died in 1607; and (b) Paṇchen Chögyen's main period of residence at Ganden was 1591 to 1601, at which point he became abbot of Tashi Lhunpo. It is of course possible that Paṇchen Chögyen wrote the text on a visit back to Ganden after he assumed the Tashi Lhunpo abbacy, but likelier that it was composed before his move.

695. For a slightly different way of dividing the root text, see *NGCS* 499–505.

Before describing an actual session of mahāmudrā meditation, Paṇchen Chögyen specifies (verse 13) that he will base his account on a sequence in which the view—that is, insight—is developed on the basis of serenity, rather than a sequence that begins with the view and develops serenity from within that. In this, he replicates the sequence of most Kagyü mahāmudrā manuals as well as of most Tibetan meditation literature in general. The session begins (verses 14–15) with the meditator's assuming the seven-point posture of Vairocana,[696] clearing the mind through the nine-round breathing,[697] going for refuge and generating the awakening mind, and practicing guru yoga: visualizing one's root guru, making fervent appeals for his or her blessing, and having the guru dissolve into one. It is at this point that serenity meditation begins. Paṇchen Chögyen describes a sequence (verses 16–24) in which one rests evenly in a state where appearances have dispersed, concepts are absent, and nothing is contrived. Without ceasing mental activity, one establishes mindfulness (*dran pa*) and alertness (*shes bzhin*), taking as one's meditative object the mind itself, whose nature is awareness and clarity (*rig gsal*). When concepts arise, one may either simply note them or cut them off, "as a skillful sword-fighter would." When they have been severed, then—as taught by Saraha and other mahāsiddhas—one should, without losing mindfulness, relax the mind. Within that relaxed state, arising concepts are seen for what they are, and naturally fade, so that "a pure vacuity dawns"; and when one looks at the abiding mind, one sees "non-obstruction, vacuity, clarity, and vividness"—this, notes Paṇchen Chögyen, utilizing Kagyü terminology, is "the merger of stillness and movement." He goes on to reiterate that one should not block concepts but, rather, observe them, letting them settle into their clear, aware nature. In concluding his instruction on serenity (verse 24), Paṇchen Chögyen describes the mind in equipoise on mind's own nature as "not . . . obscured / by anything: it is lucid and clear, / with nothing physical established anywhere within it. / It is a pure vacuity like space, / where

696. This posture (which does admit variations) typically involves sitting in vajra (or "full lotus") posture, back straight, hands at one's lap, chest open, head inclined slightly forward, tongue against the upper palate, and eyes gazing past the tip of the nose.

697. This sequence, often used at the outset of meditation to clear out "stale" air, typically involves three rounds in which one blocks the right nostril with a finger, inhales through the left nostril, opens the right nostril while blocking the left, and exhales through the right; three rounds in which one blocks the left nostril with a finger, inhales through the right nostril, opens the left nostril while blocking the right, and exhales through the left; and three rounds in which both nostrils are left open and one inhales and exhales through both. The sequence may or may not be accompanied by visualizations of, e.g., the main channels of the subtle body or by reflections on the purification of negativities of the past, future, and present, respectively.

everything appears vividly." He hastens to add, however (verses 25–27), that—contrary to what is believed by "most present-day great meditators of the Land of Snows"—the techniques he has described do *not* lead to "holding Buddha in your palm" (that is, to insight and full awakening), as they go no further than helping a beginner establish serenity and recognize (*ngo sprod*) the *conventional* nature of mind.

Paṇchen Chögyen begins the section on insight by stating (verse 28) that the real—i.e., *ultimate*—nature of mind is to be recognized on the basis of the instructions he has received from his root guru, Sangyé Yeshé. These begin (verse 29) with the meditator, still established in meditative equipoise, undertaking a subtle analysis of "the intrinsic nature of the person (*gang zag*) who meditates," in the manner of "a minnow darting about in limpid water without disturbing it." The actual analysis (verses 30–32) is predicated on two verses from Nāgārjuna's *Jewel Garland* (*Ratnāvalī*, 1.80–81), which establish that an individual cannot be found in any of the six elements,[698] nor in all of them together, nor apart from them, and that the elements themselves are empty as well. Thus, when one searches for the meditator, one does not find "even the minutest particle" of such a person, so one should settle into space-like meditative equipoise. Alternatively (verses 33–35), from within serene meditative equipoise, one may view the mind as a formless, pure vacuity, an "unceasing stream of clarity and awareness" that may appear to be independent yet is no more real than—as Śāntideva puts it[699]—"so-called 'continuums' and 'collections,' like rosaries, armies, and the like." Paṇchen Chögyen summarizes the instruction on insight (verses 36–37) by quoting Sangyé Yeshé to the effect that when one is aware that everything that arises is a mere conceptual apprehension, the Dharma realm dawns independently, and one then settles in meditative equipoise within that. He concludes (verse 38) by citing Phadampa Sangyé's famous saying: "Whirl the spear of awareness within emptiness; / the view, O Dingripas, is unobstructed."[700]

At the conclusion of the session, Paṇchen Chögyen instructs (verses 39–43), one should dedicate one's merit to "the great, unexcelled awakening." He further advises that, in the postmeditation period (*rjes thob*), any phenomenon that arises should be recognized "starkly and vividly" not as it appears (*snang tshul*) but as it truly is (*gnas tshul*): empty—and as Āryadeva insists,[701] the

698. Skt. *dhātu*: earth, water, fire, air, space, and consciousness.

699. Sd*BA* 27b (*Engaging in Bodhisattva Conduct* 8.101).

700. Ps*DRGC* 17b [34] (*Hundred Verses of Advice*, verse 51; cf. trans. Dilgo and Padampa, 95).

701. Ad*CS* 9b (*Four Hundred Verses*, verse 191 [8.16]).

emptiness of one phenomenon is the emptiness of all. With the recognition of the emptiness of appearances, elaborated extremes such as existence and nonexistence are transcended, and saṃsāra and nirvāṇa blend into a single nature. Paṇchen Chögyen tells us (verses 44–45) that another approach to postmeditative experience of the world involves seeing all appearances as merely nominal dependent arisings that are based on imputation, no more real than a dream, a mirage, the moon's reflection in water, or an illusion. When appearances do not block emptiness, and emptiness does not block appearances, dependent arising and emptiness have a single meaning, and "the excellent path . . . will be manifest." Finally (verse 46) Paṇchen Chögyen dedicates his merit, expressing the hope that by way of it, all beings may quickly awaken through the mahāmudrā path, which is second to none.

Lamp So Bright

Lamp So Bright (Bz*YSGM*), Paṇchen Chögyen's autocommentary on *Highway of the Conquerors*, was written at Tashi Lhunpo, possibly sometime between 1601 and 1603.[702] It incorporates the root verses of *Highway of the Conquerors*, isolating them into segments of varying lengths, depending on subject matter. Paṇchen Chögyen outlines his comments on the verses of the root text as follows:

1. Preface [verses 1–2]
2. Actual Instruction [verses 3–45]
   - 2.1. Preparation [verses 3–5]
   - 2.2. Main Practice [verses 6–38]
     - [2.2.1. Various Modes of Explanation, no verses][703]
     - 2.2.2. Mantra Mahāmudrā [verses 7–8]
     - 2.2.3. Sūtra Mahāmudrā [verses 9–38]

702. I base this conjecture on the fact that (a) according to the colophon, the text was requested by Gendun Gyaltsen, who died in 1607, (b) Paṇchen Chögyen took up residence at Tashi Lhunpo in 1601, and (c) Gendun Gyaltsen became Ganden throneholder in 1603, yet Paṇchen Chögyen does not mention him in this connection, referring to him—as he does in the root-text colophon—as the "limitlessly learned master of the ten topics" (*gnas bcu rab byams pa*) Gendun Gyaltsen. There is, of course, no assurance that Paṇchen Chögyen would have referred to Gendun Gyaltsen as Ganden throneholder, even if the text had been written after his ascension to the throne, nor for that matter, is it entirely certain that the text was composed while Gendun Gyaltsen still was living, though the likelihood is strong.

703. Bracketed section headings are implicit rather than explicit in Paṇchen Chögyen's text.

[2.2.3.x. The Promise to Teach Sūtra Mahāmudrā in Detail] [verses 9–10]
[2.2.3.1. The Essential Teaching] [no verses]
[2.2.3.2. Different Traditions of Mahāmudrā] [verses 11–12]
2.2.3.3. [The Actual Meditation] [verses 13–38]
2.2.3.3.1. Serenity [verses 14–27]
2.2.3.3.1.1. Preliminaries [verses 14–15]
2.2.3.3.1.2. The Main Practice [verses 16–27]
[2.2.3.3.1.2.1. The Method for Accomplishing Mental Stillness] [verses 16–23]
[2.2.3.3.1.2.2. Imprints Resulting from Maintaining Mental Equipoise in This Way] [verse 24]
[2.2.3.3.1.2.3. Identifying This Path in Terms of Its Own Nature] [verses 25–27]
2.2.3.3.2. Insight [verses 28–38]
[2.2.3.3.2.x. The Real Method for Distinguishing the Nature of Mind] [verse 28]
2.2.3.3.2.1. A General Demonstration that Distinguishes the Way of Recognizing [the Real Nature of Mind] [no verses]
2.2.3.3.2.2. A Demonstration that Summarizes the Essence of Those [Discussions] [verses 29–38]
2.3. Follow-Up [verses 39–45]
3. Dedication of the Virtue Arising from the Composition [verse 46]

Paṇchen Chögyen begins section 1, his preface, by citing the Sanskrit salutation to mahāmudrā that begins *Highway of the Conquerors*, followed by verses that celebrate the gnosis of the buddhas, pay homage to his guru, and promise to explain mahāmudrā, which is the mind elixir of the conquerors, the essential meaning of the sūtras and tantras, and the road taken by all the mahāsiddhas. Section 2, which explains the Actual Instruction, uses verse 3a to note that the text is divided into three major sections: preparation, main practice, and follow-up.

Section 2.1, on Preparation, begins by quoting verses 3b–5 of the root text, which recommend various preliminary practices as the groundwork for mahāmudrā practice. Paṇchen Chögyen goes on to explain these practices in some detail, and with copious citations from Indian and Tibetan masters. He quotes Sakya Paṇḍita and Phadampa Sangyé on the importance of going for refuge in the Triple Gem, and Śāntideva and Atiśa on the indispensability, for Mahāyāna practitioners, of arousing the awakening mind—which is the cause of a buddha's gnosis and the completion of the method side of the bodhisattva's path. Paṇchen Chögyen then specifies that most Tibetan traditions agree that there are four preliminaries to serious spiritual practice: (1) going for refuge and generating the awakening mind, (2) offering the Mount Meru maṇḍala, (3) Vajrasattva purification recitation, and (4) guru yoga. He touches explicitly on all of these except the maṇḍala offering and ties them to even more basic stages-of-the-path meditations on such topics as impermanence, death, karma and its fruits, the disadvantages of saṃsāra, the necessity of love, compassion, and the awakening mind, and the absence of self in any entity, showing along the way that different expressions of these basic understandings—from poetic exhortations by Milarepa, to the "four dharmas" of Gampopa,[704] to the Sakya master Drakpa Gyaltsen's teaching on "separation from the four clingings"[705]—all are in harmony. After some instructions on Vajrasattva practice, Paṇchen Chögyen concludes the section by emphasizing the centrality of faith in one's guru, who is the "source of all virtue and goodness," quoting for support the likes of Sapaṇ, Atiśa, Phadampa Sangyé, and Milarepa.

At the beginning of section 2.2, on "the main practice," Paṇchen Chögyen cites verse 6, to the effect that mahāmudrā is twofold: sūtra and mantra. He goes on to quote a long poem by Drigung Jikten Sumgön, which demonstrates the universality of mahāmudrā by showing how each of the four seals—usually associated with tantric Buddhism—actually may be applied to practitioners of each of the three types of vows: śrāvakas, bodhisattvas, and tantric yogīs or yoginīs. For the śrāvaka, mahāmudrā is nonabiding nirvāṇa, for the bodhisattva it is the equal taste of emptiness and compassion, for those on the tantric path of means it is the manifestation of connate gnosis, and for those on the tantric path of liberation it is spontaneity. The Paṇchen Lama also quotes Gö Lotsāwa to the effect that mahāmudrā seals all Buddhist practices, from the Prātimokṣa vows all the way up to the Guhyasamāja tantra.

There follows a section on mantra mahāmudrā (2.2.2), in which Paṇchen Chögyen quotes verses 7–8, on the nature and sources of tantric great seal traditions, then gives an etymological definition of the Tibetan term for

704. These are (1) a mind that goes to the Dharma, (2) a Dharma that takes up the path, (3) a path that clears away confusion, and (4) confusion that is severed in gnosis.

705. The four clingings (or attachments, *zhen pa*) are stated in the form of conditionals: (1) "If you cling to this life, you are not a Dharma practitioner." (2) "If you cling to saṃsāra, you are not renounced." (3) "If you cling to your own aims, you do not have awakening mind." (4) "If you grasp, you do not have the view." Drakpa Gyaltsen wrote a twenty-nine-verse explication of this teaching, hence Paṇchen Chögyen's attribution of it to him; the root verse itself, however, is said to have been transmitted by Mañjuśrī to Drakpa Gyaltsen's predecessor, Sachen Kunga Nyingpo.

mahāmudrā, *phyag rgya chen po*, whereby *phyag* equates to the gnosis of emptiness, *rgya* is freedom from saṃsāric phenomena, and *chen po* is union. He goes on to describe tantric mahāmudrā as the luminosity of great bliss resulting from the introduction of vital winds into the central channel on the completion stage of unexcelled-yoga-tantra practice, stating that this is the definition accepted by all the mahāsiddhas of India and all the great early masters of the Kagyü. Next, Paṇchen Chögyen describes the Seven Attainment Texts, paying particular attention to Padmavajra's *Secret Attainment* (*Guhyasiddhi*), which is said to be the "grandmother" of both the other attainment texts and Saraha's Essential Trilogy. The Paṇchen quotes and comments on a number of excerpts from Saraha's *People Dohās*, explaining them in terms of unexcelled-yoga-tantra concepts and techniques.[706] Finally, with quotations from the likes of Tsongkhapa, Milarepa, and Sakya Paṇḍita, he discusses the division of tantric mahāmudrā practitioners into subitists—who are able, because of previous good karma, to manifest the luminosity of great bliss instantly—and gradualists—who only can manifest it through training in such gradual Mantra Vehicle practices as the six Dharmas of Nāropa.

Most of the rest of the commentary, like most of the rest of the root text (verses 9–38), is devoted to detailed instructions on Paṇchen Chögyen's main concern: sūtra mahāmudrā (section 2.2.3). Paṇchen Chögyen begins (2.2.3.1) by identifying the "essential teaching," which, as noted in the root text (verses 9–10), is the view of emptiness expounded in the Perfection of Wisdom sūtras, especially as interpreted by Nāgārjuna and Candrakīrti. He cites Nāgārjuna, Sapaṇ, and Atiśa to the effect that there is no path to liberation other than the realization of emptiness, and he follows Sapaṇ in insisting that that there is no difference in the emptiness discussed in the Sūtra and Mantra Vehicles. He promises to point out (*ngo sprod*) the nature of mind: emptiness—which, as the *King of Concentrations Sūtra* states, "seals the nature of all things," hence is the great seal, mahāmudrā.

Paṇchen Chögyen goes on (section 2.2.3.2) to discuss in some detail the concordant Tibetan wisdom traditions asserted in the root text (verses 11–12) to have a single intention and to be equal in their capacity to effect buddhahood: the connate union, the amulet box, the fivefold, equal taste, the four letters, pacification, severance, the great perfection, and the Madhyamaka view. In discussing the *connate union*, he quotes Gampopa to the effect that everything is, in one way or another, related to the Dharma body and he breaks the practice itself down into preliminaries, serenity and insight, and applying one's experience to whatever appears. The Shangpa Kagyü *amulet box* is divided into a

706. See the discussion below in chapter 16, and the translation in part 5, section 5.

"self-descended" preliminary practice, a main practice in which faults are "self-freeing," and the resultant "self-appearing" buddha bodies; it is related, too, to the six Dharmas of Nigumā—which, as we have seen, are related to the completion stage of unexcelled yoga tantra. The *fivefold* is illustrated by a long quotation from Drigung Jikten Sumgön in which the five practices—(1) love, compassion, and the awakening mind, (2) self-generation as the deity, (3) guru devotion, (4) nonconceptual mind (or mahāmudrā), and (5) dedication of merit—are illustrated by a variety of inventive metaphors. Paṇchen Chögyen mentions three Drukpa practices: the eight great guidances, the six cycles on equal taste, and the mountain dharma; all of these involve creative combinations of sūtra and mantra practices, with a particular orientation toward transforming everyday attitudes and events into opportunities for awakening. The *four letters—a-ma-na-si*, meaning nonmentation—are said to correspond, respectively, to cutting the root of mind,[707] settling the mind, eliminating mental error, and taking the mind as the path. The *pacification* tradition is reflected in a long quote from Phadampa Sangyé, exhorting his disciples to see the true nature of whatever arises and use all circumstances, even the most negative, as a basis for realization. Paṇchen Chögyen briefly mentions Machik Labdrön's *severance* tradition, Padmasambhava's *great perfection*, and the "guidance in the profound *Madhyamaka view*," then closes by endorsing a quotation from Puṇḍarīka's *Stainless Light* to the effect that while various jewels may differ in name and function, they all have the same precious nature, as jewels.

Paṇchen Chögyen begins the description of the actual mahāmudrā meditation (section 2.2.3.3) by stating that, of the two possible ways of ordering the practice—insight followed by serenity or serenity followed by insight—he will adopt the latter approach (verse 13), citing Śāntideva and the *Jewel Heap* (*Ratnakūṭa*) *Sūtra* in support of such a "gradual" approach.

He then begins his account of serenity meditation (section 2.2.3.3.1, verses 14–27), first outlining the "preliminaries," or "requisites for yogic bliss" (section 2.2.3.3.1.1), as suggested by Maitreya and spelled out in the root text (verses 14–15): sitting comfortably in the seven-point posture of Vairocana, practicing the nine-round breathing, taking refuge and arousing the awakening mind, and meditating on and appealing to one's guru—who dissolves into light, which in turn dissolves into the meditator. The description of the main practice of serenity (section 2.2.3.3.1.2, verses 16–27) begins with a long quotation from the root text (section 2.2.3.3.1.2.1, verses 16–23), which advises one to

707. The expression *sems rtsa chod* may be translated either as "cut the root of mind" or "determine the [nature of] mind." I have opted for the former, but the reader should keep the latter in mind, as well.

rest evenly in a state free from appearances, concepts, and contrivance, and then, with the awareness and clarity of the mind itself as the meditative object, establish mindfulness and alertness—which one maintains either by noting thoughts as they arise or cutting them off. Then, while maintaining mindfulness, one should relax the mind, and within a relaxed state see arising concepts as they are and allow them to fade, such that the mind, whether moving or still, is seen as a pure vacuity. Paṇchen Chögyen elaborates on these lines by aligning the root text's instructions with the standard account of the stages and processes of serenity meditation detailed in Asaṅga's *Levels of the Śrāvakas* (*Śrāvakabhūmi*), then noting that of all the many objects of meditation taught by the Buddha, the mind itself is the object stressed in this particular lineage.

Going into detail, Paṇchen Chögyen specifies that after absorbing the guru's blessings, the meditator should maintain a mental state free from hope and anxiety, focused on the unmoving mind of the present. One must maintain strong mindfulness of the mind, falling into neither unconsciousness nor distraction, and employ alertness to keep stray thoughts at bay, either through noting (or identifying, *ngos 'dzin*) them or, alternatively, cutting them off. When thoughts have been successfully managed, one should relax the mind, as advised by Machik Labdrön and Saraha, though not too much: a balance between tautness and relaxation, as described by Candragomin and others, is ideal. When one has found the proper meditative balance and focused on mind's own clear, aware nature, one deals with remaining thoughts either (1) by immediately seeing them for what they are, or (2) by letting thoughts go where they will settle into their own nature, as described by Saraha and Yangönpa. In either case one is left with the experience of a pure and vivid emptiness.

Paṇchen Chögyen then elaborates on the procedure for settling the mind nonconceptually, citing six analogies provided by "present-day disciples," presumably Kagyüpas: the sun apart from clouds, an eagle soaring in the sky, a ship on the great sea, a child viewing temple murals, bird tracks in the sky, and loosely woven cotton or wool. In short, says Paṇchen Chögyen, citing and commenting briefly upon verse 24 (section 2.2.3.3.1.2.2), mind in equipoise on mind is "lucid and clear," a space-like vacuity where everything appears vividly. Addressing a query as to the degree to which one recognizes one's own nature on this path (section 2.2.3.3.1.2.3), the Paṇchen cites verses 25–27 of the root text, to the effect that the practice in which one focuses "gently . . . without grasping, on whatever appears," is one in which the real nature of mind is directly seen yet cannot be specified as this or that. Contrary to the claims of his contemporaries, however, this is *not* true insight, let alone buddhahood, but merely "a marvelous means for a beginner to accomplish mental stillness and a way of introducing the phenomenal (*kun rdzob*) nature of mind." In short, it is serenity and not insight.

Paṇchen Chögyen begins the instruction on insight (section 2.2.3.3.2, verses 28–38) with a citation of his root text's promise (verse 28) to explain "the way to recognize the real nature of mind" as transmitted to him by his guru, Sangyé Yeshé. He turns next to a general discussion—unrelated to the root text—of various ways of examining the nature of mind (section 2.2.3.3.2.1). He starts with quotations from Saraha and Lingrepa to the effect that mind is the source of all attainments, and that realizing its nature is therefore basic to buddhahood. He then describes five different ways of "cutting the root basis of mind": (1) as taught by Saraha, inquiring whether the mind is to be found outside or inside oneself, or as arising, abiding, or ceasing; (2) as taught by Shang Rinpoché, inquiring whether the mind is to be found in any part of the body or is in any significant way related to form; (3) as taught by Saraha and Lingrepa, ignoring past and future and settling into the "fresh, uncontrived cognition of the present"; (4) as taught by Tilopa, allowing appearances and concepts to arise and then seeing their intrinsic nature and settling into "a wakeful, pure vacuity"; and (5) as taught by Shang Rinpoché, suppressing conceptual images, then allowing them to arise and release themselves.

Paṇchen Chögyen's detailed discussion of insight (section 2.2.3.3.2.2, verses 29–38) begins with a general discussion of the indispensability of realizing emptiness on the spiritual path, with supporting quotations from a number of sources, including such sūtras as the *King of Concentrations*, *Questions of Rāṣṭrapāla* (*Rāṣṭrapālaparipṛcchā*), and *Perfection of Wisdom in Eight Thousand Lines* (*Aṣṭasāhasrikāprajñāpāramitā*), and such Indian masters as Nāgārjuna, Candrakīrti, Dharmakīrti, Śāntideva, and Atiśa. The Paṇchen stresses that a nonconceptual realization of reality is the *sine qua non* for liberation, but that nonconceptual realization must be preceded by analytical understanding. This requires, in turn, that one correctly identify the object of negation—the connate or instinctive grasping at a truly existing self of persons—neither over-determining nor under-determining it, lest the arrow stray from its target.

Turning at last to the root text's actual instruction on how to maintain meditative equipoise while subtly investigating the nature of the meditator (verse 29), Paṇchen Chögyen discusses the necessity of distinguishing entities' mode of appearance (*snang tshul*) from their mode of existence (*gnas tshul*)—which is as mere nominal designations—drawing supporting quotations from Tsongkhapa and Khedrup Norsang Gyatso, among others. He then expands on the passage from the root text (verses 30–32) that uses a direct quotation from Nāgārjuna's *Jewel Garland* to argue that because the individual (*pud-*

gala, gang zag) is neither separate from nor identical to the six elements, the meditator cannot be found—and that one should dwell stably on that not-finding. By the same token, says Paṇchen Chögyen (citing Śāntideva and the *King of Concentrations Sūtra*, among others), the individual cannot be found apart from or within either the various parts of one's body or the aggregates, and when the individual, or self, cannot be found, "all of a sudden, there is emptiness," and one joyously enters a space-like meditative equipoise focused on reality, which is tantamount to direct insight. Even after meditation ceases and ordinary appearances resume, one sees them as nominally designated, illusion-like dependent arisings, no more truly existent than a magician's trick, a son in a barren woman's dream, the moon's reflection in water, summer mirages, or the core of a plantain tree. Alternatively, says Paṇchen Chögyen (commenting on verses 33–35), one may investigate the nature of mind by recognizing that the "uninterrupted stream of clarity and awareness" that is the mind is no more real than the "continuums and collections" (e.g., rosaries and armies, respectively) refuted by Śāntideva; rather, in the words of Marpa, it is "ablaze with emptiness," or, as Phakmo Drupa teaches, "it is pure suchness from the beginning." By way of summary (verses 36–38), Paṇchen Chögyen comments on the words of his guru, Sangyé Yeshé, to the effect that when one applies single-pointed meditative equipoise to the realization of emptiness ("the ultimate Dharma realm"), it is, in a word, "marvelous"; and quoting the root text (verse 38), he concludes the section with the famous exhortation by Phadampa Sangyé to the people of Dingri: "Whirl the spear of awareness within emptiness; / the view . . . is unobstructed."

With the conclusion of section 2.2 on the main practice pursued during a meditation session, Paṇchen Chögyen turns finally to a discussion of how to apply one's insight afterward (section 2.3, verses 39–45). Having dedicated the merit at the end of one's session (verse 39), one then reengages with the everyday world (verses 40–42) on the basis of the insight developed in meditation. Keeping in mind Mitrayogin's admonition that "identification of whatever appears is the key to the view," one regards appearances not as they seem but as they truly are, as dependent arisings that are "hollow and unreal" but nevertheless appear "nakedly and vividly." Since, in the words of Āryadeva, the emptiness of one is the emptiness of all, all phenomena of saṃsāra and nirvāṇa share a single taste: emptiness. As the root text affirms (verses 43–44) and quotations from Milarepa confirm, when in equipoise on the ultimate, one is free from extremes such as existence and nonexistence, buddhahood and obstructions, or saṃsāra and nirvāṇa, and there is no meditator, no path, no realization, no action and result. The ultimate emptiness of things, however, does not impede their conventional validity as dependent arisings, for as

Milarepa observes, "in the realm of phenomenal truth, everything in saṃsāra and nirvāṇa exists." Paṇchen Chögyen adds that this is only nominally so, since a pillar, which cannot be found through any ultimate analysis, exists only on the basis of our imputation.

At this point, the Paṇchen Lama digresses briefly to criticize the typically Svātantrika Madhyamaka view that, to avoid nihilism, (a) we must distinguish between the way an entity appears to us and its true existence, with the latter to be refuted and the former to be preserved, and (b) in meditation on the lack of self of persons, we must negate only an imagined truly existent person, not the apparent person that is "us." In neither case, says Paṇchen Chögyen, is it legitimate to make such a distinction, since the way entities appear to us *is* as truly existent, and the truly existent person that is negated *is* the person that is "us." Maintaining such a distinction does not save us from nihilism but, rather, leads us down a slippery slope toward eternalism. Then the Paṇchen comments on verse 45, which affirms the unity of emptiness and dependent arising, realization of which allows "the excellent path . . . to be manifest." This point—so crucial to the Geluk outlook—is buttressed by quotations from Tsongkhapa, Candrakīrti, and Nāgārjuna and is, insists Paṇchen Chögyen, "easy to understand." In short, proper analysis rooted in equipoise developed through serenity meditation leads to "a concentration that is imbued with the bliss of physical and mental pliancy" that leaves one not far short of the direct insight into emptiness that is the beginning of the path of seeing, and of the levels traversed by a bodhisattva en route to awakening.

By way of a coda to his section on insight, Paṇchen Chögyen refers to Kagyü descriptions of the four yogas of mahāmudrā, and Shang Rinpoché's way of relating those yogas to the five paths and the ten levels,[708] as well as sudden and gradual approaches to awakening. He cites Sapaṇ's assertion that mahāmudrā systems "do not fully agree with the tantras and other scriptural collections," but does not enter into debate, pleading instead that all should "reject the hateful power of partiality and fill themselves with the precious light of seeing everything as pure."

The final part of the text (section 3) quotes the dedication of merit from the root text (verse 46) and ends with a poem in praise of mahāmudrā, which is said to be, *inter alia*, "the supreme essence churned from the sea of sūtras and tantras," "the path traversed by every supreme and holy siddha," "a plea-

708. The five paths are those of accumulation, preparation, seeing, meditation, and no-more-training. The ten levels are perfect joy, the immaculate, the luminous, the radiant, the hard-to-conquer, the clearly manifest, the far progressed, the immovable, the excellent-minded, and the cloud of Dharma.

sure grove, a resting place where pain is soothed," "the jeweled mirror in which everything appears," and "the guru who exhorts us on the ultimate path." By virtue of his having taught it, Paṇchen Chögyen requests, "may the excellent mind-vase of every being be filled with the nectar of . . . mahāmudrā, . . . and may they enjoy the great bliss of union."

Mahāmudrā Lineage Prayer

Paṇchen Chögyen's *Mahāmudrā Lineage Prayer* (Bz*PCSD*)[709] is not listed as a separate entry in his collected works but is almost invariably appended to *Highway of the Conquerors*. The prayer has been updated several times in the centuries since Paṇchen Chögyen so as to reflect the addition of further masters to the lineage. One such version was composed by Shar Kalden Gyatso in seventeenth-century Amdo. What is now the standard version was composed over several centuries in Ü-Tsang by a series of masters that includes Kachen Yeshé Gyaltsen (1713–93), Phabongkha Dechen Nyingpo (1878–1941), an unidentified lama or lamas, the Third Trijang Rinpoché (1901–81), and Thubten Zopa Rinpoché (1946–), each of whom added masters where his predecessor had left off.[710] In every case, Paṇchen Chögyen's basic text is preserved, with later editors simply expanding it to bring the lineage up to date.

Paṇchen Chögyen begins the prayer with a Sanskrit salutation to mahāmudrā. Then, in each of the first eight verses, he addresses one member of the Geden Hearing Transmission, describing their virtues and appealing to them for assistance. The fountainhead of the lineage, Vajradhara, is described as the "primordial buddha," the "head of all families," and the "pervasive lord," residing in the "mansion of the three spontaneous buddha bodies." The next figure in line, the wisdom buddha (or bodhisattva) Mañjuśrī, who resides in "the world of ten directions, this wide-spreading field," is described as "the father begetting conquerors in all three times." The first human to receive the transmission, Tsongkhapa, who resides in "the northern country, this snowy land," is praised as a second Buddha. His immediate successor, Tokden Jampal Gyatso, is said to be the "primary holder of the hearing-transmission teaching of Tsongkhapa, son of Mañjuśrī." The next in line, Baso Chökyi Gyaltsen, is said to "open the trove of hearing-transmission instruction and bring fortunate students to maturity." The mahāsiddha Chökyi Dorjé (or Dharmavajra)

709. This is translated below in part 5, section 3, with later additions. For a translation and analysis of a well-known Kagyü lineage prayer, see Thrangu 2018.

710. The additions by Yeshé Gyaltsen and Phabongkha Rinpoché are discussed in the chapter or section devoted to each.

is lauded for "completing the yogas of both tantric stages" and gaining "an awareness holder's immortal body." Paṇchen Chögyen's incarnation-lineage predecessor, Ensapa, is said to be "untouched by the bonds of the eight mundane concerns"[711] and to "bear the definitive teaching's triumphal banner." Finally, Paṇchen Chögyen's own teacher, Khedrup Sangyé Yeshé, is described as "sporting in saffron robes" and leading all beings to "the joyous palace of the three buddha bodies." Each verse is followed by this refrain:

> Please grant me blessings to cut in my mindstream
> the myriad ways of grasping at self,
> arouse love and compassion, awakening mind,
> and quickly attain supreme mahāmudrā, the unitive path.

Paṇchen Chögyen concludes the lineage prayer by appealing to his root guru, who is seen, he says, "in great splendor" in Tsongkhapa's home monastery—presumably Ganden, where, like *Highway of the Conquerors*, the text was likely composed. Then, after one more instance of the refrain, he asks for a final blessing in the following words:

> Seeing the holy guru as Buddha,
> rejecting desire for mundane abodes,
> taking the burden of freeing all motherly beings,
> may I be blessed to quickly attain
> the splendid unitive mahāmudrā
> on common and uncommon paths.

Like the first eight verses and the refrain, these final two sets of verses will be retained in each updating of the prayer—and undoubtedly retained in any future updating—so that Paṇchen Chögyen's text remains both the frame and heart of the Geluk mahāmudrā prayer, no matter how long or large it eventually becomes.

Like a Treasure Inventory

Although *Like a Treasure Inventory* is not related to the *Mahāmudrā Lineage Prayer* as explicitly as *Lamp So Bright* is to *Highway of the Conquerors*, it is in many ways a companion piece, as it supplies brief spiritual biographies of the key masters listed in the lineage prayer. The text—whose full title is *Like a*

711. Concern for pleasure and pain, loss and gain, praise and blame, and fame and shame.

Treasure Inventory: A Brief Summary of the Life Stories of the Lineage Masters of the Profound Path of the Precious Geden Oral Transmission—never explicitly states that the lineage being described is a *mahāmudrā* lineage (indeed, the term never occurs), but the exact correspondence between the masters described here and those in the lineage prayer and the use of the term "precious Geden Oral Transmission" here as in *Highway of the Conquerors* and *Lamp So Bright* make it quite clear that the lineage Paṇchen Chögyen describes is indeed the lineage that contains the mahāmudrā teachings.

At the outset, Paṇchen Chögyen divides the transmission—which is linked to mahāmudrā only implicitly—into a common (or long, or distant) transmission and an uncommon (or short, or proximate) transmission. The common transmission,[712] which relates to teachings possessed by the Kadam, includes three lines—the first two sūtra-based, the third tantric—each of which originates with Vajradhara. (1) The lineage of extensive activity includes Maitreya, Asaṅga, and other experts on love, compassion, and the awakening mind. (2) The lineage of profound view includes Mañjughoṣa, Nāgārjuna, and other experts on the nature of reality, emptiness. (3) The lineage of the blessing of practice includes Tilopa, Nāropa, and other experts in esoteric doctrine and practice. All three of these transmissions came together in Atiśa, and from there they passed down through successive masters until they reached Tsongkhapa. As noted earlier, the uncommon, or short, hearing transmission[713]—to which Paṇchen Chögyen devotes the bulk of the text—consists of Vajradhara, Mañjughoṣa, Tsongkhapa, Tokden Jampal Gyatso, Baso Chökyi Gyaltsen, Chökyi Dorjé, Ensapa Losang Döndrup, and Paṇchen Chögyen's own teacher, Khedrup Sangyé Yeshé. While Paṇchen Chögyen's version of the distant lineage would be altered slightly by later scholars, his far more important identification of the members of the short lineage became authoritative, crowding out any alternative lists that might have arisen before or after his time.

Having generally identified the lineages related to the hearing transmission, Paṇchen Chögyen goes on to give brief spiritual biographies of the key figures from Tsongkhapa down through his own teacher Khedup Sangyé Yeshé, detailing how they received, practiced, and transmitted the tradition. (As we have seen, there also is discussion of the Khedrup Jé's ambiguous relation to the lineage.) The bulk of the biographical material in *Like a Treasure Inventory* is devoted to Tsongkhapa; in describing Jé Rinpoché's place in the transmission, Paṇchen Chögyen draws on a range of early biographical material, including Khedrup Jé's *Entryway to Faith* and perhaps on oral traditions

712. Bz*TKBT* 1b–2a.

713. Bz*TKBT* 2a–11a.

as well. His accounts of lineage masters after Tsongkhapa are brief but quite interesting. In any case, between the identification of the various lineages and the accounts of the lives of the key Tibetan figures in the short transmission, *Like a Treasure Inventory* provides a vital source of information on how the Geden Oral Transmission was conceived by the Paṇchen, hence by others who practiced and wrote in his wake.

As part of its discussion of the ways in which members of the lineage received, practiced, and transmitted the secret teachings, *Like a Treasure Inventory* addresses those masters' connection to the emanated scripture, the heaven-sent text containing all the teachings of the transmission the Paṇchen says Mañjughoṣa passed on to Tsongkhapa. In doing so, it may well be the first Geluk text to claim the existence within Tsongkhapa's tradition of such a "magic book." Such texts are, of course, scattered throughout Tibetan lore; the Kadampas, for instance, are said to have had access to their own emanated scripture, as did Shabkar Tsokdruk Rangdröl, a great early modern nonsectarian master from Amdo.[714] And given the importance of the Kadam for Tsongkhapa and his followers, this may well have served as a model for Gelukpas in fashioning their own tales of an emanated scripture. Emanated scriptures bear obvious comparison to the Nyingma treasure (*gter ma*) texts left by Padmasambhava for his followers: they resemble treasure texts in having a mysterious heavenly origin and in conferring the authority and prestige of divine revelation on those who find or keep them. On the other hand, emanated scriptures are somewhat more elusive than treasure texts, which once revealed become a fixed part of the religious canon; in the case of the Geluk emanated scripture, for instance, there is general agreement that it was transmitted by Mañjughoṣa to Tsongkhapa and handed down through the masters of the hearing transmission until roughly the time of Paṇchen Chögyen (who may or may not have possessed it) but that it is no longer extant. Whether it ever was a "real," physical text is uncertain, but many of the traditions committed to writing by Geluk masters over the centuries are said to have been drawn from it. In this sense, it also resembles Indian "root tantras" of extraordinary length, such as the *Kālacakra*, that long ago disappeared but of which we have fragments on which to draw.

Offering to the Guru

Beyond the core texts outlined above, Paṇchen Chögyen composed a guru-yoga ritual, *Offering to the Guru*, that is regarded as deeply interwoven with

714. On Shabkar, see below, chapter 13.

mahāmudrā practice, and he composed a range of spiritual songs that express in poetic fashion his understanding and appreciation of the view, meditation, conduct, and fruition of the mahāmudrā path.

Ritual of Offering to the Guru (Bz*LMCP(1)*)[715] is a tantric liturgical text in the common Tibetan genre from which it takes its name (*bla ma mchod pa*), itself a sub-genre of the broader category of ritual (*cho ga*). *Offering to the Guru* is also related in important ways to the genre of *sādhana*, serving as a kind of public equivalent of the often-private visualization and recitation practices involved in most generation-stage unexcelled-yoga-tantra practices.[716] In his colophon, Paṇchen Chögyen describes how he composed the text on the basis of a comparative study of previous instances of guru-offering texts, including those of the great Sakya masters, the Second Dalai Lama, and his guru, Khedrup Sangyé Yeshé, and how he incorporated some material from earlier sources into his own composition.[717] The colophon also informs us that Paṇchen Chögyen composed it at Tashi Lhunpo at the behest of Dulzin Chökyi Drakpa and Losang Phuntsok. No date is given, and the two disciples mentioned are otherwise unknown. Given this, and given, too, that Paṇchen Chögyen was in and out of Tashi Lhunpo for the last sixty years of his life, we can only say that it probably was composed sometime in the first half of the seventeenth century.

We cannot be certain of its reception in Paṇchen Chögyen's time, but from at least the eighteenth century on, it became one of the central ritual texts of the Geluk tradition, recited in monastic assemblies semi-monthly on the tenth and twenty-fifth lunar days, as well as on such special occasions as long-life ceremonies, major Buddhist festivals, and the conclusion of major teachings. It also may serve as the focus of individual daily practice. It is commonly performed in conjunction with a ritual feast (*tshogs*), the text for which was composed

715. See translations in, e.g., Dalai Lama 1988, K. Gyatso 1992b, Kachen Yeshe Gyaltsen 2014, and below, part 5, section 8. Unusually but not uniquely for a later Tibetan text, *Offering to the Guru* is supplied not only with its Tibetan title (*Bla ma mchod pa'i cho ga*) but with a Sanskrit equivalent, *Gurupūjasyakalpa*. This is not meant to imply the existence of an Indic original so much as to indicate that the text is continuous with traditions of guru yoga found in the subcontinent.

716. For a detailed discussion of the complexities involved in identifying the genre of *Offering to the Guru*, see R. Jackson 2014.

717. See Bz*LMCP(1)* 31, trans. below, page 594. A full redaction analysis of *Offering to the Guru* remains a scholarly desideratum. A comparison of Paṇchen Chögyen's text with that of Khedrup Sangyé Yeshé (Sy*LMCP*) reveals that the first six verses of the former are drawn verbatim from the latter.

by Khedrup Sangyé Yeshé (Sy*LMCT*).[718] At the same time as it gained popularity and importance in the Geluk world, *Offering to the Guru* also came to be closely associated with the Ganden Hearing Transmission and the practice of mahāmudrā. Indeed, it came to be regarded as one of key components of the emanated scripture transmitted from Mañjughoṣa to Tsongkhapa then handed down through the lineage.[719] Its association with the hearing transmission is, as we will see, reasonable, for although the text nowhere explicitly mentions mahāmudrā, Paṇchen Chögyen does state in his colophon that he composed it in part by drawing on earlier exemplars of the guru-offering genre and in part from receiving the pith instructions of masters of sūtra and mantra. *Pith instructions* (*man ngag*) is the term usually reserved for the most rare and precious of oral teachings, including those of a hearing transmission.

In his poetic prelude to the ritual, after bowing to Vajradhara, the "wish-fulfilling jewel" who bestows upon us "the three greatly blissful bodies," Paṇchen Chögyen promises to lay out a flower garland picked from the garden of "holy instructions on sūtra and tantra," which effect the "benefit and bliss" of any disciple fortunate enough to encounter it. The ritual proper begins (verse 1) with the generation of oneself, "within a state of great bliss," as the guru-deity, who sends light to beings in all directions, purifying them. Oneself and all beings then take refuge in the guru and the Triple Gem and repeat three times the Sanskrit expressions of homage to the Guru, Buddha, Dharma, and Saṅgha (verses 2–3). One may, at this point, insert additional prayers related to refuge, the awakening mind, and the four immeasurables. One then recites three times a promise to "establish all mother sentient beings in the supreme state of a guru-deity" (verse 4) and three times a similar promise to free them from suffering and "establish them in the state of great bliss, buddhahood" (verses 5–6). Next (verses 7–8), one blesses the inner and outer offering substances, either through the complex visualizations and mantras prescribed in unexcelled-yoga-tantra traditions or simply by reciting thrice the syllables *oṃ āḥ hūṃ*. By reflecting on how the offerings' nature is gnosis and their function "to produce the special bliss-emptiness gnosis in the domain of the six senses," one comes to see them as secret offerings. One then visualizes all the offerings pervading everywhere; a later interpolation instructs us to do so with "an unwavering mind."

With the completion of the offerings, one engenders out of "the vast space

718. Modern editions of the feast text (but not Sangyé Yeshé's original) usually also incorporate a vajra song, the *Song of the Spring Queen* (*Dpyid kyi rgyal mo glu dbyangs*), which is often attributed to Tsongkhapa, though it is not found in his collected works.

719. See, e.g., Dalai Lama 1988, 16, and K. Gyatso 1992b, 33–40.

of inseparable bliss and emptiness" the ritual's main visualization (verses 9–13), which will be maintained through most of *Offering to the Guru*. At the top of a wish-fulfilling tree, surrounded by "clouds of Samantabhadra's offerings," one sees one's own guru in the guise of Lama Losang Thupwang Dorjé Chang, the form of Tsongkhapa taught to Ensapa by the great Tibetan siddha Chökyi Dorje, who received it from Tsongkhapa himself in a vision. This threefold image consists of (1) Tsongkhapa dressed as a monk wearing a yellow paṇḍita hat, (2) at his heart the Buddha Śākyamuni,[720] and (3) at his heart Vajradhara in union with his consort Dharmadhātvīśvarī. The guru sits resplendently in vajra posture. In truth, his aggregates are the five tathāgatas; his elements the four consorts; his sense fields, channels, sinews, and joints the great bodhisattvas; his pore hairs the 21,000 arhats; his limbs the wrathful protectors; and his light rays directional guardians and "secret yakṣas," or protector deities. He is surrounded by the gurus of various lineages and the deities of different levels of practice, from tantric yidams (tutelary deities), through buddhas, bodhisattvas, and arhats, down to ḍākas, ḍākinīs, and Dharma protectors. While one chants verses and a mantra of invitation, light rays emanate from a *hūṃ* at the heart of each figure, drawing down from his or her abode the corresponding "gnosis being" (*jñānasattva, ye shes pa*), the actual divine figure, whose absorption into the visualized "pledge being" (*samayasattva, dam tshig pa*) is sealed by the syllables *jaḥ hūṃ baṃ hoḥ*.

The next major section (verses 18–42) involves recitation of the sevenfold worship rite. First (verses 18–22), one mentally *bows down* to the guru in his various manifestations: as enjoyment body, emanation body, and Dharma body; as emanation of the Triple Gem; and as identical with all buddhas. Second (verses 23–37), one *makes offerings*, including jewels, flowers, incense, lamps, perfume, food, drink, and song as outer offerings; the traditional Meru maṇḍala; an offering of practice; aromatic Chinese tea; the five hooks (i.e., meats) and five lamps (i.e., nectars)[721] as inner offerings; magical consorts "skilled in the sixty-four arts of love" as secret offerings; the great blissful gnosis of the supreme awakening mind as the suchness offering; medicines to cure the ills of the world; and last but not least, one's service to the guru.

720. This second aspect is not specified in the text but is regarded as implicit.

721. The five meats are the flesh of humans, cows, horses, elephants, and dogs; the five nectars are semen, blood, urine, feces, and marrow. In Indian tantric traditions, these forbidden and forbidding substances likely were consumed by those attending ritual feasts as a way of enhancing their appreciation for the ultimate lack of difference between the pleasant and the disgusting and perhaps of inducing an experience of nondual gnosis. In later times, especially in Tibet, a small piece of meat often substituted for the five meats, while a drop of alcohol stood in for the five nectars.

Third (verse 38), one *confesses* all one's transgressions from beginningless time, regrets them, and vows not to repeat them. Fourth (verse 39), in the face of their dream-like nature, one *rejoices* in the bliss, joy, and virtue that have arisen in the mindstreams of ordinary and ārya beings, those advanced practitioners who have realized the nature of reality face to face. Fifth (verse 40), one *requests* a rainfall of "profound and extensive Dharma" to "create, sustain, and increase a moonflower garden for the benefit and bliss of infinite beings." Sixth (verse 41), one *entreats* the guru-buddhas—whose bodies are not, in fact, subject to birth and death—to remain until the end of saṃsāra. Seventh (verse 42) one *dedicates* all one's virtue to others, so that one never need be separated from the guru and will, in the end, attain the state of Vajradhara.

One next (verses 43–54) praises the guru and makes fervent appeals to him for blessing. The guru is described as an upholder of the Vinaya who is a great sea of morality; a Mahāyāna spiritual friend who is the buddhas' Dharma heir; a vajra holder who is expert in mantra and tantra; a compassionate refuge and protector who tames unruly beings, enacts the buddhas' deeds in our dark age, provides for us a field for the generation of merit, and assists beings through skillful means; a distillation of the Triple Gem, whose body is made of buddhas, bodhisattvas, and protectors; a guardian of primordial union who engages in the play of omniscient gnosis; and the awakening mind itself, pervading all, inseparable from the play of connate joy. One then repeats three times a slow, solemn prayer (verse 53) in which one identifies the guru with the yidam, the ḍākinīs, and the Dharma protectors, takes him as one's sole refuge, and appeals to him to hold one with his "hooks of compassion" in every circumstance and to protect one from fear, grant all yogic attainments, be one's friend, and guard one from interferences. At the conclusion of this special appeal (verse 54), rays of white, red, and blue light absorb into one's forehead, throat, and heart cakras, respectively, then all three rays absorb into all three cakras at once. By this, at least symbolically, one's body, speech, and mind are purified, obstacles to awakening are cleared away, empowerments are received, and buddha bodies are obtained. A double of the guru then absorbs into one, conferring blessing. If one were to practice mahāmudrā meditation as part of ritual, this would be the point at which to do so. Alternatively, one may practice a sādhana and/or recite mantras at this juncture.

This also is the point at which the congregation will typically interrupt the recitation of *Offering to the Guru* to chant and perform the tantric ritual feast, or *tsok* (verses T1–29), the core of which was composed by Paṇchen Chögyen's guru, Khedrup Sangyé Yeshé. In its most elaborate form, the tsok involves the disciples' offering the guru a multitude of substances, including food, the sculpted sacramental cakes known as tormas (*gtor ma*), and most crucially, liquor and meat, which then are redistributed to the congregation. The rite begins (T1–6) with the purification of the offerings: one visualizes all the earth and sky filled with precious substances, which produce "a special gnosis of bliss and emptiness," reflecting their true nature. "In the grand play of gnosis," the text continues, all regions are vajra fields, all houses vajra palaces, and all beings ḍākas and ḍākinīs, such that "everywhere there is only purity." One then visualizes the offering substances inside a human skull cup atop a tripod of human heads that is heated by a fire blown by the wind. When the fire heats the skull cup, the substances melt, and through the syllables *oṃ*, *āḥ*, and *hūṃ* above the cup, they emit light rays, which spread to all ten directions and then are drawn back to the syllables. The syllables melt into nectar, then melt into the liquid in the skull cup, "purifying, transforming, and increasing" it. One next (T7–8) invokes the gurus and various buddha-deities, inviting them to the offering site, where they take their place on a jeweled throne. One then requests the presiding master to bless the various substances, which they do while holding them at their throat. In verses of offering (T9–13) that are repeated thrice, one addresses, in order, one's root and lineage gurus, the hosts of yidams and deities, the Triple Gem, the hosts of ḍākinīs and Dharma protectors, and the hosts of motherly sentient beings, asking that they enjoy "this sea of uncontaminated ritual-feast offering blessed by concentration, mantra, and mudrā" and bestow great rainfalls of blessings, yogic attainments, holy Dharma, and buddha deeds, and effect an end to the suffering brought on by deceptive appearances.

Then, in the central act of the ritual (T14–15), one respectfully offers the tsok (in the form of liquor and meat) to the guru and entreats them to enjoy it; the guru responds that, seeing themselves as the guru-deity and maintaining the awakening mind, they will taste the tsok so as to satisfy the deities dwelling in their body. Uttering the mantra *a ho mahā sukha*, the guru tastes the tsok, and the congregation follows suit. In most instances, while the tsok is being consumed, all present recite the *Song of the Spring Queen* (T16–21) attributed to Tsongkhapa. These verses appeal to various deities present at the feast but above all to the "stainless ḍākinī," whose bliss-bestowing lotus (sex organ) is repeatedly celebrated, and who is asked to bestow connate great bliss and regard her devotees with mercy and beneficence. Next (T22–25), the leftover tsok is collected and offered to the oath-bound field protectors, amid requests for the success of the Dharma and the achievement of mundane enjoyments. Three additional verses (T26–28) make further requests for protection from interferences, the attainment of tantric powers, and the spread of happiness throughout the world. Finally (T29), one expresses the hope that through the merit produced by offering the tsok, one may become a "self-arisen buddha," who will "free the multitude of beings not freed by previous conquerors."

Returning to the main text of *Offering to the Guru*, one reviews in detail the stages of the path to awakening (verses 55–86). Devotion to the guru being the root of the path, one begins (verse 55) with a renewed appeal to the guru to serve as one's spiritual protector and caregiver. One then (verses 56–59) takes the perspective of beings of lesser and middle scope, requesting the guru to provide blessings so that one may recognize the value and brevity of human life; take refuge and practice virtue out of fear of the lower realms; and aspire to liberation from all of saṃsāra by adhering to the training in morality, concentration, and wisdom. One next (verses 60–71) asks the guru's blessing to adopt the great perspective of the bodhisattva and engender the essential Mahāyāna attitude, the awakening mind, by, for instance, feeling gratitude and compassion for all the beings who have been one's mother; recognizing that one is equal to others in wanting to avoid pain and enjoy happiness; overcoming self-cherishing and learning to cherish others; equalizing and exchanging oneself with others; taking on the suffering of others and giving them one's attainments (*gtong len*)[722]; transforming adverse conditions into a basis for practice of the path; and taking up the bodhisattva vows and the special Mahāyāna training in morality, concentration, and wisdom. This leads to a contemplation of the six perfections (verses 72–79) in which one asks the guru's blessing to be able to donate one's body, wealth, and virtues to all sentient beings; adhere to one's ethical precepts without the slightest lapse and with the good of others always in mind; maintain patience and equanimity in the face of the most trying circumstances; strive for awakening diligently and undiscouraged through any and every trial; meditate undistractedly and single-pointedly on the nature of reality; and arrive at true wisdom through a blissful, space-like meditative equipoise on ultimate reality that is based on an understanding that "not an atom of saṃsāra or nirvāṇa intrinsically exists, yet the dependent arising of cause and effect is unfailing." One then (verses 80–83) rehearses the stages of the tantric path, asking the guru's blessing to uphold one's vows and pledges; transform appearances through the practices of the generation stage; gain final union through the subtle-body practices of the completion stage; and, should awakening elude one in this life, be able to transfer one's consciousness to a pure land at the time of death. By way of sum-

722. A practice, traced to Indian masters like Śāntideva and developed in Kadam tradition, in which one typically visualizes sending (*gtong*) to other beings one's own happiness and spiritual attainments in the form of light and taking on (*len*) their suffering and delusion in the form of darkness or smoke. These two phases often are "mounted on" the out-breath and in-breath, respectively.

mary (verses 84–86) one appeals to the guru to care for one and accept one into their retinue in each and every birth, and in the meantime, to come to the crown of one's head and "set your radiant lotus feet firmly at the center of my heart."

In the last two verses of *Offering to the Guru* (87–88), one dedicates "whatever bright virtue"—that is, merit—one has created to the cause of fulfilling the aspirations of the buddhas and bodhisattvas, hence of gaining realizations and helping sentient beings. One prays, further, that one's merit allow one always to be in contact with the traditions of the Mahāyāna and complete one's journey from renunciation, to the awakening mind, to right view, through the two tantric stages, and to arrive at complete buddhahood. In most performances of *Offering to the Guru*, five verses of benevolence that conclude the text of the ritual feast (T30–34) are added. These verses express the wish that, through one's merit, one's own practice may be successful, the teachings and institutions of the Buddha and Tsongkhapa may flourish, the aims of beings may be realized, one may remain in contact with Tsongkhapa's teaching, and the guru may "remain in this land, as immutable as a vajra."

Before moving on, we should touch briefly but explicitly on the connection between *Offering to the Guru* and mahāmudrā. It is fourfold. First, later Geluk tradition, if not Paṇchen Chögyen himself, regarded the ritual as part of the Ganden Hearing Transmission that was transmitted—along with its emanated scripture—from Mañjughoṣa to Tsongkhapa, then passed down through several generations of lineage holders until it reached Paṇchen Chögyen. The transmission contains many important teachings, none more prominent than those of guru yoga and mahāmudrā, which have a natural association by virtue of their shared heritage. Second, because the mahāmudrā meditation explained by Paṇchen Chögyen in *Highway of the Conquerors* and *Lamp So Bright* is practiced in the context of guru yoga, *Offering to the Guru* provides a natural ritual context in which to focus on mahāmudrā. Third, in specific terms, Yeshé Gyaltsen tells us in his commentary on *Offering to the Guru* that the appropriate point to undertake the practice of mahāmudrā is just before the end of the ritual, when, having requested (in verse 86) that one's guru set his feet at one's "lotus heart," one visualizes the field of assembly dissolving into the guru and the guru melting into one's heart, then feels inseparably united with the guru's mind. From within that state of union with the guru's mind, one may proceed through serenity and insight meditation, assisted perhaps by the recitation of *Highway of the Conquerors* and the *Mahāmudrā Lineage Prayer*.[723] Fourth and finally, the entirety of *Offering to the Guru* is to be practiced with a tantric mindset, most particularly with the

723. Kachen Yeshe Gyaltsen 2014, 360–62.

luminous connate gnosis of emptiness and bliss—which for Paṇchen Chögyen, as we have seen, is the very definition of tantric mahāmudrā. Thus *Offering to the Guru* may not ever mention mahāmudrā, but it is easy to see why it came to be regarded as an important way in which one might approach the practice.

Paṇchen Chögyen's Spiritual Songs

There is no single, definitive collection of Paṇchen Chögyen's spiritual songs (*mgur*). Dozens of poems are scattered throughout a number of important texts. They are most concentrated, however, however, in two sources: his massive, posthumously completed autobiography (Bz*AFPL*) and a text I refer to as the *Mila Songs*, whose full title is *A Guru-Yoga Practice Based on the Lord of Siddhas Mila, along with Spiritual Songs Not Included in the [Author's] Life-Story* (Bz*MLNJ*). In the *Autobiography*, the songs are interspersed with far-longer passages of narrative prose, perhaps in accordance with the time in Paṇchen Chögyen's life when they were composed. The *Mila Songs*, on the other hand, is a self-conscious collection of twenty-three songs, juxtaposed (perhaps by the Paṇchen himself, perhaps by the editor of his collected works) with a guru-yoga practice devoted to Milarepa, which Paṇchen Chögyen says he composed at Tashi Lhunpo at the repeated insistence of the scholar-ascetic Sönam Yarphel. Like other Tibetan spiritual songs, Paṇchen Chögyen's poems use a variety of metrical schemes (though most commonly seven, eight, nine, or eleven syllables per line) to cover a range of themes, from beginning meditations on the preciousness of human life to Madhyamaka and tantric expressions of the nature of reality. Often quite personal, the poems employ both traditional metaphors and images unique to Paṇchen Chögyen, sometimes (as with Milarepa) drawn from nature. A significant number of the songs, which Tibetan scholars would include under the subgenre "songs of the view" (*lta mgur*), either mention mahāmudrā or take up themes typical in Tibetan mahāmudrā verse, such as emptiness, the nature of mind, and the joys of yogic life. It is on those that we will focus here.

Song 1[724] begins with a Sanskrit homage to Guru Mañjughoṣa and a celebration of Vajradhara. Paṇchen Chögyen then bemoans "the demon of delusive grasping at things," the source of our continued suffering, and encourages us to see that they are "unarisen from the start," so that both subject and object "dissolve into the Dharma realm, like ice in the vastness of the sea." In that realm, one transcends all conventionalities and conceptual elaboration,

724. The songs are translated below in part 5, section 10.

"enters into the luminous realm," and goes beyond even seeing. The Paṇchen next exhorts "beings in terror of saṃsāra" to see reality as an empty expanse in which all concepts are transcended yet "the Dharma of cause and effect is unfailing." This, he says, is the middle path, where "there is no alteration of appearance and emptiness," the primordially pure realm where action, cause, and effect do not fail. The poem ends with an appeal to Tsongkhapa to bless "even unkind beings" to attain such a realization.

Song 2 also begins with a Sanskrit homage to Guru Mañjughoṣa, followed by a verse of homage to the magician-father guru who's "like an untrue dream" to the author, his "illusory son." In the next six verses, Paṇchen Chögyen asserts the validity of the conventional in the face of its ultimate emptiness by stressing the inseparable union, in ultimate realization, of, in turn, illusion and emptiness, appearance and emptiness, conventional and ultimate truths, emptiness and dependent arising, truth and falsity, and emptiness and causality. Each of the six verses ends with a three-line chorus declaring that such union is attained through the guru's kindness and that he, Paṇchen Chögyen, is beyond the extremes of "is" or "isn't" and has "settled in the realm beyond extremes."

Song 3 begins with yet another Sanskrit homage to Guru Mañjughoṣa, followed by a verse of homage to father-guru Vajradhara, "the illusionist who makes even abstractions appear as the connate great bliss of the ineffable realm." Paṇchen Chögyen then declares that he sings a song exalting everyday appearances "in some small way." One must recognize any arising object as "unstable, impotent, false, and hollow"; with this recognition, one sees the truth: "the mind standing naked, draped in the finery of emptiness." While all conventions are empty, he adds, nevertheless the wise do consider questions of virtue and vice. They view self-grasping as the enemy and, once it is conquered, they can, like Paṇchen Chögyen, gaze into "the vast mirror without reference point" and view themselves "in a way that does not view." Phenomena may be without any basis, yet in the Dharma realm, anything can and does appear, and phenomena—beyond singularity and difference, beyond expression—all taste the same. In conclusion, says the Paṇchen, although even the Buddhist path is ultimately nonexistent, he asks to attain the three buddha bodies for the sake of sentient beings.

Song 4 begins, too, with a Sanskrit homage to Guru Mañjughoṣa and, unusually, lacks a following verse of prostration. In the opening verse, Paṇchen Chögyen celebrates "the Dharma realm where appearances are not blocked" and the enjoyment, within the mindstream, of the single taste of bliss and emptiness blended together. The next two verses bemoan the attitudes and actions of sentient beings, who are "bound by the noose of desirable things' allure," bedeviled by the "sorcerer of self-grasping," and "trembling with the fevers of attachment and anger." The fourth verse contrasts those who believe in appearances—who are "weary, remorseful, and afraid"—with those who see reality and "dissolve into laughter," their hearts glad, their minds blissful. The penultimate verse asks rhetorically and metaphorically what our discerning friends will think if we are attached to a "beautiful, barren woman." The final verse praises the āryas, who have studied and meditated, and who are "drenched with the pollen of essential deep meaning and sprinkle dewdrops on the path of words."

Song 5 lacks a Sanskrit homage, beginning directly with a request to "triply kind guru Vajradhara" to root out the enemy: "the eight mundane concerns and my clinging to shiny appearances." In the following four verses, Paṇchen Chögyen cites the aims set by most humans—long life, wealth, praise, and pleasure—and avers that even if he dies soon, is poor, is despised, and suffers, it is fine with him, because his mind is free. In the fifth verse, he states that whatever one experiences, positive or negative, "is the guru's blessing." The final verse describes the instruction—derived from Śāntideva, Atiśa, and Tsongkhapa—as "changing poison to nectar." Every verse but the first ends with one or another version of a chorus in which the Paṇchen expresses his equanimity toward whatever befalls him and asserts that, in every case, "it's delightful: it's a trove of delight."

Song 6 begins with the Sanskrit homage to Guru Mañjughoṣa followed by a verse of homage to Father Jé Tsongkhapa, who is described as one "who knows the whole extent of elaborations yet rests eternally in the unelaborated realm." In the second and third verses, Paṇchen Chögyen describes his long-term beguilement by the "evil sorcerer of self-grasping" and celebrates how "this very day," through the guru's kindness, he has seen "the original intrinsic nature, unelaborated." The fourth verse plays out a nuptial metaphor, describing how the "groom of self-arisen awareness" joins in the realm of the real with the "bride of objective luminosity," in a "marriage without union or separation." In the next two verses, the Paṇchen describes his transcendence of nihilism and eternalism, since even in emptiness causality still holds, yet all dependently arisen phenomena are illusory appearances. He goes on to describe himself as "the yogī in the sky of emptiness" who has banished "the bandit of grasping at true existence," seen through "the game of assigning names," lost his fear of birth and death, and—thanks to his guru—"reached the abode of healing and rest, the ambrosial essence, the emptiness of things." The song concludes with the assertion, "I amuse myself on the mahāmudrā path" and exhorts readers who desire liberation to do the same.

Song 7, which is one of the longest and most nature-oriented in our selection, begins with a Sanskrit homage to the guru followed by a verse of prostration to Tsongkhapa, who is said to be in actuality all the buddhas and to rob the enemy, saṃsāric existence, of its terror. Over the next five verses, Paṇchen Chögyen describes the charms of his retreat hut and its natural setting, "beside a ravine in a fruited hidden valley." He is captivated, he says, by "the seductive play of the emerald glow of every mountain and stream," by flowers of every hue, by a turquoise lake surrounded by mountains, with its leafy groves and abundant birdlife, its medicinal and sweet-smelling plants. There, says the Paṇchen, "I walk and sit, mindful and alert," and see through appearances, to the "unthinkable and empty" nature of the things he sees. The next three verses describe how the true master rejoices in the realization that phenomena ultimately are nonexistent and beyond analysis and how sentient beings similarly will rejoice when they have overcome grasping and "understand such things." This special teaching, Paṇchen Chögyen asserts, "is not found in the general transmission," so we must rely on the instruction of the gurus, whose minds are "suffused with tantric Dharma," hence cannot be "swamped by distorted views." In the last three verses, Paṇchen Chögyen concludes by requesting the fulfillment of the prayers of sentient beings and the masters, his own attainment of contentment with the fruit of every deed, and the awakening of all beings on "the path whose essence is emptiness and compassion."

Song 8 begins with a Sanskrit homage to Guru Jé—that is, Tsongkhapa—followed by an appeal to the Triple Gem for "every supreme and common yogic attainment." The next four verses are a traditional expression of topics contemplated on the first stages of the path to awakening: the rarity and preciousness of a human rebirth; the need to transcend attachment; the fragility of life; the insecurity of mundane pleasures, even those enjoyed by powerful gods; and the necessity to rely on the guru and the three trainings (in morality, concentration, and wisdom) if we are to attain liberation. The song concludes with the statement that it was set down at the request of a disciple "by the crazed bee, Chökyi Gyaltsen, a do-nothing who wanders aimlessly."

Song 9 begins with a Sanskrit homage to Guru Mañjughoṣa followed by a verse of prostration to "triply kind guru Vajradhara" and a verse describing the song as an "unwavering appeal" to the guru that its author master "the means for becoming a buddha in a single life . . . the essence of the profound path." Paṇchen Chögyen goes on to equate conventional appearances with "the unfailing dependent arising of cause and effect," and the "ultimate beyond elaboration" with the sharpness of a rabbit's horn. He emphasizes the importance, on the path, of being able to distinguish the two truths, generate the awakening mind, and balance emptiness with compassion. This path, "a sky treasury of unobstructed virtues," results in the "ultimate union," mahāmudrā, which is the "quintessence of the three buddha bodies." In meditation, one must meditate with unwavering focus, "steady as the middle of a river," and in postmeditation, one must apply the three regards—body as deity, speech as mantra, mind as buddha—and maintain pure conduct that is "a great imperturbable wave." In the last verse, the Paṇchen sings joyously that he is a yogī on this path and his song an offering to the Triple Gem.

Song 10, which begins with the simple Sanskrit expression of auspiciousness, *svāsti*, is a brief report on a dream, in which initially, Paṇchen Chögyen notes, "various instinctive delusions arose." When he saw their defects, however, his mind "dissolved in the spacious Dharma realm itself," like ice melting in the ocean, and in that "azure realm" he saw various wonders that, whether real or imagined, "were like rainbows, or like the moon reflected in water." Words, he concludes, are like a rainbow in the azure realm: they can lead us to exaggerate or understate the way things really exist. Hence, "I simply put labels away."

Song 11 begins with a Sanskrit salutation to the guru (perhaps Sangyé Yeshé, perhaps Tsongkhapa), who then is described as a sovereign of ten million maṇḍala wheels, who plays the role of a monk in "this final age," performs buddha deeds, and sees the world with the eye of gnosis. Paṇchen Chögyen then exhorts his readers not to cling to the conventions of saṃsāra and nirvāṇa but to see them as they are and thereby be freed from eternalism and nihilism. He encourages them to serve the master of the "uncorrupted blessing transmission," who provides an understanding of the sūtras and tantras and access to special instructions. Turning one's sight to "the face of reality," one should fix the mind and heart on Tsongkhapa. Learning his teachings, one should "cut the root of clinging" amid appearances and be free from "is" and "is not" within awareness, recognizing the mutual implication of dependent arising and emptiness. This yoga of the union of dependent arising and emptiness, Paṇchen Chögyen concludes, perfects view, meditation, and conduct.

Song 12 begins with Paṇchen Chögyen's request to Vajradhara, in Tibetan, to confer upon him all supreme and common yogic attainments, then recounts how one day, as the Paṇchen was on his way to Ganden to make offerings, he had a vision of "manifold objects." With his "sense doors unstopped," he analyzed the objects and found that their appearance and their emptiness were not in contradiction. Recognizing this "immeasurable union," he states, is the key to all the Buddha's teachings. Since nothing that appears has even an atom "that's not just a name that's labeled by thought," why, he asks, bother with rejections and proofs? Furthermore, even the fires of the deepest hell have no more reality than a fire we dream, so why worry? Even the great Hindu gods, he notes, are unattached to mundane splendor, so how much less should we be. This insight, he concludes, he owes to his guru, whose blessing transmission "is not a transmission of arid verbal explanation."

Song 13 begins with the exclamation, "*Ha, ha!*" Paṇchen Chögyen celebrates "the unimpeded arising of mind's clear awareness," in which nothing arises and all appearance is like "the posturing of a barren woman's daughter." If in the Dharma realm there is no arising or appearance, no subject or object, why, he asks, is he prompted to sing? Because, he replies, mahāmudrā meditation, where there is no "I" who meditates, is delightful, "it's a trove of delight." And although death may come at any moment, the mind is at base a constellation of appearance, emptiness, and bliss, so even suffering is delightful, a trove of delight. When logicians hear this, the Paṇchen concludes, "they think it's a mass of contradictions"; yogīs, on the other hand, "break out in smiles," for they have experienced the meaning behind the words.

Song 14 begins with a Sanskrit salutation to mahāmudrā and Paṇchen Chögyen's appeal to Tsongkhapa, "father unequaled in kindness," to remain at the anthers of his lotus heart. In the main verses, the Paṇchen reviews the basic points of the stages-of-the-path meditation: the rarity and transience of a human life, the need to practice diligently, the importance of refuge in the guru and the Triple Gem, and the sincere wish to deliver all beings from suffering. He observes that, although he has for eons "wandered in saṃsāra by force of deluded mind," now he no longer chases after delusions, for he is "blessed by the primordial nature of all things." His goal is the "unwavering vajra mind," and the path is mahāmudrā, where beyond hope or fear, or proof or rejection, he "gently relaxes into the Dharma realm," and his body (that of a deity) is empty appearance, his speech (vajra recitation)[725] is empty sound, and mind (the great seal) is empty clarity. He concludes by dedicating his collections of merit and gnosis to the "great awakening."

Song 15 begins with a Sanskrit salutation to Guru Mañjughoṣa. After a verse of homage to the "fatherly guru," Paṇchen Chögyen sings of the basis of practice, which is "the way the two truths abide"; the path of practice, which is the exercise of wisdom and means; and the fruition of practice, which is a state of union marked by "the unobscured inseparability of the deep and the vast." He goes on to sing of the royal view, which is starkly seeing the unarisen and stainless nature of mind; the ideal meditation, which is "settling mindfully and alertly" on the mind itself; and supreme conduct, which is the freedom we enjoy when "the stake of internal self-grasping has been removed." If you want all this, concludes the Paṇchen, then "feed on the heavenly nectar in the perfect vessel of your mind," and soon enough, the three buddha bodies "are right in your hand."

725. *Rdo rje bzlas pa* is the completion-stage form of mantra recitation, in which, typically, there is no actual vocalization.

Song 16 begins with a Sanskrit salutation to the guru followed by a verse of homage to the buddhas arrayed in their buddha fields and to the compassionate guru, who, like a dancer, appears in various forms in "this tainted age." As in the previous song, Paṇchen Chögyen focuses on view, meditation, and conduct, describing each twice. In the first iteration, the view is the recognition that, in the Dharma realm, all conventions are merely appearances in our mind; meditation is single-pointed placement on emptiness, the true nature of things; and conduct is virtuous action of body, speech, and mind performed with the understanding that, ultimately, even the awakening mind is illusory. In the second iteration, the view involves the expulsion of ego-grasping through understanding the nature of all things; meditation is "highly subtle and detailed examination" of "the original nature of all things," of which we then remain constantly aware; and conduct is a union of method and wisdom that involves recognizing that "good" and "bad" are merely names whose nature eludes all mental elaboration. In the final verse, the Paṇchen dedicates the merit arising from the necklace he has strung together "for faithful beings."

Song 17 also begins with a Sanskrit salutation to the guru and with Paṇchen Chögyen's request to his kindly root guru to reside at his heart. It also takes up the triad of view, meditation, and conduct. The "royal view" is described as a realization, beyond eternalism and nihilism, that nothing in saṃsāra or nirvāṇa—our own minds included—possesses even an atom of true existence. The "supremacy of meditation" involves resting in the Dharma realm while eliminating dullness and excitement and maintaining mindfulness and alertness, "so they flow like the Ganges." The "supremacy of conduct" is a postmeditative practice in which, from within "the illusion-like yoga," we do what we like "on the pure path," free from any vice of body, speech, or mind. The song concludes, like many others, with a dedication of merit, so that deluded beings may "win the battle against the four māras with the wisdom sword of understanding the way things are."

Song 18, the third-longest in our collection, begins with a Sanskrit homage to Mañjughoṣa and a verse celebrating Jé Matibhadra—that is, Losang (Drakpa), or Tsongkhapa—as a leonine master who wears "the mane of the Buddha's word, the sūtras and tantras," emits the roar of emptiness, and smashes the brains of "the demon elephant, grasping at things." Paṇchen Chögyen sings of how he once was "drunk on the liquor of grasping at things," but when he ceased to collect "the chaff of denying cause and effect," he saw the truth, he "experienced exuberant joy within illusion's machine, and compassion arose." "Today," he continues, "this old heap . . . has fled to the empty realm." In that vast expanse, he "spins the spear of awareness" and pierces the breast of "the enemy within," self-grasping. In the Dharma realm, all phenomena are absorbed in "naturally virtuous play," and the mind, like a she-fish darting about in the ocean's depths, "enjoys the water play, delighting in every experience." The Paṇchen declares himself "the yogī of unarisen sky," who has transcended judgments of good and evil and who sleeps "within the inseparability of saṃsāra and nirvāṇa." Indeed, the āryas see all appearances of saṃsāra and nirvāṇa as "unimpeded brilliance" and whatever arises as "illusion's grand play." Seeing that nothing anywhere can stand on its own, he realized that "the foundation of saṃsāric existence has crumbled" and experienced bliss "deep within." In the final two verses, Paṇchen Chögyen delights in the harmony between emptiness and dependent arising and once again salutes Tsongkhapa and those who uphold his lineage.

Song 19 begins with an appeal to "the great Mādhyamika, Sumati"—that is, Losang (Drakpa)—and "the exalted one inseparable from him, Ensapa," to think lovingly on their son and help him uproot self-grasping. The next two verses lament the condition of sentient beings, who, as if "afflicted by tainted food or defective vision or tumors," "grasp at self when there is no self" and hence continue to circle in saṃsāra, sowing the seeds of consciousness and moistening them with water from the river of craving, producing from them sprouts of name and form, from which all other sufferings arise. Paṇchen Chögyen then switches gears, asking rhetorically how there could be "even the name of suffering" when one has discerned "the Dharma realm face to face through discernment that realizes truthlessness." He celebrates "the king, awareness and knowledge," who soars high in the sky of "the spacious expanse of true emptiness," where "all arising things are taken as the Dharma body," and who afterward sees all appearances as like a dream, a reflection, or a substance magically charmed. He celebrates the interdependence of emptiness and dependent arising, adding that there is not "a single thing in saṃsāra or nirvāṇa" that isn't "a name that's merely labeled by thought." He goes on to celebrate how:

> Meditating on nothing but the definitive meaning,
> making no effort to squeeze out suffering,
> I rest happily in the abiding nature.

He concludes by singing that when he sees his own nature, "the friend I've known so long," then all objects of the six senses arise as his own nature, the path is a play of conceptuality, and there is no longer even a need to stop notions of true existence or to realize truthlessness: "This is the unfixed yoga. O joy!"

Song 20, the longest in the collection, begins with a Sanskrit salutation to Guru Mañjughoṣa followed by Paṇchen Chögyen's request to Tsongkhapa—"who saw as it is the meaning of emptiness and dependent arising"—to remain forever as an ornament at his crown. The main part of the song starts with a request to the guru to help him realize the "union of appearance and emptiness" implied by Tsongkhapa's central teaching. This is followed by the first instance of the refrain that will be repeated throughout the song:

> *Ha ha!* Aware of my penchant for falsehood,
> I have no cause for elsewhere attaining truth;
> attaining the meaning of having no cause for attaining,
> seeing the show where there is no cause for seeing—
> *e ma ho!* I take up this song of expansive joy.

In the verses preceding later refrains, the Paṇchen sings of how, for someone meditating on "the profound Madhyamaka path," all phenomena are "free from every elaborated sign"; good and bad are like "rainbows along their paths in the sky"; relief from saṃsāric suffering is found in maintaining "childlike awareness within suchness, reality"; whatever arises is "wide-open Dharma body"; objects of clinging are "unarisen, like a lotus in the sky"; and the yogī's mind settles in space-like meditative equipoise. In describing postmeditation, he laments the sufferings of his "age-old mothers"—sentient beings—who cling to false appearances as if they were true and generates compassion for them that is mixed with the recognition that they have no intrinsic nature. He concludes the song by playfully observing that the lies he has uttered and the yoga of truth are united "when you have the eye that sees that all is unseen" and you hoist "the Dharma banner without a Dharma." Finally, he expresses the hope that through his merit, sentient beings may understand the falsity of appearances, obtain the "dream-like three buddha bodies," and "teach the echo-like Dharma."

Song 21 begins with a Sanskrit salutation to the guru and by Paṇchen Chögyen's going for refuge to Tsongkhapa and the Triple Gem. He goes on to give advice for serenity meditation, describing in general terms the need for all practitioners to purify negativities and accumulate merit and gnosis through practice of the sevenfold worship rite, and then specifying that one should "reject desire for the vulgar body" and see oneself in deity form, uttering speech as mantra and focusing single-pointedly on the divinity of one's own mind. Whether one is focused on a divine form or the intrinsic nature of mind, it is important to maintain unwavering concentration, recognizing that the various obstacles that arise are merely projections that must be seen for what they are: manifestations of anger, attachment, or delusion whose true nature is actually that of the mind: "clear and aware."

Song 22 begins with a Sanskrit salutation to mahāmudrā and Paṇchen Chögyen's brief request to Tsongkhapa to dwell on the anthers of his lotus heart. The song proper is a concise summary of the practice of mahāmudrā detailed in *Highway of the Conquerors* and *Lamp So Bright*. Paṇchen Chögyen first acknowledges the rarity, importance, and transience of a human life and the importance of not wasting it. Next, he goes for refuge to the guru and the Triple Gem and generates love, compassion, and the awakening mind. With a "mind full of respectful devotion tinged with tenderness," he contemplates "the profound path of guru yoga." Guru yoga, in turn, is the doorway to the mahāmudrā path, in which, the Paṇchen says, "I see the mind's own open face as emptiness." There, in "uncontrived and easy placement of mind," one rests in "the actual primordial nature of all things," recognizing all appearances as nothing more than mental depictions, to be discarded within the Dharma realm. In sum, we should rest at all times in a meditative equipoise in which the body is seen as a divine body of inseparable emptiness and appearance, speech is uttered as the vajra recitation of empty sound, and mind is experienced as "the mahāmudrā of bliss and emptiness." Finally, in a state in which he is "unaffected by the poison of grasping after signs," Paṇchen Chögyen dedicates the merit of his song to "the great awakening."

Why Mahāmudrā?

Before leaving Paṇchen Chögyen so as to discuss his successors in the hearing transmission, we might briefly consider a question that begs to be asked. Given that—regardless of the *oral* tradition that may have preceded him—Paṇchen Chögyen was almost certainly the first Gelukpa to *write down* instructions for a distinctly Geluk practice of mahāmudrā, why did he choose to do so? If the human lineage of the oral tradition really did originate with Tsongkhapa, yet Jé Rinpoché felt it inappropriate to commit his instructions to writing, and if as relatively recent a holder of the lineage as Ensapa (supposedly Paṇchen Chögyen's previous rebirth) still felt it inappropriate to write the teachings down, why did Paṇchen Chögyen, late in the sixteenth or early in the seventeenth century, take it upon himself to do so? Was he instructed thus by his own guru, Khepdrup Sangyé Yeshé? Did he feel that with the disappearance of the emanated scripture, the tradition was in danger of dying out, hence required preservation in writing? Or, did he simply feel that the tradition need no longer be restricted, and could be appreciated by a wider audience? Was he searching for a Geluk practice that could compete, in Tsang and elsewhere, with the famous and popular mahāmudrā teachings of the Kagyü? Or, to take another angle on the politics of the text, was he seeking a basis for finding common ground with the Kagyü?

We probably never will know for certain, for Paṇchen Chögyen nowhere explains why he decided to bring the mahāmudrā teaching into the public domain. He does not report that Sangyé Yeshé told him to write it down, so we must assume that the decision to do so was made by the Paṇchen himself. The colophon to *Highway of the Conquerors* typically and simply informs us that the text was written at the repeated urging of his disciples, and the circumstances of the composition of *Lamp So Bright* are reported no differently. Like Tsongkhapa and Ensapa before him, Paṇchen Chögyen could have demurred and refused his disciples' requests, but he did not.

To speculate that he committed the mahāmudrā practice to writing because of the absence of the emanated scripture presupposes that he did *not*, in fact, possess that mysterious text. As we have seen, Paṇchen Chögyen and Yeshé Gyaltsen both suggest that the disappearance—or, more properly, the return to the gods—of the emanated scripture may predate Paṇchen Chögyen's receipt of the transmission, but other accounts insist that the volume was kept on earth at least through Paṇchen Chögyen's time, or perhaps that of Yeshé Gyaltsen (1713–93),[726] or even Phabongkha Rinpoché (1878–1941).[727] For however long it remained in the human realm, the emanated scripture was a token of the Ganden Hearing Transmission's unique and private nature: only one master could possess the text, and its complete teaching, at a time. Thus, if Paṇchen Chögyen did not receive it—or chose to downplay his possession of it—he may have worried that the tradition was in danger, or he may simply have interpreted the volume's eclipse as a sign that the nature of the transmission had changed, such that teachings that had been heard and seen by only six masters in two hundred years now could be made available to a wider audience, which was karmically ready to receive it.[728]

As we know, Paṇchen Chögyen came of age and rose through the Geluk hierarchy at a time and place (late sixteenth–early seventeenth century Tsang) where relations between the Geluk and Kagyü were particularly fraught. Drawn as he might have been to the hermitic life, the Paṇchen himself was

726. See Willis 1995, 161–62n114. According to Willis, "There is a humorous story told about how the First Paṇchen . . . kept an empty space on his bookshelves. When it was asked why he did this, one of the Paṇchen's disciples replied, 'That is where the [emanated scripture] is kept.'"

727. Willis 1995, 151n80.

728. The Paṇchen's decision is somewhat reminiscent of that of Sachen Kunga Nyingpo, who chose to write down for the first time, and comment upon, Virūpa's *Vajra Verses*, which had until then been handed down orally by the earliest Sakya masters. Unlike Paṇchen Chögyen, however, who seems to have decided on his own to commit the mahāmudrā root verses to writing, Sachen publicized and wrote about the *Vajra Verses* with the permission of his teacher, Shangtön Chöbar (1053–1135). See Stearns 2001, 145 and 153–55. Thanks to José Cabezón for drawing this parallel to my attention.

not above the fray, and while he used his diplomatic skills to promote harmony among Tibet's various rival factions, the interests of the Geluk were probably never far from his mind. He did, after all, help to strengthen the Geluk in the Kagyü strongholds of Tsang and Bhutan, and forged relationships with various Mongol tribes that helped assure the enthronement of the Fourth and Fifth Dalai Lamas and pave the way for the Fifth Dalai Lama's suzerainty over much of Tibet—particularly at the expense of the Kagyü and their noble allies. It is tempting, therefore, to ascribe "political" motives to his publication of texts outlining a Geluk mahāmudrā system. If we choose to see Paṇchen Chögyen as a rival of the Kagyü, we could see his mahāmudrā texts as an attempt to show that Gelukpas were invested in the prestigious great seal quite as heavily as the Kagyü, hence deserving of equal respect and patronage.

Alternatively, we might regard Paṇchen Chögyen as someone who sought to defuse tensions between the Geluk and Kagyü, in this case by showing that the two had fundamental ideas and practices in common. Certainly, that is implicit in the famous claim, in *Highway of the Conquerors*, that all the great Tibetan meditative traditions come down to the same intention, or idea (*dgongs pa gcig*). Later Gelukpas of an ecumenical bent, from Thuken Chökyi Nyima to the Fourteenth Dalai Lama, have cited this claim with approval, and a few (including the Dalai Lama) have even suggested that the mahāmudrā system Paṇchen Chögyen promulgated should be regarded as a Geluk-Kagyü synthesis. As we will see in chapter 15, we have no clear evidence for this rather less cynical explanation of the Paṇchen's promotion of a Gelukpa mahāmudrā tradition, but it certainly remains a possibility.

We must concede, I think, Paṇchen Chögyen was a complex, multifaceted figure in a tumultuous place and time, and it is probably not too far-fetched to speculate that in his decision to write about mahāmudrā, he was motivated *both* by political rivalry with the Kagyü *and* a religiously-based desire to ameliorate relations with them. In any event, Paṇchen Chögyen lived to see the Geluk triumphant, not just in Tsang, but in all of Central Tibet, as his disciple the Fifth Dalai Lama was brought to power in 1642 by the armies of the Mongol chieftain, Gushri Khan. In the end, we really do not know why Paṇchen Chögyen decided to write *Highway of the Conquerors* and *Lamp So Bright*. We do know that, by committing the Geluk mahāmudrā tradition to writing, he assured both its preservation and its wider dissemination, and it is to the figures most responsible for keeping it alive in the centuries after the First Paṇchen's death that we turn in the next several chapters.

Part 3
Later Geluk Mahāmudrā

10. Paṇchen Chögyen's Successors

PAṆCHEN CHÖGYEN'S MOST famous disciple by far was the Fifth Dalai Lama Ngawang Losang Gyatso (1617–82), and the Paṇchen did transmit mahāmudrā teachings to his illustrious student. For reasons to be explored shortly, however, the Great Fifth does not figure in the lists of lineage masters succeeding Paṇchen Chögyen. The two direct disciples of Paṇchen Chögyen who *are* on the list are Drupchen Gendun Gyaltsen (1532–1607), who also was the Paṇchen's teacher, and his contemporary, Drungpa Tsöndrü Gyaltsen (1567–1650). These two inaugurated what later came to be seen as separate branches of the hearing transmission, centered primarily in Tsang and Amdo, respectively.[729]

Important figures in the Tsang line (which also extended into Ü) include the Second Paṇchen Lama Losang Yeshé (1663–1737), the Third Paṇchen Lama Palden Yeshé (1738–81), and several masters who commented specifically on Paṇchen Chögyen's mahāmudrā tradition, including Kachen Yeshé Gyaltsen (1713–93) and Ngulchu Dharmabhadra (1772–1851). Significant figures outside the standard lineage list include Gugé Losang Tenzin (1748–1813) and Keutsang Losang Jamyang (b. eighteenth century), each of whom wrote a commentary on Paṇchen Chögyen's mahāmudrā texts. The most important master in the Tsang line was undoubtedly Yeshé Gyaltsen, who was tutor to the Eighth Dalai Lama, a powerful cleric, and a prolific author who—among many other things—wrote biographies, treatises, and manuals, all of which did much to promote Geluk mahāmudrā and what he usually called

729. See Gyatso 1982, 11, and Willis 1995, 99, for details. Gyatso lists Drungpa Tsöndrü Gyaltsen, who was himself born in western Tibet, as belonging to both lineages (first in Amdo, second in Tsang). The "standard" lineage prayer composed by Paṇchen Chögyen, then updated by Kachen Yeshé Gyaltsen, Phabongkha Dechen Nyingpo, and others, agrees, although it lists him in the Tsang lineage as Drupai Gyaltsen Dzinpa, another of his several names. He and Phurbuchok Ngawang Jampa are the only figures mentioned twice in the lineage prayer. In his account of Paṇchen Chögyen's successors (below, part 5, section 2), Yeshé Gyaltsen notes the importance of a third disciple, "Drungpa Taphukpa." It is not impossible that the second reference to Tsöndrü Gyaltsen in the prayer is to Taphukpa; see below, note 1193.

the Ganden Hearing Transmission. His works provide the most complete and coherent account of the tradition that we possess, and along with Paṇchen Chögyen's foundational texts, they have become the standard lens through which the tradition is viewed.

The Amdo line includes such luminaries as Phurbuchok Ngawang Jampa (1682–1762), Könchok Jikmé Wangpo (1728–91), and Gungthang Tenpai Drönmé (1762–1823), of whom only the last wrote much on mahāmudrā. More significant in Amdo were figures outside the lineage, who include:

- Shar Kalden Gyatso (1607–77), a direct disciple of Paṇchen Chögyen who wrote treatises on mahāmudrā, songs of realization, and a lineage prayer
- Jamyang Shepai Dorjé (1648–1721), who wrote a commentary on Saraha's *Dohākoṣa*
- The Seventh Dalai Lama Kalsang Gyatso (1708–57)
- Changkya Rölpai Dorjé (1717–84), who was the author of many texts, including a series of beloved spiritual songs
- Thuken Losang Chökyi Nyima (1737–1802), whose extraordinary history of Asian religions, the *Crystal Mirror of Tenet Systems*, discusses Kagyü mahāmudrā in considerable detail
- Tsultrim Nyima (nineteenth century), who wrote a lengthy commentary on *Highway of the Conquerors*
- Akhu Sherab Gyatso (1803–75), who commented extensively on *Offering to the Guru*, among other texts
- Choné Lama Lodrö Gyatso (b. 1816), who wrote a large number of mahāmudrā-inflected spiritual songs
- Losang Dongak Chökyi Gyatso (1903–57), who wrote penetrating works on the intersections among Madhyamaka, the great perfection, and mahāmudrā

The Tsang and Amdo lineages eventually were reunited in the dominant Gelukpa master of the early twentieth century, Phabongkha Rinpoché Dechen Nyingpo (1878–1941), and were passed on by him to the Fourteenth Dalai Lama's principal tutors, Trijang Rinpoché (1901–81) and Ling Rinpoché (1903–83). Through them, and through the Fourteenth Dalai Lama, the Ganden Hearing Transmission became well known in the Geluk community and was conveyed, as well, to practitioners of Tibetan Buddhism born outside the Tibetan cultural sphere.

In the next five chapters, we will examine several important figures from each of the main lines stemming from Paṇchen Chögyen, and attempt to bring the tradition into the present day. Rather than discussing each of the branch lineages separately, we will proceed chronologically.

The Fifth Dalai Lama

The "Great Fifth" Dalai Lama, Ngawang Losang Gyatso (1617–82), is one of the towering figures of Tibetan history.[730] With the aid of the Qosot Mongol chieftain Gushri Khan (1582–1665), he secured hegemony over most of Tibet in 1642, ushering in the regime—the Ganden Phodrang—that would rule much of the plateau, with only brief interruptions, until the 1950s.[731] He unified Tibet politically as no ruler had since the imperial period, and he did so to the considerable advantage of the Geluk order, from which he had received his monastic vows and much of his education. As we have seen, he also was schooled in various Nyingma traditions, which he studied and practiced assiduously. With their important centers in border regions and the east (Amdo and Kham), the Nyingma were a lesser presence in Ü-Tsang and, besides, were generally not much involved in "national" politics. The Kagyü, on the other hand—especially the Black Hat Karmapas—had wielded considerable power in both Tsang and Kham, and it was Gushri Khan's annihilation of their power that assured the Dalai Lama's suzerainty over Tibet. Some Kagyü monasteries were taken over by the Geluk, and the order was "de-politicized" in Central Tibet for many generations. The other big losers in the struggles of 1642 were the Jonangpas, whose philosophical view of extrinsic emptiness was anathema to Gelukpas and who—probably more to the point—had aligned themselves with the Karmapa in opposing the Dalai Lama and Gushri Khan. Most of their centers in Ü and Tsang became Geluk and, except in parts of Kham and Amdo, they became thoroughly marginalized.

As already noted, Losang Chökyi Gyaltsen was one of the Great Fifth's principal tutors. It was Paṇchen Chögyen who oversaw the Dalai Lama's novice and full ordinations, transmitted countless teachings to him, and served him in various diplomatic capacities, right up to the time of the Paṇchen's death, in 1662. It is clear from the Great Fifth's autobiography that he had

730. See, e.g., Shakabpa 1984, 100–124, Mullin 2001, 185–238, and Schaeffer 2005b.

731. Of course, given the size of the Tibetan cultural area (more or less that of Western Europe) and limitations in transportation and communication technology, the degree to which the Ganden Phodrang actually exercised control was more or less inversely proportional to a locale's distance from Lhasa; we must not imagine that the regime of the Dalai Lamas was a highly centralized governing body, even in the twentieth century.

immense respect for the Paṇchen, and indeed it was he who oversaw the search for Paṇchen Chögyen's reincarnate successor, helping thereby to solidify the Paṇchen-Dalai connection that would be so important to later Tibetan history. At the same time, though, the Fifth Dalai Lama's connection to Paṇchen Chögyen's mahāmudrā teaching appears to be complicated. He acknowledges the importance of the great seal to his tutor when, in his secret biography of Paṇchen Chögyen, he reports that the Paṇchen Lama enjoyed visions of Saraha and Chökyi Dorjé and on one occasion saw Maitreya together with his own guru, Sangyé Yeshé, who was dressed as a mahāsiddha. When the Paṇchen appealed to them, rays from Maitreya's heart melted into Sangyé Yeshé, who appeared to assume a rainbow body—at which point Paṇchen Chögyen "understood the dependent arising that accomplishes the benefit of beings on the basis of the authentic, definitive mahāmudrā."[732] In his autobiography, the Great Fifth reports that he received teachings on the Ensa Hearing Transmission—hence, presumably, mahāmudrā—from Paṇchen Chögyen in 1654,[733] though it would be surprising if he had not heard the tradition from his guru earlier in his education.

In the *Flowing River Ganges*, the Dalai Lama's record of teachings he had obtained, he records his familiarity with the Geluk mahāmudrā tradition but adds, quite critically, "Surely, it would be good if the Gelukpas kept to what Gelukpas do; what's the point of pushing in amid the Kagyüpas?"[734] Along similar lines, the Fourteenth Dalai Lama records his great predecessor as having clearly expressed the opinion that the phrase *geden kagyü* (*dge ldan bka' brgyud*) in the subtitle of Paṇchen Chögyen's root text on Geluk mahāmudrā should be understood to refer *not* to a Geluk-Kagyü synthesis but to a Geluk "oral transmission."[735] Elsewhere, the Fifth Dalai Lama expresses some disdain for Kagyü mahāmudrā—or at least for practitioners during his lifetime. In his autobiography, for instance, he particularly singles out the Drukpa Kagyü for their unwarranted pretensions to understanding mahāmudrā and comments that "this was the time when mahāmudrā, the great voidness, was becom-

732. Ng*DPST* 7a [340].

733. Karmay 2014, 335.

734. Cf. Karmay 1988, 146. It is also possible that the Fifth Dalai Lama rejected the notion—central to Paṇchen Chögyen's articulation of the tradition—that mahāmudrā was not only a tantric term and practice but also had a Sūtra Vehicle aspect; oral communication from Jangtsé Chöjé Rinpoche Losang Tenzin, July 13, 2015.

735. Dalai Lama and Berzin 1997, 107 and 232. The Dalai Lama does not provide a reference for the Great Fifth's statement. For further discussion of this issue, see below, chapter 15.

ing extinct within its own establishment."[736] At the same time, critical of the Kagyü as the Great Fifth may have been—and we cannot forget the political dimension of his relation to them—he does reject the authenticity of a treasure text, attributed to Padmasambhava, that excoriates Kagyüpas as "a flock of demon emanations," the Kagyü as a "false religion," and mahāmudrā as a "stupid meditation" that leads beings "through the wrong path."[737] Nevertheless, the Fifth Dalai Lama never seems to have evinced much affinity for mahāmudrā, and it is unsurprising that he is not included in the lineage of Paṇchen Chögyen's successors in the transmission.

Shar Kalden Gyatso

Also outside the standard line of transmission, yet far more attuned to it than the Great Fifth, was Shar Kalden Gyatso (1607–77), a scholar, siddha, abbot, and poet from Amdo who studied with Paṇchen Chögyen while residing in Central Tibet. He was the first master after the First Paṇchen to write significant texts on Geluk mahāmudrā.[738] He was born in Repkong, in the far eastern part of Amdo. He was sent at an early age to study with his considerably older half-brother (or uncle, or cousin), Chöpa Rinpoché Losang Tenpai Gyaltsen (1581–1669), also known as Rongbo Chöjé, who would guide his education through the early part of his life. When Kalden Gyatso was eleven, his brother escorted him to Central Tibet, where, based primarily at Jangtsé College of Ganden Monastery, he spent the next decade studying with some of the great Geluk luminaries of the age, including Paṇchen Chögyen, from whom he received full ordination at the Jokhang in Lhasa in 1627. He returned to Amdo the following year. There, he studied the sūtras and tantras under thirty-three masters, of whom the most important were his oler relation Chöpa Rinpoché; his main teacher in most subjects, Chöjé Tenzin Losang Gyatso (1593–1638); the mahāsiddha from Denma, Tsultrim Gyatso; and Gyalsé Losang Tenzin. Like Chöpa Rinpoché, Kalden Gyatso was inspired by Milarepa and strongly inclined to the hermitic life, but at his brother's urging he first committed himself to institution building. In 1630, he founded a Geluk college, Thösam Ling, at the formerly Sakya monastery of Rongbo. He would administer and expand it for most of the rest of his life, and it would become the third largest Geluk monastery in Amdo, after Labrang and Kumbum. Around the time

736. Karmay 2014, 461; cf. 204, 245, and 356.

737. Karmay 2014, 381.

738. For details on Kalden Gyatso, see Sujata 2004, Namgyal 2011, Zasep 2019, 40, and Sujata 2019.

he turned thirty, he began to spend longer and longer periods in retreat, and although he did take time to teach disciples and attend to official duties—and to found a hermitage and tantric college at Tashi Khyil—through much of his later life he was essentially a peripatetic yogī and poet, in the style of Milarepa. His last seven years were mostly spent in retreat at Tashi Khyil, where he died in 1677.

Although Kalden Gyatso studied with Paṇchen Chögyen in Central Tibet, and clearly regarded him as an inspiring figure,[739] it seems that he learned the Geluk mahāmudrā tradition not from the Paṇchen but from three of his own gurus in Amdo: Chöpa Rinpoché, Tsultrim Gyatso, and Gyalsé Losang Tenzin, of whom the last was the most crucial. Of the hundred or so writings in Kalden Gyatso's collected works,[740] four are devoted to the Geluk mahāmudrā tradition. In addition, a number of his songs directly or indirectly refer to mahāmudrā.

His *Appeal to the Mahāmudrā Lineage* (Kd*PCGD*) is an update of Paṇchen Chögyen's *Mahāmudrā Lineage Prayer.* Its authorship is uncertain: although it is found in Kalden Gyatso's collected works, the modern scholar who has investigated Kalden Gyatso in the greatest depth, Victoria Sujata, proposes Chöpa Rinpoché as the author. She bases her claim on a note to the effect that the text had been "spoken" by him.[741] The editions to which I have access, however, specify that the text was spoken by Losang *Chökyi* Gyaltsen (i.e., the Paṇchen), not Losang *Tenpai* Gyaltsen (Chöpa Rinpoché).[742] This makes sense, given that roughly the first half of the prayer, and most of the end, is taken directly from Paṇchen Chögyen's original version. Up to Paṇchen Chögyen, the lineage laid out—Vajradhara, Mañjughoṣa, Tsongkhapa, Jampal Gyatso, Baso Chökyi Gyaltsen, Chökyi Dorjé, Ensapa, Sangyé Yeshé—and the verses of supplication to them, are taken verbatim from the Paṇchen Lama's text. There follow then verses of appeal to four masters who will figure in the "standard" lineage prayer edited first by Yeshé Gyaltsen in the eighteenth century and then Phabongkha Rinpoché and others in the twentieth century and Lama Zopa Rinpoché in the twenty-first: Paṇchen Chögyen, Gendun Gyaltsen, Gyaltsen Dzinpa, and Tsöndrü Gyaltsen.[743] Then come verses directed

739. See Sujata 2005, 73–74 and 364–66.

740. See Sujata 2005, 384–426.

741. Sujata 2005, 66.

742. Kd*PCGD* 3a [401].

743. It is important to note that the verses to each of these four differ considerably from the verses to the same four in the standard version; this would indicate that Yeshé Gyaltsen either did not know of Kelsang Gytaso's version or chose to ignore it.

to three men who do not figure in the standard list: Gyalsé Losang Tenzin, Kalden Gyatso himself, and Losang Tenpai Gyaltsen (Chöpa Rinpoché). It is unlikely that Kalden Gyatso composed a verse of supplication to himself, but he could well have written the others, including that to his older relation, Chöpa Rinpoché. Also, at the very end of the prayer, he adds four beautiful lines not found in Paṇchen Chögyen's version:

> Your holy body and my body, father,
> your holy speech and my speech, father,
> your holy mind and my mind, father—
> please bless me to know they're inseparably one.

Whether Kalden Gyatso composed these lines himself or drew them from elsewhere I do not know. We do know that, whether through the influence of *Appeal to the Mahāmudrā Lineage* or some other source, they were appended to the "standard" update of the Paṇchen's prayer credited to Yeshé Gyaltsen, Phabongkha, and others.

The *Guidebook on Mahāmudrā* (Kd*PCKY*), which appears to be Kalden Gyatso's own composition,[744] is in certain respects a gloss on Paṇchen Chögyen's *Highway of the Conquerors*. It cites some of the same sources, and like *Highway*, is divided into sections on preliminaries; a main practice consisting of rituals, serenity meditation, and insight meditation; and a concluding dedication of merit. The section on preliminaries (1b–2a) briefly discusses four practices that must be undertaken before one is fit to meditate on mahāmudrā: going for refuge, which is the door to the teaching; generating the awakening mind, which is the door to the Mahāyāna; reciting the hundred-syllable mantra of Vajrasattva, which purifies vices and obscurations; and guru yoga, which builds up merit and brings blessings.[745] The discussion of the main practice includes detailed instructions on the rituals preceding meditation, concise presentations of serenity and insight meditation, and advice on the follow-up to meditation. The rituals preceding meditation (2a–5b) include adopting the ninefold posture of Vairocana; performing the nine-round purification breathing exercise; reciting verses of refuge and the awakening mind; visualizing

744. See Sujata 2005, 66.

745. This list effectively overlaps with the standard list of "uncommon" preliminaries: refuge and the awakening mind (usually accompanied by prostrations), Vajrasattva meditation, offering of the Meru maṇḍala, and guru yoga. To the degree that guru yoga here includes the sevenfold worship rite and that the Meru maṇḍala practice is an instance of offering, it seems that the usual preliminaries are, in fact, contained in Kalden Gyatso's list.

one's guru, in the form of Mañjughoṣa, in the space before one; receiving the guru's blessings of one's body, speech, and mind in the form of light rays; inviting gurus and deities from Akaniṣṭha Heaven to absorb into one's guru; making offerings to the guru and requesting blessings and empowerments from him; receiving the four empowerments in the form of light rays; and absorbing the guru into oneself, so that his mind and one's own become inseparable. One then performs serenity meditation (5b–7a), settling into concentration on the clear, aware conventional nature of mind, applying mindfulness and alertness so as to maintain concentration and fend off thoughts, then relaxing into clear and empty space-like awareness and eventually attaining the mental and physical pliancy that are the signs of true serenity. Then, one moves to insight meditation (7a–8a) using a corner of the mind settled serenely in space-like awareness to investigate the ultimate nature of the one performing the meditation, basing one's investigation on Nāgārjuna's proof (in the *Jewel Garland*) that no self can be found either within or apart from the six elements, then resting in the experience of the absence, or emptiness, of the self one has sought. In the postmeditative experience of everyday life (8a–b), one is instructed to see each and every appearing object as empty and illusion-like but to understand that emptiness and appearances, and emptiness and dependent arising, do not contradict each other in the slightest. At the end (8b–9a), one dedicates the merit of one's practice.

Quotations from Kalden Gyatso's Ocean of Instructions on the Profound Teaching on Geden Mahāmudrā (Kd*SLDN*) consists of notes written by a disciple of Kalden Gyatso and edited by the master for oral presentation.[746] Like the *Guidebook*, it roughly follows the order of *Highway of the Conquerors*, quoting it directly on two occasions.[747] Also like the *Guidebook*, it is notable for its detailing of ritual preliminaries to meditation. In its thorough presentation of analytical approaches to insight meditation and its extensive discussion of postmeditation, however, it goes beyond even the Paṇchen's autocommentary, *Lamp So Bright*. The preliminaries that are detailed (1b–4a) include taking refuge and generating the awakening mind, then visualizing, and receiving blessings from, one's root guru at the center of a visualized divine assembly, appealing to the gurus of the mahāmudrā lineage[748] and absorb-

746. See Sujata 2005, 66.

747. Kd*SLDN* 10a [421] and 14a [429].

748. These are Vajradhara, Mañjughoṣa, Tsongkhapa, Jampal Gyatso, Baso Chökyi Gyaltsen, Chökyi Dorjé, Ensapa, Sangyé Yeshé, and Paṇchen Chögyen, followed by several of Kalden Gyatso's gurus, including Tenzin Losang Gyatso, Chöpa Rinpoché, and Gyalsé Losang Tenzin, and finally Kalden Gyatso himself. Kd*SLDN* 3a–b [407–8].

ing Mañjughoṣa into oneself, then resting in meditation. In Paṇchen Chögyen's root text, this is the point at which serenity meditation is described, but Kalden Gyatso proceeds immediately to a detailed exposition of various ways of gaining insight into emptiness (4a–9a). These include searching within and apart from the aggregates to see if a self is to be found; applying Candrakīrti's famous sevenfold reasoning with regard to the ways in which a chariot—and by implication, the self—might exist;[749] using the "royal reasoning" that establishes the equivalence between dependent arising and emptiness; employing the "vajra slivers" to determine whether things are produced from themselves, from something else, both, or neither; and understanding—and experiencing—emptiness as analogous to space. As we might expect, the section on postmeditation (9a–14b) stresses the importance of seeing everyday appearances as illusion-like, supporting this advice with numerous quotations from Indian texts and Tibetan masters. Notable among the Indian texts quoted are the *Death-Time Gnosis (Ātijñāna) Sūtra*, the *Epitome (Kā dpe)*, and the *Sublime Continuum*, all of which were important to Kagyü mahāmudrā tradition; and notable among the Tibetan masters cited are Marpa, Milarepa, and Phakmo Drupa, who as we know are key figures in Kagyü mahāmudrā lineages. Kalden Gyatso closes the text with definitions of "outer perfection" and "inner mantra" mahāmudrā that differ little from Paṇchen Chögyen's, a discussion of the relation between view and meditation that stresses flexibility in the ordering of the two, and an endorsement of Paṇchen Chögyen's insistence that all the great Tibetan philosophical systems come down to the same point.

An Experiential Teaching on Mahāmudrā in the Geden Oral Transmission (Kd*PCNK*), which was written by Kalden Gyatso on the advice of Chöpa Rinpoché,[750] follows the order of Paṇchen Chögyen's two mahāmudrā texts—especially *Lamp So Bright*—fairly closely, focusing most of its attention on instructions for serenity and insight meditation, though when it comes to insight meditation, it adds an interesting wrinkle, as we will see. The text starts with a brief "chronicle" of the members of the Geden Oral Transmission (1b–2b) beginning with the now-familiar list of Vajradhara, Mañjughoṣa, Tsongkhapa, Jampal Gyatso, Baso Chökyi Gyaltsen, Chökyi Dorjé, Ensapa, Sangyé Yeshé, and Paṇchen Chögyen. In turn, says Kalden Gyatso, Paṇchen Chögyen taught the tradition to such figures as Gendun Gyaltsen, Sherab Sengé,

749. The seven points are to the effect that a chariot (1) is not identical to its parts, (2) is not separate from its parts, (3) does not have its parts as its basis, (4) does not depend on its parts, (5) does not possess its parts, (6) is not the collection of the parts, and (7) is not the configuration of the parts.

750. See Sujata 2005, 66.

and Tsultrim Gyatso,[751] who practiced it assiduously and gained realization of the ultimate. It is for the sake of conveying the essence of their realization, says Kalden Gyatso, that these instructions are being set forth. The instructions themselves (2b–12a) include encouragement to meditate in an isolated place; adopt the sevenfold posture of Vairocana; review the basic points of the stages of the path and mind training; practice the extraordinary preliminaries of refuge, confession to Vajrasattva, the maṇḍala offering, and guru yoga; and absorb one's guru into oneself. At that point, one begins serenity meditation. Kalden Gyatso's instructions follow closely the pattern established in *Highway of the Conquerors* and *Lamp So Bright*, using some of the same examples and quotations to describe a sequence in which one rests in nonconceptuality, then, with the clear, aware conventional mind as the object, first applies mindfulness and alertness then relaxes into an open, aware, and empty state.

One then shifts to insight meditation, investigating the way in which an intrinsically existent mind might exist, in terms of shape, color, relation to aggregates, and so forth. Kalden Gyatso places particular emphasis on ascertaining the proper object of negation of such an investigation, underscoring the point with a lengthy quotation on the topic from Tsongkhapa's *Essence of Excellent Explanation*. Insight meditation proceeds with a careful analysis of the modes of appearance and existence of various entities and concepts, including the mind, and issues in the realization that, however they may appear, none of them exists as anything more than a mere nominal designation. This realization then is experienced as a nondiscursive, nonintentional, space-like meditation. At this point,[752] Kalden Gyatso raises the question of the sort of negation involved in experience of the mind's natural emptiness. He cites a teaching apparently given by Tsongkhapa to his disciple Gungru Gyaltsen Sangpo to the effect that even if a beginner initially meditates properly on the mind's emptiness as a nonaffirming—or absolute—negation, it is possible that later, when momentary events are under scrutiny, the correct understanding of emptiness may be lost and nihilism may ensue. The upshot—not stated explicitly by Kalden Gyatso—seems to be that it may be necessary at first to regard the mind's emptiness as an affirming negation, as an absence in which certain positive qualities—such as empty clarity or luminosity—are naturally entailed. He goes on to quote the *Perfection of Wisdom in Eight Thousand Lines* and *Jewel Heap* sūtras, as well as a poem by Marpa, to the effect that the mind's nature is both emptiness and luminosity, which can-

751. The first two are the monks at whose behest Paṇchen Chögyen wrote *Highway of the Conquerors*; the last was one of Kalden Gyatso's three main mahāmudrā teachers.

752. Kd*PCNK* 10a [449]. See Dalai Lama and Berzin 1997, 230–31.

not easily be separated. In his brief, concluding discussion of postmeditation, Kalden Gyatso asserts that "in our system, meditation on mahāmudrā is not different from meditation on emptiness, because mahāmudrā is not different from emptiness, and because the natural emptiness of any and every phenomenon is explained as mahāmudrā."[753] He goes on to recommend that the reader learn further details from Tsongkhapa's stages-of-the-path texts and Paṇchen Chögyen's *Lamp So Bright*.

Like many a Tibetan practitioner of mahāmudrā, Kalden Gyatso was inspired by his practice to compose spiritual songs (*mgur*), and as we have seen, like Paṇchen Chögyen, both he and his older relation Chöpa Rinpoché felt a particular affinity for Milarepa, who served for them, as he has for so many Tibetans, as a paragon of the peripatetic and ascetic poet-yogī. Kalden Gyatso's songs have been thoroughly studied and partially translated by Victoria Sujata,[754] so we will touch on them only briefly here. In one particularly revealing song,[755] he sings of his initial uncertainty about practicing mahāmudrā, especially of the tantric variety, but adds that because he desired to see the nature of mind, appealed to gurus and deities, focused on the oral instructions while in retreat, and sought to preserve his commitments and purify his mind, he now has become "an old monk with firm faith in the mantra path." In another song, he advises a disciple to analyze his own experience and, discovering that it has no more reality than a sky flower, to "settle unwaveringly on mind itself as it arises, free from all elaboration, and quickly attain the view."[756] In yet another song, which has an especially Kagyü ring to it, he sings,

> When you see the real nature of mind, you bar the door of saṃsāric birth.
> The Dharma body arises within, but you must seek it again and again.
> Deep primordial emptiness exists pervading everything.
> When you see a sight like that, the mind on its own is blissful and
> splendid.[757]

In two other songs, Kalden Gyatso employs the joyous but hard-to-translate interjections used by Indian and Tibetan yogīs to emphasize the extraordinary nature of their experience, singing, for instance,

753. Kd*PCNK* 11b–12a [452–53].

754. Sujata 2005; for her translations of selected songs, see 267–369 ; see also Sujata 2019.

755. No. X-22; Sujata 2005, 67–68.

756. No. VIII-13, my translation; cf. Sujata 2005, 69–70.

757. No. XII-26, my translation; cf. Sujata 2005, 70–71.

O O, the way all things originally exist:
Auu, the Dharma realm free from extremes;
Kho Re, meditate on it as space-like;
Heh Heh, mind is blissful and splendid—do you understand?[758]

Or, again,

O O, the view of mahāmudrā:
Auu, understanding won't suffice—you have to meditate;
Kho Re, maintain it like a river's flow;
Heh Heh, mind is blissful and splendid—do you understand?[759]

Jamyang Shepa

Jamyang Shepai Dorjé (1648–1721/22),[760] also known as Ngawang Tsöndrü, was neither a direct disciple of Paṇchen Chögyen nor a main lineage holder of the Geluk mahāmudrā tradition, yet he bears brief mention for his interest in the tradition and for his general importance within the Geluk: he was among the first Gelukpa lamas from Amdo to play a significant role in central Tibetan political and religious affairs, and he left a lasting imprint on Geluk intellectual life with his great treatise on tenet systems and his textbooks for Gomang College of Drepung Monastery. He spent his first two decades in Amdo, taking novice vows at thirteen and quickly becoming an assiduous student of both Buddhist and secular subjects. At twenty-one, he traveled to Central Tibet, where he entered Gomang. He progressed rapidly in his studies and gained fame for his prowess in debate. He received full ordination from the Fifth Dalai Lama in 1674—he was given the name Ngawang Tsöndrü—and two years later entered Gyümé Monastery, where he devoted himself to tantric study and practice for a number of years. In 1680, he received the Geden or Ensa Hearing Transmission, along with special instructions on Guhyasamāja, from the great master of the Sé tantric lineage, Könchok Yarphel (b. 1602), who designated him as his successor at Riwo Gephel, a hermitage above Drepung. Jamyang Shepa spent most of the next two decades at the hermitage, where he is said to have received a vision of Mañjughoṣa, which in turn led to his being designated as "smiled upon by Mañjughoṣa": Jamyang Shepa. He also continued his studies, composed most of the texts for which he is best

758. No. IV-8, my translation; cf. Sujata 2005, 71–72.

759. VIII-24, my translation; cf. Sujata 2005, 72–73.

760. Information in this paragraph is based primarily on Chhosphel 2011b.

known, and began instructing a growing circle of students. In 1697, he was made a tutor to the young Sixth Dalai Lama, and in 1700, he became abbot of Gomang. Now near the center of the Tibetan power, he became embroiled in a variety of religious and political disputes involving, among others, various factions within the Geluk, the regent Desi Sangyé Gyatso, and the Qosot Mongol chieftain Lajang Khan. Forced to step down from the Gomang abbacy in 1707, he led Phabongkha Hermitage, above Sera, until 1709, when he returned to Amdo. There, he founded what would become the largest of all the Geluk institutions in Amdo, Labrang Tashikhyil. He also founded a tantric college at Gönlung Jampaling, at that point the most important Geluk monastery in the region. He spent his last years instructing a multitude of disciples, many of whom rose to great prominence in the Geluk hierarchy, and passed away in 1721 or 1722.

Jamyang Shepa left behind nearly 150 works, which were collected into fifteen volumes. The most famous is undoubtedly his root text and massive autocommentary on Indian tenet systems,[761] but he also is renowned for his informative autobiography, his textbooks for the Drepung monastic curriculum, and many works on the Indian Buddhist classics and on tantric practice. As noted, he received the Geden, or Ensa, Hearing Transmission from the Sé lineage master Könchok Yarphel. That he would receive the Ensa transmission from a Sé master is intriguing, and seems to reflect tendencies in his era toward a fusion of different hearing transmissions traced to Tsongkhapa. Indeed, as noted earlier, he, along with the Second Changkya tulku and the Mongolian master Thangsakpa Ngödrup Gyatso, is credited with combining the Sé, Mé, and Ensa transmissions into a single stream of teachings.[762] Later, Jamyang Shepa composed interlinear notes on *Offering to the Guru*, the *Chariot Leading to Union*, which draws heavily on the special teachings on Guhyasamāja he had learned through this uncommon, combined "proximate lineage."[763] Although he wrote nothing of significance about Geluk mahāmudrā, he was interested enough in that classic source of great seal traditions, the *People Dohās* of Saraha—often quoted by both Norsang Gyatso and Paṇchen Chögyen—that he wrote a textual outline of the Great Brahman's verses, which will be discussed below.[764]

761. For a complete English translation, see Hopkins 2003.

762. Thuken 2009, 287, and Dalai Lama and Berzin 1997, 231. Sources differ as to whether the trio received teachings from Könchok Yarphel in Ü or in Amdo, with Chhosphel 2011 asserting the former and Thuken 2009 and Dalai Lama and Berzin 1997 opting for the latter.

763. Dalai Lama and Berzin 1997, 232. See Jz*ZJST*.

764. See below, chapter 16.

Of his Tibetan forerunners, Jamyang Shepa seems to have felt a special affinity for Machik Labdrön. Her Chö tradition—itself closely related to mahāmudrā—had, of course, made its way into the Geluk centuries earlier and had become part of the Ensa Hearing Transmission. Jamyang Shepa's unique contribution seems to have been his claim to have discovered, at Labrang, a treasure text left by Machik, which, with help, he then decoded. Treasure discoveries are quite unusual among Gelukpas—many of whom are critical of the practice—so Jamyang Shepa was in this regard, as in so many others, exceptional.

Kalsang Gyatso, The Seventh Dalai Lama

Among Jamyang Shepa's many disciples was a master from Amdo, Ngawang Chokden (1677–1751),[765] who spent most of his life in Central Tibet. His studies were concentrated first at Sera, then at Tashi Lhunpo—where he ordained and studied with the Second Paṇchen Lama Losang Yeshé—and eventually at Gyümé, where he became disciplinarian and then abbot. Later in life, he reached the apex of the Geluk world, assuming the post of the Ganden throneholder. More importantly, he served, from 1728 until his death, as chief tutor to the Seventh Dalai Lama Kalsang Gyatso (1708–57),[766] a fellow easterner, who although born in Kham, received his early education in Amdo. The early part of the Seventh Dalai Lama's reign was caught up in the whirlwind of events surrounding the abduction and death of the Sixth Dalai Lama, repeated interventions in Tibetan affairs by competing Mongol chieftains and the Kangxi emperor in Beijing, and struggles for power among various elements of the Tibetan nobility. Although he became active and successful as a national leader late in life, for the most part, Kalsang Gyatso eschewed politics and focused on the spiritual and scholarly pursuits for which he is most renowned. He ordained or taught many of the most important Geluk lamas of the eighteenth century and left behind a considerable number of texts,[767] of which perhaps the most renowned are his spiritual songs.[768]

Although none of the Seventh Dalai Lama's works is explicitly devoted to Geluk mahāmudrā, his contemporary Yeshé Gyaltsen—with whom he was

765. See Chhosphel 2011c.

766. For biographical information on the Seventh Dalai Lama, see, e.g., Kalzang Gyatso 1982, 166–80, Kapstein 2005, and Chhosphel 2011c.

767. For a listing, accompanied by brief synopses, see Kanakura et al. 1953, 279–95.

768. For a translation, see Kalzang Gyatso 1982.

acquainted[769]—reports that he received the hearing transmission from Ngawang Chokden, and there are occasional references in his spiritual songs both to mahāmudrā and to the transmission. In one song, in the context of a discussion of tantric practice, he describes how:

> . . . the apparitions of people and things
> dissolve into light, and the waves
> of misconception are stilled. . . .
>
> In the realms of both semblance and connate mahāmudrā,
> empty images appear as rainbows.[770]

Elsewhere, in a song addressed to Tsongkhapa, he sings of how "the oral teachings of the Ganden patriarchs / contain . . . all of the Buddha's methods," and adds:

> Your mahāmudrā lineage, blissful and beyond intellect,
> cannot be reached by mere samādhi, but
> only by the meditation on bliss and radiance
> that reveals the real nature of one's own mind.[771]

Kalsang Gyatso also has a number of songs on the Madhyamaka view that in their appreciation for nature and their celebration of the yogī's life and realizations, recall those of Paṇchen Chögyen and Kalden Gyatso. For instance, he sings of how

> . . . mind . . . is beyond birth and death,
> abiding in the ultimate mode of being.
> *Eh-ma-ho:* Most wondrous! . . .
>
> In the vision of my mind as being inseparably one with emptiness . . .
> all mental entanglements subsided:

769. Kalzang Gyatso 1982, 51–52. This assumes that the Yeshé Gyaltsen to whom the "precept" poem is directed is the Yeshé Gyaltsen so important to the Geluk mahāmudrā tradition.

770. Kalzang Gyatso 1982, 83 (translation adapted). *Semblance* mahāmudrā is a realization of emptiness in which some conceptuality still remains, while *connate* mahāmudrā is the full, direct experience of the nature of things.

771. Kalzang Gyatso 1982, 126 (translation adapted).

I, an unborn yogī of space.[772]

Elsewhere, he advises a practitioner, "During meditation, keep the mind unobstructed as space; / after meditation, regard the flow of events as a rainbow."[773] In another song, he invokes:

An image of a kingly eagle gliding high in space:
were one's mind to glide without grasping
in the space of truth itself clear and void,
how excellent!"[774]

And, like his two predecessors, the Seventh Dalai Lama also shows a deep devotion to Milarepa, who "soared in the sky of truth, / the way things are,"[775] and provided a model for all beings to emulate.

772. Kalzang Gyatso 1982, 49.

773. Kalzang Gyatso 1982, 54.

774. Kalzang Gyatso 1982, 68

775. Kalzang Gyatso 1982, 156.

11. Yeshé Gyaltsen

ALTHOUGH THE PREVIOUS chapter should make it clear that many figures besides Shar Kalden Gyatso studied and mastered Geluk mahāmudrā in the century-plus after Paṇchen Chögyen published his two seminal texts, it was not until well into the eighteenth century that the practice again received detailed written exposition.[776] When it did, it was at the hands of one of the greatest Geluk intellectuals of the age, Yeshé Gyaltsen (1713–93), variously known as Kachen Yeshé Gyaltsen for his mastery of four difficult scholastic topics,[777] Yongzin Yeshé Gyaltsen for his role as tutor to the Eighth Dalai Lama, and Tsechokling Yeshé Gyaltsen for the monastery just south of Lhasa that was his abbatial seat near the end of his life. Yeshé Gyaltsen would shape subsequent understandings of Geluk mahāmudrā more than any master apart from Paṇchen Chögyen himself, for it was he who expanded the lineage prayer written by Paṇchen Chögyen, composed biographies of the masters of the tradition, brought mahāmudrā practice into close alignment with Paṇchen Chögyen's *Offering to the Guru*, and expounded mahāmudrā practice both at length and in shorter texts. It is also he who seems to have standardized the name of both the hearing transmission and the mahāmudrā practice within it, changing the Geden used by most of his predecessors to Ganden, while retaining the alternative designation of the tradition as the Ensa Hearing Transmission.

Most of what we know about Yeshé Gyaltsen is found in a long biography written by his student the Eighth Dalai Lama Jampal Gyatso (1758–1804).[778] He was a native of the Kyirong area of southwestern Tsang, not far from the Nepal border. His parents were an ill-matched couple who often argued

776. For information on Yeshé Gyaltsen, see Willis 1995, 125–30, Smith 2001, 171–76, Kachen Yeshe Gyaltsen 2014, 9, and Zasep 2019, 38–39.

777. Abhidharma, Vinaya, the Perfection of Wisdom, and either Madhyamaka or Pramāṇa. The title of *kachen* is the Tashi Lhunpo equivalent of the designation of *geshé* granted by the three main Lhasa-area Geluk monasteries.

778. Willis 1995, 126, and Smith 2001, 171–72.

violently and provided a less-than-stable upbringing for their son. At seven, he persuaded his father to take him to the nearby Rikhu Monastery, where he was cared for and taught to read by a nun named Tsewang. Two years later, he enrolled at Tashi Lhunpo, where he received his novice ordination from the Second Paṇchen Lama and began study with such luminaries as Kachen Yeshé Thokmé, Phurbuchok Ngawang Jampa (1682–1762), and Drupai Wangchuk Losang Namgyal (1670–1741). He advanced quickly in his studies, won his Kachen degree, and in 1735 took full ordination and began a period in which he alternated between further education and extended solitary retreat. He began to attract disciples and patrons, and although much in demand at Tashi Lhunpo, he chose instead in 1751 to move back to the Nepal-Tibet border region, where in 1756 he founded a small monastery, Kyirong Samten Ling. There, he took on a number of disciples, including the great Changkya Rölpai Dorjé (1717–84), and wrote many of the numerous religious, literary, and philosophical works for which he is famous. Besides the hearing-transmission and mahāmudrā texts we will examine shortly, these include works on the Madhyamaka view, a concise description of the elements of Buddhist psychology,[779] eloquent retellings of Buddhist legends,[780] works promoting the cult of the sixteen arhats,[781] a massive collection of biographies of the masters of stages-of-the-path lineage,[782] and of course, many works on tantric ritual and meditation. He stayed mostly in Kyirong until 1782, when, with the death of the Third Paṇchen Lama Palden Yeshé (1738–81) and the incapacitation of the Ganden throneholder, the Eighth Dalai Lama asked him to come to Lhasa to be his tutor. Yeshé Gyaltsen agreed and was installed in a newly built monastery across the river from the Potala, Tsechok Samten Ling, where he remained—serving faithfully as the Dalai Lama's preceptor—until his death in 1793.

Yeshé Gyaltsen counted among his teachers three recognized holders of the Ensa Hearing Transmission (none of whom seems to have written much on the topic): the Second Paṇchen Lama, Phurbuchok Ngawang Jampa,[783] and Drup-

779. See Guenther and Kawamura 1975.

780. See Willis 1995, 130.

781. See Smith 2001, 175–76.

782. For a translation of material related to masters of the Geden Hearing Transmission, see Willis 1995, 33–96.

783. Phurbuchok actually comes *after* Yeshé Gyaltsen in the standard lineage listing, suggesting that (as with Paṇchen Chögyen and Drupchen Gendun Gyaltsen) the junior lama may have transmitted the tradition to one of his own teachers. Phurbuchok did write a short commentary on Tsongkhapa's vision-suffused and mahāmudrā-tinged *Synopsis of the Spiritual Practice Taught by the Exalted Mañjughoṣa* (Ts*JBDD*, translated below, part 5, section 1), entitled

wang Losang Namgyal. Drupwang seems to have been his primary instructor in mahāmudrā and other practices of the hearing transmission[784]—on which Yeshé Gyaltsen focused intently during his periods of retreat and on which, eventually, he wrote a passel of important and influential works. Among his works on the hearing transmission that are not focused primarily on Geluk mahāmudrā are a brief account of the six Dharmas of Nāropa, a commentary on a text by Ensapa on severance practice, and a number of guru-yoga manuals, several of which are related to Paṇchen Chögyen's *Offering to the Guru.*

Works Focused Mainly on Mahāmudrā

Yeshé Gyaltsen wrote at least ten works that are significantly related to mahāmudrā—the most, so far as I can tell, of any single Gelukpa writer. By far the most important of these is *Bright Lamp of the Excellent Path of the Hearing Transmission: A Letter of Instruction on Ganden Mahāmudrā* (Yg*LZGM*), a 122-folio masterwork written at the request of Changkya Rölpai Dorjé that provides both a history of the tradition, told through the lives of its lineage holders, and a highly detailed set of instructions on the preliminaries to, and actual practice of, mahāmudrā. About a fifth of the text is given over to a discussion of the preliminaries and an eighth to serenity meditation, while the discussion of the Madhyamaka view—corresponding more or less to the First Paṇchen's section on insight meditation—takes up almost half the text. *Bright Lamp of the Excellent Path* is replete with supporting quotations from Indian sūtras and śāstras, and from Tibetan masters, mostly Geluk—of whom the most frequently cited are Tsongkhapa and Paṇchen Chögyen. Although *Bright Lamp of the Excellent Path* is not a commentary on Paṇchen Chögyen's *Highway of the Conquerors* as such, it does quote, partly or in whole, from twenty-four of the root text's forty-six verses.[785] Yeshé Gyaltsen also draws liberally from Paṇchen Chögyen's spiritual songs, occasionally from his mahāmudrā lineage prayer, and on several occasions from his commentary on Tsongkhapa's *Queries from a Pure Heart*; Tsongkhapa's text, as we may recall, is taken by many scholars as a critique of Kagyü mahāmudrā practices. On the other hand, *Lamp So Bright*, Paṇchen Chögyen's autocommentary to

A Commentary Briefly Clarifying the Meaning of the Instruction Directly Given to Jé Lama by Mañjughoṣa; see Pb*NDSB*.

784. Yeshé Gyaltsen asserts this explicitly in Yg*LZGM* (15b–16a [230–31]). There, he states that Drupwang learned mahāmudrā from Jatang Trinlé Chöphel (b. seventeenth century), himself a student of Paṇchen Chögyen's direct disciple Drungpa Tsöndrü Gyaltsen.

785. These are verses 1–2, 6, 14–24, 29–35, 39–41, and 44–45.

his mahāmudrā root verses, which includes ample quotations from Tibetan Kagyü sources, is rarely cited. Thus, while not especially polemical, *Bright Lamp of the Excellent Path* is a highly Geluk-centric text, in which the familiarity—and even sympathy—displayed toward the Kagyü by Paṇchen Chögyen and Kalden Gyatso is little in evidence.

The text begins with an account of "the origins of the instruction" (Yg*LZGM* 3b–16a). Yeshé Gyaltsen identifies the main textual sources of Ganden mahāmudrā as the Perfection of Wisdom sūtras and the unexcelled yoga tantras (both of them collections that were explicated in Nāgārjuna's philosophical and tantric works) as well as the *Dohās* of Saraha and the Seven Attainment Texts attributed to one or another tantric mahāsiddha. The background of the transmission also includes the Mahāyāna "profound view" lineage of teachings on emptiness—stretching from the Buddha, to Mañjughoṣa, to Nāgārjuna, to Candrakīrti, thence eventually to Atiśa and down to Tsongkhapa—and the "extensive activity" lineage teachings on love, compassion, and the awakening mind—which begin with the Buddha and are transmitted through, among others, the coming buddha Maitreya, Asaṅga, Vasubandhu, Atiśa, and finally Tsongkhapa. Yeshé Gyaltsen identifies two separate lineages specifically dedicated to mahāmudrā that culminated in Tsongkhapa. The long or distant lineage runs as follows: Buddha, Maṇjughoṣa, Saraha, Nāgārjuna, Śavaripa, Lūipa, Dārikapa, Diṅkaṃpa, Tilopa, Nāropa and Maitrīpa, Marpa, and Milarepa, from whom it descended through various Kagyü masters, until it was transmitted to Tsongkhapa by his Drigung Kagyü guru, Chenga Chökyi Gyalpo. Tsongkhapa also received relevant teachings from a number of masters, none more important than Rendawa, who taught him cycles related to Madhyamaka and Guhyasamāja. The near or uncommon proximate lineage came to Tsongkhapa directly from Mañjughoṣa, who, as we know, appeared to him in the 1390s in a series of increasingly intense visions, which culminated in Jé Rinpoché's direct realization of emptiness—which is, of course, synonymous with mahāmudrā. In the course of that decade, Mañjughoṣa granted Tsongkhapa specific instructions on mahāmudrā practice and bestowed upon him the emanated scripture that would be handed from one transmission holder to another for the next two centuries. Yeshé Gyaltsen goes on to relate in brief the life stories of Tsongkhapa's successors—Tokden Jampal Gyatso, Baso Chökyi Gyaltsen, Chökyi Dorjé, Ensapa, Khedrup Sangyé Yeshé, and Paṇchen Chögyen—followed by brief notes on Paṇchen Chögyen's successors, through whom the tradition eventually descended to Drupai Wangchuk, who taught it to many disciples, including Yeshé Gyaltsen.

The next section of *Bright Lamp of the Excellent Path* is a detailed discussion of "the greatness of the instruction" (16a–23b), which begins with the assertion that the root of saṃsāra and all its troubles is grasping at the existence of an intrinsically existent self, and that self-grasping only can be uprooted by adopting the Madhyamaka view expounded in the Perfection of Wisdom sūtras and by Nāgārjuna and his successors, a view that leads to the direct realization of emptiness, hence eventually to liberation and buddhahood. On the "ordinary" level of Perfection Vehicle practice, emptiness is realized by a relatively coarse consciousness. In the "uncommon" teachings of unexcelled yoga tantra, that very same emptiness is realized by an extremely subtle consciousness, which is referred to as the "connate gnosis of luminous mahāmudrā," said to be all-pervading, the nature of everything, and the "vajra of mind." Whether on the common Perfection Vehicle or the uncommon Mantra Vehicle path, the Madhyamaka view to be realized is exactly the same. It cannot be attained without prior meditation on the stages of the path as expounded by Tsongkhapa, practice of guru yoga, and some sense of the nature of the mind, as expounded for instance in the *Perfection of Wisdom in Eight Thousand Lines:* "Mind does not exist in mind; the nature of mind is luminous."[786]

Turning to the "actual instruction" on mahāmudrā, Yeshé Gyaltsen first outlines the preliminaries to the serenity and insight meditation that form the core of the practice (23b–49b). After finding a suitable spot for practice, one sets up an altar replete with offerings and establishes an altruistic motivation. One seats oneself in the posture of Vairocana and performs the nine-round breathing purification practice. Alternatively, one may count out seven breaths, holding the breath at the end for as long as is comfortable. One next reflects on the importance of going for refuge to the Guru, Buddha, Dharma, and Saṅgha on the grounds that only they can offer oneself and all other sentient beings permanent relief from the vicissitudes of saṃsāra, including the prospect of rebirth not just in the lower realms but in the alluring heavens of the gods as well. One then visualizes the objects of refuge: one's own guru in the form of Lama Losang Thupwang Dorjé Chang, encircled by various gurus, tantric deities, buddhas, bodhisattvas, pratyekabuddhas, śrāvakas, and Buddhist texts. One is oneself surrounded by a vast number of sentient beings, also intent on refuge. As one chants verses of refuge to Guru, Buddha, Dharma, and Saṅgha, radiant nectar streams into one from the appropriate

786. Cited in Yg*LZGM* 22b [244]. The Tibetan of the sūtra passage (*de ltar sems de ni / sems ma mchis pa ste / sems kyi rang bzhin ni / 'od gsal ba lags so*)—which differs somewhat from that cited by Yeshé Gyaltsen (*sems la sems ma mchis te / sems kyi rang bzhin 'od gsal ba'o*)—is found at, e.g., *ASP*t (*ka*) 4b. The Sanskrit (*taccittamacittam / prakṛtiścittasya prabhāsvarā*) is found at *ASP*s 3; cf. trans. Conze 1973, 84.

visualized figures. Reflecting next on one's obligation as a bodhisattva to liberate "mother sentient beings" from suffering, one recites a prayer for the generation of the awakening mind, during which oneself and all sentient beings are filled with light emanating from the guru. After expressing the four immeasurable attitudes—love, compassion, sympathetic joy, and equanimity—one visualizes the objects of refuge dissolving into the guru and the guru dissolving into oneself. One then briefly reflects on the importance of perfecting the three principal aspects of the path articulated by Tsongkhapa: renunciation, awakening mind, and right view. This is followed by Vajrasattva absolution meditation, which involves visualization of Vajrasattva, in union with his consort, at one's crown, acknowledgment of one's broken vows, and recitation of Vajrasattva's hundred-syllable mantra, during which purifying nectar flows down into one's body, resulting in the complete purification of all transgressions.

The final preliminary is the practice of guru yoga, which begins, in the manner of *Offering to the Guru*, with a fresh visualization of Lama Losang Thupwang Dorjé Chang seated on a great, jeweled throne in the space before one. His aggregates, elements, senses, and various body parts are identified with corresponding tathāgatas, female consorts, bodhisattvas, arhats, wrathful protectors, and other divinities. In the space above him are the gurus of three major transmissions: that of the profound view of emptiness, that of the extensive practice of the awakening mind, and that of the "blessings of practice," above which is the proximate lineage of mahāmudrā with Mañjughoṣa at its head. In ranks below one's guru are yidams, buddhas, bodhisattvas, śrāvakas, pratyekabuddhas, ḍākas and ḍākinīs, and Dharma protectors. One invites the gnosis beings of each visualized member of the assembly to absorb into his or her respective visualized deity. One then reflects on the kindness, greatness, and indispensability of the guru and develops a special desire to receive from him (or her) the basis for the mahāmudrā attainment, or buddhahood. One next recites the sevenfold worship rite. This is followed by an "outer" offering of the Meru maṇḍala, the physical execution of which, involving circular metal layers and various substances, is described here in considerable detail. Then follow brief descriptions of the inner, secret, and suchness offerings, which are more tantric in orientation, involving, for instance, a visualized offering of five nectars (urine, excrement, semen, blood, and marrow) and five meats (human, cow, horse, elephant, and dog) or of the gnosis in which emptiness and bliss are inseparable. One then makes fervent appeals to the guru, reciting the great prayer to Tsongkhapa composed by Rendawa, the *Miktsema*, as well as the beautiful verses from *Offering to the Guru* in which one identifies the guru with the yidam, ḍākinīs, and Dharma protectors and asks that the guru grant protection and friendship now, at the time of death, and in the intermediate state and bestow all yogic attainments, whether mundane or transmundane. One then requests from the guru the four unexcelled-yoga-tantra empowerments, which one receives in the form of light rays. After this, the members of the assembly absorb into the guru and the guru melts into one's heart, where one feels that one's guru, one's yidam, and one's own mind are inseparably fused. Yeshé Gyaltsen concludes this section with a reflection on how attainment of mahāmudrā requires the preliminaries, whether on the Perfection Vehicle level of a realization of emptiness as taught by Nāgārjuna and other Mādhyamikas or on the Mantra Vehicle level, where the realization of emptiness is referred to in terms of the primordial mind, great bliss, and so forth. He ends by citing an unidentified passage from Paṇchen Chögyen that speaks of mahāmudrā as threefold: *ground mahāmudrā* is mind itself, the connate abiding nature of mind, the mother luminosity of the time of death; *path mahāmudrā* is a meditative equipoise achieved through mixing a contemplatively derived luminosity with the ground luminosity; and *fruitional mahāmudrā* is a direct and unmistaken encounter with the reality contemplated in path mahāmudrā.[787]

Bright Lamp of the Excellent Path's section on mahāmudrā meditation itself begins with a discussion of the two options for ordering serenity and insight, noting that in this case, following the model established by Tsongkhapa in his stages-of-the-path texts, serenity will precede insight. In the section on serenity (49a–69b), Yeshé Gyaltsen begins by outlining the requisites for successful serenity practice, such as an isolated abode, having few desires, being satisfied with what one has, consorting with few people, living virtuously, and ridding oneself of passion and evil thoughts. He also stresses the necessity of having a foundation in renunciation and the awakening mind, and of overcoming such impediments as laziness, forgetfulness of the instruction, and mental dullness and agitation. The text goes on to discuss the extrasensory perceptions that may ensue from the attainment of serenity and the various types of objects one may select for meditation. Yeshé Gyaltsen notes that, given its role in the perpetuation and transcendence of saṃsāra, the mind itself is a particularly important object of meditation, which may be identified either at the general level, as in Perfection Vehicle practices, or more subtly, as in tantric practices involving deity yoga and the revelation of the connate luminous gnosis. In the context of a mahāmudrā practice session, says Yeshé Gyaltsen, one begins serenity meditation at the point where the guru has dissolved into one's heart cakra, and one feels oneself inseparable from him. Within that context, one

787. Yg*LZGM* 49a [297].

maintains a focus on the mind itself as clear and aware, a pure vacuity. As appearances subside, the mental factor of mindfulness keeps one focused on the object, while the factor of alertness fends off distractions and is cognizant of the mind's tendency toward agitation or dullness. In an aside, Yeshé Gyaltsen comments on the oft-encountered Buddhist rhetoric of "not thinking," suggesting that it is meant not as a condemnation of thought in general or meditative recollection in particular but only as an indication that we should not concern ourselves with any object other than the one we have selected—in this case, the bare nature of mind. The text goes on to exhort the practitioner to maintain a balance between excessive tightness and excessive slackness in fixing on the object of meditation, and noting that advice by Saraha and other mahāsiddhas to relax the mind must be understood against the background of the mind's tendency at times to hold the object too tightly. Yeshé Gyaltsen describes various techniques for counteracting agitation and dullness (e.g., tightening the mind for the former or a forceful utterance of *phaṭ* for the latter), then concludes the section on serenity by outlining the relation among the five faults, the eight antidotes, and the nine stages of serenity, as described originally by Asaṅga and emphasized by Tsongkhapa.[788]

The very long section on insight meditation (69b–119a) is devoted almost entirely to a discussion of "seeking the view," which reads like a précis of the Geluk approach to Madhyamaka. It begins with a general description of the indispensability of wisdom for the attainment of omniscient buddhahood, and the necessity, in the acquisition of wisdom, of both the guidance of a guru and serious study of key texts, such as the treatises of Nāgārjuna. Yeshé Gyaltsen next advises the practitioner to reflect on the source of saṃsāric suffering—which is "self-grasping," the apprehension of a truly existing self—and the necessity to develop its antidote: the wisdom that realizes no-self. No-self is the case for both persons and phenomena; here, notes Yeshé Gyaltsen, the analysis is primarily directed toward a self of persons. Some Tibetan meditators, he observes, think that no-self can be realized instantaneously; the approach he favors, however, requires gradual investigation, starting with careful identification of the object of negation, a self of persons, which should be defined neither too broadly nor too narrowly, and must be observed as to how it appears, how one apprehends it, and how it actually exists in vari-

788. The five faults are laziness, forgetfulness, agitation or dullness, nonapplication, and overapplication. The eight antidotes are physical and mental pliancy, enthusiastic effort, desire, faith, mindfulness, alertness, application, and equanimity. The nine stages are focus, continual focus, patch-like focus, close focus, controlled focus, pacified focus, complete pacification, single-pointed focus, and equipoise.

ous contexts. Yeshé Gyaltsen then subjects the self of persons to a variety of dichotomous analyses, questioning whether it is identical to or disconnected from such all-embracing categories as the aggregates, physical elements, subject and object, or—the one on which he focuses most—mind and body. In each case, the self's complete oneness with a complex category would entail that it is multiple and impermanent, which by definition it cannot be, while its utter disconnection from that complex would simply take it beyond the realm of comprehension or expression. Through such analyses, one comes to understand that a self of persons is no more real than a snake that is *not* in the corner of a room, or a conjured elephant, or an image in a mirror, or the events of a dream. It is, instead, merely a label, a name, a designation, a sign, a mental construct, without true existence—yet that lack of true existence does nothing to negate the validity of the dependently arising conventional world. With the recognition that there is not an atom of true existence in a self of persons, one may move on to a search for a self of phenomena. By investigating one's own body or external objects, one will conclude that there is no self of phenomena either—and, again, that this fact does not cancel out the conventional world.

Eventually, Yeshé Gyaltsen homes in on the particular meditative object whose way of existing is the focus of Paṇchen Chögyen's mahāmudrā system: the mind, which, whether through Madhyamaka analysis or tantric techniques, must be seen as it actually is. Although the mind appears to be truly existent and is grasped as such, when subjected to philosophical analysis it turns out to be just another dependently arisen phenomenon, another label, another concept in a web of concepts—hence to be ontologically null and void. At the same time, it is no more unreal conventionally than any other concept or entity we might consider, since the fact of its emptiness, far from negating its conventional validity, actually helps to assure it, such that there is no contradiction at all between the emptiness of things and the appearance of things. Yeshé Gyaltsen brings his *Bright Lamp of the Excellent Path* toward a conclusion by describing how meditative equipoise on emptiness can be the basis for developing a union of serenity and insight, which will, in turn, lead to irreversible progress on the path to awakening. In describing the practitioner's postmeditative encounter with the world, he stresses the importance of seeing all persons, things, and events as "illusion-like," that is, as only *appearing* to one as if they were truly existent, when one knows very well that they are not. Whether one is sleeping, eating, studying, or engaged in any other mundane activity, one must see through it and appreciate its ultimate emptiness. That way, when one is practicing on the higher reaches of the tantric path, the luminous mahāmudrā connate gnosis will easily manifest, and the mahāmudrā attainment, buddhahood, will be ours.

Yeshé Gyaltsen also wrote at least two other accounts of mahāmudrā practice: the medium-length *A Profound Teaching on the View of the Geden Hearing Transmission: The Source of All Attainments* and the brief *Advice of Mañjughoṣa Lama, Which Teaches Clearly the Key Points of the Special Instruction on Ganden Mahāmudrā.* Though they differ from *Bright Lamp of the Excellent Path* by omitting the life-stories of masters of the hearing transmission, and by their greater economy in the deployment of quotations, they otherwise replicate the longer text's structure and most of its key points

The twenty-six-folio *Profound Teaching on the View* (Yg*TKZM*) is divided into a long section on the meditation session itself and a short discussion of how to act between sessions. About two-thirds of the account of the actual session is devoted to the preliminaries, which begin with finding a comfortable and isolated spot for meditation and adopting the seven-point Vairocana posture before images of the Buddha, Mañjughoṣa, and Tsongkhapa, then undertaking a purifying breath meditation, at the end of which one rests as best one can in clarity and awareness—which are, Paṇchen Chögyen has reminded us, the mind's conventional nature. One next reflects on the various themes of the stages-of-the-path teachings: the perfect human rebirth, impermanence and death, the miseries of the lower realms, the inadequacy of the upper realms, the kindness shown us in the past by "mother sentient beings," and the resolve to repay that kindness by liberating them from suffering—on the basis of one's own mastery of wisdom and development of the awakening mind. One then visualizes, as refuge objects, an array of gurus, buddhas, deities, and Dharma texts before one (with one's own guru in the center) and imagines oneself and all sentient beings praying to them; they purify one and melt into one, and one's body becomes transparent. One next takes specific refuge in the Guru, Buddha, Dharma, and Saṅgha and is purified and blessed by light from each set of refuge objects in turn. Refuge-taking complete, one recites a prayer to generate the awakening mind, using the prayer as a springboard for a detailed meditation in which one develops love, compassion, the awakening mind, and the resolve to master wisdom and method. After this, Vajradhara melts into one, and one sees oneself as Vajradhara, in whose form one reviews the four immeasurables: first, equanimity, then love, compassion, and sympathetic joy. One is filled with light from the various refuge objects, and contemplating important sayings by Khedrup Sangyé Yeshé, one develops a special resolve to awaken for the sake of beings. Finally, the objects of refuge melt into the central guru, the guru melts into light, which melts into oneself, and one rests for a while in the view of emptiness.

One then assumes the form of Yamāntaka, blesses offering substances, and absorbs the gnosis being into oneself. One then generates the merit field described in *Offering to the Guru*, with Lama Losang Thupwang Dorjé Chang at the center and the three guru lineages and ranks of deities described as in *Bright Lamp of the Excellent Path*. After the gnosis beings are absorbed into the members of the visualized assembly, one makes offerings, recites the sevenfold worship rite, offers the Meru maṇḍala, appeals to the gurus—including those of the mahāmudrā lineage—to grant one yogic attainments, recites the *Miktsema*, reflects on the virtues and kindness of one's guru, then requests and receives the four unexcelled-yoga-tantra empowerments from him. Then, one makes specific requests to attain various advanced realizations and, after death, to go to Tuṣita Heaven so as to meet Maitreya, Tsongkhapa, and his spiritual sons and to receive a prophecy of enlightenment. After one utters a final prayer to attain the state of Vajradhara so as to assist all beings, the retinue dissolves into the guru, the guru comes to one's crown and, melting into light, descends through one's central channel as far as the heart cakra, where one feels that one's own mind and the guru's mind are indissolubly merged.

At this point, one begins the actual practice of mahāmudrā, first establishing serenity by taking the mind itself as the object and focusing nonconceptually, "without hope or fear," on its nature: clear and aware, a pure vacuity. If one begins to lose focus, one is advised to apply mindfulness and alertness, and once stability has been regained, to tighten or relax one's concentration so as to find a proper balance between stability and clarity, beset by neither agitation nor dullness. Eventually, one will attain the special pliancy of body and mind that is the definition of serenity. With serenity attained, one moves on to insight meditation, which presupposes the prior instruction of one's guru. One prays to the guru for blessing and undertakes a set of general reflections on the way in which grasping at an "I" is the root of suffering in saṃsāra, realization of the absence of self is the key to reversing such suffering, and absence of self is divided into that of persons and phenomena. Focusing on the lack of self of persons, one identifies the object of negation: the "I" we impute to our aggregates, which appears to be truly existent. When, however, we inquire whether that "I" is identical to the body, identical to the mind, or separate from them, we see that none of these is a sustainable position and that there is no self. But that absence of self, whether in ourselves or in phenomena, does not negate their conventional validity, for they are dependent arisings. Within a meditation session, one starts from the previously established stable focus on the mind's clarity and awareness and then, without losing concentration, alternates between analysis and nonconceptual focus, until insight founded on serenity is achieved. At the end of meditation, one is urged to recite the *Mahāmudrā Lineage Prayer* and dedicate one's merit. In between sessions, one is generally encouraged to guard one's senses, maintain awareness in everyday activities, rely on one's guru and friends, and read scripture; in tantric terms, one is told to see all events as the play of the guru's body, speech, and mind. The text concludes with verses of dedication.

The shorter (eight-folio) *Advice of Mañjughoṣa Lama* (Yg*JLZL*) discusses all the features of mahāmudrā practice but is weighted more heavily toward the actual meditation, with the preliminaries receiving less attention. It also follows Paṇchen Chögyen's *Highway of the Conquerors* fairly closely. The preliminaries begin with the now-familiar advice to find an isolated place and assume a comfortable position. One slows down and purifies the mind through the ninefold breathing practice, then rests briefly in the mind's natural clarity and awareness. One then forcefully develops the awakening mind, reflecting on the sufferings that beings undergo and vowing to relieve them. Having generated great faith, one visualizes the objects of refuge (not described in detail here) and recites prayers of refuge, the awakening mind, and the four immeasurables, after which the objects of refuge melt into one, and one meditates on emptiness "with the pride of the Dharma body."[789] From that emptiness, one sees oneself in the form of one's yidam at the center of a maṇḍala of other deities. As the deity, one visualizes one's own guru as Lama Losang Thupwang Dorjé Chang in the space before one, with deities below him and gurus above him (again, not described in detail). After the gnosis beings absorb into the assembled deities, one offers the sevenfold worship rite and the Meru maṇḍala and supplicates Tsongkhapa and the lineage gurus, especially those related to the mahāmudrā transmission. Remembering the kindness of one's own guru, one requests—and receives—the four unexcelled-yoga-tantra empowerments. In thanks, one then recites the mantras of Śākyamuni, Vajradhara, and Tsongkhapa. The members of the assembly absorb into the central guru, who in turn absorbs into oneself, and one rests stably in the experience of the inseparability of one's own mind and the guru's mind.[790]

The actual mahāmudrā practice begins from here, with a serenity meditation rooted in a state of nondiscursive absorption on the clear, aware nature of the mind. One applies mindfulness and awareness as necessary, and when thoughts arise, one gazes starkly at their nature and relegates them to their "own place," then settles back into single-pointed meditative equipoise on the nature of mind. This, notes Yeshé Gyaltsen, is a method found in the Seven Attainment Texts and the *Dohās* of Saraha. Alternatively, one may, like a spear

789. Yg*JLZL* 2a [355].

790. Yeshé Gyaltsen mentions in an aside (Yg*JLZL* 3a [357]) that the preliminaries just described implicitly include three of the four tantric preliminary practices—refuge and generation of the awakening mind, the Meru maṇḍala offering, and guru yoga—with only Vajrasattva recitation not being folded in.

wielder, cut off thoughts as they arise—a practice Yeshé Gyaltsen traces to the Maitreya texts and Asaṅga's *Levels of the Bodhisattva* (*Bodhisattvabhūmi*). Or, drawing from Saraha, one may—like a vulture[791] that flies around and then settles down where it began—let thoughts go for a time, and allow them to return to their source, in clarity and awareness. After a brief digression on how to practice single-pointedness in completion-stage meditations within the subtle body (an instruction he attributes to Paṇchen Chögyen), Yeshé Gyaltsen articulates the necessity of overcoming tendencies toward agitation and dullness and cites Tsongkhapa's various stages-of-the-path texts, along with certain special instructions (*gdams ngag*), as source texts. If one keeps at this meditation from session to session, month to month, and year to year, Yeshé Gyaltsen continues, eventually one will attain the pliability of body and mind that is definitive of serenity.

The section on insight meditation begins with the recognition that success depends on generally learning the Madhyamaka view from one's teacher, supplicating one's guru and Mañjughoṣa, maintaining one's vows purely, and above all, receiving special instructions on the view from one's guru. The actual search for the view requires that one observe—from the vantage point of a mind in equipoise on the clear, aware nature of mind—how the mind naturally appears. Although all appearances, including the mind, are merely labels, they *seem* to truly exist, and our belief in their true existence is a form of self-grasping, the root of saṃsāra. This mistaken apprehension is refuted rationally by ascertaining that the self is not identical to either the body or mind, nor is it completely separate from them. Once one sees that the "I" is a mere label, one can see the aggregates, on which the concept is based, in the same way, and then focus in on the mind—the basis of saṃsāra and nirvāṇa—and recognize that it, too, is merely a label without true existence. Seeing the emptiness of all phenomena, one effortlessly sees as well the harmony between emptiness and dependent arising, the crucial point that avoids the extremes of eternalism and nihilism. The actual meditation, briefly described, involves examining the nature of mind with a corner of the mind in equipoise: one settles the mind on that nature then undertakes an analysis of the sort described above; in the end, on the basis of seeing the mind's emptiness with a concentrated mind, one attains insight. After the session, Yeshé Gyaltsen advises, one should regard all events as illusion-like, without negating their conventional validity; appearance and emptiness are simply two sides of the same coin. This advice is buttressed by a long poetic quotation from the *King of Concentrations Sūtra* (quoted also in Paṇchen Chögyen's *Lamp So Bright*), which gives

791. In most sources, the bird is described as a raven (*bya rog*) rather than a vulture (*bya rgod*).

many examples of the illusion-like nature of things: magically conjured beasts, dream experiences, reflections, mirages, and so forth. Before concluding with verses of dedication and auspiciousness, Yeshé Gyaltsen praises the hearing transmission, emphasizing that one must hear its teachings directly from a lama, but noting as well that Paṇchen Chögyen's mahāmudrā root text and autocommentary are helpful guides.

Works Focused Mainly on the Madhyamaka View

Yeshé Gyaltsen also composed at least two texts on the Madhyamaka viewpoint that are indirectly related to mahāmudrā practice: the *Advice of Losang [Drakpa]: An Uncommon Instruction on the View of the Profound Madhyamaka* and *Source of All Attainments: A Very Secret Short Letter Teaching the Key Points of the View* (Yg*LZZL*).

The *Advice of Losang*[792] is not framed as a mahāmudrā manual per se; it focuses instead on the three principal aspects of the path identified by Tsongkhapa: renunciation, awakening mind, and right view. It does, however, quote extensively from the writings of Ensapa and the spiritual songs of Paṇchen Chögyen,[793] which themselves sometimes refer to the great seal, and the detailed Madhyamaka meditations that occupy the central part of the text easily could be applied by a practitioner of mahāmudrā. The teaching begins with verses of homage to the gurus, the buddhas, and Tsongkhapa and then describes the importance of mastering both wisdom and method, as these are the basis of the Dharma body and form bodies of a buddha, respectively. The practitioner then is exhorted to develop renunciation, "like a swan flying away from a frozen lake," and the awakening mind, "like . . . a merciful leader who . . . sets out in a ship to fetch the wish-fulfilling gem" for the sake of sentient beings.[794] This encouragement is supplemented by quotations about the value of the awakening mind drawn from such sūtras as the *Splendid Array* (*Gaṇḍavyūha*) and *King of Concentrations* and such masters as Nāgārjuna, Śāntideva, Tsongkhapa, and Paṇchen Chögyen. Then begins the extensive exposition of the Madhyamaka view, which Yeshé Gyaltsen defines as "the wisdom realizing the empty nature of all phenomena."[795] He goes on to identify the apprehension of or grasping at a permanent self (*bdag 'dzin*) as the root

792. See the translation in Guenther 1976, 104–27.

793. All the songs by Paṇchen Chögyen excerpted by Yeshé Gyaltsen are translated in their entirety below, where the reader will find page references for Guenther's 1976 translations.

794. Guenther 1976, 106 and 107.

795. Yg*LZZL* 7a [173]; cf. Guenther 1976, 112.

of our troubles and then undertakes a careful philosophical search to determine if such a self exists. If the self were identical with the body, then it would perish when a corpse is cremated. If it were identical with the mind, then we should not be susceptible to the mental vicissitudes brought on by changes in the body. Similarly, it is illogical to translate "my mind" as "I's I." If the self were separate from either body or mind, its separateness should be evident upon examination, but it is not, since the only tools of examination are within the mind-body complex. The text goes on to cite a series of examples of how we may misconceive, then properly understand, the nature of things: a distant scarecrow that is mistaken for a person then recognized for what it is, animals that either frighten or delight us in our dreams that are recognized as illusory when we awake, and a rope mistaken at twilight for a snake but seen as a rope on closer inspection. Yeshé Gyaltsen further supports his analysis with lengthy quotations from Āryadeva, Tsongkhapa, and most prominently, Ensapa and Paṇchen Chögyen; works by the latter that are cited include numerous poems and *Lamp So Bright*. The text goes on to make the familiar and all-important point that emptiness does not entail nihilism, since it is harmonious with the dependent arising of conventional phenomena; this claim, too, is supported by extensive quotations, most of them from Tsongkhapa's *Praise for Dependent Arising* and Paṇchen Chögyen's spiritual songs. The text then briefly describes an actual practice session, in which one begins with guru yoga and then applies to the nature of phenomena both placement and investigative meditation (the former being inadequate on its own). The resulting recognition of emptiness is celebrated as the "life of the path"[796] and the basis for all serious practice of the Mantra Vehicle. Yeshé Gyaltsen concludes with a long quotation from the *King of Concentrations Sūtra* about the illusory nature of phenomena and, of course, a poetic dedication of merit and expression of auspiciousness.

Key Points of the View (Yg*TBYC*) is a brief teaching from the tradition of Ensapa and his spiritual sons (presumably Sangyé Yeshé and Paṇchen Chögyen) that focuses on realization of the Madhyamaka view as a basis for tantric meditation. It begins with expressions of refuge and awakening mind followed by a brief meditation on the stages of the path, which leads to the recognition that (1) self-grasping is the root of defilements, on the basis of which one performs actions whose consequence is saṃsāric suffering, and (2) if one ends self-grasping, then defilements, negative actions, and suffering will cease as well. Next, one analyzes the possible relations a self might have to the aggregates: it cannot be identical with them, or it would arise and cease with them, and cannot be apart from them, or there could be no effect on oneself if something

796. Guenther 1976, 124.

affected the aggregates. One must be certain that nothing truly exists—not oneself, not others, not things—and recognize, too, that our sense that these are real is no more accurate than the yellow hue the world takes on for someone afflicted with jaundice. In short, there is no essence to anything, a point we must reinforce again and again, while also remembering that there is no contradiction at all between emptiness and appearances, which are "friends."[797] Having determined that there is no self, one settles stably upon the empty nature of one's own mind, then—in a practice reminiscent of severance but not identified as such—offers up one's flesh and blood, and body and aggregates, to various demons, which consume and enjoy them. One sees them all as buddhas, and they all disappear into emptiness, and one's own mind becomes clear and empty, like the sky. When one rises from meditation, all appearances are to be seen as like illusions.

A further practice, the most advanced, which is the "essence of the ocean of unexcelled yoga tantras,"[798] involves seeing oneself and all beings in the form of Heruka, or Cakrasaṃvara, and all environments as his pure land. These all dissolve into light, which absorbs into one's Heruka body, and one's own body dissolves into the heart cakra. There the mind rests in space-like awareness, which becomes the gnosis of connate inseparable bliss and emptiness. From within that gnosis, one experiences all reality as having the single taste of bliss-emptiness in the form of Heruka Cakrasaṃvara and his consort, Vajrayoginī. One imagines joining with her in sexual union, meditates single-pointedly on the nature of the mind, and then, after meditation, sees all appearances as the divine couple. Finally, in verse, Yeshé Gyaltsen requests that the realizations he has outlined come to pass so that, for instance, he sees all phenomena as mere empty mental designations; his own mind abides in the Dharma realm; "through experiencing the play of connate bliss-emptiness," he may dance amid the heroes and ḍākinīs;[799] and through closely embracing the Dharma realm from which he is inseparable, he reaches the unitive stage—a synonym, as we know, for mahāmudrā.

Works Focused Mainly on Guru Yoga

Finally, Yeshé Gyaltsen is credited with several guru-yoga texts that are regarded as preliminary or supplementary to mahāmudrā meditation:

797. Yg*TBYC* 4b [346].

798. Yg*TBYC* 6b [350].

799. Yg*TBYC* 7a [351].

- *A Guidebook on "Offering to the Guru": A Treasury of Hearing Transmission Special Instructions That Distinguishes the Secret Key Points*
- *Source of All Yogic Attainments: Words of Supplication Related to Ganden Mahāmudrā*
- *A Magic Key that Opens the Hundred Treasures of the Hearing Transmission: Summary of the Guru Yoga Preliminary to Ganden Mahāmudrā*
- *Cluster of Yogic Attainments: The Essence of Guru-Deity Yoga*
- *Mahāmudrā Lineage Prayer*

The most important of these is the *Guidebook on "Offering to the Guru,"*[800] a massive, meticulously outlined, and erudite commentary on Paṇchen Chögyen's *Offering to the Guru*. Yeshé Gyaltsen works verse by verse through the text of the ritual (providing a separate explanatory heading for almost every verse), with digressions, as seem appropriate, into the life stories of the masters of the hearing transmission; the details of the iconography of various unexcelled-yoga-tantra deities; instructions on how to generate renunciation, awakening mind, and right view; and lengthy exhortations to guru devotion—all buttressed by a large apparatus of supporting quotations from Indian sūtra and tantra literature and a variety of Tibetan masters, almost all of them Gelukpa; the most frequently quoted are Tsongkhapa, Ensapa, Sangyé Yeshe, and Paṇchen Chögyen. The commentary mentions mahāmudrā a few times in passing, usually as treated in key texts such as Paṇchen Chögyen's *Highway of the Conquerors* or Yeshé Gyaltsen's own *Bright Lamp of the Excellent Path*, though it also refers on one occasion to the "mahāmudrā attainment."[801] The most significant comment on mahāmudrā, and the one that seals a connection between *Offering to the Guru* and mahāmudrā meditation forevermore, comes toward the end of the commentary, right after the request (in verse 86) that the guru plant his feet firmly at one's "lotus heart." According to Yeshé Gyaltsen,[802] the visualization that accompanies this request involves the dissolution of the field of assembly into the central guru (Lama Losang Thupwang Dorjé Chang) and then the absorption of the guru into one's own heart cakra, as a result of which one experiences the inseparability of one's own mind and the guru's mind. At this point, says Yeshé Gyaltsen, the practitioner may meditate on either (Sūtra) mahāmudrā or the completion stage of unexcelled yoga tantra. If one opts for mahāmudrā, then it is appropriate to recite *Highway of the Conquerors*, presumably using it as a basis for applying

800. Yg*LCKY*, translated in Kachen Yeshe Gyaltsen 2014, 13–380.

801. Kachen Yeshe Gyaltsen 2014, 192.

802. Kachen Yeshe Gyaltsen 2014, 360–62.

the techniques of serenity and insight meditation—as well as recommendations for encountering the world in the post-meditative state—described in Paṇchen Chögyen's root verses. The practitioner also is encouraged to seek the blessings of the hearing transmission lineage by reciting the *Mahāmudrā Lineage Prayer*—in the revision of which, of course, Yeshé Gyaltsen himself had an important hand.

The *Source of All Yogic Attainments* (Yg*PCMT*) is a stages-of-the-path prayer directed to Tsongkhapa and other hearing-transmission lineage holders. In it, Yeshé Gyaltsen writes of how he has fallen time after time in his saṃsāric sojourn and that this time, having achieved a perfect human rebirth, he must work night and day to make it meaningful, since it is as evanescent as a dewdrop at the tip of a lotus blossom. Recognizing that he is prone to deception by the "demoness of saṃsāric existence," he asks for help to arouse disgust for the world and also to generate compassion and the awakening mind toward the myriad sentient beings who have been his mother and father, requesting in particular that they be able to enter the Vajrayāna and "quickly attain the jewel of great bliss." He petitions Mañjughoṣa Lama (i.e., Tsongkhapa) for protection from defilements and asks to be able fully to practice guru yoga, which has the power to grant ultimate attainments. He requests assistance in taking to heart the guru's instructions, in developing renunciation, awakening mind, and right view, and in assiduously practicing the two stages of unexcelled yoga tantra. Recognizing that he is distracted, focusing on the wrong things and drunk with desire for them, Yeshé Gyaltsen next asks to be restrained by the ironclad training in mindfulness and alertness described in the hearing transmission, and he seeks concentration through focusing on a virtuous object and traversing the stages of serenity meditation. He then asks to realize the profound Madhyamaka view by understanding the true meaning of dependent arising, avoiding the extremes of nihilism and eternalism, and analyzing phenomena with the "stainless eye of realization" so as to overcome false conventions, see things as they are, and realize the unity of the two truths. He appeals for help in seeing that all arising phenomena are mere conceptual labels, without an atom of true existence, and in realizing their unborn nature. Next, he asks to be able to "seize the royal throne" of awakening in this very life by meditating on "unitive mahāmudrā, the quintessence of the special instructions of the hearing transmission of Losang the second Conqueror, which collects the essential meaning of all the scriptures of sūtra and mantra."[803] In short, he requests that, when faith dawns and the sunlight of the guru shines in the sky, all his delusions may be cleared away. He concludes by appealing for the

803. Yg*PCMT* 3a [449].

strength to maintain his vows and expressing the hope that all beings complete the five paths and the ten bodhisattva levels and attain the rank of Vajradhara.

The Magic Key (Yg*PGDM*) is a brief and heavily outlined summary of the guru-yoga ritual to be performed prior to mahāmudrā meditation, clearly modeled on Paṇchen Chögyen's *Offering to the Guru*. It begins by identifying the four uncommon preliminaries that are the background to any actual practice: refuge and the awakening mind, purification meditation on Vajrasattva, the Meru maṇḍala offering, and guru yoga—which is said to fulfill the other three as well as itself.[804] The actual practice of guru yoga begins, as usual, with (1) taking refuge and generating the awakening mind, after which one generates out of emptiness a deity in the space before oneself, (2) receiving blessings of body, speech, and mind, and (3) purifying offering substances. The core practice involves an external visualization of one's own guru in the form of Lama Losang Thupwang Dorjé Chang. As in *Offering to the Guru*, the guru's aggregates, elements, sense organs, and so forth all are identified with buddhas and other deities. He is surrounded by gurus of the main lineages and by deities of various classes.[805] After the "real" gurus and deities of the assembly (gnosis beings) are absorbed into their visualized counterparts (pledge beings), the practitioner offers them the sevenfold worship rite followed by a Meru maṇḍala offering, then reflects on the guru's virtues and kindness and requests the four unexcelled-yoga-tantra empowerments, which are duly received in the form of light. One then requests blessings to master renunciation, the awakening mind, the seven-point mind training,[806] and the six perfections and to

804. Yg*PGDM* 1b–2a [268–69].

805. His retinue here includes five sets of lineage gurus—those of extensive activity (i.e., method) on a petal to his right, those of the profound view (i.e., wisdom) on a petal to his left, those of the blessing of practice on a petal to thc rear, those of attaining a Dharma connection on a petal to the front, and those of the hearing transmission—from Vajradhara to one's lama—in the space above him. In ranks below him, then, are eleven grades of buddhas and deities: (1) the three main Geluk unexcelled-yoga-tantra deities—Guhyasamāja, Cakrasaṃvara, and Yamāntaka—along with Hevajra, (2) other unexcelled-yoga-tantra deities, (3) yoga tantra deities, (4) performance tantra deities, (5) action tantra deities, (6) buddhas, (7) bodhisattvas, (8) pratyekabuddhas, (9) śrāvakas, (10) "heroes" and ḍākinis, and (11) Dharma protectors.

806. The Kadam seven-point mind training is said to have originated with Atiśa, but its fully developed version is credited to Chekawa Yeshé Dorjé (1102–76). It consists of a set of approximately sixty slogans for Buddhist practice, divided among seven categories: (1) preliminaries, (2) training in the awakening mind, (3) bringing adverse conditions onto the path to awakening, (4) a lifetime's worth of practice summarized in the practice of transference of consciousness, (5) criteria for knowing when the mind has been trained, (6) the commitments of mind training, and (7) the precepts of mind training. For a translation of the root text and a commentary by Sé Chilbu Chökyi Gyaltsen (1121–89), see Jinpa 2006, 83–132.

receive empowerments, preserve one's vows, succeed in generation-stage and completion-stage practices, practice transference of consciousness at the time of death, and be close by the guru in all one's lives. Afterward, one is to maintain unstinting awareness during everyday activities, see appearances as the play of the guru's secret yogic attainments of body, speech, and mind, and transform all objects of the mind and senses into offerings to the guru. The text concludes with a very brief instruction on mahāmudrā meditation. Perfection Vehicle mahāmudrā meditation involves settling the mind in a stable state on the basis of common instructions on serenity meditation, then contemplating the profound Madhyamaka view. Mantra Vehicle mahāmudrā meditation involves a highly secret method of blocking karmic winds through piercing the vital points of the subtle body. These secret practices, of course, only can be practiced on the basis of oral instruction from a guru and are not detailed in the text.

Cluster of Yogic Attainments (Yg*NGNM*) also situates mahāmudrā meditation in relation to guru-yoga practice. Combining passages from Paṇchen Chögyen's *Offering to the Guru* with his own compositions, and alternating verse with prose, Yeshé Gyaltsen describes the text as a "special instruction of the supreme siddha Ensapa and his spiritual sons, from the hearing transmission of Mañjughoṣa Lama."[807] It begins with preliminary meditations on the role played by the mind in effecting bondage and liberation and the need to practice guru yoga. Then, as in *Offering to the Guru*, one goes for refuge and generates the awakening mind, then visualizes one's own guru as Lama Losang Thupwang Dorjé Chang, clear and luminous in the space before one, surrounded by offerings and a retinue of gurus and deities. After the usual absorption of the gnosis beings into the pledge beings, one makes offerings, performs the sevenfold worship rite and offers the Meru maṇḍala. With increasing fervor, and while extolling their virtues, one then appeals for blessings to the gurus of the hearing transmission in general and to one's own guru in particular. They respond by bestowing the four empowerments, which will become the basis for the future attainment of the four buddha bodies. One then requests blessings to traverse the stages of the path to awakening; among the last is an appeal to "bless me to seize the royal throne through meditation on unitive mahāmudrā, the essential special instruction of the hearing transmission of Losang the second Conqueror."[808] After a few further requests, the guru comes to one's crown, melts into light, and settles at one's heart cakra—at which point mahāmudrā meditation would commence. The practice is cel-

807. Yg*NGNM* 1b [186].

808. Yg*NGNM* 5b [194].

ebrated for planting the seeds for accomplishing the path and, in particular, mastering "the profound uncommon mahāmudrā path explained by the precious Ganden Oral Lineage" and the generation and completion stages of unexcelled yoga tantra.[809] At the completion of the session, one is instructed to guard the sense doors and see all appearances as the play of the guru's secret yogic attainments of body, speech, and mind. The text concludes with verses of dedication and auspiciousness.

Last, but far from least, among the guru-yoga texts is the expanded version of Paṇchen Chögyen's *Mahāmudrā Lineage Prayer*,[810] which is not found in Yeshé Gyaltsen's collected works but is universally credited to him. In recent times, it has been published both as an independent work[811] and as an appendix to Paṇchen Chögyen's *Highway of the Conquerors*.[812] The latter makes sense, since, as we know, the lineage prayer was composed in its basic form by Paṇchen Chögyen, then supplemented by later members of the lineage. Kalden Gyatso's updating remained limited to certain circles in Amdo, while Yeshé Gyaltsen's version, as supplemented by Phabongkha and others, has become the standard version used as part of Geluk mahāmudrā practice. Because Yeshé Gyaltsen's version of the prayer is, so far as I know, unavailable without the material contributed by Phabongkha and other modern lamas, we do not know exactly which lineage gurus he added to Paṇchen Chögyen's basic prayer. It would be reasonable to assume that he filled in the lamas between Paṇchen Chögyen's time and his own, but whether these would include teachers in Amdo as well as those in Ü and Tsang is difficult to know. We might expect that, minimally, Yeshé Gyaltsen composed the verses of supplication to Paṇchen Chögyen (who is described as omniscient and inseparable from Tsongkhapa's teaching), Drupchen Gendun Gyaltsen (1532–1607, who condensed the Buddha's multiple teachings into a single practice), Drupai Gyaltsen Dzinpa (sixteenth–seventeenth centuries, who "tasted the very essence" of Tsongkhapa's teachings), Könchok Gyaltsen (1612–87, who was a skillful teacher of "the distillate nectar of deep and vast Dharma"), the Second Paṇchen Lama (1663–1737, who is Paṇchen Chögyen reborn "for the good of the teachings and beings"), Losang Trinlé (b. seventeenth century, who

809. Yg*NGNM* 6a [195].

810. Yg*PCSD(2)*. This is included in the translation below, part 5, section 3. For alternative translations, see Gyatso 1982, 227–34, Willis 1995, 101–6, Kachen Yeshe Gyaltsen 2014, 445–54, and Zasep 2019, 13–25.

811. See Willis 1995, 253.

812. E.g., Yg*PCSD(2)*, which is a blockprint in my possession bearing no bibliographic information.

has "plumbed the depths of the hearing transmission path"), and Drupwang Losang Namgyal (1670–1741, who fully practiced the heart of Tsongkhapa's hearing transmission). In the absence of textual evidence, however, we really cannot be sure which of those verses Yeshé Gyaltsen wrote and which were composed by Phabongkha. In short, most the verses in the middle section of the *Mahāmudrā Lineage Prayer*—those postdating Paṇchen Chögyen and preceding Yeshé Gyaltsen—are nowadays attributed primarily to Yeshé Gyaltsen, but we do not know how much of a hand he actually had in shaping the version of the prayer prevalent in the modern era.

Final Remarks

In concluding our discussion of Yeshé Gyaltsen, a couple of comparative observations bear making. One is that his works display scant evidence of interest in or familiarity with Kagyü mahāmudrā traditions. Unlike Paṇchen Chögyen and Kalden Gyatso, who were conversant with Kagyü literature in general and inspired by Milarepa in particular, Yeshé Gyaltsen almost never quotes Kagyüpa masters in support of his analyses. Also, while he does occasionally cite the Indian mahāsiddhas that so influenced Tibetan mahāmudrā traditions, Kagyü and otherwise, he draws on them far less often than Paṇchen Chögyen and Kalden Gyatso. He also departs from his predecessors in his descriptions of the serenity and insight practices that form the heart of Geluk mahāmudrā practice. He typically describes serenity meditation according to the traditional stages, obstacles, and antidotes established by Asaṅga and endorsed by Tsongkhapa in the *Great Stages of the Path*, without recourse to the Kagyü techniques emphasized by Paṇchen Chögyen and Kalden Gyatso. By the same token, his description of insight meditation hews quite closely to the standard Geluk emphasis on identifying the object of negation and showing how the "I" cannot be found in either the body or the mind, nor outside them. In short, while there is no question that Paṇchen Chögyen and Kalden Gyatso made mahāmudrā a distinctly Geluk practice in a number of ways, Yeshé Gyaltsen, by reducing his reliance on Kagyü sources and models and aligning key mahāmudrā practices with orthodoxies traceable to Tsongkhapa, managed to "Geluk-ize" the tradition far more thoroughly. And to the degree that Yeshé Gyaltsen's great enthusiasm for and extensive writing about the Ganden mahāmudrā transmission helped shape all subsequent Geluk understandings of the tradition, his approach partially eclipsed the efforts of his great predecessors—or, at least, provided a particular lens through which to view them.[813]

813. For further reflection on these issues, see R. Jackson 2019.

12. Four Later Commentators

THE NEXT TWO chapters track Geluk writings about mahāmudrā from the time of Yeshé Gyaltsen to the beginning of the twentieth century. We will first consider briefly the works of four masters who wrote close commentaries on Paṇchen Chögyen's *Highway of the Conquerors*. In the next chapter, we will survey a number of eastern Tibetan lamas from the same era who did not write commentaries on Paṇchen Chögyen's root verses but nevertheless knew the tradition and either discussed it or expressed its spirit.

The four who wrote verse-by-verse commentaries on Paṇchen Chögyen's *Highway of the Conquerors* are Gugé Losang Tenzin, Gungthang Tenpai Drönmé, Ngulchu Dharmabhadra, and Keutsang Jamyang Mönlam. Of these, only the second and third are recognized as part of the hearing-transmission lineage, but the first and fourth were also important figures. The first two were direct disciples of Yeshé Gyaltsen, while the last two were grand-disciples.

Gugé Losang Tenzin

Losang Tenzin (1748–1813),[814] whose full, formal name is Gugé Yongzin Losang Tenzin Gyatso, was a direct disciple of Yeshé Gyaltsen and is closely associated with Tashi Lhunpo Monastery, where he spent most of his life. A native of Gugé in far western Tibet, he received his novice ordination at the age of eight and a year later entered the Kyilkhang regional monastic house of Tashi Lhunpo and began academic study there under the tutelage of Yeshé Gyaltsen and other masters. In 1775, he received full ordination and was granted a *kachu* (*dka' bcu*) degree, Tashi Lhunpo's highest scholarly achievement, signifying mastery of ten difficult texts or topics. He spent most of the next fourteen years in meditative retreat at Paljor Lhunpo, the main hermitage of Tashi Lhunpo, and then in 1792 returned to the Kyilkhang regional house as master of studies. Two years later, he was named tutor to the Fourth Paṇchen Lama,

814. Information in this paragraph is derived from the BDRC website: http://www.tbrc.org/#!rid=P308. See also Zasep 2019, 40.

Tenpai Nyima (1782–1853). Before his death in 1813, Losang Tenzin produced enough works to fill five volumes. Most of them are focused on the tantras, but he also produced the longest single work on Geluk mahāmudrā, his 227-folio, verse-by-verse commentary on *Highway of the Conquerors* entitled *Storehouse of Attainments Concordant with the Supreme: An Explanatory Commentary on the Root Verses and [Auto]commentary of the Mahāmudrā Teaching Tradition of the Precious Ganden Oral Transmission* (Gg*NGBM*).

This massive treatise, divided into nearly 150 sections, subsections, and sub-subsections,[815] reflects a tendency we already saw at work in the mahāmudrā writings of Yeshé Gyaltsen, namely, to front-load the analysis with more and more detailed exposition of the preliminaries leading up to serenity and insight meditation. Indeed, nearly two-thirds of Losang Tenzin's text is given over to preliminary practices, mostly the various phases of guru yoga, of which a subset is a detailed set of meditations on the stages of the path, especially regarding the awakening mind. Only the last third of the work—covering seventy-plus folios—is given over to the meditative and postmeditative practices in which the typically mahāmudrā concern with the nature of mind and phenomena is the focus. Apart from its extraordinary length and detail, and its status as the first verse-by-verse commentary on *Highway of the Conquerors* since Paṇchen Chögyen's own *Lamp So Bright*, there is little in *Storehouse of Attainments* to set it apart from earlier Geluk mahāmudrā works: its quotations are familiar and predictable, and it takes no particularly new or original angles on the preliminaries, the process of serenity meditation, the philosophical reasoning behind insight meditation, or the perspectives to adopt in postmeditation.

To summarize briefly, the text's first eight folios (Gg*NGBM* 2b–10b) discuss the importance of mahāmudrā, the meaning of the term, its division into sūtra and mantra, and the general contours of the Ganden Hearing Transmission as detailed in the works of Yeshé Gyaltsen. The long section on preliminaries (10b–153a)—which, like those of Yeshé Gyaltsen, is rooted in Paṇchen Chögyen's *Offering to the Guru*—includes instructions on posture, the nine-round breathing practice, and the visualizations and prayers required for taking refuge and generating the awakening mind. That leads into a lengthy exposition of the practice of guru yoga (35b–92b), with the now-familiar visualization of one's own guru as Lama Losang Thupwang Dorjé Chang with his retinue of gurus and deities and, after that, the absorption of the actual dei-

815. Indeed, it is so complex that Losang Tenzin himself seems to lose track of his own categories at times, leaving the reader who is keeping a "scorecard" a bit perplexed, especially toward the end of the text.

ties into the imagined deities and the performance of the sevenfold worship rite (which subsumes multiple offerings and the Vajrasattva meditation and recitation). As usual, this is succeeded by praises of and appeals to the assembled gurus and receipt of the four unexcelled-yoga-tantra empowerments. At that point, Losang Tenzin provides more than fifty folios of instructions (92b–144a) on how to contemplate the "ordinary Mahāyāna," which cover the expected topics of the stages-of-the-path tradition, from the perfect human rebirth through the six perfections, with a special focus on meditations aimed at generating the awakening mind.

Following his description of the absorption of the visualized assembly into the central guru, and the guru's dissolution into one's heart, the author at long last gets to mahāmudrā. Following the order of Paṇchen Chögyen's root verses, he discusses mahāmudrā's importance, its divisions, the different ways it has been taught, and the unity among different traditions of practice (153a–167b). Turning to serenity meditation (167b–185a), he details the various ways in which one may focus on the nature of mind as clear and aware, and maintain that focus through the proper application of mindfulness, alertness, and other antidotes to such faults as agitation and dullness, or excessive tightness or laxity. The discussion of insight meditation that follows (185a–216a)[816] consists primarily of an exposition of the absence of self in persons and phenomena, respectively, with the former receiving the most attention. Before his concluding verses and colophon, Losang Tenzin provides standard instructions on how to see and act when not engaged in formal meditation—namely, by seeing all phenomena as like illusions (216a–227a).

Gungthang Könchok Tenpai Drönmé

Like Losang Tenzin, Gungthang Könchok Tenpai Drönmé (1762–1823)[817] was a student of Yeshé Gyaltsen, though within Tibet he hailed from Amdo in the northeast rather than Gugé in the far west. At the age of six, he was recognized by the great scholar-monk Könchok Jikmé Wangpo as the third tulku in the Gungthang line and taken to Labrang Monastery to receive his novice vows and begin his education in Buddhist and secular sciences as well as the Chinese and Mongolian languages. At sixteen, he moved to the Lhasa area, continuing his education at Gomang College of Drepung Monastery, where

816. It is not entirely clear where this discussion begins, as this is a place where Losang Tenzin's text divisions do not seem entirely consistent.

817. Information in this paragraph is drawn primarily from Chhosphel 2010c. See also Zasep 2019, 39–40.

he received full ordination and studied under a number of major teachers, including the Eighth Dalai Lama, Thuken Losang Chökyi Nyima, Könchok Jikmé Wangpo, and Yeshé Gyaltsen. (The last two are both lineage holders in the Ganden Hearing Transmission.) He became a *lharampa* geshé at the unusually early age of twenty and, after further study, returned in 1786 to Labrang, where he began to gain fame as a teacher. Under the guidance of Könchok Jikmé Wangpo, he assumed a series of abbatial seats in Amdo, first at Tsakhoi Datsang, then at the newly founded Ngawa Gomang. He went on to preside at Labrang itself and at another great Geluk institution in the area, Gönlung Jampa Ling. He traveled throughout Amdo, giving teachings and empowerments, raised funds for the construction of a great stūpa, and began composing texts of his own. From 1806 until his death in 1823, he resided primarily at Labrang and its hermitages, spending time in retreat and writing, and occasionally teaching his large band of disciples. Gungthangsang (as he often is known) left behind eleven volumes of writings, which reveal the extraordinary breadth and depth of his learning. He wrote analyses of important Indian Buddhist philosophical texts; tantric sādhanas and commentaries; biographies; texts on "secular sciences" like astrology, medicine, and painting; guru-yoga practices; poetic aphorisms employing water and tree imagery; a commentary on some songs of Milarepa; and a large number of still-popular songs of spiritual experience.[818]

Gungthangpa's one work on Geluk mahāmudrā, *Garland of Nectar Drops: Notes on an Oral Instruction on Geden Mahāmudrā* (Gt*DTTP*), seems to be based on a discourse delivered by Yeshé Gyaltsen, who was, as mentioned, one of two Geluk mahāmudrā lineage holders he counted among his teachers. It is not, properly speaking, a verse-by-verse commentary on Paṇchen Chögyen's *Highway of the Conquerors*, but it does allude to nearly all of the root text directly or indirectly, hence may be read fruitfully in conjunction with it. At twenty-nine folios, it is barely a tenth the size of Losang Tenzin's massive commentary, yet it covers all the same bases, in roughly the same order and with the same proportion of discussion devoted to preliminaries and actual practice—yet it has a number of distinctive passages and perspectives that make it among the more rewarding Geluk mahāmudrā texts to study. Since the order of such texts is well known to us by now, I will not summarize it here but will simply mention a few of the more striking points Gungthangpa makes along the way.

Toward the beginning of the text, when discussing the history of the tradition's transmission (Gt*DTTP* 40), Gungthangpa makes the point that

818. See, e.g. Jinpa and Elsner 2000, 33–37 and 51–60.

Tsongkhapa did *not* write down any mahāmudrā instructions, using as his sources the same texts by Jé Rinpoché cited by Yeshé Gyaltsen in his *Bright Lamp of the Excellent Path*. In commenting on Paṇchen Chögyen's description of mahāmudrā in verse 1 of *Highway of the Conquerors* (41–42), he carefully aligns its designation as "the all-pervasive nature of everything" with "objective mahāmudrā" (*yul phyag chen*), which is consonant with the sūtra-mahāmudrā tradition; and its designation as "the inseparable, inexpressible vajra realm of the mind" with a mantra-oriented "subjective mahāmudrā" (*yul can phyag chen*), which is described as "the gnosis that starkly sees the abiding nature [of everything]" (51). When describing the sources of mantra mahāmudrā (52), he notes the controversy over whether Saraha did, in fact, compose all three *Dohā Treasuries*, or whether, as claimed by Butön, the *People Dohās* is genuine and those addressed to the king and queen spurious; he does not pass judgment on the question. In commenting on Paṇchen Chögyen's list of different Tibetan practices, all of which are determined to have the same view or intention (55–56), Gungthangpa cites, without further comment, the suggestion by the Third Paṇchen Lama, Losang Palden Yeshé (1738–81), that Paṇchen Chögyen must have been joking when he attributed the same intention to those who assert emptiness as an affirming negation (e.g., Jonangpas, most Nyingmapas, and many Kagyüpas) and those who insist it is a nonaffirming negation (e.g., Gelukpas and most Sakyapas).[819] In quoting the lines for visualizing the field of assembly found in *Offering to the Guru* ("in the vast space of inseparable bliss and emptiness"), Gungthangpa explicates bliss as the gnosis that dwells in the ultimate (i.e., the Dharma body), and emptiness as the inseparability and essential emptiness of the two form bodies (57). Just before the dissolution of the assembly, at the culmination of a stages-of-the-path meditation, he gives a lucid summary of the two stages of mantra practice (70–71).

In introducing the section on insight meditation, he cites Kagyü distinctions (not generally emphasized by Gelukpas) between gradual and sudden approaches to mahāmudrā and tells a long story about the realizations attained by the early Kagyü master Phakmo Drupa (76–77). He goes on to mention, on the authority of Yeshé Gyaltsen, Tsongkhapa's study with Umapa of Lama Barawa's Kagyü mahāmudrā technique for recognizing the nature of mind (which Tsongkhapa may have passed on to Gungru Gyaltsen Sangpo as part of a special mahāmudrā teaching) and notes Khedrup Jé's critique of this position, in his biography of Tsongkhapa, as leading only to serenity, not

819. See the Fourteenth Dalai Lama's mention of this point in Dalai Lama and Berzin 1997, 124–25.

insight. In discussing the mahāmudrā insight practice of mind meditating on mind, Gungthangpa raises doubts about whether the idea is at all coherent, since as Mādhyamika critics of the Mind-Only position have noted, mind cannot see mind any more than an eye can see itself or a finger touch itself; his response, keyed to distinctions made by Changkya Rölpai Dorjé and Yeshé Gyaltsen, specifies that "mind seeing mind" begins with a mental image[820] of mind separate from the apprehending cognition, and that that image becomes the basis for moment-by-moment meditation on the nature of the mind thus imagined (81). He closes out the section on insight meditation by quoting the quatrain of Khedrup Sangyé Yeshé cited by Paṇchen Chögyen in *Highway of the Conquerors* (verse 37):

> When you're fully aware that whatever appears is conceptually
> apprehended,
> then the Dharma realm appears independent of anything else;
> when awareness rests within this appearing
> and you settle in single-pointed meditative equipoise—*E ma*![821]

This, says Gungthangpa, condenses the entire point of mahāmudrā into a single verse.

Ngulchu Dharmabhadra

Ngulchu Dharmabhadra (1772–1851)[822] was born to a family of impoverished shepherds in the Yeru region of Tsang, west of Shigatsé. He did not learn to read or write until he was eleven but was so dedicated to literacy that he would spend hours scratching on slates while tending his flock. At thirteen, he received lay ordination, then novice vows, at Tashi Gephel Ling Hermitage. Shortly thereafter, his brother, mother, and maternal aunt died, and he retreated to Ngulchu Hermitage, where he received full ordination in 1793. At Ngulchu, he

820. *Don spyi* is difficult to translate comprehensibly. Sometimes rendered as "generic image" or "meaning generality," it is a technical epistemological term, especially prominent in the Sautrāntika and Pramāṇa schools, that refers to the way we commonly apprehend objects indirectly, through images, concepts, or representations. Only buddhas are capable of seeing all things directly; ārya bodhisattvas can see emptiness directly while in meditative equipoise, but when not in equipoise they still perceive the world—and the world's emptiness—indirectly, through a mental image.

821. Gt*DTTP* 82–83.

822. Information in this paragraph is drawn from Chhosphel 2010a and Ngulchu Dharmabhadra and Vth Ling Rinpoche 2010, 3–6.

studied with Losang Kalsang Chögyal (dates unknown) and Khedrup Ngawang Dorjé (1720–1802); the latter is part of the Ganden mahāmudrā lineage, though he wrote nothing on the topic. From 1794 to 1804, Dharmabhadra spent considerable time at Tashi Lhunpo, where he studied with a number of eminent teachers, including Drongtsé Losang Tsultrim (1745–1800), Jedrung Losang Dedun, and Gugé Losang Tenzin, author of the massive commentary on mahāmudrā discussed above. He mastered a wide range of Buddhist and secular branches of knowledge and became especially renowned for his understanding of grammar, composition, and poetics, in both Sanskrit and Tibetan. He spent most of the last half of his life at Ngulchu, teaching and writing, and attracting a number of disciples who themselves attained eminence, including his nephew and successor in the mahāmudrā lineage, Yangchen Drupai Dorjé (1809–87).[823] Dharmabhadra left behind nearly two hundred written works, which are usually collected in six or eight volumes.[824] Besides his well-known texts on grammar and poetics, he composed dozens of works on tantra, including highly respected commentaries on the six Dharmas of Nāropa and the practices of Cakrasaṃvara and Yamāntaka,[825] and numerous works as well on guru yoga, the stages of the path, and mind training.

His single text on mahāmudrā, which appears to have been written in 1827, is *Clearing Away All Delusion: Notes on the Occasion of Bestowing Profound Instructions Based on "Highway of the Conquerors," the Root Text for the Profound Path of Mahāmudrā* (Db*KPKS*). While it lacks the detail of Gugé Losang Tenzin's *Storehouse of Attainments* or the provocative asides of Gungthangpa's *Garland of Nectar Drops*, Dharmabhadra's commentary has the twin virtues of manageable length (28 folios) and scrupulous but not excessive imposition of text divisions. In addition, it hews fairly closely to the proportions and details of Paṇchen Chögyen's root text. The outline of Dharmabhadra's commentary follows that of *Lamp So Bright* but is a bit more detailed. For instance, it divides the discussion of serenity meditation (11b–17b) into subsections on the object of meditation (covering root verses 16–17), the meditative process (root verses 18–23), and the essence of serenity (root verses 24–27). The actual instructions on insight (18a–22a) are subdivided into sections on analyzing the self of persons (root verses 29–32), a

823. For a listing of his works that includes a description of each text, see Kanakura et al. 1953, 399–412. As best I can ascertain, he wrote nothing about mahāmudrā.

824. For a listing that includes descriptions of each text, see Kanakura et al. 1953, 371–99.

825. Translated in Ngulchu Dharmabhadra and the First Panchen Lama 2014, 17–105, Ngulchu Dharmabhadra and the First Panchen Lama 2010, 11–114, and Ngulchu Dharmabhadra and Vth Ling Rinpoche 2012, 19–210, respectively.

discussion of the nature of mind (root verses 33–35), and a summary (root verses 36–38). And, the section on postmeditative practice (22a–25a) is subdivided into the dedication of merit (root verse 39), a summary of refutations of true existence (root verses 40–43), a description of how to see all phenomena as "illusion-like" (root verse 44), and a summary of the Madhyamaka view (root verse 45). Appended to *Clearing Away All Delusion* is a text entitled *Outline of Mahāmudrā*,[826] which eschews all commentary and simply provides a detailed set of text divisions and subdivisions for *Highway of the Conquerors*. Interestingly, it mirrors almost verbatim the text divisions found in Keutsang Losang Jamyang Mönlam's *Excellent and Completely Virtuous Path to Freedom*, to be discussed below. Because Keutsang's commentary is undated, we cannot be sure whether Dharmabhadra copied Keutsang's outline or the other way around; neither master mentions the other. In any case, Dharmabhadra's gloss provides a brief, useful overview of the structure of Paṇchen Chögyen's root text in relation to particular groups of verses, doing so in greater detail than the Paṇchen himself but not on the baroque scale found in the commentary by his own teacher Gugé Losang Tenzin.

Keutsang Losang Jamyang Mönlam

Keutsang Losang Jamyang Mönlam is a master on whose life we have little reliable information.[827] He was born sometime in the last quarter of the eighteenth century, perhaps in 1791.[828] He was a scion of the Doringpa, a wealthy family of Lhasa aristocrats, and was recognized at some point as the rebirth of Jampa

826. *Phyag chen sa bcad*; found at Db*KPKS* 26a–28a [53–57].

827. The most reliable information is found at "Blo bzang 'jam dbyangs smon lam" at https://www.tbrc.org/#!rid=P308 and "Keutsang Hermitage (Ke'u tshang ri khrod)" at thlib.org. Keutsang Losang Jamyang Mönlam should not be confused, as he sometimes is, with the Losang Jamyang Mönlam from eastern Tibet known as Drakgo Lama (Brag mgo bla ma, b. 1689; see http://www.tbrc.org/#!rid=P1513), nor with the Losang Jamyang Mönlam, also from Kham, who became the sixty-seventh Ganden throneholder (1750–1814/1817; see http://www.tbrc.org/#!rid=P307). Unfortunately, in the fine collection of Geluk mahāmudrā texts issued by Drepung Loseling in 1999, the brief biography of Keutsang preceding his commentary (*LZGM* 89) is that of the Ganden Tripa Losang Jamyang Mönlam rather than the Losang Jamyang Mönlam who wrote the text that follows.

828. According to the information on the BDRC website, Keutsang's father, Doring Tenzin Paljor, was born in 1760 and fathered a younger sibling of Keutsang's, Doring Mingyur Sönam Paljor, in 1784. Assuming (perhaps unsafely) that his father was sixteen or older when Keutsang was born, the range of likely birthdates based on this evidence would run from 1776 to 1783. This is not a lot to go on, though, and the preponderance of opinion in recent Tibetan sources (*LSGT* 87, *DKTD* 92–93) supports a birthdate of 1791. I want to thank José Cabezón, expert on

Mönlam (1729?–90), who served as the seventeenth abbot of Sera Jé Monastic College and spent his later years at the Keutsang Hermitage above Sera.[829] The name of the hermitage came to be attached to Jampa Mönlam's incarnate successors, making Losang Jamyang Mönlam the Second Keutsang Tulku. We may assume that, as the Keutsang Tulku, Losang Jamyang Mönlam was based primarily at Sera Jé, and at Keutsang in particular. Indeed, it has been suggested that, coming from a family of considerable means, he may have helped sponsor the expansion of the hermitage in the late eighteenth and early nineteenth centuries.[830] His teachers—several of whom he mentions in his mahāmudrā commentary[831]—included the Second Radreng Tulku Losang Yeshé Tenpa Rabgyé (1759–1815), who was a student of both Yeshé Gyaltsen and the Third Paṇchen Lama Palden Yeshé; a Sera master named Rinchen Wangyal (1741–1812), who studied with both Yeshé Gyaltsen and Tenpa Rabgyé; and Losang Namdröl (dates unknown), a student of Tenpa Rabgyé whom Keutsang credits with the approach to mahāmudrā he takes in his commentary. Keutsang had numerous disciples, of whom the most important seems to have been Yeshé Thupten Gyatso, who lived from 1806 to 1846. Assuming the dates for this disciple are correct, it is unlikely that Keutsang died before 1815, and it may well have been much later. He left behind a relatively small collection of twenty-two writings, including texts on guru yoga, an exposition of Tsongkhapa's views on Yogācāra, a biography of his teacher Rinchen Wangyal, analyses of the stages of the path, discussions of monastic discipline, several tantric sādhanas, and a variety of letters, prayers, and question-and-answer texts.[832]

Keutsang's largest text by far is his mahāmudrā commentary, the undated *Excellent and Completely Virtuous Path to Freedom: Notes on the Mahāmudrā Oral Tradition of the Geden Hearing Transmission* (Kt*GBLZ*). Consisting of seventy-two folios, it is exceeded in length among Geluk mahāmudrā works only by Gugé Losang Tenzin's *Storehouse of Attainments* (which is three times longer) and Yeshé Gyaltsen's *Bright Lamp of the Excellent Path* (which is not quite twice as long). It reproduces and comments upon every line of *Highway of the Conquerors* and draws liberally, as well, from Paṇchen Chögyen's autocommentary, *Lamp So Bright*. Its general outline follows that of *Lamp So Bright*, but like other commentaries, it adds far more subdivisions than Paṇchen

all things Sera, for providing valuable information on this question (personal correspondence, March 24, 2015).

829. See "Keutsang Hermitage (Ke'u tshang ri khrod)," 50.

830. "Keutsang Hermitage (Ke'u tshang ri khrod)," 50.

831. Kt*GBLZ* 1b [8] and 71b–72a [148–49].

832. For a listing that includes descriptions of each text, see Kanakura et al. 1953, 413–17.

Chögyen himself did, especially in the sections on serenity and insight meditation. Its proportions are similar to those of Paṇchen Chögyen's texts, with a major focus on serenity meditation, insight meditation, and postmeditative awareness—though Keutsang does pay more attention to preliminary practices and less to postmeditative training than does the First Paṇchen.[833]

The early part of *Excellent and Completely Virtuous Path to Freedom* (Kt*GBLZ* 3b–7b) includes useful perspectives on the importance of mahāmudrā but goes into little detail on the history of the hearing transmission itself. The section on the preliminaries (7b–23b) includes long and interesting discussions of refuge, the awakening mind, purification, and guru devotion; it is loosely keyed to Paṇchen Chögyen's *Offering to the Guru* but does not follow it as closely as many other commentaries. It does include a pithy and pointed comment on the Paṇchen's use of the term "the real nature of mind" (verse 4), as follows:

> In this context, "the real nature of mind" (*sems kyi chos nyid*) is not in fact the final, abiding nature of the mind.... Other schools assert that the term refers to the final nature, but according to our school, it simply refers to direct perception of the awareness and clarity that are the mind's conventional nature.[834]

The brief section on mantra mahāmudrā (23b–24b) says relatively little about the textual sources of the tradition but gives an eloquent summary of the meaning of mahāmudrā in the context of completion-stage practices, based on the analysis in Paṇchen Chögyen's *Lamp So Bright*. When it comes to the various Tibetan "views" identified by Paṇchen Chögyen—the connate union, pacification, the great perfection, and so forth (25a–27b)—Keutsang provides brief summaries of each and then, like Gungthangpa, raises questions as to how to interpret the First Paṇchen's assertion that all the various views come down to the same point, alluding to Tsongkhapa's critiques of Kagyü mahāmudrā in *Queries from a Pure Heart* and the Third Paṇchen's comments on the irreconcilability of systems that see emptiness as an affirming negation and those that see it as a nonaffirming negation. He suggests that Paṇchen Chögyen held back from criticizing other systems so as to maintain "pure vision," and that we must be very careful, when comparing soteriologies, to distinguish provisional from definitive, and inferior from superior perspec-

833. For Keutsang's outline as applied to *Highway of the Conquerors*, see appendix C.

834. Kt*GBLZ* 13a–b [31–32].

tives; the clear implication is that the Geluk perspective is superior to that of other traditions.

Of interest in Keutsang's discussion of serenity meditation (27b–41a) is his broad division of the topic into "the way of maintaining stability at the time of the cause" and "the way things appear at the time of fruition." The former, covering the actual procedures for focusing on the clear, aware nature of mind, identifies five techniques for maintaining stability: (1) "new mindfulness" (identifying thoughts as they arise; root verse 18a–b), (2) "old mindfulness" (cutting off thoughts as they arise; verse 18c–d), (3) "timely demarcation" (relaxing the mind; verses 19–20), (4) applying "conventions known to others" (being aware, Kagyü style, of the mind's stillness and movement within a state of pure vacuity; verse 21), and (5) "the self-stopping of concepts" (letting thoughts arise and subside on their own; verses 22–23). The section on the way things appear at the time of fruition (verses 24–26) describes the unobstructed, limpid, and clear state in which one abides when one has completed the causal processes. In line with verse 27 of *Highway of the Conquerors*, Keutsang notes that, contrary to common opinion in Tibet, this meditative equipoise is *not* insight into the ultimate nature of the mind.

The section on insight (44b–66a) also includes nuanced divisions, covering such procedures as a general analysis establishing lack of self, examination of the constituents that comprise self and other, investigation of the ultimate nature of the mind, and training in how to respond to objects that arise during meditation. Throughout, there is a strong emphasis on the superiority of Tsongkhapa's particular approach to Madhyamaka, with its emphasis on seeing emptiness as a nonaffirming negation that is harmonious with dependent arising, and seeing dependently arisen phenomena in terms of increasing subtlety, as produced by causes and conditions, as interdependent, and as mere nominal designations. The section on postmeditation (66a–70a) is relatively brief but covers the main points made by Paṇchen Chögyen with regard to seeing postmeditative appearances as illusion-like dependent arisings, and understanding the profound point of Tsongkhapa's system: that there is no contradiction at all between emptiness and dependently arisen appearances. As is typical, Keutsang ends with the dedication of merit, final verses, and a colophon, which as noted mentions his indebtedness to various gurus but does not specify the date of the commentary's composition. While the lack of such a date makes it hard to know whether the outline of mahāmudrā written by Ngulchu Dharmabhadra in 1827 that is identical in nearly every respect predates or follows Keutsang's text, the close correspondence is probably not a coincidence. Either way, it provides a useful way of structuring Paṇchen Chögyen's root verses.

13. Later Lamas from Amdo and Kham

As already noted, the Ganden Hearing Transmission after Paṇchen Chögyen bifurcated into Ü-Tsang and Amdo branches. With the exception of Gungthangpa, who studied for a number of years at Drepung but spent most of his life in Amdo, the great commentators on *Highway of the Conquerors* were situated in the Lhasa area or in Tsang. Through the eighteenth and nineteenth centuries, however, Amdo continued to produce great masters who were drawn to mahāmudrā. They may not figure in the official lineage lists, and may not have written texts explicitly dedicated to mahāmudrā, but figures such as Changkya Rölpai Dorjé, Thuken Losang Chökyi Nyima, Shabkar Tsokdruk Rangdröl, Gyalrong Tsultrim Nyima, Akhu Sherab Gyatso, Choné Lama Lodrö Gyatso, and Losang Dongak Chökyi Gyatso all should be acknowledged for their contributions to Geluk discourse on the great seal.

Changkya Rölpai Dorjé

Changkya Rölpai Dorjé (1717–86)[835] was one of the most important Gelukpa lamas of the eighteenth century, in part on the basis of his extensive and influential writings, but far more because, in his role as chief lama in Beijing, he supervised the translation of major portions of the Tibetan canon into Mongolian and Manchu and served as the eyes and ears on Tibetan affairs for the powerful Qianlong emperor (1711–99). Born of Mongour (mixed Tibetan-Mongolian) parents in the Tsongkha region of Amdo, he was recognized at age four by Jamyang Shepa as the third incarnation of the Changkya line, whose main seat was Gönlung Jampaling Monastery, near Lake Kokonor. Not long after his installation at Gönlung, the monastery was destroyed by a Chinese army and Changkya was brought to Beijing. His predecessor, Ngawang

835. Material in this paragraph is drawn from Jinpa and Elsner 2000, 221, Smith 2001, 133–46, Brunnhölzl 2007, 391–92, Townsend 2010, and Namgyal 2012. See also Wang 1995 and Illich 2006.

Losang Chöden, had spent much of his later life in Beijing, giving teachings and empowerments and founding temples, so there was a well-established connection between the Changkya line and the seat of Chinese power. There, Changkya received his education. A student of the second Thuken tulku, Ngawang Chökyi Gyatso (1680–1736), and schoolmate of the future Qianlong emperor, he mastered Buddhist philosophical and tantric systems and learned to speak and write the Tibetan, Chinese, Mongolian, and Manchu languages.

He visited Central Tibet for the first time at seventeen, accompanying the Seventh Dalai Lama to Lhasa. He spent nearly two years there, studying with the Dalai Lama and other masters, and receiving his monastic vows from the Second Paṇchen Lama Losang Yeshé. He was recalled to Beijing in 1736, upon the sudden death of the Yongzheng emperor, and Changkya's childhood friend the Qianlong emperor was next in line. Though Changkya was barely twenty, the emperor made him chief lama of Beijing and asked him to oversee the translation of the Tibetan Tengyur into Mongolian, a project that took eight years to complete. Later, he would oversee the translation of the Tengyur into Manchu. During his long periods of residence in Beijing, Changkya taught and translated to and from the multiple languages he knew, served as the emperor's preceptor on Buddhist thought and practice, helped found numerous temples and monasteries (including the famous "Lama Temple," Yonghegong), and repeatedly helped persuade the emperor to grant Tibetans sovereignty over important aspects of their own affairs. He visited Central Tibet again from 1757 to 1760, helping to identify the Eighth Dalai Lama and establish a regency for him, and traveled to Amdo in 1763 upon the death of his father, spending some time in retreat at Gönlung, which had been rebuilt. Although his visits to Tibet were few and brief, he attracted a number of disciples, of whom the most important were Könchok Jikmé Wangpo[836] and the Third Thuken, Losang Chökyi Nyima, who would write his biography. Changkya's later years were divided between Beijing and Mañjuśrī's holy mountain, Wutai Shan, where he established a retreat center at which he spent at least four months a year, and where he passed away in 1786. Changkya left behind over two hundred texts collected into seven volumes. His most famous and influential work is a long doxography, *Ornament Beautifying the Meru of the Sage's Teaching: A Clarifying Explanation of the Arrangement of Tenet Systems*, which among Geluk tenet-system texts is second in prestige only to the *Great Exposition of Tenet Systems* by Jamyang Shepa, though it actually is

836. He was recognized as the reincarnation of Jamyang Shepa and hence is sometimes referred to as the Second Jamyang Shepa or the Jamyang Shepa Tulku.

broader in scope, touching as it does on a number of issues not just in Indian but in Tibetan Buddhist thought.[837]

Although Changkya is not counted among the main lineage holders of Geluk mahāmudrā, he studied with the Second Paṇchen Lama and was acquainted, as well, with his own close contemporary, Yeshé Gyaltsen, who credits him with requesting the composition of his most important mahāmudrā text, *Bright Lamp of the Excellent Path*.[838] Changkya did not himself write any texts dedicated to Geluk mahāmudrā, but it is evident from a number of his question-and-answer texts that he was interested in the transmission's origins and nature. In *Answers to the Questions of Gomang Gungru Rabjampa Lodrö*, he discusses the literary history of the tradition, and wrestles with questions of the compatibility of Geluk mahāmudrā with other systems and of the sort of emptiness realized in mahāmudrā meditation.[839] In *Answers to the Questions of the Jamyang Shepa Tulku* (Ck*JSDL*), he begins with the famous quote from Sangyé Yeshé—cited by Paṇchen Chögyen in *Highway of the Conquerors*—to the effect that the Dharma realm appears on its own when one sees all appearances as mere conceptual apprehensions, and he goes on to analyze the way in which this pithy summary of mahāmudrā tallies with the Prāsaṅgika Madhyamaka viewpoint in general and Tsongkhapa's emphasis on the concordance between emptiness and dependent arising in particular. In yet another question-and-answer text, Changkya asserts that Tsongkhapa transmitted a special tradition of mahāmudrā in which the Madhyamaka view was explained in a somewhat different manner than in his best-known philosophical texts—a possible reference to an instruction he may have received from Lama Umapa and passed on to Gungru Gyaltsen Sangpo.[840]

Changkya's familiarity with the tradition also is evident from a number of his spiritual songs, the most famous of which is *A Profound Song on the View*, better known as *Recognizing My Mother* (Ck*TBSG*),[841] composed on Wutai Shan. In this complex, allegorical poem about the process of realizing emptiness, Changkya relies on the common Buddhist gender-polarity symbolism that equates the male with method and the conventional and the female with wisdom and the ultimate. He refers repeatedly to his father as dependent

837. For a full translation of Changkya's great treatise by Donald S. Lopez, Jr., see Changkya 2019.

838. Yg*LZGM* 122a [443].

839. Ck*LGDL* 9a–12a (question 6).

840. Dalai Lama and Berzin 1997, 164 and 231.

841. This has been translated into English at least twice: Jinpa and Elsner 2000, 109–13, and Brunnhölzl 2007, 393–97.

arising or skillful means and to his mother as emptiness—that is, the way things really are. After homage to his guru, he begins the poem proper by describing himself as a "lunatic child" who long ago lost his mother, and gently chiding her for deceiving him with her display of duality. Only through the whispers of his father, dependent arising, can he begin to find her traces, since "this world of diversity and change / is actually my changeless mother's moods."[842] His father, being conventional, cannot actually be found, yet in the wake of this not-finding, "Lo! Father's found in mother's lap. / That, is how the parents create us, I'm told!"[843] In the second part of the poem, Changkya expresses confidence in the transmissions coming to him from Nāgārjuna and Candrakīrti and reflects through pointed metaphors on the excessive realism entailed by the views of Vaibhāṣikas, Sautrāntikas, Vijñānavādins, and Svātantrikas, and wonders whether the descriptions of the ultimate put forth by masters of the Sakya ("self-cognition of void and clear"), Nyingma ("pristine purity and spontaneity"), Kagyü ("mahamudra, the coemergent uncontrived mind"), and Drukpa ("the viewless view") really hit the target at which they aim.[844] He goes on, in a gently mocking tone, to reassure these Indian and Tibetan thinkers that their views may be justified through recognition of the inseparability of emptiness and dependent arising, adding, "please forgive me if I've offended."[845] In the last part of the poem, Changkya alludes to the kindness of his forefathers, especially Nāgārjuna, Tsongkhapa, and his own guru, and asserts that because of them he is confident he can guide his steed across "the impassable cliff," relax into freedom from the two extremes, and come close to seeing his mother's face, even as "I see in front of me / the kind parents so long lost."[846] He concludes by expressing the hope that the meeting of the son—his own awareness—with "the unborn, inexpressible mother" will help lead beings to bliss, and singing:

> *E ma la!* I, Rölpai Dorjé
> *A o la!* pounding out here
> *O na la!* this happy dance
> *Ma ho ya!* I offer it to the Triple Gem.[847]

842. Jinpa and Elsner 2000, 110.

843. Jinpa and Elsner 2000, 110.

844. Jinpa and Elsner 2000, 111.

845. Jinpa and Elsner 2000, 112.

846. Jinpa and Elsner 2000, 113.

847. Ck*TBSG* 3b [390]; cf. trans. Jinpa and Elsner 2000, 113, and Brunnhölzl 2007, 426.

Recognizing My Mother became one of the best-loved and most studied poetic works in the Geluk canon, and received attention from a number of later commentators, including the great nineteenth-century Nyingma master Mipham Gyatso (1846–1912), who reads Changkya as not being especially critical of other Tibetan schools and, in fact, as using the song to propound the idea that emptiness is an affirming negation—precisely as claimed by many Sakya, Nyingma, and Kagyü masters, but in opposition, of course, to the standard Geluk view that it is a nonaffirming negation.[848] Among Geluk commentaries, perhaps the most extensive and wide ranging is that by Gungru Geshé Tenpa Tenzin (1917–2007), the *Jewel Heart of the Four Tenet-Systems*, which includes detailed doxographical analyses of the various Indian and Tibetan traditions mentioned by Changkya. It includes, as well, a long chapter on the mahāmudrā of the early Kagyü masters in which he addresses various issues in mahāmudrā theory and practice, such as the sūtra-mantra debate, the ways in which mahāmudrā meditation can go astray, and the nature of the four yogas. And he has a shorter chapter on the views of later Kagyüpas, which touches, among other topics, on attempts to synthesize mahāmudrā and the great perfection.[849]

Thuken Losang Chökyi Nyima

Thuken Losang Chökyi Nyima (1737–1802)[850] was, like his teacher Changkya, a recognized tulku—the third—in one of the Mongolian Amdo incarnation lineages that were so vital to Chinese-Mongolian-Tibetan cultural and political relations during the Qing dynasty. His predecessor, Ngawang Chökyi Gyatso, was one of Changkya's main teachers, and like both his predecessor and his guru, Thuken Chökyi Nyima would live a peripatetic, cosmopolitan life, residing at various times in Amdo, Beijing, Mongolia, Lhasa, or Tsang. He was born to Mongour parents in 1737 in a part of Amdo now in Gansu province. Recognized as an incarnate at an early age, he began his education at Gönlung Monastery. At thirteen, he received novice vows there from Changkya Rölpai Dorjé, with Sumpa Khenpo Yeshé Paljor (1704–88) also in attendance. A brilliant student, he was sent at eighteen to Drepung Monastery in Lhasa, where he studied with Könchok Jikmé Wangpo, also a disciple of Changkya,

848. See Brunnhölzl 2007, 399–427.

849. See Tt*GZNN* 89–103 and 221–27, respectively.

850. Information in this paragraph is drawn primarily from Thuken 2009, 3–13, which in turn is based, *inter alia*, on Wang 1995, 186–89, Kapstein 2000, 130, and Smith 2001, 147–70. For further references, see Thuken 2009, 412n26.

and with the Third Paṇchen Lama Palden Yeshé, both members of the Ganden mahāmudrā lineage. At the completion of his studies in 1759, he served for two years as abbot of the ancient Shalu Monastery in Tsang. He returned to Amdo in 1761 to become abbot of Gönlung but was summoned two years later to Beijing, where he was feted by the Qianlong emperor and spent time with Changkya. Finding the Beijing climate unhealthy, he returned to Gönlung by way of Mongolia in 1768 but was brought back to Beijing three years later. For the next dozen years, he divided his time among Beijing, Inner Mongolia, and Gönlung. He returned to Amdo for good in 1783, presiding over Jakhyung Monastery and teaching at Kumbum but spending most of his time at Gönlung, where he devoted himself to writing and to instructing his numerous disciples, including Gungthang Könchok Tenpai Dronmé, who would write Thuken's biography after his master's death in 1802.

Thuken was a prolific author, his roughly 250 works collected in ten volumes. Like so many great masters, he devoted the largest number of texts to aspects of tantric practice,[851] but he also wrote biographies of the Second Thuken and of Changkya,[852] monastery chronicles, catalogs of images, various poetic works, and a defense of the authenticity of the Nyingma treasure traditions.[853] The text for which he is by far the best known is his *Crystal Mirror: An Excellent Explanation Showing the Sources and Assertions of All Tenet Systems* (Tk*SGML*),[854] a grand survey of the history, doctrines, and practices of the religions of India, Tibet, China, Mongolia, and Shambhala. The *Crystal Mirror* includes, in the long chapter on the Geluk, a relatively brief account of the Ensa Hearing Transmission,[855] which focuses on the sequence of lineage holders from Tsongkhapa to Paṇchen Chögyen but says nothing about the contents of the lineage and does not mention mahāmudrā. Although Thuken does touch on mahāmudrā in passing in the chapters on the Kadam, Sakya, and Chan traditions,[856] his main discussion of the topic, as we might expect, comes in his section on the Kagyü. This substantial chapter,[857] the longest on any non-Geluk Tibetan tradition, is divided into three major parts: a historical account of the Kagyü in general and its various subschools in particular; an

851. See R. Jackson 1997 for a translation of an Avalokiteśvara fasting-ritual text.

852. For a source partially based on the latter, see Wang 1995.

853. See Kapstein 2000, 121–37.

854. For a full English translation, see Thuken 2009.

855. Tk*SGML* 238–40; trans. Thuken 2009, 291–92.

856. See the index references in Thuken 2009, 624a.

857. Tk*SGML* 76–113; trans. Thuken 2009, 117–56.

exposition of view and meditation among the Kagyü, with a special emphasis on different approaches to mahāmudrā; and an investigation of certain problems in the interpretation of Kagyü mahāmudrā.

The final two sections in particular[858] contain much of interest for understanding later Gelukpas' views of the great seal—both that of the Kagyü and their own. Amid accounts of different mahāmudrā systems and practices (often drawn from Norsang Gyatso's *Bright Lamp of Mahāmudrā* or Paṇchen Chögyen's *Lamp So Bright*), Thuken makes a number of striking points about Kagyü mahāmudrā:[859]

(1) The great Indian and Tibetan forefathers of the Kagyü—Nāropa, Maitrīpa, Marpa, and Milarepa—occasionally expressed themselves in a manner consonant with the views of Cittamātra or Svātantrika Madhyamaka but were fundamentally committed to the Prāsaṅgika Madhyamaka view of Nāgārjuna and Candrakīrti.

(2) Early Tibetan Kagyü mahāmudrā is divisible into sūtra, or gradualist, and mantra, or subitist, approaches. The former involves a single-pointed investigation of the nature of mind, which is discovered to be—and contemplated as—an affirming negation, while the latter is the luminous mind of great bliss resulting from the introduction of the vital winds into the central channel of the subtle body.

(3) Later Kagyü techniques for "seeking the mind," as described by Paṇchen Chögyen in *Lamp So Bright*,[860] are valuable for giving a meditator a sense of the nature of the coarse conventional mind but do not probe the subtlest levels of mind, and often are vitiated by an anti-intellectual attitude, in which analytical investigation of the ultimate nature of mind is dismissed as unnecessary.

(4) Kagyüpas are correct to assert, *contra* Sakya Paṇḍita, that there does exist a sūtra-based system of mahāmudrā, which is vouchsafed in such sūtras as the *King of Concentrations* and in the treatises of Jñānakīrti.

(5) The Tsalpa Kagyü mahāmudrā tradition of the white panacea is not, as Sapaṇ claims, mere quietism, such as was preached by Heshang Moheyan at the Samyé debate.

(6) Contrary to the assertions of the renegade Geluk-turned-Nyingma scholar Losang Rinchen (seventeenth–eighteenth century), Khedrup Norsang Gyatso's *Bright Lamp of Mahāmudrā* should *not* be seen as an attempt to show the unity of Kagyü and Geluk, as it focuses almost entirely on the

858. An excerpt of this is translated below in part 5, section 9.

859. Tk*SGML* 99–112; trans. Thuken 2009, 137–54.

860. Thuken overtly draws his description of these practices from the First Paṇchen's text: Tk*SGML* 105; trans. Thuken 2009, 144.

former—yet much of what it does present of Kagyü mantra mahāmudrā is in harmony with the teachings of Tsongkhapa.

(7) The four yogas of mahāmudrā described by Maitrīpa and the Kagyü traditions are, *contra* Losang Rinchen, *not* the set of four yogas discussed in certain Cittamātra texts but are instead based on Prāsaṅgika Madyamaka principles.

(8) Losang Rinchen also is incorrect to reject Paṇchen Chögyen's famous statement, in *Highway of the Conquerors*, to the effect that all the great Tibetan philosophical systems come down to the same idea.

(9) It is difficult to decide one way or the other whether Tsongkhapa actually was the author of the purportedly anti-Kagyü *Queries from a Pure Heart*, but most scholars, both inside and outside the Geluk, have treated it as a genuine work by Jé Lama.

Broadly speaking, the upshot of Thuken's analysis is to reinforce a sense of unity—if not unanimity—between the Geluk perspective on view and meditation and that of the great early Kagyüpa masters, though their successors are treated with some skepticism. The unity is especially apparent when it comes to tantric approaches to mahāmudrā, but even on the sūtra level, the common foundation in Prāsaṅgika Madhyamaka thought helps to override any differences that may crop up because of Kagyüpa masters' occasional use of Cittamātra terminology as a skillful means or their tendency to view the ultimate emptiness of the mind as an affirming negation, which may, again, be seen as an exercise in skillful means.

Shabkar Tsokdruk Rangdröl

The great nonsectarian peripatetic yogī Shabkar Tsokdruk Rangdröl (1781–1851)[861] does not fit cleanly into our survey of Geluk mahāmudrā masters but merits our attention nonetheless. He was born in the Repkong area of Amdo, also the land of Shar Kalden Gyatso, of whom he was well aware. He was drawn to Buddhist practice from an early age, joining a group of wandering tantric practitioners, or *ngakpas*, when he was only eleven. Throughout his teen years, he studied with a number of Nyingmapa and Gelukpa lamas in the area, receiving teachings on the great perfection, various treasure cycles, mind training, and other important practices. Dharma, he once remarked, always came easily to him. Over his mother's objections, he took monastic vows at twenty, from the Gelukpa master Arik Geshé Jampa Gelek Gyaltsen (1726–1803), who had spent thirteen years in Central Tibet. Arik Geshé's two main

861. Material in this paragraph is drawn from Ricard 1994, xiii–xxiv, and Ricard 2007.

teachers there were Phurbuchok Ngawang Jampa and the Third Paṇchen Lama Palden Yeshé, both members of the "standard" Ganden mahāmudrā lineage. On Arik Geshé's advice, Shabkar traveled to Urgé Tratsang Monastery to seek out the renowned Nyingmapa master Chögyal Ngakyi Wangpo (1736/40–1807), who became his principal teacher. Over the course of six years, Chögyal granted Shabkar nearly every important Nyingma empowerment and teaching but also instructed him in mind training, mahāmudrā, and other practices not strictly of Nyingma provenance. Following Ngakyi Wangpo's death in 1807, Shabkar spent eight years in retreat at various wilderness sites in Amdo, including the remote forest of Tseshung and Tsonying Island, in the middle of Lake Kokonor. He then began a pilgrimage of many years' duration that took him to nearly every corner of Tibet, from Kham to Mount Kailash, and from the great monasteries of Lhasa to Everest-region caves once inhabited by Milarepa, and even to the Kathmandu Valley. With his wandering lifestyle, his penchant for long, cave-bound retreats, and his talent for instructing others through spontaneous spiritual songs, he came to be regarded as a "second Milarepa"—though eventually he would be regarded as the emanation of many other figures, as well, including Avalokiteśvara and a number of masters from the Nyingma, Kadam, Kagyü, and Geluk traditions.[862] Although he never abandoned the yogic way of life, Shabkar did return to Amdo in 1828 and lived out his last two decades in the region, instructing numerous disciples, acting as a peacemaker in local disputes, and writing the texts for which he would become famous:[863] his series of "emanated scriptures" on various aspects of Buddhist thought and practice; his brilliant poem on the great perfection, *The Flight of the Garuda*;[864] his treatise on avoiding the consumption of meat;[865] and his massive autobiography, which also serves as a repository of many of his spiritual songs.[866]

Although Shabkar is most closely associated with the great perfection and other Nyingma traditions, his impartiality toward the various Tibetan traditions—his insistence on envisioning them as pure—seems to have been deep-seated and genuine. They mirrored developments during the nineteenth century in Kham, where such nonsectarian (*ris med*) lamas as Jamyang Khyentsé, Jamgön Kongtrul, and Mipham Gyatso sought to preserve and promote

862. Ricard 1994, 471.

863. For a description of his writings, see Ricard 1994, 577–88.

864. English translations are found in Dowman 1994, 65–135, and Kunsang 2008, 13–99.

865. An English translation is found in Padmakara Translation Group 2004.

866. This is fully translated in Ricard 1994. Further translations of Shabkar's songs may be found in Jinpa and Elsner 2000, 66–67, and Sujata 2012.

endangered teachings from all the major Tibetan orders. Shabkar's own nonsectarianism is most evident in his frequent references to two different triads that inspired him. The first is the triad of views: middle way, great seal, and great perfection, which, Shabkar says:

> Are like sugar, molasses, and honey:
> one is as good as the other.
> For this reason, I have listened to
> and practiced all of them without partiality.[867]

The other triad contains three spiritual teachers: Padmasambhava, Atiśa, and Tsongkhapa, who represent, respectively, the teachings on the great perfection, mind training, and the stages of the path.[868] The inclusion of Tsongkhapa (and Atiśa, who inspired Jé Lama) points to Shabkar's sense of indebtedness to his Gelukpa teachers and the master whose tradition they transmitted. In the poetic preface to his autobiography—after verses celebrating the Buddha, Samantabhadra, Vajradhara, Padmasambhava, and Atiśa—Shabkar addresses Tsongkhapa, saying:

> Losang, the second Buddha,
> manifestation of Lord Atiśa in this degenerate age,
> to you who spread the teachings of the conquerors
> and made them bloom like the sun rising in the sky, I bow down.[869]

At various points, Shabkar studied many of Tsongkhapa's works, especially his stages-of-the-path treatises, of which Shabkar himself wrote a summary; he also mentions such well-known texts as *Praise for Dependent Arising*, the *Three Principal Aspects of the Path*, and Jé Rinpoché's tantric commentaries on the five stages of the Guhyasamāja completion stage and the six Dharmas of Nāropa, and he is aware of Tsongkhapa's connection to the Nyingma teacher Namkha Gyaltsen (a.k.a. Lekyi Dorjé), who we may recall transmitted great-perfection teachings from Vajrapāṇi to Tsongkhapa, as recorded in the *Garland of the Supremely Medicinal Nectar*.[870] Shabkar also encountered Tsongkhapa in a visionary dream, where he listened to a teaching on the con-

867. Ricard 1994, 138 (translation adapted).

868. Ricard 1994, xv, 3, 584.

869. Ricard 1994, 3 (translation adapted).

870. Ricard 1994, 584; for the *Garland*, see above, pages 155–56.

densed text on the stages of the path and was presented with a copy of the text by Jé Rinpoché.[871] Later, Padmasambhava appeared to Shabkar in a vision, and told him that it had been he, Guru Rinpoché, who had appeared in the form of Tsongkhapa on the earlier occasion.[872]

Although Shabkar referred to mahāmudrā often, and wrote a number of songs focused on it,[873] his approach to the topic seems squarely based on Kagyü perspectives on the great seal. He was deeply familiar with the dohās of the Indian mahāsiddhas and the songs of Milarepa, and studied with a number of Kagyü lamas of his own era. We do know that he also had been exposed to the Ganden Hearing Transmission and its emanated scripture, which helped inspire him to write his own emanated scriptures,[874] and he reports that when he visited the Geluk monastery at Chubar—the site of Milarepa's passing away—he received from Chubar Khen Rinpoché Yönten Lhundrup a set of teachings on key Kadam and Geluk texts, including *Highway of the Conquerors*.[875] Shabkar mentions a number of other texts by Paṇchen Chögyen, as well, including *Offering to the Guru*, *Path to Bliss*, and the Paṇchen Lama's commentary on the six Dharmas of Nāropa, and he seems generally quite familiar with, and quite reverential toward, important Geluk teachers and practices. It is interesting to note, however, that the Geluk texts to which Shabkar refers are, for the most part, practice texts. With the possible exception of the *Great Stages of the Path*, he does not mention any of the philosophical works composed by Tsongkhapa and his successors, and while we cannot doubt that he found the middle way, mahāmudrā, and the great perfection to be equally valid views, he does not allude to the differences, let alone the controversies, that have been part of Tibetan intellectual life as far back as we can see—perhaps for fear it might undermine the vision of unity to which he wanted to subject *all* traditions.

871. Ricard 1994, 138.

872. Ricard 1994, 583.

873. For instance, Ricard 1994, 255–59.

874. Ricard 1994, 307. He mentions the transmission holders only from Tsongkhapa through Ensapa, though there is no reason to suppose he was unaware of the place of Sangyé Yeshé and Paṇchen Chögyen in the lineage. As we have seen, Geluk authors are not of one mind as to whether the Ganden Hearing Transmission's emanated scripture was extant by Shabkar's time, but if, as is sometimes claimed, it was still available at the time of Yeshé Gyaltsen (who died when Shabkar was in his teens) or even Phabongkha Rinpoché (who lived until the mid-twentieth century), it is not impossible that Shabkar could have been exposed to it in some fashion.

875. Ricard 1994, 434.

Gyalrong Geshé Tsultrim Nyima

Relatively little is known about Gyalrong Geshé Tsultrim Nyima (eighteenth–nineteenth centuries).[876] He was born in the Gyalrong region of Kham, making him one of the few Geluk mahāmudrā commentators from that region. He is known to have spent time at Drepung and to have studied there, or elsewhere in Ü, with Lhatsewa Yeshé Tenzin (b. eighteenth century), himself a student of Yeshé Gyaltsen. Tsultrim Nyima left behind only a handful of works, but among them is a 126-folio discussion of mahāmudrā within the context of guru yoga entitled *A Letter of Final Testament Cast to the Winds: A Guidebook of Pith Instructions and Oral Advice on Mahāmudrā* (Gr*LKPY*). Of the works on Geluk mahāmudrā we have surveyed, Tsultrim Nyima's *Letter of Final Testament* is perhaps the most heavily weighted toward the preliminaries to mahāmudrā meditation. Indeed, the first 104 folios are an extended commentary on Paṇchen Chögyen's *Offering to the Guru*, understood as the necessary preliminary to actual contemplation of the great seal. Tsultrim Nyima begins by laying out in some detail the distant and proximate lineages related to *Offering to the Guru*[877] and by emphasizing the importance of guru yoga for both sūtra and mantra practice. With the help of numerous quotations from Indian Buddhist texts, especially the tantras, he explains how and why it is the swiftest path to awakening, regardless of one's orientation within Buddhism. The next ninety folios are devoted to an extraordinarily detailed set of instructions for the practice of every phase of *Offering to the Guru*, with a special emphasis on auxiliary practices involving the three main Geluk unexcelled-yoga-tantra deities—Guhyasamāja, Cakrasaṃvara, and Yamāntaka—and an equally strong focus on the complex, nested figure at the center of the ritual's visualized field of assembly, Lama Losang Thupwang Dorjé Chang. The section on preliminaries also

876. See "Tshul khrims nyi ma."

877. Gr*LKPY* 2b–16b. The distant lineage (Gr*LKPY* 7b–8b) begins with Śākyamuni and Vajradhara, who transmit it to Maitreya, Mañjughoṣa, and Vajrapāṇi, who in turn pass it on to Asaṅga, Nāgārjuna, and Indrabodhi, respectively. These three transmissions (that of extensive activity, profound meaning, and special tantric blessing, respectively) were combined by the likes of Atiśa and Marpa and eventually made their way to Tsongkhapa. Tsongkhapa obtained the proximate lineage from Mañjughoṣa, and transmitted it to Khedrup Jé and Tokden Jampal Gyatso, from whom it descended through the familiar sequence of Baso Chökyi Gyaltsen, Chökyi Dorjé, Ensapa, Sangyé Yeshé, and Paṇchen Chögyen (11a–12a). This account differs slightly from the standard description of the lineage established by Paṇchen Chögyen and Yeshé Gyaltsen, in that it (a) establishes a highly symmetrical relation among the three major types of transmission and (b) reintroduces Khedrup Jé to the list of lineage masters.

includes detailed discussions of the four empowerments one receives from the visualized guru and of the various stages-of-the-path topics, including the disadvantages of saṃsāra, the advantages of renunciation, mind training, the four immeasurables, giving and taking (*gtong len*),[878] the awakening mind, the six perfections, and the two stages of unexcelled-yoga-tantra practice. As in every other text that connects mahāmudrā to *Offering to the Guru*, meditation on the great seal commences near the very end of the ritual, at the point where one absorbs the guru into one's own heart cakra.

The section on mahāmudrā in the *Letter of Final Testament* (Gr*LKPY* 106b–123b) follows the general structure, and includes many of the specifics, of Paṇchen Chögyen's *Highway of the Conquerors*, but it is not a verse-by-verse commentary on the root text, which it quotes only occasionally. Although for the most part it replicates accounts of serenity meditation, insight meditation, and postmeditation practice found in the works of Paṇchen Chögyen or Yeshé Gyaltsen, it does have at least five distinctive features.

(1) On the level of mantra mahāmudrā, it includes fairly detailed descriptions of unexcelled-yoga-tantra meditations, with a special emphasis on practices involving visualizations at the heart cakra on the generation stage and experience of the connate bliss and emptiness in the indestructible drop within the heart cakra on the completion stage (106b–108a).

(2) In the context of the completion stage, it makes a distinction between a realization of the conventional nature of the "coarse primordial mind" and a "final" realization of emptiness by the "subtle primordial mind" (108a–b), which as the Fourteenth Dalai Lama remarks, "gives much to think about in terms of the First Paṇchen Lama's presentation of the mahamudra technique of recognizing first the conventional nature of luminous primordial mind as its mere clarity and awareness—which is undoubtedly coarse primordial mind—and then coming to recognize the deepest nature of that luminous mind—its voidness. . . ."[879]

(3) It argues, in the context of serenity meditation, that the mind's ability to hold on to an object through the factor of mindfulness and its ability to maintain awareness of the object through the factor of concentration are simply two ways of describing the same event (110a–b).[880]

(4) In the discussion of insight meditation, it mounts a lengthy defense of the standard Geluk contention that all instances of emptiness, including

878. See above, note 722.

879. See Dalai Lama and Berzin 1997, 227.

880. See Dalai Lama and Berzin 1997, 282.

those related even to the subtlest level of cognition, are nonaffirming negations rather than negations that imply some "positive" reality (117b–119b).

(5) In the context of a retreat, it provides an outline of the practices to be undertaken in each of the day's sessions, though the key, of course, is to maintain the mahāmudrā view throughout all one's practice periods (123a–b). Following a lengthy set of final verses (125b–126b), the author, describing himself as "the Do-Nothing Tsultrim Nyima," credits Yeshé Tenzin as the source for the teachings he has written down and reports that the text was composed at Lophel Hermitage near Ganden Monastery (126b5).

Akhu Sherab Gyatso

Akhu Sherab Gyatso (1803–75) was one of the more prolific Geluk scholars of the nineteenth century. A native of Tseshung in Amdo, he seems to have spent most of his life in that part of Tibet. He studied at Labrang Tashi Khyil and eventually settled at a smaller monastery not far to the south, Dzögé Ling. He studied with many of the major Amdo lamas of the era, including Tsultrim Nyima, Palmang Könchok Gyaltsen (1764–1853), and Jamyang Thupten Nyima (1779–1862). The last two were students of Gungthang Tenpei Drönmé, and it appears that Akhu studied with Gungthangpa, as well, though he does not cite him as a major influence. He left behind over a hundred works, which were collected into seven volumes. Although he did write commentaries on the *Vinaya Sūtra*, *Ornament of Higher Realization*, and *Entry to the Middle Way*, most of his texts focus on matters of practice rather than philosophy. In addition to many works related to tantric maṇḍalas, deities, and rituals, he wrote on such key Geluk themes or texts as the stages of the path (including Paṇchen Chögyen's *Path to Bliss*), the six Dharmas of Nāropa, and the *Hundred Deities of Tuṣita*. The texts of greatest interest to us are two sizeable compilations of notes to discourses on how to combine *Offering to the Guru* with mahāmudrā delivered, respectively, by Balmang Könchok Gyaltsen and Jamyang Thupten Nyima.

The longer of the two, in ninety-five folios, is *Notes on a Teaching on Combining "Offering to the Guru" with Mahāmudrā* (Ak*LPZB*), based on discourses he heard from Palmang Könchok Gyaltsen. Like many other Geluk mahāmudrā texts, it is structured along the lines of Paṇchen Chögyen's *Highway of the Conquerors*. The introductory section (1–15b) covers the expected topics: sūtra and mantra mahāmudrā, objective and subjective mahāmudrā, the meaning of the term *mahāmudrā*, the long and short Geluk mahāmudrā lineages, and so forth. Akhu does make two points in this opening section that are unusual, hence noteworthy. First, he identifies the Five Maitreya

Texts as an important source for sūtra mahāmudrā, on the grounds that they reveal the hidden meaning of the Perfection of Wisdom sūtras.[881] The association of mahāmudrā with the Maitreya texts is not uncommon in Kagyü circles but is rare among Gelukpas, who tend to regard Nāgārjuna, Candrakīrti, and other Prāsaṅgika Mādhyamikas as the most authoritative interpreters of the ultimate purport of the Perfection of Wisdom, with the Maitreya texts being useful mainly for uncovering the conventional practices of the path implicit in the sūtras. Akhu does not expand on his point, so it is hard to know what to make of it. His second unusual—though not unprecedented—observation leaves open the possibility that, quite apart from the standard Geluk mahāmudrā lineage traced from Tsongkhapa to Tokden Jampal Gyatso down to Paṇchen Chögyen and beyond, there might be a special practice tradition stemming from Tsongkhapa's transmission of a "hidden Dharma" (*lkog chos*) to Gungru Gyaltsen Sangpo.[882] Although Akhu does not give details of this practice, the Fourteenth Dalai Lama speculates that it may involve an approach to mahāmudrā rooted in teachings Tsongkhapa received from his teacher Umapa, who in turn had learned them from the Kagyü master Barawa Gyaltsen Sangpo. As we know, the Fourteenth Dalai Lama has suggested that this approach may involve an unconventional, mahāmudrā-specific manner of conceiving of emptiness as a nonaffirming negation, or perhaps even as an affirming negation.[883] Since *Notes* is focused above all on *Offering to the Guru*, it is unsurprising that over half the text (15b–66b) covers the preliminaries to mahāmudrā meditation. About half of the discussion of preliminaries is dedicated to the visualizations, offerings, and prayers associated with *Offering to the Guru* and half to a detailed exposition of the stages-of-the-path topics covered in the text, with a special focus on such mind-training meditations as giving and taking. In this context, Akhu invokes Gampopa, whose teaching has commonly been described as merging the two streams of Kadam mind training and Kagyü mahāmudrā.[884] The account of mahāmudrā meditation and postmeditation occupies the last twenty-five folios. It follows *Lamp So Bright* fairly closely and is distinct from other texts of its era only in the liberality with which it cites and discusses the Kagyü literature mentioned by Paṇchen Chögyen in his autocommentary.

881. Ak*LPZB* 2b.

882. Ak*LPZB* 15a.

883. Dalai Lama and Berzin 1997, 230–31. As noted above (p. 162), Khedrup Jé is said to have criticized Gungru on precisely this point.

884. Ak*LPZB* 55a; cf. 66b.

Akhu's shorter text, covering forty-three folios, is *A Nectar Stream Clearing Away the Miseries of Saṃsāric Existence and Peace: Notes on a Teaching on Combining "Offering to the Guru" with Mahāmudrā* (Ak*DTCG*), based on discourses delivered by Thupten Nyima. *Nectar Stream* covers the expected topics in the usual order but, like its longer companion text, displays a number of distinctive features. For instance, in its discussion of the preliminaries to mahāmudrā meditation, it mentions the *Hundred Deities of Tuṣita* as an alternative to *Offering to the Guru* as a context for the practice,[885] and it also details a special, tantra-inflected method for offering the Meru maṇḍala.[886] Akhu focuses considerable attention on historical and philosophical questions. As he does in *Notes*, he mentions an alternative approach to mahāmudrā transmitted from Tsongkhapa to Gungru Gyaltsen Sangpo, specifying that the teaching was imparted at Jangtsé College of Ganden Monastery.[887] He cites or quotes from a number of important Gelukpa predecessors, including Jamyang Shepa, Changkya Rölpai Dorjé, Longdöl Lama Ngawang Losang (1719–94), and Thuken Chökyi Nyima. He also considers at times the positions propounded by other Tibetan schools on various points of theory and practice. He notes that the philosophical view adopted by many early Kagyüpa and Nyingmapa masters was more in accord with Yogācāra than with Prāsaṅgika Madhyamaka,[888] but he adds later that Geluk practices do—in many but not all instances—harmonize with those of their Kagyü and Sakya predecessors[889] and makes the vital point that, whatever their differences on other matters, all four schools agree on the centrality of guru yoga to Tibetan Buddhist practice.[890]

Choné Lama Lodrö Gyatso

Little is known about our penultimate premodern figure, Choné Lama Lodrö Gyatso, except that he was born in Amdo in 1816 and that, apart from some time at Drepung, he spent most of his life in or near Labrang and other monasteries in Amdo, devoting considerable time to solitary retreat. His works include a popular commentary on Tsongkhapa's *Praise for Dependent Arising*

885. Ak*DTCG* 22a and 29b.

886. Ak*DTCG* 22a; cf. Dalai Lama and Berzin 1997, 192–94.

887. Ak*DTCG* 25b; cf. Dalai Lama and Berzin 1997, 230.

888. Ak*DTCG* 26a.

889. Ak*DTCG* 28a, 28b, 35a, and 36a–b.

890. Ak*DTCG* 40a.

and a number of spiritual songs.[891] His songs are very much in the tradition of poet-yogīs such as Milarepa, Paṇchen Chögyen, and Shar Kalden Gyatso. They do not, for the most part, mention mahāmudrā explicitly, and Choné Lama is not listed as a member of the Ganden lineage, but his songs are very much in the spirit of the hearing transmission, expressing the joys of the hermitic life in general and experience of the natural mind in particular, often in erotic—or, more properly, tantric—terms.

He laments in one song, for instance,

> How I wish to look to my heart's content
> at the smiling face of the great bliss queen—
> the dawning of the view that no objects are real—
> by seeing through the illusion of a solid world.
> May I rest at will in the space free of clinging.[892]

Elsewhere, he requests,

> May the youthful *rikpa* of my natural mind
> unite with the beautiful woman, emptiness,
> in a bond never to be parted again.
> How I seek to be nurtured by eternal bliss![893]

Elsewhere, he asks,

> Great bliss, the union of wisdom and method
> engaged in the play of the unmoving with movement,
> young coral maiden with beautiful eyes,
> vajra queen, embrace me with your arts of love.

He goes on to ask, "When will I be immersed in the glory of sexual play / through the secret act of conjoining space and vajra?" and further requests,

> May my mind be always intoxicated by drinking insatiably the
> nectar—
> the delicious taste of sexual play

891. Jinpa and Elsner 2000, 222.

892. Jinpa and Elsner 2000, 158.

893. Jinpa and Elsner 2000, 41. *Rikpa* (*rig pa*) is "awareness," here meant in the deep sense of primordial pristine awareness—a usage common in the Nyingma great perfection tradition.

> between the hero in his utter ecstasy
> and his lover, the lady emptiness.[894]

His emphasis on the radiance of the natural mind—reminiscent of Kagyü and even Nyingma modes of expression—is articulated in other ways, as well, as when he sings of how "from the space of void's nature / arises the multiplicity of the dependent world,"[895] and of how:

> From multiple, interacting causes and conditions
> in the empty space of the radiant mind,
> fruits diverse both pure and impure
> arise as sentient beings and their world.[896]

At the same time, Choné Lama frequently expresses more typical Geluk positions, as when he sings that:

> Appearance . . .
> seemingly tangible to the deluded mind,
> when probed by the question "What is real?"
> offers nothing to withstand the search.[897]

At the same time,

> It's not that nothing exists: there are phenomena,
> but nothing is as it seems in the mind;
> those who stride the middle way free of being
> and nonbeing, they are called Mādhyamikas. . . .
>
> When form reveals the content of the void
> and the void makes way for spontaneous appearance,
> then you have entered the delight of the sages,
> never again to fall prey to extreme views.[898]

894. Jinpa and Elsner 2000, 144–45.

895. Jinpa and Elsner 2000, 94.

896. Jinpa and Elsner 2000, 90.

897. Jinpa and Elsner 2000, 87.

898. Jinpa and Elsner 2000, 103–4.

Losang Dongak Chökyi Gyatso

Strictly speaking, Losang Dongak Chökyi Gyatso (1903–57)[899] is a twentieth-century figure, hence a proper subject for the next chapter, but his life and work were rooted in a thoroughly premodern setting and sensibility, so it is fitting to have him conclude this chapter on premodern masters from eastern Tibet. A native of the nomadic Golok region west of Amdo, while still in his teens he was recognized by his main teacher, Amdo Geshé Jampal Rölpai Lodrö (1888–1936), as an incarnation of Japa Dongak Gyatso (1824–1902). Japa Dongak was a Gelukpa master said to be the tulku of Gungthangpa and was a student of both Shabkar and the great Nyingmapa master Patrul Rinpoché (1808–87). The latter supposedly arranged a debate between Japa Dongak and another student of his, the great Mipham Gyatso (1846–1912), who, according to Mipham's biography, defeated Japa.[900] Like his predecessor, Losang Dongak Chökyi Gyatso studied not only with well-known Gelukpa teachers, such as Amdo Geshé and Drakar Geshé Losang Tenzin Nyendrak (1866–1928), but with Nyingmapa masters as well, including Tertön Sogyal Lerab Lingpa (1856–1926). He became a main teacher, and eventually abbot, at Pal Nyenmo, a monastery established in Golok by Amdo Geshé Jampal Rölpai Lodrö; he was associated with a number of other monasteries in the region as well. Recognized for his abilities by both the Sixth/Ninth Paṇchen Lama Losang Thupten Chökyi Nyima (1883–1937) and the Thirteenth Dalai Lama Thupten Gyatso (1876–1933), he was throughout his later life a highly respected teacher in Amdo who attracted many notable disciples.

Not all of Dongak's writings survive; those that do comprise three volumes. Amid a raft of practice instructions, sādhanas, panegyrics, guru-yoga texts, experiential songs, letters, biographies, and bits of advice, his most notable contributions include two commentaries on Śāntarakṣita's Madhyamaka masterpiece, *Ornament of the Middle Way* (*Madhyamakālaṃkāra*), and a text that analyzes the combined principles of grammar and logic. His writings touch on both Geluk and Nyingma topics and show familiarity, as well, with the literature of the Kagyü and Sakya schools. He also wrote three texts that, in the nonsectarian spirit of nineteenth- and twentieth-century eastern Tibet, argue for the ultimate harmony between the New and Old translation schools, and/or among the three principal oral traditions (*bka' srol*) of Tibetan Buddhism: mahāmudrā, the great perfection, and Madhyamaka.[901]

899. Biographical information is based on Pearcey 2013.

900. See Pearcey 2014.

901. I am grateful to B. Alan Wallace, who kindly alerted me to the existence of these texts and

A Cloud of Ambrosial Offerings: Proving the Unity of the Systems of Scholars of the Old and New [Translation Schools][902] is a versified treatise that argues that the Prāsaṅgika Madhyamaka viewpoint of Nāgārjuna and Candrakīrti is, protestations to the contrary notwithstanding, the basis of theory and practice for both Nyingma and Geluk—and was accepted as such by the great Nyingmapa philosophers Rongzom Chökyi Sangpo (1012–88) and Longchenpa. *A Jeweled Mirror of Pure Appearances: Proving the Unity of the Views of the Old and New [Translation Schools] of Secret Mantra*[903] is a prose treatise that argues the same general idea in twenty-one specific theses. Each thesis begins with an assertion of the Prāsaṅgika standpoint of Tsongkhapa, followed by lengthy quotations from the works of Rongzom and Longchenpa and the discussion of possible objections.

For us, the most interesting of Dongak's three "harmonizing" texts is *Advice from the Wise: Questions and Answers on the Views of Mahāmudrā, the Great Perfection, and Madhyamaka*.[904] After some prefatory verses, *Advice from the Wise* begins with the assertion that the three great oral traditions include most of the teachings of the Buddha. Mahāmudrā and the great perfection are identified as the "ultimate vajra yogas" of the New and Old translation schools, respectively, in which the realizations of method and wisdom related to the unexcelled yoga tantras cannot be differentiated (Dn*STSG* 68). Madhyamaka is described as the acme of all tenet systems with regard to the wisdom side of the path, a viewpoint, Dongak asserts, shared by Rongzom and Longchenpa from among the Nyingmapas, by Sakya Paṇḍita from among the Sakyapas, and Tsongkhapa and his two spiritual sons (Gyaltsab Jé and Khedrup Jé) from among the Gelukpas (68). He supports his assertion with quotations from Rongzom, Longchenpa, Atiśa, Sapaṇ, Tsongkhapa, and Jamyang Shepa and then goes on to insist that not only do Rongzom and Longchenpa accept Madhyamaka as the highest viewpoint, relevant in both sūtra and mantra contexts, but with respect to questions like the proper object of negation, the relation between the two truths, and the definitions

shared with me drafts of his translations of all three, which now have appeared in final form in Wallace 2017.

902. *Gsar rnying mkhas pa'i dgongs bzhed gcig tu sgrub pa rigs lam bdud rtsi'i chu sprin*. Found at Dn*STSG* 51–64; English translation in Wallace 2017, 289–310.

903. *Gsang sngags gsar rnying gyi lta ba gcig tu sgrub pa dag snang nor bu'i me long*. Found at Dn*STSG* 15–48; English translation in Wallace 2017, 241–88.

904. *Phyag rdzogs dbu gsum gyi lta ba'i dris lan mkhas pa'i zhal lung*. Found at Dn*STSG* 67–81; English translation in Wallace 2017, 209–24. I am grateful to Donna Brown for allowing me to work with her on some difficult passages in her own draft translation of this text.

of eternalism and nihilism, they adhere to the same Prāsaṅgika viewpoint as Tsongkhapa (68–72).

The section on mahāmudrā briefly summarizes the Kagyü tradition of Marpa, Milarepa, and Gampopa, describing it as divisible into sūtra and mantra. In the sūtra system, mahāmudrā is synonymous with meditation on emptiness, while in the mantra system, it refers both to the consort with whom one practices sexual yoga and to the luminous realization of emptiness that is entailed by such practices—whether with a flesh-and-blood or visualized consort. Like all Buddhist meditation, it requires a union of serenity and insight focused on an ultimate object (72). Dongak also briefly mentions important teachers and texts in the Ganden tradition of mahāmudrā, then details the ways in which both Kagyü and Geluk traditions can be traced to Saraha, Nāropa, and Maitrīpa. He mentions that many scholars believe a misunderstanding of Maitrīpa's nonmentation doctrine led some practitioners of both Kagyü mahāmudrā and the great perfection into the discredited quietism of the Chinese Heshang (72–73). He goes on to list the four yogas of mahāmudrā, and to recommend that his readers consult Paṇchen Chögyen's *Highway of the Conquerors*; interestingly, he recommends as well that beginning practitioners should first, in a Yogācāra manner, learn to see all appearances as mind, since—though the ultimate view in all mahāmudrā systems is Prāsaṅgika Madhyamaka—the pointing-out instructions transmitted by Kagyüpa masters often involve at least a provisional adoption of the Yogācāra perspective, a perspective that can be useful if it is not taken as ultimate (73–74).

The section on the great perfection (74–76) need not detain us; Dongak summarizes some of the sources, structures, perspectives, and practices central to the tradition, insisting along the way that the great-perfection view rejects Yogācāra and embraces Prāsaṅgika Madhyamaka. He goes on to cite a range of Tibetan masters, including the Kagyüpa Rangjung Dorjé, the Gelukpa Losang Chögyen, and the Nyingmapa Jikmé Lingpa (1729–98) to the effect that all the great oral traditions of Tibet converge on the same point (76–77). Next (77–80), he advises that those intent on practice of any of these traditions base themselves in an appreciation for the perspectives of the stages-of-the-path tradition inaugurated by Atiśa, providing supporting quotations from various Kadam, Nyingma, and Kagyü masters, and insisting that this may be "even more profound than mahāmudrā, the great perfection, or Madhyamaka" (79). *Advice from the Wise* concludes with Dongak's prayer that we be able to realize the Madhyamaka view taught in the Perfection of Wisdom sūtras and explained by Nāgārjuna and Candrakīrti; cultivate the unfixed, nonconceptual, space-like mahāmudrā meditation taught in the tradition of Saraha, Maitrīpa, Marpa, Milarepa, and Gampopa; and attain awakening through the atiyoga path of the great luminosity of primordial pristine awareness (*rig pa*), which is the essence of the teachings of Padmasambhava and Vimalamitra (80–81).

14. The Twentieth Century and Beyond

THE CENTURIES THROUGH which we have traced the development of Geluk mahāmudrā literature often were politically tumultuous, and witnessed significant cultural and religious shifts as well. The period from 1500 to 1900 saw the rise of the Geluk order in Central Tibet and its spread to a position of influence and, eventually, one or another degree of political power throughout the whole plateau. The expansion of the Geluk came at the expense of the Kagyü, especially the Karma Kagyü, who were relegated to secondary roles on the political stage, though they continued to develop religiously and intellectually. The Sakya and Nyingma were similarly marginalized, though their diminished political influence did little to blunt their vitality, either. Indeed, all three major non-Geluk schools not only sustained their creativity in the shadow of Geluk sovereignty but continued to exercise strong cultural influence in various regions outside Central Tibet: the Sakya in their home territory of Tsang, the Kagyü through southern Tibet and Bhutan, and the Nyingma in Kham and Amdo, as well as in various border regions. In the nineteenth century, a number of major non-Geluk masters in Kham affiliated themselves loosely around a series of scholarly projects and efforts at cultural preservation that came to be known as the Rimé, or nonsectarian, movement, so at the turn of the twentieth century all the major Tibetan traditions were relatively healthy.

The developments just described occurred within the larger sphere of international politics, however, and it was that particular history that would prove most decisive for the fate of Tibetan religion and culture after 1900. From Mongol interventions in Tibetan affairs in the seventeenth and early eighteenth centuries (it was Mongols who brought the Fifth Dalai Lama to power and deposed the Sixth), to regular displays of power by the Chinese Qing dynasty in the eighteenth century (installing the Seventh Dalai Lama, posting proconsuls in Lhasa, fighting Nepalese Gurkhas on behalf of Tibet), to nineteenth-century commercial and diplomatic overtures from European powers such as Russia and Britain (culminating in a British incursion in 1904), Tibet seemed regularly to be embroiled in international intrigue. These regional and transregional political trends would come to a head in the middle of the twentieth century, when, uncontested by the world's great powers or the United Nations, the newly victorious Communist regime in China revived claims to Tibet dating at least as far back as the Qing period. Chinese forces invaded the country in 1950 and established full control in 1959, in the wake of an abortive revolt that began in Kham and spread to Lhasa. With the ensuing flight into exile in India by the Fourteenth Dalai Lama and, following him, nearly a hundred thousand other Tibetans, Tibetan culture—and nationhood—was bifurcated, with an influential minority of diaspora Tibetans doing their best to preserve their language, culture, and religion outside their homeland, mostly in India, but also elsewhere in South Asia and in the West, while the majority of Tibetans, still ensconced on the plateau, endured the vagaries of Chinese policies aimed at modernizing the region and integrating it with the "motherland." The most trying period within Tibet was that of the Cultural Revolution, which convulsed China between 1965 and 1976 and which hit Tibet especially hard: religious expression was almost completely quashed, and the material culture of Tibetan Buddhism—its monasteries, images, and texts—was decimated. Although the period since 1980 has seen occasional relaxation of restrictions on religious life, the vitality of Buddhism—especially of the great monasteries that were its lifeblood—has largely been sapped, and there is no indication that, so long as China remains in control, religion will regain its place at the center of Tibetan culture.

It is against this background of catastrophic change that our brief consideration of Geluk mahāmudrā in the period after 1900 is set. Although little changed on the surface in the first half of the twentieth century, after the Chinese occupation and the exile of a large number of Tibetans, the circumstances in which mahāmudrā practices might be pursued and mahāmudrā texts might be produced were in many cases straitened—and certainly were changed. The first figure we will consider here, Phabongkha Rinpoché, still operated more or less within the traditional dispensation, but the others—Geshé Rabten, Geshé Acharya Thubten Loden, Gelek Rinpoché, Geshé Kelsang Gyatso, and the Fourteenth Dalai Lama—were working within the exile community, and teaching in a very different cultural context than that of their predecessors, to the point where the mahāmudrā works for which they are celebrated, though often originally spoken or written in Tibetan, are most widely known through their English-language versions.[905]

905. The late twentieth-century lamas on which I focus here all have published books in English relating to mahāmudrā, but they represent only a small percentage of Gelukpa teachers who have given oral discourses on the great seal. Among other teachers known to have lectured

Phabongkha Rinpoché

Phabongkha Rinpoché Dechen Nyingpo (1878–1941)[906] is widely regarded as the most religiously influential Gelukpa lama of the early twentieth century. A native of northern Tsang, he was initially recognized as an incarnation of Changkya Rölpai Dorjé, who had spent most of his life at the Qing court in Beijing, but this identification was reconsidered in light of political tensions between China and Tibet, and the child eventually was declared to be the reincarnation of the abbot of the small, well-established hermitage atop Phabongkha, a massive rock formation near Sera Monastery just outside Lhasa. Phabongkha Rinpoché, as he commonly was known, entered Gyalrong House of Sera Mé College, and there earned his geshé degree—at the second level, *tsokling*, rather than the highest, *lharampa*. He spent two years studying at Gyütö Tantric College and then traveled to the mountains and caves of Lhokha, in southern Tibet, for nearly a decade of meditation on the stages of the path under the guidance of his main teacher, Dakpo Rinpoché Jampal Lhundrup (1845–1919), his devotion to whom was legendary. Early in the twentieth century, Phabongkha returned to Sera Mé, where he quickly gained a reputation for his sanctity, his learning, and his extraordinary eloquence as a teacher. His popularity as an expounder of Buddhist texts resulted in his becoming one of the first modern Tibetan lamas to give large, public discourses—sometimes to an audience of up to ten thousand monastics and laypeople. Phabongkha's reputation was so formidable that when the Fourteenth Dalai Lama was identified in 1937, he was asked to become one of the child's two tutors. Although he declined the honor, the task did eventually devolve upon three of his disciples: Takdrak Rinpoché (1874–1952), Ling Rinpoché (1903–83), and Trijang Rinpoché (1901–81).[907] Many of his other disciples, at Sera Mé and elsewhere, went on to become influential Gelukpa teachers in the second half of the twentieth century.

Through his discourses, his disciples, and his voluminous writings—which are collected in ten volumes, and focused heavily on tantric topics—

on the topic just in the United States are Lama Thubten Yeshe (California, 1981; a teaching of his given in Australia has been published in Yeshe 2019), Ven. Lobsang Namgyal (Vermont, 1987), Geshé Lobsang Tharchin (New Jersey, 1990), Lochö Rinpoche (Minnesota, 2004), Yangsi Rinpoche (Oregon, 2006, 2007), and Jangtsé Chöjé Rinpoché (Wisconsin, 2015). Undoubtedly, there are many others.

906. For biographical information, see, e.g., Tsongkhapa 1988, 4–13, Phabongkha 1991, 10–15, Sharpa 2018, and Kilty 2019, 119–98.

907. On Ling Rinpoché, see especially Dalai Lama 2017; on Trijang Rinpoché, see especially Sharpa 2018.

Phabongkha deeply influenced the course of modern Geluk thought and practice. He placed strong emphasis on study of the stages of the path, on which he lectured regularly.[908] More distinctively, he promoted two deities whose role had previously been relatively minor among the Geluk: Vajrayoginī and Dorjé Shukden. The Vajrayoginī practice had been brought into the Geluk from the Sakya tradition, where it is one of the "thirteen golden Dharmas." A few earlier Geluk masters had written on her as a stand-alone deity rather than in her role as Cakrasaṃvara's consort, but Phabongkha gave her status as a solitary Geluk deity equal or even superior to Yamāntaka, suggesting that she was actually Tsongkhapa's innermost, secret yidam. The great popularity of Vajrayoginī practice among contemporary Gelukpas is directly attributable to Phabongkha's dissemination of her practice.[909] Dorjé Shukden, also known as Dölgyal, was a Gelukpa wrathful protector deity as far back as the time of the Fifth Dalai Lama and was invoked over the centuries for various purposes, including, most controversially, protection of the Geluk against the magic employed by other Tibetan Buddhist traditions, particularly the Nyingma. Despite opposition from the abbot of Drepung and the Thirteenth Dalai Lama, Phabongkha actively promoted Dorjé Shukden during his lifetime and initiated his disciples into the practice. So influential were he and his disciples on twentieth-century Geluk thought and practice that by the 1970s Shukden practice was nearly universal among Gelukpa monks, and observed by many laypeople as well. The Fourteenth Dalai Lama, however, rejected the practice, on the grounds that it was contrary to the ecumenical spirit he wished to foster among the Tibetan Buddhist schools, and also because he regarded Shukden as a mundane deity given to punishing those who stand in his way. Most Gelukpas followed the Dalai Lama's lead in rejecting Shukden—though not without hesitation on the part of many, resistance on the part of a few, and one terrible episode of bloodletting: the murder of the head of the Dialectics School in Dharamsala, Losang Gyatso (1928–97).[910]

Phabongkha's promotion of the propitiation of Dorjé Shukden must be understood against the background of his outspoken Geluk exclusivism, which was marked by relatively frequent and pointed critiques of other Tibetan traditions, especially Bön and Nyingma. His exclusivism may be seen

908. See, e.g., Tsongkhapa 1988, Phabongkha 1990–2001, Phabongkha 1991,and Tsongkhapa 1995.

909. See Dreyfus 1998, 246, English 2002, xxv, and Phabongkha 2011, ix–x; for translations of relevant texts, see Phabongkha 2011 and K. Gyatso 1991, 267–425, 437–93.

910. Among the many discussions of this controversy, see especially Dreyfus 1998 and Kilty 2019.

as based in part on a fear that if Gelukpas—as they sometimes did—accepted empowerments and undertook practices rooted in other traditions, the purity of Tsongkhapa's teachings would be lost. His exclusivism also may have been a reaction to the rise of the Nyingma-Kagyü-Sakya nonsectarian movement in eastern Tibet in the nineteenth century. Jamgön Kongtrul and his colleagues may have considered themselves nonsectarian, but they were not necessarily perceived as such by politically minded Gelukpas, who saw the movement as an attempt to form an anti-Geluk resistance in Kham and Amdo. Phabongkha's rancor toward non-Geluk traditions was not limited to written polemics. In the late 1930s, he served for a time as the overseer of Geluk monasteries in Kham, which were in a weakened state in the wake of the success of the Rimé movement. Although Phabongkha was remembered by Khampas for his personal saintliness and his concern for their problems, he was also recalled for having overseen the destruction of statues of Padmasambhava, the burning of ancient texts, and the forcible conversion of several Nyingma monasteries to the Geluk.[911] Even three-quarters of a century after his death in 1941, Phabongkha remains a polarizing figure, revered by most Gelukpas but an embarrassment to some, and still regarded by members of non-Geluk traditions as the face of Geluk evangelical intolerance.[912]

The controversies surrounding him notwithstanding, Phabongkha also was heir to the Ganden Hearing Transmission in general and the mahāmudrā lineage in particular. Although he may well have received mahāmudrā teachings from Dakpo Rinpoché, his two main teachers in the tradition appear to have been Khedrup Tenzin Tsöndrü (b. nineteenth century) and Palden Tenpai Nyima (nineteenth–twentieth century). We know little about either master, but they are said to be, respectively, the termini of the Ü-Tsang and Amdo branches of the lineage that had separated shortly after the time of Paṇchen Chögyen. Phabongkha himself is credited with reuniting the two branches and is said, too, to have added verses to the *Mahāmudrā Lineage Prayer* celebrating the lineage holders between Yeshé Gyaltsen and his own two mahāmudrā teachers. He also is the author of the *Six-Session Guru Yoga* text that is recited daily by nearly all Gelukpa practitioners and of an important commentary to the *Hundred Deities of Tuṣita*. He further is credited with establishing the form of the merit field in *Offering to the Guru* that is most widely recognized in the Geluk world today, with its detailed visualization of Lama Losang Thupwang

911. See, e.g., Beyer 1978, 239, and Kay 2004, 43.

912. As an example, in the early 2000s, when a Geluk-sponsored collection of relics of Buddhist masters was considered for display at a Kagyü monastery, it was rejected on the grounds that it included some relics of Phabongkha. (Personal communication, Amanda Russell, May 2017.)

Dorjé Chang, three major sets of guru lineages in the sky above him, and eleven rows of deities on the tree below him.[913] Although he was instrumental in uniting and transmitting the Geluk mahāmudrā tradition, Phabongkha seems not to have written much about it; he does, however, discuss it in passing in various texts. For instance, he specifies that the *Offering to the Guru* merit field will be visualized somewhat differently depending on whether one is reciting the ritual in the context of mahāmudrā meditation or not,[914] and he describes elsewhere the techniques offered by Paṇchen Chögyen for practicing serenity meditation with the mind as a formless object of focus,[915] while criticizing enthusiasts for mahāmudrā and the great perfection who neglect to develop the awakening mind, thinking that mere single-pointed concentration on the clear and aware conventional nature of mind is genuine insight into mind's ultimate nature.[916] He also shows the influences of the mahāmudrā poetic tradition in his spiritual songs, where he sings, for instance, of the joy induced by a proper understanding of emptiness by "merely hearing the deep instruction / that points out directly the primordial face of mind," and

> . . . encountering . . .
> the teachings of the Oral Lineage of Losang Drakpa
> that deliver buddhahood right into the palm of one's hand
> even quicker than quickly. . . .[917]

Elsewhere, he refers to the "uncontrived, self-arising, and primordial" nature of mind, which is "inherently pure,"[918] and prays for help in

> seeing the true face of the nature of mind . . .
> entering into the unconditioned Dharma realm . . .
> [and] dwelling in the state of luminous clarity.[919]

913. For a detailed key to this particular field of assembly, see Phabongkha 1990–2001, 1:235–43. For description and analysis of its general structure, see, e.g., Phabongkha 1991, 187–96, and R. Jackson 1992.

914. Tsongkhapa 1988, 146. It is clear from Trijang Rinpoché's discussion of him in his autobiography that when Phabongkha taught mahāmudrā, it often was in the context of *Offering to the Guru.*

915. Phabongkha 1991, 656–57 and 667.

916. Phabongkha 1991, 675–76.

917. Sujata 2015, 204 (translation adapted).

918. Sujata 2015, 206.

919. Sujata 2015, 207 (translation adapted).

Phabongkha passed on the mahāmudrā teachings to many of his disciples, including the two most prominent, Trijang Rinpoché (1901–81) and Ling Rinpoché (1903–83), who in turn transmitted them to their many students, including five lamas whose approaches to the tradition have found their way into English-language publications.

Geshé Rabten

Geshé Tamdrin Rabten (1920–86)[920] was born to a farming family in eastern Tibet. He longed for monastic life from an early age and left home at eighteen for Lhasa, where he entered Sera Jé Monastery. With only the occasional visit home, he would remain there for the next two decades. He took as his main teacher Geshé Jampa Khedrup, studying as well with other luminaries at Sera and the other great monasteries, including Trijang Rinpoché, as he moved steadily through the curriculum leading to the geshé degree. He was poor, and his inclinations ascetic, so he sometimes was referred to as Milarepa. Eventually, though, his scholastic prowess won him a position as tutor to a young tulku, Gonsar Rinpoché, after which his material conditions improved. When the Chinese crushed the Lhasa uprising of March 1959, he—along with Gonsar Rinpoché and a number of other monks—escaped to India, where in 1963 he completed his education, attaining the highest rank, that of lharampa geshé. He attracted a large number of young Tibetan disciples, whom he would continue to teach over the next two decades. In 1964, he was chosen as a philosophical-debate partner for the Fourteenth Dalai Lama, who had established his exile headquarters in Dharamsala in the Indian Himalayas. In 1969, as Westerners interested in Buddhism began finding their way to Dharamsala, Geshé Rabten was asked by the Dalai Lama to teach them the basics of the Dharma. In 1975, the Dalai Lama sent him to Switzerland, where he founded an educational and monastic center, Tharpa Choeling, which served the dual purpose of ministering to a Tibetan refugee community and training Westerners (most of them ordained at the time) to translate and interpret Buddhist teachings for the wider world. Geshé Rabten died in 1986.

Amid a life of travel and change, Geshé Rabten produced a number of works in Tibetan, including a set of annotations to Tsongkhapa's *Essence of Excellent Explanation*, and a song on the Madhyamaka view along with his own commentary on that song. In addition, a number of his writings, oral teachings, and interviews have been edited by his Western students and pub-

920. For biographical information, see Wallace 1980, 3–120.

lished in English. Of these, the two most notable for our purposes are *Echoes of Voidness* and *Song of the Profound View*.[921]

As the title indicates, *Echoes of Voidness* is a work on emptiness, consisting of a commentary on the *Heart Sūtra*, a translation, with brief annotations, of portions of the sixth (wisdom) chapter of Candrakīrti's *Entry to the Middle Way*, and a summary of Geluk mahāmudrā practice. The teaching on mahāmudrā, which was first given in Dharamsala in 1979,[922] covers much of the same ground as a typical pre-twentieth-century Geluk mahāmudrā commentary—although in its edited form, it discusses neither the mahāmudrā lineage nor any tantric forms of the practice. It begins (Rabten 1983, 97–100) with a brief section on the meaning of the term *mahāmudrā*, which is followed by a substantial discussion of the five extraordinary practices (prostration, Vajrasattva meditation and recitation, refuge, the Meru-maṇḍala offering, and guru yoga) that are necessary preliminaries to mahāmudrā practice (100–112)[923] and a detailed description of the serenity and insight meditations that form the core of mahāmudrā (113–37). The section on serenity—called "mental quiescence" (113–28)—includes analyses of the proper ordering of serenity and insight, the nature and value of objectless meditation, the crucial role of mindfulness (or "recollection") as a factor for maintaining focus, the obstacles to proper concentration, the importance of untensing once a certain focus has been achieved, six common images for a calm and relaxed mind, and the nature of serenity—and how it should not be confused with insight. The section on insight—simply titled "Mahamudra" (128–37)—deals first, in classic Geluk style, with the importance of identifying the proper object of negation, the "I" that appears in experience. It then investigates, in sequence, whether the body or cognition exists intrinsically. Upon examination, neither is found, hence both are empty, yet the conventional "I" is not negated by this not-finding. Geshé Rabten concludes the text by discussing the two ways in which we may establish the emptiness of *any* object of negation—by seeing it as a mere conceptual designation or as a dependently arisen phenomenon—and detailing the ways in which we may experience events in everyday life as like illusions. Throughout the book, he resorts to analogies to make his point, bringing the at times recondite teaching on mahāmudrā within the purview of his audience.

Song of the Profound View consists of twelve verses of poetry on the Madhya-

921. Rabten 1983 and Rabten 1989, respectively.

922. He himself says he received the tradition from the Fourteenth Dalai Lama (Wallace 1980, 113).

923. The preliminaries typically are said to be four, but Geshé Rabten has here separated prostration and refuge (including generation of the awakening mind).

maka view written by Geshé Rabten during a retreat in Dharamsala and his own later commentary on those verses. Although the term *mahāmudrā* never is mentioned, the sorts of meditations undertaken by Geshé Rabten are very similar in style to those described in the Geluk mahāmudrā literature, and the first-person song style echoes that of earlier poets, from Paṇchen Chögyen, to Kalden Gyatso, to Changkya, to Choné Lama. The songs, combined with their commentary, give the reader a good feel for the nature of Geshé Rabten's retreat, which involved careful investigation of the real nature of the phenomena he encountered and freely admitted moments not only of insight, gratitude, and joy but also fear, sadness, doubt, and desire. In typical style, Geshé Rabten recounts his experiences, both mundane and spiritual, and reflects on various examples that drive home key doctrinal points, such as a hundred-rupee note held up to him by Trijang Rinpoché, a pillar in his hut that helped support the ceiling, and the invisible tracks of birds in the sky. Through Geshé Rabten's deft use of metaphor and first-person description, the poetry and commentary in *Song of the Profound View* provide at least a glimpse of what it must actually be like to undertake a retreat involving the mahāmudrā meditations described more schematically in *Echoes of Voidness* and elsewhere in the literature of the Ganden Hearing Transmission—very much as the spiritual songs of Paṇchen Chögyen and other masters add vitality to the precise but prosaic treatises in which mahāmudrā is laid out systematically.

Geshé Acharya Thubten Loden

Geshé Acharya Thubten Loden (1924–2011)[924] was, like Geshé Rabten, a native of Kham. Inclined to the religious life from an early age, he entered his local monastery, Drombu Thupten Dargyé Ling, at age seven, focusing primarily on study of the stages of the path and mastering basic rituals and sādhanas. At fourteen, he moved to the larger Sershul Monastery, also in Kham, where he followed a more philosophically oriented curriculum. Three years later, a series of visionary experiences and prophetic dreams made it clear that he was destined to go to Lhasa, and so he did, entering Sera Jé College in 1941. For the next eighteen years, he worked his way through the geshé program, studying with some of the great masters of the Geluk tradition, including his root guru, Geshé Jampa Chöphel, and the Dalai Lama's junior tutor, Trijang Rinpoché. He fled Tibet in 1959 and settled eventually in Dharamsala, where

924. Biographical information is taken from the "Geshe Acharya Thubten Loden in Tibet," "Geshe Acharya Thubten Loden in India," and "Geshe Acharya Thubten Loden in Australia" pages at www.tibetanbuddhistsociety.org, accessed June 2015.

he was made part of a special class of young scholars charged with continuing the tradition of study and debate in exile, while beginning to learn about the outside world. At the Dalai Lama's instigation, he attended Sanskrit University in Varanasi from 1968 to 1970, learning Sanskrit and Hindi, meeting Westerners for the first time, and receiving an *acharya* degree. He completed his geshé studies in in the early 1970s, attaining the high rank of *lharampa*, and went on to study for several years at Gyümé Tantric College. In 1976, he was asked by Lama Thubten Yeshe (1935–84), head of the westward-looking Foundation for the Preservation of Mahayana Tradition, to take up residence at a center in Melbourne, Australia. Geshé Loden taught there for three years, leaving a strong impression on many students in various parts of the country. He returned for a time to India in 1979 but was persuaded before long to return to Australia, which would be his home until his death in 2011. In some thirty years there, he founded the Tibetan Buddhist Society and the numerous centers affiliated with it throughout Australia, gave countless teachings and empowerments, and published a number of books for the guidance of his disciples, covering everything from the stages of the path, to buddha nature, to the six Dharmas of Nāropa and other advanced tantric teachings.

The last-published of these books is *Great Treasury of Mahamudra*,[925] a compendious overview that spans the Geluk cosmos, from the life of Śākyamuni Buddha to the highest reaches of the completion stage of unexcelled yoga tantra, drawing liberally from a wide range of Indian Buddhist literature, both sūtra and mantra, and from Tibetan masters of both the Geluk and Kagyü traditions. The first part of the book (Loden 2009, 19–73) is devoted to stories of the Buddha and his successors in the Indian tradition, as handed down through Tibetan historical literature. Part 2 (75–151) introduces some key Buddhist categories: the three turnings of the Dharma wheel, the three vehicles, and the four buddha bodies; the last of these sets is given particularly detailed treatment. The third part of the book (153–62) is a brief account of the four preliminary practices: taking refuge and generating the awakening mind, the Meru maṇḍala offering, Vajrasattva recitation and meditation, and guru yoga. Part 4 (163–257) focuses on sūtra mahāmudrā. It omits a discussion of serenity meditation, focusing exclusively on the approach to insight taken by Tsongkhapa, with its strong reliance on the works and perspectives of the Perfection of Wisdom sūtras and the treatises of Nāgārjuna and Candrakīrti. Geshé Loden does, however, dedicate separate chapters to poetic expressions of mahāmudrā by Maitrīpa and Milarepa. These passages are quoted in Tsong-

925. Loden 2009. Access to the book is restricted to those who have received an empowerment into an unexcelled-yoga-tantra system.

khapa's six Dharmas of Nāropa commentary, the *Book of Three Inspirations*. However they might be interpreted by others, Geshé Loden reads them in light of the axiomatic Geluk assumption that the Indian and early Kagyüpa masters of mahāmudrā were Prāsaṅgika Mādhyamikas, completely in line with Nāgārjuna and Candrakīrti as interpreted by Tsongkhapa. The fifth and final part of the book, "The Mahayana of the Vajrayana System" (259–403), moves systematically through the stages of unexcelled-yoga-tantra practice, often using Yamāntaka as the representative yidam. The generation stage is discussed only briefly. Most attention is focused on the completion stage, which is analyzed in great detail and from a variety of perspectives, including those of the Guhyasamāja literature and the six Dharmas of Nāropa. Whatever one's approach, the final fruit is the state of Vajradhara.

Geshe Loden's book provides a deeply learned overview of the Buddhist path from start to finish. While the discussion is framed in terms of mahāmudrā, Geshe Loden actually ignores many of the elements we have come to expect in Geluk mahāmudrā texts: he does not discuss the Ganden Hearing Transmission at all, he says little about the nature of mind, he passes over serenity meditation in silence, and he avoids any and all controversy associated with mahāmudrā, whether over the shifting line between serenity and insight, the sort of negation that is involved in meditation on emptiness on the tantric level, or anything else. It is probably safe to conclude that Geshe Loden—in this context, at least—thinks of mahāmudrā as being synonymous with meditation on emptiness, pure and simple. In that sense, his book is about mahāmudrā in the broadest possible sense, not about mahāmudrā as a specific term and system within the broad compass of Buddhist approaches to the path.

Gelek Rinpoché

Ngawang Gelek Demo (1939–2017)[926] was born in Lhasa to a noble family—the Thirteenth Dalai Lama, had he lived longer, would have been his uncle. He was recognized at the age of four as a tulku by Phabongkha Rinpoche and entered Drepung Loseling, where he studied with Ling Rinpoché, Trijang Rinpoché, and Song Rinpoché (1905–84). At twenty, not long before the Lhasa uprising, he became one of the youngest monks ever to attain the advanced degree of geshé *lharampa*. He fled Tibet in 1959 and soon thereafter gave up monastic life. He attended the Young Lamas' Home School in Delhi with the likes of Chögyam Trungpa Rinpoche, Chökyi Nyima Rinpoché,

926. Biographical information is based on "Gelek Rimpoche" (Jewel Heart), "Gelek Rimpoche" (Wikipedia), "Gelek Rinpoche" (FPMT), and my own personal recollections.

and Thubten Zopa Rinpoche and became proficient in English. He lived in Delhi for over two decades, working primarily as a publisher of Tibetan texts, many of which had been spirited out of Tibet and were in danger of being lost. He also began teaching in English at centers of Lama Thubten Yeshe's Foundation for the Preservation of Mahayana Tradition (FPMT) in Delhi and Dharamsala, where students immediately were attracted to his knowledge, humor, and ability to communicate with them in their own language and idioms. In the early 1980s he moved to Ann Arbor, Michigan, where he soon established Jewel Heart, a Buddhist center that eventually had branches in other American cities, including New York, and in Europe and Asia. In New York, he became a teacher of the musician and composer Philip Glass, who in turn introduced him in the late 1980s to poet Allen Ginsberg. Ginsberg, who had worked previously with the recently deceased Chögyam Trungpa Rinpoche, studied with Gelek Rinpoché for ten years, and when Ginsberg died in 1997, Gelek Rinpoche was present to ease the transition.

Over the years, Gelek Rinpoché led many courses and retreats on a variety of Geluk texts and practices, many of which have been published in lightly edited form. He was perhaps best known for his lucid expositions of Geluk ritual and meditative practices, such as the sādhanas of Yamantaka, Tārā, and Vajrayoginī, the *Hundred Deities of Tuṣita*, and the six-session guru-yoga prayer. He also published two general-interest books: *Good Life, Good Death* and *The Tara Box*. He died in 2017.

Gelek Rinpoché was well versed in the Ganden Hearing Transmission in general and mahāmudrā in particular, offering courses on the latter a number of times over the years. His most detailed published teaching on the great seal is found in a transcript called *Gom: A Course in Meditation*, whose final main chapter, simply entitled "Mahamudra," takes up over sixty pages. The chapter is a relatively detailed commentary on the first twenty-seven verses of *Highway of the Conquerors*, those running from the beginning of the text through the instructions on serenity meditation, covering what Gelek Rinpoché calls "relative Mahamudra."[927] The chapter is replete with information and observations drawn from the Ganden Hearing Transmission, as well as anecdotes from Gelek Rinpoché's own life. It is especially notable for its focus on the qualities of experience a meditator ought to expect when practicing Geluk mahāmudrā. In his discussion of the Sanskrit homage to the great seal, Gelek Rinpoché emphasizes that one possible meaning of the term *mahāmudrā* is "commitment," in the sense of commitment to the guru—not just the human guru

927. Gelek 2005, 219. Rinpoché also draws at times on Paṇchen Chögyen's autocommentary, *Lamp So Bright*, and on Dalai Lama and Berzin 1997.

who imparts instructions to us but the absolute guru, which is our primordial mind.[928] In commenting on the poetic preamble (verses 1–2), he focuses on the core connotation of *mahāmudrā* as emptiness, the all-pervasive nature of all phenomena, which obviates neither conventional realities nor compassion, and may be said to be the "creator of all" in the sense that it is the condition for the possibility of all conventionalities.[929] Turning to the preliminary practices (verses 3–5), Gelek Rinpoché stresses that these are not to be taken lightly but given serious attention.[930] Gelek Rinpoché's discussion of the distinction between sūtra and mantra mahāmudrā (verses 6–10, covered on pages 234–41) is quite concise but does reiterate Paṇchen Chögyen's point that the former is synonymous with the emptiness taught in the Perfection of Wisdom sūtras and the latter focuses primarily on revealing the primordial nature of mind; although the latter is the more powerful technique, it is the former, of course, that the Paṇchen Chögyen's text describes in most detail. Rinpoché goes on to endorse briefly but unambiguously the First Paṇchen Lama's views on the unity of intention among the major Tibetan traditions (verses 11–12).[931]

In considering the actual practice of mahāmudrā, Gelek Rinpoché first focuses on the preliminaries (verses 14–15), placing special emphasis on the crucial role played by guru yoga. He discusses the different liturgical contexts in which mahāmudrā may be practiced—principally *Offering to the Guru*, the *Hundred Deities of Tuṣita*, the *Six-Session Guru Yoga*, or a special Mañjuśrī visualization[932]—and extols the state to be attained after the visualized guru, to whom one has been making fervent appeals, dissolves into one's heart cakra. He calls this state, which in Tibetan is pronounced *nangwa ben bun* (*snang ba ban bun*), "the NBB state": a natural state in which the mind rests joyously in its own nature.[933] The NBB state, which is akin to the feeling of falling in love, is the baseline for the serenity meditation to follow. Gelek Rinpoché goes on to specify six basic instructions for achieving serenity:

928. Gelek 2005, 220–21.

929. Gelek 2005, 224–27.

930. Gelek 2005, 229–34. To illustrate the point, he relates a story told to him by Ling Rinpoché (231–33) of a high-level tantric teaching session offered in Lhasa by Phabongkha Rinpoché. It was scheduled to begin at noon but for various reasons did not begin until nine at night. Everyone assumed that Phabongkha would hurry through the preliminaries so as to get to the "meat" of the teaching, but he went through them with great care, only turning to the main topic after midnight, and then spending very little time on it.

931. Gelek 2005, 241–43.

932. Gelek 2005, 247–48 and 254.

933. Gelek 2005, 246–47 and 252–54; cf. 103–4.

1. "Actually leave the mind as it is and meditate" by applying mindfulness and "meta-alertness" (what I am calling "alertness," *shes bzhin*) to its natural NBB state (verses 16–17d).[934]
2. "Focus on the clear and lucid nature of mind and meditate," making sure to keep the mind from wandering or dullness, or from growing too tight or too loose (verse 17ef).[935]
3. "Whatever thoughts come up, recognize them and meditate," either by simply recognizing them or by cutting them off, like a swordsman fends off arrows, or suppressing them, like an elephant tromping on someone's head (verse 18).[936]
4. "Loosen . . . the tightness of mindfulness" by relaxing the mind's grip on its own nature as clear and aware—without, however, losing alertness, let alone relaxing moral discipline (verses 19–20).[937]
5. "Merge the steady and moving" by learning to discern moments when the clear, aware mind is moving—as when new thoughts arise—from those when it is still and stable, and resting in the vacuity that is the nature of both (verse 21).[938]
6. "Recognize the movement of your mind" by letting thoughts go; at this stage, they will naturally subside into their own ground, as a crow released by a ship to find land will return to the ship when it finds none (verses 22–23).[939]

Gelek Rinpoché concludes his discussion by articulating nine qualities of the state of serenity that results from following the six steps (verses 24–26a). Such a mind is: (1) void, (2) clear, (3) lucid or knowing, (4) capable of developing all the qualities of awakening, (5) continuously present, (6) unchanging regardless of our karmic circumstances, (7) "pure like sunshine," (8) beyond all faults, which are only temporary and inessential, and (9) "pure like pure water."[940] He goes on to discuss the differences among the various experiences of emptiness entailed by serenity meditation on the nature of mind and the

934. Gelek 2005, 252–59.

935. Gelek 2005, 260–61.

936. Gelek 2005, 261–64.

937. Gelek 2005, 264–66.

938. Gelek 2005, 266–71.

939. Gelek 2005, 271–73.

940. Gelek 2005, 271–76.

ways in which they can be misinterpreted as true realizations of emptiness,[941] and he ends by underscoring Paṇchen Chögyen's contention (verses 26b–27) that the meditation just detailed familiarizes us only with the conventional nature of mind, as clear and aware.[942] The ultimate nature of mind, which is simply emptiness, is covered by *Highway of the Conquerors* (verses 28–45), but Gelek Rinpoché does not discuss it in this context.

Geshé Kelsang Gyatso

The highly controversial Kelsang Gyatso[943] was born in Tsang in 1931 and began his monastic training at Ngamring Jampa Ling, near Shigatsé, taking novice ordination at the age of eight. At some point, he moved to Lhasa and entered Sera Monastery, where he resided in Tsangpa House of Jé College, beginning study toward a geshé degree. Among his contemporaries at Sera Jé were Tamdrin Rabten and Lhundub Sopa (1923–2014), both his seniors, and Thubten Yeshe, his junior by four years. Like so many Lhasa-area monastics, he fled Tibet in 1959 and took refuge in India, where he spent time in study and retreat while also suffering bouts of ill health. His main teachers in India were Geshé Sopa and, especially after the latter's departure for America in 1962, the Dalai Lama's junior tutor, Trijang Rinpoché. He claims to have completed his geshé degree at some point after going into exile, though the claim has been disputed, and in any case the date and rank he attained are uncertain. In 1977, at the invitation of Lama Yeshe, now head of the burgeoning FPMT, he took up residence at Manjushri Institute, an FPMT center in Ulverston, Cumbria, England. At some point in the late 1970s or early 1980s, he split from the FPMT, maintaining control over Manjushri Institute, distancing himself from other Gelukpas, and developing his own program of study, which was institutionalized in 1991 under the name his organization still bears, the New Kadampa Tradition (NKT). NKT claims to preserve the teachings of Tsongkhapa in their undiluted purity and to have 1,100 centers worldwide, staffed by the large number of Western monks and nuns ordained by Kelsang Gyatso.[944] The reasons for his split from mainstream Geluk probably include both

941. Gelek 1005, 277–81.

942. Gelek 2005, 281–82.

943. Completely reliable information about Kelsang Gyatso is hard to find. For a somewhat disorganized and tendentious but nonetheless useful compilation of various perspectives and sources, see "Geshe Kelsang Gyatso." For a perspective from within Kelsang Gyatso's organization, see "Venerable Geshe Kelsang Gyatso."

944. For a scholarly study of the NKT, see Kay 2004, part II.

personality conflicts and philosophical differences, but the point of contention that has been most publicized is his public opposition to the Dalai Lama's ban—at least for students who wish to receive empowerment from him—on the practice of the protector deity Dorjé Shukden, which, as we have seen, was promoted by Phabongkha Rinpoché and was endorsed, as well, by Trijang Rinpoché until late in his life. Kelsang Gyatso's open defiance of the ban led to his expulsion from Sera Jé College in 1996 and to the spectacle of his followers picketing talks in the West by the Dalai Lama in the late 1990s and again in 2007–8. As of this writing, Kelsang Gyatso is mostly retired from public life, but his New Kadampa Tradition appears to be thriving.

Kelsang Gyatso has published over a score of books in English—some based on oral teachings, others produced collaboratively with Anglophone disciples—that outline various aspects of NKT thought and practice. These include commentaries on such Indian classics as the *Heart Sūtra*, *Entry to the Middle Way*, and *Engaging in Bodhisattva Conduct*, detailed instructions on the NKT's favored tantric deity, Vajrayoginī, general accounts of meditation practice or of the different levels of tantric practice, specialized writings on such topics as the structure and function of the mind, and several texts that touch on aspects of the Ganden Hearing Transmission—a lineage with which Kelsang Gyatso clearly feels a strong affinity.

Great Treasury of Merit[945] is his detailed commentary on Paṇchen Chögyen's *Offering to the Guru*, set within the context of the Ganden Hearing Transmission and keyed to the practice of such unexcelled-yoga-tantra deities as Heruka, Vajrayoginī, and Guhyasamāja. As do many of the texts we have reviewed, he links *Offering to the Guru* to mahāmudrā meditation, encouraging the practitioner to contemplate the great seal at the point where the field of assembly has dissolved into the guru and the guru has dissolved into one's heart cakra, leaving one with an experience of spontaneous great bliss, a mental state with which we meditate single-pointedly on emptiness. This bliss-emptiness meditation, says Kelsang Gyatso, "is Definitive Guru Yoga."[946] He goes on to describe the ways in which this mahāmudrā meditation can be applied to the completion-stage practices of various deities, and extols the purity of Tsongkhapa's tantric mahāmudrā teachings, which, he says, rescued the great seal from the disrepute that had come its way after self-styled mahāmudrā meditators indulged in consort practices without sufficient mastery of renunciation, awakening mind, right view, and the generation and completion stages—the requisites insisted upon by such early mahāmudrā masters as Saraha, Marpa,

945. K. Gyatso 1992b.

946. K. Gyatso 1992b, 272.

and Milarepa.[947] An appendix to *Great Treasury of Merit* includes a translation of the late-twentieth-century version of the *Mahāmudrā Lineage Prayer*, with one important change: the most recent masters in the lineage are not, as in the standard version, Phabongkha Rinpoché, Trijang Rinpoché, Ling Rinpoché, and the Fourteenth Dalai Lama, but Phabongkha Rinpoché, Trijang Rinpoché, and Kelsang Gyatso himself—the verse of supplication to whom is said to have been composed and transmitted, at the request of Kelsang Gyatso's students, by none other than Dorjé Shukden.[948]

Kelsang Gyatso has published two books on mahāmudrā in English, *Clear Light of Bliss* and *Mahamudra Tantra*.[949] The two texts cover much the same ground, though in a different order and with slightly different emphases. Their common denominator is an exposition of the serenity and insight meditations associated with sūtra mahāmudrā within the context of unexcelled-yoga-tantra practice, especially on the completion stage.[950]

Clear Light of Bliss, first published in 1982, was among the first English-language texts to detail completion-stage practices from the standpoint of the Geluk school. In his preface, Kelsang Gyatso specifies that his main sources for understanding Geluk mahāmudrā are the two basic texts by Paṇchen Chögyen as well as commentaries by Yeshé Gyaltsen and Keutsang. The introduction (K. Gyatso 1982, 3–16) discusses mahāmudrā in general, and its tantric aspect in particular, which is defined as "the union of connate great bliss and emptiness,"[951] and said to be divided into causal-time and fruitional-time mahāmudrā; the latter is buddhahood, while the former "is divided into two successive stages: the mahamudra that is the union of connate great bliss and emptiness and the mahamudra that is the union of two truths,"[952] the two truths in this case being the illusory body (conventional) and the direct experience of luminosity (ultimate). The introduction also outlines the Ganden

947. K. Gyatso 1992b, 274–75.

948. K. Gyatso 1992b, 340. This shift also is reflected in K. Gyatso 1992a, a revised edition of K. Gyatso 1982 (233); in the earlier version, Ling Rinpoché's place in the lineage is intact.

949. These are K. Gyatso 1982 (revised as K. Gyatso 1992) and K. Gyatso 2005, respectively.

950. Kelsang Gyatso also has published a book on mahāmudrā in Tibetan: *Meaningful to Behold: A Collection of Pith Instructions from the Hearing Transmission, including "An Excellent Explanation of the Mahāmudrā of the Geden Hearing Transmission" and Other [Texts]* (*Mthong ba don ldan zhes pa dge ldan snyan brgyud phyag rgya chen po'i legs par bshad pa sogs snyan brgyud kyi man ngag phyogs bsdus*). I have not had a chance to read the text, but some of the controversy surrounding its alleged claims to be the only pure repository of Geluk mahāmudrā may be gleaned from "The Last Upholder of the Gelug Mahamudra Tradition: Kelsang Gyatso."

951. K. Gyatso 1982, 9.

952. K. Gyatso 1982, 9–10.

Hearing Transmission and the preliminaries required for serious tantric practice. The first four chapters (17–129) present, respectively, a detailed discussion of the channels, vital winds, and drops that are the physical basis for completion-stage practice; instructions on the "inner fire" practice derived from the six Dharmas of Nāropa; an account of the central-channel experience of the four joys and semblance luminosity (as opposed to actual, or connate, luminosity); and guidance on the integration of the three buddha bodies with various aspects of waking, dreaming, and dying, via the "nine mixings," along with an explanation of the achievement of connate great bliss through an action seal—a sexual consort. The next three chapters (130–82) are closest in style to the sūtra-oriented Geluk mahāmudrā texts we have reviewed above. They deal, in order, with the nature of mind, serenity (here called "tranquil abiding"), and emptiness. These chapters summarize clearly the perspectives on these matters of Paṇchen Chögyen and others in the hearing transmission without adding anything particularly new. In the last three chapters (183–226), Kelsang Gyatso returns to the completion stage and outlines illusory-body practices, the experience of "objective" luminosity, the stage of union, and the "fruitional mahāmudrā" that is buddhahood itself.

Despite its title, *Mahamudra Tantra* actually focuses more or less equally on Perfection and Mantra Vehicle meditations. Part 1 of the book, entitled "What Is Tantra?" (K. Gyatso 2005, 1–74) focuses on Vajrayāna mahāmudrā practices. The first two chapters cover the basic view and intention required for tantric practice: the understanding of karma and the generation of the awakening mind, respectively. The next chapters cover, in order, the nature of tantra (defined as "an inner realization that functions to prevent ordinary appearances and conceptions and to accomplish the four complete purities"),[953] the general nature of generation-stage and completion-stage practices, and the basics of mahāmudrā, understood in its tantric sense as "a mind of fully qualified luminosity that experiences great bliss and realizes emptiness directly."[954]

Mixing sūtra and mantra perspectives, part 2 (77–114) discusses "How to Train in Mahamudra," beginning with the preliminary practices of going for refuge, generating the awakening mind, and then practicing guru yoga—

953. K. Gyatso 2005, 19. The four purities are the purity of place, body, enjoyments, and deeds.

954. K. Gyatso 2005, 55. Kelsang Gyatso goes on to note (72–74) that the particular tantra mahāmudrā meditation taught by Tsongkhapa, in which the focus of practice is the indestructible drop at the heart, rather than, e.g., the navel cakra, allows the swiftest and easiest access to awakening. The fact that Gelukpa adepts focusing on the indestructible drop, such as Dharmavajra and Ensapa, mastered the great seal with ease, whereas Milarepa, who focused on the navel cakra, underwent many hardships, suggests to Kelsang Gyatso the superiority of Tsongkhapa's technique.

which includes visualizing one's guru as Tsongkhapa at the center of a field of assembly,[955] performing the sevenfold worship rite, offering the Meru maṇḍala, requesting attainment of the stages of the path, and absorbing blessings. Kelsang Gyatso then turns to the "six stages of training in mahāmudrā": (1) identifying our own mind, (2) realizing our mind directly, (3) identifying our subtle mind, (4) realizing our subtle mind directly, (5) identifying our very subtle mind, and (6) realizing our very subtle mind directly.[956] Traversing each of the three pairs of stages requires that one seek the level of mind in question, find it, hold it, and remain in it—then realize it directly. In this sense, the practice covers the serenity portion of mahāmudrā meditation, with the first two stages involving sūtra-level focus on the mind as clear and aware, and the last four requiring—especially in the context of deep sleep—work within, first, the heart cakra within the subtle body, and then the indestructible drop within the heart cakra.

Part 3 of the book, "What Is Emptiness?" (117–73), moves through a by-now familiar sequence of reflections: on the importance of realizing emptiness; the crucial role played in that realization by identifying the object of negation, self-grasping; the way in which our body and mind are both unfindable and empty; the unfindability and emptiness of our "I"; the harmony between emptiness and dependent arising; mixing one's mind indissolubly with emptiness; and bringing realization of emptiness into everyday activities. In short, Kelsang Gyatso concludes, "Mahamudra Tantra is a single mind that has two parts: (1) experiencing great bliss, and (2) realizing emptiness directly. We can accomplish the first part through Buddha's tantric teachings . . . and we can accomplish the second part through Buddha's Sutra teachings. . . ."[957]

The Fourteenth Dalai Lama

The life story of the Fourteenth Dalai Lama (b. 1935) is too well known to repeat here in detail. Through his multiple autobiographies, two Hollywood films, numerous biographies by others, his own voluminous writings, and unrelenting media attention wherever he goes, people throughout the world have become familiar with the story of Tenzin Gyatso's discovery and identification in Amdo; his enthronement as Dalai Lama; his often-lonely life in Lhasa; his attempts to balance Buddhist study and dealing with an increasingly

955. Here, Tsongkhapa is seen as Lama Losang Thupwang Heruka, rather than Lama Losang Thupwang Dorjé Chang (Vajradhara).

956. I have not yet located a textual source for these six trainings.

957. K. Gyatso 2005, 173.

aggressive Communist China; his desperate flight to India in 1959; his work to preserve Tibetan cultural traditions in exile and unify the disparate elements of the Tibetan Buddhist community; his growing interest in Western ways of thinking, whether religious, political, or scientific; his travels to all corners of the planet to teach and learn, and to meet people; his authorship of dozens of works, in English and other languages, on Tibetan Buddhist philosophy and meditation as well on topics of general interest, such as science, comparative religion, ethics, or the pursuit of happiness; his frequent bestowal of the esoteric Kālacakra empowerment to large public gatherings; his consistent advocacy of nonviolence in general and a peaceful solution to the China-Tibet impasse in particular; his receipt of the Nobel Peace Prize in 1989 and a U.S. Congressional Medal of Honor in 2007; his eschewal, in 2011, of his political role in the Tibetan exile government; and his open questioning of the very future of the institution of Dalai Lama.

As this précis indicates, the Dalai Lama has filled a multitude of roles in his lifetime. Far from the least of these, of course, is that of Tibetan Buddhist teacher. He completed his geshé training just before the Lhasa uprising of 1959, when he was only twenty-four, and is well versed not just in the Indian and Tibetan texts favored by the Geluk school but in the writings of masters of other Tibetan traditions as well, especially the Nyingma. For many decades, he has offered multi-day lecture series to Tibetan communities in India and to audiences in the West. Usually—as is typical in Tibetan tradition—he bases his discourses on a particular Indian or Tibetan text, most often from the Sūtra Vehicle. Among his favorites are the *Heart Sūtra*, Nāgarjuna's *Verses on the Middle Way*, Śāntideva's *Engaging in Bodhisattva Conduct*, Kamalaśīla's *Stages of Meditation*, Atiśa's *Lamp on the Path to Awakening*, and a wide range of works by Tsongkhapa. He also has commented from time to time on texts steeped in the Mantra Vehicle, including the unexcelled-yoga-tantra systems favored by Gelukpas and the great perfection teachings of the Nyingmapas. As a well-trained Gelukpa monk, he is familiar as well with the various hearing transmissions that provide so much of the ritual and meditative lifeblood of Geluk practice. Of practices related to the Ganden Hearing Transmission, he has discoursed on Paṇchen Chögyen's *Offering to the Guru* as well as *Highway of the Conquerors* and *Lamp So Bright*, and at least some of these discourses have been translated and published in Western languages.[958]

In his commentary on *Offering to the Guru* delivered in Dharamsala in

958. The commentary on the first is found in Dalai Lama 1988, on the last two in Dalai Lama and Berzin 1997.

1986 and published as *The Union of Bliss and Emptiness*, the Dalai Lama situates *Offering to the Guru* within the broader compass of Geluk hearing transmissions, of which three are prominent: those in the Khedrup Transmission, which are related to meditations on emptiness; those in the Sé Transmission, of which the most notable is the *Hundred Deities of Tuṣita*; and those in the Ganden or Ensa Hearing Transmission, of which *Offering to the Guru* is by far the most important. Of these, the Dalai Lama notes, only *Offering to the Guru* requires a prior empowerment into unexcelled yoga tantra.[959] In his actual explanation of the text, the Dalai Lama explicitly links its procedures to mahāmudrā meditation only once, when in the context of describing the tantric gurus directly above the central figure in the field of assembly, he mentions the mahāmudrā lineage and notes that *Offering to the Guru* "is like an uncommon preliminary practice to Mahamudra meditation."[960] He does, however, explicate the meaning of the gnosis of bliss and emptiness on the basis of which the practitioners are supposed to (1) imagine themselves as a deity at the outset of the ritual so as to take refuge and (2) generate the field of assembly that is the focal point of the main part of the ritual,[961] noting that, in a profound sense, everything in existence is a manifestation of this gnosis, since all appearances ultimately arise at the very subtlest level of mind, which itself is of the nature of a spacious, blissful, nondual experience of emptiness.[962] This gnosis, as we know, is synonymous with tantric mahāmudrā. Otherwise, he recommends briefly that a mahāmudrā practitioner of *Offering to the Guru* should (a) focus on the last part of the text—implicitly, the point where the guru dissolves into one's heart cakra[963]—(b) recite the *Mahāmudrā Lineage Prayer* at the beginning of the section in which one praises and appeals to the guru,[964] and (c) at the point where the guru finally dissolves into one's heart cakra, hasten the process by reciting the final verses of the same lineage prayer:

> Your holy body and my body, Father,
> your holy speech and my speech, Father,

959. Dalai Lama 1988, 16.

960. Dalai Lama 1988, 80; he notes here, as well, that one may call this mahāmudrā lineage Geluk only or Geluk and Kagyü.

961. Dalai Lama 1988, 53–54 and 63–64.

962. Dalai Lama 1988, 63–64.

963. Dalai Lama 1988, 99–100.

964. Dalai Lama 1988, 122. This is prior to verse 43 of *Offering to the Guru*.

> your holy mind and my mind, Father—
> please bless me to know they're inseparably one.[965]

As noted, the Dalai Lama has discoursed multiple times on Paṇchen Chögyen's mahāmudrā texts, which were transmitted to him by his junior tutor, Trijang Rinpoche,[966] who had in turn received them from Phabongkha Rinpoché. At least two such discourses have been brought together in English in *The Gelug/Kagyü Tradition of Mahamudra*, which consists of a long introduction to Geluk mahāmudrā by Alexander Berzin, a prose translation of Paṇchen Chögyen's *Highway of the Conquerors*, and translations of the Dalai Lama's commentary on *Highway of the Conquerors*, delivered orally in 1978, and on *Lamp So Bright*, delivered orally in 1982. We will focus here on the Dalai Lama's two commentaries, treating them synoptically and thematically rather than sequentially.

What strikes the reader first about the two commentaries is how deeply learned they are: quite apart from his familiarity with Indian sources, the Dalai Lama clearly has read a great deal of the Geluk literature on mahāmudrā, and some texts by non-Gelukpa teachers as well. He makes reference to the writings and ideas of such Gelukpa masters as Tsongkhapa, Khedrup Jé, Gungru Gyaltsen Sangpo, Khedrup Norsang Gyatso, the Fifth Dalai Lama, the Third Paṇchen Lama, Jamyang Shepa, Yeshé Gyaltsen, Changkya Rölpai Dorjé, Gungthang Tenpai Drönmé, Gyalrong Tsultrim Nyima, and Akhu Sherab Gyatso, as well as such non-Geluk figures as Padmasambhava, Marpa, Milarepa, Gampopa, Phakmo Drupa, Jikten Sumgön, Sakya Paṇḍita, Longchenpa, Lingrepa, Götsangpa, and Barawa. A survey of the structures of his two commentaries shows that while the Dalai Lama is interested in everything that Paṇchen Chögyen has to say, and reports it faithfully, he is especially focused on material from the First Paṇchen's sections on mantra mahāmudrā, devoting a greater portion of his discussion to the topic than Paṇchen Chögyen himself does. He explicates in some detail, and with reference to both sūtra and mantra, the meaning of such basic sets as ground, path, and fruit and the four seals[967] and repeatedly investigates the claim that all appearances of saṃsāra and nirvāṇa are the play of primordial luminous mind—or the gnosis of bliss and emptiness—finding that it is in the experi-

965. Dalai Lama 1988, 175. For the place of this verse within the lineage prayer, see below, part 5, section 3.

966. On Trijang Rinpoché's relation to mahāmudrā, see Sharpa 2019, 79, 123, 140, 154, 172, 179, 230, 271, and 408n170.

967. Dalai Lama and Berzin 1997, 173 and 216, respectively.

ence of the subtlest level of cognition, accessible only through tantric practice, that this assertion may truly be understood.[968]

Another striking feature of the Dalai Lama's commentaries is his evident delight in trying to resolve various disputes that have arisen in the discussion of mahāmudrā, whether among Gelukpas or between different traditions. For instance, he wades into an intra-Geluk debate on whether the tradition ought to be regarded as strictly Geluk or a Geluk-Kagyü synthesis, favoring the latter view, on the grounds that

- Geluk mantra mahāmudrā is based on Guhyasamāja traditions learned by Tsongkhapa from his Kagyüpa masters, while Geluk sūtra mahāmudrā is based on Tsongkhapa's unique perspective on emptiness.[969]
- The tradition as a whole "takes as its basis the oral guidelines of the great Kagyü masters of the past and supplements it with the profound techniques for gaining a decisive understanding of voidness that Tsongkhapa has uniquely presented in his great texts concerning the madhyamaka view."[970]
- The Fifth Dalai Lama's pointed rebuke of those Gelukpas who would mix with Kagyü provides indirect evidence that Paṇchen Chögyen may have been attempting just that in his mahāmudrā works.[971]

This debate turns, in part, on the meaning of the term *kagyü* (*bka' brgyud*) in the title of Paṇchen Chögyen's *Highway of the Conquerors*, a question we will consider in the next chapter. The foregoing dispute is related to another, and more basic, intra-Geluk disagreement, over the First Paṇchen's oft-cited assertion that all of the great Tibetan traditions of practice, when seen by a yogī who is learned, philosophically acute, and meditatively adept, have a single intention, or come down to the same idea. As we have seen, there was considerable debate among Gelukpas as to whether this assertion by Paṇchen Chögyen should be taken as provisional or definitive. Those whom we might term Gelukpa exclusivists, such as the Third Paṇchen Lama, admit that we cannot be certain what Paṇchen Chögyen meant but feel that, given the deficiencies of thought and practice evident in the positions and practices of other schools, he must have intended the statement provisionally. On the other hand, ecumenical

968. See, e.g., Dalai Lama and Berzin 1997, pp. 127, 195, 226, and 252.

969. Dalai Lama and Berzin 1997, 169.

970. Dalai Lama and Berzin 1997, 230.

971. Dalai Lama and Berzin 1997, 232–33.

Gelukpas, like Thuken Chökyi Nyima, insist that Paṇchen Chögyen must be taken at his word, and that his statement is, indeed, definitive. The Dalai Lama clearly sides with the ecumenical position, arguing that (1) the First Paṇchen was well known for speaking forthrightly when he felt another school's position was mistaken, and (2) it is highly unlikely that he would blunt his opinion on such a crucial point, "which if we understand properly we gain liberation and if we misunderstand we remain caught in the . . . cycle of rebirth."[972]

Motivated by this vision of the unity of Tibetan Buddhist traditions, the Dalai Lama addresses a number of intersectarian Tibetan disputes related to mahāmudrā. For instance, despite the obvious differences in terminology and philosophy among the Geluk, Kagyü, and the great-perfection traditions, he finds that, in the end, they amount to the same thing. Thus, while the Geluk mahāmudrā tradition focuses on the empty object realized by the luminous mind, the Kagyü mahāmudrā tradition focuses on the luminous mind itself, and the great-perfection tradition focuses on the foundational awareness at the base of all appearing phenomena, nevertheless, "when, through mahamudra meditation, we realize the unification of appearance and voidness in terms of our conviction in the subtlest primordial mind's lack of an inherently findable nature, we come, I believe, to the same essential point at which we arrive through dzogchen meditation."[973]

As we have seen, an important basis of the divide between Gelukpas on the one hand and many Kagyüpas and Nyingmapas on the other is the controversy over the intrinsic-emptiness view—*rangtong*—propounded by nearly all Gelukpas and the extrinsic-emptiness view—*shentong*—advocated by many in the other schools. This in turn is related to a controversy over just what sort of negation emptiness is, with Gelukpas insisting that all phenomena, from matter to buddha mind, are empty in the same way—intrinsically and nonaffirmatively, and the others claiming that buddha mind is empty in a different way than mundane phenomena: it is empty of everything mundane and extrinsic to it, and that very emptiness implies the presence of the mind's natural luminosity and a full complement of buddha qualities.[974] While upholding the standard Geluk view that all phenomena are empty in the same way—intrinsically and nonaffirmatively—the Dalai Lama strives mightily to find ways in which assertions about extrinsic emptiness and affirming negations may at least be provisionally accepted. He distinguishes, for instance, between an unacceptable, substantialist version of shentong and an acceptable version, in

972. Dalai Lama and Berzin 1997, 124.

973. Dalai Lama and Berzin 1997, 223, 226.

974. Dalai Lama and Berzin 1997, 126ff. and 234ff.

which the primordial luminous mind is "devoid of everything other, namely, it is devoid of all fabricating levels of mind and their mental fabrications. . . . The fact that the clear light mind is a level of mind that is devoid of all fleeting levels . . . affirms that clear light mind is something . . . other than this; the clear light mind, as an other-voidness, is an affirming negation."[975] The Dalai Lama also suggests that, at the deepest level of tantric meditation on the primordial mind, one may explicitly contemplate the luminous nature of mind as an affirming negation while recognizing implicitly that the ultimate nature of this mind is a nonaffirming negation, its emptiness of any intrinsic existence.[976]

Whether members of other schools—or even his own Geluk tradition—would find persuasive the Dalai Lama's grand attempt at an ultimate harmonization of all Tibetan Buddhist views and practices is beside the point; for him, it is the key not only to understanding Paṇchen Chögyen's mahāmudrā tradition but to uniting the disparate traditions of his homeland at the deepest possible level, thereby helping assure cohesion not just at the level of religion but of society more generally.

A Note on Recent Tibetan Editions

While the works of the lamas mentioned in this chapter have become well known to Western readers, it is important to recall that Geluk mahāmudrā remains, centrally, a Tibetan practice. Despite the dislocations entailed by the Tibetan diaspora and the depredations visited upon Tibet during the Chinese Cultural Revolution, most of the great religious literature of Tibet has survived the traumas of the late twentieth century and continues to circulate in Tibetan communities both inside and outside the plateau. The heroic efforts of a variety of Tibetan and Western publishers, including Gelek Rinpoché, Mongolian Lama Gurudeva, E. Gene Smith of the U.S. Library of Congress, and many others have assured that both blockprints and large-format bound volumes of photostatic reproductions of the texts could find their way to selected libraries in Asia and the West. Later, when cultural repression eased in Tibet, the Chinese increasingly began to publish Tibetan works, usually in standard book format. And, most recently, electronic archives like the Buddhist Digital Resource Center, the Tibetan Himalayan Library, and the Asian Classics Input Project have made the classics of Tibetan literature, including those on Geluk mahāmudrā, more broadly and easily available than ever before.

At the same time, several useful Tibetan-language anthologies of Geluk

975. Dalai Lama and Berzin 1997, 235.

976. Dalai Lama and Berzin 1997, 126 and 239.

mahāmudrā texts have been published in India and Tibet. Three of these bear brief mention. In 1999, the Mundgod, Karnataka–based Drepung Loseling Educational Society brought out the *Lamp Illuminating the Excellent Path of the Conqueror: A Collection of Special Instructions on the Profound-Path Mahāmudrā of the Hearing Transmission* (*LZGM* in my bibliographic system), which includes Paṇchen Chögyen's *Highway of the Conquerors* and *Mahāmudrā Lineage Prayer* (Bz*GBZL*), Yeshé Gyaltsen's *Source of All Attainments* (Yg*TKZM*), Gungthangpa's *Garland of Nectar Drops* (Gt*DTTP*), and Keutsang's *Excellent and Completely Virtuous Path to Freedom* (Kt*GBLZ*). Each anthologized text is preceded by a brief biography of the author.

In 2005, Geshé Thupten Jinpa's Library of Tibetan Classics issued from Delhi the *Dharma Cycle on the Stages of the Path and the Hearing Transmission of the Glorious Gedenpa* (*NGCS*). This compilation of Geluk stages-of-the-path and hearing-transmission texts includes such guru-yoga works as the Seventh Dalai Lama's *Guidebook on the "Hundred Deities of Tuṣita,"*[977] Paṇchen Chögyen's *Offering to the Guru*, and Tsultrim Nyima's *Letter of Final Testament Cast to the Winds: A Guidebook on "Offering to the Guru."*[978] Among the mahāmudrā texts included are Paṇchen Chögyen's *Highway of the Conquerors* and *Lamp So Bright*, Shar Kalden Gyatso's *Guidebook on Mahāmudrā* (Kg*PCKY*), and, again, Yeshé Gyaltsen's *Source of All Attainments* (Yg*TKZM*).

In 2010, the Lhasa-based Bod ljongs mi dmangs dpe skrun khang (Tibetan People's Publishing House) brought out the *Collection of Guidebooks for Thoroughly Identifying the General View of Mahāmudrā* (Pn*KYPS*), which includes Khöntön Paljor Lhundrup's *Wish-Fulfilling Gem of the Hearing Transmission Guidebook for Thoroughly Identifying the General View* (Ph*NGKY*),[979] Paṇchen Chögyen's *Highway of the Conquerors* and *Lamp So Bright*, Changkya Rölpai Dorjé's *Recognizing My Mother: A Song on the View* (Ck*TBSG*), and Achithu Nomenhan's *Commentary on "Recognizing My Mother."*[980] Biographies of the contributors are found at the beginning of the volume.

No doubt, with time, further compilations will appear, making Geluk mahāmudrā—a tradition that began in solitude, secrecy, and visionary experience—that much more a part of the Tibetan community's, and the world's, cultural mainstream.

977. *Dga' ldan lha rgya ma'i khrid yig.*

978. Despite the differing title, this is identical to Gr*LKPY*, discussed above, pages 302–4.

979. As already observed (note 678), this text is mistakenly attributed by the editors to *Nyaltön* Paljor Lhundrup, who lived a century and a half before *Khöntön* Paljor Lhundrup, the actual author.

980. A chi thu no man han, *Lta ba'i nyams mgur a ma ngos 'dzin gyi 'grel ba.*

Part 4
Perspectives on Geluk Mahāmudrā

15. Three Issues in Geluk Mahāmudrā

In this chapter, we will consider in depth three questions about Geluk mahāmudrā that have arisen in the course of our historical survey: (1) What is the proper name of the tradition? (2) What are the key similarities and differences between Geluk mahāmudrā and Kagyü mahāmudrā? and (3) What is the place of mahāmudrā in Geluk institutional life?

The Name of the Tradition

As noted in the preceding chapter, the Fourteenth Dalai Lama has argued strongly that the Geluk mahāmudrā tradition ought to be considered a Geluk-Kagyü synthesis. The key to determining whether he is correct in this claim lies in the interpretation of the titles of Paṇchen Chögyen's two texts on mahāmudrā—and these, it turns out, permit at least two competing answers. The full Tibetan title of the root verses he composed on mahāmudrā is *Dge ldan bka' brgyud rin po che'i phyag chen rtsa ba rgyal ba'i gzhung lam*, or *Highway of the Conquerors: The Root Text for the Mahāmudrā of the Precious Geden Kagyü*. The autocommentary to the root text is entitled *Dge ldan bka' brgyud rin po che'i bka' srol phyag rgya chen po'i rtsa ba rgyas par bshad pa yang gsal sgron me*, or *Lamp So Bright: An Extensive Explanation of the Root Text of the Mahāmudrā Teaching Tradition of the Precious Geden Kagyü*. The ambiguity comes from the fact that "Kagyü," apart from being the name of a Tibetan Buddhist school, can be translated as "oral transmission." Thus the Kagyü in the title may not refer to the Kagyü school at all but simply to a lineage of orally transmitted teachings. For instance, when Sangyé Yeshé refers to an Ensa Kagyü, he means an oral transmission practiced at Ensa Monastery in Tsang. Quite obviously, one reading suggests that Paṇchen Chögyen believed his tradition to be a combined Geluk-Kagyü lineage, while the other reading does not preclude an exclusively Geluk identity.

Three translations of the *Highway of the Conquerors* issued in the last forty years make it clear from their titles and their texts that their authors regard Geluk mahāmudrā as a combined tradition. The 1975 Library of Tibetan

Works and Archives translation is entitled *The Great Seal of Voidness: The Root-Text for the Ge-lug/Ka-gyu Tradition of Mahamudra*. The 1997 translation and discussion by the Fourteenth Dalai Lama and Alexander Berzin is entitled *The Gelug/Kagyü Tradition of Mahamudra*. The 2014 translation by David Gonsalez, in an appendix to his translation of Yeshé Gyaltsen's *Offering to the Guru* commentary, is entitled "The Root Text on the Precious Ganden-Kagyu Mahamudra Entitled 'The Main Path of the Conquerors.'" In each case, not only the title of the text, but the one passage in the root text that refers to the Geden Kagyü that was imparted well by the transmission masters—*legs par 'doms mdzad dge ldan bka' brgyud pa*[981]—is taken to refer to a combined tradition,[982] even though the line retains the same ambiguity as to the meaning of Geden Kagyü as does the text's title. We might expect that Paṇchen Chögyen's autocommentary would shed light on the issue; unfortunately, he merely remarks that "because it is not difficult to understand the meaning of these two verses, I will not write about them in detail."[983] On the other hand, an unpublished translation by Geshé Thupten Jinpa translates the full Tibetan title as "The Main Path of the Conquerors: Root Stanzas on the Mahamudra according to the Precious Lineage of the Sacred Words of Geden Masters."[984] By separating "Geden" from "Lineage" in his translation of the title, Jinpa makes clear his belief that Paṇchen Chögyen considered the Geden Kagyü a strictly Geluk lineage or transmission.[985]

Paṇchen Chögyen's direct disciple, the Fifth Dalai Lama, did not comment on his teacher's mahāmudrā texts but is, as we have seen, reported to have insisted that the phrase "Geden Kagyü" referred *not* to a Geluk-Kagyü synthesis but to a Geluk oral transmission.[986] When we arrive at the significant commentarial literature on Paṇchen Chögyen's mahāmudrā system, we have traversed nearly a century since the First Paṇchen's time and so must be wary of any claims in the literature to expose Paṇchen Chögyen's "true purport." Be that as it may, we find virtually no indication that Gelukpas of later centuries considered the mahāmudrā tradition to be a combined one. In his *Bright Lamp of the Excellent Path*, Yeshé Gyaltsen refers not to a Geden-

981. Bz*GBZL* 1b [82] (verse 2).

982. First Paṇchen 1975, 3, Dalai Lama and Berzin 1997, 97, and Kachen Yeshe Gyaltsen 2014, 435.

983. Bz*YSGM* 2b [95].

984. Jinpa n.d., 1.

985. Jinpa also has communicated this view in conversation, e.g., on December 14, 2013.

986. Dalai Lama and Berzin 1997, 107 and 232.

Kagyü mahāmudrā tradition but to a Ganden mahāmudrā teaching (*dga' ldan phyag rgya chen po'i khrid*).[987] Gugé Losang Tenzin also refers to it as Ganden mahāmudrā (*dga' ldan phyag rgya chen po*) and gives an elaborate gloss on the term *kagyü* to the effect that the tradition was developed by Paṇchen Chögyen "according to the *word* of Tsongkhapa" (*rje bla ma'i bka' bzhin du*) and was an instruction in the "hearing *transmission*" (*snyan brgyud*).[988] Similarly, Ngulchu Dharmabhadra glosses the line from Paṇchen Chögyen's root text thusly: "The heart or essence [of the sūtras and tantras] having all been well collected, it was made into the instruction, the uncommon orally descended transmission of Mount Geden" (*de rnams kyi snying po'am bcud mtha' dag legs par bsdus te 'doms par mdzad pa ri bo dge ldan bka' babs kyi brgyud pa thun mong min pa*).[989] Finally, Keutsang Losang Jamyang specifies that the Geden Kagyü, i.e., the Geden Oral Transmission (*bka' brgyud*) descending from Tsongkhapa, is the general subject of Paṇchen Chögyen's text, while the particular subject is the instruction on mahāmudrā, the uncommon oral tradition of Dharmavajra, father and sons.[990] Thus later commentators are virtually unanimous in regarding the Geluk mahāmudrā tradition as a Ganden Oral Transmission rather than a combined Ganden-Kagyü practice.

The Fourteenth Dalai Lama concedes this point[991] and does not speculate as to why this might have been, simply observing that the Great Fifth's view may have affected that of later commentators.[992] Indeed, as we know, the Fifth Dalai Lama did observe that ". . . it would be good if the dGe lugs pas kept themselves to themselves. What is the good of pushing in among the bKa' brgyud pa!"[993] This is not an explicit comment on the purport of Paṇchen Chögyen's text, but it certainly is suggestive of guru-disciple differences over attitudes and policy toward the Kagyü, and perhaps, by extension, over the place of Kagyü practices such as mahāmudrā in the Geluk tradition.

The commentaries we have just examined do not specifically debate whether there exists a combined Geluk-Kagyü mahāmudrā tradition; they announce their negative decision indirectly, through their glosses on Paṇchen Chögyen's root text. Evidence that such a debate must have occurred, however, may be

987. Yg*LZGM* 1a [201].

988. Gg*NGBM* 9a [17].

989. Db*KPKS* 4a [9].

990. Kt*GBLZ* 6b [18].

991. Dalai Lama and Berzin 1997, 107.

992. Dalai Lama and Berzin 1997, 232.

993. Karmay 1988, 146.

gleaned from Thuken Losang Chökyi Nyima's *Crystal Mirror of Tenet Systems*. As we saw above, in his chapter on the Kagyü, Thuken discusses a number of controversial issues regarding mahāmudrā in general and the relation between Geluk and Kagyü in particular. Most importantly for our purposes here, he asks the question: Do the Kagyü and Geluk have the same purport? He cites a critique of Khedrup Norsang Gyatso by a renegade student of Jamyang Shepa named Losang Rinchen (sixteenth–seventeenth century). Norsang had insisted in his *Bright Lamp of Mahāmudrā* that the mahāmudrā systems of the early Kagyüpas—including the white panacea (*dkar po gcig thub*) of Gampopa and Shang Rinpoché—were fully Mahāyāna practices and also in conformity with the tradition of Saraha.[994] Losang Rinchen takes Norsang's real point to be a demonstration that mahāmudrā has the same purport as the teachings of Tsongkhapa, and Losang Rinchen ridicules this idea, citing familiar Sakya critiques of the white panacea. Thuken is in turn highly critical of Losang Rinchen, insisting that he has misrepresented Norsang's position (and, for that matter, the title of his text), which is not at all an attempt to argue that the Geluk and Kagyü have the same intention. He adds, however, that there exists not the slightest disagreement between the early mahāmudrā practices described by Norsang and Tsongkhapa's teaching—thereby implicitly endorsing the idea that Geluk and Kagyü do have the same intention.[995]

Thuken further criticizes Losang Rinchen for his attack on Paṇchen Chögyen's view that the various traditions of mahāmudrā, as well as the Madhyamaka and the Nyingma great perfection, all come down to the same idea.[996] Losang Rinchen was not alone among Gelukpas in his rejection of this ecumenical stance: the Fifth Dalai Lama, Paṇchen Chögyen's disciple, was sympathetic to the great perfection but, as we know, was critical of Paṇchen Chögyen's interest in Kagyüpas and their doctrines, while the Third Paṇchen Lama Losang Palden Yeshé, who is a member of the Geluk mahāmudrā lineage, argued that the great perfection was inferior to the other traditions listed,[997] whereas Losang Rinchen believed it superior. Thuken further strengthens his ecumenical credentials by equivocating on the attribution to Tsongkhapa of the controversial question-and-answer text, *Queries from a Pure Heart*, which

994. See Nz*PCSG* 10–12, and below in part 5, section 7.

995. Tk*SGML* 109–11; trans. Thuken 2009, 152, and below in part 5, section 9.

996. Tk*SGML* 111–12; trans. Thuken 2009, 153–54, and below in part 5, section 9.

997. Dalai Lama 1984, 205.

may, as we have seen, be read as criticizing Kagyü mahāmudrā theories and practices.[998]

It should be noted that while these passages from Thuken demonstrate that there was a great deal of intra-Geluk discussion about the school's relationship to other traditions, and while we probably can conclude that Thuken himself believed that the Geluk and Kagyü have the same purport, they do not provide any evidence that Paṇchen Chögyen's mahāmudrā system actually was a combined Geluk-Kagyü tradition—at best, they provide evidence that at least some Gelukpa thinkers saw no contradiction between early Kagyü mahāmudrā traditions and the teachings of Tsongkhapa. This is a far cry, however, from maintaining that the Ganden Hearing Transmission is actually a deliberately syncretic tradition.

Still, if there is little positive evidence that Paṇchen Chögyen regarded his mahāmudrā system as a combination of Geluk and Kagyü, the question cannot be considered closed. As we have seen, the present Dalai Lama has insisted that the tradition should be regarded as a Geluk-Kagyü synthesis, because (a) while the view of reality presented in the tradition is uniquely that of Tsongkhapa, the tradition of Guhyasamāja interpretation that underlies the tantric portion of the system was received by Tsongkhapa via the Kagyü,[999] (b) Paṇchen Chögyen's account of mahāmudrā, while clearly indebted to Tsongkhapa, also owes a great deal to earlier Kagyü traditions of explanation,[1000] and (c) the Fifth Dalai Lama's critique of mixing with Kagyüpas is an indication that that is exactly what his guru, Paṇchen Chögyen, must have been attempting.[1001] The possibility thus is left open that Paṇchen Chögyen did intend to describe his system as a joint one. One other small piece of evidence—albeit circumstantial and grammatical—may be adduced at this point: the title of Paṇchen Chögyen's autocommentary already refers to a "mahāmudrā oral tradition" (*phyag rgya chen po bka' srol*); thus, if the *kagyü* of Geden Kagyü meant "oral transmission," it would be largely redundant. Hence, it must refer to the school, the Kagyü.

Probably, we will never know exactly what Paṇchen Chögyen meant by the expression *geden kagyü*, but another perspective on the relationship between Geluk and Kagyü in his system—indeed, the most important of all—is

998. Tk*SGML* 112; trans. Thuken 2009, 154, and below in part 5, section 9.

999. Dalai Lama and Berzin 1997, 169–70.

1000. Dalai Lama and Berzin 1997, 233 and 234.

1001. Dalai Lama and Berzin 1997, 232–33.

provided by at least a brief examination of the contents of his texts vis-à-vis the Kagyü, which follows.

Geluk and Kagyü Mahāmudrā Compared

We cannot, in this brief section, responsibly compare the entirety of Geluk mahāmudrā with the vast and varied body of Kagyü literature on the great seal.[1002] Nevertheless, we may be able to gain some sense of the relative mix of Geluk and Kagyü elements in the Ganden Hearing Transmission by focusing specifically on Paṇchen Chögyen's treatment of five topics in *Highway of the Conquerors* and, especially, *Lamp So Bright*: (1) the sources he quotes, (2) his position on the question whether there is a sūtra-level mahāmudrā, (3) his ordering of the stages of mahāmudrā meditation, (4) the procedures he outlines for serenity meditation, and (5) the procedures he outlines for insight meditation. The major Kagyü sources we will use for comparative purposes are from the generation immediately preceding Paṇchen Chögyen: Tashi Namgyal's *Moonbeams of Mahāmudrā*, Pema Karpo's *Notes on Mahāmudrā*, and the Ninth Karmapa Wangchuk Dorjé's *Mahāmudrā Eliminating the Darkness of Ignorance* and *Ocean of Definitive Meaning*.

(1) *Sources*. Even a cursory examination of Paṇchen Chögyen's *Lamp So Bright* reveals how conversant he was with Kagyü literature, and how influenced by that literature he must have been in formulating his mahāmudrā system. Of the slightly more than one hundred quotations or citations in the text, approximately half are from Indian sources and half from Tibetan sources. Of those from Indian sources, nearly a quarter are from texts or persons that figure prominently in the mahāmudrā lineage preserved in Tibet by the Kagyü, most notably Saraha, who is cited eleven times. More impressively, of the citations from Tibetan sources, nearly two-thirds are from the Kagyü: Milarepa is quoted nine times, Lama Shang four times, and Drigungpa Jikten Gönpo, Phakmo Drupa, Yangönpa, and Lingrepa twice each, just to name the most frequently cited. By comparison, among non-Kagyüpas, Sakya Paṇḍita is cited seven times, Atiśa five times, Tsongkhapa—surprisingly—only four times, and Phadampa Sangyé (who was Indian but whose works are only known in their Tibetan versions) thrice.

The vast majority of the Kagyüpas cited by Paṇchen Chögyen belong

1002. For the perspective of Paṇchen Sönam Drakpa on the similarities and differences between the two traditions, see above, pages 192–93. For nuanced analysis of the multiplicity of Kagyü perspectives on mahāmudrā, see, e.g., D. Jackson 1994, Mathes 2008, and Higgins and Draszczyk 2016.

to what he and other Gelukpas refer to as the "early Kagyü" (*gong ma bka' brgyud*), those seminal figures of the eleventh to thirteenth centuries who established the great Kagyü lineages and monasteries on the basis of teachings recently transmitted from India. In spite of the fact that Kagyüpas in the generation immediately preceding Paṇchen Chögyen had produced a tremendous amount of literature on mahāmudrā, he ignores them almost entirely, focusing his attention instead on the masters of centuries past. Why is this so? One possibility is that he was unaware of the efforts of his contemporaries. Certainly, he makes no specific acknowledgment of their work, yet he does make occasional oblique references to contemporaneous Kagyü practices,[1003] and as we will see, the structure of his text seems to have been influenced by the general style of mahāmudrā manuals produced in the immediately preceding generation. In fact, it is likely that Paṇchen Chögyen was aware of some, if not all, of the recent Kagyü literature on mahāmudrā, but did not cite it explicitly because (a) at least part of his purpose was to establish that there is a convergence of the stages-of-the-path tradition so important to the Geluk and the mahāmudrā tradition so central to the Kagyü, and it is in the ancient antecedents of the two modern schools—with Atiśa for the stages of the path and the early Kagyüpas for mahāmudrā—that such a convergence is to be found;[1004] and (b) there were both views and practices among contemporaneous Kagyüpas with which he probably disagreed, and emphasizing such disagreements would both involve him in scholastic disputes beyond the purview of a meditation manual and undercut his assertion of the commonality among mahāmudrā, the great perfection, and Madhyamaka.[1005]

Although we do not know whether Paṇchen Chögyen found his quotations from the early Kagyü masters in the original texts themselves or in some more recent compendium or anthology, the number and importance of those quotations would have to be counted as evidence for the idea that he was attempting to combine Geluk and Kagyü, much in the same way, perhaps, as Gampopa, the fountainhead of Dakpo Kagyü, combined the "two streams" of the Kadampa stages-of-the-path tradition and the mahāmudrā tradition he had received from Milarepa.[1006]

(2) *Sūtra Mahāmudrā.* Probably the most hotly debated issue in mahāmudrā exegesis in Tibet was whether there existed a sūtra-based

1003. For instance, Bz*YSGM* 16a–b [123–24] and 17a [125]; translation below in part 5, section 5.

1004. Bz*YSGM* 2b–5a [96–99].

1005. Bz*YSGM* 10b–12b [112–16].

1006. Bz*YSGM* 3b [98].

tradition of mahāmudrā practice in addition to the obviously tantric, or Mantra Vehicle, practices in connection with which the term generally had been used in India. As we have seen, the idea that there existed such a Sūtra Vehicle (or Perfection Vehicle) mahāmudrā tradition may have been suggested by members of Maitrīpa's circle, and in Tibet it seems to derive from the great systematizer of the early Kagyü, Gampopa, who, as we know, believed that the mahāmudrā connected with advanced tantric practice (the completion stage, or path of means) was suitable only for subitist practitioners while sūtra mahāmudrā, based on "pointing-out instructions" from one's guru, was suitable for even the most dull-witted gradual practitioner. The opinion further developed among Kagyüpas that this sūtra mahāmudrā was equivalent to Madhyamaka—whatever that meant—with some suggesting that it found its most perfect Indian expression in the great buddha-nature treatise, the *Sublime Continuum*.[1007] It is important to recall that for many Kagyüpas there is no essential difference between the fruits of sūtra and mantra mahāmudrā practice; it is only the methods that differ. The methods of sūtra mahāmudrā center on a direct realization of the mind's true nature; the methods of mantra mahāmudrā are based primarily on the six Dharmas of Nāropa. This distinction of methods, it should be added, is not always maintained faithfully: not only do Kagyüpas tend to frame their discussions of mahāmudrā more along the lines of the gradualist-subitist division than the sūtra-mantra division, but also there is no one-to-one correspondence between gradualism and sūtra on the one hand and subitism and mantra on the other. Furthermore—and quite importantly—mind-realization practices with no explicit link to the six Dharmas of Nāropa often are regarded as tantric. As we also have seen, these practices sometimes are assigned to a category of their own: essence mahāmudrā.

As we know, the idea that there could exist a mahāmudrā outside the tantric context, let alone that it could issue in the same result as advanced tantric practice, was severely criticized by Sakya Paṇḍita, who insisted in his *Clear Ascertainment of the Three Vows* that mahāmudrā (a) must be considered primarily as an *achievement*, the result of a path rather than a technique on the path, and (b) must be preceded by tantric empowerment, most specifically the four empowerments recognized in the unexcelled yoga tantras. As a consequence, he regarded Kagyü mahāmudrā systems of his own time—especially the white panacea promoted by Shang Rinpoché and the Single Intention of the Drigungpas—as the long-discredited Chinese Heshang

1007. See Roerich 1976, 724–25, Seyfort Ruegg 2010, 348–49, Broido 1985a, Broido 1987, Brunnhölzl 2004, and Brunnhölzl 2014.

quietism in disguise.[1008] Later Kagyüpas like Tashi Namgyal and Pema Karpo, of course, expended considerable ink in the attempt to defend their doctrine from Sapaṇ's attacks, pointing out the many ways in which they differed from the Heshang doctrine[1009] and providing evidence that *mahāmudrā* had a much broader meaning than that assigned to it by Sapaṇ.[1010]

It is quite evident from both the content and structure of his two texts on mahāmudrā that Paṇchen Chögyen essentially sides with the Kagyü on the question of the legitimacy of sūtra mahāmudrā. Not only does he criticize Sapaṇ for his partiality,[1011] but he cites approvingly both Jikten Gönpo and Gö Lotsāwa in their insistence that mahāmudrā is to be found at all levels of the path, from the most elementary to the most advanced.[1012] Paṇchen Chögyen states quite explicitly that there are two divisions of mahāmudrā practice, sūtra and mantra, and as we know, he divides the main portion of both *Highway of the Conquerors* and *Lamp So Bright* into a brief analysis of mantra mahāmudrā and a considerably longer discussion of sūtra mahāmudrā. Thus he is in general accord with the Kagyüpas, over against the Sakyapas, that there does exist both a sūtra mahāmudrā and a mantra mahāmudrā.

We will revisit the contents of Paṇchen Chögyen's version of sūtra mahāmudrā shortly, but it should be noted with regard to his version of mantra mahāmudrā that it differs from that of the Kagyü in at least two ways. First, it is demarcated from sūtra mahāmudrā more sharply than by the Kagyüpas, who as noted above, sometimes seem to combine the two systems and disassociate the concepts of gradual and sudden practice from specific relation to one or the other system. For Paṇchen Chögyen, on the other hand, (a) the gradual and sudden practice are closely aligned with sūtra and mantra levels of practice, respectively, (b) mantra-level meditations always are preceded by empowerment and entail practices within the subtle body like those involved in the six Dharmas of Nāropa, and (c) it is only through the completion stage of an unexcelled yoga tantra that buddhahood can be achieved. Thus, sūtra mahāmudrā can be neither conflated nor confused with the tantric level, for there is a clear difference in practice and a clear difference in the result. On this last point, at least, Paṇchen Chögyen is aligned with Sapaṇ, for though

1008. See Rhoton 2001; see also R. Jackson, 1982, D. Jackson 1990, D. Jackson 1994, and D. Jackson 2015, 489–511.

1009. Dakpo Tashi Namgyal 1986, 105ff., Broido 1987, and Higgins and Draszczyk 2016, 2:179–94.

1010. Dakpo Tashi Namgyal 1986, 124.

1011. Bz*YSGM* 30b [152].

1012. Bz*YSGM* 5a–b [101–2].

he rejects the latter's narrow interpretation of the term *mahāmudrā*, he does maintain that the mantra mahāmudrā system is separate from and superior to the sūtra approach.

Second, Paṇchen Chögyen and subsequent Gelukpas specify that tantric mahāmudrā is practiced through completion-stage yogas originating with such mother—or yoginī—tantra-rooted practices as the inner-heat meditation fundamental to the six Dharmas of Nāropa, or the generation of the gnosis of inseparable bliss-emptiness, which are well known to Kagyüpas. Nevertheless, Gelukpa masters differ subtly from Kagyüpas in their understanding of these practices: influenced by Tsongkhapa, Gelukpas interpret virtually every completion-stage practice—even those developed in mother tantras—through the five-stage yoga articulated in the tradition of Guhyasamāja (a father tantra), whereas Kagyüpas rely more on structures suggested by the mother tantras themselves. This—in addition to certain differences in the interpretation of Madhyamaka, to be noted below—will lead to variations in the interpretation of such crucial terms as *connate* (*lhan skyes*) and *union* (*gzung 'jug*)—and even *completion stage* itself—hence to subtle disagreements in reading such seminal texts as the *Dohā Treasury* of Saraha.[1013]

Regardless of these differences, however—and Paṇchen Chögyen alludes to neither of them—the central point of this analysis is that the First Paṇchen is more or less closely aligned with the Kagyü in his view of the scope and divisions of mahāmudrā.

(3) *Ordering of stages.* The arrangement of mahāmudrā meditation primarily in terms of the practices of serenity and insight probably goes back to the time of Gampopa and is common in the works of later figures like Rangjung Dorjé and the sixteenth-century scholars under examination here: Tashi Namgyal, Pema Karpo, and Wangchuk Dorjé. The later systematizers agree that there are two possible orderings of serenity and insight, and that the system in which insight comes first is the more advanced and the system in which serenity has precedence is the more elementary. All of them order their texts for the elementary practitioner, describing first serenity then insight. By and large, the practices that are included under serenity involve bringing the mind to single-pointedness through a progressive series of ever-more finely attenuated concentrations, starting with visual objects, and moving from there to other sensory objects, the breath, and—finally—the mind itself, which is gradually brought to perfect serenity. The practices that are included under insight are quite various but tend to involve analyses of the nature of that mind that has been brought to serenity, e.g., in terms of its movement or rest, its materiality

1013. Broido 1985a, 30–31.

or immateriality, its oneness or multiplicity, or its ultimacy or non-ultimacy—followed by a nondual realization of the mind as it truly is, a stage that is beyond meditation in the usual sense of the word.

Paṇchen Chögyen, too, divides his account of sūtra mahāmudrā into the practices of serenity and insight—though it should be noted in passing that he ignores other important Kagyü ways of ordering mahāmudrā, such as the triads of view, meditation, and conduct and of ground, path, and fruit.[1014] He also specifies that there are two traditions for ordering serenity and insight, and that (following Tsongkhapa) he will describe that in which serenity comes first.[1015] Unlike his Kagyü predecessors, however, he does not specify which type of practitioner practices in which order, for as we have seen, Paṇchen Chögyen takes the terms *gradual* and *sudden* to demarcate sūtra from mantra mahāmudrā, not those who practice serenity first from those who practice insight first. Generally, Paṇchen Chögyen's assignment of various practices as conducing to serenity or insight also is similar to that of his immediate predecessors in the Kagyü: serenity meditation begins with the mind as object and proceeds through various stages of calming until single-pointed fixation upon the mind's clear, aware nature is attained; phenomenologically, this is described as a pure vacuity (*gsal stong*). Insight begins with an analysis of the nature of the meditator and of the mind and proceeds to a nondual experience of the mind's empty nature, which also is described as a pure vacuity.

We will examine particular differences between Paṇchen Chögyen's and Kagyü accounts of serenity and insight in the following two subsections. Here let us simply note in general that Paṇchen Chögyen seems to have more rigid standards for what may be classified as "insight" than do some Kagyüpas, especially his contemporaries. First, the examination of the mind in stillness and movement, which is taken by most Kagyü systematizers to be part of insight,[1016] is included by Paṇchen Chögyen as an aspect of serenity.[1017] Further, one of the techniques apparently taken by many of Paṇchen Chögyen's Kagyüpa contemporaries to be an advanced stage of insight, namely, "settling gently, without grasping, on whatever appears," is regarded by Paṇchen Chögyen as merely "a marvelous method for a beginner / to accomplish mental stillness," a technique that "is a way of recognizing the phenomenal

1014. He does, however, refer to these in his spiritual songs; see, e.g., songs 15–17, translated below in part 5, section 10.

1015. Bz*YSGM* 12b–13a [116–17].

1016. See, e.g., Roberts 2014, 115–16, and Wangchuk Dorjé 1981, 69–93.

1017. Bz*YSGM* 15b–16a [122–23].

nature of mind," which is clear and aware.[1018] The technique at issue is not dissimilar to methods, listed without comment in the section on insight, that will be considered below. These and other subtle differences in assignment indicate that Paṇchen Chögyen upholds a typically strict Geluk standard for what counts as insight into the ultimate: if it does not lead to a realization of emptiness—rather than of some conventional aspect of an object—a practice cannot count as ultimate insight, though it may aid in achieving serenity or understanding conventionalities. This disagreement with his Kagyüpa contemporaries notwithstanding, we see that Paṇchen Chögyen's ordering and distribution of serenity and insight is generally quite similar to that of the Kagyü tradition of his own time.

(4) *Serenity.* When we examine the particular sequence of practices that Paṇchen Chögyen includes in his section on serenity, we find that much of his material is like that found in Kagyü texts. As we already know, the sequence he establishes is as follows: after seating oneself and purifying via the nine-round breathing, one should go for refuge and generate awakening mind, then engage in guru-yoga practice. At the point where, following repeated fervent requests, one's guru is visualized as dissolving into oneself, one actually begins serenity meditation. One first abides in a nonconceptual, uncontrived, contentless state that nevertheless is not unconsciousness; then, applying mindfulness and alertness against wandering thoughts, one gazes intently at the clear and aware conventional nature of mind. Thoughts are to be cut off either by noting them as mere thoughts or by suppressing them. When some meditative equipoise on the aware, clear nature of mind has been established, then one should relax one's effort a little: conceptualizations are permitted to arise, but when they do, one's continued, natural mindfulness and alertness assure that they will dissipate on their own, leaving a pure vacuity. The same vacuity is experienced when one observes the settled mind. The state in which there is no duality between active thought and mental stability is termed "the merger of stillness and movement." The mind that has achieved meditative equipoise on the aware, clear nature of mind is "a pure vacuity like space," without the slightest trace of material form, and anything that arises within it is similarly to be seen as beyond designations such as "existent" or "nonexistent," and as formless and space-like.

Most of the techniques organized thus by Paṇchen Chögyen are found in Kagyü mahāmudrā literature, too, and the Kagyüpas have in most cases derived them from Indian antecedents. The emphasis on suppressing thought

1018. *Highway of the Conquerors*, verses 26–27. Bz*GBZL* 3a–b [85–86]; translation below in part 5, section 4.

through the application of mindfulness and alertness is rooted in the Maitreya-Asaṅga tradition common to both Geluk and Kagyü, while the methods of alternately tightening and loosening the mind, of mixing awareness of stillness and movement, and of remaining space-like in clear awareness, can all be found in the writings of such mahāsiddhas as Saraha, Maitrīpa, Śavaripa, and others.[1019] Not only are the elements chosen by Paṇchen Chögyen securely grounded in Kagyü literature, but also his particular ordering of it is generally like that of Tashi Namgyal[1020] and quite similar to that of Pema Karpo, who also—once he begins his discussion of mind as the object of mahāmudrā meditation—describes a procedure that moves from the suppression of thought to its allowance, to an alternation of tightening and loosening and of stillness and movement, and culminates in a nondual, nonconceptual, space-like state.[1021] This does not prove that Paṇchen Chögyen derived his discussion of serenity from Pema Karpo or some other Kagyüpa predecessor; it does suggest, however, that whatever the specific sources Paṇchen Chögyen may have used, both the elements and ordering of his section on serenity do have strong precedents in Kagyü tradition—and these precedents are not likely coincidental.

Though there are considerably more similarities than differences between Paṇchen Chögyen's and at least some Kagyü accounts of mahāmudrā serenity meditation, it ought to be recollected that there are differences, too. First, as noted above, some of what is considered by certain Kagyüpas to be a part of insight meditation is regarded by Paṇchen Chögyen as falling more properly under the rubric of serenity. Second, his specification of awareness and clarity as the two characteristics of mind on which one single-pointedly focuses does not really convey the range of characteristics that one encounters in the Kagyü literature. Wangchuk Dorjé, for instance, like many Kagyüpas, pays considerable attention to three experiences (*nyams*) typically accompanying serenity meditation—bliss, clarity, and nonconceptuality[1022]—that either implicitly or explicitly point to how Kagyü masters understand the nature of mind. Paṇchen Chögyen, on the other hand, maintains a "bare" definition of mind as mere clarity and awareness. Third, the Paṇchen's insistence that the various experiences he classifies as serenity only relate to the conventional nature of the mind, not its ultimate reality, is somewhat at variance with

1019. See, especially, the various references in Dakpo Tashi Namgyal 1986 and Wangchuk Dorjé 2001.

1020. Dakpo Tashi Namgyal 1986, 146–74.

1021. Roberts 2014, 111–22.

1022. Wangchuk Dorjé 1981, 62.

the Kagyü tendency not to distinguish so strictly: where Paṇchen Chögyen is careful to treat references to (for instance) nonconceptuality or clarity as referring to the mind's conventional nature, many Kagyüpa writers take them as indicators of its ultimate nature,[1023] hence as in some sense related to insight.

(5) *Insight.* If Paṇchen Chögyen's discussion of serenity has more similarities than differences relative to Kagyü accounts of the same procedure, his section on insight is the reverse: it only superficially resembles Kagyü accounts and is, in the final analysis, the most unequivocally Geluk part of his instruction. He first outlines five Kagyü methods for "determining the root basis of mind": (1) seeking the mind within or without, or in arising, abiding, or ceasing, (2) seeking the mind in materiality, (3) settling in uncontrived awareness in the present, (4) observing the nature of whatever object arises, and (5) allowing images to arise and pass freely into "self-liberation."[1024] Neither criticizing nor endorsing these techniques, Paṇchen Chögyen goes on to spell out the "essential" method for gaining insight he has learned from his guru, Khedrup Sangyé Yeshé. In an actual meditation session, this involves, first of all, analyzing whether the meditator who has achieved serene meditative equipoise can actually be found in an ultimate sense. Seeking the meditator both within and apart from the various elements, one encounters it nowhere; seeking ultimacy in phenomena, one encounters it nowhere. Thus, one comes to abide in a space-like awareness of the empty nature of both the person and phenomena. Next (or alternatively), one examines more carefully whether the mind itself can be found in an ultimate sense: it is discovered to have the conventional nature of a flow of awareness and clarity but no ultimacy, no true existence. In short, one should recognize that any existent that arises, whether an object of the mind or the mind itself, is merely conceptual; it is empty, and—as Paṇchen Chögyen quotes Sangyé Yeshé as saying—"When . . . you settle in single-pointed meditative equipoise on that—*E ma*!"[1025] In the periods between meditation sessions, one should see all appearances as illusion-like—that is, as existing differently than they appear—but one must at the same time recognize that their ultimate emptiness does not preclude their conventional functioning, any more than their conventional functioning gives them true existence.

There is little in this general account that would not find acceptance by a Kagyüpa: certainly Kagyüpas will deny as readily as Gelukpas that an ultimately existent person can be found that is either identical to or different from that

1023. See, especially, Dakpo Tashi Namgyal 1986, chaps. 6 and 8.

1024. Bz*YSGM* 17b–19a [126–29].

1025. *Highway of the Conquerors*, verse 37. Bz*GBZL* 4a [87].

person's constituents, and they also will insist that, as surely as entities may be reduced to mind, mind too is ultimately empty. It is when we begin to examine Paṇchen Chögyen's emphases and his particular terminology—especially in his commentary—that the idiosyncratically Geluk nature of his account of insight begins to emerge. In terms of his emphases, we already have seen that he mentions, but does not specifically endorse, a variety of Kagyü methods of "determining the root basis of mind," most of which center on taking the present ordinary mind as equivalent to the enlightened mind. These methods, while grounded in statements by either the mahāsiddhas or early Kagyü masters, may, if taken out of context, lead to mistaking the conventional for the ultimate: it is for this reason that later Gelukpas[1026] criticized the practices, and it may be for this reason that Paṇchen Chögyen does not pattern his system upon them. Indeed, the technique of "settling, without grasping, on whatever appears," whose relegation by Paṇchen Chögyen to the rubric of serenity we already have noted, bears a more than passing resemblance to the five techniques listed at the beginning of his section on insight. In passing over these techniques, Paṇchen Chögyen ignores an element of mahāmudrā considered crucial by many Kagyüpas. One modern writer goes so far as to say that what is unique about mahāmudrā is precisely its "extraordinary theory that an individual's 'ordinary mind' represents his original stream-consciousness, defined as being an unaltered natural state. . . . The ordinary mind is identified with a pure and valid perception regarded as natural enlightenment and usually called 'buddha nature.'"[1027]

What Paṇchen Chögyen does emphasize in his section on insight is the sort of analysis of the person and the mind that was central to the Geluk version of Madhyamaka, in which a great deal of attention is paid to identifying the object of negation, all entities are said to exist only nominally, no entity is truly existent, and emptiness and dependent arising not only do not negate each other but actually imply one other. The language Paṇchen Chögyen uses, though only moderately technical, is still quite specific to the Geluk. His analysis of an object's "modes" of appearence, apprehension, and existence; his discussion of nominal existence; his mention of a mental image of emptiness as a nonaffirming negation; his refutation of particular versions of Madhyamaka that either over- or under-specify the degree of sentient beings' delusion; and his strong insistence on the perfect complementarity of emptiness and dependent arising—all these are quite particularly Geluk and cannot really be

1026. For instance, Thuken; see Tk*SGML* 105; cf. trans. Thuken 2009, 145, and below in part 5, section 9.

1027. Dakpo Tashi Namgyal 1986, xxxviii–xxxix.

understood without some familiarity with Geluk thought. Indeed, they differ from the standard, non–hearing transmission Geluk treatment of emptiness meditation[1028] only in their focus on the mind as the main meditative object.

It is hardly surprising that it is in the area of insight—or correct view—that Paṇchen Chögyen's text emerges as least Kagyü and most Geluk, for—political differences aside—it is on the level of correct view, especially on the interpretation of Madhyamaka, that Tibetan schools tend to have the most serious disagreements. They may concur on the greatness of Nāgārjuna and assert with equal conviction that all entities are empty by nature, but what this means is a subject of almost limitless wrangling. Some of it is no doubt scholastic hairsplitting, but much of it is crucial. Such issues as (a) the relative priority of the second and third turnings of the Dharma wheel, (b) the place of rationality en route to the realization of emptiness, (c) the relation between the conventional and the ultimate levels of truth, (d) the type of negation involved in emptiness, and (e) whether all instances of emptiness are intrinsic emptinesses or whether some are extrinsic emptinesses all bear significant philosophical import—and of course they are philosophically important because they touch, finally, on the great issues of bondage and liberation. We cannot detail here all the ways in which the Geluk differed from the Kagyü—let alone from other schools—on these matters. We might note in passing, however, the following:

(a) On the question of the relative priority of the second and third turnings of the Dharma wheel, Gelukpas uniformly assert that the second turning of the wheel, in which the Buddha taught the Perfection of Wisdom sūtras (and which became the basis for Nāgārjuna's Madhyamaka) is definitive because it presents all entities' emptiness of intrinsic existence in a straightforward and uncompromising way, while the third turning, whose sūtras emphasize such doctrines as mind-only, the natural purity of mind, or buddha nature (and which became the basis for Maitreya-Asaṅga's Yogācāra), must, by and large, be interpreted, because a literal reading of their viewpoint might lead to eternalism. Many but not all Kagyüpas assert that because of its negative rhetoric, the second turning must be interpreted, lest one fall into nihilism, while the third turning is definitive because it distinguishes clearly what is real (e.g., the empty and luminous nature of mind) from what is not (mental designation and elaboration); others assert that the second and third turnings both are definitive and must be used in complementary ways.

(b) On the question of the place of rationality en route to the realization of emptiness, Gelukpas assert that a direct realization cannot occur unless

1028. See, e.g., Hopkins 1996.

one has first determined with great precision the object of negation for a meditation on emptiness, and then, once that object (the connate grasping at self) has been determined, investigated all the ways in which it might possibly exist, with the result that it is not found; when one undertakes such analysis on the basis of serenity, the not-finding of the object of negation (which heretofore was a mental image of emptiness) will become a direct realization of emptiness. Kagyüpas agree that rational analysis is a part of the contemplative path but tend to see it not as a *sine qua non* for a direct realization of emptiness but as a tool for sharpening the mind as it prepares for such a realization, with realization being seen not as the final outcome of a rational process but as a complete transcendence of it.

(c) On the question of the relation between the conventional and ultimate levels of truth, Gelukpas assert that the ultimate and conventional entail each other in a perfectly noncontradictory way, such that the ultimate—emptiness—serves as a demonstration of the conventional—dependent arising—and vice versa, with the conventional determined through the avenues of valid cognition, perception, and inference. Kagyüpas agree that the two truths are noncontradictory, in that emptiness does not prevent appearances nor the other way around, and accept that the avenues of valid cognition are useful for settling mundane disputes, but they are more inclined to see the ultimate as thoroughly transcending the conventional, which does not, in the end, have real status as a "truth."

(d) On the question of the type of negation involved in emptiness, Gelukpas uniformly assert that all phenomena, "from form to omniscience," are ultimately empty in the sense of being nonaffirming negations, which lack intrinsic existence, period, and do not imply through that negation any "positive" entities or characteristics at all. Most Kagyüpas accept that Madhyamaka reasoning applied to conventionalities produces a recognition of those conventionalities' emptiness as a nonaffirming negation, but when it comes to the awakened realm beyond conception and description, they maintain that the distinction between the two types of negation, which itself is a form of conventional discourse, does not apply. And if it does, we must consider the possibility that both buddha nature and buddha mind are best described as affirming negations, whose lack of defilements implies the presence of awakened qualities.

(e) On the question of whether all instances of emptiness are intrinsic emptinesses or whether some are extrinsic emptinesses, the Gelukpas, in line with their stance on negation, insist that all phenomena, including buddha nature and buddha mind, are empty in exactly the same way, in that they lack intrinsic existence, and they argue as well that the extrinsic-emptiness view both denigrates the conventional world and absolutizes the awakened state. Almost all Kagyüpas accept that conventionalities are intrinsically empty, but they apply different standards to buddha nature and buddha mind, asserting that they are empty of everything extrinsic to them—namely defilements and their traces—but possess the full array of awakened qualities, either explicitly or implicitly; they fault proponents of intrinsic emptiness for bringing the ultimate down to the level of the conventional rather than seeing it as utterly transcending the mundane.

Gelukpas and Kagyüpas criticized each other on all these questions, and others besides,[1029] and the differences between them, while pointedly not emphasized by Paṇchen Chögyen, nevertheless subtly or overtly determined the shape he and later Gelukpas gave to their accounts of insight meditation, hence of mahāmudrā.

The Place of Mahāmudrā in Geluk Life[1030]

In the summer of 2015, I asked Jangtsé Chöjé Rinpoché Losang Tenzin (who in 2017 become the 104th Ganden throneholder) about the place of mahāmudrā meditation in Geluk institutional life. In response, rather than detailing the way in which the great seal is transmitted or practiced, or relates to the Geluk educational or ritual traditions, he simply answered, somewhat gruffly, "How am I supposed to know what people are meditating on?" The answer was surprising, but illuminating in a number of ways. Broadly, it reminds us that unlike in, for instance, Zen Buddhist monasteries, in Tibetan monasteries, "meditation" is typically regarded as a private ritual practice, usually to be undertaken in the confines of one's own room, or perhaps pursued intensively for a time at a specifically designated retreat center. To the degree that monasticism is the dominant form of religious life for many of the most committed Tibetan Buddhists, and to the degree that Tibetan monastic life is essentially a communal form of existence dominated by collective activities such as participating in religious ceremonies, hearing discourses from a lama, eating meals, and debating in the courtyard, meditation may, to a surprising degree, be a

1029. Other issues include which of Nāgārjuna's writings ought to be given priority in Madhyamaka; how to read the phrases "*x* exists" and "*x* does not exist" in Madhyamaka discourse; whether Mādhyamikas actually hold a philosophical position; and the differences between Svātantrika and Prāsaṅgika Madhyamaka. See, e.g., Williams 1983, Broido 1985b, Brunnhölzl 2004, 553–97, Thakchoe 2007, *passim*, and Seyfort Ruegg 2010, 345–46.

1030. The observations in this section are based in part on conversations, over the course of a number of years, with several Geluk monks and former monks, most notably Ganden Tri Rinpoché Losang Tenzin, Geshé Thupten Jinpa, and Yangsi Rinpoché Gendun Tenzin.

marginal activity within the larger compass of the monastery. Granted, both in rhetoric and real life, there are differences in the place that different Tibetan orders accord to meditation. To mention only the two traditions most pertinent to this book, the Kagyü tend to place meditation at or near the center of their self-description, with mahāmudrā being the key to their meditative theory and practice, while the Geluk tend to present themselves (and be seen by others) as a tradition in which philosophical study and debate, especially of Madhyamaka, is the centerpiece. In this sense, using Geoffrey Samuel's terminology, we might regard the Kagyü as a more "shamanic" tradition and the Geluk as more "clerical."[1031] It is important to remember, however, that over the centuries the "charismatic" and "practice-oriented" Kagyüpas have maintained high intellectual standards and developed their own systems of study and debate and that, conversely, the "schematic" and "scholastic" Gelukpas have placed considerable value on contemplation rooted in both the sūtras and tantras. And, to reiterate an earlier point, the rhythms of life and the sorts of activities in a Kagyü monastery—or that of the Nyingma, Sakya, or Jonang—will differ only slightly from those in a Geluk institution.

Still, it would be misleading to suggest that mahāmudrā meditation has anywhere near the importance in Geluk settings as it does for the Kagyü. The great seal is an absolutely central topic of discourse for the Kagyü and the focus of much practice, both in and outside the monastery, whereas for the Geluk it is—compared to the study and debate of Indian philosophical classics or the performance of tantric rituals—relatively marginal.[1032] For Kagyüpas, mahāmudrā is synonymous with Madhyamaka and provides an important basis for view, meditation, and conduct. For Gelukpas, Prāsaṅgika Madhyamaka is the supreme view, and the Prāsaṅgika approach to reality articulated by Nāgārjuna, Candrakīrti, and Tsongkhapa is the key focus of study and

1031. Samuel 1993. Not all critics are comfortable with Samuel's use of the word "shamanic," which has fairly specific connotations in the field of religious studies. He defines it as "a category of practitioners found in differing degrees in almost all human societies [whose practices involve] the regulation and transformation of human life and human society through the use (or purported use) of alternate states of consciousness by means of which specialist practitioners are held to communicate with a mode of reality alternative to, and more fundamental than, the world of ordinary experience" (Samuel 1994, 8). By this definition, I think we can allow that the Kagyü, with their strong focus on the attainments, discourses, and deeds of charismatic masters, are somewhat more shamanic than the scholastic Geluk, while recognizing that (a) the Kagyü has had a strong clerical side for a millennium and (b) the life stories and teachings of members of the Geluk hearing transmissions provide ample testimony as to the shamanic side of that tradition.

1032. Indeed, non-Gelukpa Tibetan teachers—not to mention their Western followers—are sometimes surprised to learn that there is any sort of mahāmudrā practice in the Geluk tradition.

debate—not to mention meditation. Mahāmudrā may be one way Gelukpas can describe Madhyamaka, but it is far from the most common way, perhaps because it still is seen as part of an esoteric hearing transmission that—although better publicized than it was in the early years of the tradition—is still restricted in certain ways. Thus, when Jangtsé Chöjé Rinpoché couldn't say whether monks in Geluk monasteries were meditating on mahāmudrā, it wasn't just because an individual's personal practice is beyond the ken and control of his superiors but because in a Geluk setting one would typically expect personal practice to involve reflection on the stages of the path, contemplation of standard arguments for emptiness, or the performance of a tantric sādhana, not meditation on the great seal.

To assert this, however, is to overlook the pervasiveness of the Ganden and other Geluk hearing transmissions in the religious life of Tsongkhapa's tradition. There are at least three guru-yoga texts absolutely basic to Geluk ritual that are derived from one or another hearing transmission.

(1) The most important is *Offering to the Guru*.[1033] Although this pūjā was written down by Paṇchen Chögyen, it is said to have been part of the Ganden Hearing Transmission conveyed to Tsongkhapa by Mañjughoṣa. It is inarguably the most important single Geluk liturgy, recited regularly, and sometimes daily, in both large assemblies of monks and private rooms. As we know, from the time of Yeshé Gyaltsen, if not earlier, *Offering to the Guru* came to be closely tied to Paṇchen Chögyen's mahāmudrā texts, such that one could engage in great-seal meditation at certain points in the ritual, especially the moment toward the end when the visualized assembly field dissolves into one's guru as Lama Losang Thupwang Dorjé Chang, and the lama comes to the crown of one's head, dissolves into light, and dissolves into one's heart cakra. Following this one would move through the prescribed sequences of serenity meditation and insight meditation with the mind itself as the object of meditation.

(2) The Sé-transmission prayer *Hundred Deities of Tuṣita*[1034] is centered on the worship of Tsongkhapa and, to a lesser degree, his two main disciples, Gyaltsab Jé and Khedrup Jé. It is sūtra-based where *Offering to the Guru* is tantric and short where *Offering to the Guru* is long, but it is believed to be equally effective for the cultivation of guru devotion, and like *Offering to the Guru*, it has (at least in its ten-line version) a moment toward the end when the guru absorbs into one—and that absorption, too, may become the basis for engaging in mahāmudrā meditation. Perhaps because of its brevity, the *Hundred Deities of Tuṣita* is often the focus of retreats, in which guru yoga

1033. See, e.g., Dalai Lama 1988, and the discussion above in chapter 9.

1034. See, e.g., Chöden 2013, and the discussion above, pages 144–45.

and mahāmudrā meditation may at times be given equal emphasis. Its ten-line version also includes the famous prayer to Jé Rinpoché, the *Miktsema*, which is recited with particular fervor on Ganden Ngamchö, the festival (usually in December) that commemorates Tsongkhapa's final nirvāṇa.

(3) The *Six-Session Guru Yoga*[1035] was, like *Offering to the Guru*, supposedly a part of the Ganden Hearing Transmission that came down to Paṇchen Chögyen and was written down by him, though the version presently recited by Gelukpas seems to derive from Phabongkha Rinpoché. The practice, which like many Tibetan sādhanas is found in longer, medium-length, and extremely abbreviated versions, must be recited six times daily by anyone who has received an unexcelled-yoga-tantra empowerment from a Gelukpa master. At a Geluk monastery, this will be virtually everyone. Apart from worship and contemplation of the guru (in the form of either Vajradhara or a figure appropriate to a particular tantric tradition), it serves the purpose of reiterating the tantric vows and pledges associated with each of the five buddha families—those of Akṣobhya, Vairocana, Ratnasambhava, Amitābha, and Amoghasiddhi. Ideally, the *Six-Session Guru Yoga* is to be practiced three times in the morning and three times at night, though variations are permissible. Like other guru-yoga rituals, it includes a moment when the guru comes to the crown of one's head and dissolves into one. At that point, before one goes on to visualize oneself as Vajrasattva or some other tantric deity, mahāmudrā meditation may be practiced.

These, then, are three common, hearing-transmission–based ritual contexts in which Gelukpas might—and undoubtedly sometimes do—practice mahāmudrā meditation as described by Paṇchen Chögyen and his successors. While one rarely reads or hears of Gelukpa monks explicitly making mahāmudrā their central practice, or "going on a mahāmudrā retreat," it is quite clear that the tradition and its texts—which after all were promoted by the widely influential Phabongkha Rinpoché—still are actively taught and studied within Geluk monasteries. Furthermore, to the degree that any serenity or insight meditation that dwells on the conventional or relative nature of mind is mahāmudrā, and any simulation or realization of the state of luminosity in tantric practice is mahāmudrā, there may be more mahāmudrā among the Geluk than meets the eye. Thus, whether Gelukpa monks contemplate it in passing as part of their sādhana practice or other ritual routines or take the time to consider it specifically and carefully as a way to calm the mind and see reality, the great seal is an important part of Geluk life—not perhaps at the very core of that life, but subtly and powerfully permeating the ideas, attitudes, and actions of those who participate in it.

1035. See, e.g., Gelek 2006.

16. Archer Among the Yellow Hats: Geluk Uses of Saraha

As we know from Gö Lotsāwa's *Blue Annals* and other sources, when Atiśa taught in Tibet in the mid-eleventh century, he sought to promulgate the *People Dohās* of the Great Brahman, Saraha,[1036] but was discouraged from doing so by his disciple Dromtönpa, who feared that Saraha's radical critique of religious conventions and celebration of tantric bliss would be taken literally by Tibetans—who were, Drom believed, more in need of a dose of old-time religion than of paradoxical poems that might be taken as a license to antinomian behavior.[1037] As a result, Atiśa transmitted the *Dohās*—and other tantric traditions—only in secret. Saraha's songs rarely became prominent among the Kadampas, gaining their importance in Tibet instead through the efforts of such figures as Vajrapāṇi, Balpo Asu, Kor Nirūpa, Phadampa Sangyé, and, above all, Marpa and his successors in the Kagyü lineage, for whom, as we know, the *Dohās* became seminal texts in the transmission of ideas and practices related to mahāmudrā.

Three centuries after Atiśa, Tsongkhapa sought to revive the Kadam and, like his exemplary predecessor, possessed in his arsenal of traditions those surrounding Saraha's *Dohās*, which he probably had received from one of his numerous Kagyüpa teachers.[1038] And just as there had been ambivalence among the Kadampas about the proper place of Saraha in public religious discourse in Tibet, Tsongkhapa, too, seems to have been concerned to limit the dissemination of the *Dohās*' teachings, specifying in his *Lamp to Illuminate the Five Stages* that "the *Treasury of Dohās* and other works of the Great Brahman take as their essence the collections of teachings on the high paths

1036. For a discussion of Saraha within his Indian context, see R. Jackson 2004, 3–51, and above, pages 44–48.

1037. For references, see Schaeffer 2005a, 61–62.

1038. Precisely how Tsongkhapa received the transmission of the *Dohās* is unclear; it is not mentioned in his *Record of Teachings Received* (Ts*TKSY*) or in any biographical material I have examined.

of connate exalted wisdom in which all other elaborations have been cast aside."[1039] In other words, the title of his most famous text notwithstanding, Saraha's sayings are not for popular consumption, for they only can be understood in the context of advanced Mantra Vehicle practices, especially those of such unexcelled yoga tantras as the Guhyasamāja.

This statement would seem to bode as ill for Saraha's place among Gelukpas as Drom's censorship did for Kadampas, yet in fact the Great Brahman has ended up playing a more significant role for the Gelukpas than we might expect—not, certainly, as important as among the Kagyü, but a noteworthy one nevertheless. In what follows, I will—based on the writings of Tsongkhapa, Khedrup Norsang Gyatso, Paṇchen Chögyen, Khöntön Paljor Lhundrup, and Jamyang Shepa—present a preliminary sketch of a number of ways in which the most conservative of Tibetan orders has harnessed one of the most radical figures produced by Indian Buddhism, in the hope that it will illuminate how Gelukpas assimilate potentially antinomian texts and figures into their worldview, deal with influences from Kagyü traditions, and construct their ideas about the theory and practice of mahāmudrā.

Tsongkhapa and Saraha

As just mentioned Tsongkhapa insisted that Saraha's *Dohās* are to be understood and practiced within the context of the "high paths of connate exalted wisdom," that is, the tantras. Clearly Tsongkhapa wished to confine the interpretation of Saraha's songs to a circle of initiates and to keep the songs, as much as possible, from the eyes and ears of the public. Nevertheless Saraha *was* significant for Tsongkhapa, and did have a place—albeit solely tantric—within the new dispensation that was the Geluk. Indeed, Saraha appears in a number of texts both by and about Tsongkhapa.

I have not had the opportunity to survey all of Tsongkhapa's writings for references to or quotations from Saraha, but all the passages I have found—with one intriguing exception—support his characterization of Saraha as a teacher within tantric contexts. Tsongkhapa quotes Saraha three times in his text on tantric vows, *Fruit Cluster of Attainments* (*Dngos grub kyi snye ma*), in each case drawing from the mahāsiddha's commentary on the *Buddha Skull Tantra*.[1040] He also cites Saraha in the *Great Exposition of the Stages of Secret Mantra* (*Sngags rim chen mo*). Of the thirty-four mentions of Saraha in Tsongkhapa's tantric masterpiece, all occur in the section on unexcelled yoga tan-

1039. Ts*RNSG* 65; trans. Tsongkhapa 2013b, 122 (translation adapted).

1040. Tsongkhapa 2005a, pp. 38, 97, and 115–16.

tra, and all but a handful of these are in chapters 6–8, which focus primarily on rites related to the maṇḍala. In many cases, Saraha is simply listed as part of a lineage of instruction; in others, he is mentioned as endorsing a specific action, as when, for instance, he is said to have advocated the offering of flowers and incense in a certain maṇḍala ritual.[1041] In chapter 10, which deals with the second, third, and fourth empowerments, he is said to have explained that the third, or wisdom-gnosis, empowerment is conducive to the gnosis connate with great bliss.[1042] Although Tsongkhapa clearly was aware of Saraha's role in various unexcelled-yoga-tantra lineages, the only text by the Great Brahman that he mentions in the *Great Exposition* is the *Buddha Skull* commentary;[1043] nowhere does he cite or mention any of Saraha's *Dohās*.

Tsongkhapa does, however, quote the *Dohās* numerous times in his Guhyasamāja commentary, *A Lamp to Illuminate the Five Stages*. For instance, he cites Saraha's insistence that a practitioner cannot one-sidedly focus only on wisdom or compassion but must combine both in the pursuit of awakening, and he glosses Saraha's reference to compassion as implying "great bliss," which is the tantric transformation of compassion.[1044] Tsongkhapa goes on to encourage his readers not to be satisfied with shallow wisdom or ordinary bliss, citing to bolster his point Saraha's observation that people talk a great deal about great bliss but really don't know what it is.[1045] In discussing the ways in which different tantric systems instruct us to bring vital winds into the central channel, he quotes Saraha's celebration of a state where, through appropriately timed enjoyment of food, drink, and sex, one will reach a state where "the vital winds and the mind do not flow" and "the sun and the moon do not engage," preparing one for the final stages of tantric realization.[1046]

1041. Ts*NRCM* 229b. I am grateful to Tom Yarnall for providing me with an easily searchable electronic version of the text and highlighting for me passages that mention Saraha.

1042. Ts*NRCM* 263a. The source is not given, though it likely is from the *Buddha Skull Tantra* commentary.

1043. Ts*NRCM* 304a.

1044. Ts*RNSG* 28b [56]; trans. Tsongkhapa 2013b, 109. The verse, in Kilty's translation, is: "Dwelling in emptiness devoid of compassion, / such persons have not found the supreme path. / But those meditating on compassion alone / will not become free from abiding in this samsara. / Those who bring these two together / will not abide in samsara or nirvana." Cf. trans. Schaeffer 2005a, 137, and R. Jackson 2004, 61.

1045. Ts*RNSG* 30a [59]; trans. Tsongkhapa 2013b, 113. The verse, in Kilty's translation, is: "In house after house they talk about it, / but there is no complete knowledge / of the principles of great bliss." Cf. trans. Schaeffer 2005a, 149, and R. Jackson 2004, 97.

1046. Ts*RNSG* 35b [70]; trans. Tsongkhapa 2013b, 127. The verse, in Kilty's translation, is: "Eating, drinking, the joy of conjoining / again and again fill the cakras. / With this Dharma

Encouraging his readers to see all appearances as having the single nature of bliss and emptiness, he quotes Saraha's advice to transform everything in the three realms into "the color of the one great desire," a great bliss in which there is neither self nor other, neither saṃsāra nor nirvāṇa.[1047] Commenting on the relation between the vital winds and consciousness, Tsongkhapa twice quotes Saraha's observation that the mind is influenced by the vital winds: when mind controls them, it will succeed in its aims, but when moved by the vital winds, it will be uncontrolled.[1048] Finally, in his exposition of tantric activities, Tsongkhapa cites Saraha's warning not to confuse ordinary sexual bliss with the great bliss generated through proper sexual yoga; the latter will bring realization, while the former will result only in spiritual frustration.[1049]

Saraha turns up eight times in the lineage lists contained in Tsongkhapa's *Record of Teachings Received*. Seven of these lineages are clearly tantric, relating, for instance, to the Gö system of Cakrasaṃvara interpretation, Lūipa's system of explaining empowerments and root tantras, the *Vajra Peak Tantra*, and Kṛṣṇācārya's instructions on secret suchness related to the completion stage.[1050] The one exception is the very last lineage listed, that for the philosophical and devotional texts of Nāgārjuna, where Saraha is sixth in line, after Nāgārjuna, Buddhapālita, Bhāviveka, Candrakīrti, and Vidyākokila the

you will transcend the world. / Trample on the head of the world of ignorance and go. / Where the winds and the mind do not flow, / there the sun and moon do not engage. / Penetrate with the mind those places of unknowing. / Saraha, having taught all the core teachings, has gone." Cf. trans. Schaeffer 2005a, 141–42, and R. Jackson 2004, 66.

1047. Ts*RNSG* 62b [124]; trans. Tsongkhapa 2013b, 209. The verse, in Kilty's translation, is: "Do not make it plural, make it one. / Of types, do not divide into specifics. / The entirety of these three realms / transform into the color of the one great desire. / In it, there is no beginning, middle, or end, / no samsara, no going beyond suffering. / In this supreme and great bliss, / there is no self or others." Cf. trans. Schaeffer 2005a, 142, and R. Jackson 2004, 67.

1048. Ts*RNSG* 69b [138] and 76b [152]; trans. Tsongkhapa 2013b, 231 and 251. The verse, in Kilty's translation, is: "Gathering the mind is influenced by the winds; / moving and carried, it becomes uncontrolled. / If it knows the nature of the innate, / that will make it of stable nature." The last two lines are cited in the latter instance but not in the former. Cf. trans. Schaeffer 2005a, 150–51, and R. Jackson 2004, 80.

1049. Ts*RNSG* 169a [339]; trans. Tsongkhapa 2013b, 523–24. The verse, in Kilty's translation, is: "Those not knowing the nature of all things / who at all times are engaged in great bliss / are like the thirsty chasing a mirage. / Even if they are dying of thirst, / will they find water from the sky? // If those who sport in the bliss / that dwells between the vajra and the lotus / are unable to make use of it, / how will they fulfill the hopes of the three worlds?" Cf. trans. Schaeffer 2005a, 166, and R. Jackson 2004, 105 and 107. Note that in the Apabhraṃśa version, there are two intervening verses, not translated into Tibetan, between the first five lines and the last four.

1050. Ts*TKSY* 3a, 9a, 14a, 24a. The other three are found at 10a, 13b, and 14b.

Elder.[1051] However, the fact that Saraha possessed a sūtra-level teaching lineage does not make him any less tantric a figure, especially since the lineage in question is not one that he himself founded. Indeed, it is notable that Tsongkhapa lists no transmission primarily traceable to Saraha, mentioning him only in lineages of which the Great Brahman is a transmitter rather than a founder.

When we turn from Tsongkhapa's own writings to biographical literature about him, we find that Saraha again plays a small but not negligible role. The panegyric *Secret Life Prayer* of Tsongkhapa by Jamyang Chöjé Tashi Palden reports that he had visionary encounters with a variety of Indian mahāsiddhas, including Indrabhūti, Saraha, Lūipa, Ghaṇṭapa, and Kṛṣṇācārya, who "constantly cared for him" (*rgyun du rjes bzung ba*).[1052] These encounters are not as crucial as Tsongkhapa's visions of Mañjughoṣa or Buddhapālita, but they are further evidence that his life was infused with such meetings and that Saraha was among those he encountered. Similar encounters are reported in Khedrup Jé's *Entryway to Faith*, which also details Tsongkhapa's studies with a range of teachers from virtually every extant Tibetan tradition, including, as we have seen, numerous teachers who instructed him in a variety of crucial Kagyü traditions, such as the fivefold mahāmudrā, the six Dharmas of Nāropa, and the works of Phakmo Drupa and Drigung Jikten Sumgön. Although Khedrup Jé does not specify that Tsongkhapa received teachings on the *People Dohās*, Jé Rinpoché's citations of the text in his Guhyasamāja commentary and the later affirmation by Paṇchen Chögyen and Yeshé Gyaltsen that he was heir to a mahāmudrā "distant lineage" that included Saraha make it clear that he knew the text, and it seems reasonable to suppose that he received teachings on it (or at the very least a reading transmission of it) from his Kagyüpa teachers, even if he never specifically mentioned the fact.

Khedrup Norsang Gyatso and Saraha

Khedrup Norsang Gyatso's *Bright Lamp of Mahāmudrā* was, as we know, a text primarily concerned with expounding the mahāmudrā system of the early Kagyü, and that primarily from a tantric perspective. Norsang specifies at the outset that the primary subject of his text is "the way of meditating on primordial mind intended in Śrī Saraha's *Dohā*."[1053] The major focus, therefore, is on the establishment of the nature of primordial mind according to Indian tan-

1051. Ts*TKSY* 27b. This runs contrary to the more common Tibetan tradition in which Nāgārjuna is Saraha's direct disciple.

1052. Kp*NTSD* 3a [206]; cf. Thurman 1982, 50.

1053. Nz*PCSG* 1; translation below in part 5, section 7.

tric tradition, and the ways in which sudden and gradual practitioners, respectively, meditate upon it. Norsang makes it quite clear that true mahāmudrā practice—the manifestation of primordial mind—is possible only for those with great experience in the completion stage of unexcelled yoga tantra, while those with lesser experience must be content with settling nonconceptually on the nature of mind or, if they are rank beginners, following the common path that develops renunciation, awakening mind, and right view. For Norsang, therefore, mahāmudrā is primarily a matter of tantra, and while he does not deny that mahāmudrā-like practices are possible for those without empowerment, he does not specify that there exists a Sūtra Vehicle mahāmudrā, as both the Kagyü and the Geluk mahāmudrā tradition do.

In any case, Saraha—quite apart from being credited for being the human source of mahāmudrā practice—is quoted seven times in *Bright Lamp of Mahāmudrā*. All of the quotations are from the *People Dohās*, and whether coincidentally or not, more than half of them are passages also quoted by Tsongkhapa in his *Lamp to Illuminate the Five Stages*. The first three citations are found in the initial discussion of the nature of primordial mind,[1054] where Saraha's verses are cited to demonstrate, respectively, the fact that the primordial mind (a) is unseen by fools,[1055] (b) cannot be pointed out by anyone,[1056] and (c) may be seen through the guru's instruction.[1057] The next three citations from Saraha speak of attaining joy through eating, drinking, and sex;[1058] stopping mind and the vital winds;[1059] and turning everything into the single color of great desire.[1060] Norsang uses them to support his claim that the essence of sudden practice is "settling single-pointedly on the nature of mind, so that the vital winds are made to enter, abide, and dissolve within the cen-

1054. Nz*PCSG* 1–2.

1055. "The primordial nature is not seen by the childish; / by delusion are the childish deceived, says Saraha." Cf. trans. Schaeffer 2005a, 139, and R. Jackson 2004, 63.

1056. "No one points to the primordial nature." Cf. trans. Schaeffer 2005a, 145, and R. Jackson 2004, 70.

1057. "The primordial nature is inexpressible, / but it is visible through the guru's instruction." Cf. trans. Schaeffer 2005a, 146, and R. Jackson, *Tantric Treasures*, 72.

1058. "Eating and drinking and enjoying sex, / always filling the cakras more and more: / through such a Dharma, you'll reach the world's far shore; / step on the heads of deluded worldlings and go on your way." Cf. trans. Schaeffer 2005a, 141–42, and R. Jackson 2004, 66.

1059. "Where breath and mind are unmoving, / and sun and moon do not enter in: / there, idiots, stop the inbreath and outbreath; / Saraha has taught all these instructions and gone away." Cf. trans. Schaeffer 2005a, 142, and R. Jackson 2004, 66.

1060. "This entire triple world without exception: / turn it the single color of great desire." Cf. trans. Schaeffer 2005a, 142, and R. Jackson 2004, 67.

tral channel, and the primordial mind arises in the nature of great bliss."[1061] The last verse he cites, Saraha's famous assertion of the importance of meditating on both compassion and emptiness,[1062] is, as with Tsongkhapa, given a distinctly tantric reading:

> The compassion taught here is the greatly blissful compassion of the uncommon highest yoga mantra system . . . any yogī who is able to join both great bliss and emptiness into natural inseparability will attain the highest stage, in which one does not abide in saṃsāra and does not abide in the lower nirvāṇa.[1063]

In short, for Khedrup Norsang Gyatso, Saraha is a vital figure in the articulation of the practice of tantric mahāmudrā as he understands it to have been taught by the early Kagyüpas. Although he focuses on Kagyü traditions, there is nothing in his account that could be gainsaid by a Gelukpa, and indeed Norsang's text influenced later Gelukpa discussions of mahāmudrā, including those of the author to whom we turn next, Losang Chögyen.

Paṇchen Chögyen and Saraha

Where Norsang's mahāmudrā text focused on the tantric sense of mahāmudrā, Paṇchen Chögyen's seminal Geluk mahāmudrā texts, *Highway of the Conquerors* and *Lamp So Bright*,[1064] acknowledge a division into sūtra and tantra approaches to mahāmudrā but, as we have seen, focus primarily on the sūtra-based tradition. The sūtra tradition is said to include such Kagyü practices as the connate union, the amulet box, the fivefold, the equal taste, and the four letters, as well as pacification, severance, and the great perfection—along with the "Madhyamaka view" (*dbu ma'i lta ba*) of the Geluk. All are said to be based on the Perfection of Wisdom sūtras and the teachings of Nāgārjuna

1061. Nz*PCSG* 10.

1062. "Whoever enters emptiness bereft of compassion / does not reach the supreme path; / and if you cultivate only compassion, / you'll remain here in saṃsāra, and not obtain liberation." Cf. trans. Schaeffer 2005a, 137, and R. Jackson 2004, 61.

1063. Nz*PCSG* 9–10.

1064. The citations here will all be from *Lamp So Bright*, which incorporates the root-verses of *Highway of the Conquerors*; where appropriate, the number(s) of the verse(s) from the root text addressed by the commentary will be mentioned.

and Candrakīrti, and to have a single intention, or come down to the same point.[1065]

In Paṇchen Chögyen's scheme, Saraha is mentioned or quoted over a dozen times, initially in connection with tantra mahāmudrā, which is described in *Highway of the Conquerors* as follows:

> It is the great bliss-luminosity [mind] arising
> from skill in the methods of penetrating the vital points
> in the vajra body.
> The mahāmudrā of Saraha and Nāgārjunapāda,
> of Nāro and Maitrī,
> is taught in the Seven Attainment Texts and the Essential Trilogy
> and is the quintessence of the unexcelled tantras.[1066]

In the discussion that follows, Paṇchen Chögyen identifies the Essential Trilogy as the three *Dohā*-collections of Saraha, noting the controversy in Tibet over their authorship.[1067] He quotes several passages (at least one from Saraha) about relaxing the mind, only to emphasize that such practices are to be undertaken only in the appropriate contemplative context and not made one's main mode of meditation.[1068] He then goes on to analyze six different excerpts from the *People Dohās*,[1069] touching on such themes as the inseparability of compassion and wisdom;[1070] the need for the guru's teaching if one is to understand

1065. Bz*YSGM* 10b–12b [112–16], on *Highway of the Conquerors* verses 11–12 in translation in part 5, section 5.

1066. Bz*GBZL* 2a [83] (verses 7–8).

1067. Bz*YSGM* 6b [104], on verses 7–8.

1068. Bz*YSGM* 6b [104]. Paṇchen Chögyen cites a passage from Saraha's *Secret Vajra Teaching Instruction* (Sa*VG* 61a): "As brahmans spin the sacred thread, / the yogī puts his mind at ease. / This very mind that's bound by worldly cares, / when loosed, will be free—no doubt." Translation below in part 5, section 5. He also cites a verse (untraced so far) to the effect that "the fresh, uncontrived [mind] is best," along with a passage purportedly from Maitrīpa's *Ten Stanzas on Thatness* (but not present in any edition I have seen): "Non-investigation [is the mind] of the supreme guru." All these, notes Paṇchen Chögyen, are liable to misinterpretation if taken out of context.

1069. Bz*YSGM* 7a–9b [105–8].

1070. Bz*YSGM* 7a [105]: "Whoever enters emptiness bereft of compassion / will not reach the supreme path; / and if you cultivate only compassion, / you'll remain here in saṃsāra and not obtain liberation." Cf. trans. Schaeffer 2005a, 137, and R. Jackson 2004, 61; and below (in part 5, section 5).

that the real is everywhere;[1071] the elusiveness and inexpressibility of the connate primordial mind;[1072] the absence from ultimate reality of tantra, mantras, or contemplation and the ability of the yogī to use eating, drinking, and sex on the path;[1073] and the ubiquity of discussion of great bliss while all remain in ignorance of its meaning.[1074] Throughout this analysis, Paṇchen Chögyen is intent on showing how Saraha's verses lead to confusion if read literally but make sense within the context of Madhyamaka philosophy and unexcelled-yoga-tantra meditation practice.

The second major locus for quotations from Saraha is in the long section on serenity meditation, in which the mind itself is the focal object. Here, Paṇchen Chögyen quotes in two different forms Saraha's advice to relax the mind and simply let it go, which may have the paradoxical effect of helping to keep awareness settled and truly concentrated.[1075] For Paṇchen Chögyen, these verses are *not* to be taken as an invitation to let the mind run wild. Rather, they must be understood as pointing out the necessity, on the path of serenity, to

1071. Bz*YSGM* 7a [105]: "If you have realization, then all [things] are that; / no one knows anything other than that; / reading is that; apprehension and meditation are also that. / Studying the treatises is also that. / There is no view not indicated by that, / but it depends on the words of the guru alone. / Taking the words of the guru to heart / is like seeing a treasure in the palm of your hand. / The primordial nature goes unnoticed by the fool; / fools are deceived by delusion—so says Saraha." Cf. trans. Schaeffer 2005a, 138–39, and R. Jackson 2004, 62–63; and below.

1072. Bz*YSGM* 7b [106]: "If it's manifest, what's the point of meditation? / If it's hidden, you only encounter darkness. / That connate nature / is neither entity nor nonentity." Cf. trans. Schaeffer 2005a, 140, and R. Jackson 2004, 64; and below. And Bz*YSGM* 8a [107]: "Since it's separate from meditation, what is there to think? / How can you explain the inexpressible? / All beings are deceived by the seal of saṃsāric existence; / no one takes up the primordial nature." Cf. trans. Schaeffer 2005a, 141, and R. Jackson 2004, 65; and below.

1073. Bz*YSGM* 8a [107]: "No tantra, no mantra, nothing on which to think or meditate: / all those cause your own mind to be confused. / The naturally pure mind is unpolluted by meditation. / Abide in your own bliss and don't make yourself miserable: / there's joy in eating, drinking, and sex. / Always, again and again, fill the cakras. / By a dharma such as this you'll transcend the world; / treading on the head of mundane confusion, go on. / Where wind and mind no longer move, / where sun and moon do not enter, / the minds of the ignorant will find relief. / The archer has taught all these pith instructions and gone on." Cf. trans. Schaeffer 2005a, 141–42, and R. Jackson 2004, 65–66; and below.

1074. Bz*YSGM* 8b [108]: "In this house and that house they talk about it, but / the point of great bliss is completely unknown." Cf. trans. Schaeffer 2005a, 149, and R. Jackson 2004, 76; and below.

1075. Bz*YSGM* 15a [121]: "This mind, bound by worldly entanglements, / is freed when relaxed—there is no doubt." Cf. trans. Schaeffer 2005a, 149, and R. Jackson 2004, 78; and below. Bz*YSGM* 16a [123]: "It's like a raven that flies from a ship, / circles in every direction, and alights there again." Cf. trans. Schaeffer 2005a, 158, and R. Jackson 2004, 93; and below.

let the mind relax a bit after periods of intense concentration, so as to maintain the proper balance between tautness and slack in the musical string that is the concentrated mind.

The final three quotations come at the beginning of the section on insight, where Paṇchen Chögyen seeks to generally establish "the real nature of mind," which is the reality to be uncovered by the insight meditation procedures whose description will follow. Paṇchen Chögyen quotes two Kagyüpa masters, Lingrepa and Shang Rinpoché, and two Indian mahāsiddhas, Tilopa and Saraha. The passages from Saraha describe how (a) mind is the seed of everything in saṃsāra and nirvāṇa, the wish-granting jewel to which we must bow;[1076] (b) there is no true nature to mind, which has the nature of great bliss, or its appearances, which are the Dharma body;[1077] and (c) one must settle in one's meditation on the fresh, uncontrived mind.[1078] Paṇchen Chögyen then proceeds to describe the actual procedures for insight meditation, which are, as we have seen, heavily Geluk in orientation, and Saraha is not heard from again for the rest of the text. His omission from the central discussion of insight practice is not really surprising, for despite Paṇchen Chögyen's contention that various Tibetan practice traditions (including those heavily dependent on Saraha) come down to a "single intention," the rhetorical style of Saraha's *Dohās*—with their focus on the fundamental purity of mind and depiction of the ultimate in positive imagery—does not mesh easily with the negative approach favored by Gelukpa versions of Prāsaṅgika Madhyamaka. Indeed, to the most conservative, Saraha's approach might seem an invitation to the dreaded shentong—or extrinsic emptiness—view.

Paṇchen Chögyen, then, sees Saraha in three different roles: as a gnomic exponent of the mahāmudrā of unexcelled yoga tantra; as a guide to certain aspects of calm-abiding meditation; and as a celebrant of the centrality and emptiness of the mind that is the object of insight meditation. By employing Saraha outside the purely tantric realm to which he seems to have been

1076. Bz*YSGM* 17b [126]: "Mind itself alone is the seed of everything, / whence worldly existence and nirvāṇa are projected / and which bestows all desired results— / to the mind like a wish-fulfilling jewel, I bow down." Cf. trans. Schaeffer 2005a, 147, and R. Jackson 2004, 73; and below.

1077. Bz*YSGM* 18a [127]: "When sought, no mind or appearance / is found, nor is there anywhere a seeker; / The nonexistent does not arise or cease at any time, / so it cannot become something else— / it is the abiding nature of natural great bliss. / Thus, all appearances are the Dharma body." The passage is from the *Dohā Treasury Instruction*, which sometimes is attributed to Mahāśabara Saraha or to Śavari. For a slightly different reading, based on a different recension, see above, page 49. Cf. trans. Thaye 1990, 81; and below p. 513.

1078. Bz*YSGM* 18b [128]: "Settle gently on the fresh, uncontrived [mind]." SNL.

consigned by Tsongkhapa and Norsang Gyatso, Paṇchen Chögyen gives him something to say about such sūtra-level concerns as serenity and insight, but he still keeps the actual procedures of insight meditation—the key to liberation—firmly within the confines of standard Geluk ideas and practices.

A brief comparative note: Kagyü mahāmudrā manuals—of which a multitude had appeared by Paṇchen Chögyen's time—tend to weave Saraha seamlessly into all areas of discussion and find his verses relevant to every type of practice. Thus, for instance, Dakpo Tashi Namgyal's *Moonbeams of Mahāmudrā*, written perhaps half a century before Paṇchen Chögyen's texts, quotes Saraha at least sixty times, more than any other individual except Gampopa. Tashi Namgyal quotes not just the *People Dohās* but other poetic texts as well and cites Saraha most frequently in his sections on insight meditation and "maintaining absorption and post-absorption." Because Kagyü approaches to Madhyamaka and insight meditation differ from those of the Geluk, for instance in their greater enthusiasm for positive characterizations of the ultimate, Tashi Namgyal, unlike Paṇchen Chögyen, does not feel the need to keep Saraha at a distance when he discusses such matters. By the same token, because many Kagyüpas regard mahāmudrā as a practice that transcends the sūtra-tantra distinction, Tashi Namgyal does not, as is the wont of some Gelukpas, consider Saraha to be primarily an exponent of Mantra Vehicle mahāmudrā, for in mahāmudrā, sūtra and tantra are indistinguishably interfused, and Saraha's texts are the *locus classicus* for that perfect blend, hence eminently quotable in virtually any mahāmudrā-related context.

Khöntön Paljor Lhundrup and Saraha

As we have seen, the *Wish-Fulfilling Gem of the Hearing Lineage*[1079] of Paṇchen Chögyen's contemporary, Khöntön Paljor Lhundrup, is a self-conscious attempt to integrate mahāmudrā, the great perfection, and Geluk "Great Madhyamaka,"[1080] into a single integrated meditation practice. It places Geluk

1079. See above, chapter 8. It is not clear which hearing lineage Khöntönpa has in mind. He does not figure in the hearing lineage of which Paṇchen Chögyen is the great exponent. It is likely that the lineage is that of the fifteenth-century Nyingmapa master Sangyé Tsöndrü, who is mentioned prominently in the final verses, and that Khöntönpa received it from his own Nyingma teacher, Nyinda Sangyé, who is singled out in the colophon; see Dalai Lama et al. 2011, 138.

1080. As we have seen, "Great Madhyamaka" (*dbu ma chen po*) is a term employed variously by Tibetan authors. In Nyingma and Kagyü contexts, it often refers to the extrinsic emptiness (*gzhan stong*) view, but for Khöntönpa, as for Gelukpas in general, it appears to connote the approach to Madhyamaka taken by Nāgārjuna, Candrakīrti, Atiśa, and Tsongkhapa. There are,

teachings in noncontradictory juxtaposition to mahāmudrā (and the great perfection) views and practices, but it does not synthesize them even to the degree that Paṇchen Chögyen does in his classic texts on Geluk mahāmudrā. Khöntönpa mentions Saraha seven times in the *Wish-Fulfilling Gem*. The Great Brahman initially appears in the verses of homage, where he is listed first among the great lineage holders of the New Translation schools.[1081] His subsequent appearances—all in the form of quotations from one or another of his *Dohās*—are scattered throughout the text and introduced, like other quotations, to buttress a particular point that Khöntönpa wishes to make.

Thus, in an early section where he stresses the fundamental importance of the mind for both saṃsāra and nirvāṇa, Khöntönpa quotes Saraha first to the effect that there is no phenomenon apart from mind and immediately afterward to the effect that mind is the seed of everything. The first passage is from the *Dohā Treasury of Instruction on Mahāmudrā*,[1082] the second from the *People Dohās*.[1083] Saraha next is quoted in support of Khöntönpa's contention that it is possible for concentration and mental fluctuations to coincide, and that this view is common to Madhyamaka, mahāmudrā, and the great perfection. The passage, from the *People Dohās*,[1084] simply states that relaxation of a mind tightly bound is the assurance of freedom; the implication in this context is that a truly concentrated state need not involve the suppression of thought. In the section on serenity, a verse from Saraha's *Song of Secret Vajra Instruction on Mahāmudrā* enjoining yogīs to ease the mind in the same way that brahmans spin the sacred thread (also quoted by Paṇchen Chögyen in *Lamp So Bright*), is used to encourage the reader to ease into a concentrated state where the object, the nature of mind, is held but not too tightly.[1085] In his discussion of postmeditative awareness, in a subsection entitled "Recog-

of course, many non-Gelukpas—and many modern scholars—who would dispute that the Madhyamaka of Candrakīrti and that of Tsongkhapa are the same.

1081. Dalai Lama et al. 2011, 64.

1082. Dalai Lama et al. 2011, 67: "Every phenomenon is your own mind; / apart from the mind, there is no phenomenon, / not even the slightest." Cf. trans. Thaye 1990, 80. Recall that the text is also attributed to Mahāśabara Saraha and to Śavari.

1083. Dalai Lama et al. 2011, 67–68: "The mind alone is the seed of everything; / existence and nirvana are projected out of mind. / I bow down to the mind that, like a wish-fulfilling jewel, / brings me to my desired goal." Cf. trans. Schaeffer 2005a, 147, and R. Jackson 2004, 73.

1084. Dalai Lama et al. 2011, 85: "If you let go of the mind bound by ordinary mental concerns, / there is no doubt that you will be free." Cf. trans. Schaeffer 2005a, 147, and R. Jackson 2004, 74.

1085. Sa*VG* 61a; trans. Dalai Lama et al. 2011, 67: "Brahman, just like spinning thread, / the yogī should rest the mind by loosening it."

nizing that Appearances are Mind," Khöntönpa quotes a passage from Saraha's *King Dohās* that underscores how, despite the appearance of duality, there is only unity; this is important to bear in mind in the postmeditative state, where dualistic appearances reassert themselves.[1086] Saraha is cited one final time later in the discussion of the postmeditative state, in support of the idea that, whether sentient beings realize it or not, their minds are the basis of attaining the Dharma body of a Buddha; the passage, from the *People Dohās*,[1087] asserts that the childish are deceived because they fail to appreciate their primordial nature.

Unlike most Gelukpas, then, Khöntönpa quotes from a wide range of Saraha's *Dohās*—at least four separate texts—and does not confine the mahāsiddha to a particular pigeonhole as, for instance, only relevant to tantric practice, only useful in the context of mahāmudrā serenity meditation, or only philosophically interesting in his insistence on the importance of mind. At the same time, as we have seen, the *Wish-Fulfilling Gem* is a Geluk text only in the sense that it has a Gelukpa frame to it, while the core of teaching derives from and deploys the terminology of Kagyü and Nyingma traditions related to mahāmudrā and the great perfection, both separately and at their intersection. In this sense, Khöntönpa is not constrained in his use of Saraha, because he is evoking him from a standpoint that is, for the most part, not really Geluk.

Jamyang Shepa and Saraha

The final take on Saraha we will consider is that of Jamyang Shepai Dorjé, among whose minor compositions is a text entitled *Annotations to the People Dohās* (Jz*DDCG*), which is, so far as I know, the only extant Geluk treatment of Saraha's seminal poem in its entirety. Lest the reader faint with anticipatory excitement, it must quickly be added that Jamyang Shepa's annotations are decidedly *not* a commentary on the *People Dohās* of the sort produced in abundance within Kagyü circles but simply a detailed outline of the text (*sa bcad*), with the section titles inserted at appropriate places in the Tibetan

1086. Dalai Lama et al. 2011, 104–5: "Just as unperturbed waters turn into turbulent waves / when they are agitated by wind, / likewise you, O King, create diversity in regard to the image of the archer [Saraha] / even though there is only unity here. / Just as the deluded see a single lamp as two / due to having faulty vision, / likewise there is no distinction between the seer and the seen. / How amazing, then, that the mind should give rise to dualities." Cf. trans. Guenther 1993, 150; Thrangu 2006, 125–26.

1087. Dalai Lama et al. 2011, 67: "'Erring on account of not seeing the nature of the primordial state, / the childish are deceived.' So says the archer." Cf. trans. Schaeffer 2005a, 139, and R. Jackson 2004, 63.

translation of the poem. Thus, any clues to Jamyang Shepa's view of Saraha must be inferred from his outline.[1088]

Most broadly, Jamyang Shepa takes the *People Dohās* as a text about the connate mind/reality and its realization. His discussion of the connate is divided into a brief section refuting the approaches to reality of non-Buddhist schools (Jz*DDCG* 1b–2b)[1089] followed by "vajra songs for our own system," which take up most of the rest of the text (2b–13b). The section on vajra songs includes Saraha's critiques of various mistaken approaches to practice taken by Buddhists (2b–3a) and a massive subsection on "establishing the unsurpassed connate" (3a–13b). This is, as is common in commentarial literature, divided into a brief demonstration (3a–b) and an extensive explanation (3b–13b). The extensive explanation is broadly divided into analyses of the nature of suchness (*de nyid*) or reality (*chos nyid*) (3b–5b) and of the intrinsic primordial nature (*rang bzhin gnyug ma*) (5b–13b). The latter, which includes a brief demonstration (5b), an extensive explanation (5b–9a), and a very extensive explanation (5b–13b), includes, at one or another level of specificity, such headings as "how to abide like space," "binding the vital winds," "the body as the supreme locus," "how the guru's instruction is supreme," "the nature of mind as free," "particulars of the paths of the two stages," "stopping concepts through seeing reality," "the nature of mahāmudrā," "the reality of the unelaborated realm," "blazing of great bliss through pure meditation," "the bliss of nonemission as the cause of liberation," and "settling into one's own luminosity."

The brief section explicitly addressing mahāmudrā (10b–11a) is subdivided into three topics. The first, "contemplation of the mind as unsullied," covers the lines in Saraha that run:

> By eating one, you consume all.
> You go outside to look for the master of the house:
> he comes but you don't see him; he goes and he isn't here;
> even when he's right before you, you don't recognize him.
> The glorious supreme lord, who is waveless,
> becomes untroubled contemplation.[1090]

1088. This inherently difficult task is not made any easier by the fact that the outline is not always consistent, with some promised subsections never appearing and others improperly numbered.

1089. Translations of the relevant verses in Saraha are found in, e.g., Schaeffer 2005a, 133–71, and R. Jackson 2004, 53–115.

1090. Sa*PD*t 75b; cf. trans. in Schaeffer 2005a, 162, and R. Jackson 2004, 100.

The second topic is "mahāmudrā meditation," which, according to Jamyang Shepa, is covered by the lines in Saraha that run:

> Let water [become clear] and the lamp shine on its own.
> Whatever comes or goes, I do not accept or reject.
> You meet a sensuous woman who didn't exist before,
> but the sleeping mind is founded on the baseless.[1091]

The third mahāmudrā section demonstrates how "that is great bliss" by referring to the lines of Saraha that run:

> Don't see her as different from your own nature;
> that way, you find Buddha in your hand.
> When body, speech, and thought are inseparable,
> then the connate nature is beautiful.[1092]

It is unfortunate that Jamyang Shepa did not provide us with an explanation for these intriguing ways of thinking about mahāmudrā. At the very least, it is clear that (a) mahāmudrā is being conceived in a thoroughly tantric manner and (b) to practice mahāmudrā requires inward contemplation of our inborn stainless and radiant awareness, which may work best if it simply is allowed to shine on its own.

From all this—and this summary barely scratches the surface—it is clear that Jamyang Shepa, like most of his Gelukpa predecessors, sees the *People Dohās* as a text that is relevant primarily to completion-stage practices as described in the unexcelled yoga tantras, for the vocabulary he employs in developing his outline originates from those especially advanced and esoteric Indian textual systems. Beyond this unsurprising general observation, however, it is not at all evident that, for all his efforts, Jamyang Shepa succeeds in bringing Saraha's text into any semblance of useful order. For all the apparent tidiness of his divisions—into brief and extensive analyses; ground, path, and fruit; non-Buddhist systems and Buddhist systems; and so forth—the outline as a whole does not really add up to a logical sequence. The reason for this is obvious: Saraha's text simply is not amenable to the categories of the scholastic mind. It is, after all, a compilation of couplets, some thematically related and others quite distinct, that was redacted long after the time of Saraha, whenever that may have been; and it does not seem to have been redacted with any

1091. Sa*PD*t 75b; cf. trans. in Schaeffer 2005a, 162, and R. Jackson 2004, 100.

1092. Sa*PD*t 75b; cf. trans. in Schaeffer 2005a, 162, and R. Jackson 2004, 100.

grand scheme in mind. Jamyang Shepa's outline does not fully make sense of the *People Dohās* because there is no sense to be made—at least not of the sort that philosophers prefer.

It should be noted that Jamyang Shepa is not alone in struggling—and perhaps failing—to impose order on an essentially unruly text. The outlines provided in such famous Tibetan commentaries as those of Chomden Raldri (1227–1305)[1093] and Karma Trinlepa (1456–1539)[1094] are not markedly more coherent than that of Jamyang Shepa. It is hardly surprising that one of the earliest Tibetans to comment on the *People Dohās*, the great Lingrepa Pema Dorje (1128–88), simply rearranged the text so that it fit into his outline.[1095] Like modern topical reorderings of the Qur'ān, such commentarial efforts may make a text more accessible to readers, but the text to which they are given access is not the one that has been received, and the illusion of coherence that is generated by reading it seems, if I read him rightly, to be precisely what Saraha preached against.

Final Remarks

What, in sum, may we say about the place of Saraha in Geluk tradition? With the caveats that (a) my survey has been far from complete and (b) Khöntön Paljor Lhundrup stands as an interesting, if understandable, counterexample to the generalizations that follow, I would hazard these conclusions:

First, Saraha is among the most influential Indian mahāsiddhas for Geluk tradition, as he is for nearly every tradition traceable to the later spread of Buddhism in Tibet. However, of the many texts attributed to Saraha in the Tengyur, only the *People Dohās* (and to a lesser degree the commentary on the *Buddha Skull Tantra*) seems to have exerted major influence on Gelukpas, who only occasionally cite the rest of his corpus. It is worth remarking, however, that the *People Dohās* is by far Saraha's best-known work and is his most oft-quoted text in non-Geluk sources, as well.

Second, Saraha's writings are seen by Gelukpas as relevant mainly to the practice of the Mantra Vehicle and are read primarily in terms of completion-stage practices in the unexcelled yoga tantras; they are rarely cited in Sūtra Vehicle contexts. At the same time, because Saraha did not write commentaries on the tantric traditions most studied by Gelukpas—the Guhyasamāja,

1093. See Schaeffer 2005a, 129–73.

1094. See Guenther 1993, 189–222.

1095. See Schaeffer 2005a, 115–19 and 187–89.

Cakrasaṃvara, Hevajra, and Kālacakra—his work is not often cited in standard Geluk presentations of unexcelled yoga tantra.

Third, within the Geluk mahāmudrā tradition, Saraha is seen as a seminal figure in the distant lineage that descended to Tsongkhapa through a succession of Indian and Tibetan masters; he is especially revered as the main Indian exponent of mantra mahāmudrā, which is a particular way of accomplishing completion-stage practices within the subtle body in the context of meditating on the nature of mind. Saraha's verses also may sometimes be cited in sūtra mahāmudrā discussions of the nature of mind or techniques for serenity meditation, but they do not provide a basis for the practice of Geluk mahāmudrā insight meditation, which remains almost entirely within the compass of the Madhyamaka approach developed by Tsongkhapa.

Fourth and finally, this careful circumscription of Saraha, even in the mahāmudrā tradition, is typical of the caution that Gelukpas exercise in dealing with the antinomian elements of their Indian Buddhist tantric heritage. As Tibetan Buddhists, they cannot deny that heritage or the countercultural elements within it, but like the Kadampas from whom they drew their original inspiration, they can make sure that there is no leakage between the watertight compartments they feel they must maintain so as to separate sūtra from tantra. Saraha's writings may seem to defy such compartmentalization—and they have often been read as pertaining to both sūtra and tantra by those outside the Geluk fold—but the maintenance of a sharp sūtra-tantra distinction has always been crucial to Geluk discourse, so Saraha probably will remain for Gelukpas a marginal figure, revered as an inspiring forefather, honored for his place in certain lineages, quoted carefully in the appropriate context, but never given sufficient space in which to draw his bow and unleash every arrow in his rich and dangerous quiver.

17. The Big Picture: Sixteen Questions

TIBETAN DISCUSSIONS OF mahāmudrā over the centuries, both within and outside the Geluk fold, raised important questions, which were—and in many cases still are—much debated. While the questions take on a distinctive character in the context of mahāmudrā discourse, they are not unique to it. Indeed, they are particular instantiations of problems that, in one form or another, arise in nearly all Buddhist traditions, from the Foundational schools of South and Southeast Asia to Mahāyāna settings in India and elsewhere in northern Asia.[1096] Nor are the deeper issues implied by these questions solely the province of Buddhism; indeed, the problems raised by mahāmudrā discourse and practice find echoes in other religious traditions, both East and West—especially in those areas of religion that pertain to "mysticism": the most direct possible human encounter with ultimate reality, however that reality may be construed.[1097] In the final chapter of this section—and of the narrative portion of the book—we will touch briefly on sixteen questions about mahāmudrā that have explicitly or implicitly animated Tibetan scholars and siddhas for the past millennium but bear in significant ways on larger problems in Buddhist culture and thought, and in religious studies (and sometimes philosophy) more generally.

The discussion here must perforce be laid out in general terms, and the reader seeking definitive answers to any of the questions will come away disappointed. Nevertheless, if these final reflections succeed in bringing a modicum of closure to the preceding analysis of Geluk mahāmudrā, and in showing some of the key issues raised within the tradition and their wider implications and resonances, I will rest content.[1098]

1096. See, especially, Hookham 1991, D. Jackson 1994, Seyfort Ruegg 1989, Dalai Lama and Berzin 1997, R. Jackson 2001, and Sakya Pandita 2002.

1097. See, especially, Stace 1960, Katz 1978, Proudfoot 1987, Forman 1997, and Taves 2009.

1098. Because these chapters serve as a sort of conclusion to the narrative portion of the book, I will annotate them less thoroughly than the chapters preceding them, only occasionally

1. Is There Scriptural Warrant for Mahāmudrā?

One of Sakya Paṇḍita's accusations against the Kagyü mahāmudrā traditions he targeted—especially the white panacea of Lama Shang and the single intention of the Drigung—was that they lacked scriptural warrant in the Indic tradition. He was not arguing, of course, that the term *mahāmudrā* cannot found in Indian Buddhism, only that using it in the ways favored by many Kagyüpas—to describe a single, nondual realization that is found in both Sūtra and Mantra Vehicle sources and suffices for liberation—is inappropriate, and most likely derived from Chinese Chan traditions rather than those of India. Sapaṇ's critique was rejected not only by a long series of Kagyüpa masters but by Paṇchen Chögyen and other Gelukpas as well, all of whom insisted that the sūtras, treatises, and commentaries produced in both sūtra and mantra circles in India pointed to multiple and complex concepts of the great seal, not simply to the buddhahood ensuing upon tantric empowerment that Sapaṇ insisted was mahāmudrā's sole legitimate denotation. Thus, according the Kagyü and Geluk, mahāmudrā was employed in many different ways by the masters of later Indian Buddhism, who in turn based themselves on explicit or implicit teachings on the subject delivered by the Buddha in either the sūtras or the tantras. It is important to remember, too, that the authoritative teachings accepted widely in the Tibetan world include those based on visionary encounters with buddhas or past masters, or the special oral instructions transmitted by one's own guru. Thus, for Gelukpas, the teachings received by Tsongkhapa during his visionary encounter with the wisdom-buddha Mañjughoṣa, including mahāmudrā, are effectively the word of the Buddha. Yes, mahāmudrā can be (and is) traced back into the Indic textual tradition, but Tsongkhapa's vision and the chain of oral transmission he initiated are equally, if not more, authoritative. Much the same could be said of the oral traditions celebrated within Kagyü mahāmudrā circles, of which Tilopa's transmissions to Nāropa and Marpa's visionary encounters with Saraha are just two prominent examples.

Within Buddhism more broadly, authority ultimately rests on *buddhavacana*, the word of the Buddha: if the Buddha described some reality or encouraged some attitude or delineated some practice, then that reality, attitude, or practice is said to bear the Buddha's imprimatur, hence to be warranted.[1099] Broadly speaking, therefore, ultimate authority within Buddhism rests with

suggesting a Buddhist studies or religious studies resource that may deepen the reader's understanding of the issues I am addressing.

1099. On this topic, see, e.g., Davidson 1990.

Indian texts attributable to the Buddha. Justification on the basis of *buddhavacana*, however, begs a number of important questions for Buddhists, who cannot even agree among themselves on the extent and content of the Buddha's teachings. Theravāda Buddhists in South and Southeast Asia accept as Buddha's word only the discourses contained in the Pāli canon, while Mahāyāna Buddhists in East and Inner Asia accept not only the "Hīnayāna" Sanskrit *āgama*s that are close equivalents of the Pāli canon but also a vast and varied corpus of Mahāyāna sūtras and tantras, most of them originally in Sanskrit. Theravādins hold to a closed canon, which has been inalterable since early in the first millennium CE, while many Mahāyānists conceive of their canon as open, such that, for instance, a visionary encounter with a buddha (and in Mahāyāna tradition buddhas are well-nigh infinite) may result in a fresh revelation, which is no less authoritative for its occurrence at a time and place far removed from those of the historical Buddha. By the same token, in certain contexts, as in Chan/Zen and tantric settings, oral transmissions (all of which are traced to some form of buddha) may be regarded as equally or even more valuable relative to written traditions. In any case, Mahāyāna canons—which are found in their most complete and fixed form in Chinese and Tibetan translations—never reached the same degree of closure as the Pāli canon. In Tibet, in particular, there were significant debates about the legitimacy of the Nyingma tantric canon, whose texts were not, typically, accepted by the New Translation school scholars as Indic in origin. Similarly, the Tibetans, like the Chinese and most other non-Indians, created "grey texts" that purported to be Indian but were, in fact, composed in a non–South Asian setting. For a strict Theravādin, neither the sūtras nor the tantras of the Great Vehicle—let alone later visionary revelations—are *buddhavacana*; hence, from a Foundational standpoint, the Ganden Hearing Transmission and its teachings on mahāmudrā are quite illegitimate.

The larger question within religious studies is: by what authority are religious ideas and practices justified? Nearly every religious tradition, whether solely oral or written as well, looks to some collection of authoritative narratives and doctrines in order to regulate its community and the practices of its members.[1100] Restricting ourselves here to heavily written traditions like Buddhism, we may generally, if cautiously, observe that nearly every literate religion has, over the course of time, separated out a body of narratives and doctrines as being uniquely authoritative, that is, as being "scripture" or "canon." Among and within the various written traditions, conceptions of scripture are quite various, ranging from Hindu notions of *śruti*, the divine

1100. See, e.g., Levering 1989.

in verbal form as received and transmitted orally by visionary sages (*ṛṣis*); to Christian assertions that the Old and New Testaments were written by humans but prompted by the Holy Spirit; to Muslim ideas about the existence of a primordial, preverbal Qur'ān that was instantiated in the Arabic language in the revelations received by Muhammad between 610 and 632 CE. However conceived, each of these scriptures is ultimately authoritative for the tradition that has identified it, hence is the most important single basis of justification for any idea or practice that may arise within the community. Of course, most communities also identify "secondary" sources of authority that supplement the primary scripture(s)—whether Hindu remembered tradition (*smṛti*), the Judaic Talmud, Christian commentarial literature, or Islamic Sunna—and in certain cases, as in Buddhist Chan/Zen or mahāmudrā circles, will insist that oral traditions supersede anything written. Still, whatever their importance, these secondary sources of authority, whether written or oral, still will refer back to the primary scriptures—the interpretation of which is probably the most important single task of commentators or theologians, whatever their tradition.

2. *To Which Dharma Wheel Does Mahāmudrā Belong?*

Although Sakya Paṇḍita and his followers attempted to limit discussion of mahāmudrā to the late Indian tantric contexts in which it refers to the fruit of the Mantra Vehicle path, most Tibetans took the great seal to refer as well to the ultimate nature of reality, the fundamental luminosity of the mind, and meditative techniques for realizing these. Correspondingly, they found discourse on mahāmudrā not only in Indian tantric literature but in the sūtra tradition, too. Kagyüpas, for instance, find teachings on the great seal as empty luminosity in buddha-nature sūtras and such treatises as the *Sublime Continuum*, while Paṇchen Chögyen identifies sūtra mahāmudrā with the teaching on emptiness in the Perfection of Wisdom sūtras and the treatises of Nāgārjuna and Candrakīrti. In terms of the influential hermeneutical categories established in chapter 7 of the *Unraveling the Intention Sūtra*,[1101] Tibetans accept the latter, "negative" perspective (roughly that of Madhyamaka) as comprising the second of the Buddha's three turnings of the Dharma wheel, while the former, "positive" perspective, roughly that of Yogācāra, is said to have been articulated during the third turning of the Dharma wheel.[1102] The hermeneutical question on which Tibetan traditions often disagree is which

1101. See, e.g., Powers 1995, 93–146.

1102. There is general agreement that the first turning of the Dharma wheel (a) corresponds

turning, the second or third, is definitive (*nges don*), acceptable at face value as an expression of the ultimate, and which is provisional (*drang don*), requiring further interpretation as an expression of the ultimate. Since mahāmudrā is a teaching on the ultimate for both Kagyüpas and Gelukpas, it is not surprising that Kagyüpas most often identify the great seal with the third turning, as it is there that the ultimate is expressed in terms most congenial to them, while Gelukpas identify the great seal with the second turning, for the same reason. By the same token, Kagyüpas often find the second turning provisional, while Gelukpas typically think the same of the third turning.

Within Buddhism more broadly, hermeneutical problems are raised by the fact that the Buddha is often said to have delivered 84,000 different teachings.[1103] The extant collections of *buddhavacana* translated into Chinese and Tibetan run to well over a hundred volumes, and even the relatively compact Pāli canon and its equivalent non-Pāli *āgama*s cover more than thirty volumes. Given the vast array of teachings attributed to the Buddha in even the most conservative version of the canon, apparent contradictions abound: here the Buddha denies there is a self, but there he seems to affirm one; here he describes ultimate reality in negative terms, but there he describes it positively. According to tradition, however, the Buddha cannot possibly contradict himself, and it is from this basic assumption that Buddhists in various places and times developed hermeneutical principles, whereby interpreters could determine which of the Buddha's statements should be taken literally and which taken figuratively, as mere examples of skillful pedagogy (*upāya*). The principles developed ranged from Theravāda articulations of a gradual path to *nibbāna* as the basis for understanding the Buddha's various statements; to the Chinese Tiantai school's concept of five stages of progressively deeper revelation by the Buddha (*panjiao*), culminating in the *Lotus Sūtra*; to the Tibetan tradition's embrace of the *Unraveling the Intention Sūtra*'s notion of the three turnings of the Dharma wheel and the identification of each as definitive or provisional. And as we have seen, it is in disputes about the assignment of definitive and provisional status to particular texts or teachings that hermeneutical debates about mahāmudrā are most likely to arise.

The larger question within religious studies is: how do we interpret scripture when it seems to be imprecise or even contradictory?[1104] Just as nearly every religious tradition sets apart certain texts (whether oral, written, or both) as

to the "Hīnayāna" perspective and (b) requires further interpretation because it can be read as espousing a subtle ontological realism.

1103. See, e.g., Lopez 1992.

1104. See, e.g., Kaiser and Silva 2007, Von Denffer 2009, and Sherma and Sharma 2008.

canonical, every tradition that possesses a canon is faced with the problem of interpretation, and with determining proper principles for assessing the various descriptions and prescriptions found within its body of authoritative discourse. Among the general hermeneutical principles typically adduced to weigh a particular assertion are such criteria as conformity with statements in other parts of the canon, susceptibility to rational analysis, and confirmability in everyday experience. Another principle sometimes cited is agreement with the deliverances of mystical experience, whether attained through systematic techniques, the action of divine grace, or some combination of the two. Specific hermeneutical approaches outside Buddhism include Talmudic linguistic and semantic rules for interpreting the Torah; Sufi conceptions of the Qur'ān as covered by seven veils, each more esoteric than the one outside it; or medieval Daoist methods for reading the philosophical classics of Laozi and Zhuangzi in terms of inner alchemical practices. As European philosophers of the early nineteenth century onward pointed out, all interpretive activity is caught up in a "hermeneutical circle," whereby the specific contents of a text can only be based on one's understanding of the whole, but the whole cannot be understood separately from the parts. Beyond this paradox is the key observation that no interpreter comes to a text without prior assumptions and biases, so that all reading is contextual, and all interpretations must be qualified. In the context of the interpretation of scripture, then, hermeneutical principles like the seven veils of the Qur'ān or the three turnings of the Dharma wheel may seem to function perfectly well within a particular tradition, but on closer examination turn out to be less than decisive, infected as they are by the circularity of the interpretive process. Thus Kagyü and Geluk debates over which mahāmudrā teachings are definitive and which provisional are rooted in a fundamentally circular process that makes a final determination effectively impossible.

3. Is There Mahāmudrā outside the Tantras?

Starting with Gampopa—who himself may have drawn on suggestions made by late Indian thinkers like Maitrīpa and Jñānakīrti and his own Tibetan predecessors, Marpa and Milarepa—Kagyü thinkers insisted that mahāmudrā practice and realization need not be confined to tantric contexts, since in its deepest sense, the great seal is about the nature of mind and reality, which is addressed in all Buddhist traditions: not just in the Perfection Vehicle of the Mahāyāna but in Foundational Buddhism as well. Thus Gampopa would teach mahāmudrā even to disciples who lacked tantric empowerment—with a master's "pointing-out instructions" sufficing as permission for the student to practice the great seal. Sakya Paṇḍita, on the other hand, insisted that *mahāmudrā* was a strictly Mantra Vehicle term, referring primarily to the final gnosis of buddhahood ensuing upon tantric empowerment, though it also could denote a symbolic hand gesture or a consort in sexual yoga practices. In this sense, Sapaṇ restricted mahāmudrā to the esoteric context in which it was explicitly discussed in Indian Buddhist literature, while Gampopa and his Kagyüpa successors accepted that it had an exoteric dimension as well, revealed implicitly in a wide range of Indic writings on the nature of mind/reality and how to realize it—to the point where *any* discussion the ultimate nature of reality could be regarded as mahāmudrā discourse. As we have seen, later Kagyüpas, as well as Gelukpas, drew on a variety of historical and textual evidence to refute Sapaṇ and uphold Gampopa's position.

Within Buddhism more broadly, the question long has been debated whether the tradition admits of an esoteric dimension, and if so, what the place of that dimension ought to be. While the Foundational tradition reflected in the Pāli canon is generally regarded as exoteric in the sense that the Buddha is depicted there as freely sharing his teachings with all comers—indeed, he specifically denies that he teaches "with a closed fist"—he also remarks that the teachings he has imparted are as few compared to what he knows as are a handful of leaves compared to all the leaves in a forest. This statement does not imply the existence of a secret teaching the Buddha revealed only to selected disciples, but it does imply that he has not shared publicly everything that is worth knowing; this notion, in turn, helps open the way to the later development, within the Mahāyāna, of various types of lineage-based or esoteric teachings and communities. Among the most notable are those of the Chan/Zen and tantric traditions.[1105] Although primarily developed in China, Chan/Zen traces its lineage back to the Buddha, who, according to later legend, gave a special, extra-scriptural, "mind-to-mind" transmission to his disciple Mahākāśyapa, from whom it descended through a series of masters to Bodhidharma, who carried it to China in the sixth century CE. The various Buddhist tantric communities that arose in India starting in the mid-first millennium focused their efforts on practices that could be undertaken only after receiving an empowerment from a qualified guru. These traditions grew increasingly influential in later Indian Buddhism, and were of great cultural significance elsewhere in Buddhist Asia, not only in such Mahāyāna centers as Tibet, Mongolia, and East Asia, but in Sri Lanka and Southeast Asia, as well, where their importance prior to the consolidation of Theravāda has often been understated. It is noteworthy that although esoteric traditions were in

1105. See, e.g., McRae 2004 and Davidson 2002a.

principle highly restricted, they often had a major public role in the cultures where they took root: Japanese Zen, for instance, became closely associated with a variety of artistic theories and practices, while tantric Buddhism, in Tibet and elsewhere, provided grand rituals for state occasions and wove tantric concepts and practices into the very fabric of everyday life. In this sense, although *mahāmudrā* strictly speaking was an esoteric term, the esoteric often was not really hidden in Buddhist culture, so it is unsurprising that so rich a concept would take on resonances well beyond its original, restricted milieu.

The larger question within religious studies is: how restricted must religious insights and practices be if they originate in esoteric contexts?[1106] There is a sense, perhaps, in which many, if not all, religions have esoteric origins, in that they begin with an with an individual or group of individuals who impart a novel set of ideas and practices to a small circle of "those with ears to hear." The early Vedic sages with their students, the Buddha with his first five followers, Jesus with his twelve disciples, Muhammad with the first believers in Mecca: all these origin narratives describe a moment at which a vital teaching is shared only with a small group, hence is esoteric. However, if the teaching is vital—and religious teachings often are regarded as being uniquely true and important, uniquely conducive to human flourishing—it must be shared more widely and hence shift from an esoteric mode to an exoteric mode. Such a shift is crucial if a movement is to grow into an institutionalized "religion." Once a tradition has become exoteric, institutional, and complex, however, at least some its adherents will begin to feel that the purity in which the tradition originated has been compromised, and that deep truths have been trivialized. Returning to what they see as the true roots of the tradition, certain sages will insist that they have privileged access to an insight not vouchsafed to everyone and begin teaching that insight to a small circle of like-minded people, thereby instituting an esoteric community within the larger religious community. These esoteric communities, in turn, often take on an institutional power of their own, such that *their* restricted teachings become widespread in the community, reshaping religious culture in the process. This certainly happened with the teachings of the Upaniṣadic sages, the various Sufi and Shi'i orders of premodern Islam, Kabbalist circles in Judaism, and as we have seen, tantric Buddhism in India, Tibet, and elsewhere. Thus Gampopa's—and Panchen Chögyen's—promulgation of an exoteric, sūtra-based mahāmudrā may be seen as part of a larger pattern within religions of the "popularization" of the esoteric.

1106. See, e.g., Bolle 1987.

4. Is Sudden Realization Possible?

Among the various styles of mahāmudrā described by Gampopa and his Kagyüpa successors were gradual approaches to awakening, such as the connate union, and practices like the white panacea and the lightning strike in which realization is attained suddenly or instantaneously—and perhaps independently of any previous effort. In his critique of Kagyü mahāmudrā, Sakya Paṇḍita, insisted that realization never occurs out of the blue and always must be preceded by gradual progress along one or another Buddhist path. Sapaṇ also suggested that the Kagyü enthusiasm for sudden realization was an indication of the degree to which their mahāmudrā discourse had been infected by the discredited Chan views of the Chinese representative at the Samyé debate, Heshang Moheyan. For Sapaṇ, promotion of sudden realization, whether by Heshang or Lama Shang, threatened to undermine the ethical and contemplative groundwork that he saw as essential to Buddhist life and to life in society more generally. Later Kagyüpas defended their view by noting that (a) there are numerous Indian texts that identify sudden realization as a category just as legitimate as the gradual path, (b) *all* realizations are sudden, in the sense that they occur in a specific instant prior to which there was no realization, and (c) all realizations nevertheless must be preceded by some sort of gradual path, however short or long it may be. Thus subitists—those practitioners who seem to attain realization swiftly and suddenly—do so only because they are karmically prepared to do so by their mastery of gradual-path practices—including conventional morality and meditation—in previous lives or perhaps earlier in this life.

Within Buddhism more broadly, the question of how quickly or suddenly one might reach awakening preoccupied contemplatives and scholars from the early years of the tradition.[1107] Thus, while the path to arhatship in Foundational Buddhism is generally represented as a gradual one, the early texts articulate a number of different ways of approaching awakening. The two most notable involve (a) sequential progress through four, eight, or nine meditative absorptions and (b) direct attainment of insight into one or another liberating truth, such as the four noble truths, dependent arising, or no-self. The former approach would appear to be more gradual, the latter rather more sudden, but in either case it seems that the moment of awakening only occurs after significant preparation, whether contemplative or analytical. The Abhidharma traditions of the early centuries CE, such as that described by Vasubandhu in his *Treasury of Higher Knowledge*, also assumed that the path to liberation

1107. See, e.g., Gregory 1987 and Seyfort Ruegg 1989.

was gradual, and although they allowed that one might approach arhatship by uprooting defilements either slowly or quickly, they nowhere described a scenario in which liberation is instantaneous and independent of all previous effort. After the appearance in India first of Mahāyāna sūtras—with their striking accounts of bodhisattvas' flashes of realization—then of tantric literature—especially the songs of mahāsiddhas like Saraha, with their insistence on a direct and dramatic assault on buddhahood—scholarly discussion of sudden and gradual paths became more common, as for instance in the writings of Kamalaśīla and Vimalamitra. Such discussions were even more significant in the Buddhist schools that developed in China and Tibet. The Chan/Zen traditions of East Asia are famous for their exploration of the meaning of sudden awakening, and the topic was analyzed in other schools as well, such as the Tiantai and Huayan. The Chan sudden-realization approach was defended at the Samyé debate by both Heshang Moheyan the Indian master Vimalamitra, and although Chinese influence in Tibet waned soon thereafter, the sudden-gradual distinction continued to be used by Tibetan masters, and to be especially influential within the Nyingma and Kagyü schools. Since mahāmudrā was, for many Tibetan traditions, synonymous with both reality and buddhahood, the speed and style with which it would be realized became subject to debate, as seen in the disagreement between Sapaṇ and the Kagyüpas. Gelukpas, as noted above, recognize the sudden-gradual distinction but do not tend to employ it much.

The larger question within religious studies is: does religious experience, especially mystical experience, have to be preceded by particular practices, or is it sudden, unique, and independent of all effort? Modern scholars are divided as to how important "experience" is within the realm of religion: some, like William James, assert it as the central element of any religion, while others, like Robert Sharf, assail such assertions on the grounds that they are based on projections of a modern, Western preoccupation onto traditions that may be more concerned with other matters.[1108] These debates notwithstanding, it seems hard to deny that human encounters with the sacred or divine—what can we call these but "experiences"?—have proven a powerful motivator in the development and maintenance of religious traditions everywhere. There are, of course, many types of religious experiences that are (usually) quite ordinary, such as reciting scripture, participating in ritual, or listening to a discourse. There are, however, extraordinary experiences, in which individuals feel themselves drawn into the closest possible relation with ultimate reality, however that is conceived—and this is what we typically term *mysticism*.

1108. See, e.g., James 1983, Sharf 1998, and Martin and McCutcheon 2012.

Many of the issues surrounding mysticism will be discussed in the sections to follow; the question here—whether mystical experience is the outcome of systematic practice or occurs independent of such practice—has received various and complex answers in the world's religious traditions.[1109] The discussions in theistic settings are particularly rich and interesting. In Christianity, for instance, mystics have laid out many different techniques conducive to an encounter with God, from Dionysius the Aereopagite's way of subtraction, to Ignatius Loyola's spiritual exercises, to Teresa of Avila's seven mansions, yet no Christian will claim that spiritual striving alone will suffice for the mystic, for the ultimate experience is granted only by the grace of God, who by definition cannot be compelled. Similarly, for all the "stations" of mystical ascent described by Sufis over the centuries, reaching the final mystical outpost is not a matter of human choice but divine will. In each instance, we might argue that the mystical attainment is sudden, and independent of any process that pointed toward it; at the same time, though, the mystic's efforts are not utterly irrelevant, since they make of him or her a suitable vessel for realization. Many Buddhists do not concern themselves with divine grace, and they often are confident that their path, if properly followed, will naturally issue in awakening, but as we have seen, even in a nontheistic tradition, the precise relation between path practices and ultimate realization may not be clear cut. As a result, though mahāmudrā realization is an ideal for many Tibetan Buddhists, the way in which it is achieved remains a topic of serious and sometimes contentious debate.

5. Can a Single Realization Suffice?

In their discussions of such subitist approaches to mahāmudrā as the white panacea, many Kagyüpas asserted that the single, sudden realization of reality that is the great seal is itself an attainment of wisdom sufficient to complete the entire Buddhist path. In his critique of Kagyü mahāmudrā, Sakya Paṇḍita argued that the subitist approach makes buddhahood impossible, because the Mahāyāna path cannot be completed without the accumulation of both wisdom and compassionate methods: properly applied, the former leads to the Dharma body of a buddha and the latter to the form body. The claim that a single realization can suffice to make one a buddha, says Sapaṇ, is yet another example of the Kagyü penchant for adopting the discredited Chan position of Heshang Moheyan. As with other such attacks by Sapaṇ, later Kagyüpas cited Indian precedents for their rhetoric, ranging from the Perfection of Wisdom

1109. See, e.g., Katz 1978.

and other Mahāyāna sūtras to the songs of Saraha, and pointed out, as well, that they did not claim that mahāmudrā realization precludes the exercise of compassion—only that, rather that preceding realization, it may be achieved suddenly and will flow naturally from it.

Within Buddhism more broadly, there has long been ambiguity as to whether awakening, however described, can be brought about through a single, vital realization, or whether it always requires multiple causes and conditions.[1110] From the early scriptures on, Buddhist literature is replete with stories of disciples who seem to have "broken through" to a profound realization of some simple, central truth or truths and thereby become ārya beings, or even arhats or buddhas. Any number of early disciples of the Buddha achieved realization or arhatship on hearing an exposition of the four noble truths or dependent arising, and the early Mahāyāna sūtras are filled with laypeople, monks, and bodhisattvas who as a result of some profound teaching or other—for instance, on emptiness—either conceive the awakening mind or attain a direct realization of the nature of reality. In the East Asian Chan/Zen tradition, the sudden attainment of insight is sometimes seen to suffice for manifesting all the qualities of liberation, while some Pure Land traditions in Japan claim that a single, sincere recitation of the name of Amitābha Buddha will assure our rebirth in Amitābha's western paradise, Sukhāvatī. And in the tantric literature of India and Tibet, especially the songs of the mahāsiddhas, direct realization of the emptiness and luminosity of the mind often seems to be the sole requirement for buddhahood. At the same time, more conservative Buddhist masters always have insisted that progress toward awakening is a multifaceted process, requiring not just moments of profound insight but the discipline of ethical living, skill in meditation, and the cultivation of various virtues. For Mahāyāna scholars, in particular, buddhahood requires the cultivation of both wisdom and method, so while a direct realization of the nature of reality is a necessary condition for awakening, it is *not* a sufficient condition, and claims to the effect that it is all we need in order to awaken, such as are found in the literature of Indian and Tibetan mahāmudrā, must not be taken literally, lest we think that the path is easier to traverse than it really is. Nevertheless, adherents of either position can find plentiful support in Buddhist literature.

The larger question within religious studies is: can any single realization or practice ever be regarded as sufficient for salvation or spiritual liberation? Although much of religious experience is quite quotidian, extraordinary experiences do occur, whether in moments of dramatic conversion or of mystical

1110. See, e.g., Gregory 1987 and Seyfort Ruegg 1989.

rapture, and such experiences prompt reflection on whether they are so utterly transformative for the experiencer as to eliminate all problems and manifest all virtues at a single blow.[1111] The convert or mystic, of course, often feels thus transformed, but members of the tradition within which they operate may not always be so certain. The disciple of a Hindu tantric swami may receive from him or her the energized blessing that is *śaktipat* and feel like a completely new person; or a Christian may be "born again" through unstinting acceptance of Jesus Christ as savior and be confident that all obstacles to living a perfect life have been overcome in an instant; or a nature mystic may feel that, in a moment of communion with the great, starry cosmos, everything suddenly makes sense and life can be lived fully and meaningfully forever after. But are such momentary experiences, however profound and convincing, fully adequate to the spiritual transformation of the experiencer? Whatever the convert or mystic may feel about the adequacy of their experience, most of us will acknowledge their spiritual transformation only on the evidence of words uttered and deeds performed when they are *not* absorbed in religious ecstasy. In short, we will only know them by their fruits—and even if their words and deeds are laudably virtuous, we cannot say for sure that those virtues were all completed at the moment of the transformative experience. Indeed, their practice almost certainly preceded that moment, and still must be developed after the moment has passed. Thus an experience like that of mahāmudrā realization may be pivotal in a person's spiritual development, and convey the subjective sense that everything has been accomplished in a single, dramatic moment, but in fact, such moments are not really separable from what precedes and follows them, and what one does outside the momentary, overwhelming experience is just as important to real transformation as what happens in the moment itself. Transformation may require extraordinary experience, but that experience alone does not, in the end, suffice to effect the transformation.

6. Are We All Already Buddhas?

Among the key Mahāyāna concepts with which mahāmudrā came to be associated was the idea of buddha nature, the notion that all beings eventually will become fully awakened buddhas, replete with buddha bodies and buddha qualities and residing amid a great entourage at the center of a splendid pure land. Because buddha-nature discourse is rooted in the conviction that the mind is fundamentally pure and luminous, and that purity and luminosity

1111. See, e.g., James 1983.

are beginninglessly and endlessly natural to all beings, mahāmudrā rhetoric, especially among Indian mahāsiddhas and subitist Kagyüpas, sometimes veered in the direction of insisting that all beings are already buddhas and that there really is nothing to be done on the spiritual path. Critics of this view, including Sakya Paṇḍita and many others, were quick to point out that if this were so, then there would be no need for practice—or, for that matter, for Buddhism itself. Defenders of mahāmudrā refuted the criticism in various ways. Kagyüpas often pointed out that we do possess natural buddhahood but that it has been forever obscured by delusion and afflictions, and our naturally awakened state will only be revealed through practice of the perfections and other aspects of the path. Gelukpas typically took the claim that we are all already buddhas as a metaphorical way of referring to the mind's conventional qualities of awareness and clarity and its ultimate emptiness of intrinsic existence; it is because of the mind's emptiness that buddha qualities—which are not present prior to awakening—can be developed through gradually practicing the path over the course of time. In either case, proponents of mahāmudrā took the rhetoric of preexisting buddhahood more or less provisionally and thereby provided a rationale for practice of the path, and the continued existence of Buddhism.

Within Buddhism more broadly, the idea that we might all already be buddhas, or any kind of awakened being, is found almost exclusively in Mahāyāna traditions. It is true that Foundational Buddhist literature asserts both the natural luminosity of the mind and the capacity of all beings to attain arhatship—though not buddhahood, which is a rare and special form of arhatship confined to those who have a historical mission to rediscover and propagate the Dharma at regular, widely spaced intervals in cosmic time. Traditional commentators, however, did not, as a rule, interpret these concepts to imply that we are all already arhats; to become an arhat required systematic practice of ethics, concentration, and wisdom, or the eightfold noble path, or the thirty-seven limbs of awakening. In some early Mahāyāna literature, on the other hand—for instance the Perfection of Wisdom, *Teaching of Vimalakīrti*, or *Flower Ornament* sūtras[1112]—the authors' indulgence in paradoxical extremes of negation and affirmation often resulted in the apparent claim that all beings are, in fact, already buddhas, whether because they truly possess buddha qualities from the beginning or because buddhahood is equivalent to emptiness and all beings are by nature empty. Such rhetoric was especially common in the Chan/Zen tradition, whose masters delighted in the paradoxical assertion that all beings are buddhas and no being is buddha.

1112. See, respectively, e.g., Conze 1973 and Conze 1993; Thurman 1976; and Cleary 1993.

As late as the thirteenth century, the Japanese Sōtō Zen master Dōgen took as his animating question, why, if all beings are buddhas, is practice necessary? (His answer: as an expression of the awakening we already possess.) The assertion that all beings already are buddhas also is prominent in tantric literature, especially in such "higher" tantras as the Hevajra and Kālacakra, and in the songs of Saraha, Tilopa, and other mahāsiddhas. Sometimes the claim is deployed there as another of way of talking about emptiness and/or buddha nature; at other times it is used, in a quasi-cosmogonic sense, to imply that the entire cosmos, with its inhabitants, is itself merely an emanation of a primordial buddha—which itself is indistinguishable from emptiness, however that may be conceived. Although, as noted, approaches such as these found some purchase among proponents of mahāmudrā in Tibet, they were, and are, especially important in the discourse of the Nyingma great perfection, which is more amenable to notions of the cosmos-as-divine-emanation than are the New Translation schools.

The larger question within religious studies is: is the basic state of our mind, or soul, truly pure and free, and merely waiting to be uncovered, or is our nature sufficiently deluded or sinful that our purity and freedom must be cultivated? In such Asian-based traditions as Mahāyāna Buddhism, Advaita Hinduism, and philosophical Daoism, it is perfectly reasonable—if perhaps problematic—to assert that all beings not only have the capacity to realize and identify with the ultimate nature of reality but that they may already be at one with it. Thus, a Hindu may cite the Upaniṣads to affirm, "I have always been Brahman"; a Buddhist, as we have seen, may say, "I am already a buddha"; and a Daoist may claim, "I have forever been one with the Dao." Each will, in their own way, have to qualify these radical claims so as to allow room for the recognition that our present situation does not, at first blush, seem to justify the claim, and that spiritual practice therefore is required—yet for each there is some sense that we all have within us, indeed we *are*, the fundamental reality with which we must consciously identify if we are to be free. This sort of claim, which is either explicitly or implicitly monistic—is not so easily made within the confines of, for instance, the Abrahamic traditions. No theologically observant Jew, Christian, or Muslim can claim "I am God" without risking charges of blasphemy, for the orthodox ontology of each of these religions is fundamentally dualistic, in the sense that a basic distinction must be maintained between God and God's creation. To assert that God and God's creation are identical—to see God as immanent but not transcendent—is to succumb to pantheism, which robs God of his metaphysical dignity by equating him with the phenomenal, conditioned world of which he is the creator. At the same time, each tradition acknowledges that humans have within them something like the "image" of God, which allows us to know him, if not become him. Further, certain mystics within these traditions risked (and sometimes received) censure by going even further, as when Meister Eckhart talked of the Godhead within each person, or Ibn 'Arabi spoke of the cosmos, including humans, as being a mere reflection, or even emanation, of God's perfect qualities. However radical their rhetoric, though, even the mystics, not to mention more orthodox thinkers, admitted that humans have been alienated from God and that reconciliation with the divine requires some effort, some cultivation. In this sense, then, despite differences in ontology, a range of religious traditions agree that, on the one hand, we all possess the divine within us to some degree and, on the other, we have strayed from our divinity and can only be freed to enjoy it through some degree of spiritual cultivation.

7. What Sort of Negation Is Emptiness?

One of the most vigorously debated questions among Madhyamaka philosophers was whether emptiness—the true nature of things that must be realized in mahāmudrā meditation—is a simple, nonaffirming negation, which implies nothing positive at all, or an implicative, affirming negation, which suggests that something is "left over" after phenomena—or their falsely imputed true existence—have been negated. In a mahāmudrā context, this is particularly important with reference to the cognition that realizes the emptiness of the mind. Proponents of emptiness as an affirming negation, including many Kagyüpas (not to mention Nyingmapas and Jonangpas), argued that taking emptiness as a negation pure and simple—especially in the case of the luminosity/emptiness of the awakened mind—fails to do justice to "positive" interpretations of emptiness found in many sūtras, the treatises of Maitreya and Asaṅga, and tantric literature. They feared, as well, that such an understanding of negation might lead to a nihilistic reading of emptiness in general and to a denigration of the awakened state in particular. Proponents of emptiness as a nonaffirming negation, like the Gelukpas (and many Sakyapas), asserted that such a reading is most consistent with discourse in the Perfection of Wisdom sūtras and the writings of Nāgārjuna and Candrakīrti. They expressed the fear that if anything is "left over" in emptiness—even the emptiness of the awakened mind—then what is left over—for instance luminous, empty awareness—may become an object of self-grasping, hence take us further from awakening rather than closer to it. As a result, say Gelukpas, descriptions of emptiness as an affirming negation must be taken as provisional claims, requiring further interpretation in light of the definitive assertion that, in the final analysis, it is only and ever a nonaffirming negation.

Within Buddhism more broadly, there long have been two strands of discourse about ultimate reality and the ultimate attainment. The tradition is perhaps best known for its negative rhetoric, but from the very outset positive descriptions have been common as well. In Foundational Buddhism, for instance, a permanent self, or *ātman*, like that asserted in Hindu traditions is commonly refuted, and the person analyzed into five impermanent constituent factors, or aggregates, but the Buddha and his interpreters were quite willing to speak of a conventional person who "bears the burden" of being born, suffering, dying, and being reborn.[1113] By the same token, the liberated state of nirvāṇa means "extinction." It often is said to be indescribable, and when it is described, it often is described negatively, as, for instance, the absence of ignorance and other defilements. At the same time, nirvāṇa is described positively, too, whether as bliss, or knowledge, or an island, or a lamp; it also is typically regarded as pure and unchangeable.[1114] These two rhetorical tendencies are found in Mahāyāna Buddhism as well. Negative descriptions of reality and buddhahood abound in the Perfection of Wisdom and many other early Great Vehicle sūtras, and in the writings of such early Mādhyamika thinkers as Nāgārjuna, Āryadeva, Buddhapālita, and Candrakīrti. There, all phenomena, "from form to omniscience," are empty of intrinsic existence in the sense of a nonaffirming negation—realization of which is the *sine qua non* for awakening, which itself must be seen as utterly devoid of self-existence. At the same time, more positive accounts of reality and realization arose in the literature of the Yogācāra school: while accepting the centrality of the concept of emptiness, such sūtras as the *Descent to Laṅkā* and *Unraveling the Intention* and such treatises as the *Ornament of Mahāyāna Sūtras* and the *Sublime Continuum*[1115] tended to articulate emptiness as an affirming negation, especially in the case of the mind, which typically was described as pure and luminous, and often asserted to be primordially awakened, or even to be the true source and substance of everything in the cosmos. These positive and negative strands of discourse became intertwined in subsequent Buddhist philosophy, culture, and aesthetics, whether in Yogācāra-Svātantrika-Madhyamaka thought in India; tantric traditions of theory and practice in India, Tibet, and East Asia; major East Asian schools such as Tiantai/Tendai, Huayan/Kegon, and Chan/Zen; and even Theravāda in Southeast Asia. Thus recondite issues of the nature of negation, which resonated through philosophical discussions of mahāmudrā in Tibet, turn out to reflect major trends in Buddhist thought.

1113. See, e.g., Collins 1990.

1114. See, e.g., Collins 2006.

1115. See, respectively, e.g., Suzuki 1978, Powers 1995, Thurman 2014, and Brunnhölzl 2014.

The larger question within religious studies is: what is the relation between "negative" and "positive" descriptions of the ultimate or divine?[1116] Just as Buddhist discourse is woven from strands of both negative and positive ways of imagining reality and realization, so it seems are the discourses of virtually all religious traditions. All definitions of religion are necessarily limited and debatable, but a case may be made that one common characteristic of the world's religions is their attempts to imagine and articulate a higher or ultimate reality that stands as the measure of human striving and an ideal toward which we ought to strive. Typically, this ultimate—whether we call it God, Brahman, Buddha, Dao, or Wakan Tanka—is said to radically transcend ordinary human thinking and striving, and to be more true, more real, more beautiful, and more good than anything else. It is, in short, the most important thing there is. Because it transcends ordinary thought and speech, it beggars description, or requires negative descriptions; but because knowledge and appreciation of it is vital to human flourishing and freedom, it must be described, and must at times be described in positive terms, lest it seem completely inaccessible. Discourse about God in Christian mystical theology illustrates well the perils and possibilities of each type of discourse. The apophatic way, or *via negativa*, of figures like Dionysius the Aereopagite, Meister Eckhart, or the author of *The Cloud of Unknowing* covers God in a "divine darkness" that allows us to see how utterly different from the world God is, and to enter into states of mind that are devoid of ordinary ideas, attitudes, and emotions. At the same time, such a way is deep and difficult, and the potential for getting lost in the metaphysical or meditative shadows, or even of losing God altogether, is very real. The cataphatic way, or *via positiva*, of the likes of Teresa of Avila, Ignatius Loyola, or Thomas Traherne tries to make God accessible through images and descriptions that are easily accessible to human thought and emotion, whether in Teresa's passionate love mysticism, where Christ is the bridegroom and we the brides; Ignatius's spiritual exercises, where we visualize ourselves amid scenes of Christ's life; or Traherne's quasi-pantheism, where all of nature is said to be an expression of God. At the same time, such ways of "figuring" God run the risk of making the divine too accessible, and lulling us into the complacent belief that God is *just like* love, or imagination, or nature. One Christian mystic in whom the apophatic and cataphatic are combined is St. John of the Cross, who composed some of the most eloquent accounts of divine darkness ever expressed yet also wrote passionate lyrics about Christ as lover. We could adduce comparable examples

1116. See, e.g., Sells 1994 and Egan 1978.

from many other traditions,[1117] but for now suffice it to say that the problem of whether to describe reality and the divine in positive or negative terms is one faced not just by Tibetan mahāmudrā masters but by religious thinkers everywhere.

8. Of What Is Buddha Mind Empty?

At the end of the path, buddhahood and mahāmudrā are synonymous. Buddha mind is, of course, regarded as empty, but there was disagreement among Tibetans as to what it is empty *of*. Those propounding *shentong*, or "extrinsic emptiness" (Jonangpas above all, but also many Kagyüpas and Nyingmapas, and the occasional Sakyapa), claimed that buddha mind is empty of anything saṃsāric but is itself intrinsically pure, real, and possessed of all the qualities of awakening. Those upholding the *rangtong*, or "intrinsic emptiness," view (Gelukpas, most Sakyapas, and some Kagyüpas and Nyingmapas) said that buddha mind is empty in exactly the same way as saṃsāric phenomena are, in the sense of lacking intrinsic existence. In the language of the previous section, shentongpas tend to view buddha mind's emptiness as an affirming negation, while rangtongpas see it as a nonaffirming negation. Shentongpas accused rangtongpas of bringing buddhahood down to the level of conventional phenomena and of failing to understand the profound nature of the mind and mahāmudrā experience. Rangtongpas accused shentongpas of absolutizing buddhahood to the point where their view was little more than crypto-Hinduism, and of denigrating the conventional world. Over the centuries, a number of attempts were made to mediate the dispute, for instance by pointing out that the shentong view comes in many varieties, some more subtle and philosophically defensible than others; or by arguing that rangtongpas and shentongpas inhabit different realms of discourse, with the former focusing on purely philosophical argumentation and the latter most concerned to provide a way of making sense of meditative experience, especially in the context of such advanced tantric systems as the great perfection or the completion stage of unexcelled yoga tantra. Such attempts at harmonizing the two views may or may not be compelling, but they do carry with them the message that, whatever one's view of mahāmudrā as emptiness or mahāmudrā as buddhahood, there may be more agreement than meets

1117. Examples might include the tension in Hinduism between unqualified (*nirguṇa*) Brahman and qualified (*saguṇa*) Brahman or the Daoist distinction between the Dao as it is, empty, and the Dao as manifest in "the world of ten thousand things."

the eye, and in any case, finding room for both perspectives may be spiritually salubrious.

Within Buddhism more broadly, the problem of the relation between the conventional world and states of realization or awakening has been endlessly debated.[1118] Foundational Buddhist traditions tended to equate the conventional world with saṃsāra, seeing it as utterly impure, and pervaded by the "three characteristrics" of all phenomena: impermanence, suffering, and absence of self. By contrast, nirvāṇa was marked by its *lack* of everything saṃsāric: in it, there are no five aggregates, nor is there any suffering—and while it is not asserted to be or possess a self, it is often said to be completely pure and beyond temporality and change, hence in some way, perhaps, "permanent." Despite this bifurcation, Foundational Buddhist traditions recognized that the transition from saṃsāra to nirvāṇa cannot, typically, be made in one fell swoop, and that the body, and conventional ideas and practices, however "corrupt" they may be, must be utilized in the service of awakening. If the earlier traditions tended, at least on a conceptual level, to radically separate nirvāṇa from saṃsāra, in Mahāyāna literature the divide was to some degree bridged. In the Perfection of Wisdom sūtras and the writings of Nāgārjuna, for instance, nirvāṇa is negated—that is, regarded as empty—as surely as is saṃsāra; conversely, in sūtras like the *Teaching of Vimalakīrti* and the *Flower Ornament*, the conventional world often is identified as a pure land, and its inhabitants as incipient, if not actual, buddhas.[1119] In this sense, for at least some Mahāyānists, the difference between saṃsāra and nirvāṇa is not between two separate realms, but between two different ways of seeing the single realm inhabited by all beings, whether they are ordinary or awakened. The rhetorical tendency to collapse saṃsāra into nirvāṇa, and vice versa, became prominent in the Chan/Zen traditions of East Asia and the tantric traditions that originated in India and spread to Tibet and other parts of Inner Asia. It is worth recalling, however, that even the most radical Mahāyāna thinkers—such as Nāgārjuna, Huineng, or Saraha—still operated within a basic soteriological framework in which saṃsāra and nirvāṇa were valid, and distinct, categories: there might, ultimately speaking, be no difference between the two, but conventionally speaking, sentient beings find themselves in an unsatisfactory condition ("saṃsāra") and must attain a satisfactory state ("nirvāṇa") through conventional practices and realizations—including the realization that there is no ultimate difference between saṃsāra into nirvāṇa! Thus Tibetan debates

1118. See, e.g., Cowherds 2010.

1119. See, respectively, Thurman 1976 and Cleary 1993.

about mahāmudrā in terms of rangtong or shentong reflect broader patterns of argumentation in Buddhist traditions as a whole.

The larger question within religious studies is: how does the phenomenal world stand in relation to the sacred, or the ultimately real? As Western scholars of religion such as Émile Durkheim and Mircea Eliade have noted, one of the characteristics of religions wherever we find them, and whatever their metaphysics, is an explicit or implicit assertion that the cosmos is divisible into two realms, the sacred and the profane.[1120] The latter is the quotidian, more or less unsatisfactory world we inhabit most of the time, while the former is that which is most real, most true, and most good: the ultimate. One way, then, to understand what we call "religion" is as a set of processes whereby humans mark out certain places, times, persons, words, and actions as stemming from or related to that which is most real, true, and good—the sacred. The deepest purpose of human life, thus, is to gain access to the sacred as often and in as many ways as possible, tapping the deepest wellsprings of one's being so as to make life in the profane realm fully meaningful. On this, most religions more or less agree. Where they tend to part company, both among and within themselves, is on the question of how closely related the sacred and profane are. It is tempting to assert that many Asian (and indigenous) traditions—whose ontologies frequently are monistic, nondualistic, or naturalistic—tend to see the boundary between the sacred and profane as fairly permeable, while Abrahamic traditions, with their dualist ontologies, maintain a strict division between the two. However, it may well be that particular ontologies are less significant for the practice of religion than we think. Asian traditions, including Buddhism, Hinduism, and Daoism, typically are divided internally on how to demarcate the sacred-profane distinction—and even when they seem to soften or collapse it, they still maintain it to some degree. Abrahamic traditions also vary within and among themselves on the question. Christians may divide the cosmos sharply into God and God's creation, but they do believe that the incarnation of Christ provides a connecting point between two otherwise irreconcilable realms, and they are far from unanimous on the value of the world and how to live within it. Muslims, asserting a similar basic ontology, see the Qur'ān as a bridge between the incomparable majesty of God and those of us living in God's creation and, like Christians, vary in their attitude toward the conventional world, with some loathing it and others exalting it. In all religious settings, then, from Tibetan mahāmudrā debates about extrinsic and intrinsic emptiness to Abrahamic discussions of the value of the world, the tension between the sacred and the profane must remain: if the sacred is

1120. See, respectively, Eliade 1987 and Durkheim 2008.

absolutely transcendent, then we have no access to it, while if it is collapsed into the profane, then life may turn out to be without foundation or purpose. For most religions, maintaining a sensible balance between the two is the key to a meaningful and fruitful existence.

9. What Is Serenity and What Is Insight?

Serenity and insight are the two major goals of meditation in nearly all Buddhist traditions, and a "union" of the two is often thought necessary for attaining direct realization of the nature of reality and the awakening that stems from that realization. Unsurprisingly, then, most Tibetans who wrote about mahāmudrā as a meditation system (rather than as, say, a tantric consort, primordial luminosity, emptiness, or buddhahood) framed the practice in terms of the attainment of serenity and insight on the basis of placement meditation and investigative meditation, respectively, with the mind itself as the object. Since most meditation manuals were written for "beginners," placement meditation leading to serenity was generally the starting point, with investigative meditation leading to insight following on that. More advanced practitioners might aim first at insight, then develop serenity on the basis of that. Whatever their order, when the mind itself is made the object of meditation, both serenity and insight are attained by resting in an open and formless state, so the lines between the two are sometimes hard to draw. Thus, for instance, Paṇchen Chögyen describes the experience of both serenity and insight as a "pure vacuity" (*stong sang*), raising phenomenological questions as to whether the pure vacuity experienced in serenity meditation is the same as or different from the pure vacuity experienced in insight meditation. Along somewhat similar lines, Kagyüpas often considered such experiences as vacuity, bliss, clarity, and nonduality as byproducts of *both* serenity and insight, leading to similar questions about what difference there might be between identically described serenity-based experiences and those rooted in insight.

Paṇchen Chögyen and his Gelukpa successors argued that experiences of vacuity, bliss, clarity, and nonduality (at least as described by certain latter-day Kagyüpas) were functions of "mere" serenity meditation, useful for introducing the conventional nature of the mind but not impinging on the ultimate. For their part, Kagyüpas did acknowledge that such experiences could mislead a meditator into thinking that he or she had progressed further than was the case, but they were able to defend their association of those experiences with the attainment of insight by appealing to scriptural sources, especially the tantras and the songs of the mahāsiddhas—which, of course, were cited copiously by Gelukpas, as well. Disagreements on such boundary questions aside, Tibetan mahāmudrā masters were unanimous in recognizing that meditational experiences—from vacuity, bliss, clarity, and nonduality to the "blank" state supposedly championed by Heshang Moheyan—could easily deceive the meditator into a false sense of accomplishment, and unanimous as well in instructing their disciples to practice both serenity and insight meditation, as well as the combination of the two, in their pursuit of mahāmudrā as the outcome of a proper Buddhist path.

Within Buddhism more broadly, the categories of serenity and insight are ancient and pervasive, having become standard not long after the tradition's founding, and shaping discourse about meditation throughout the Buddhist world ever since. In the scriptures taken as canonical by the Foundational Buddhist schools, however, the necessity of cultivating both kinds of meditative experience is not always immediately apparent. In the Pāli canon, for instance, a text like the *Discourse on the Noble Quest* (*Ariyapariyesanā Sutta*) seems to endorse the attainment of arhatship solely through placement meditation that leads one through states of absorption (*jhāna*), with no real mention of insight; conversely, the *Great Discourse on Mindfulness* (*Mahāsatipaṭṭhāna Sutta*) focuses more or less exclusively on meditative investigation into the body, sensations, mental states, and the categories of reality, with little indication of the importance of serenity.[1121] Regardless of whether such textual disparities indicate the presence of multiple and perhaps incompatible approaches to awakening in early Buddhism, scholastic traditions within the Foundational schools soon bridged the gap with their insistence that neither serenity nor insight alone was sufficient for liberation. Rather, a meditator must master each and then combine them, such that one views the deepest truth—whether the four noble truths, dependent arising, or no-self—with a mind of serenity. When one does so, one is transformed from an ordinary person to an *ārya*, a noble being, and begins the process of uprooting one's defilements rather than merely suppressing them—which is all that serenity meditation can accomplish on its own.

This approach became generally accepted in all subsequent Buddhist traditions, including Indian Mahāyāna, the various East Asian schools, and Indian and Inner Asian tantric lineages. That did not mean, however, that there were no tensions or complexities to resolve. Advanced meditation is a difficult and sometimes unpredictable process, and Buddhists debated among themselves whether this or that style of meditation (say, observing the breath, or visualization) was better classed as serenity or insight; whether serenity ought to

1121. These are, respectively, *Majjhima Nikāya* suttas 26 and 10; see, e.g., Ñāṇamoli and Bodhi 1995, 253ff. and 145ff., respectively.

precede insight or vice versa; at precisely what point they ought to be combined; and whether this or that "profound" experience truly had salvific value or was merely a byproduct of deep states of concentration or absorption, useful for suppressing defilements or gaining yogic attainments but not sufficiently steeped in the nature of things to lead to awakening. As with mahāmudrā, many of the subtlest Buddhist meditations involved states of mind that were highly attenuated, or even entirely vacuous, and it was not always easy to determine whether an experience of vacuity was a genuine realization of emptiness or simply a case of "spacing out." By the same token, it was hard to know, at times, whether the bliss often accompanying meditation was the bliss of realization or liberation, or just a "blissed out" state of concentration. Such questions are at the heart of Foundational Buddhist discussions of the importance of the absorptions over against mindfulness meditation, Mahāyāna discourse about the meditations of a bodhisattva, the Samyé debate between Chan and Indian masters in eighth-century Tibet, and considerations of the nature of contemplative experience in tantric traditions, so it is to be expected that such matters would come to the attention of mahāmudrā masters—as, indeed, they did.

The larger question within religious studies is: what kinds of inner experience are liberative and which are not, and why? Buddhists were far from alone in asking which sorts of inner experiences were genuinely mystical or transformative and which were delusive or even destructive. Other traditions, as surely as Buddhism, recognized the rarity, delicacy, and difficulty of real visionary or contemplative states, and they recognized, as well, the human capacity for self-deception in the face of the overwhelming sense of conviction that often accompanies extraordinary experiences. They recognized, too, that such events can have powerful influence not just on those who experience them but in the religious community as a whole. And given the importance of maintaining certain boundaries and standards within a community, the determination of which experiences are authentic and which spurious became an important priority. The claim, frequent in the early twentieth century, that mystics inevitably pose a threat to the religious status quo, has long since been debunked, by citing the common instances in which (a) mystics were themselves upholders of orthodoxy and (b) the orthodox have used the reports and writings of mystics to uphold their viewpoint.[1122] However, the power and persuasiveness of mystical experience has at times led mystics to speak or write in ways that appear to counter orthodoxy. From the Sufi "martyr" al-Hallaj, to the German friar Meister Eckhart, to Saraha and other Hindu and Buddhist tantric

1122. See, e.g., Katz 1984.

siddhas, to the Jewish antinomian prophet Sabbatai Zevi, mystics sometimes have been held to go beyond the limits of acceptable speech and behavior, and to threaten the community. If their unorthodox ways are rooted in their mystical experiences, then there is all the more reason to assure that boundaries and standards are established for such experiences. But the delineation and regulation of extraordinary experience is just as much a concern of mystical communities, such as monasteries, as of the religious community writ large, precisely because it is particularly within those communities that mystical experience is taken most seriously.

Hence, it becomes vitally important for scholars and mystics alike to discern which experiences might be helpful to the spiritual quest and which might be unhelpful or even deleterious. Depending on their particular theologies, anthropologies, and institutional concerns, different communities will determine these matters in different ways. Hence, Muhammad wondered whether his encounters with the angel Gabriel were genuine or a sign of madness; Teresa of Avila debated, both to herself and with her spiritual director, whether her visions of Christ were God-sent, a product of her own fevered imagination, or truly diabolical; and the Japanese Zen master Hakuin repeatedly doubted the validity of his enlightenment experiences, some of which were rejected by his master as delusive and others of which were acknowledged as genuine. Tibetan debates about serenity and insight in relation to mahāmudrā meditation may seem a far cry from these concerns, but the concern is really the same: to determine which sorts of practice and experience are conducive to freedom and which are not. In a context where the attainment of a spiritual *summum bonum* is the highest human goal, few questions could be more crucial.

10. Is There a Place for Reason in Mahāmudrā?

In both India and Tibet, mahāmudrā masters often embraced a rhetoric that was dismissive of conceptuality in general and of philosophical analysis in particular. The great poet-siddha Saraha was especially emphatic on this score, mocking scholars and philosophers alike while insisting that mahāmudrā is utterly inaccessible to reason or analytical thought. His critique of rationality and insistence on the inconceivability of the ultimate reality and realization was echoed by other mahāsiddhas, and by a range of Tibetan masters, including Milarepa, Gampopa, Lama Shang, and many others, both within and outside the Kagyü fold. In Tibet, anti-rational rhetoric was perhaps most pronounced in the mahāmudrā masters' spiritual songs, but it is also found at times in their treatises and meditation manuals as well—and in any case it is undeniably a key theme in great-seal discourse. At the same time, few if any mahāmudrā masters saw philosophical analysis as totally useless. Figures like Maitrīpa, Gampopa, Rangjung Dorjé, Gö Lotsāwa, and Pema Karpo, to name just a few, were first-rate scholars and thinkers, and asserted the need for rational analysis at certain points along the mahāmudrā path, most often in the context of ascertainment of the view in general and the practice of insight meditation in particular. For none of them, though, was rational understanding a sufficient condition for the realization or attainment of the great seal—and there is some question as to whether they even regarded it as a necessary condition.

Gelukpa mahāmudrā masters from Paṇchen Chögyen onward agreed that rational analysis is not a sufficient condition for realizing or attaining the great seal but, inspired by Tsongkhapa, they were more likely than their Kagyüpa counterparts to suggest that it is a necessary condition. Indeed, they tended to insist that the direct realization of mahāmudrā as emptiness *must* be preceded by proper philosophical analysis along the lines suggested by Nāgārjuna and Candrakīrti, and that despite the apparent gulf between conceptual thought and direct, nondual realization, the former in fact naturally flows into the latter. Kagyüpas, for their part, were more likely to see realization as possible only when analytical reasoning is dropped. These differences aside, it should be reiterated that all Tibetan traditions accept that direct realization of the truth transcends rationality, and that nearly all of them agree that there is *some* role for rationality on the path to that realization, even if they disagree on just how important that role should be.

Within Buddhism more broadly, the place of philosophy and rationality has long been debated. The Buddha depicted in the discourses of the Foundational Buddhist tradition seems quite familiar with the philosophical traditions of his day. He frequently engages in debate with members of other communities, pointing out defects in their doctrines. Indeed, the *Net of Brahmā*, the very first sūtra of the first, "long" collection of sūtras,[1123] consists mostly of a critique of sixty-two actual or possible philosophical views. The Buddha, however, is also presented as a pragmatist who resists philosophy for its own sake. He insists on several occasions that all he teaches is "suffering and its ending" and famously refuses to answer a set of metaphysical questions—about the nature of the world, the "soul," and final nirvāṇa—on the grounds that they are irrelevant to spiritual liberation. Further, in a number of Pāli texts regarded by scholars as quite early—the "Chapter of Eights"

1123. *Dīgha Nikāya* sutta 1, trans., e.g., Walshe 1995, 67–90.

in the *Sutta Nipāta*[1124]—the Buddha seems to eschew philosophy, stating that the Tathāgata is free from all opinions and views. None of this is to say that the Buddha dismissed rationality entirely, but his strong emphasis on attaining truth and freedom through direct experience rather than hearsay, faith, or reason established from the outset of the tradition a tension that has remained until the present day.

Subsequent Buddhists, in South Asia and elsewhere, tried to make sense of the reason-experience divide in a variety of ways. The Abhidharma masters of both Foundational and Mahāyāna Buddhism created vast analytical superstructures in order to make sense of the world, persons, and the path to liberation in terms that did not require a cosmic or individual self, and in so doing they often seemed to let rationality override other concerns, yet they saw themselves as creating analytical tools that would promote realization and liberation. Read a certain way, the Perfection of Wisdom sūtras seem aimed at the destruction of the Abhidharma edifice, and perhaps of reason itself—everything, after all, is empty—yet they gave rise to a vast commentarial and philosophical literature. Similarly, the writings of Nāgārjuna seem to use reason to undermine our confidence in reason, leaving us only with nonconceptual realization of reality, yet they too became the root of a vast philosophical enterprise, the Madhyamaka. As its name suggests, the Yogācāra ("practice of yoga") school grew out of an interest in experience and realization, yet it produced some of the most erudite and complex philosophical treatises ever written by Buddhists. By the same token, traditions that employ a "rhetoric of immediacy,"[1125] such as the Chan/Zen school of East Asia or the radical tantric movements to which many Indian mahāsiddhas belonged, both arose from and were interpreted within the great intellectual traditions against which they appeared to react. In the end, we can only say that the problem of the relation between reason and experience in Buddhism has never been fully solved: each tradition, or individual, finds a balance that seems appropriate in their own context. All Buddhists agree that liberation finally transcends mere rationality, but they disagree over the proper role that philosophical analysis ought to play in moving us toward liberation. The final word, perhaps, should be Nāgārjuna's: "The ultimate is not taught without recourse to conventions, but nirvāṇa is not attained without proceeding by way of the ultimate."[1126]

The larger question within religious studies is: does rationality have a place in religious traditions that insist that reason must be transcended, and if so,

1124. See, e.g., Fronsdal 2016 and Bodhi 2017, esp. 294–312.

1125. See Faure 1994.

1126. *Root Verses on the Middle Way* 24.10, in, e.g., Ng*MKs* 273.

what is that place? It is very nearly definitive of a religion that its adherents believe that the ultimate reality they take as their pole star cannot fully be comprehended by reason; indeed, if they believed that reason could encompass the ultimate, they would be philosophers rather than religious folk. Along similar lines, religious people typically assert that the profoundest experiences accessible to humans, whether those be visions, divine revelations, or states of mystical absorption, only are possible when philosophy ends and rational processes are short-circuited. At the same time, all religious traditions have a doctrinal and philosophical component, and in most cases, rational reflection upon, and incorporation of, doctrines is an important part of living religiously and attaining whatever the *summum bonum* may be.[1127] The question that is begged by this last observation, however, is *how* important rational reflection is to religious life and spiritual realization.

Reading the hagiographic literature of various traditions, we might be inclined to answer, "Not much." Such literature is full of stories of men and women who had to transcend mundane conventions and intellectual structures in order to gain true religious experience. It is said, for instance, that Thomas Aquinas, on having a mystical experience late in life, declared all his theological writings to be no more valuable than straw. The great Islamic legal scholar and theologian, al-Ghazzali, gave up his post at the University of Baghdad to live with Sufi mystics for a decade. In a similar fashion, as we have seen, the Indian Buddhist scholar Nāropa gave up the abbacy of Nālandā University to go in search of the mahāsiddha Tilopa—and himself eventually became a mahāsiddha. These are only a few of many examples that can be found in religious literature that illustrate, or argue for, the primacy of direct experience rather than intellect in religious life. Yet the philosophical and commentarial writings of an Aquinas, Ghazzali, or Nāropa remain, and are treasured in the traditions to which they belong, so we have to wonder, to what degree did they, or their traditions, truly abandon reason? Indeed, as was the case in mahāmudrā traditions and in Buddhism generally, so in other religious settings, rationality—whether it is regarded as integral to the spiritual life from beginning to end or merely a necessary evil to be transcended as soon as possible—is an inescapable part of being human, hence an element that must be weighed as one goes about attempting to live in proper harmony with the nature of reality.

1127. See, e.g., Katz 1978 and Katz 1984.

11. Is There a Place for Devotion in Mahāmudrā?

Since it often described as the empty nature of the mind, the inconceivable buddhahood that awaits at the end of the path, or a meditation system for realizing the former and attaining the latter, mahāmudrā can seem to inhabit a sort of "negative space," in that it typically is viewed in terms of absence rather than presence, openness rather than concreteness, and coolness rather than emotion. On the face of it, therefore, it does not give much scope for amazement, devotion, joy, or other affective elements of religious life. Such an impression may be heightened by a selective reading of the songs of such Indian mahāsiddhas as Saraha and Tilopa, who mock the devotion shown to their deities by Hindus and are willing to negate the Buddha, as well, in the service of cutting through appearances so as to realize the nature of reality. It is easy, too, for someone outside the tradition to read mahāmudrā literature—especially meditation manuals—so as to "cut to the chase" and focus only on instructions for gaining serenity and insight, or practicing the four yogas, while ignoring the preliminary practices that set one up for such "actual" meditations.

What we miss when we find in the songs of the mahāsiddhas little or no religious sentiment, or read mahāmudrā manuals solely for their instructions on contemplating the nature of mind, is the crucial role that religious emotions—especially devotion—actually do play in mahāmudrā practice. Thus, when we read the songs of Saraha more fully, we cannot ignore the degree to which—however much he may criticize religious devotion in other contexts—he is openly and absolutely beholden to his guru for receiving instructions on how to realize mahāmudrā, and unabashed in his expression of amazement and joy at the fruits of realization. Along similar lines, the hagiographies of the mahāsiddha Nāropa detail the intensely devoted service he performed for his guru Tilopa so as to receive instruction on mahāmudrā and other tantric topics. Guru devotion is just as evident in Tibetan mahāmudrā meditation manuals. Not only do nearly all manuals—like much Tibetan religious literature—begin with obeisance to the guru, but the practice of mahāmudrā meditation, whether sudden or gradual in approach, is necessarily preceded by guru yoga. While guru yoga takes many forms, in a mahāmudrā context it typically requires that we visualize the guru before us, request blessings from the guru with intense devotion, and eventually absorb the guru into us, feeling that our minds have merged. That then becomes the basis for mahāmudrā meditation and realization. In their oral instructions and writings, Tibetan masters often differed on the relative emphasis they placed on guru yoga and the actual mahāmudrā meditation on the nature of mind, but they were unanimous in seeing devotion to one's master as a *sine qua non* for practicing and attaining the great seal. What's more, the lives and writings of both Indian and Tibetan siddhas make it clear that they extended devotion not only to their gurus but to various tantric deities as well—that indeed, their lives were steeped in devotion to one or another embodiment of buddhahood.

Within Buddhism more broadly, just as in mahāmudrā, the place of devotion—and religious emotion more generally—may appear to be uncertain, but such is not the case. The Buddha of the Foundational canons does not typically display a strongly affective side. Calm and controlled, he rarely seems prey to the emotional ups and downs of ordinary beings, and to the degree that, as the ideal being, he is a model for others to follow, his disciples would be expected to keep their emotions in check in a similar way. In his teachings, too, the Buddha seems to discourage excessive emotion, and to be as suspicious of claims to religious realization based on faith and devotion as he is of claims based solely on reason, asking simply that his students "come and see" the truth for themselves.[1128] At the same time, disciples who had not yet attained the direct realization enjoyed by an arhat or ārya only could proceed on the basis of some sort of faith in what the Buddha taught. And indeed faith, or confidence (*śraddhā*), was from quite early on listed as the first of five cardinal Buddhist virtues, along with energy, mindfulness, concentration, and wisdom. Also, while the Buddha may have hoped that his disciples would gain realization without recourse to either faith or reason, it is evident from the early texts that many of his students were deeply devoted to him, that their devotion facilitated, or even brought about, their realization, and that realization itself often was accompanied by such affective states as joy and contentment.

Similarly, certain early Mahāyāna texts—such as the Perfection of Wisdom sūtras and the writings of Nāgārjuna— seem to employ negative rhetoric to deconstruct virtually any idea or emotion ever entertained by a Buddhist, including devotion, so as to look unblinkingly at the empty nature of things. Once again, though, a more complete reading undermines this impression. The bodhisattvas who are the heroes of the Great Vehicle sūtras and models for us all are passionately devoted both to the Buddha and to the welfare of all sentient beings, while Nāgārjuna, despite his often relentlessly analytical style, is also the author of devotional songs directed to the Buddha.[1129] It is worth noting that later traditions that revel in critical, negative rhetoric, such

1128. See, e.g., the famous discourse to the Kālāmas in the *Kesaputtiya Sutta; Aṅguttara Nikāya* 3.65, trans., e.g., Bodhi 2012, 279–83.

1129. These include the *Four Praise Songs* (*Catuḥstava*); see, e.g., Tola and Dragonetti 1985.

as Chan/Zen and (as we have seen) the tantra of the mahāsiddhas, take devotion and service to the spiritual master as a given, and while the affective styles of the two movements differ—with Chan/Zen being more laconic and tantra more expressive—it is clear that some element of devotion is crucial to spiritual success in each, and that such success brings with it other emotions, too, like amazement and joy. Needless to say, when we add the overtly devotional approach of the Indian, Central Asian, and East Asian Pure Land traditions to the mix, we have even stronger evidence that Buddhism, for all its emphasis on detachment, is in fact suffused with emotions, of which devotion may be the most important.

The larger question within religious studies is: what role does devotion play in the deepest of religious experiences? The Enlightenment-era German theologian Friedrich Schleiermacher characterized religion as being based on a "feeling of absolute dependence,"[1130] and although his definition is limited by its indebtedness to idiosyncratically Christian (or theistic) assumptions about humans' relation to a divine other, namely God, it does point up the degree to which religious life is deeply rooted in affect in general and devotion in particular. Since well before Schleiermacher (and not only in the West), it has been observed that most people do not have the time, discipline, or inclination to live a life of renunciation and meditation, and that the surest route to spiritual satisfaction for the noncontemplative majority is devotion to some sort of "externalized" anthropomorphic or theriomorphic deity, however that deity may be named or imagined. Such an approach to religion—whose emblems include Mexican grandmothers telling their rosary beads, Tibetan pilgrims prostrating their way from the borderlands to Lhasa, or Shi'ite penitents flagellating themselves in memory of the martyred imam Husayn on the tenth of Muharram—often is dismissed as "popular," and is contrasted with the "higher," elite religion of theologians and mystics.

This dichotomy is, in fact, quite misleading: apart from reflecting the biases of a certain strand of Protestantism, it simply is not borne out by the history or anthropology of religion. However analytical the style of most theologians, we must remember that they are, to begin with, devout men and women who are "seeking understanding," such that their entire intellectual struggle is motivated by religious emotions. Furthermore, the mystics of various traditions—however ascetic their lifestyle or apophatic their rhetoric—are typically no less devout or emotional than "ordinary" practitioners; indeed, if mystics can be distinguished from ordinary people, it is not because they possess or lack devotion but because they are more deeply and intensively devout. The importance

1130. See, e.g., Schleiermacher 1996.

of devotion in mystical life is obvious in the "love mysticism" of the Jewish author of the "Song of Songs," a Rabi'a or Rumi within Islam, a Bernard or Teresa in Christianity, and a Mirabai or Surdas in Hinduism, yet the more negatively inclined mystics—a Śaṃkara or Eckhart or Ibn 'Arabi—are themselves typically just as driven by devotion, and just as likely to express emotion, as their cataphatic counterparts. Indeed, in most mystical settings, devotion is a necessary condition for spiritual progress, and in many cases may even be sufficient on its own. We might do best to conclude with the perspective of the *Bhagavad Gītā*, whose author recognized two millennia ago that the divine may equally be approached by way of works, knowledge, or devotion but that to follow one way inevitably entails following the others as well.[1131] Thus, whatever the religious context, from Kṛṣṇa *bhakti* to mahāmudrā, the devotion of the devotee leads to knowledge of the divine, while gnostics may only gain true knowledge when they are sufficiently devout. And in every case, because religious processes are human processes, human emotions, however they may be regarded, are inevitably felt and expressed by those who experience them.

12. Does Mahāmudrā Transcend Ritual?

One major reason for mahāmudrā's appeal to people in the modern West is that, as a meditation practice, it appears to be devoid of ritual. If all that is required to practice the great seal is to gaze inward so as to realize the nature of one's own mind, then presumably it can be undertaken by anyone, regardless of metaphysical or religious commitments or cultural background. Similar claims have been made about the transcultural accessibility of Theravāda mindfulness and Zen meditation techniques, which similarly seem to be free of ritual concerns. For Westerners, the problem with ritual, especially religious ritual stemming from a faraway culture, is that it enmeshes us in mythologies, ideologies, aesthetics, and bodily practices that are quite foreign to us. Conversely, the appeal of mahāmudrā as a ritual-free practice is that it allows us, we believe, to shed what is superfluous and culture-bound and focus on the essential nature of the mind, which transcends culture. As with the question of devotion, there is some support for such an approach in mahāmudrā literature, and as before, it is the mahāsiddhas that supply the evidence. The songs of Saraha, Tilopa, and others are full of admonitions that such rituals as going on pilgrimage, bathing in holy rivers, performing ascetic penances, making fire offerings, contemplating maṇḍalas, and even following the way of mantra or tantra are all beside the point, for they don't do what is essential: give us direct

1131. See, e.g., Patton 2008.

access to our own connately empty and luminous mind. In short, they take us away from the great seal. Once again, however, such statements are misleading if read out of context. We must recall that the mahāsiddhas' critical stance on ritual draws on a long tradition of Buddhist religious critique and negative ontological rhetoric, and that they themselves were in fact steeped in the mythology, ideology, and rituals of esoteric Buddhism, especially the yoginī tantras. Thus, rhetoric to the contrary, their practice of mahāmudrā meditation was almost certainly set within a ritual frame that derived its meaning from a particular, culturally specific understanding of the world and how to live within it. And even if, somehow, their meditation lay outside any obvious ritual frame, meditation itself is a ritual practice as surely as are pilgrimage, prostration, or circumambulation of holy objects. Except when they were echoing the mahāsiddhas, Tibetan mahāmudrā masters seldom tried to distance great seal-meditation instruction from ritual. They did emphasize the interrelation between meditation and "outward" ritual to varying degrees. Just within the Geluk, for instance, some commentators focused more on Paṇchen Chögyen's instructions for attaining mahāmudrā serenity and insight than on his prescriptions for preliminary rituals, while others gave greater attention to meditating on the great seal in the context of such rites as *Offering to the Guru* or the *Hundred Deities of Tuṣita*. In general, however, proponents of mahāmudrā in Tibet seem to have been quite comfortable with the idea that ritual and contemplation were complementary rather than conflicting elements of spiritual life—and indeed, few of them would have imagined that contemplation would be practiced in any other context than a ritual one.

Within Buddhism more broadly, the apparent tension between ritual and contemplation has been articulated from the beginning. As with the question of devotion, there is considerable evidence from a range of Buddhist traditions that ritual sometimes was disparaged, but as with critiques of devotion, such anti-ritualism is not quite as it appears. The Buddha depicted in the Foundational *āgamas* and *nikāyas* certainly seems to promote a life of ethical and contemplative practice above any kind of ritual observance. He spends little time describing or prescribing outer rituals for his disciples, and in many cases he re-valorizes common rituals in ethical or contemplative terms, as when, in the *Discourse to Sigala* (*Sigālaka Sutta*),[1132] he reinterprets the Brahmanical tradition of offering fires to the six directions in terms of proper comportment toward family, friends, and teachers. Moreover, the Buddha frequently lists as an example of wrong view the belief that ritual practices such as bathing in sacred rivers or performing austerities can result in liberation. At the same

1132. *Dīgha Nikāya* sutta 31; trans., e.g., Walshe 1995, 461–70.

time, the Buddha did prescribe some rituals for his followers, including the ordination ceremony, daily almsround, and fortnightly confession required of monastics and certain practices recommended to laypeople, such as going for refuge to the Buddha, Dharma, and Saṅgha and observing basic moral precepts, either for life or occasionally. He also is said to have conceded near the end of his life that it would be acceptable after his passing to erect stūpas to commemorate him and hold his ashes and to have given instructions on how this was to be done. Regardless of the Buddha's own attitude toward ritual—he seems ambivalent—the nascent Buddhist movement required regular, repeated observances to help bind the community together, and there is strong evidence that not long after the Buddha's passing, his followers, both monastic and lay, began erecting stūpas in his memory, undertaking pilgrimages to sites important in his life, making offerings at the various shrines that began to appear, and in some cases, practicing meditation on a regular basis. In short, the Buddha's followers developed a recognizably Buddhist ritual life.

The importance of ritual seems even more pronounced in the early literature of the Mahāyāna, which abounds in references to a multitude of recommended practices, including pilgrimage, prostration, circumambulation, offering, image bathing, sūtra copying, stūpa worship, and so forth, and as noted already, tantric traditions usually involve elaborate, highly symbolic ritual practices. At the same time, the anti-ritual rhetoric sometimes employed by the Buddha found its way into later literature, as well. The Perfection of Wisdom sūtras made it clear that realizing emptiness was far more valuable than any ritual practice, the writings of East Asian Chan/Zen masters advertised the "meditation" school as beyond ritual, and the songs of the tantric mahāsiddhas, as we know, were often dismissive of ritual. However, even the Perfection of Wisdom sūtras depict a wide range of ritual practices to be undertaken by a bodhisattva. By the same token, the "essential" meditative practices of both Chan/Zen and tantra clearly are undertaken within ritual contexts. Thus, while ritual at times seems to have troubled Buddhists on the grounds that it might distract us from what is most important, it was in the end an unavoidable part of their religious life and hence, *mutatis mutandis*, a part of the practice of mahāmudrā as well.

The larger question within religious studies is: how important is ritual to religious life, especially to the mystical life sometimes regarded as the quintessence of religious practice?[1133] It is clear from anthropological and zoological literature that ritual—regular, patterned behavior—is a fundamental aspect of both human and much other animal life. Religious ritual is only a subset

1133. See, e.g., Driver 2006 and Bell 2009.

of a broader tendency in *homo sapiens*, but it is nonetheless a crucial category for understanding religious phenomena. Many rituals are publicly observable, hence provide a window onto a particular religious culture. But more importantly they take the mythology and ideology of a given community and instantiate them in specific, more or less routinized, verbal and bodily actions, which in turn help shape the behavior and experience of the members of the community. Religious ritual, then, is a powerful way of consolidating community harmony, promoting individual identification with the community and its ideology and enriching the interior life of those individuals. To take some obvious examples, participation in the Muslim pilgrimage to Mecca, or the Christian eucharist, or the Lakota sun dance, or a Buddhist worship ritual, or a Hindu *kumbha melā*, encapsulates a great deal of what is most vital about the tradition that practices each, and serves to unite and motivate the participants, often in extraordinary ways. Consider, for example, the transformative effect of the Hajj on the thought of Malcolm X or the mystical vision attained by the Jesuit theologian Pierre Teilhard de Chardin by his contemplation of the Eucharist.

Yet any oft-repeated activity may become rote and meaningless, and ritual often devolves into ritual*ism*. It is a concern with ritualism that probably lay behind the Buddha's critique of Hindu observances and Luther's objections to Roman Catholic liturgy, and such a concern, as well, likely lies behind mystical writings that either ignore, downplay, or overtly criticize religious ritual. Thus, such figures as Eckhart, Śaṃkara, and the early Daoist sages seem largely to overlook ritual, while Zen masters and Buddhist and Hindu tantric great adepts often mock it. Yet none of them is (or can be) entirely free from ritual, and for all of them, undoubtedly, it is ritual*ism* that is "death to the spirit," whereas ritual itself, properly and deeply observed, may in fact enhance the possibility for having deeply meaningful and even transformative experiences, including those we designate as "mystical." Thus, in religious contexts more generally and in the specific case of Tibetan mahāmudrā, ritual may at times prove problematic for the cultivation of inwardness, but it is inescapable, and for most contemplatives and mystics, ritual was as natural as the air they breathed, and often served to deepen their visions and realizations.

13. Is There Room for Ethics in Mahāmudrā?

If mahāmudrā is above all a gnostic realization of the emptiness of mind and reality, in which not only conceptual thought but all conventions are transcended, the question naturally arises as to whether there is a place in it for ethics. The rhetoric of the great mahāmudrā adepts of India, and of the tantric traditions within which they operated, was often overtly transgressive and antinomian, with their insistence that sex, wrath, and power might be crucial to the attainment of buddhahood; their mockery of standard morals and moralists, especially ascetics; and their celebration of acting exactly as they pleased—as Saraha puts it, like an elephant in rut.[1134] Because such rhetoric was deeply embedded in the tantric traditions adopted by Tibetans, it could not easily be extracted from the Buddhism that developed on the plateau. Indeed, it found its way into the writings—especially the spiritual songs and pith instructions—of many a Tibetan master, from Padmasambhava and his Nyingmapa successors to proponents of mahāmudrā such as Shang Rinpoché, Thangtong Gyalpo, and the notorious Drukpa "madmen" (*smyon pa*) of the fifteenth and sixteenth centuries, to name just a few. Even establishment figures like Rangjung Dorjé, the Second Dalai Lama, Pema Karpo, Paṇchen Chögyen, and Phabongkha Rinpoché sometimes represented themselves in their songs as carefree, crazy do-nothings.

Just as the mahāsiddhas met with resistance from more conservative Indian Buddhists—recall the legend that Atiśa had Maitrīpa expelled from Vikramaśīla Monastery for immorality—so Tibetans with antinomian tendencies were criticized by their compatriots. Thus Dromtönpa reportedly tried to prevent Atiśa (an Indian who adopted Tibet as his final home) from teaching Saraha's *dohās* in Tibet, and Sakya Paṇḍita asked, in *Clear Ascertainment of the Three Vows*, whether the subitist, negative rhetoric of some early Kagyüpa mahāmudrā masters wasn't simply a cover for immorality. Tsongkhapa may have had similar concerns about the Kagyüpa practitioners to whom he directed his critical *Queries from a Pure Heart*. Proponents of mahāmudrā defended such rhetoric by pointing out that emptiness not only does not negate ethics but may serve as a basis for it, and that the unconventional behavior of certain Indian and Tibetan mahāsiddhas was in fact an expression of compassionate skillful means rooted in the gnostic understanding that emptiness entails the interrelationship of all beings, who must be helped to achieve awakening through whatever methods are most appropriate to their particular situation.

Furthermore, as has been noted by Christian Wedemeyer, the transgressive behavior described in Indian tantric literature should be seen not as an utter rejection of standard morality but as a particular phase of religious training in which, for a time, the practitioner cultivates nonduality quite viscerally, so as to expedite the final realization and attainment of mahāmudrā.[1135]

1134. See Sa*PQ* 31b; trans. R. Jackson 2012, 180.

1135. See Wedemeyer 2013.

Indeed, even conservative monastics like Tsongkhapa conceded that there was—at least for non-monks—a proper time and place for transgressive practices, including sexual yoga, and that one could not reach buddhahood in this body without them. Still, there is no doubt that, from mahāmudrā's origins in India until the present day, both the rhetoric of transgression that formed part of its discourse and the actions of some of its proponents have been problematic and controversial for those trying to make sense of the great seal.

Within Buddhism more broadly, antinomian rhetoric and the rejection of conventional morality are virtually unknown in the Foundational traditions, only making their appearance in the literature of the Mahāyāna. It is quite clear from the sūtras and commentaries of the early schools that the Buddha himself lived an utterly blameless life and that his followers were expected to do the same. Ethics or morality (*śīla*)—as codified in, but not limited to, lay and monastic vows—is regarded as the foundation of the path, without which neither fortunate future rebirths nor the contemplative life conducive to liberation are possible. Although strictly speaking the awakened state of nirvāṇa is utterly beyond mundane categories, conventions, or concepts, there is no suggestion in the Foundational texts that the path to attaining it is paved with any behavior that is even remotely nonvirtuous, nor that awakened arhats ever behave with anything but probity. By the same token, the key ontological doctrine of no-self could in principle be read as negating fixed morality as surely as it negates a permanent self, but there is no indication that such an implication ever was drawn. Similarly, although the Buddha was regarded from the earliest times as an immensely skillful and flexible teacher, able to understand his pupils' needs and instruct them accordingly, he never is depicted as using or condoning any methods that involve duplicity or immorality.

In the literature of the Great Vehicle, on the other hand, we often see a universalization and radicalization of doctrines established within the Foundational traditions. In particular, the doctrine of no-self was universalized into emptiness, which was seen to apply to all concepts, including such previously unquestioned "goods" as ethics and nirvāṇa. Also, the doctrine of skillful means was extended in such a way as to suggest that the Buddha's—or bodhisattva's—pedagogical skill and compassionate work for the sake of sentient beings may, in certain instances, require the overt transgression of standard moral rules, which, viewed through the lens of emptiness, have no more ultimacy than anything else. Thus a buddha or bodhisattva may lie, or engage in sex, or even kill if it is for the spiritual benefit of others. It should quickly be added that the types of transgressive methods described in, for instance, the

Lotus Sūtra, the *Teaching of Vimalakīrti*, and the *Sūtra on Skillful Means*[1136] are only possible for highly advanced practitioners, and only in extraordinary circumstances. Furthermore, though they attract a lot of attention, such passages are few and far between in Mahāyāna literature, most of which emphasizes the practice of a more conventional type of morality. Still, the twin notions of emptiness and skillful means provided a rationale for the antinomian rhetoric and occasionally transgressive behavior that are especially prominent in the Chan/Zen and tantric traditions. Especially in the case of tantra, what was exceptional in "standard" Mahāyāna became quite common. Still, it is important to recognize that, however counter to the norm the discourse or behavior of Zen masters or tantric adepts might have been, they still operated within contexts that were most often monastic, and almost always presupposed on the part of their practitioners the exercise of generosity, compassion, and other elements of standard morality.

The larger question within religious studies is: do transcendental ontological discourses obviate ethical attitudes and behavior, and if not, why not?[1137] Whether ultimate reality is described "positively" as, say, a loving personal God or a powerful impersonal force, or "negatively" as, say, emptiness or the Dao, it typically is conceived as transcending—perhaps even falsifying—all mundane conventions and ideas. At least in principle, however, such a transcendental ontology puts into question not just "the wisdom of the world" but mundane categories and distinctions as well—including ethical distinctions. Thus, as basic as the divide between good and evil may be to human life, it may be threatened by the larger ontology in which it is embedded. By the same token, phenomenologically unmediated encounters with the ultimate—that is, mystical experiences—sometimes take the mystic into states of consciousness where everything known and valued before is erased in nondual ecstasy or luminous incomprehensibility. What then is the connection, if any, between an experience of the transcendent ultimate and the moral categories and actions that guide most people's ordinary lives?

Even in theistic traditions where God's absolute goodness is supposed to inspire and undergird at least relative goodness in his worshipers, the status of "goodness" as a meaningful concept may at times be brought into question, although more commonly in the context of apophatic rather than cataphatic theologies and discourses. It hardly need be said, then, that the disconnection between ultimacy and morality may be even more pronounced in thoroughly nondualistic or monistic settings, where the ultimate appears either to negate

1136. See, respectively, e.g., Watson 1994; Thurman 1976; Tatz 2016.

1137. See, e.g., Katz 1984.

conventional distinctions—in which case the good-evil dichotomy is negated, too—or to incorporate all of them—in which case good cannot be said to be any more ultimate than evil.

That being so, the question becomes: if the ultimate is "beyond good and evil," then why should we be good? Over the course of religious history, a few have simply replied, "We don't have to be," and gone on to live lives unmoored from ethics. Most, however, have insisted that goodness still is crucial to living a proper human life and gaining access to the *summum bonum*, whatever that may be. In most Abrahamic traditions, it is recognized that God transcends all our categories yet may provisionally, with relative accuracy, be described as possessing to the maximum extent such qualities as knowledge, love, and power, so that our earthly attempts to develop such traits do reflect the nature of the divine, however imperfectly. Morality, thus, is justified.

In a number of Asian traditions, including many Hindu and Buddhist schools, the ultimate truly is bereft of moral distinctions (since neither emptiness nor Brahman permits *any* distinctions), but the saṃsāric world operates according to its own laws, such as karma—whereby conventionally negative actions lead to negative results and positive actions to positive results, including (perhaps indirectly) realization of the ultimate. Morality in this scheme is justified on purely conventional grounds, despite the nature of the ultimate. There are other Hindu and Buddhist schools, of course, that regard reality as fundamentally good, such that, e.g., everything is Śiva, or everything is Buddha, although as in Abrahamic traditions, the goodness of reality may be well beyond our comprehension. Any of these rationales, of course, leaves open the question of what the "good" or the "positive" is on a conventional level, and as a result, there still remains, in every religious tradition, some scope for debate about which behavior truly is conducive to the spiritual good; this, in turn, opens some leeway for speech and behavior that, while contravening generally accepted norms, may—like the transgressive words and deeds of some mahāmudrā masters—turn out to be spiritually effective and appropriate, hence "good" in an extended sense of the term.

14. Is Mahāmudrā Expressible?

Whether as the realization of emptiness or the attainment of buddhahood, the experience of mahāmudrā is said to transcend duality, conceptuality, and predication and therefore is, strictly speaking, ineffable. Both the mahāyoga and yoginī tantras that fueled mahāmudrā discourse and the songs of the Indian and Tibetan mahāsiddhas that celebrated it are laced with reminders that the great seal is a state, or a reality, that cannot adequately be described, for description requires language, and language does violence to the nature of things. Texts such as the *Drop of Mahāmudrā* and the lyrics of Saraha, Tilopa, and Nāropa repeatedly insist that mahāmudrā is inconceivable and incommunicable and can only be understood when concepts are dropped and it is experienced directly. At the same time, the very authors who stressed the great seal's ineffability wrote voluminously about it. The reason is simple: as the ultimate reality and attainment, mahāmudrā is the most important single thing a person can know; to be denied it is to continue to circle in saṃsāra, while to realize it to open the door to buddhahood. Thus, though the great seal is inconceivable and inexpressible, it is too vital *not* to be thought and spoken, however imperfectly.

Kagyüpa and Gelukpa exponents of mahāmudrā sometimes differed as to just how conceivable and expressible mahāmudrā is, with the former putting greater emphasis on its utter indescribability, the latter granting language somewhat greater power to capture its contours, if not all of it. Yet all of them agreed that in the final analysis, because it is the ultimate, and the ultimate transcends conceptual thought, mahāmudrā *is* inconceivable, yet expression of it is *not* impossible or even paradoxical, since—Madhyamaka negative rhetoric notwithstanding—the conventional world and activity within it, including speech, are *not* negated by the ultimate but enabled by it. Furthermore (as Kagyüpas pointed out more often than the rationalist Gelukpas), the conventional world itself may be no more conceivable or expressible than mahāmudrā. In any case, despite the rhetoric of ineffability that pervades mahāmudrā literature, masters of the great seal in both India and Tibet felt justified in speaking of it, whether on pragmatic or philosophical grounds, and they spoke of it in some of the most compelling and evocative poems and treatises ever produced by Buddhists—works that only were deepened and enriched by their authors' acknowledgment of the groundlessness of all that they said and did.

Within Buddhism more broadly, the tension between, on the one hand, the sense that contemplative experience and the transcendent ultimate are inconceivable and inexpressible and, on the other, the need to communicate vital truths to suffering sentient beings led to a long-standing ambivalence within the tradition about the role of language.[1138] As far back as the sūtras of Foundational Buddhism, a key epithet of the Buddha is the *muni*, the "silent sage," and most early narratives of the Buddha's life emphasize that following his awakening under the bodhi tree, he concluded at first that his achievement was so profound that it could not be communicated. On further reflection, however, he realized that there were some in the world, "whose eyes were cov-

1138. See, e.g., Cabezón 1994.

ered with but a little dust," that might understand what he had to say, so he set out for Sarnath, where he "turned the wheel of Dharma" for his first five disciples—and continued teaching for the next forty-five years. All of the Buddha's many teachings were supposed to aid his followers in attaining nirvāṇa, a transcendent, unconditioned state that cannot be grasped by those who have not attained it. But because it is the final, necessary outcome of beginningless eons of sentient spiritual striving, it *must* be grasped. Because it cannot be described literally, it is best approached through metaphors, both positive and negative. Hence, as we have seen, in the early literature nirvāṇa is described negatively as the unconditioned absence of all defilements and positively as true knowledge, real happiness, or an island, or a light, or the cool that ensues when a fire has been put out.

Similar tensions are evident in Mahāyāna traditions, where the Perfection of Wisdom sūtras and the writings of Mādhyamika philosophers stress the degree to which the ultimate nature of things, emptiness, and the ultimate being, buddha, are utterly beyond comprehension or predication—yet demand expression. And in Mahāyāna, more than in Foundational traditions, the ultimate is not radically separable from the conventional. The *Heart Sūtra* reminds us that "form is emptiness, emptiness is form," with the consequence that even mundane words and deeds may, if understood aright, serve as an avenue to deeper realization. Given, too, the Mahāyāna celebration of the multitude of skillful pedagogical means employed by buddhas and bodhisattvas, it is not surprising that the Great Vehicle produced a wealth of stories, songs, images, and other artistic forms that were intended to bring their audience closer to a final realization that no piece of art could capture perfectly but that each work, appreciated properly, nevertheless could suggest. Whether we consider the koans, poems, paintings, gardens, and other art forms inspired by the Chan/Zen tradition; or the melodious chants and impressive Buddha images of Pure Land Buddhism; or the profound, playful, and popular songs sung by mahāmudrā masters from Saraha, to Milarepa, to Paṇchen Chögyen, to Chögyam Trungpa, we see the same process at work: Buddhists giving form to that which they know has no form and giving words to that which they know cannot be spoken, simply because a master's suggestion, their need for expression, and their own deep compassion prompt them to do what cannot be done but must be done.

The larger question within religious studies is: does mystical experience silence the mystic, and if not, then what sort of expression is appropriate to the significance of the experience and the reality encompassed by it? The tensions over the place of language that we have encountered in connection with mahāmudrā and with Buddhism writ large are played out as well in most of the world's religious traditions, for it is a common, if not universal, trait of religions that they posit an ultimate reality that transcends worldly existence and human conceptions and yet may be partially understood through language and other communicative forms, and may be approached and encountered by those with sufficient dedication and discipline—those we call mystics.[1139] And, as William James pointed out at the beginning of the twentieth century, what mystics discover, and report, is that the encounter with the ultimate is so powerful, so convincing, so visceral, so different from everyday states of consciousness as to be ineffable. Yet, as many scholars of mysticism have observed, even the claim that the mystical experience or its referent is indescribable is itself a description—albeit a negative one—that does convey something about what the mystic has understood.

That ironic observation aside, the alleged ineffability of the mystical experience—or of the ultimate reality that is the "object" or "content" of that experience—does not at all silence the mystic. Quite to the contrary, mystics have said a great deal in attempting to describe the indescribable.[1140] Moses may have been dumbfounded by his encounter with God on Mount Sinai, Teresa of Avila rendered speechless by seeing the "sacred humanity" of Christ, Dante stunned into momentary silence by his vision of the fiery rose of the triune God, or Ramana Maharshi overwhelmed by his realization of Brahman—yet all of them did speak in some way of what they had experienced. Why? Because it was essential to do so: what they experienced could not be communicated, but it *had* to be communicated, because it was the single truth without which struggling humans had no hope of redemption or liberation. And, as in the Buddhist cases discussed above, the communication of the ultimate—both as reality and realization—could take many forms, whether autobiographical, philosophical, exhortatory, or artistic.

Although some have suggested that—given the intangibility and elusiveness of the ultimate—art forms such as music (think of Bach or John Cage) or painting (think of Hakuin or Kandinsky) may capture it best, at some point it will have be rendered in language. And while philosophy may succeed in bringing linguistic order, even a provisional sense of rationality, to the transcendent, it is perhaps poetry, with its metaphors, its verbal playfulness, and its deliberate ambiguities, that comes closest to "re-presenting" the unrepresentable ultimate. Not all mystics were poets, of course, but a remarkable number of them—including Saraha, Rumi, Lallā, St. John of the Cross, and countless others—were prompted to express in the images, insights, and rhythms of verse the incomprehensible reality they had seen and understood, thereby

1139. See, e.g., Katz 1992.

1140. See, e.g., Katz 1978.

bringing both themselves and their readers closer to tasting that reality. In short, it is fundamental to religious traditions everywhere that they accept the inconceivability and inexpressibility of the ultimate yet conceive it nonetheless and express it, as best they can, in words, images, sounds, and signs.

15. Is All Mahāmudrā Realization the Same?

Over the course of time, all Tibetan orders came to house both exclusivist and inclusivist factions, and they often debated among themselves and with other orders the question whether ultimate experiences such as the realization of mahāmudrā were identical across sectarian lines, or whether one particular approach (presumably that of one's own lineage) was superior to others, or even uniquely salvific.[1141] Nyingmapas and Kagyüpas, for instance, argued about whether mahāmudrā and the great perfection were the same or different, with exclusivists from each school asserting the superiority of its own doctrine, and inclusivists—the Third Karmapa Rangjung Dorjé is a conspicuous example—insisting that although terms and methods might differ, reality is indivisible in the end, so all true realizations of it must be the same.

The Geluk tradition witnessed significant internal disagreement over whether a Geluk mahāmudrā realization could be the same as that of a Kagyüpa, given differences between the orders in terms of lineage, ritual, meditation, and, most crucially, philosophy and hermeneutics. Tsongkhapa's own view of other traditions is hard to pinpoint: he borrowed liberally from many sources in forging his grand synthesis yet was strongly critical of many aspects of the traditions from which he drew, whether on matters of ontology, ethics, meditation practice, or tantric theory. Yet Paṇchen Chögyen, who publicly articulated the mahāmudrā tradition he attributed to Tsongkhapa, stated clearly in *Highway of the Conquerors* his conviction that all the great Tibetan contemplative traditions—whatever their differences is style, terminology, or philosophical underpinnings—come down in the end to the same idea and experience—which was, as it happened, the realization of all phenomena's emptiness of intrinsic existence, as described in Prāsaṅgika Madhyamaka. The First Paṇchen's inclusivism was called into question by his own second successor, the Third Paṇchen Palden Yeshé, who could not imagine that his great predecessor would affirm the spiritual realizations of contemplatives whose view of reality, and especially of emptiness, was incorrect. The inclusivist position was reaffirmed by Thuken Chökyi Nyima, who noted that the exclusion of non-Gelukpa masters from the ranks of the realized could

1141. See, e.g., Komarovski 2015.

threaten the coherence of Mahāyāna soteriology, not to mention open political and cultural fissures among the Tibetan orders. Thus, from the standpoint of Thuken and other Gelukpa inclusivists, Buddhist masters whose philosophical affiliation was non-Prāsaṅgika (or even non-Mahāyānist) could have their realization certified as long as it was understood that their actual experience of reality was that described in Prāsaṅgika Madhyamaka: as empty of intrinsic existence. Whether or not this is an adequate solution to the problem, it is a common inclusivist move, and it allowed Gelukpas (or others who might use a similar argument) to assert that all mahāmudrā realization is the same because *their* account of the subjective and objective elements of that realization is the only plausible one. Hence, all realized masters must by definition have encountered reality in the way described by Gelukpas, whether they thought of it that way or not.

Within Buddhism more broadly, exclusivist and inclusivist strains are evident from the very beginning.[1142] The Buddha depicted in Foundational Buddhist literature is severely critical of a wide range of doctrines and practices asserted by other traditions—Brahmanical, Jain, Ājivaka, and so forth—whether on grounds of their philosophical incoherence or because they are soteriologically impotent. As arguably a pragmatist, the Buddha was particularly concerned with soteriology, reserving his strongest condemnations for religious practices he thought ineffective, including ritual bathing, fire sacrifices, and extreme asceticism. He was critical as well of contemplative practices that tranquilized the mind and led to psychic powers but failed to provide proper insight into the nature of things. Because the question of ignorance and knowledge is, for most Buddhists, the linchpin on which our spiritual failure or success depends, no teaching that does not give its practitioners access to proper, salvific knowledge—for instance of the four noble truths, dependent arising, or no-self—was worth pursuing. In these respects, the Buddha was clearly an exclusivist.

At the same time, though, the Buddha recognized that those who had attained liberation—arhats—might differ in their degree of meditative absorption or psychic power but still share exactly the same insight into reality and possess the same degree of spiritual freedom. The Buddha also recognized the existence of a class of awakened beings, solitary buddhas (*pratyekabuddha*), who—at least in their final life—neither listened to Buddhist teachings nor imparted them; it has been suggested by certain scholars that the Buddha acknowledged them so as to include at least some non-Buddhist experiences

1142. See, e.g., Vélez de Cea 2013.

of realization under the umbrella of the Dharma.[1143] Mahāyānists often were preoccupied not only with criticizing the soteriologies of non-Buddhist traditions (consider, for instance, the works of Āryadeva, Dharmakīrti, and Saraha) but with distancing themselves from the approach taken by "Hīnayāna" schools, which in many cases were dismissed as insufficiently profound and as leading to "mere" personal liberation, whereas the wise, compassionate, and fully mature practices of Great Vehicle bodhisattvas would lead beyond arhatship to full buddhahood, a state from which one could work with maximum effectiveness for the welfare of all beings.

It is worth noting, however, that Mahāyāna thinkers agreed almost unanimously that Foundational Buddhist practices lead to freedom from saṃsāra; the question on which they differed was whether arhatship was a final destination or whether all beings sooner or later would have to become bodhisattvas and eventually buddhas. The general consensus that eventually emerged—expressed most forcefully in the *Lotus Sūtra* and the buddha-nature literature—was that there is only one final vehicle, that which leads to buddhahood. Because, however, any form of liberation is dependent upon a proper realization of the nature of reality, and the arhat's liberation, however "incomplete," still was liberation, those on the path to arhatship must have understood the nature of reality correctly, hence—their own "Hīnayāna" rhetoric notwithstanding—have attained a direct realization the ultimate as described in Mahāyāna, whether that ultimate be designated as emptiness, mind-only, buddha nature, or by some other term. In this sense, most Great Vehicle traditions (indeed, all Buddhist traditions) were inclusivist at least within the bounds of Buddhism, asserting that the realizations enjoyed by all Buddhists are, at base, identical; nor is it impossible that the criteria they applied within the tradition might be extended to realizations in other traditions as well, such that, for instance, Eckhart or 'Arabi might be seen as realizing emptiness in a different context or Jesus might be seen, in some sense, as a bodhisattva.

The larger question within religious studies is: are mystical experiences the same cross-culturally, or even intra-traditionally, and how might we ascertain whether they are or are not? The question of exclusivism and inclusivism has often preoccupied thinkers in the world's religious traditions. While it is common to identify, say, Abrahamic traditions as exclusivist and, say, Asian traditions as inclusivist, this facile generalization is belied by the complexity found in every religion, where centrifugal and centripetal tendencies constantly are at play with each other. Thus the religion most often said to be inclusivist, Hinduism, long has harbored factions that reject the validity of differing Hindu

1143. See Vélez de Cea 2013, 91–104.

traditions, not to mention the ideas and practices of those outside the Hindu fold. By the same token, Islam, which too often is caricatured as denigrating all those outside the community of the faithful, has in fact proven extraordinarily flexible over the course of its history, accommodating non-Muslim, and even non-Abrahamic, beliefs and practices to a greater degree than often is recognized.

In the case of Islam, and in the case of many traditions, it is the mystics who often have proven most open to other traditions, and most likely to take an inclusivist stance. Because of this, the modern study of mysticism has proven a particularly interesting site of contestation over the question of the sameness or difference among experiences of spiritual realization. In mystical studies, the problem is usually framed not in terms of exclusivism and inclusivism (which are theological categories) but in terms of "perennialism" (or universalism) and "pluralism" (or particularism). The perennialist position, whose best known exponents include Aldous Huxley, W. T. Stace, and Robert Forman,[1144] holds that the world's mystics—whatever their cultural, linguistic, or even metaphysical differences—experience in the end the same, single reality, however it may be named or interpreted. The perennialist view is defended (a) by appealing to the phenomenological similarities evident in many, if not all, mystical reports, and (b) on the philosophical grounds that the ultimate described by mystics and mystical theologians could not really be ultimate if it is not singular. The pluralist view—as represented most notably by Steven Katz, Wayne Proudfoot, and Robert Sharf[1145]—maintains that the world's mystics may be identified as "mystics" in the general sense that they claim, or are recognized, to have experienced the most intense possible relation to the ultimate but that we cannot go beyond this to assert that they all experience the same ultimate. The argument here is that we have no privileged access to the minds of mystics, living or dead, and can only rely on the reports they give or the theologies they frame—all of which point to irreducible differences in their experience. This is not the place to adjudicate this dispute, which, despite the ascendancy of the pluralist view in recent decades, shows no signs of ending. It should be clear, however, that the issues faced by mystics and those who seek to make sense of them are in many respects the same ones faced by Buddhists throughout their history, including Tibetan mahāmudrā masters, as they sought to understand the points of similarity and difference between their own deep realizations and those of others, whether coreligionists or those well outside the fold.

1144. See, respectively, Huxley 2009, Stace 1961, and Forman 1997.

1145. See, respectively, Katz 1978, Proudfoot 1987, and Sharf 1998.

16. What Is Mind?

If there is a single phrase that summarizes the meaning of mahāmudrā for the Indian mahāsiddhas and their Tibetan successors, it is "the nature of mind": the mind is, in one sense or another, the foundation of the world and our spiritual efforts within it, and it is the ultimate nature of mind that we must realize if we are to transform ourselves from ordinary beings into buddhas—or rediscover the buddha mind we have always possessed. Tibetan mahāmudrā theorists did not, of course, always agree on the definition of mind, debating, for instance, which of mind's characteristics are conventional and which are ultimate, or how many types of cognition sentient beings possess. For instance, shentong-oriented Kagyüpas who conceived of emptiness as an affirming negation and buddha mind as empty of everything mundane but replete with buddha qualities tended to see the mind's conventional nature as its saṃsāric nature and its ultimate nature as empty and inconceivable yet pervaded by positive attributes. Thus, to realize the ultimate nature of mind was to realize its primordial lack of afflictive states and its unchanging purity and luminosity. Gelukpas, as we now well know, insisted that emptiness was in all instances a nonaffirming negation, such that even the Dharma body of a buddha, and the qualities attributed to it, are empty in precisely the same way as a pillar or a person is empty: as devoid of intrinsic existence. Thus to realize the ultimate nature of mind is simply to recognize, first analytically and then experientially, that the mind—whose conventional nature is clarity and awareness, whether in a sentient being or a buddha—is empty of intrinsic existence, hence capable of transformation.

In considering the structures of the mind, some Kagyüpas (like many Nyingmapas) promoted the Yogācāra-based view that beings have eight or more consciousnesses, including the usual six "sense" consciousnesses, an afflictive mind (*kliṣṭamanas*), and a storehouse consciousness (*ālayavijñāna*), sometimes adding an even more basic "ground" (*ālaya*), which is the pure awareness (*vidyā*; *rig pa*) that is the source of everything. Gelukpas, following Tsongkhapa and most Prāsaṅgika Mādhyamikas, rejected the existence of a storehouse consciousness and reaffirmed the more common Buddhist claim that beings possess six consciousnesses, which, they say, are perfectly adequate for giving an account of the various sorts of cognitive activity that mark our mental life. Whatever their differences, however, Tibetan proponents of the great seal agreed that, conventionally speaking, the mind is the key to our place in the cosmos and that the most vital of human concerns is with mind's *ultimate* nature, an understanding of which, however described, is not just a matter of academic interest but an experience that leads to genuine freedom and joy, to a creative and compassionate engagement with the world.

Within Buddhism more broadly, the importance of mind for the world and for human endeavor within it has never seriously been questioned. One of the most popular and influential of all Foundational Buddhist texts, the Pāli *Dhammapada*, asserts its very first verse that "phenomena are preceded by mind, they are founded on mind, they are composed of mind."[1146] Although the notion that phenomena are "composed of mind" (*manomayā*) might suggest the subjective idealism (or at least the phenomenalism) evident later in many strands of Yogācāra, the *Dhammapada*'s primary claim seems not to be ontological but metaphysical: the world and its phenomena are shaped, or brought into being, by the positive and negative actions of sentient beings, and because actions are defined by their being volitional or intentional, and intention is an aspect of mental life, all things are "preceded by" and "founded on" the mind. This being so, the key to release from the sufferings of saṃsāra is the redirection of the mind away from nonvirtuous mental states and toward the virtuous, such that the fruits of the actions prompted by those states will themselves be increasingly virtuous. And because, as the *Aṅguttara Nikāya* reminds us, the mind is naturally clear and luminous, and its defilements only incidental,[1147] it is possible, through proper training, to eventually reach a condition—a state of mind—in which one is utterly free and need not take rebirth. Because the liberation of the mind was the overriding, normative goal for Buddhist practitioners, Buddhist thinkers—especially in the Abhidharma and Yogācāra schools—devoted a great deal of time to delineating the structures of mentality, from the six (or eight, or even nine) types of consciousness, to the various mental factors (*caitta*) that accompany a primary moment of awareness (*citta*), to the various refined states of mind achievable through meditation. Despite their differences on these matters, almost all Buddhists agreed that the mind was *the* key factor in the cosmos, and its transformation the most important single task a human being could undertake.

Some traditions, especially within the Mahāyāna, went even further: in the sūtras and treatises of the Yogācāra, in the poems and puzzles of Chan/Zen, and in the later tantras and the songs of the mahāsiddhas, mind was seen not only metaphysically, as shaping the cosmos, but often ontologically, as *being* or becoming the cosmos. And the mind that *is* the cosmos, that emanates it, is nothing less than the Dharma body, or buddha mind, or pure awareness—of which our conventional states of mind, our bodies, and our envi-

1146. *DHP* 1–2.

1147. *Aṅguttara Nikāya* 1.52; trans., e.g., Bodhi 2012, 97.

ronment are all simply projections. Not all Buddhists went so far, of course, nor did all mahāmudrā masters. In particular, Prāsaṅgika Mādhyamikas like Candrakīrti and the Gelukpas in Tibet were consistently dubious regarding such claims about the relation between mind and cosmos. Ontological disagreements aside, though, in many Buddhist traditions, and certainly in those propounding the great seal, to rest in and realize the true nature of mind is the heart of practice, the surest method for making us free.

The larger question within religious studies but perhaps even more so within philosophy more generally, is simply: what *is* mind, and can a real understanding of it make us free? Although Buddhists may have concerned themselves with the description and classification of mental states to an unusual degree, thinkers in other religious traditions certainly recognized the importance of understanding and cultivating the mind in pursuit of whatever their spiritual aims might be. Thus sophisticated descriptive psychologies arose in various Hindu lineages, and in Judaism, Christianity, Islam, and other traditions as well, and in all these traditions, methods of exercising, training, and transforming the mind were developed, particularly for purposes of entering into the deeper levels of the spiritual life. Still, in most non-Buddhist traditions, the mind and its faculties often are quite distinct from, and ultimately less important than, the immortal substance designated as the "self," or "soul"—however that might be conceived, and however its relation to the mind might be described. Buddhism differed from nearly every other religious tradition in denying the existence of such a self or soul and focusing only on the mind—which was, typically, regarded as an impermanent series of mental events that happens to be beginningless and may well be endless. This distinguishing feature aside, Buddhists tend to be in accord with adherents of most other religions in asserting that (a) there is *some* factor in human beings (whether "soul" or "mind," whether substance or process) that is distinct enough from the body to survive death and serves as the locus for the most important spiritual work we are called upon to perform, and (b) such spiritual work may, in fact, be fruitful because the soul or mind has as its essential nature a purity, or an element of the divine, that allows its ascent to the *summum bonum*, whether in this life or sometime in the future.

In these respects, however, Buddhism and most other religions are at considerable odds with much of modern philosophy, which asserts that (a) the mind (or soul) is not separate or separable from the body—more specifically, the brain—but a property or function of it, and (b) by virtue of its being a function of a limited body and brain and also subject to cultural and linguistic influences, the mind (or soul) is constrained in its cognitive capacity, hence incapable of attaining the sort of perfection claimed for it in one or another spiritual tradition. If, in this regard, we return to a consideration solely of Buddhism in general and mahāmudrā traditions in particular, we find that although Buddhist descriptive psychology and Buddhist meditation practices may fascinate and even edify modern non-Buddhists, especially in the West, when it comes to more basic matters of ontology, metaphysics, epistemology, and human potential, Buddhism is not nearly as "science friendly" as its enthusiasts claim.[1148]

Thus, where Buddhists assert that materialist arguments for the mind's identity with or dependence upon the body are indefensible while arguments for its independence of the body are compelling, modern philosophers view the mind as identical with or dependent for its existence upon a functioning brain. Where Buddhists assert the beginningless and possibly endless continuity of individual minds across a multitude of lives, modern philosophers believe that the mind originates with the development of the brain of a unique person in a single life and comes to an end when that life ends. On a broader evolutionary scale, where Buddhists assert that the "bodies, enjoyments, and environments" experienced by sentient beings have as their principal cause mind—which is the root of intention, action, and result in the mental, moral, and physical realms—modern philosophers, influenced by evolutionary biology, see mind as an emergent property within an developmental process that is material and random. Where Buddhists are epistemological "optimists," asserting that the nature of mind is "pure"—that is, able to know things clearly and correctly—modern philosophers, at least since the Enlightenment, have often been epistemological "pessimists," doubting the capacity of the human mind to know the world (or the mind itself) as it actually is—whether because our perceptions deceive us (Hume), we are constrained by the *a priori* categories of understanding (Kant), we are subject to cultural and psychological conditioning (Nietzsche), we are trapped in language games that misrepresent reality (Wittgenstein), or our mind is a hopelessly distorted "mirror of nature" (Rorty). Finally, then, where Buddhists assert that the fundamental purity of the mind assures the possibility of true realization and full awakening, modern philosophers reject the possibility of such an attainment. In a material and relativistic universe, they argue, perfect knowledge is impossible for any being, and any claims that person X or Y has in fact attained such perfection are impossible to prove, their "truth" simply a matter of consensus within a given community.

There are further arguments to be made by both sides on all of these points, but perhaps the question that matters most in the present context is whether any of this is at all important for the practice of mahāmudrā, especially in the present day. Does it matter to a practitioner of the great seal whether mind is

1148. See, e.g., Lopez 2012.

dependent on matter or the other way around, whether there "really" are past and future lives, whether objectively true knowledge is possible, or whether humans are capable of physical, moral, and cognitive perfection? Many a traditional (or neo-traditional) Buddhist, committed to a more or less literal interpretation of the saṃsāra-karma-nirvāṇa cosmology, will insist that it *does* matter, arguing that if the long-standing, distinctive features of the Buddhist worldview are rejected, muted, or modernized, then practice of the Buddhist path—with its deep wellsprings of devotion, ritual, ethics, and meditation—will be pointless, because it will be impossible to attain a "maximal" state of buddhahood from which to work to benefit the countless sentient beings who have been circling beginninglessly from life to life and even now cry out for help. Indeed, say the neo-traditionalists, if traditional Buddhist cosmology, metaphysics, and soteriology are soft-pedaled, or reinterpreted psychologically or existentially, we may as well just admit that we are secular humanists in Buddhist guise and be done with it. In defense of their more or less literal interpretation of traditional Buddhist beliefs, some neo-traditionalists will simply revive or rework classical arguments—like those of Dharmakīrti—for mind's separability from the body, the reliable functioning of karma within and across lives, the mind's capacity for the infinite development of positive qualities, and the salvific power of a realization of no-self.[1149] Others may appeal to the fringes of physics and other sciences to show the primacy of mind in the cosmos and its potency in affecting, and even effecting, events within it. Still others will exploit the uncertainties admitted by modern cognitive philosophers—for instance over solutions to the "very hard problem" of accounting for the subjectivity of experience on a physicalist model of mind—to drive home the limits of materialist assumptions and the scientific methods based upon them.[1150]

Other Buddhists, however—the modernists, pragmatists, or "agnostics"[1151]—will assert that we simply do not know whether traditional cosmology, metaphysics, and soteriology describe the world as it actually is; it may in fact be wrong—and perhaps that does not matter. In framing their approach, they will invoke the Buddha's oft-stated objections to metaphysical speculation and epistemic arrogance and his pragmatic, psychological approach to ending anxiety and suffering. They also will cite the repeated insistence by certain Yogācāra philosophers, Chan/Zen masters, and Indian and Tibetan adepts of the tantras, the great perfection, and mahāmudrā that all that really matters in spiritual life is to realize the nature of mind, which in the ultimate sense

1149. See, e.g., R. Jackson 1993 and Dalai Lama 2006.

1150. See, e.g., Wallace 2003 and Wallace 2013.

1151. See, e.g., Batchelor 2017.

is emptiness, however conceived; the rest, as T. S. Eliot puts it, "is not our business."[1152] From this perspective, Buddhist life in general, and mahāmudrā in particular, is in the final analysis *only* about realizing the final, empty nature of mind—and of the world it subsumes. Thus, whatever the "facts" may turn out to be about the wondrous, violent, and passingly strange universe in which we live and the "actual" place within that universe of the mind by which we know it, as meaning-seeking beings we nevertheless must bring all our passion, compassion, discipline, intelligence, humor, and skill to the great task of delving as deeply as we can into the ultimate nature of things—and minds. In doing so, we may, like many "post-religious" moderns, eschew the mythology, cosmology, imagery, prayers, and meditations described in Buddhism more broadly and mahāmudrā literature specifically.

Alternatively, though, we may continue to invoke and employ these same myths, cosmologies, images, prayers, and meditations, even without full confidence that the traditional worldview from which they originated corresponds exactly to "the way things are," or that the practices we undertake will turn us into buddhas in the maximal sense of the term, for we may remain confident that our rational and contemplative inquiries will inevitably lead to the conclusion that all things are empty. Further, we may trust that the experiential realization of emptiness can be profoundly transformative in the mind and life of someone who has gained that realization, and that the stories we tell and the practices we employ to structure our practice may be profoundly helpful in that transformation.

Regardless of our approach, when we break open the great seal imprinted on all phenomena, and see the world and the mind in their natural emptiness, our desperate and deluded grip on things may start to loosen, as we relax into a spacious and open state—mind's natural condition—that is pervaded by a calm that is not just empty-headed, a contentment that is not complacent, a knowledge that is not merely intellectual, a confidence that is not arrogant, and a joy that is not simply self-indulgent. These inner qualities, in concert with deeply cultivated love and compassion, will, to quote Eliot again, "fructify in the lives of others,"[1153] and give meaning to our own and others' strivings. Thus, in the course of our brief and groping passage through this uncertain and ultimately inconceivable cosmos, cracking open the great seal to see the emptiness beneath it all, and behind the mind that sees, may take us as close to real freedom as we will ever get—and in the modern milieu, that may be quite close enough.

1152. *Four Quartets*, "East Coker," part V.

1153. Eliot, *Four Quartets*, "The Dry Salvages," part III.

Part 5
Translations

1. Synopsis of the Spiritual Practice Taught by the Exalted Mañjughoṣa[1154]

Tsongkhapa Losang Drakpa

I bow down to the exalted treasure of knowledge [Mañjughoṣa].

You who are the supreme body that arises by virtue of accumulating the two collections,
you who see everywhere in the ten directions with the eye that delights in compassion,
you who tear out by the root the delusions that are the basis of worldly existence:
please bestow on beings the great wisdom that is the life tree of liberation.

In the city of Katara,[1155]
the flowers of the pleasure garden bloom;
swarms of bees play there,
drinking up the supreme nectar.

Thus the omniscient exalted Tsongkhapa praised the exalted Mañjughoṣa when he had an extraordinary vision at Gyasok Hermitage in which the deity taught a synopsis of spiritual practice. On that occasion, the exalted Mañjughoṣa himself taught the synopsis of spiritual practice thusly:

1154. *Rje btsun 'jam pa'i dbyangs kyis gsungs pa'i nyams len mdor bsdus* (Ts*JBDD*). For context, see above, pages 159–60. The roman-text portions of the following are assumed to be the words of Tsongkhapa, whether his own or quoting Mañjughoṣa. The italicized portions are likely interpolations by the editor who compiled the text. The bracketed subheadings have been inserted by me based on the analysis of commentator Phurbuchok Ngawang Jampa (1682–1782) in Pb*NDSB*.

1155. See note 573 above.

[Identifying the path][1156]
Without abiding anywhere,
contemplate mind itself as like space.
Be assiduous in all the related practices.
Live like a rhinoceros.
Abandon all distractions.
Attain meditative equipoise within.
Obtain great awakening.

[Common methods]
Do not doubt the fruition of karma.
Meditate on renunciation and the awakening mind.

[Uncommon methods: The actual point and the way of meditating on it]
Keep the great fire of mindfulness continuously ablaze,

[Uncommon methods: Benefits]
and the kindling of the six sense objects will certainly be consumed.

[Wisdom: A brief summary]
All things in saṃsāra and nirvāṇa
are boundless like space:
they never have been nor will they ever be perceived by anyone.

[Wisdom: An extensive explanation]
[Refuting the object]
Appearing objects are like a sky flower,

[Refuting the subject]
and what sugata has found the subject, the mind?

[Refuting the self-awareness that is the oneness of awareness and the Dharma realm]
The oneness of awareness and the Dharma realm is proven to be like a rabbit's horn.

1156. This first text division is supplied by Phurbuchok, at Pb*NDSB* 314–15; the rest are those listed by Tsongkhapa near the end of the text, though their specific location in the poem is supplied not by Jé Lama but by Phurbuchok, at Pb*NDSB* 315–20.

> *[Showing the greatness of the path]*
> Whatever is practiced like that is the path of the conquerors.

This is just what he said.

The path that leads to awakening is twofold: method and wisdom. Methods are twofold: common and uncommon. The uncommon are threefold: the main point, the way of meditating on it, and the benefits. Wisdom is twofold: a brief summary and an extensive explanation. The extensive explanation is fourfold: refuting the object, refuting the subject, refuting the self-awareness that is the oneness of awareness and the Dharma realm, and showing the greatness of the path.

Thus this synopsis of the spiritual practice taught by the exalted Mañjughoṣa, which is condensed into these four and a half ślokas, was composed by the exalted omniscient Tsongkhapa himself.

2. Bright Lamp of the Excellent Path: An Excerpt[1157]

Kachen Yeshé Gyaltsen

Showing the Sources of the [Ganden Mahāmudrā] Instruction

Seeing the gradations of his disciples' elements, thoughts, latent propensities, and faculties, the perfectly complete Buddha expounded countless, unlimited definitive and provisional scriptures. From among all those, the scriptures that are superior, clear, and uppermost, that explain the Conqueror's own intention and the ultimate definitive meaning, are the precious Perfection of Wisdom sūtras and the precious unexcelled yoga tantras, such as the root and explanatory tantras of Śrī Guhyasamāja. Thus the ultimate explanatory sources for this mahāmudrā instruction are the extensive, middle-length and concise Mother [Prajñāpāramitā] and the precious unexcelled yoga tantras. Later disciples, however, did not rely upon the instructions of scholar-siddhas authoritative in commenting on the intentions of the Conqueror. They approached the Buddha's words on their own, [207] so they could not get the key point of the profound definitive meaning and could not understand the key points of how to practice on the path at the beginning, end, or in between. In commenting on the Conqueror's intention, they were mired in confusion about the sūtras and tantras.

The Conqueror himself, authoritative in every way, predicted in many sūtras and tantras that his great charioteer would be Ārya Nāgārjuna. Ārya Nāgārjuna composed the Six Collections of Madhyamaka Reasoning, which are ultimate instructions set forth according to the meaning intended by the Conqueror himself in the Mother sūtras. He also composed the *Five Stages* and other ultimate-level pith instructions that plainly extract the essential meaning of the Guhyasamāja and other unexcelled yoga tantras.

1157. *Dga' ldan phyag rgya chen po'i khrid yig snyan brgyud lam bzang gsal ba'i sgron me* (Yg*LZGM* 3b–16a). For context, see above, chapter 11. See also *Collected Works (gsuṅ 'bum) of Tshe mchog gliṅ yongs 'dzin ye shes rgyal mtshan*, 22:206–31 (New Delhi: Tibet House Library, 1974). For an English translation of a lengthier account by Yeshé Gyaltsen of the lineage masters from Tokden Jampal Gyatso to Losang Chögyen, see Willis 1995, 31–96.

The splendid guardian Mahāsukha [i.e., Padmavajra] taught that the essence of the countless unexcelled yoga tantras is the gnosis of connate luminosity; he composed the *Secret Attainment* (*Guhyasiddhi*), which is an ultimate-level pith instruction on how to put that into practice. In the wake of that, others of the Seven Attainment Texts, such as the *Attainment of Certainty about Wisdom and Means* (*Prajñopāyaviniścayasiddhi*), appeared. The mahāsiddha Saraha gained proficiency in the mahāmudrā gnosis of the great bliss-luminosity and explained it by composing *dohā* instructions on its essential meaning. Thus the Six Collections of [208] Madhyamaka Reasoning composed by the guardian Nāgārjuna, the Seven Attainment Texts such as the *Secret Attainment* by the guardian Mahāsukha, and the dohā texts of the mahāsiddha Saraha are the ultimate root texts for this instruction on the profound mahāmudrā path. As the mahāmudrā root text *Highway of the Conquerors* states:

> The main practice of mahāmudrā,
> has many modes of explanation,
> but they are divisible into two: sūtra and mantra.
> The latter is the great bliss-luminosity mind arising
> from skill in the methods of penetrating the vital points
> in the vajra body.
> The mahāmudrā of Saraha and Nāgārjunapāda,
> of Nāro and Maitrī,
> is taught in the Attainment Texts and the Essential Trilogy
> and is the quintessence of the unexcelled tantras.
> As for the former, it is a way of meditating on emptiness
> directly taught in the three Mothers: the extensive, middle-length, and concise.
> The supreme ārya, Nāgārjuna, has stated that there is
> no path to liberation apart from this.[1158]

The way in which [the teaching] arose from a single guru and was ordered into a single lineage

With respect to the uncommon proximate lineage, although it was given directly to the omniscient Jé Tsongkhapa by the exalted Mañjughoṣa, the omniscient Jé did not openly boast that it had been given to him by a high deity. That alone does not suffice, and so he said that he received it [209] from

1158. Bz*GBZL* 2a [83] (verses 6–9); see translation below in part 5, section 4.

the Buddha. It is an uninterrupted lineage of great renown, and if one cannot touch upon the Buddha's word that is the root of the special instruction, one should at least, having seen a little the benefits of the general teaching, rely definitively upon a spiritual friend who holds the transmitted instruction in a succession from the Buddha. As Jé Rinpoché himself says:

> In general nowadays in Tibet, countless instructions on the Secret Mantra and Definitional vehicles have appeared, but since they were not transmitted in lineages of buddhas and bodhisattvas and do not appear there, there is no reason to disseminate them apart from their having been spoken by some yidam. The minds of their transmitters go only this way and that; they are unable to extract the principles of the path and have no method for producing definitive purification. Thus when the intelligent properly seek an unmistaken path, they do not contradict at all the undisputed sūtras and tantras. Instead, drawing from them, they follow the reasoning of the single vehicle [the Mahāyāna] and correctly distinguish definitive from provisional scriptures. In this way, not inappropriately, they are not harmed by poor reasoning that would lead them to extremes. They prize the stainless door of reasoning that seeks out the classic texts and their meaning, and although many [210] ways of organizing the tantras have previously appeared, they are not satisfied with those and are consumed solely by thoughts of the teaching. Without distinguishing yidam from guru, they strive continuously in the many approaches to beseeching, amassing, and purifying. Apply your knowledge to practicing not just fragments but the entire corpus of the general scriptures and the great treatises that comment upon their meaning.[1159]

[Mahāyāna lineages][1160]

As for the way of seeking suchness, which is the profound meaning of the precious Perfection of Wisdom sūtras, and, having sought it, the stages of the path one cultivates: the Teacher, the Mighty Sage granted it to the exalted Mañjughoṣa, and the exalted Mañjughoṣa granted it to the guardian Nāgārjuna. The latter granted it to Candrakīrti, who granted it to Vidyākokila the Elder, who granted it to Vidyākokila the Younger, who granted it to Jowo

1159. SNL.

1160. Here and elsewhere, bracketed section headings represent my own interpolations.

Jé Atiśa. The guardian Nāgārjuna showed the way of putting into practice the complete corpus of the Mahāyāna path, composing the *Jewel Garland* on Madhyamaka and the *Compendium of Sūtras*, which establishes the nature of reality scripturally. Because he composed the *Condensed Sādhanas*, the *Mixture of Sūtras*, and the *Five Stages*, which show the way of meditating on the two stages of the [unexcelled] yoga tantra path and their ancillaries on the basis of the ordinary path, [211] Nāgārjuna's texts fully contain every key point of meditation on the Mahāyāna [path].

There also is an orally transmitted lineage taught by those proficient in the stages of the path of greatly extensive activity. The Mighty Sage granted it to the exalted Maitreya. The latter granted it to Ārya Asaṅga, who granted it to the master Vasubandhu, from whom it was transmitted eventually to the great guru Serlingpa, who granted it to Jowo Jé Atiśa.

The pith instructions on secret mantra, the four classes of tantras, were extant in the Land of the Āryas, and Jowo possessed most of them. Jowo Jé was a lord of the complete teaching of the Sage. Jé Rinpoché heard the instructions of the Jowo lineage from Lhodrak Drupchen and Drakor Khenchen, but he also was blessed directly by Jowo Jé himself: from the time when, as a youth, he dwelled in eastern Tibet, Jé Rinpoché was blessed with teachings again and again by Jowo. Most importantly, when at the royal retreat center at Radreng Jé Rinpoché made forceful and intensive appeals to the image of Jowo known as Facing Left, he saw the lineage gurus of the stages of the path amid a moon disk and received many instructions and follow-up teachings. In the end, the gurus absorbed progressively into Jowo. Atiśa himself [212] placed his hand on Jé Rinpoché's head and said, "You must perform far-reaching deeds for the teaching, become awakened, and help sentient beings achieve their aims." Then he blessed him as a lord of the teaching.

[Mahāmudrā lineages descending to Tsongkhapa]

With reference to this profound teaching of Ganden mahāmudrā, it is essential to explicate the transmission of the stages of the path to awakening; the reason is shown below.

[The distant lineage]

Vajradhara granted the mahāmudrā teaching to the lord of secrets, Vajrapāṇi. The latter granted it to the mahāsiddha Saraha, who granted it to the guardian Nāgārjuna, and Saraha and the guardian Nāgārjuna both granted it to Śrī Śavaripa. In accordance with the meaning of the Great Brahman Saraha's *Dohā Treasury*, Śavaripa composed the *Answer That Teaches the View and Meditation of Mahāmudrā*.[1161] He granted the teaching to Lūipa, who granted it to Dārikapa, who granted it to Diṅkaṃpa, who granted it to Tilopa. As for the mahāsiddha Tilopa, his biography says that he possessed the transmissions known as the four orally descended transmissions and that he heard the mahāmudrā cycle from Diṅkaṃpa. The mahāsiddha Tilopa taught a verse instruction on mahāmudrā to the great paṇḍita Nāropa by the banks of the river Ganges; it is known as the *Mother Ganges Mahāmudrā*. Tilopa granted the teaching to Nāropa, who granted it to Marpa. The glorious Śavaripa also granted the teaching to Maitrīpa, and the mahāsiddha Maitrīpa composed [213] a lengthy work that summarized the advice of earlier mahāsiddhas, the *Golden Garland of Mahāmudrā*, as well as many shorter works on the mahāmudrā view—the *Ten Verses on Thatness* and so forth. Maitrīpa also granted the teaching to Marpa, so Marpa the translator heard the instruction on mahāmudrā from both Nāropa and Maitrīpa—although it is said that he gained the ultimate Madhyamaka view, the profound meaning of Nāgārjuna, from Maitrīpa. As Marpa himself says:

> I came to the banks of the Ganges River in the east.
> Through the kindness of Lord Maitrīpa,
> I realized the ground, unborn reality.
> My mind was ablaze with emptiness;
> I saw the primordial nature, reality free from elaboration;
> I met the three mother buddha bodies face to face.
> From then on, this man's elaborations were severed.[1162]

Combining into a single body the instructions on meditation of the four orally descended transmissions transmitted from the great paṇḍita Nāropa, the translator Marpa granted to the exalted Milarepa the complete instructions on the six Dharmas of Nāropa as well as the mahāmudrā transmitted from the mahāsiddha Maitrīpa. Mila says:

> I heard from afar the renown of the father-translator,
> said to be blessed by Nāro and Maitrī

1161. *Phyag chen gyi lta sgom ston pa'i kha ya*; there is no work by this name attributed to Śavaripa in the Tengyur. There is a work by Saraha entitled *Lta bsgom spyod pa 'bras bu'i do ha'i glu* (*Bhāvanādṛṣṭicaryāphaladohāgītikā*), Toh 2345.

1162. Th*MPNT* 134. Cf. trans. Nālandā Translation Committee 1982, 144–45. This passage also is quoted by Paṇchen Chögyen and Thuken.

and living in the upper village by the southern river.
Traversing a difficult road, I came before him.
I, Milarepa,
dwelt at the feet of that kind father
for six years and eight months
and, as purification, constructed singlehandedly [214]
a nine-story tower and its courtyard.
Seized by compassion, the kindly father
granted me the ultimate view, mahāmudrā,
which introduces the profound abiding nature,
the path of means that is the six Dharmas of Nāro,
and the ripening path that is the flowing river of the four
empowerments,
together with the oral precepts entrusted
into the hands of Śrī Nāro.
I, not acting lazy,
used my mind for meditation and in this life
first and foremost established lasting happiness.[1163]

The omniscient Jé Tsongkhapa received the profound teachings transmitted from the exalted Mila from Chenga Chökyi Gyalpo and Drakpa Jangchub. Moreover, Tsongkhapa received the stream of empowerments, scriptural transmissions, and pith instructions primarily from Chöjé Döndrup, Khyunglepa, Chökyi Palwa, and the exalted Rendawa. Above all, he heard from the exalted Rendawa countless cycles of teaching on Madhyamaka and Guhyasamāja.

The uncommon proximate lineage

Jé Rinpoché received the complete pith instructions of the various lineage seats from the exalted Mañjughoṣa. Also, measureless eons ago, Jé Lama had been the favorite pupil of the exalted Mañjughoṣa, and from then on in the presence of mighty conquerors in countless buddhafields, he apprehended in general all the holy Dharmas of the conquerors. Above all, [215] he aroused the thought, and made a great and powerful vow, to spread widely the profound Madhyamaka view and the teachings on the two stages of the unexcelled-yoga-tantra path. He arrived at this intention for the purpose of spreading in this earthly field the essential teachings of the sūtras and tantras. In general, his realiza-

1163. Th*MLGB* 274; cf. trans. Chang 1989, 1:267–68, and Tsangnyön Heruka 2016, 277.

tion of countless teachings, and above all of the ultimate view of the profound Madhyamaka, went as far as possible,[1164] but overwhelmed by the degeneration of the essence of the teaching in Tibet, he decided to seek the view among the mahāsiddhas who had attained the rainbow body in the wooded mountains of India. He prepared to leave alone to seek the essence of the teaching, without regard for either body or life and despite the hundreds of difficulties he would encounter. At that time, the lord of secrets Vajrapāṇi and various other deities and gurus thought that if Jé Rinpoché went to India, Tibet would become an island of darkness, while if he remained in Tibet, the situation would improve, so they formally requested him to remain. Then Jé Rinpoché said, "I ask only that the exalted Mañjughoṣa explain to me this profound view," and when importuned again and [216] again, the exalted one taught him in detail the key points of the pith instructions. When he had been taught again and again the way required for realization of this ultimate view by relying solely on the pith instructions of the great charioteer Nāgārjuna, Jé's mind became thoroughly immersed in the object. When he asked Mañjughoṣa what should be done if those teachings known as the "profound pith instructions of Tibet" did not accord with the textual systems of the great charioteers, the exalted one taught that if a pith instruction is authentic, it will certainly accord with the textual systems of the great charioteers, while if it happens that a pith instruction does not accord with the classic texts, it is flawed and should be rejected, for it is improper to reject the texts of the great charioteers in any respect.

When Jé asked what methods were necessary for attaining nondeceptiveness in this profound view, Mañjughoṣa taught him that, having taken the guru and the principal deity as inseparable, it is necessary to combine three activities: making appeals, striving to collect merit and purify nonvirtues, and examining the meaning of the classic texts—and he granted him in detail the pith instructions on how to do those things. Also at that time, the exalted one said:

> For these savage sentient beings so hard to train,
> what great good can come through explanation?
> Through it, they will devote themselves to practice and resort to solitude
> and will think of attaining the path that satisfies both [217] self and others.[1165]

1164. Lit. "reached the very limits of existence" (*srid mtha' tsam du song*).

1165. SNL.

Saying this, he urged upon Jé the necessity to strive for the requisite causes of attaining the profound view while abiding in solitude, and so, following the exalted one's advice, Jé immediately went to a solitary place.

When he strove as continuously as a river for the requisite causes of those immeasurable collections and purifications, he had visions of many buddhas and bodhisattvas. He was visited and blessed by countless paṇḍitas and siddhas, such as the Six Ornaments and the Two Supremes,[1166] Saraha and Lūipa, and others. Of those, he was visited repeatedly by the quintet of the Ārya father and his sons.[1167] Most importantly, one night, the master Buddhapālita placed an Indian text on top of his head, and a special sign of the purity of the blessing occurred. First thing[1168] the next day, Jé examined the Buddhapālita commentary in detail, and all reference points for apprehending signs were destroyed. Then the profound Madhyamaka view free from all elaborated extremes appeared to him. It came to mind in accordance with Nāgārjuna's elucidation of the Conqueror's intended meaning: that the ultimate profound view is that emptiness dawns as dependent arising and dependent arising as emptiness, which clears away the appearance-based extreme of "is" and clears away the emptiness-based extreme of "is not." His mind was thoroughly satisfied, and he composed [218] a wondrous marvel of a text, the *Essence of Excellent Explanation that Praises the Mighty Sage for His Teaching of Profound Dependent Arising.*[1169] Then he once again made extensive outer, inner, secret, and suchness offerings to the exalted Mañjughoṣa, and when he prayed for the spread of this essence of the teaching, the exalted one conferred upon him many common and uncommon instructions. Most importantly, he granted Jé Rinpoché himself, along with the exalted Jampal Gyatso and some fortunate deities, the pith instructions of the hearing lineage, together with an emanated scripture. Thenceforth, Jé Rinpoché granted countless pith instructions on sūtra and mantra to numberless disciples and gave many unprecedented excellent explanations, mainly on the two aspects of the stages of the path—according to sūtra and mantra, respectively.

Thinking that at that time the obstacles were too great, Jé limited his instruction on the profound path of mahāmudrā to the hearing transmission; without putting it in writing, he merely indicated it symbolically by saying, "It

1166. The Six Ornaments are Nāgārjuna, Āryadeva, Asaṅga, Vasubandhu, Dignāga, and Dharmakīrti; the Two Supremes are Guṇaprabha and Śākyaprabha.

1167. Nāgārjuna and his four main followers: Āryadeva, Buddhapālita, Bhāviveka, and Candrakīrti.

1168. Literally, "without even making offerings" (*dngos su 'bul ma byung bar*).

1169. *Thub pa'i dbang po la zab mo rten 'byung gsung ba'i sgo nas stod pa legs par bshad pa'i snying po*, better known as the *Rten 'brel stod pa* (*Praise for Dependent Arising*). See translation at, e.g., Thurman 1982, 99–107, and Kilty 2001, 216–45.

is like this." Also, in *Queries from a Pure Heart*, at the end of a section where he poses many questions regarding the sufficiency of the cycle of teachings on mahāmudrā view and meditation, he says:

> Well why, you may wonder, did the Conqueror state that seeing nothing is the highest seeing and looking nowhere is the highest looking? It was intended [219] for those who are sincerely intent on really deepening themselves, not for the coarse. It seems that the time is not right for us at this point to impart to those who desire it the original pith instruction of the wise father guru.[1170]

Also, in the *Reply to Statements by Rendawa*, he says:

> Since it does not appear at present that there is any rationale for teaching these systems that elicit the experience of renunciation, arousing awakening mind, and the view, they are uncommon. In particular, this system that imparts the experience of the view is recognized as being a definitive [teaching]; it is an instruction that penetrates to the marrow, but it is not a teaching for the present time. It is stated that if one practices this technique, one may hope to obtain precisely the fruits of that path, while if one meditates on other instructions, one's possibilities will not be as great. As for guidance in the trio of renunciation, arousing awakening mind, and the view in this system of ours: I have granted teachings on the system along with its fine details, and it has not occurred to me to write about it extensively. Even though I could have written about the system, I have not done so, because its practice is dependent on its being taught by certain gurus.[1171]

Many variant statements of this type appear in Jé Rinpoché's work.

1170. Ts*LSRK* 79b [356].

1171. Ts*RDSL* 44b [326].

[The Ganden Hearing Lineage after Tsongkhapa]

Tokden Jampal Gyatso[1172]

Jé Rinpoché then granted the pith instructions of the hearing transmission to Tokden Jampal Gyatso and the omniscient Khedrup, and he placed the emanated scripture in the hands of Tokden Jampal Gyatso. Then, so as to [220] reach the headwaters of the teaching of the hearing lineage of Jé Lama, Jé Jampal Gyatso rejected the turbulence of this life and absorbed himself single-mindedly in practice in a solitary place. He had continual visions of the exalted Mañjughoṣa and asked the exalted one what actions to undertake and then performed them. He explained the pith instructions to a fortunate few, and most importantly, he granted to Baso Chökyi Gyaltsen the complete pith instructions of the hearing transmission along with the emanated scripture.

Baso Chökyi Gyaltsen[1173]

In order to single-pointedly practice the pith instructions of the hearing transmission of father Jé and his spiritual sons, Paṇchen Baso Chökyi Gyaltsen formed the intention to model himself on the life of Śrī Śavaripa in an unpeopled, empty valley, but it fell to him that he had to assume the Ganden throne so that the central pillar[1174] of Jé Lama's teaching could grasped; thenceforth, Jé's teaching spread widely. Most importantly, as prophesied to Paṇchen Baso Chökyi Gyaltsen by a ḍākinī, the mahāsiddha Chökyi Dorjé arrived at Ganden at the age of eleven, accompanied by his parents. Baso donated many material goods to the boy's parents and then ordained him, giving him the name Chökyi Dorjé. Then, for five years, Baso treated Chökyi Dorjé as his prize pupil and conferred on him countless instructions on sūtra and mantra. Most importantly, he granted him the complete pith instructions of the hearing transmission, together with the [221] emanated scripture, and sealed his oral transmission by saying, "It is necessary that you perform the essential practice in an unpeopled, solitary place, and in the future, you should teach these pith instructions of the hearing lineage to a fortunate few. One thing more: pith instructions like these should not be allowed to proliferate."

1172. See also Willis 1995, 33–40, and above, chapter 7.

1173. See also Willis 1995, 43–47, and above, chapter 7.

1174. Literally, "life tree" (*srog shing*).

Chökyi Dorjé[1175]

Then the mahāsiddha Chökyi Dorjé fulfilled the advice of Paṇchen Baso Chökyi Gyaltsen and, living austerely amid isolated mountains and forests, applied himself to the essential practice. Once, he saw the exalted Tsongkhapa directly, and Jé Rinpoché granted him the common and uncommon precepts in their entirety. Most importantly, he fully granted him teaching on the guru yoga connected to the three-tiered being[1176]—which is a preliminary practice for the pith instructions of Ganden mahāmudrā—along with the key points of both the sūtra and mantra paths. Then, when the mahāsiddha applied himself single-pointedly to the commitments of this guru yoga, he had visions of numberless buddhas and bodhisattvas, such as the exalted Padmapāṇi and others. Realizations on the common and uncommon paths arose one after the other, and he attained the rainbow body, the state of union, the vajra body.

Wondering to whom [222] he should entrust these hearing lineages of Jé Lama, the mahāsiddha looked inward with his gnostic power and came to know that the great Gyalwa Ensapa would be lord of the hearing-transmission teaching. When the great Gyalwa Ensapa reached the age of seventeen, he was stricken with smallpox. While he was living in isolation, the mahāsiddha Chökyi Dorjé arrived at his door and said: "I have the ultimate pith instructions of profound meaning." As a sign of this, he recited Tsongkhapa's *Praise for Dependent Arising* and made as if asking for alms. Just from hearing the sound of the teaching, the great Ensapa thought that Chökyi Dorjé was unique, and he invited him inside. He thought, "Here is a monk with a wispy white beard. Even wearing this dusty teaching robe, he is greatly resplendent. It is absolutely certain that he is a great lord." Then, when he analyzed in detail, he came to know that Chökyi Dorjé was a mahāsiddha who held the complete hearing transmission of Jé Lama. His request to be the transmission's next holder was gladly accepted. Chökyi Dorjé said, "Come right now to Jomo Lhari," and the mahāsiddha went to Jomo Lhari. Then, following the mahāsiddha's advice, the great Ensapa arrived at Jomo Lhari before long; he met Chökyi Dorjé in

1175. See also Willis 1995, 43–47, and above, chapter 7.

1176. As we have seen, *sems dpa' gsum brtsegs* evokes the external visualization of one's guru in the guise of Tsongkhapa, with Śākyamuni Buddha at his heart, and Vajradhara and his consort at Śākyamuni's heart. Also, in unexcelled-yoga-tantra contexts more broadly, the term may also refer to oneself visualized as a complex pledge being, the two-armed, one-faced deity at one's heart as the gnosis being, and the seed syllable at the gnosis being's heart as the concentration being.

the Gulgarmo [223] Dharma castle on Jomo Lhari.[1177] Within his means, he offered Chökyi Dorjé a ritual feast together with a maṇḍala. When he asked for instructions, Chökyi Dorjé granted him countless Dharma teachings of sūtra and mantra and, most importantly, the complete pith instructions of the hearing transmission of Jé Lama together with the emanated scripture.

Gyalwa Ensapa[1178]

Now the great Gyalwa Ensapa, from the days of his youth, had repeatedly been taught directly by the Teacher and Mighty Sage [i.e., the Buddha] and by Jé Lama and had been blessed by them. Most importantly, one evening, Jé Lama placed a hat on Ensapa's head and blessed him as a lord of the teaching of the hearing transmission. Then, following the advice of his guru, the mahāsiddha Chökyi Dorjé, the great Ensapa resorted to austere living in isolated places such as the palace of Drakgya Dorjé, and applied himself to the essential practices of the pith instructions of the hearing transmission. At that time, with his feet in the vajra posture, he sat unmoving all day and all night, and although the flesh on his thighs became rotten, he merely smeared his body with soft ash-dung. He remained fixed single-pointedly on the yidam and successively manifested realizations of the common and uncommon paths. He gained a special concentration, which entailed the power in which one knows many hundreds of thousands of one's own and others' rebirths; [224] the special ability to pass at will through anything: Mount Meru, the walls of a house, and so forth; and the arising, as a great treasury, of the measureless attributes of scripture and realization described in the *Perfection of Wisdom in Eight Thousand Lines* and other Sanskrit texts he recited. Most importantly, based on the pith instructions of the hearing transmission, he perfected the concentrations of the two tantric stages and attained the body of union. As the conqueror Ensapa the Great himself says:[1179]

In early times Milarepa,

1177. A prominent snow-capped mountain, 24,035 feet high, on the Tibet-Bhutan border. The implication of this passage is that as a mahāsiddha Chökyi Dorjé was able to go to the mountain instantaneously, while Ensapa had to get there by more conventional means.

1178. See also Willis 1995, 57–70, and above, chapter 7.

1179. The text clearly indicates that the two quotes that follow are attributable to Ensapa, but their unabashed third-person celebration of his spiritual accomplishments suggests that perhaps they were spoken or written by a contemporary.

at the present time Losang Döndrup:[1180]
except for the food and clothing of immediate Dharma,
they needed nothing; they seized the jewel directly.
To achieve buddhahood in a single life,
may I properly abide in such practices,
and in solitude, with attachment and aversion abandoned,
take up the essence of this free and favored life.[1181]

And:

The supreme disciple of the snowy ranges
is said to be Losang Döndrup:
by putting into practice this supreme path,
he achieved buddhahood in this very life.[1182]

As for the uncommon supreme secret, it was entrusted amid the oceanic assembly of the Teacher and Mighty Sage to the supreme ārya, Subhūti, who was peerless and unrivaled in proclaiming the sweet words of the profound view. At the time of being taught how the body [225] weakens on the verge of death, some in that fortunate retinue offered a maṇḍala and made a single-pointed appeal, saying:

We intend to be chief of those who travel the path
to liberation; to be śrāvakas who grasp
the Mahāyāna teaching; to achieve the supreme
realization of the śrāvakas of the Great Sage.[1183]

Thus, in this final age of impurity—so as to illumine these profound pith instructions arranged by Ārya Nāgārjuna to show the Conqueror's meaning and to uphold and disseminate the hearing transmission of Jé Lama—things will doubtless come to pass as they intended. As Ensapa himself says:

In this present time, please bestow upon just us

1180. This is Ensapa's monastic name.

1181. SNL.

1182. SNL.

1183. SNL.

apprehension of the hearing transmission that is the essence of the speech
of the guru known as Losang Drakpa,
the supreme, chosen pupil of Mañjughoṣa.[1184]

Thus the lord of the teaching of the hearing transmission, the great Ensapa, widely disseminated the teaching of Jé Lama's hearing transmission. Most importantly, he granted the complete pith instructions of the hearing transmission to his heart son, the holy Khedrup Sangyé Yeshé. He taught Khedrup Sangyé Yeshé the great emanated scripture in its entirety face to face, and [226] Khedrup Sangyé Yeshé learned it by heart in its entirety. When, however, he requested that the book itself be directly given to him, Ensapa said, "Since it is an emanated scripture, you will see it if the time is right; if the time is not right, then even if, this very day, it is unconcealed, you will not see it." It is not clearly stated whether the emanated scripture was extant after that.

Khedrup Sangyé Yeshé[1185]

When Khedrup Sangyé Yeshé undertook the essential practice of the pith instructions of the hearing transmission as advised by the mahāsiddha Ensapa, he gradually attained supreme realizations. Most importantly, it is said that when he focused single-pointedly upon the yidam in practicing the uncommon guru yoga, he attained the level of luminosity mahāmudrā. Khedrup Sangyé Yeshé granted the complete pith instructions of the hearing transmission to the omniscient Paṇchen Losang Chökyi Gyaltsen.

Paṇchen Losang Chökyi Gyaltsen[1186]

The omniscient Paṇchen Chökyi Gyaltsen also applied himself single-pointedly to the practice of the pith instructions of the hearing transmission. He practiced the liberating teachings of the great Ensapa at the Ensa Dharma palace, the Drakgya Dorjé palace, and other places. Based on the pith instructions of the profound path of mahāmudrā, he came to realize the ultimate, profound Madhyamaka view, and he progressively [227] gained common and uncommon special realizations. He dispensed such inspiring utterances as this:

1184. SNL.

1185. See also Willis 1997, 73–82, and above, chapter 7.

1186. See also Willis 1997, 85–96, and above, chapter 9.

> Serving the guru who holds the meaning transmission
> of scholar-siddhas who manifest this
> supreme path taken from the noble Buddha,
> I uphold the transmission of general vows[1187] and dwell in utter bliss.[1188]

And this:

> Well, apart from the game of assigning names
> to every phenomenon of saṃsāra or nirvāṇa,
> there is nowhere a realm with intrinsic nature,
> so I have no fear of either birth or death.
>
> I once wandered compulsively, but now I've reached the abode
> of healing and rest, the ambrosial essence, the emptiness of things.
> I think this is the kindness of my exalted guru;
> he's certainly most kind, my noble guru.
>
> I, a son of Losang the second Conqueror,
> amuse myself on the mahāmudrā path
> and take up this song of the Dharma view.
> All you friends who seek liberation should do the same.[1189]

Having obtained the complete pith instructions of the hearing transmission, Chökyi Gyaltsen cut all ties to this life and went to a secluded forest: he went so far as to equate life with practice, emulating the mahāsiddha Śavaripa and others. When his practice became continuous, he received teachings directly from Jé Tsongkhapa, who prophesied that, to disseminate the essence of the teaching, he would have to study even more extensively [228] and would have to disseminate many instructions to other fortunate beings. Then, following the advice of Jé Lama, he received countless empowerments, scriptural transmissions, and pith instructions from many holy spiritual friends. He became a lord of the Sage's complete teaching and imparted the pith instructions of the hearing transmission to countless fortunate beings. Seeing that the time was right, he composed the root verses for the pith instructions of Ganden mahāmudrā, *Highway of the Conquerors*, together with its commentary, *Lamp So Bright*, and gave guidance to countless disciples intent

1187. Reading *dam tshig* for *da tshig.*

1188. SNL.

1189. This is from song 6, translated below in part 5, section 10; cf. trans. Guenther 1976, 123.

on the final goal. Moreover, he set forth in guidebooks the pith instructions of the hearing transmission relating to the stages of the path to awakening and the pith instructions on the two stages of the profound unexcelled-yoga-tantra path. By virtue of his great waves of previous arousal of awakening mind, as well as prayer, he received offerings from all beings throughout the expanse of Jambudvīpa and had countless beings, regardless of doctrinal preference, take the dust of his feet upon their heads. Because all those beings were encompassed by his Dharmic kindness, his dissemination of Jé Lama's teaching was tantamount to the deeds of Jé Lama himself.

The Ganden mahāmudrā lineage after Paṇchen Chögyen

When Jé Losang Chökyi Gyaltsen had granted these instructions on Ganden mahāmudrā to many fortunate beings, his various holy heart sons disseminated them widely in every direction. Those [229] whom he advised mainly about action were: Nechu Rabjampa Gendun Gyaltsen,[1190] Drungpa Tsönsdrü Gyaltsen,[1191] Dorjé Dzinpa Könchok Gyaltsen,[1192] and Drungpa Taphukpa.[1193] Furthermore, the tradition also was extensively disseminated by Drupchen Losang Yarphel, Drupai Wangchuk Namkha Dorjé, and Shabdrung Losang Tenpai Dargyé. Drungpa Tsönsdrü Gyaltsen, Dorjé Dzinpa Könchok Gyaltsen, and Drungpa Taphukpa granted it to a hidden yogī named Jatang Trinlé Chöphel, who was cherished dearly by most of the heart sons of Jé Losang Chökyi Gyaltsen. Most importantly, Drungpa Tsönsdrü Gyaltsen considered Jatang his heart son and granted him the complete special instructions. Jatang Trinlé Chöphel cut his ties to this life, and when he applied himself single-pointedly to solitary practice, he gained confidence in the profound path. That holy being granted the profound teaching of Ganden mahāmudrā many times to my guru, the great Drupai Wangchuk.[1194]

My guru, the great Drupai Wangchuk, came to the decision to dissemi-

1190. See lineage prayer, verse 10, translated below in part 5, section 3.

1191. See lineage prayer, verse 11, translated below in part 5, section 3, where he is identified as Drupai Gyaltsen Dzinpa.

1192. See lineage prayer, verse 12, translated below in part 5, section 3.

1193. This may be another name for the Losang Tsöndrü Gyaltsen mentioned in the lineage prayer, verse 23 (translated below in part 5, section 3), but I have not yet found textual confirmation of this.

1194. Willis 1995, 127. His full name, as noted below, is Drupai Wangchuk Chenpo Losang Namgyal Palsang (1640–1741). See verse 15 of the lineage prayer, translated below in part 5, section 3.

nate this pith instruction of the hearing transmission. From the time [230] he was small, having memorized them, he recited the root verses on Ganden mahāmudrā continually. Even when conducting himself according to the textual tradition,[1195] everything he did he did solely as a method for realizing the meaning of these pith instructions and generating them in his mindstream. Exerting himself relentlessly in seeking the pith of these pith instructions, he served many holy spiritual instructors. Drupai Wangchuk received many pith instructions, including guidance on mahāmudrā and other practices, from the heart son of Losang Yarphel named Losang Tsewang. He received many pith instructions on this profound teaching's uncommon guru-deity yoga preparatory practices from Dorjé Dzinpa Losang Rikdröl. He received guidance on mahāmudrā from many other spiritual friends as well. Most importantly, he received the pith instructions of the hearing transmission in detail from Shabdrung Lhapa Losang Trinlé in the hermitage of Jangchen. When he devoted himself to the teaching, he came to realize the ultimate, profound uncommon view explained by the guardian Nāgārjuna and the conqueror Tsongkhapa. This lama and the great omniscient Second Paṇchen, the exalted Losang Yeshé, were the matchlessly kind crown holders [of the lineage]. Over the course of a month, that very lama, the great Drupai Wangchuk [231] Losang Namgyal Palsangpo, gladly conferred upon me the Ganden mahāmudrā tradition together with guidance in its four preliminaries[1196]—and I obtained it well.

1195. That is, the Sūtra Vehicle.

1196. Presumably, as described above, the practices of (1) taking refuge and generating the awakening mind while prostrating to visualized buddhas and bodhisattvas, (2) purifying via Vajrasattva recitation and meditation, (3) offering the Meru maṇḍala, and (4) performing guru-yoga meditation. Each would be performed 100,000 times.

3. Mahāmudrā Lineage Prayer[1197]

Namo mahāmudrāya!

1

In the mansion of the three spontaneous buddha bodies,
you're the primordial buddha, head of all families—
to the pervasive lord, great Vajradhara, I appeal:

Please grant me blessings to cut in my mindstream
the myriad ways of grasping at self,
arouse love and compassion, awakening mind,
and quickly attain supreme mahāmudrā, the unitive path.

2

In the world of ten directions, this vast expanding field,
you're the father begetting conquerors in all three times—
to all-wise Ārya Mañjuśrī, I appeal:

Please grant me blessings to cut in my mindstream
the myriad ways of grasping at self,
arouse love and compassion, awakening mind,
and quickly attain supreme mahāmudrā, the unitive path.

1197. *Phyag chen brgyud pa'i gsol 'debs.* Reproduced in Willis 1995, 107–10. Cf. trans. Willis 1995, 101–6, Kachen Yeshe Gyaltsen 2014, 445–54, and Zasep 2019, 13–25. For context, see the discussion of Paṇchen Chögyen, Yeshé Gyeltsen, and Phabongkha Rinpoché above, in chapters 9, 11, and 14, respectively. Verses 1–8 and 37–38 represent Paṇchen Chögyen's original prayer, while additions are by Yeshé Gyaltsen (9–15, 39), Phabongkha Rinpoché (16–32), an unknown lama or lamas (33–34), Trijang Rinpoché (35), and Thubten Zopa Rinpoché (36). For a chart that gives the dates (so far as they are known) of all members of the lineage, see appendix A. I would like to acknowledge the assistance of Ven. Tenzin Gaché in puzzling out the identities of several of the figures in this list.

3
In the northern country, this snowy land,
you are [1b] Jé, a second sage for the Sage's teaching—
to the exalted Losang Drakpa, I appeal:

Please grant me blessings to cut in my mindstream
the myriad ways of grasping at self,
arouse love and compassion, awakening mind,
and quickly attain supreme mahāmudrā, the unitive path.

4
You're primary holder of the hearing-transmission teaching
of Tsongkhapa, son of Mañjuśrī—
to Tokden Jampal Gyatso, I appeal:

Please grant me blessings to cut in my mindstream
the myriad ways of grasping at self,
arouse love and compassion, awakening mind,
and quickly attain supreme mahāmudrā, the unitive path.

5
You open the trove of hearing-transmission instruction
and bring fortunate students to maturity—
to Baso Chökyi Gyaltsen, I appeal:

Please grant me blessings to cut in my mindstream
the myriad ways of grasping at self,
arouse love and compassion, awakening mind,
and quickly attain supreme mahāmudrā, the unitive path.

6
Completing the yogas of both tantric stages,
you've won an awareness holder's immortal body—
to the supreme siddha, Dharmavajra, I appeal:

Please grant me blessings to cut in my mindstream
the myriad ways of grasping at self,
arouse love and compassion, awakening mind,
and quickly attain supreme mahāmudrā, the unitive path.

7
Untouched by the bonds of the eight mundane concerns,
you bear the definitive teaching's triumphal banner—[2a]
to Losang Dönyö Drupa [Ensapa], I appeal:

Please grant me blessings to cut in my mindstream
the myriad ways of grasping at self,
arouse love and compassion, awakening mind,
and quickly attain supreme mahāmudrā, the unitive path.

8
Sporting in saffron robes, you lead every being
to the joyous palace of three buddha bodies—
to the scholar-siddha Sangyé Yeshé, I appeal:

Please grant me blessings to cut in my mindstream
the myriad ways of grasping at self,
arouse love and compassion, awakening mind,
and quickly attain supreme mahāmudrā, the unitive path.

9
You guard Jé Losang the Conqueror's teaching;
inseparable from it, you know everything—
to the exalted Losang Chögyen, I appeal:

Please grant me blessings to cut in my mindstream
the myriad ways of grasping at self,
arouse love and compassion, awakening mind,
and quickly attain supreme mahāmudrā, the unitive path.

10
Each sūtra, tantra, and treatise of Buddha's word
you condensed to one meaning and put into practice completely—
to the mahāsiddha Gendun Gyaltsen, I appeal:

Please grant me blessings to cut in my mindstream
the myriad ways of grasping at self,
arouse love and compassion, awakening mind,
and quickly attain supreme mahāmudrā, the unitive path.

11
Through great exertion you tasted the very essence
of Jé Losang the conqueror's teaching and gained the supreme—
to Drupai Gyaltsen Dzinpa, I appeal:

Please grant me blessings to cut in my mindstream
the myriad ways of grasping at self,
arouse love and compassion, awakening mind,
and quickly attain supreme mahāmudrā, the unitive path.

12
You're skilled [2b] at instructing fortunate students
in the distillate nectar of deep and vast Dharma—
to the great tantric master, Könchok Gyaltsen, I appeal:

Please grant me blessings to cut in my mindstream
the myriad ways of grasping at self,
arouse love and compassion, awakening mind,
and quickly attain supreme mahāmudrā, the unitive path.

13
You are Jé Losang Chökyi Gyaltsen himself
come again for the good of the teachings and beings—
to the exalted Losang Yeshé,[1198] I appeal:

Please grant me blessings to cut in my mindstream
the myriad ways of grasping at self,
arouse love and compassion, awakening mind,
and quickly attain supreme mahāmudrā, the unitive path.

14
You're blessed by the noble Lord Buddha himself
and have plumbed the depths of the hearing-transmission path—
to Jé Losang Trinlé, I appeal:

Please grant me blessings to cut in my mindstream
the myriad ways of grasping at self,

1198. The Second Paṇchen Lama.

arouse love and compassion, awakening mind,
and quickly attain supreme mahāmudrā, the unitive path.

15
You put into practice completely the heart of the meaning
of Jé Losang the Conqueror's hearing transmission—
to the supreme siddha Losang Namgyal, I appeal:

Please grant me blessings to cut in my mindstream
the myriad ways of grasping at self,
arouse love and compassion, awakening mind,
and quickly attain supreme mahāmudrā, the unitive path.

16
Out of benevolence you gave unerring instruction
on the precepts of Jé Lama's oral transmission—
to kindly Yeshé Tsenchen,[1199] I appeal:

Please grant me blessings to cut in my mindstream
the myriad ways of grasping at self,
arouse love and compassion, awakening mind,
and quickly attain supreme mahāmudrā, the unitive path.

17
The essential inerrant teaching of the entire path [3a]
you spread far and wide, from the center to the border lands—
to the exalted Ngawang Jampa,[1200] I appeal:

Please grant me blessings to cut in my mindstream
the myriad ways of grasping at self,
arouse love and compassion, awakening mind,
and quickly attain supreme mahāmudrā, the unitive path.

18
Splendid primordial buddha, sporting in saffron robes,

1199. That is, Yeshé Gyaltsen.

1200. This is Phurbuchok Ngawang Jampa, who also appears in verse 26.

through Dharma you ripened China, Tibet, and every land—
to Paṇchen Palden Yeshé,[1201] I appeal:

Please grant me blessings to cut in my mindstream
the myriad ways of grasping at self,
arouse love and compassion, awakening mind,
and quickly attain supreme mahāmudrā, the unitive path.

19
With mind single-pointed, to the utmost you practiced
the utterly perfect paths of sūtra and mantra—
to the scholar-siddha Ngawang Dorjé, I appeal:

Please grant me blessings to cut in my mindstream
the myriad ways of grasping at self,
arouse love and compassion, awakening mind,
and quickly attain supreme mahāmudrā, the unitive path.

20
With steadfast wisdom, like a second Sage,
you illumined the Conqueror's teaching by discourse and writing—
to the exalted Dharmabhadra,[1202] I appeal:

Please grant me blessings to cut in my mindstream
the myriad ways of grasping at self,
arouse love and compassion, awakening mind,
and quickly attain supreme mahāmudrā, the unitive path.

21
Like those of Mañjuśrī, your greatly benevolent eyes
beyond conceiving are never closed, and your knowledge is
deep and vast—
to Yangchen Drupai Dorjé, I appeal:

Please grant me blessings to cut in my mindstream
the myriad ways of grasping at self,

1201. The Third Paṇchen Lama.

1202. That is, Ngulchu Dharmabhadra, author of a major commentary on *Highway of the Conquerors*, discussed above in chapter 12.

arouse love and compassion, awakening mind,
and quickly attain supreme mahāmudrā, the unitive path.

22
Completing the yoga of [3b] emptiness and bliss,
you went right to the stage of a conqueror's union—
to the scholar-siddha Tenzin Tsöndrü, I appeal:

Please grant me blessings to cut in my mindstream
the myriad ways of grasping at self,
arouse love and compassion, awakening mind,
and quickly attain supreme mahāmudrā, the unitive path.

23
The path so profound you understand to the utmost,
and you bear the triumphal banner of both expository and practical teachings—
to Losang Tsöndrü Gyaltsen,[1203] I appeal:

Please grant me blessings to cut in my mindstream
the myriad ways of grasping at self,
arouse love and compassion, awakening mind,
and quickly attain supreme mahāmudrā, the unitive path.

24
Untouched by flaws or downfall of vows,
you grasp the heart of the teachings of all the three trainings—
to Losang Dönyö Drupa, I appeal:

Please grant me blessings to cut in my mindstream
the myriad ways of grasping at self,
arouse love and compassion, awakening mind,
and quickly attain supreme mahāmudrā, the unitive path.

25
Disporting in saffron robes, you resemble
Jé the second Conqueror, Losang Drak, come again—
to the exalted Gelek Gyatso, I appeal:

1203. As mentioned above (note 729), this probably represents a second appearance of Drupai Gyaltsen Dzinpa, but it may refer to Taphukpa Losang Damchö Gyaltsen.

Please grant me blessings to cut in my mindstream
the myriad ways of grasping at self,
arouse love and compassion, awakening mind,
and quickly attain supreme mahāmudrā, the unitive path.

26
For fortunate minds you illumined completely
the treasure of Dharma, its paths deep and vast—
to kindly Ngawang Jampa,[1204] I appeal:

Please grant me blessings to cut in my mindstream
the myriad ways of grasping at self,
arouse love and compassion, awakening mind,
and quickly attain supreme mahāmudrā, the unitive path.

27
With laughter of stainless realization,
you're skilled at lighting the path [4a] that's beyond extremes—
to the supreme scholar Jikmé Wangpo,[1205] I appeal:

Please grant me blessings to cut in my mindstream
the myriad ways of grasping at self,
arouse love and compassion, awakening mind,
and quickly attain supreme mahāmudrā, the unitive path.

28
You're unmatched in spreading the exposition and practice
of the supreme tradition of the protector, Losang the conqueror—
to the exalted Tenpai Drönmé,[1206] I appeal:

Please grant me blessings to cut in my mindstream
the myriad ways of grasping at self,
arouse love and compassion, awakening mind,
and quickly attain supreme mahāmudrā, the unitive path.

1204. Phurbuchok Ngawang Jampa also appears in number 17 above.

1205. That is, Könchok Jikmé Wangpo, the Second Jamyang Shepa tulku.

1206. That is, Gungthang Könchok Tenpai Drönmé, discussed above in chapter 12.

29
Tasting the nectar of the hearing transmission of Jé the gentle protector,
you strengthened the body of understanding within—
to the exalted Könchok Gyaltsen, I appeal:

Please grant me blessings to cut in my mindstream
the myriad ways of grasping at self,
arouse love and compassion, awakening mind,
and quickly attain supreme mahāmudrā, the unitive path.

30
Dwelling single-pointedly in the unfixed abode,
you bear the practice-transmission teaching's triumphal banner—
to the mahāsiddha Ngödrup Rabten, I appeal:

Please grant me blessings to cut in my mindstream
the myriad ways of grasping at self,
arouse love and compassion, awakening mind,
and quickly attain supreme mahāmudrā, the unitive path.

31
In attributes of rejection and realization, you've reached the utmost
and freely sent down a Dharma rain of excellent explanation—
to Yongzin Gendun Gyatso, I appeal:

Please grant me blessings to cut in my mindstream
the myriad ways of grasping at self,
arouse love and compassion, awakening mind,
and quickly attain supreme mahāmudrā, the unitive path.

32
Receiving coronation [4b] as wisest among the wise,
you rose to the rank of adept of the two tantric stages—
to the splendid Tenpai Nyima, I appeal:

Please grant me blessings to cut in my mindstream
the myriad ways of grasping at self,
arouse love and compassion, awakening mind,
and quickly attain supreme mahāmudrā, the unitive path.

33
Under the sway of love for all living beings,
you bear the triumphal banner of sūtra and mantra teachings—
to the exalted Trinlé Gyatso,[1207] I appeal:

Please grant me blessings to cut in my mindstream
the myriad ways of grasping at self,
arouse love and compassion, awakening mind,
and quickly attain supreme mahāmudrā, the unitive path.

34
You're the friend who dispenses to fortunate students
the mind-essence of the second Conqueror, Jé—
to kindly Losang Yeshé,[1208] I appeal:

Please grant me blessings to cut in my mindstream
the myriad ways of grasping at self,
arouse love and compassion, awakening mind,
and quickly attain supreme mahāmudrā, the unitive path.

35
As the Conqueror intended, you augment in manifold ways
the Sage's vast teaching, the holy Dharma of scripture and realization—
to the matchless Trinlé Damé,[1209] I appeal:

Please grant me blessings to cut in my mindstream
the myriad ways of grasping at self,
arouse love and compassion, awakening mind,
and quickly attain supreme mahāmudrā, the unitive path.

36
Refuge who is a treasure of compassion of all the conquerors,

1207. That is, Phabongkha Rinpoché Dechen Nyingpo; see above, chapter 14.

1208. That is, Trijang Rinpoché, junior tutor to the Fourteenth Dalai Lama, on whom see, e.g., Sharpa 2019.

1209. That is, Ling Rinpoché, senior tutor to the Fourteenth Dalai Lama, on whom see, e.g., Dalai Lama 2017. Perhaps working from a different edition, Gonsalez (Kachen Yeshé Gyaltsen 2014, 453) presents the verses dedicated to Trijang Rinpoché and Ling Rinpoché in reverse order.

appearing as the guardian of all disciples—
to the exalted Tenzin Gyatso,[1210] I appeal:

Please grant me blessings to cut in my mindstream
the myriad ways of grasping at self,
arouse love and compassion, awakening mind,
and quickly attain supreme mahāmudrā, the unitive path.

37
For faithful disciples, in splendor you're seen
in Jé the mahāsiddha's home monastery—
to my kindly [5a] root guru, I appeal:

Please grant me blessings to cut in my mindstream
the myriad ways of grasping at self,
arouse love and compassion, awakening mind,
and quickly attain supreme mahāmudrā, the unitive path.

38
Seeing the holy guru as Buddha,
turning away desire for mundane abodes,
taking the burden of freeing all motherly beings,
may I be blessed to quickly attain
the splendid unitive mahāmudrā
on common and uncommon paths.

39
Your holy body and my body, father,
your holy speech and my speech, father,
your holy mind and my mind, father—
please bless me to know they're inseparably one.[1211]

1210. That is, the Fourteenth Dalai Lama. This verse, so far as I am aware, appears in no published Tibetan text except as a marginal addendum. It does not appear in the version published by Willis (1997, 110), but I have interpolated my translation of it here, in its logical place in the text. It was composed by Thubten Zopa Rinpoché (1946–). In Tibetan, it runs: *skyabs rgyal ba kun gyi snying rje gter / yongs gdul bya'i mgon du legs shar ba / rje btsun bstan 'dzin rgya mtsho la gsol ba 'debs.*

1211. This final verse, which is found in Yeshé Gyaltsen's edition, is also found in the earlier version of the prayer composed in the seventeenth century by Shar Kalden Gyatso.

4. Highway of the Conquerors[1212]

Paṇchen Losang Chökyi Gyaltsen

This is *Highway of the Conquerors: The Mahāmudrā Root Text of the Precious Geden Oral Transmission.*

Namo mahāmudrāya.

1

I bow respectfully to the feet of my peerless guru,
the sovereign master and lord of siddhas, who plainly[1213] teaches
mahāmudrā, the all-pervasive nature of everything,
the indivisible, inexpressible realm of the vajra mind.

2

Collecting the vital essence of the sea of sūtras, tantras, and pith instructions,
I will write the instructions of the mahāmudrā oral tradition

1212. Blo bzang chos kyi rgyal mtshan. *Dge ldan bka' brgyud rin po che'i phyag chen rtsa ba rgyal ba'i gzhung lam* (Bz*GBZL*). Cf. trans. Dhargyey 1975, Dalai Lama and Berzin 1997, 97–102, Kachen Yeshe Gyaltsen 2014, 435–42, and Yeshe 2018, 115–35. For context and a summary, see above, chapter 9. Besides the published sources mentioned, I have benefited from consulting unpublished translations by Thupten Jinpa and Glen Svensson.

1213. The Tibetan expression *rjen par*, which occurs here and in verse 40, literally means "nakedly" or "in its naked state." It implies that the meditating subject cognizing the real nature of things and/or the real nature cognized by the meditating subject is bare of any elaboration or complication, i.e., is unclothed by conceptuality. Although in this instance I have rendered it as "plainly," in general I have translated the phrase as "starkly" when it seems to refer primarily to a manner of subjective apprehension, and "nakedly" when it seems to refer to the manner in which reality presents itself to the apprehending mind. Admittedly, however, the distinction is not always clear; here, for example, it seems equally plausible to talk about the guru as teaching mahāmudrā in a plain or stark manner or as teaching mahāmudrā as it is, "in its naked state." (The synonymous phrase *gcer gyis*, which occurs in verse 17, is more straightforwardly adverbial, hence can be translated with confidence as "starkly," but it occurs less frequently in the literature than *rjen par*.)

of the supreme siddha Dharmavajra, father and son,[1214]
who possessed the Geden Oral Transmission and imparted it well.

3
From among the three—preparation, the main practice, and follow-up—
first, in order to enter the gateway and erect the supporting pillar
of the teaching in general and the Mahāyāna in particular,
exert yourself in going for refuge and arousing awakening mind,
not just by paying lip service with words alone.

4
Also, since seeing the real nature of mind
depends on collecting merit and purifying obscurations, [83]
prepare as much as possible through reciting the hundred-syllable mantra
a hundred thousand times, confessing your moral lapses hundreds of times,
and making as many prostrations as possible.

5
Then make heartfelt appeals again and again
to your root guru, who is inseparable from
all the buddhas of the three times.

6
The main practice of mahāmudrā
has many modes of explanation,
but they are divisible into two: sūtra and mantra.

7
The latter is the great bliss-luminosity mind arising
from skill in the methods of penetrating the vital points
in the vajra body.

8
The mahāmudrā of Saraha and Nāgārjunapāda,
of Nāro and Maitrī,
is taught in the Seven Attainment Texts and the Essential Trilogy
and is the quintessence of the unexcelled tantras.

1214. This refers to Dharmavajra/Chökyi Dorjé and his successor in the hearing transmission, Ensapa.

9
As for the former, it is a way of meditating on emptiness
directly taught in the three Mothers: the extensive, middle-length, and concise Perfection of Wisdom sūtras.
The supreme ārya, Nāgārjuna, has stated that there is
no path to liberation apart from this.

10
Here, in accordance with his thought,
I will give guidance on sūtra mahāmudrā,
expounding the way to recognize the mind
according to the teaching of the lineage gurus.

11–12
The connate union, the amulet box,
the fivefold, equal taste, the four letters,
pacification, severance, [84] the great perfection,
and guidance in the Madhyamaka view: these and other teachings
are called by many names individually,
but when examined by a yogī who has mastered
definitive-meaning scriptures and reasoning and possesses
inner experience, they come down to a single intention.

13
Thus, of the two systems—
seeking meditation based on the view and
seeking the view based on meditation—
the [explanation] here is according to the latter system.

14
On a platform conducive to contemplation,
your body in the seven-point posture,
clear away stale breath through the nine-round breathing,
distinguishing well between clear and sullied awareness.

15
With a mind that is perfectly virtuous,
give yourself over to going for refuge and arousing awakening mind,
then meditate on the profound path of guru yoga.

After hundreds of fervent appeals,
your guru dissolves into you.

16
Within a state where appearances are indistinct,[1215]
do not alter anything at all
by thoughts of hope, fear, or other [delusions], but
settle for a while in unwavering meditative equipoise.

17
Do not cease mental activity,
as in swoon or sleep:
post the sentry of undistracted mindfulness,
and station alertness to be aware of any movement.
Hold tightly to that clear and aware
nature of mind, and starkly behold it.

18
Any thought, anything that arises,
should be noted as that and just that.
Alternatively, sever arising thoughts abruptly,
as a skillful sword fighter would.

19
When, after severing thoughts, [your mind] is stable,
then, without losing mindfulness, loosely relax:
"Tightly focus [85] and loosely relax;
that's the ground on which to place your mind."[1216]

20
So it is said, and elsewhere it says:
"This mind, bound by worldly entanglements,

1215. *Snang ba ban bun* is very hard to translate into English. Among the suggestions I have read are "[a state of] miscellaneous appearances," "a state of fleeting appearances," "the state of diverse perceptions," "[a state of] evanescent appearances," "that state which is without the gurgle-gurgle of appearance-making and appearances (of 'this' and 'not that')," "a state where you are indistinct [from your guru]," and "this state in which all haphazard appearance-making and appearances have been contracted until they have disappeared." My own translation is based on a conversation with Yangsi Rinpoche on December 12, 2017.

1216. In *Lamp So Bright* (below, page 508), this statement is attributed to Machik Labdrön, but I have not, so far, been able to locate it.

is freed when relaxed—there is no doubt."[1217]
As taught here, you should relax without distraction.

21
When thoughts arise, and you observe their nature,
then they naturally disappear, and a pure vacuity dawns;[1218]
likewise, when you examine the settled mind,
you see nonobstruction, vacuity, clarity,
and vividness: this is known as "the merger of stillness
and movement". . . .[1219]

22
. . . Whatever thoughts may arise,
do not stop them, but recognize
their movement, and place your attention
upon their nature. . . .

23
. . . It's the same as in the example
of the flight of a ship's captive bird:
"It's like a raven flies from a ship,
circles in every direction, and alights there again."[1220]

24
When you practice in this way,
the nature of meditative equipoise will not be obscured
by anything: it is lucid and clear,
with nothing physical established anywhere in it;
it is a pure vacuity like space,
where everything appears vividly.

1217. Saraha in Sa*PD*t 73a; cf. R. Jackson 2004, 78 (verse 42h).

1218. The term *stong sang* contains the syllable that means "empty," or "emptiness," which is, of course, the nature of all things—including the mind—for most Mahāyāna Buddhists, but because the referent in this and subsequent occurrences is epistemological rather than ontological, I translate it as "vacuity" so as to indicate the phenomenology of the experience. The verb *shar* may be translated as either "appear" or "dawn." I have rendered it as one or the other, as seemed to me to suit the context.

1219. Ellipses at the end or beginning of a verse indicate places where I have separated parts of the same Tibetan poetic line into two different English verses.

1220. Sa*PD*t 74b; cf. R. Jackson 2004, 93 (verse 70).

25
Thus, though the real nature of mind
may be seen through higher perception,
it cannot be apprehended or taught as "this."

26
Gently place the mind, without grasping, on whatever appears:
"This," it is singlemindedly proclaimed by most
present-day great meditators of the Land of Snows,
"is the special instruction that leads
to holding Buddha in your palm."

27
That may be, but this way,
say I, Chökyi Gyaltsen,
is merely a marvelous means for a [86] beginner
to accomplish mental stillness
and a way of recognizing the phenomenal nature of mind.

28
Now, the way to recognize
the real nature of mind
is as set forth in the oral instructions of my root guru,
who is all the gnoses of the buddhas[1221]
but has taken the guise of a saffron wearer
and dispelled the gloom of my mental confusion.

29
From within the foregoing meditative equipoise,
like a minnow darting about
in limpid water[1222] without disturbing it,
analyze wisely with subtle awareness[1223]
the intrinsic nature of the person who meditates.

1221. This is a play on the name of Paṇchen Chögyen's teacher, Sangyé Yeshé (*sangs rgyas rnams kyi ye shes kun*).

1222. Reading *chu* for *tshu*.

1223. Reading *shes* for *shis*.

30
The protector himself, Ārya Nāgārjuna, says:
"An individual is not earth, is not water,
is not fire, is not air, is not space,
is not consciousness—nor is it all of them.
And what individual can there be apart from these?

31
"Just as an individual does not really exist
because it is a composite of the six elements,
in the same way, the individual elements
do not really exist because they are composites."[1224]

32
In accordance with that statement, when you search,
you do not find even the minutest particle
of meditative equipoise, the one who rests in equipoise, and so forth.
At that time, maintain a space-like meditative equipoise,
single-pointedly and without distraction.

33
Alternatively, within that state of meditative equipoise
the mind is nothing physical: it is a pure vacuity,
unobscured, where various things appear and proliferate,
an unceasing stream of clarity and awareness.

34
The mind engaging ceaselessly with objects
appears to be independent, but the objects of fixation
we apprehend are as stated by the guardian Śāntideva:
"So-called 'continuums and collections,'
such as rosaries, armies, [87] and the like, are false."[1225]

35
That said, informed by scripture and reasoning,
settle in single-pointed meditative equipoise in the state
where things do not exist in the way they appear.

1224. Ng*RA* 109b (verses 1, 80–81).

1225. Sd*BA* 27b (verse 8.101).

36
In brief, as related by my
spiritual friend, Sangyé Yeshé,
who knows everything as it really is:

37
"When you're fully aware that whatever appears is conceptually apprehended,
then the Dharma realm dawns independently of anything else;
when awareness rests within this dawning
and you settle in single-pointed meditative equipoise—*E ma*!"[1226]

38
Along the same lines,[1227] Dampa Sangyé says:
"Whirl the spear of awareness within emptiness;
the view, O Dingripas, is unobstructed."[1228]
This and the other sayings make the same point.

39
Afterward, the virtue[1229] that has arisen
from meditating on mahāmudrā—
together with the sea of virtues collected in the three times—
should be dedicated to great, unexcelled awakening.

40
Having familiarized yourself thusly, you must realize
precisely the mode of appearance of any object
appearing to the six types of consciousness.
Its mode of being will then nakedly and vividly appear;
identification of whatever appears is the key to the view.

41
In short, whatever appears—whether your own mind
or something else—should not be taken
to be real; you should ascertain

1226. Sy*SGDL* 67.

1227. Literally, "in accord with that statement" (*gsungs de bzhin*).

1228. Ps*DRGC* 17b [34] (*Hundred Verses of Advice*, verse 51; cf. trans. Dilgo and Padampa, 95).

1229. Literally, "whiteness" (*rnam dkar*).

its mode of being and always maintain that awareness.
Knowing this, subsume all phenomena
of saṃsāra and nirvāṇa into a single nature.

42
Also, as stated by Āryadeva:
"The viewer of one entity
is explained as the viewer of all.
The emptiness of one
is the [88] emptiness of all." . . .[1230]

43
. . . Thus, within a proper
meditative equipoise on reality,
you are free from elaborated extremes
of saṃsāra and nirvāṇa, such as existence, nonexistence, and so forth.

44
Yet when you arise from that equipoise and analyze,
it is undeniable that dependently arisen actions and agents
naturally appear as mere names,
only labels—like a dream,
a mirage, the moon in water, or an illusion.

45
When the empty is not obscured
by appearances, and appearances are not negated
by the empty, the excellent path—where emptiness
and dependent arising have a single meaning—will be manifest.

46
I, who am called Losang Chökyi Gyaltsen,
a renunciant who has heard many discourses, say:
by my virtue, may all beings quickly become conquerors through this path,
the door to peace, apart from which there is no second.

1230. Ad*CS* 9b (verse 191 [8.16]). Cf. trans. Lang 1986, 83.

[Colophon]

This method for pointing out mahāmudrā was initially requested by both the limitlessly learned master of the ten topics Gendun Gyaltsen and the master of the ten difficult texts Sherab Sengé of Hatong, who have seen the eight mundane concerns as a mad spectacle and dwell in the mountains, behaving like sages and making this path their essential practice. I was repeatedly entreated by them and beseeched as well by many of my own disciples who wished to practice the mahāmudrā of definitive meaning.

In one of his songs of experience for the instruction of himself and others, the noble lord of siddhas, the omniscient Ensapa the Great himself, gives instruction according to the Kadam stages of the path on topics ranging from reliance on [89] a spiritual friend to serenity and insight. At the end, he says:

> There is a path that is not the one I have just explained,
> the ultimate, special instruction on mahāmudrā;
> it is not at present public knowledge in the Land of Snows,
> so I could not commit it to writing at this point.[1231]

What cannot be set forth on account of present obstacles may be intended for a later time. As it says in the *Lotus Sūtra*:

> This method was spontaneously devised
> for the sake of beings' realization of what is to be realized by a buddha's
> gnosis,
> but for the time being you should not say to them,
> "You will be buddhas."
> Why is that? The Protector factors in the timing.[1232]

1231. I have been unable to locate this passage in Ensapa's writings, and *NGCS* provides no reference. This leaves open the question of how much of the passage is a direct quote from Ensapa and how much a summary by Losang Chögyen. Some English-language translators would begin the quoted passage with the account of what Ensapa has discussed (giving instruction according to the Kadam stages of the path), while others would limit it to the four poetic lines at the end. I side with the latter, on the grounds that a *song* is being cited, songs are almost always versified, and only the last four lines are in verse.

1232. *SDP*t 30a. Cf. *SDP*s 20, which reads, in translation: "That method is promulgated for the sake of the spontaneous awakening of gnosis. / Do not ever say to them, 'You will be buddhas in the world.' / What is the reason for that? Factoring in the timing and having perceived the moment, [the Buddha] will only speak later."

In order that wishes such as those stated above be fulfilled, I, Losang Chökyi Gyaltsen—who (a) have not undermined this lineage, which blesses one to properly experience the path directly, and which runs from the Peerless Teacher, the Śākya Conqueror, down to my own root guru, the all-knowing and all-seeing Sangyé Yeshé, from whom I heard it; (b) have joined the [Buddha's] family and not allowed its pledges to be lost; and (c) uphold the pith instructions on sūtra and mantra—have composed this at Geden Nampar Gyalwai Ling [Ganden Monastery].

5. Lamp So Bright[1233]

Paṇchen Losang Chökyi Gyaltsen

This is *Lamp So Bright: An Extensive Explanation of the Mahāmudrā Root-Text of the Teaching Tradition of the Precious Geden Oral Transmission.*

Namo mahāmudrāya.
The gnosis of all the ubiquitous buddhas
is the joyous dance of one in saffron robes.
To the lotus feet of the exalted guru,
triply kind, I respectfully bow down.

I will explain the lamp shining brightly on mahāmudrā,
which is the vital essence of the conquerors of the three times,
the essential meaning of the sea of sūtras and tantras,
the road traversed by all the lordly siddhas.

Here, the instruction on the mahāmudrā oral tradition of those wise and accomplished holy beings is threefold: (1) preface to the composition, (2) explanation of the composition's actual instruction, and (3) dedication of the virtue arising from the composition.

1. [Preface to the composition] [verses 1–2]

In order to show oneself in accord with those whose behavior [95] is quintessentially holy, one bows down to the special object; and in order to complete the composition, one makes a general promise to compose:

1233. Blo bzang chos kyi rgyal mtshan, *Dge ldan bka' brgyud rin po che'i bka' srol phyag rgya chen po'i rtsa rgyas par bshad pa yang gsal sgron me* (Bz*YSGM*). For context and a summary based on Paṇchen Chögyen's outline, see above, chapter 9. In addition to the detailed feedback I received from Alan Wallace, I have benefited from consulting an unpublished translation of the entire text by Thupten Jinpa and a partial translation by Glen Svensson.

Namo mahāmudrāya.

1

I bow respectfully to the feet of my peerless guru,
the sovereign master and lord of siddhas, who plainly teaches
mahāmudrā, the all-pervasive nature of everything,
the indivisible, inexpressible realm of the vajra mind.

2

Collecting the vital essence of the sea of sūtras, tantras, and pith instructions,
I will write the instructions of the mahāmudrā oral tradition
of the supreme siddha Dharmavajra, father and sons,
who possessed the Geden Oral Transmission and imparted it well.

Because it is not difficult to understand the meaning of these two verses, I will not write about them in detail.

2. Explanation the composition's actual instruction [verses 3–45]

3a

From among the three—preparation, the main practice, and the follow-up . . .

The actual explanation of the instruction that has been composed is threefold: (1) preparation, (2) the main practice, and (3) the follow-up.

2.1. Preparation [verses 3–5]

3b–e

. . . first, in order to enter the gateway and erect the supporting pillar
of the teaching in general and the Mahāyāna in particular,
exert yourself in going for refuge and arousing awakening mind,
not [96] *just by paying lip service with words alone.*

4

Also, since seeing the real nature of mind
depends on collecting merit and purifying obscurations,
prepare as much as possible through reciting the hundred-syllable mantra
a hundred thousand times, confessing your moral lapses hundreds of times, and making as many prostrations as possible.

5
Then make heartfelt appeals again and again
to your root guru, who is inseparable from
all the buddhas of the three times.

The great master Śāntipa, the guru Serlingpa, the great and divine Jowo Atiśa, and many other scholar-siddhas of the Land of the Āryas have distinguished Buddhists from non-Buddhists purely on the basis of going for refuge. In accord with them, the exalted Sapaṇ says, "If you do not go for refuge, you are not a Dharma practitioner."[1234] It is necessary to make going for refuge part of your mindstream, because, as Dampa Sangyé says:

> If you commit yourself mind, heart, and breast to the Triple Gem,
> blessings will arise from their power, O people of Dingri.[1235]

Along the same lines, the guardian Śāntideva says:

> When they have aroused awakening mind even for an instant,
> those tormented by bondage in the prison of saṃsāra
> will be called children of the sugatas
> and will be revered by mundane gods and by humans.[1236]

Also, as the great lord Atiśa says:

> Those desiring to enter the door of the Mahāyāna Dharma
> should strive for an eon to arouse
> the awakening mind, which, like the sun and moon,
> illumines darkness and pacifies torment.[1237]

Not only is awakening mind the gateway of [97] the Mahāyāna, but as stated in the *Awakening of Vairocana* (*Vairocanābhisaṃbodhi*) *Tantra*:

> O Lord of Secrets, the gnosis of the omniscient ones arises from a

1234. Sp*DSRB*t 25b.

1235. Ps*DRGC* 16b [32] (*Hundred Verses of Advice*, verse 3; cf. trans. Dilgo and Padampa 2006, 8).

1236. Sd*BA* 2a (verse 1.9).

1237. At*MS* 300a.

> cause that is awakening mind; it arises from a root that is compassion; it is the culmination of skillful means.[1238]

Awakening mind is the essence of the Mahāyāna. Generally, all of the supreme sources of the individual doctrinal systems of the Land of Snows designated four teachings as preparation for either explaining or meditating on the profound teaching: (1) going for refuge and arousing awakening mind, (2) the maṇḍala offering, (3) Vajrasattva purification meditation, and (4) guru yoga. On this, there is no disagreement among practice traditions. In particular, the supreme disciple of unexcelled mantra, the lord of yoga Milarepa, first contemplated love, compassion, and the awakening mind; renunciation and karma and its fruits; and death and impermanence and then gave instructions on them. He says:

> Terrified of the eight unfortunate states,[1239]
> I contemplated the disadvantages of impermanence and saṃsāra,
> strove in the Dharma of karmic cause and effect,
> and committed my inmost mind to the Three Jewels of refuge.
> When my mindstream was trained in the method of awakening mind,
> I cut the continuum of obscurations and the propensities thereto,
> realized all arising appearances as deceptive,
> and had no fear of the three lower realms.[1240]

Milarepa also says:

> If you do not think clearly on the causes and effects
> of virtuous and nonvirtuous actions,
> you will not be able to bear the sufferings of the lower realms.
> So try to be [98] careful and mindful
> of the very subtle fruitions of deeds.[1241]

He also says:

> If you see the many faults in things we desire
> and do not inwardly reverse your clinging to them,

1238. *VAT* 153a.

1239. These are: being born as a hell being, hungry ghost, animal, demigod, or god; being born at a time when no buddha has appeared; holding erroneous views; and having defective sense faculties.

1240. Th*MLGB* 317; cf. trans. Chang 1989, 1:302–3, and Tsangnyön Heruka 2016, 315.

1241. Th*MLGB* 341; cf. trans. Chang 1989, 1:321, and Tsangnyön Heruka 2016, 336.

> you will not be freed from saṃsāra's prison.
> So with a mind that knows all things as illusions,
> try to rely on the antidote to clinging's arisal.[1242]

He also says:

> If you do not repay the kindness shown you
> by parent sentient beings of the six realms,
> you incur the fault of straying into Hīnayāna.
> Therefore, with great benevolence,
> seek training in the awakening mind.[1243]

In this and other statements, Milarepa speaks according to the stages-of-the-path system.

Also, Dakpo Rinpoché—the main follower of the exalted Milarepa and the pioneer in mixing the two streams of Kadam and mahāmudrā—is in accord with the Kadam mind-training tradition in his extensive explanations of the famous "four Dharmas of Dakpo": (1) a mind that goes to the Dharma, (2) a Dharma that takes up the path, (3) a path that clears away confusion, and (4) confusion that is severed in gnosis.[1244]

Similarly, the great vajra holder Drakpa Gyaltsen says:

> In separating from the four clingings, (1) if you cling to this life, you are not a Dharma practitioner, (2) if you cling to saṃsāra, you have no renunciation, (3) if you cling to your own aims, you have no awakening mind, and (4) if you grasp, you do not have the view.[1245]

Having directly taught the four inverted tendencies in negative terms, he discusses their positive counterparts: (1) As the antidote to clinging to this life, a person of lesser scope should think about the free and favored life, impermanence, the suffering of the lower realms, and other topics. (2) As the antidote to clinging to saṃsāra, a person of middling scope must know the suffering nature of all saṃsāra and train in [99] the three path-trainings.[1246] (3) As an

1242. Th*MLGB* 341; cf. trans. Chang 1989, 1:321, and Tsangnyön Heruka 2016, 336.

1243. Th*MLGB* 341; cf. trans. Chang 1989, 1:321–22, and Tsangnyön Heruka 2016, 336.

1244. Dakpo Rinpoché is better known as Gampopa. Gp*CZDD* 10a.

1245. Dg*ZZBD* 1b.

1246. That is, the three higher trainings in morality, concentration, and wisdom.

antidote to striving solely for personal peace and happiness, a person of higher scope should contemplate love, compassion, and the awakening mind. (4) As an antidote to the self-grasping that is the root of saṃsāra, such a person must contemplate the lack of a self in both persons and phenomena.

Thus all the Indian and Tibetan scholar-siddhas who comment authoritatively on the sūtras and tantras rightly praise those paths, explaining them when they explain the preliminaries. But do not think that they are only preliminaries; you also need to keep them in mind throughout the main practice. In general, directly seeing the mind's real nature depends on amassing a great, extensive collection of merit and purifying vices and obscurations. Strive therefore to collect and purify during sessions, between sessions, and at all times.

In particular, the *Ornament of the Essence* says:

> According to the rite of the hundred-syllable mantra,
> it should be recited twenty times;
> it is said that through the blessing of such recitation
> downfalls and so forth will not increase.
> The supreme siddhas explain it thus,
> so you should practice both during and after sessions,
> and if you recite the mantra a hundred thousand times,
> the utterly pure self-nature will come to be.[1247]

Thus, since the quote says that if you recite the mantra just twenty times you prevent an increase in downfalls, and if you recite it a hundred thousand times you also wash away the root downfalls, you must exert yourself in the recitation meditation of Vajrasattva. Moreover, you must confess your downfalls hundreds of times while making prostrations and strive sincerely to disclose and refrain from such downfalls through fully applying the four opponent powers.[1248]

Then, your own triply kind root guru[1249]—who is the source of all virtue and goodness [100] here and hereafter and the essence of the liberation of all the conquerors, their children, and the lordly siddhas—should be imagined as being inseparable from the buddhas of the three times, or as the quintessence

1247. Mk*GA* 238a.

1248. Although the components and ordering of the lists vary, typically these involve: (1) regretting a nonvirtuous action, (2) relying on the sources of refuge, (3) promising not to repeat the offense, and (4) applying a purifying antidote, such as Vajrasattva visualization/recitation or meditation on emptiness.

1249. The guru's triple kindness is most commonly explained as his or her kindness in conferring empowerments, explaining the details of tantric practice, and transmitting pith instructions.

of the Triple Gem: cultivate the so-called "guru practice" or the profound-path guru yoga. Appealing to the guru continuously again and again from the bottom of your heart is the truly meaningful key point. When Dromtön loudly requested of the great Jowo, "Atiśa, I request instruction!" Atiśa said, "Ha, ha, I have good ears, and my instruction is: faith, faith, faith."[1250] Also, the Dharma lord Sapaṇ says:

> Thus people who have received empowerment,
> seeing that the whole Triple Gem
> is collected in the guru, will incur blessings
> when they appeal to the guru.[1251]

Also Dampa Sangyé says:

> When you are carried by the guru, you arrive at your desired destination.
> O people of Dingri, offer admiration and reverence as your fee.[1252]

The exalted Mila says:

> When you've gone to Central Tibet as a teacher,
> a vision of the guru may at some point appear.
> If a vision of the guru appears,
> appeal to him as inseparable from you at your crown,
> and without forgetting, contemplate him at your heart cakra.[1253]

2.2. [Main practice] [verses 6–38]

6
The main practice of mahāmudrā
has many modes of explanation,
but they are divisible into two: sūtra and mantra.

1250. Cited in Ts*LRCM* [Zhol ed.] 29a.

1251. Sp*DSRB*t 27b.

1252. Ps*DRGC* 17a[33] (*Hundred Verses of Advice*, verse 23; cf. trans. Dilgo and Padampa, 47).

1253. Th*MLGB* 590 and 591; cf trans. Chang 1989, 2:491 and 492; Tsangnyön Heruka 2016, 518 and 519. In the original, the first line is separated from the last four lines by several verses.

[2.2.1. Modes of explanation]

There are many ways of explaining the main practice of [101] mahāmudrā. The conqueror Drigungpa, explicating the thought of Drogön Rinpoché, arranged mahāmudrā according to the three vehicles and the four seals. As he says:

> In his discussion of the four profound seals,
> the eminent Drogön clearly taught
> that the four seals of the path
> are methods for achieving the three aspects of awakening.
> The four seals are characterized in terms of the three vows.
>
> The inseparability of the srāvaka's body, speech,
> and mind is the action seal,
> their realization of the lack of self of persons
> is taught as the Dharma seal;
> their freedom from defilement is the pledge seal; and
> the nirvāṇa without remaining aggregates
> is the great seal, mahāmudrā.
>
> The inseparability of the bodhisattva's
> three doors from the six perfections
> is the action seal;
> their freedom from illusion and elaboration
> is the Dharma seal;
> their not being tainted by the stain of self-interest
> is the pledge seal; and
> the equal taste of emptiness and compassion
> is the great seal, mahāmudrā.
>
> According to the path of secret mantra,
> reliance on the messenger[1254] is the action seal,
> the inseparable joining of vital winds and mind
> is the Dharma seal,
> the non-degeneration of vows is the pledge seal,
> and the manifestation of the connate gnosis
> is the great seal, mahāmudrā.

1254. A common metaphor for the consort with whom one associates in advanced tantric practice.

On the path of freedom, the pith instruction on inner fire,
concentration on the physical exercises,
and manipulation of the vital winds are the action seal;
the arising of blissful gnosis
is said to be the Dharma [102] seal;
dispassion is the pledge seal; and
spontaneous actualization is the great seal, mahāmudrā.[1255]

The great Gö Lotsāwa Shönu Pal explains that the nonconceptual gnosis that ascertains emptiness is mahāmudrā. At the very beginning of his history of mahāmudrā in the *Blue Annals*,[1256] he explains:

> Now I will speak of mahāmudrā, which seals all practices and attainments, from the prātimokṣa vows that are the basis of the Buddha's teaching right up to the glorious Guhyasamāja.[1257]

In short, although there are various modes of explanation, mahāmudrā is twofold, divided into sūtra and mantra. Of these, I will explain the former rather extensively here; because I will say less about the latter, I will explain it first.

[2.2.2. Mantra mahāmudrā] [verses 7–8]

7
The latter is the great bliss-luminosity mind arising
from skill in the methods of penetrating the vital points
in the vajra body.

8
The mahāmudrā of Saraha and Nāgārjunapāda,
of Nāro and Maitrī,
is taught in the Seven Attainment Texts and the Essential Trilogy
and is the quintessence of the unexcelled tantras.

And why is it called the *great seal—phyag rgya chen po*? According to the *Drop of Mahāmudrā*:

1255. SNL.

1256. Reading *deb sngon* for *deng sngon*.

1257. Gz*DTNP* 983; cf. trans. Roerich 1976, 839.

Phyag is the gnosis of emptiness,
rgya is freedom from saṃsāric phenomena,
chen po is union;
this expresses the meaning of the term *great seal*.[1258]

As for the mahāmudrā of the mantra system: On a foundation of obtaining the four pure empowerments, guarding your vows and pledges properly, and stabilizing your familiarity with the generation stage, you should penetrate the vital points of the vajra body [103] through skill in various internal and external methods to make the vital winds enter, abide, and dissolve within the central channel. When the gnosis of connate great bliss that arises from that realizes emptiness by way of its mental image, that is semblance luminosity; when such a gnosis realizes emptiness directly, that is actual luminosity. That mind that has come to have the essential nature of those two types of luminosity is given such names as "the short *a* of definitive meaning," "the indestructible drop," "the uncontrived mind," "ordinary cognition," "the primordial mind," and so forth. The mahāsiddhas of the Land of the Āryas—the splendid guardian Mahāsukha or Saroruhavajra,[1259] the mahāsiddha Saraha, Nāgārjuna, Lord Śavari, Telo, Nāro, Maitrī, and others—as well as the early Kagyüpa masters—Marpa, Mila, Gampopa, Phakmo Drupa, and others—all explain the ultimate mahāmudrā as the luminosity of great bliss arising from having made the vital winds enter, abide, and dissolve within the central channel. That is the principal topic of the Seven Attainment Texts and the Essential Trilogy and is the innermost essence of the unexcelled yoga tantras, vast as the ocean.

The Seven Attainment Texts:[1260] (1) The guardian Mahāsukha[1261] composed the *Secret Attainment* (*Guhyasiddhi*). This is a commentary on the main ideas of the Guhyasamāja root tantra. Mahāsukha expresses the greatness of the Guhyasamāja by such statements as "There is no tantra greater than the [104] glorious *Guhyasamāja*; / it is a jewel unique in all the worlds."[1262] He then explains the Guhyasamāja generation stage a little, and teaches in particular

1258. As noted above (note 82), this passage does not appear in the *Drop of Mahāmudrā*, though it does occur in Tilopa's *Dharma of the Bodiless Ḍākinī* (Tp*VD* 84b).

1259. Saroruhavajra is also known as Padmavajra, and here, at least, seems also to be known as Mahāsukha, though whether these three names all in fact designate a single individual in uncertain.

1260. See above, chapter 2.

1261. The author of the *Secret Attainment* is usually said in Indic sources to be Padmavajra; I am uncertain of the genesis or significance of the tradition of referring to him as Mahāsukha.

1262. Pv*GSt* 5a.

the direct meaning of the root tantra, the powerful path of inseparable bliss-emptiness when one practices on the lofty completion stage. The *Secret Attainment* became like the "grandmother" of all the other Attainment Texts and the Essential Trilogy. (2) Mahāsukha's disciple Anaṅgavajra composed *Attainment of Certainty about Wisdom and Means* (*Prajñopāyaviniścayasiddhi*); (3) Anaṅgavajra's disciple Indrabhūti composed the *Attainment of Gnosis* (*Jñānasiddhi*); (4) Indrabhūti's lady, Lakṣmīṅkarā, composed the *Attainment of the Nondual* (*Advayasiddhi*); (5) Ḍombī Heruka composed the *Attainment of the Connate* (*Sahajasiddhi*); (6) Dārikapa composed the *Attainment of the Principle of the Great Secret* (*Mahāguhyatattvasiddhi*); and (7) Yoginī Cintā composed the *Attainment of the Principle that Follows the Illumination of Entities* (*Vyaktabhāvānugatatattvasiddhi*).

The Essential Trilogy:[1263] With respect to the three *Dohā* collections of Saraha, some masters, such as the omniscient Butön, teach that the *People Dohās* (*Dohākoṣagīti*) are purely Saraha's composition while the other two are spurious.[1264] Also, some say that it cannot be accepted that there is no difference between the *dohās'* way of teaching and the guardian Nāgārjunapāda's way of teaching the five stages of the completion stage. Some say that passages from the *Dohās* such as

> As brahmans spin the sacred thread,
> the yogī puts his mind at ease;
> this very mind that's bound by mundane cares,
> when loosed, will be free—there is no doubt[1265]

and "the fresh, uncontrived mind is best"[1266] and, from Maitrīpa's *Ten Verses on Thatness*, "Non-investigation is the mind of the supreme guru"[1267] are written for the purpose of explaining that if from the beginning you settle without analysis and cease mental activity, you will be [105] free. This and similar basic[1268] mistakes regarding the Seven Attainment Texts and the Essential Trilogy occur, but even if they are true, then they are not in accord with the omniscient Jé's

1263. See above, pages 44–45.

1264. Bt*TGKC* 47a.

1265. Sa*VG* 61a. *Contra NGPS* 634n24, this passage is not found in Saraha's *People Dohās*.

1266. Sv*MU* 123b. Recall that this text (Dergé 2273) is attributed by most Tibetan writers to Saraha rather than Śavaripa.

1267. This phrase is not found in Maitrīpa's *Ten Verses* but does appear in Sahajavajra's commentary to it: Sh*TT* 172b.

1268. Following *NGPS* 634n27 in reading *gzhi* for *bzhi*.

statement—in the *Illuminating Lamp* and elsewhere—that "The sayings in the *dohās* and so forth are to be practiced / on the high mantra path."[1269]

Let us explain the meaning through examples from the *Treasury of Dohās* (*Dohākoṣagīti*) just a little.[1270] Saraha says:

> Whoever enters emptiness bereft of compassion
> will not reach the supreme path;
> and if you cultivate only compassion,
> you'll remain here in saṃsāra and not obtain liberation.
> Whoever is able to conjoin the two
> will not abide in saṃsāra and will not abide in nirvāṇa.[1271]

Thus it is necessary to join the subject, compassion, which is the connate great bliss, with the object, emptiness. Also, from that same text:

> If you have realization, then all things are that;
> no one knows anything other than that.
> Reading is that; apprehension and meditation are also that.
> Studying treatises is also that.
> There is no view not indicated by that,
> but it depends on the words of the guru alone:
> taking the guru's words to heart
> is like seeing a treasure in the palm of your hand.
> The primordial nature goes unnoticed by the fool;
> fools are deceived by delusions—so says the archer.[1272]

This says that when yogīs directly experience and realize the primordial mind, then all phenomena are [106] seen as the emanations of that primordial nature. No person knows anything that is not an emanation of that primordial nature. That direct realization of the primordial mind is also a direct realization of the essence of reading, apprehension, and meditation, and it is also the main purpose of studying treatises. There is no other view superior to the view indicated by that essence. However, the direct experience of that essence occurs by virtue of meditation that depends on instruction from the mouth

1269. Ts*RNSG* 58b.

1270. See also above, pages 369–73.

1271. Sa*PD*t 71b; cf. R. Jackson 2004, 60–61 (verses 15a–b).

1272. Sa*PD*t 71b; cf. R. Jackson 2004, 62–63 (verses 16b–18).

of the holy guru, who is part of an uninterrupted lineage of holy beings beginning from Vajradhara. When the words of the guru who has such instructions and experience enter your heart, if you settle upon and meditate in single-pointed meditative equipoise upon the essence—emptiness—then you will directly see the meaning of emptiness as if it were a treasure within the palm of your hand. Foolish ordinary individuals, not directly perceiving the primordial nature because they cling to true existence—"these fools are deceived by delusions—so says the archer," Saraha.

Moreover, the *Treasury of Dohās* says:

> If it's manifest, what's the point of meditation?
> If it's hidden, you only encounter darkness.
> That connate nature
> is neither entity nor nonentity.[1273]

This says: if the nature of the connate, primordial mind is revealed by the power of meditation, then what is the point of [107] investigative meditation? On the other hand, if the primordial nature is hidden, then you only encounter the darkness of ignorance. That essence is neither a truly existent entity nor a nonexistent nonentity. The *Treasury of Dohās* also says:

> Since it's separate from meditation, what is there to think?
> How can you explain the inexpressible?
> All beings are deceived by the seal of saṃsāric existence;
> no one takes up the primordial nature.[1274]

Moreover, the *Treasury of Dohās* says:

> No tantra, no mantra, nothing on which to think or meditate:
> all those cause your own mind to be confused.
> The naturally pure mind is unpolluted by meditation.
> Abide in your own bliss and don't make yourself miserable:
> there's joy in eating, drinking, and sex:
> always, again and again, fill the cakras.
> By a Dharma such as this you'll transcend the world;
> treading on the head of mundane confusion, go on.
> Where wind and mind no longer move,

1273. Sa*PD*t 71b; cf. R. Jackson 2004, 64 (verse 20).

1274. Sa*PD*t 71b; cf. R. Jackson 2004, 65 (verse 22).

where sun and moon do not enter,
the minds of the ignorant will find relief.
The archer has taught all these pith instructions and moved on.[1275]

Let us explain the meaning of the passage a little. The natural, primordial, connate mind of luminosity is known as the ground Dharma body. When, through the power of meditation, that is directly experienced, it is free from analysis, investigation, [108] or verbal expression, so what is the point of meditation involving analysis and investigation? What is there to be said? Since they have not ascertained that primordial mind by the power of meditation, all beings are deceived by the seal of saṃsāric existence. Although they are deceived, no one else can take or steal their natural primordial mind. For all sentient beings of the three realms in general and womb-born beings of the six realms in particular, the appearance, spread, near attainment, and luminosity appear at the time of death.[1276] Although they thus appear, ordinary individuals are unable to transform them into the path. Not only that, most desire-realm beings enjoy joining the two sex organs and talking about sex, though they have no knowledge of the import of great bliss. As it says in the *Treasury of Dohās*:

In this house and that house they talk about it,
but the import of great bliss is completely unknown.[1277]

When yogīs have made emptiness the object of that primordial mind that has the essential nature of great bliss, they simply settle there and do not engage in any mental elaboration regarding good and bad. With respect to the arising of such a realization of mahāmudrā, when a person has trained before on the path in previous lives or earlier in this life, and has made the vital winds enter and be purified within the central channel, then even if the person's mind settles as if it were not thinking anything at all and meditates on any object whatsoever, then the person

1275. Sa*PD*t 71b; cf. R. Jackson 2004, 65–66 (verses 23–25).

1276. These are technical terms for the final four phases of the death process, which follow upon the sequential dissolution of the four physical elements and of the coarser level of consciousness, and the absorption of all the vital winds into the central channel. The experiential counterparts to these four phases are, respectively, a vision of whiteness resulting from the wind-impelled descent of the white drop from the crown cakra to the heart chakra, a vision of redness resulting from the wind-impelled ascent of the red drop from the navel cakra to the heart cakra, a vision of blackness resulting from the dissolution of the winds into the heart cakra, and a vision of luminosity or clarity resulting from the dissolution of winds into the indestructible drop at the center of the heart cakra.

1277. Sa*PD*t 73a; cf. R. Jackson 2004, 97 (verse 78).

will directly perceive the mahāmudrā [109] of luminosity. That person is designated by the early Kagyüpas as a subitist. This verse occurs in the *Epitome* (*Kā dpe*):

> A person who has progressed in training
> is said to be a subitist.[1278]

The omniscient Jé also says in his *Illuminating Lamp*:

> It is apparent that for one who is experienced in making the vital winds enter the central channel, the vital winds will gather within the central channel no matter the object of focus.[1279]

This makes the same point as the previous passage.

To manifest the mahāmudrā of this path, disciples who are not [subitists] must certainly meditate on inner fire and other topics. The exalted Mila says that by first meditating chiefly on the six Dharmas of Nāro in accordance with the oral tradition of Nāro and Marpa, one will manifest mahāmudrā:

> Mahāmudrā is the fortress of the view,
> Nāro's six Dharmas are the fortress of meditation,
> the profound path of method is the fortress of conduct,
> the spontaneous actualization of the three bodies is the fortress of fruition.[1280]

The Dharma lord Sapaṇ agrees with those who praise and magnify Mila's "short *a* of inner fire" and says:

> Guidance on the so-called six Dharmas of Nāro
> is none other than that [stemming] from Mila.[1281]

Also, Jé Gampopa says that by meditating first on the inner fire, a great many

1278. Nr*AP* 271a.

1279. Ts*RNSG* 194b. This also is quoted by Khedrup Norsang Gyatso and Thuken.

1280. Th*MLGB* 403. As noted in *NGCS* (635n36), where Paṇchen Chögyen reads *rdzong* ("fortress") at the end of each line, the original has *bzang* ("good"). This reading is to be preferred, since Milarepa advertises in the line just before the quoted passage that he will sing of his six *goodnesses.* The stanza just before this describes Mila's six fortresses, so it may be that Paṇchen Chögyen misremembered the passage, or was working from an erroneous edition. Cf. trans. at Chang 1989, 1:364, and Tsangnyön Heruka 2016, 386.

1281. Sp*DSRB*t 41a cf. trans. Sakya Pandita 2002, 162.

practitioners have manifested the primordial mind. There are other examples, as well.

Accordingly, with respect to the meditation on mantra mahāmudrā taught here, it is necessary to obtain the four pure empowerments and also to train in the generation stage, the completion stage, and [110] the common paths. The *Epitome* teaches:

> A person who is a novice
> is said to be a gradualist.[1282]

This person is designated as a gradualist. Thus most of the mahāsiddhas of this path also entered into the empowerment lineage of the various unexcelled yoga tantras. The Dharma lord Sapaṇ teaches:

> Nārotapa made empowerment
> and the two stages the chief Dharmas.[1283]

For, the exalted Milarepa teaches:

> If you listen to the things I've said and act upon them,
> Son, you'll be fortunate in the divine Dharma.
> I'll give you empowerment and blessings, which are the gateway,
> and I'll give you the special instructions of the profound hearing
> transmission.[1284]

In a similar manner, Sapaṇ's *Clear Ascertainment of the Three Vows* says:

> My mahāmudrā is
> the gnosis arising from empowerment;
> it is the self-emergent gnosis arising
> from concentrations on the two stages.[1285]

Accordingly, no authoritative scholars and siddhas are in disagreement with respect to these ideas.

1282. Nr*AP* 271a.

1283. Sp*DSRB*t 41a cf. trans. Sakya Pandita 2002, 162.

1284. Th*MLGB* 182–83. Cf. trans. Chang 1989, 1:183, and Tsangnyön Heruka 2016, 184–85.

1285. Sp*DSRB*t 25b.

2.2.3. Sūtra mahāmudrā [verses 9–38]

Now, there is the promise to teach sūtra mahāmudrā in detail.

[2.2.3.x.[1286] The promise to teach sūtra mahāmudrā in detail] [verses 9–10]

9
As for the former, it is a way of meditating on emptiness
directly taught in the three Mothers: the extensive, middle-length, and concise
Perfection of Wisdom sūtras.
The supreme ārya, Nāgārjuna, has stated that there is
no path to liberation apart from this.

10
Here, in accordance with his thought,
I will give guidance on sūtra mahāmudrā,
expounding the way to recognize the mind
according to the teaching of the lineage [111] *gurus.*

[2.2.3.1. The essential teaching]

Of the two ways of meditating on mahāmudrā, the way of meditating on the former, the sūtra system, is as follows. It is the way of cultivating the wisdom realizing emptiness that is shown directly in the three Mother sūtras: the extensive, middle-length, and concise. This way of meditating is praised in the Mother of the Conquerors as the true life of the paths of all three vehicles; it is said that, apart from this way, there is no other appropriate path that leads to liberation. The supreme ārya, Nāgārjuna, teaches:

> It is said that the path to liberation
> that is definitively upheld
> by the buddhas, pratyekabuddhas, and śrāvakas
> is this one alone, and no other—this is certain.[1287]

1286. In Paṇchen Chögyen's text, this seems to be a brief subsection, consisting solely of two transitional verses, that has not been integrated into his outline; because the next subsection is 2.2.3.1, I have designated this one 2.2.3.x.

1287. Ng*PS* 76b. The text is more commonly attributed to Rahulabhadra, sometimes said to be a teacher of Nāgārjuna , and sometimes identified as Saraha.

Not only that, in the Vajrayāna, too, there is no different view that is other or greater than this. As the exalted Sapaṇ teaches,

> When it comes to perfection of wisdom and secret mantra,
> there is no distinction in explanations of the view.
> If there exists a view that is greater
> than the nonelaboration that is the perfection of wisdom,
> that view would entail elaboration;
> since it is unelaborated, there is no distinction.[1288]

Thus, in his commentaries of definitive meaning the prophesied guardian Nāgārjuna opened the way for the scriptures taught by the conquerors. One of his followers, the great Jowo Atiśa teaches:

> Who has realized emptiness?
> The ones prophesied by the Tathāgata—
> Nāgārjuna and his student Candrakīrti—
> who saw the true reality.
> The instructions transmitted from them
> are the Buddha's—[112] no one else's are.[1289]

Thus, this mahāmudrā instruction is given according to Candrakīrti's discussion of the thought of Ārya Nāgārjuna. The way of recognizing the nature of mind is to be expressed according to the precious oral teaching of the holy gurus who possess the uninterrupted blessing transmission of the holy scholar-siddhas.

If you ask, "Well why is what is taught here called 'the great seal'?" it is because, as taught in the *King of Concentrations Sūtra*: "The intrinsic nature of all phenomena is the seal."[1290] Also, "Emptiness, the intrinsic nature of all phenomena, is the seal, and when you realize that, you are freed from all troubles, so the seal is great or supreme. That which is great is said to be supreme and immeasurable."[1291]

1288. Sp*DSRB*t 29b.

1289. At*SA* 72b.

1290. *SRS*t 59a.

1291. SNL.

[2.2.3.2. Different traditions of mahāmudrā] [verses 11–12]

Now, the Sage's teaching was found in eighteen schools,[1292] equally able to accomplish the fruit of the path, freedom. Although there are numerous tenet systems that explain mahāmudrā, it is taught that they are equal in effecting obtainment of the ultimate fruit, the unitive mahāmudrā; it is explained thus so that one may gain mastery in categorizing the countless excellent systems promulgated by holy persons.

11–12
The connate union, the amulet box,
the fivefold, equal taste, the four letters,
pacification, severance, the great perfection,
and guidance in the Madhyamaka view: these and other teachings
are called by many names individually,
but when examined by a yogī who has mastered
definitive-meaning scriptures and reasoning and possesses
inner experience, they come down to a single intention. [113]

Jé Gampopa developed students by way of the six Dharmas, the fivefold, and connate union. Although there are some discrepancies in versions of the root text for connate union, [I read it as follows]:

> Connate mind itself is the Dharma body,
> connate concepts are waves of the Dharma body,
> connate appearances are the light of the Dharma body,
> appearances and mind are connately inseparable.[1293]

The meaning of this statement is that from the point of view of acting mainly to develop respectful devotion and to counter craving, there are three divisions: (1) the four preliminary practices, (2) the two aspects of introducing the main practice, and (3) afterward, applying your experience to whatever appears. The preliminary practices are those that are generally taught,[1294] while the two main practices are indicated as serenity and insight.

1292. These are the eighteen schools of Foundational Buddhism as identified by later traditions.

1293. Gp*PCBT* 3a.

1294. That is, the common preliminaries of basic stages-of-the-path meditations and the uncommon preliminaries of performing prostrations while generating refuge and the awakening mind, Vajrasattva meditation/recitation, Meru maṇḍala offerings, and guru yoga.

The amulet box is the oral tradition of the scholar-siddha Khyungpo Naljor. It is shown by way of (1) the threefold self-descended preliminary practice, (2) the main practice, which is the self-freeing of the four faults, and (3) the fruit, the self-dawning three bodies. The main practice is also said to be "recognizing the thief." The principal instruction of the Shangpa Kagyü is the six Dharmas of Nigumā. The six Dharmas are: (1) inner heat, the foundation stone of the path, (2) illusory body, the self-freeing of desire and anger, (3) dream yoga, the self-awakening of the deluded mind, (4) luminosity, the dispeller of the darkness of ignorance, (5) transference, buddhahood without meditation, and (6) the intermediate state, the enjoyment body of the conquerors. Of these six Dharmas, the amulet box is principally the way of meditating on luminosity.

The fivefold is a major practice [114] of those in the Drigung lineage. It is proclaimed in the *Root Song* of Jikten Gönpo:

1 As for the stallion of the awakening mind:
if you do not race it along the course of altruism,
the cheers of the crowd of gods and humans will not arise,
so earnestly apply your mind to this preliminary practice.

2 As for seeing your own body as the royal divine body:
if you do not hold fast to your immutable throne,
the hosts of ḍākinīs will not gather,
so earnestly apply yourself to seeing your body as the divine yidam.

3 As for the snow mountain of the guru's four bodies:
if the sun of respectful devotion does not rise,
the river of blessings will not flow,
so earnestly apply yourself to this mind of respectful devotion.

4 As for the vast sky of mind itself:
if the cloud mass of concepts is not cleared away,
the planets and stars of the two types of knowledge[1295] will not shine,
so earnestly apply your mind to nonconceptuality.

5 As for the wish-fulfilling jewel of the two collections:
if it is not polished by your aspiration,

1295. These are a buddha's knowledge of the ultimate nature of all things (*ji lta mkhyen*) and of every detail of knowable things (*ji rnyed mkhyen*).

the results you need and desire will not arise,
so earnestly apply yourself to this final dedication.[1296]

Those with the transmissions from Dharma lord Tsangpa Gyaré [i.e., Drukpas] practiced and gave instruction on the eight great guidances, the six cycles on equal taste, and the mountain Dharma.

The eight great guidances are: (1) guidance on the guru's three buddha bodies, (2) guidance on love and compassion, (3) guidance on the dependent arising of cause and effect, (4) guidance on the nectar-drop-like fivefold [mahāmudrā], (5) guidance on connate union, (6) guidance on the six Dharmas of Nāropa, (7) guidance on equalizing the eight mundane concerns, and (8) guidance on meditating to reverse ill fortune through secret practices.

The six cycles on equal taste are:[1297] (1) taking thoughts as the path, (2) taking defilements [115] as the path, (3) taking sickness as the path, (4) taking gods and demons as the path, (5) taking sufferings as the path, and (6) taking death as the path.

In the mountain Dharma, there are (A) four ornaments of the profound Dharma and (B) the ornaments of the oral instructions on the three spheres. Of these, the first consists of (1) the mountain Dharma, the source of all attributes, (2) the great boat of secret empowerment, (3) the hidden explanation of the vajra body, and (4) guidance on the intermediate state—these are the four. The second consists of (1) the ornament of direct guidance for clearing away hindrances, (2) the ornament of the catalogue of manifold spiritual songs, and (3) the ornament of minor scattered categories.

The four letters: The explanation is drawn from the word *amanasi*, which is the Sanskrit for "nonmentation." Its meaning is shown by way of the word's four letters. Thus, the first (*a*) is cutting the root basis of mind, the second (*ma*) shows the method of settling the mind, the third (*na*) cuts off mental error, and the fourth (*si*) shows how to take the mind as path.

The holy Dharma of Dampa Sangyé is the pacification of suffering. Thus, he says:

This holy Dharma, the pacification of suffering:
when subduing harmful male and female demons,
bind them in a magic circle of austerities.
When sickness arises in the body,
merge awareness and the Dharma realm into one.

1296. Js*NDTG* 87, 8. This poem also is cited by Khedrup Norsang Gyatso and Thuken.

1297. See Abboud et al. 2017, 63–72.

When subtle conceptualization arises,
cut the defilements out.
When sleeping alone in private,
place yourself in bare awareness.
When out amid a crowd,
behold the nature of whatever arises.
When your mind is dull, rouse yourself by saying *phaṭ*.
When your mind is dispersed, cut the root.
When your mind is excited, place yourself in [116] the Dharma realm.
When consciousness goes out after an object,
look at the real nature of the object.

This holy Dharma, the pacification of suffering:
when bad omens occur, take them as auspicious;
whatever concepts there are, delight in them.
When sicknesses occur, take them as boons;
whatever happens, delight in it.
When death occurs, take it as the path;
whatever the Lord of Death may be, delight in him.

This holy Dharma, the pacification of suffering:
it's the thought of the conquerors in the three times![1298]

So Dampa taught when he met the exalted Milarepa.

Then there are severance, which is well known as the instruction of Dampa and the profound Dharma of Machik Labdrön; the great perfection, the vital essence extracted from the mind of Master Padmasambhava in the *Garland of Views: A Pith Instruction*[1299] and other texts; guidance on the profound Madhyamaka view; and so forth. Although all these teachings are given various different names that designate their individual instructions or purposes, when the wise examine them well through scripture and reasoning that distinguishes how they are provisional or definitive, they see that they come down to a single intention and, as in the case of the complementarity of hot and cold, are not in contradiction. *The Stainless Light* (*Vimalaprabhā*) says:

It is like jewels in the earth, which are described
by distinctive and differing names

1298. Ps*ZBDG* 18b–19a [36–37].

1299. For a discussion and translation of this text, see Karmay 1988, 137–71.

from one region to the next
but do not differ in being jewels.[1300]

[2.2.3.3. The actual meditation] [verse 13]

How, then, is mahāmudrā meditation ordered?

13
Thus, of the two systems—
seeking meditation based on the view and
seeking the view based on meditation—
the explanation here is according to the latter system. [117]

How is it that one acts according to the second system? Well, as the guardian Śāntideva says:

> Knowing that insight possessed
> of serenity destroys defilements,
> you must first seek serenity.[1301]

Also, the *Jewel Heap* (*Ratnakūṭa*) says:

> Abiding in morality, you obtain concentration;
> and obtaining concentration, you cultivate wisdom.[1302]

As stated, this is the system in which one seeks the view on top of meditation.

2.2.3.3.1. Serenity [verses 14–27]

Since that is the case, what is the way to cultivate serenity first? There are preliminaries and the main practice.

2.2.3.3.1.1. [Preliminaries] [verses 14–15]

The exalted Maitreya explains:

1300. Pn*VP* 18b (*khams* chapter).

1301. Sd*BA* 23b (verse 8.4).

1302. *KPS* 252a–b. The *Jewel Heap* is a collection of sūtras; the specific sūtra (or "chapter") from which this is drawn, the *Questions of Kāśyapa*, is text 43 in the collection.

In what sort of place do the wise practice?
It should be easily accessible and have a pleasant environment,
good land, good companions,
and the requisites for yogic bliss.[1303]

Abiding with pure morality in a location thus described, with few desires and content with what you have, you must rely on the branches or collections of serenity and definitely accomplish the six preliminaries.[1304]

14
On a platform conducive to contemplation,
your body in the seven-point posture,
clear away stale breath through the nine-round breathing,
distinguishing well between clear and sullied awareness.

15
With a mind that is perfectly virtuous,
give yourself over to going for refuge and arousing awakening mind,
then meditate on the profound path of guru yoga.
After hundreds of fervent appeals,
your guru [118] *dissolves into you.*

The "mind that is purely virtuous" is the awakening mind, and the "profound path of guru yoga" is the guru yoga that completes a portion of the path. This is summary; the rest can be understood straightforwardly.

[2.2.3.3.1.2. The main practice] [verses 16–27]

[2.2.3.3.1.2.1. The Method for Accomplishing Mental Stillness] [verses 16–23]

Therefore, having begun with the preliminary stages, I will explain the method for accomplishing mental stillness:

16
Within a state where appearances are indistinct,

1303. Ma*MA* 17b (verse 14.7).

1304. These are cleaning the room and establishing a shrine, obtaining offerings, sitting in the proper posture, visualizing the merit field, offering the seven-limb prayer and the Meru maṇḍala, and appealing for inspiration.

do not alter anything at all
by thoughts of hope, fear, or other delusions, but
settle for a while in unwavering meditative equipoise.

17
Do not cease mental activity,
as in swoon or sleep:
post the sentry of undistracted mindfulness,
and station alertness to be aware of any movement.
Hold tightly to that clear and aware
nature of mind, and starkly behold it.

18
Any thought, anything that arises,
should be noted as that and just that.
Alternatively, sever arising thoughts abruptly,
as a skillful sword fighter would.

19
When, after severing thoughts, [your mind] is stable,
then, without losing mindfulness, loosely relax:
"Tightly focus and loosely relax;
that's the ground on which to place your mind."

20
So it is said, and elsewhere it says:
"This mind, bound by worldly entanglements,
is freed when relaxed—there is no doubt."[1305]
As taught here, you should relax without distraction.

21
When thoughts arise, and you observe their nature,
then they naturally disappear, and a pure vacuity dawns;
likewise, when you examine the settled mind,
you see nonobstruction, vacuity, clarity,
and vividness: this is known as "the merger of stillness
and movement". . . .

1305. Sa*PD*t 73a; cf. R. Jackson 2004, 78 (verse 42h).

22
. . . Whatever thoughts may arise,
do not stop them, but recognize [119]
their movement, and place your attention
upon their nature. . . .

23
. . . It's the same as in the example
of the flight of a ship's captive bird:
"It's like a raven that flies from a ship,
circles in every direction, and alights there again."[1306]

As for the nature of the concentration to be accomplished, concentration has two limbs: it possesses intense clarity and it possesses single-pointed nonconceptuality. The characteristic of such serenity is that it arises from a single-pointed concentration of a desire-realm mind of someone on a stage that is not yet that of complete meditative equipoise. The guardian Maitreya says:

> It arises from a cause that is abandonment
> of the five faults and reliance on the eight formations.[1307]

It is taught that the mind that arises through reliance on the eight formations that are the antidotes to the five faults is accomplished through the nine stages. Those nine mental stages are also taught by Ārya Asaṅga, in the Treatises on the Levels, as accomplished through the six powers and possessing the four types of mental application.[1308]

What sort of object does one focus on to cultivate concentration? In general, the Blessed One taught countless objects for accomplishing flawless concentration, such as pervasive objects, objects that purify analysis, objects for

1306. Sa*PD*t 74b; cf. R. Jackson 2004, 93 (verse 70).

1307. Ma*MV* 4a (verse 3). The five faults, as noted above, are laziness, forgetfulness, agitation or dullness, nonapplication, and over-application. The eight "formations," or antidotes, are physical and mental pliancy, enthusiastic effort, desire, faith, mindfulness, alertness, application, and equanimity.

1308. As*YB* 133b. Also to reiterate, the nine stages are focus, continual focus, patch-like focus, close focus, controlled focus, pacified focus, complete pacification, single-pointed focus, and equipoise. The six powers are study, reflection, mindfulness, alertness, effort, and thorough habituation. The four types of mental application are effortful mental application, intermittent mental application, uninterrupted mental application, and effortless mental application.

the wise, objects that purify defilements, and so forth.[1309] However, because the previous gurus of this lineage of instruction usually explained that one should focus on the mind [120] and then recognize it, we will do the same here.

Tears in your eyes, your hair standing on end, appeal to the guru with strong, respectful devotion from the depths of your heart for a long time without ceasing, and when, at the end, the guru dissolves into you, think that you have been blessed. Then, within a state where appearances are indistinct, do nothing by way of conceptual contrivance. Entertain no hopeful thoughts: "If only I could accomplish this temporary or ultimate goal." Have no anxious thoughts: "May undesirable events not befall me in the present or future." Neither chasing the past nor anticipating the future, settle for a while in unwavering meditative equipoise on the nature of the present.

At the time of focusing the mind, you do not cease all mental activity as if fainting or sleeping. Rather, without wavering in the slightest from resting in that motionless mind, you establish mindfulness from afar without even the slightest forgetfulness. Though the object may be tied with the rope of mindfulness, if mindfulness weakens, there is great danger that the thoughts of the moving mind will proliferate. So when the power of mindfulness declines, you need to have posted the sentry of alertness, which notices how the mind moves or does not move, and focus there. As it says in Bhāviveka's *Essence of Madhyamaka* (*Madhyamakahṛdaya*):

> The wandering elephant of mind
> should be bound to the fixed pillar
> of the object with the rope of mindfulness
> and subdued [121] by the iron hook of alertness.[1310]

In brief, the attainment of flawless concentration occurs by way of nothing but the maintenance of mindfulness and alertness. Mindfulness is the principal one: when mindfulness has arisen, alertness is taught as its result and so is derivative.

At that time, when you have stopped all other thoughts and that aware, clear mind has definitely emerged, fasten mindfulness tightly just on its nature and behold it starkly and single-pointedly. Observing thus, note any movement or thought that occurs as that and just that; doing so depends on alertness. Alternatively, as taught in a Vinaya text, meditate in the way that an archer and a swordsman fight: when you have aroused the power of mindfulness and

1309. As described in, e.g., *SNS* 26a.

1310. Bv*MH* 4a (chap. 3).

alertness, any concept that arises is, at its occurrence, severed abruptly and not allowed to proliferate further.[1311]

When you rest motionless after the proliferation of thoughts has been severed, then, without losing mindfulness and alertness, remaining inwardly vigilant, you should relax into the present, relaxing into meditative equipoise. Machik says:

> Tightly focus and loosely relax:
> that's the ground on which to place your mind.[1312]

Also, as is taught elsewhere by the Great Brahman Saraha:

> This mind, bound by worldly entanglements,
> is freed when relaxed—there is no doubt.[1313]

Inwardly vigilant, you relax. [122] Thinking, "If mind is too tight, agitation will occur," relax a little; and thinking, "if it's too loose, dullness will occur," tighten your mind a little—that way, it will be just right. Between those two extremes, release your mind from the movements of thought, and on the lookout for dullness when stillness occurs, you settle the mind. According to Master Candragomin:

> If I resort to effort, agitation will occur;
> if I abandon that, slackness will arise.
> When it is difficult to find a proper balance,
> my mind is perturbed, so what should I do?[1314]

1311. SNL. The story, as found in, e.g., Kt*GBLZ* 179, and which is probably Indian in origin, tells of a duel between a great archer who is able to launch countless arrows in the blink of an eye and a swordsman so skilled he can deflect any and every arrow with his sword. At the height of their battle, the swordsman is distracted for a split second by the archer's beautiful wife and is killed. Thus the price of losing mindfulness and alertness! As my colleague Matt Robertson has reminded me, the tropes of both preternaturally skilled sword-wielders and ascetics distracted from their contemplations by beautiful women are common in Indian literature (e.g., the *Mahābhārata* and *Rāmāyaṇa*), but I have not identified the source of this particular tale, which combines both elements. Incidentally, the two possible approaches to dealing with thoughts that are mentioned here—noting them and cutting them off—are described by later commentators (e.g., Kt*GBLZ* 178–79) as "new mindfulness" and "old mindfulness," respectively.

1312. SNL.

1313. Sa*PD*t 73a; cf. R. Jackson 2004, 78 (verse 42h).

1314. Cg*ST* 205b.

At the time when you are suppressing thoughts and observing the nature of each thought as it arises, a pure vacuity dawns right where those thoughts have naturally disappeared. Likewise, if you examine the mind when it remains thus without wavering, there also is an unobstructed, pure, and vivid vacuity. Seeing the former and the latter as indistinguishable is known and designated by the great meditators as "the merger of stillness and movement."

Alternatively, there is a method for maintaining mental stillness that is to be practiced thus: whenever a thought arises, you do not stop it but you note when it moves and where it moves, observing and engaging with the nature of that thought. When you settle thus, movement will eventually cease and there will be stillness. It is the same as in the example of the flight over the great sea by a bird that has long been held captive on a seagoing ship. [123] The *Treasury of Dohās* says:

> It's like a raven that flies from a ship,
> circles in every direction, and alights there again.[1315]

So should you maintain concentration. Also, there is this from Yangönpa:

> The mind should not see thoughts as faulty.
> Without meditating for the sake of nonconceptuality,
> rest the mind in its natural state and watch it from afar,
> and your meditation will alight upon serenity.[1316]

Moreover, when present-day disciples maintain serenity by way of the six methods of settling the mind, they become kings of instruction. How are they practiced? It is said:

> (1) Settle like the sun free from clouds.
> (2) Settle like a garuḍa soaring in the sky.
> (3) Settle like a ship on the great sea.
> (4) Settle like a small boy looking at temple paintings.
> (5) Settle like the tracks of a bird flying in the sky.
> (6) Settle like spread-out raw cotton.
> By these methods of settling the mind,
> you will get the point of yoga.[1317]

1315. Sa*PD*t 74b; cf. R. Jackson 2004, 93 (verse 70).

1316. Yn*PCTC* 11a.

1317. Citing the same items in a slightly different order, Dakpo Tashi Namgyal (Kn*PCOZ*

(1) For example, just as the sun that is free from the clouds remains supremely luminous and bright, in the same way, the luminous nature of mind is not obscured[1318] by conceptual apprehension of signs, agitation, dullness, and so forth.

(2) For example, just as a garuḍa moving through the sky moves on its own, soaring naturally without needing to exert much effort in flapping its wings and so forth, in the same way, the mind—without too much tightening or too much relaxation—possesses the sharpness of the clarity aspect of internal [124] vigilance, and by relaxing slowly into the present, it maintains an unbreakable seal of mindfulness and alertness.

(3) For example, just as waves arise a little when the great sea is buffeted by winds, but the sea cannot be moved in its depths, in the same way, the mind may be moved a little by subtle thoughts when it is focused on its object, but its focus is not moved in the slightest by coarse thoughts.

(4) For example, just as a small child looking at temple paintings does not investigate or analyze the subtle details of the picture but looks unwaveringly at the painting in a general way, in the same way, when the mind is focused on its object, pleasant or unpleasant objects of the five sense consciousnesses may appear, but [the mind] remains focused single-pointedly on the object, without investigation or analysis, attachment or aversion.

(5) For example, just as a bird flying in the sky leaves no tracks, in the same way, whatever feelings of pleasure, pain, or indifference may occur, [the mind] remains in meditative equipoise, without falling under the sway of any attachment, anger, or confusion.

(6) For example, just as raw cotton, when spread out, is soft and very loose, in the same way, the mind settled in meditative equipoise rests evenly, free from the manifest three poisons and the coarse sensations of agitation and dullness.

[2.2.3.3.1.2.2. Imprints Resulting from Maintaining Mental Equipoise in This Way] [verse 24]

What sort of imprints result from maintaining meditative equipoise in this way?

257a) attributes this list to Milarepa's *Mahāmudrā Instruction in Four Letters* (*Phyag rgya chen po yi ge bzhi pa'i gdams*), which is found in Lt*DNDZ* vol. 8; for further particulars, see Dakpo Tashi Namgyal 2019, 613n1137.

1318. Reading *sgribs* for *sgrigs*.

24
When you practice in this way,
the nature of meditative equipoise will not be obscured
by anything: it is lucid and clear,
with nothing physical established anywhere in it;
it is a pure vacuity like space,
where everything appears vividly.

When you practice in this way, the nature of the meditative equipoise, unobstructed by anything, is lucid [125] and very clear. There is no physical entity established anywhere within it, so it is a pure vacuity like that of space. Also, any good or bad objects of the five senses that appear will appear as clear and vivid, as if they were reflections in a lucid mirror. An experience occurs that is free from such identifications as "this is" or "this is not." However stable such a concentration may be, if it is not imbued with the bliss of mental and physical pliancy, it is said to be single-pointedness of mind of the desire realm. On the other hand, a concentration that is imbued with mental and physical pliancy is said to be serenity. Serenity will be the source of many positive attributes, such as yogic attainments, special prowess, and so forth. In particular, the ārya paths of all three vehicles are obtained in dependence upon it.

[2.2.3.3.1.2.3. Identifying This Path in Terms of Its Own Nature] [verses 25–27]

Well, how is this path to be identified in terms of its own nature? It is said:

25
Thus, though the real nature of mind
may be seen through higher perception,
it cannot be apprehended or taught as "this."

26
Gently place the mind, without grasping, on whatever appears:
"This," it is single-mindedly proclaimed by most
present-day great meditators of the Land of Snows,
"is the special instruction that leads
to holding Buddha in your palm." [126]

27
That may be, but this way,
say I, Chökyi Gyaltsen,

is merely a marvelous means for a beginner
to accomplish mental stillness
and a way of introducing the phenomenal nature of mind.[1319]

This is how the answer is expressed.

[2.2.3.3.2. Insight] [verses 28–38]

Now, I promise to specifically demonstrate the method for recognizing the real nature of mind:

[2.2.3.3.2.x.[1320] The real method for distinguishing the nature of mind] [verse 28]

28
Now, the way to recognize
the real nature of mind
is as set forth in the oral instructions of my root guru,
who is all the gnoses of the buddhas
but has taken the guise of a saffron wearer
and dispelled the gloom of my mental confusion.

Knowing other sources is easy, and since this promise is unlike the earlier one, there is no fault such that I will repeat previous explanations. Thus here there is: (1) a general demonstration that distinguishes the way of recognizing the real nature of mind and (2) a demonstration that summarizes the essence of those discussions.

2.2.3.3.2.1. [A general demonstration that distinguishes the way of recognizing the real nature of mind]

The Teacher has said that when there is realization of the nature of mind, that is Buddha, so Buddha is not to be sought elsewhere. Saraha says:

1319. Although Paṇchen Chögyen does not expand on the root verses here, this is as close to a critique of Kagyü mahāmudrā practices as he comes. Other commentators, such as Keutsang (Kt*GBLZ* 189–91), have more to say about the verses, but they too avoid explicitly identifying the "present-day meditators of the Land of Snows." We may recall that Tsongkhapa was similarly oblique in his *Queries from a Pure Heart.*

1320. As before, there is an implicit, unnumbered text-division here that I have made explicit.

Mind itself alone is the seed of everything
whence saṃsāric existence and nirvāṇa are projected
and which bestows all desired results—
to the mind like a wish-fulfilling jewel, I bow down.[1321]

Also, as explained by Lingrepa:

When you realize the real nature of your mind, that is Buddha;
when you sever superimpositions from within, that is fulfillment.[1322]

It is from realizing or not realizing the real nature of one's own mind that the loss and profit that are dichotomized as saṃsāra and nirvāṇa are magnified. In accordance with the meaning [127] of all the holy sūtras and tantras, ways of meditating by cutting the root basis of mind are as follows:

(1) Some examine from within meditative equipoise whether their own mind is established anywhere outside or inside, or as arising, abiding, or ceasing, and when they see that it is not established anywhere, they cut the root basis of mind, recognize the mind, and attain the goal, mahāmudrā. This is asserted as the meaning of this passage from the *Dohā Treasury of Mahāmudrā Instruction*:

When sought, no mind or appearance
is found, nor is there anywhere a seeker;
the nonexistent does not arise or cease at any time,
so it cannot become something else—
it is the abiding nature of natural great bliss.
Thus all appearances are the Dharma body.[1323]

(2) Also, some, when seeking the mind, do not find it established in any part of their own bodies, from the top of the head to the soles of the feet, and seeing that it is nowhere established as a material entity with color, shape, and so forth, they see the real nature of mind and so forth. Shang Rinpoché says:

The abiding nature of your own mind is the seed of all.
The minds of all the conquerors and their children
appear primordially as the invariant gnosis, the Dharma body:

1321. Sa*PD*t 72b cf. R. Jackson 2004, 73 (verse 41).

1322. Lr*GGRP* 28a.

1323. Sv*MU* 122b.

it is not matter, and is clear by its own nature;
unestablished as a thing, it is empty of color and dimension.[1324]

This statement should be kept in mind.

(3) Still others, neither pursuing past cognitions nor anticipating future cognitions, settle naturally into the fresh, uncontrived [128] cognition of the present and directly perceive the bare essence of mind; at that time they cut the root of mind and recognize the nature of mind.[1325] Saraha says, "Settle gently on the fresh, uncontrived mind,"[1326] and as the mahāsiddha Lingrepa says:

When you are settled in a fresh, uncontrived state, realization occurs;
when you maintain realization like a flowing river, fulfillment occurs.
Abandoning all reference points and signs,
remain always in meditative equipoise, O yogī.[1327]

(4) Others say: Whatever aspects of such objects as form, sound, and so forth arise in the mind, and whatever thoughts of virtue and nonvirtue or good and bad arise, starkly behold their intrinsic nature without acting in the least to deny or affirm them, and they will disappear on their own. Following that, settle yourself in that wakeful, pure vacuity in which there is no identifiable entity; seeing thus is realization of reality and recognition of the nature of mind. It is as explained in Tilopa's *Mother Ganges*:

If you want to realize the truth that transcends thought, with nothing to do,
then cut the root of your own mind and rest in bare awareness:
the water polluted by thoughts will turn clear.
Don't deny or affirm appearances, leave things alone:
when you do not reject or accept, that is mahāmudrā.[1328]

(5) Also, many others say: Any thought-images that arise should be suppressed without being allowed to disappear on their own; then, when they are allowed to rise back up, they release themselves—that is the simultaneity

1324. Zr*LCTT* 2b. Cf. trans. Martin 1992, 257, and Roberts 2011, 85.

1325. Zr*PCNG* 8b.

1326. SNL.

1327. Lr*GGRP* 28a.

1328. Tp*GM* 243a; cf. trans. Brunnhölzl 2007, 100.

of appearance and release. Thus there are as many Dharma bodies as there are [129] thoughts. As Guru Shang instructs:

> When thoughts suddenly arise
> from a state that is thusly settled,
> do not think that they are something
> other than the luminous Dharma body. . . .
>
> Therefore, the projection of thoughts
> is emptiness projecting from emptiness,
> Dharma body projecting from Dharma body,
> union projecting from union.[1329]

2.2.3.3.2.2. [A demonstration that summarizes the essence of those discussions] [verses 29–38]

It says in the *Questions of Rāṣṭrapāla*:

> Those who do not know the way of emptiness,
> peace, and nonarising wander in saṃsāra's realms;
> one who has compassion effects their entry into truth
> through hundreds of methods and reasons.[1330]

This states that those who do not know the profound way of emptiness and lack of self are wanderers in the realms of saṃsāra, and for the sake of freeing those saṃsāric wanderers from saṃsāra, the teacher who possesses great compassion effects their entry onto the path to realization of lack of self through hundreds of methods for realizing lack of self and arguments that establish lack of self taught directly and indirectly. Similarly, the guardian Śāntideva says:

> All these limbs of practice
> were taught for the sake of wisdom.[1331]

Also, Jowo Atiśa says:

> All the eighty-four thousand collections

1329. Zr*LCTT* 7a; cf. trans. Martin 1992, 267 and 268, and Roberts 2011, 97 and 98.

1330. *RPS* 252b.

1331. Sd*BA* 30b (verse 9.1).

of Dharma that have been taught
are for arriving at this reality.[1332]

All the eighty-four thousand collections of Dharma taught by the Conqueror were taught so as to establish [130] methods whereby disciples can, in the end, realize reality, or lack of self, by direct perception.

As for the realization of lack of self by direct perception: having previously established lack of self through hearing and reflection, you must meditate. Further, by meditating only on serenity, you will be like an extremist, unable to abandon all defilements. The *King of Concentrations* teaches:

Although the worldly cultivate concentration,
they will not destroy perceptions of self;
because they are defiled, they will be disturbed,
like Udraka Rāmaputra cultivating concentration.[1333]

Well, what is the concentration that directly effects the obtainment of liberation? The same sūtra says:

If you discern the lack of self of phenomena
and meditate on what has been discerned,
it is the cause of obtaining the fruit, nirvāṇa;
no other cause will bring about peace.[1334]

This states that one who discerns that phenomena lack self and meditates on the meaning thus discerned will obtain the fruit, nirvāṇa.

Also, in such meditation on lack of self there is no inherent division into subtle and coarse, but there is a division into lack of self of phenomena and persons. As Śrī Candrakīrti teaches:

For the sake of freeing beings, this lack of self
is taught as twofold, since it is divided into phenomena and persons.[1335]

1332. At*SA* 72b (verses 16–17).

1333. *SRS*t 27a. According to early biographies of the Buddha, Udraka was—after Ārāḍa Kālāma—the second teacher visited by the future Buddha after his departure from the palace. Udraka taught the concentration state of "neither perception nor nonperception" as the highest spiritual achievement. Gautama found this insufficient for liberation, and so moved on.

1334. *SRS*t 27a.

1335. Ck*MA* 213a (verse 6.179).

Although of these two, the lack of self of phenomena is presented first in the scriptures and their commentaries, when it comes to meditation, it is necessary to meditate first on the lack of self [131] in persons. As taught in the *King of Concentrations*:

When you perceive a self in one,
that perception applies to all.
The nature of all things
is utterly pure, like the sky,
so by knowing one, you know all,
by seeing one, you see all.[1336]

Thus, in meditating on the lack of self of persons, you need to identify at the outset the object of negation that is to be negated. As it says in *Engaging in Bodhisattva Conduct*:

Without perceiving a postulated entity,
you cannot apprehend its nonexistence.[1337]

If the object of negation is not identified, then with the target unseen, the arrow will stray; with the enemy unidentified, the army cannot be led—it is like that.

Also, if the excess that is overpervasion in identifying the object of negation occurs, you fall to the extreme of nihilism; if there is the excess that is underpervasion, then, without refuting the subtle object of negation, you fall to the extreme of eternalism. The danger is very great. Nāgārjuna's *Root Verses on Wisdom* states:

If their view of emptiness is wrong,
those of little wisdom will be destroyed:
it is like a snake seized in the wrong way
or a spell wrongly executed.

Therefore, knowing that the Dharma is deep,
and hard for the feeble-minded to understand,
the Sage turned his mind away
from teaching the Dharma.[1338]

1336. *SRS*t 44a.

1337. Sd*BA* 36a (verse 9,140).

1338. Ng*MK*t 15a (verses 24.11–12).

Also, as stated in the *Perfection of Wisdom in Eight Thousand Lines*, the circling of all sentient beings because of grasping at "I" and "mine" [132] is saṃsāra.[1339]

The ultimate root of all flaws is connate self-grasping or the connate grasping at "I." In general, the mind that has the thought "I am" either (1) takes the "I" as distinguished by being truly existent, (2) takes the "I" as not truly existent or as a mere name or merely designated by thought, or (3) does not take the "I" as real in either of those two ways. Of these three ways of thinking of "I," the last is the designation validly applied to some mere conventional "I"; the middle occurs only in the mindstream of one who has definitively attained the Madhyamaka view and does not occur in others; and the first is grasping at a self of persons.

Taking *another* person as your referent object and grasping that as truly existent is grasping at a self of persons but it is not the connate grasping at "I." The connate grasping at "I," or the view of the transitory, is the defiled discrimination that grasps as intrinsically existent the object that has been intended, the "I" of your *own* mindstream. That latter is produced by its own cause, a subtle grasping at the self of phenomena. As stated by the guardian Nāgārjuna:

> As long as there is grasping at the aggregates,
> there will be grasping at an "I" in them;
> when there is grasping at "I," there also is karma,
> and through karma, there is rebirth.[1340]

Since it is the root of saṃsāra, you cannot abandon self-grasping without repudiating the object of fixation that is the referent of that grasping, for the king of reasoning [Dharmakīrti] states:

> Without repudiating its object,
> you will not be able to abandon self-grasping.[1341] [133]

The objects of fixation of (1) grasping at a truly existent individual, (2) grasping at a truly existent "I," and (3) grasping at a truly existent person are, respectively, (1) a truly existent individual, (2) a truly existent "I," and (3) a truly existent person. Thus it is necessary to eradicate them.

As for eradicating them: They are to be viewed as not truly existent, because, having ascertained that a person is not truly existent, you accustom yourself to

1339. *ASPt* (*kha*) 353a.

1340. Ng*RA* 108a (verse 1.35).

1341. Dk*PV* 116a (verse 2.223).

that view and reverse grasping at the person as truly existent. For these reasons, I will first demonstrate, on the basis of experiential pith instructions, the way the object of negation appears and the way it is apprehended.

29

From within the foregoing meditative equipoise,
like a minnow swimming
in limpid water without disturbing it,
analyze wisely with subtle awareness
the intrinsic nature of the person who meditates.

Thus, without wavering in the slightest from the previous meditative equipoise that is settled single-pointedly in serene concentration—as, for example, a minnow that swims in a pool of limpid water without disturbing it—from within that meditative equipoise you should analyze with a subtle consciousness the quintessential nature of the individual or "I" who meditates in concentration: its mode of existence, its mode of appearance to the mind, and its mode of being apprehended. Analyze all this subtly and astutely with a precise and [134] discriminating mind.[1342]

When you analyze thus, you see that the mode of being of an individual, an "I," a person, and so forth—of all phenomena—is as mere names, mere designations by thought, merely imputed as a snake is imputed upon a striped rope or a person is imputed upon a cairn or a pile of sticks. A sūtra says:

> It appears just as does a gandharva city:
> that city exists in none of the ten directions.
> In other words, that city is merely nominal;
> thus is this realm seen by the Sugata.[1343]

1342. To highlight the discrepancy between appearance and reality, Gelukpa philosophers use the Prāsaṅgika Madhyamaka vocabulary of "modes" or "ways" (*tshul*) to describe the various manners in which epistemic objects and subjects may be analyzed. An object's mode of appearance (*snang tshul*) is the way it appears to us. The mode of apprehension or grasping (*'dzin tshul*) is the way it is taken to exist, as intrinsically real. Our inability to let go of such an incorrect apprehension of the object is the mode of fixation (*zhen tshul*). The ultimate nature of the object—its emptiness of intrinsic existence—is its mode of being (*gnas tshul*) or mode of existence (*yod tshul*). In less technical language, as long as we are not buddhas, things appear to us as intrinsically existent, so we apprehend them as existing in that way and fixate on that apprehension. When we are buddhas, things still appear to us, but they are not apprehended or fixated upon as intrinsically real, and their ultimate nature—their emptiness—is perceived simultaneously with their conventional qualities and their status as dependently arisen phenomena.

1343. *PPS* 43a.

We should see things as the Tathāgata does.

Thus, when we are unmistaken, all phenomena should appear as nominal, with merely designated existence; when they do not appear thus, we are possessed by the demon of ignorance, and the way they exist appears mistakenly. Through fixating on that, we collect karma, and by the power of this karma, we wander in saṃsāra and experience various sufferings. Now when the essence is nakedly revealed, then such a mode of appearance and such a mode of fixation are asserted, respectively, as "the appearance of the object of negation" (its mode of appearance as truly established) and the mode of apprehension of true existence (that is, the way of fixation). For us ordinary individuals, the object of negation cannot appear to reasoning in any way other than the way present appearances arise; all cognitions in the mindstream of an ordinary individual are corrupted by ignorance, so any object that appears, appears as truly existent.

Thus, based on the ascertainment that persons and phenomena exist merely [135] as designations, you ascertain accordingly that the root of saṃsāra is our mode of apprehending an "I" that is connate grasping at "I." Based on such a realization, you are able to thoroughly ascertain your mode of apprehending the subtle object of negation. The omniscient Jé Tsongkhapa stated this in many places, as for instance:

> There is the demonstration of how all phenomena exist as designations and—opposed to that—of the way to identify the object of negation.[1344]

With regard to these modes, some of those reputed as lordly scholars, who claim to be guides for many sentient beings, are ambiguous in their writings; only those holy ones who have made practice essential have sufficient greatness of mind to come across clearly. As Khedrup Norsang Gyatso says:

> The constellations of arrogant scholars trailing
> the mighty sun of the excellent mind [Losang][1345]
> say that things truly exist by their own characteristics and intrinsic
> nature.
>
> Through your own mind's settled awareness, seeing the meaning
> of negating objects of negation bound by conventional words—
> that is asserted to be the Great Madhyamaka free from extremes.

1344. Ts*GPRS* 75b.

1345. That is, Losang Drakpa, or Tsongkhapa.

Like some dream form or illusory horse or cow,
appearances do not exist in the slightest
other than as appearances in the mind.

From the peak of saṃsāric existence all the way to hell,
if sentient beings do not negate a subtle object of negation
that is designated through discrimination
of individual conventionalities, then
however much they examine, they do not in the slightest
 transcend
a superficial view, and they are slain by the self.[1346] [136]

Thus, if under analysis the "individual" and so forth exist as they appear in the mind that conceives "an individual," or "person," or "I," it would not be suitable for them to exist other than as truly existent. Thus an "individual" does not exist as it appears: (1) an individual does not exist as body and mind taken singly, (2) an individual does not exist as body and mind taken together, (3) an individual does not exist as the six elements taken singly, (4) an individual does not exist as the six elements taken together, and (5) an individual does not exist other than as the six elements. In teaching that, the unexcelled protector, the guardian Nāgārjuna himself, says:

30
"An individual is not earth, is not water,
is not fire, is not air, is not space,
is not consciousness—nor is it all of them.
And what individual can there be apart from these?[1347]

Also, in accord with that, *Engaging in Bodhisattva Conduct* says:

Teeth, hair, and nails are not the self;
the self is not the bones or blood;
it is not snot, it is not phlegm;
it is not lymph, it is not pus.

The self is not fat or sweat;
nor are lungs and liver the self;

1346. SNL.

1347. Ng*RA* 109b (verse 1.80).

nor are internal organs the self.
The self is neither excrement nor urine.

Heat and breath are not the self;
the pores are not, nor, in all their aspects,
are the six consciousnesses the self.[1348]

Thus, with respect to an individual, or self, or I, the bone and other earth elements of the body, the solid parts, are not the I. The blood and other water elements, the liquid parts, are not the self. From the crown of the head to the soles of the feet, the fire element, the warm [137] part, is not the self. The wind constituent of the body, shifting and moving within the channels, is not the individual. The inner hollow regions and other cavities of the body are not the individual. All consciousnesses—the eye consciousness and the others—are not the self, and the self is not them. The collection of those is not the self, and the I is not the collection of those, nor is it other than those; for in the mind holding the idea of "the individual who is meditating," there is no individual that exists as it appears. Also, as stated in a sūtra:

> Form is not the self, feeling is not the self, discernment is not the self, formations are not the self, consciousness is not the self.[1349]

Since that is the case, the five aggregates of the individual who meditates, or the six elements, or the collection of these, or the shape of the collection—none of these is the individual who meditates. If they were, then the basis of designation and the thing designated, the appropriated and the appropriator, the parts and the whole, would all be one. Also,

If the aggregates were the self, then
they would be multiple and selves would be multiple.[1350]

Such statements are faulty. In particular, if consciousness were the individual, it would be unacceptable that the individual hear, speak, see, or procreate. Also, although the individual is singular, just as there are six consciousnesses, so there would be six individuals; conversely, just as the individual is one, so the six consciousnesses [138] would be a partless one. If the shape of the col-

1348. Sd*BA* 33a (verses 9.57–59).

1349. *ANS* 62a.

1350. Ck*MA* 210b (verse 6.127).

lection of elements was the individual, then the individual would be material, and there would be no individuals in the formless realm.

Nor is the individual separate from the five aggregates. If it were, it would exist as inherently unconnected and separate, so the collection of aggregates would not possess the characteristics that define the aggregates. It is said:

> If it were separate from the aggregates,
> then it would not have the characteristics of the aggregates.[1351]

Also, there would be the faults taught in the *Sūtra on the Elephant's Exertion*:

> If things existed intrinsically,
> the conquerors and the śrāvakas would know it;
> there would be no immutable[1352] phenomena, nor transcendence of sorrow,
> and the wise would never be free from conceptual elaboration.[1353]

Thus, when you examine with a subtle consciousness from within meditative equipoise, you yourself appear such that not even an atom exists of the individual or self or person who is resting in equipoise: all of a sudden, there is emptiness. When the mental image of that pure vacuity is clear in your mind, then, without further conceptual elaboration, not bringing anything to mind, you rest in single-pointed meditative equipoise. If your apprehension of that pure vacuity, which is a nonaffirming negation, weakens a little, then meditate single-pointedly from within meditative equipoise, examining as before—that is the way to maintain space-like meditative equipoise. It is taught that when you first ascertain things in this way, if you are not [139] already familiar with the view, fear will arise; if you are acquainted with it, joy will arise.

To demonstrate the features of post-meditation, it is stated:

31ab
"Just as an individual does not really exist
because it is a composite of the six elements . . ."[1354]

1351. Ng*MK*s 10b (verse 18.1).

1352. Reading *ther zug* for *thar zug*.

1353. A search of the *HKS* does not turn up this passage; it is, however, found in the *Sūtra on the Concentration of the Gnosis Seal of the Tathāgatas* (*TJS* 251b).

1354. Ng*RA* 109b (verse 1.81a).

When you arise from meditative equipoise and analyze what appears, no "individual" mistakenly appears due to your being in the grasp of the demon of the ignorant idea of selfhood. However, a mere conventional individual or person or I is definitely there. Its mode of being is like that of a person imputed onto a cairn or like a snake imputed onto a rope. Having produced a consciousness ascertaining that an "individual" is a mere name designating a mere collection of one's own six elements or five aggregates, a mere sign, a mere designation by thought, a mere not-really-existent dependent arising that is empty like an illusion, meditate with that certainty. This also is to be remembered through the profound songs in the sūtras. The *King of Concentrations* says:

> An illusionist creates imaginary forms:
> various horses, elephants, and chariots.
> Just as those do not exist as they appear,
> so should you understand all things.
>
> Just as a young woman, in a dream,
> sees her son being born and dying,
> and is happy when he is born and sad when he dies,
> so should you understand all things.
>
> Just as the moon's reflection at night
> appears in water that is limpid and unmuddied [140]
> yet the moon's reflection is empty and unreal, ungraspable,
> so should you understand all things.
>
> Just as, at noon in the summer,
> beings are tormented by thirst and travelers
> see mirages as bodies of water,
> so should you understand all things.
>
> In a mirage, no water exists, but
> deluded sentient beings wish to drink it.
> There can be no drinking of unreal water:
> so should you understand all things.
>
> Just as people cut through the waterlogged trunk
> of a plantain because they desire its core,

> though inside and out there is no core,
> so should you understand all things.[1355]

Thus, when you have practiced repeatedly and have understood in your mindstream the absence of a self of persons, there is another saying, from the *Condensed Perfection of Wisdom*:

> Know that all sentient beings exist as the self exists;
> know that all phenomena exist as all sentient beings exist.[1356]

For the purpose of demonstrating the way to meditate on the lack of self in other persons and phenomena, the root text explains:

31b–d
"In the same way, the individual elements
do not really exist because they are composites."[1357]

32
In accordance with that statement, when you search,
you do not find even the minutest particle
of meditative equipoise, the one who rests in equipoise, and so forth.
At that time, maintain a space-like meditative equipoise,
single-pointedly and without distraction.

Also, when all phenomena of saṃsāra and nirvāṇa—all ordinary and ārya beings, the outer and inner earth element, and likewise the water, fire, air, space, and consciousness [141] elements—have been ascertained as individual or collective appearances in your mind, then analyze the aforementioned individual's mode of appearance and mode of apprehension and establish yourself in meditative equipoise. When you do not find even the minutest particle that is truly existent, that not-finding is said to be the supreme finding, and not-seeing to be the highest seeing. So when you see the real nature of the mind—when you recognize the mind—maintain a space-like meditative equipoise, unwavering and single-pointed, directly on the mere absence of true existence, which is the real nature of mind.

Alternatively, the subtle basis for designating a self is said to be the very sub-

1355. *SRS*s chap. 9, 26b.

1356. *PPG*t 191a; cf. trans. in Conze 1973, 12. For the Sanskrit (verse 1.12), see *PPG*s 353.

1357. Ng*RA* 110a (verse 1.81b).

tle vital winds and mind, and those who have given special instructions state that establishing the abiding nature of the mind is tantamount to recognizing the mind.

33
Alternatively, within that state of meditative equipoise
the mind is nothing physical: it is a pure vacuity,
unobscured, where various things appear and proliferate,
an unceasing stream of clarity and awareness.

34
The mind engaging ceaselessly with objects
appears to be independent, but the objects of fixation
we apprehend are as stated by the guardian Śāntideva:
"So-called 'continuums and collections,'
such as rosaries, armies, and the like, are false."[1358]

35
That said, informed by scripture and reasoning,
settle in single-pointed meditative equipoise in the state
where things do not exist in the way they appear.

Alternatively, [142] Candrakīrtipāda says:

> Mind itself variously brings forth the world
> of sentient beings and the physical world.[1359]

Since it is taught that mind is the root of all the worlds and their inhabitants, when you cut the root basis of mind, it is not like cutting other delusions, it's like this: when you analyze your own mind from within the previous continuous meditative equipoise, it is not established as any kind of form, so there is a pure vacuity, as when the sun is unobscured by clouds. Various thoughts and memories continually appear and spread outward. Unlike a lamp that has been doused, the mind is an uninterrupted stream of clarity and awareness that does not cease, and to the mind apprehending one's own mind, it seems somehow independent, under its own power. The objects of fixation that are apprehended as existing the way they appear and the mind that apprehends

1358. Sd*BA* 27b (verse 8.101).

1359. Ck*MA* 208b (verse 6.89).

objects of fixation the way they appear are as stated by the protector Śāntideva in the *Engaging in Bodhisattva Conduct*:

> So-called "continuums and collections,"
> such as rosaries, armies, and the like, are false.[1360]

When we have strung together the individual beads of a rosary, the "rosary" is just a designation, and when we have collected individuals who bear arms, the "army" is merely nominal, just a designation; apart from that, they do not exist. On the basis of scripture and reasoning that teach this, you should rest in single-pointed meditative equipoise within the certainty that the mind does not exist in accord with its mode of appearance. Thus the *Perfection of Wisdom in Eight Thousand Lines* also says:

> Mind does not exist as mind; the nature of mind is luminous.[1361] [143]

This states that no intrinsically established mind exists, and the nature of mind is luminous emptiness. Also, the *Jewel Heap* states:

> Mind is not seen, was not seen, and will not be seen by any of the buddhas of the three times.[1362]

Also, Jé Marpa states metaphorically that when he ascertained the real nature of the mind as it is, his mind in meditation was ablaze with emptiness and, as he says:

> I came to the banks of the Ganges River in the east.
> Through the kindness of Lord Maitrīpa,
> I realized the ground, the unborn reality.
> My mind was ablaze with emptiness;
> I saw the primordial nature, reality free from elaboration;
> I met the three mother buddha bodies face to face.
> From then on, this man's elaborations were severed.[1363]

1360. Sd*BA* 27b (verse 8.101).

1361. *ASP*t (*ka*) 4b. For further details, see note 786, above.

1362. SNL.

1363. Th*MPNT* 134. Cf. trans. Nālandā Translation Committee 1982, 144–45. This passage also is quoted by Yeshé Gyaltsen and Thuken.

Also, Drogön Phakdru teaches:

> Mind is the root of both saṃsāra and nirvāṇa.
> Mind is pure suchness from the beginning;
> since from the beginning it is peaceful and unproduced,
> mind is forever free from elaborated extremes.[1364]

In brief, it is not as if our spiritual friend is reputed to be omniscient even though he isn't; indeed, I have set forth the oral instructions I received directly from Sangyé Yeshé, who knows everything as it really is.

36
In brief, as related by my
spiritual friend, Sangyé Yeshé,
who knows everything as it really is:

37
"When you're [144] *fully aware that whatever appears is conceptually apprehended,*
then the Dharma realm dawns independently of anything else;
when awareness rests within this dawning
and you settle in single-pointed meditative equipoise—E ma!"[1365]

Whatever appears is conceptually apprehended. When you are aware that whatever appears is merely designated by thought, the ultimate, the Dharma realm, dawns as a mental object without depending on other conditions, and you enter it. As Candrakīrti states, "conventional truth is the method; ultimate truth emerges from the method."[1366] Awareness enters into this dawning, and when you single-pointedly unite reality, which has appeared as the mental object, with the objectifying consciousness, and rest in meditative equipoise on that, it's wonderful! The [root text's] "*along the same lines*" harmonizes the meaning of the previous and following lines:

38
. . . Dampa Sangyé says:
"Whirl the spear of awareness within emptiness;

1364. Pg*RCGD* 2b.

1365. Sy*SGDL* 67.

1366. Ck*MA* 207a (verse 6.80).

the view, O Dingripas, is unobstructed."[1367]
This and the other sayings make the same point

as stated above.

2.3. Follow-up [verses 39–45]

The virtues of meditative equipoise on mahāmudrā should be dedicated to unexcelled awakening. In the root text the passage "*From among the three divisions—preparation, the actual session, and follow-up*" (verse 9) teaches this directly. When to apply the way of following up is implicit but unclear; in fact, it is to be applied at this juncture. In order to delineate boundaries from here on out, I set forth what is in the root text:

39
Afterward, the virtue that has arisen
from meditating on mahāmudrā—
together with the sea of virtues collected in the three times—
should be dedicated to great, unexcelled [145] *awakening.*

It is fitting that this be applied.

Now, in order to summarize how to continue practicing in the postmeditation state after you have arisen from the meditative equipoise that is in equipoise on mahāmudrā, how to ascertain inerrantly the mental image of the object of negation when you return to meditative equipoise, and how to dispel concerns regarding either equipoise or postmeditation, the root text teaches thus:

40
Having familiarized yourself thusly, you must realize
precisely the mode of appearance of any object
appearing to the six types of consciousness.
Its mode of being will then nakedly and vividly appear;
identification of whatever appears is the key to the view.

41
In short, whatever appears—whether your own mind
or something else—should not be taken
to be real; you should ascertain

1367. PsDRGC 17b [34] (*Hundred Verses of Advice*, verse 51; cf. trans. Dilgo and Padampa, 95).

its mode of being and always maintain that awareness.
Knowing this, subsume all phenomena
of saṃsāra and nirvāṇa into a single nature.

Thus, after familiarizing yourself with meditative equipoise in this way, in post-meditation you should use precise and discerning examination to realize well the mode of appearance of anything—form and so forth—that appears as an object of the six types of consciousness—visual and the others. When you have analyzed it thus, although the object appears as truly existent [to sense consciousness], it is [seen by mental consciousness as] hollow and unreal, like a dream, a mirage, or a reflection of the moon in water. Its mode of being—as a dependent arising without an independent essence—appears nakedly and vividly. On that basis, your certainty about reality grows greater, for as Jé Mitrayogī [146] says, "Identification of whatever appears is the key point of the view."[1368]

What need is there for more? Let me summarize briefly. For those of us of who are shortsighted, it is precisely the way this or that subject—one's own mind and so forth—appears that is the mode of appearance of the object of negation. Thus, without grasping at or fixating on that appearing object, you must ascertain that its mode of being is simply its lack of existing as it appears. Thus you should always maintain [your realization] by alternating between a meditative equipoise in which the mind is like space and—once you have arisen from that meditative equipoise—the yoga of postmeditation, in which, when you observe whatever remains in the absence of true existence, [those things] appear unmistakably as dependently arisen events that are merely nominal, brought about by mere designation. Knowing thus the way to practice during meditative equipoise and in the postmeditative state, rest in equipoise by indivisibly subsuming the real nature of each and every phenomenon of saṃsāra and nirvāṇa under the mere absence of true existence. During the postmeditative state, establish the phenomenal natures of things as illusion-like appearances and familiarize yourself with this perspective.

42
Also, as stated by Āryadeva:
"The viewer of one entity
is explained as the viewer of all.
The emptiness of one
is the emptiness of all."[1369]...

1368. SNL.

1369. Ad*CS* 9b (verse 191 [8.16]); cf. trans. Lang 1986, 83.

When you are in meditative equipoise on reality, do dependently arisen phenomena appear as just nominal, as mere designations? The reply is expressed thusly:

43
. . . Thus, within a proper
meditative equipoise on reality,
you are free [147] *from elaborated extremes*
of saṃsāra and nirvāṇa, such as existence, nonexistence, and so forth.

The exalted Mila says:

> Where ultimate truth holds sway,
> there is no buddhahood separate from obstacles;
> there is no meditator, object of meditation,
> levels to be traversed, or path to be realized;
> there are no fruitional buddha bodies or gnosis,
> and therefore there is no nirvāṇa—
> everything is merely designated by names and words.
> The three worlds, animate and inanimate,
> from the beginning do not exist, so there is no arising.
> There is no basis, there is no connate;
> there is no action or ripening of action.
> Therefore not even the name of saṃsāra exists.
> The final reality appears like that.[1370]

It is said that "the perfection of wisdom cannot be described, thought, or expressed,"[1371] and, as the scholar-siddha Khyungpo teaches, "Mundane appearances are self-releasing, like illusions or dreams."[1372]

If that is so, are actions and their fruits and so forth utterly nonexistent? It is said that because things' ultimate nonexistence does not assure their [conventional] nonexistence, actions and their fruits and so forth very much exist.

1370. Th*MLGB* 347–48; cf. trans. Chang 1989, 1:325, and Tsangnyön Heruka 2016, 340–41.

1371. This phrase occurs at least five different times in the Tengyur, but without an identification of the author, we cannot be certain of Paṇchen Chögyen's source. See, e.g., Ck*VS* 91a.

1372. SNL.

44
Yet when you arise from that equipoise and analyze,
it is undeniable that dependently arisen actions and agents
naturally appear as mere names,
only labels—like a dream,
a mirage, the moon in water, or an illusion.

Jé Mila also states:

> *E ma*! If there were no sentient beings,
> whence would come the buddhas of the three times?
> Since a result without a cause is impossible,
> in the realm of phenomenal truth
> everything in saṃsāra and nirvāṇa [148]
> exists—so said the Sage.
> Existence—the appearance of entities—
> and nonexistence—the ultimate reality that is emptiness: these two
> have natures that are inseparable and of a single taste,
> so [the distinction between] our own awareness and others' awareness does not exist.
> All is vast and unified.[1373]

It suffices, then, to say that entities' mode of existence is to exist as mere names, as mere designations, for the supreme ārya, Nāgārjunapāda, states:

> Because a physical thing is merely nominal,
> space also is merely nominal.[1374]

Thus the final significance of the mahāmudrā view as described by the ārya father Nāgārjuna and his spiritual son Āryadeva was clearly explained by saying "designated existence, just nominal." For example, it must be acknowledged that there are pillars in a house of four pillars, because it has four pillars. "Pillar" is a universal that pervades each of the four pillars. What, then, is the definitional basis of the substance universal, "pillar"? When you search, none of the four pillars is individually suitable as the definitional basis, nor are the four collectively its definitional basis. Nor is its definitional basis a cause shown to be anything other than just the four individually and collectively. Thus the

1373. Th*MLGB* 348; cf. trans. Chang 1989, 1:325, and Tsangnyön Heruka 2016, 341.

1374. Ng*RA* 80b (verse 1.99); cf. trans. Nāgārjuna 1997, 24.

substance universal, pillar, that is inside the pillars is the mere nominal designation "pillar" on the four pillars. If you search for something apart from what is sufficiently described as a mere nominal designation, it is not found, so all phenomena equally are to be described as "designated existence, just nominal."

Now, there is a qualm [149] that must be cleared away. Some earlier and later writers connected with this [Madhyamaka] school say, "All cognitions of ordinary individuals are mistaken cognitions, and for that reason, any and all appearances that arise in the minds of ordinary individuals arise and appear as if they were intrinsically existent." Yet they go on to assert that the object of negation is apprehended as having an extra mode of appearance as truly existent that is separate from its present mode of appearance. This error may be due to their inability to state that appearances in the minds of us ordinary beings do not exist as they appear. If so, they should think well about how Śrī Candrakīrti refuted the assertions of those Svātantrika scholars who asserted that form and so forth exist by virtue of their appearance to an undefective mind. Nevertheless, it is also necessary to understand (a) that the five ordinary sense-consciousnesses are mistaken because although the five sense objects do not exist self-sufficiently they nonetheless appear to exist self-sufficiently, (b) that the five sense objects are validly cognized in their appearance as existing by their own characteristics, and (c) because of that they are accepted as valid posits on the level of convention.

Also, many think that it is said that the truly existent person, not the person as such, is negated, so while in meditative equipoise they keep aside this whole person and try to negate a truly existent person created by the mind. This is completely unacceptable, because it entails the extreme of permanence. Although there is much more to discuss, [150] I fear going on too long, so this must suffice.

Showing the way to manifest the excellent path free from the extremes of eternalism and nihilism by meditating thusly, the root text says:

45
When the empty is not obscured
by appearances, and appearances are not negated
by the empty, the excellent path—where emptiness
and dependent arising have a single meaning—will be manifest.

In accord with this, the omniscient Jé Tsongkhapa says:

> As for the belief that undeceiving dependent appearances
> and the empty are two separate things:
> as long as they appear individually,
> the Sage's meaning will not be realized.

> But when they are concurrent and simultaneous,
> then simply seeing unfailing dependent arising
> brings certain knowledge that destroys all manner of grasping at things,
> and the investigation of the view will be complete.[1375]

Also, it says in Candrakīrti's *Entry to the Middle Way*:

> Although all phenomena thus are empty,
> they actually arise from emptiness.
> Although there are two truths, there is no intrinsic nature,
> so phenomena are neither permanent nor destroyed.[1376]

Also, the guardian Nāgārjuna says:

> Someone who knows the emptiness of phenomena
> and yet accepts cause and effect:
> this is more marvelous than marvelous!
> This is more wonderful than wonderful![1377]

This is easy to understand.

When, through the power of an examination focused on emptiness, you obtain a concentration that is imbued with the bliss of physical and mental pliancy and sustain mahāmudrā while mounted on the steed of serenity, you thus reach the heat stage of the path of [151] preparation.[1378]

Some earlier Kagyüpa masters systematize mahāmudrā into four yogas. (1) When you focus the mind single-pointedly, there is *single-pointedness*. (2) When you realize that the mind is free from mental elaboration, there is *nonelaboration*. (3) When you realize that appearances and mind are of a single taste, there is *single taste*. (4) When meditation is without signs, there is *nonmeditation*. Those are the four. In terms of correlating these with the five paths and ten bodhisattva levels, Götsangpa explains that, essentially, the first

1375. Ts*LTNS* 194b; cf. trans. Thurman 1982, 58.

1376. Ck*MA* 206a (verse 6.38).

1377. Ng*BV* 41b (verse 88); cf. trans. Lindtner 1982, 211. See also Thupten Jinpa's translation, available online at http://www.tibetanclassics.org/html-assets/Awakening%20Mind%20Commentary.pdf.

1378. This is the first of four stages on the second of the five Buddhist paths to liberation, that of preparation (*prayogamārga, sbyor lam*), on which the meditator approaches the direct realization of emptiness—and the attainment of ārya status—that is achieved on the path of seeing.

yoga is the aspirational practices, the second is the path of seeing, the third is the second through the seventh bodhisattva levels, and the fourth is the pure levels.[1379] Shang Rinpoché teaches:

> When the single mahāmudrā is cut up,
> the fool is misled into listing levels and paths.
> Still, for those who enjoy delusion,
> the paths and levels of the definitional vehicle
> will be listed explicitly here.[1380]

His way of listing is like that of Götsangpa.

Some textual systematizers say it is unacceptable to equate nonelaboration to the first bodhisattva level because [according the *Sūtra on the Ten Levels* (*Daśabhūmika*)] the 112 attributes of a buddha will not appear in postmeditation. This is contradictory. Shang Rinpoché states:

> The mighty garuḍa is complete within the egg;
> when freed from the egg, it flies high in the sky.
> The attributes of the three buddha bodies are complete in the mind;
> when the illusory body has vanished, they arise for the sake of others.[1381]

And Jikten Gönpo states:

> If you find scriptural support in commentaries that ascertain that, I'll give you a good horse; what is stated in the *Sūtra on the Ten Levels* is written with regard to future lives.[1382]

It seems reasonable [152] that he should say this.

The exalted Sapaṇ says in his *Answers to the Questions of the Kadampa Namkha Bum*:

1379. SNL. The aspirational practices are the paths of accumulation and preparation. The path of seeing is equivalent to the first bodhisattva level. The remaining nine bodhisattva levels (2–7 being "impure" because in them defilements remain and 8–10 being "pure" because in them only the traces of defilements remain) comprise the path of cultivation, while the path of no-more-training is equivalent to liberation or buddhahood.

1380. SNL.

1381. Zr*LCTT* 22a; cf. trans. Martin 1992, 279, and Roberts 2011, 114.

1382. SNL.

> The Dharma systems of the Drigungpa, Taklungpa, and other mahāmudrā practitioners do not fully agree with the tantras and the scriptural collections. You should consider whether or not they are correct paths—and not spread them to others.[1383]

Although he makes this statement, nevertheless the life stories of ārya beings transcend the scope of ordinary beings, and negativity directed to the Dharma and holy beings is most unbearable, so I, Chökyi Gyaltsen, make this appeal: I ask that you reject the hateful power of sectarianism and fill yourself with the precious light by which everything is seen as pure.

3. [Dedication of the virtue arising from the composition] [verse 46]

Thus,

46
I, who am called Losang Chökyi Gyaltsen,
a renunciant who has heard many discourses, say:
by my virtue, may all beings quickly become conquerors through this path,
the door to peace, apart from which there is no second.

This is the way of fulfilling the promise made at the beginning of the text and is dedication of the virtue entailed by composing the work so that beings may gain victory in the battle with the two obscurations. I say:

> It's the supreme essence churned from the sea of the sūtras and tantras,
> the key point fully intended by the scholar-siddhas of India and Tibet,
> the path traversed by every supreme and holy siddha—
> may the sun of mahāmudrā teaching rise here today.
>
> Embodied beings whose minds are drunk on the wine
> of ignorant delusion and enter the prison

1383. Sp*KDZL* 244a; cf. trans. Sakya Pandita 2002, 270. The version of this passage used by Rhoton is less overtly critical in tone than that cited by Paṇchen Chögyen; he translates: "Various points in the religious traditions of the Drigungpas, Taklungpas, and other mahāmudrā adherents agree or disagree with the tantras and the basic scriptural collections. You yourself should investigate them carefully to determine whether or not they constitute a correct path." The injunction against spreading them to others does not appear. Whether Paṇchen Chögyen misremembered the quotation or was working from a different version is hard to say.

of fearsome mundane existence, [153] where they're tormented by the three sufferings—
for them, mahāmudrā is a pleasure grove, a resting place where pain is soothed.

The eye that sees the excellent path for every being,
the tradition of explanation of great and holy beings,
the clear and beautiful form of undiluted mahāmudrā—
this is the jeweled mirror in which everything appears.

For those many fortunate Buddhists who have cut the binding fetters
of the eight mundane concerns and who practice in desolate places,
bending their will toward the bliss of concentration,
it is also the guru who teaches the unmistaken excellent path.

In this way, the mass of virtue that has arisen from effort,
like jasmine opened by the moon's cool rays—
any supremely white karma I have amassed—
I dedicate to great awakening so motherly beings may be free.

By virtue of that, may the excellent mind-vase
of every being be filled with the divine nectar
of mahāmudrā, which unites sūtra and mantra,
and may they enjoy the great bliss of union.

[Colophon]

Now as for this *Lamp So Bright: An Extensive Explanation of the Mahāmudrā Root-Text of the Teaching Tradition of the Precious Geden Oral Transmission*: My student, Nechu Rabjampa[1384] Gendun Gyaltsen—who has attained

1384. This title translates roughly as "limitlessly learned master of the ten topics" (*gnas bcu rab byams pa*), possibly referring to Gendun Gyaltsen's expertise in the ten difficult (*dka' bcu*) topics or texts in the curriculum at Tashi Lhunpo, or perhaps to his mastery of the ten sciences (*rig gnas*) recognized by Tibetans as part of a complete education. The latter are divided into five minor sciences (grammar, poetics, metrics, drama, and lexicography) and five major sciences (language; logic; medicine; "construction" of objects, dwellings, and works of art; and inner science, or Buddhism). Earlier Gelukpas also recognized and conferred Kadam- and Sakya-based academic degrees that predated Tsongkhapa, including *rabjampa* (*rab 'byams pa*, or "limitlessly learned [master]") and *kashipa* (*dka' bzhi pa*, or "[master] of the four difficult [topics]"; the four usually are listed as the Perfection of Wisdom, Logic and Epistemology, Abhidharma, and Vinaya). The best-known Gelukpa academic degree is, of course, *geshé* (*dge*

certainty about this path, undertaken the essential practice, and made perfect offerings of the flowers of practice unsullied by the weaknesses of the eight mundane concerns—asked me: "Would you yourself please compose an extensive commentary on this root text, which severs extreme views, clarifies the essential meaning that is to be taken to heart, provides authoritative backing for the combination of scripture and reasoning, and is [154] adorned with instructions from the hearing transmission?" Based on his enthusiastic exhortation, I, the renunciant Chökyi Gyaltsen, who have gone to the far shore of the sea of individual mahāmudrā tenet systems, have written this quickly, under prodding, at the temple in the great Dharma school of Tashi Lhunpo. By this, may the precious teaching be a banner of victory that never is lowered.

Oṃ svāsti.

The fully branching wish-fulfilling tree of the Conqueror's teaching, which is the source of
benefit and bliss, is planted at the great Dharma school of spontaneous auspiciousness (Tashi Lhundrup)[1385] so that
all beings may practice for the excellent fruit of supreme liberation.
May this inexhaustible cloud of Dharma spread like a slow-moving stream.

Sarva jagataṃ.[1386]

bshes), which signifies mastery of the four difficult topics along with Madhyamaka. It largely superseded the other degrees in the eighteenth century and is conferred to this day (whether in Tibet or south India) by the three great seats of Gelukpa scholasticism, Ganden, Drepung, and Sera. For a discussion of academic degrees in the Geluk and other Tibetan monastic systems, see Tarab 2000, and Dreyfus 2003, 144–45.

1385. This is, of course, a play on the name of the Paṇchen Lama's monastery, Tashi Lhunpo.

1386. This is Sanskrit for "all beings," or "the whole world." It is frequently found as part of a longer benediction, *śubhamastu sarva jagatam*, meaning "may all beings be happy."

6. The Hundred Deities of Tuṣita[1387]

Dulnakpa Palden Sangpo

I go for refuge, until I'm awakened,
to the Buddha, the Dharma, and the Supreme Assembly.
By the merit from my practicing generosity and so forth,
may I become a buddha for benefit of beings. (*3x*)

Oṃ svasti.

1
From the heart of the guardian of the hundred deities of Tuṣita[1388]
comes a cloud resembling a heap of fresh, white curd; atop it
sits the Dharma king, the omniscient Losang Drakpa,
with his spiritual sons. I appeal to you to come here.

2
Exalted gurus with your bright, delighted smiles,
in the space before me on lotus and moon seats on lion thrones:
I appeal to you to remain for a hundred eons to spread the teaching
as the supreme field of merit for my faithful mind.

3
Your intelligent minds comprehend all objects of knowledge,
your eloquent speech is an ear ornament for the fortunate,
and your beautiful bodies blaze with the glory of your fame:
to you who are meaningful to see, hear, and recall, I bow down.

1387. 'Dul nag pa Dpal ldan bzang po. *Dga' ldan lha brgya ma* (Dl*GDHG*). Cf. trans. Berzin et al. 1979, 61ff., and Chöden 2013, 263–65. For context, see above, pages 144–45. As noted there, some versions of the prayer only contain the first eight verses, while others, including the version translated here, contain all ten.

1388. That is, Maitreya.

4
I offer to you, supreme field of merit,
this cloud sea of actually displayed and mentally created offerings,
such as pleasant water offerings, various flowers,
sweet-scented incense, bright lamps, and fragrant water.

5
Every nonvirtuous act of body, speech, or mind
I have accumulated from beginningless time,
especially those contrary to the three vows,
each one I confess with wholehearted regret.

6
In this degenerate age, you strove in study and practice
and took full advantage of your free and favored life by rejecting the eight mundane concerns.
O Protector, I rejoice with all my heart
in the great waves of your deeds.

7
Exalted holy guru, I appeal to you:
from the billowing clouds of love and wisdom in the sky of your Dharma body,
please send down a rain of profound and extensive Dharma
to care for your disciples in the most fitting way.

8
Whatever the extent of the virtue I have collected,
may it fully benefit the teaching and all beings,
and in particular, may the essence of the teaching
of the exalted Losang Drakpa shine forth for a long time to come.

9
Great treasure of nonreferential love, Avalokiteśvara;
lord of stainless wisdom, Mañjughoṣa;
destroyer of all the forces of Māra, Guhyapati;[1389]
crown ornament of sages of the Land of Snows, Tsongkhapa:
at the feet of Losang Drakpa I appeal.

1389. That is, Vajrapāṇi.

10

Precious and glorious root guru,
I appeal to you: please sit on the lotus
at my heart, care for me with your great kindness,
and grant me all the yogic attainments of body, speech, and mind.

7. The Bright Lamp of Mahāmudrā[1390]

Khedrup Norsang Gyatso

Namo gurubhyāḥ.

To those who through long-time practice attained the supreme path
of mahāmudrā, the summit of all yogas,
the supreme path that starts with primordial mind—
to the feet of the early Kagyüpas, I bow down.

Having thus offered homage, I will articulate just a little, by way of a brief summary, the ways of meditating on mahāmudrā taught by those holy spiritual friends so that their teaching may remain unbroken. The early Kagyüpas' way of meditating on mahāmudrā is explained as the way of meditating on primordial mind intended in Śrī Saraha's *Dohā Treasuries*. The explanation of the meaning of that is threefold: (1) establishing the Indian tantric source texts that demonstrate primordial mind, (2) explaining the meaning of those texts a little, and (3) briefly summarizing and demonstrating the way of meditating on mahāmudrā and other topics.

1. [Establishing the Indian tantric source texts that demonstrate primordial mind]

The "Gnosis" chapter of the *Condensed Kālacakra Tantra* says:

> Sentient beings are buddhas; in this world sphere, there are no other great buddhas.[1391]

1390. Mkhas grub Nor bzang rgya mtsho. *Bka' dge dgongs pa gcig bsgrub kyi phyag rgya chen po'i gsal ba'i sgron ma*. Dharamsala: Library of Tibetan Works and Archives. Accession no. 20379, n.d. For context and a summary, see above, chapter 8.

1391. *KCT* 87a.

The "Empowerment" chapter of *Stainless Light* says:

> Dwelling here within the hearts of all sentient beings is gnosis; it is the indestructible sound, the characteristic of the eternal *nāḍa*.[1392]

The first summary of the "Inner" chapter says:

> For the teacher, gnosis is blended: the gnosis that definitively dwells here in the body as the conventional connection between pervader and pervaded—and that dwells in the bodies of all sentient beings—is empty.[1393]

Similarly, the *Hevajra* says:

> The great gnosis dwells in the body.[1394]

The same text says:

> Sentient beings possess buddhahood, but it is obscured by incidental stains. When they are cleared away, that is buddhahood.[1395]

Vajragarbha's commentary on that says:

> Because all sentient beings possess the connate nature from the beginning, they are buddhas.[1396]

Similarly, the *Dohā Treasury* says:

> The primordial nature is unseen by fools; [2]
> fools are deceived by delusions—so says Saraha.[1397]

Also, the *Five Stages*, on Guhyasamāja, says:

1392. Pn*VP* 127a.

1393. Pn*VP* 223a.

1394. *HVT* 1:1.12; cf. trans. 1:48.

1395. *HVT* 2:4.69; cf. trans. 1:107.

1396. Vg*HP* 102a.

1397. Sa*PD*t 71b; cf. R. Jackson 2004, 63 (verse 18).

All beings lack independence;
they do not arise independently.
Their cause is luminosity,
and luminosity is utterly empty.[1398]

This passage explains the luminosity of death as the primordial mind. The same text says:

The mind that, when bound,
binds fools to saṃsāra,
that same mind takes yogīs
to the tathāgatas' abode.[1399]

The *Thorough Exposition of Valid Cognition* says:

The nature of mind is luminous;
the stains are incidental.[1400]

Consider these and other such statements as much as possible.

2. Explaining the meaning of those texts a little

The primordial mind thus explained is the ultimate basis for training in the generation and completion stages according to the Indian tantric texts. The explanation of the meaning of this primordial mind is sixfold: (1) recognizing the intrinsic nature of the primordial mind, (2) listing its names, (3) the way it is naturally pure, (4) the way its stains are incidental, (5) how to train on the path, and (6) the time frame for manifesting it.

2.1. Recognizing the intrinsic nature of the primordial mind

The very subtle mind, at the time it manifests itself, is utterly free of all mentally elaborated extremes. Its objects appear in such a way that their emptiness is directly realized. It also has the power to produce all the attributes of a buddha. It has dwelt in the mindstreams of all sentient beings beginninglessly, without even a moment's interruption. It is directly experienced at the

1398. Ng*PK*t 57b.

1399. Ng*PK*t 52b.

1400. Dk*PV* 115b (verse 2.208).

time of death and through the vital winds' absorption into the central channel by virtue of cultivating the path. When one's own intrinsic nature is purified of stains, it will become the Dharma body. Also, although it may be indicated partially, the way it actually exists cannot be expressed by those who have perceived it directly—let alone by others. Thus, the *Treasury of Dohās* says:

> No one can point to the primordial nature.[1401]

Also, the same text says:

> Although primordial nature cannot be expressed by words,
> it may be seen through the master's pith instruction.[1402]

Drawing on scripture, the *Dohā* commentator Advayavajra, Swamī Maitrīpa, writes:

> Beings are forever free from causes and conditions.
> Someone [3] pure may at times express reality,
> but the omniscient ones have discarded words.[1403]

There are many passages like these.

2.2. Listing its names

It is designated by many names in the Indian tantric texts: the connate nature, the mind of luminosity, the mind of the Dharma realm, the natural luminosity, the primordial mind, the indestructible mind, the basic Dharma body, the vajra mind, and so forth.

2.3. The way it is naturally pure

This is twofold: (1) it does not become good or bad through extrinsic conditions, and (2) its own intrinsic nature is not naturally stained.

1401. Sa*PD*t 72b; cf. R. Jackson 2004, 70 (verse 35).

1402. Sa*PD*t 72b; cf. R. Jackson 2004, 72 (verse 38).

1403. Mt*DP* 191b.

2.3.1. [It does not become good or bad through extrinsic conditions]

For example, just as the rays of the sun shine alike on good things like jewels and bad things like filth yet they do not become good or bad through those conditions, so the very subtle mind of luminosity occurs alike in good rebirths like the god realm and bad rebirths like the hells but is not good or bad by virtue of those rebirths. Like the rays of the sun, the mind is naturally pure.

2.3.2. Its own intrinsic nature is not naturally stained

Gold may on occasion be tarnished, but its intrinsic nature is not tarnished; water may on occasion be muddy, but its intrinsic nature is not muddy. Likewise, the very subtle luminous mind may be stained by defilements, concepts, and so forth, but its intrinsic nature is not stained by defilements, concepts, and so forth. Being different from them, the mind of luminosity cannot be affected by its antitheses, defilements and concepts; and likewise, when the stains of defilements and so forth are abandoned by the mind of luminosity, their continuum is severed. Precisely because of that, the primordial mind is naturally pure.

2.4. The way its stains are incidental

An example: when water and mud occur together, the water has the intrinsic nature of great lucidity through its own substantial cause, while the mud, occurring through conditions such as earth and dust that are different from the substantial cause of water, is naturally separate from the nature of water—it is incidental to it. Likewise, (4) although the primordial mind and the stains of the two obscurations have occurred together from beginningless time, the primordial mind has an intrinsic nature of purity through a substantial cause that is a previous event of the same type, while the stains, occurring through such improper conditions as mental engagement, are—like a fish is separable from water—separable from the primordial mind; they are incidental.

Also, just as water, disconnected from earth and dust, is seen to have an intrinsic nature that is very pure, so too the primordial mind, disconnected from conditions for the occurrence of stains, possesses the aspects of clarity and limpidity, which are isolated from the elaborations of dualistic appearance. Thus, when the primordial mind occurs together with attachment and other stains, which are effected by such improper conditions as mental engagement, the real situation will not be evident to fools, because they are obscured by such stains as attachment and do not see.

2.5. How to train on the path

This will be explained below [in section 2.6.2.2].

2.6. The time frame for manifesting it

This is twofold: (1) manifesting it by way of effortless spontaneity and (2) the way of manifesting it through force of concentration.

2.6.1. Manifesting it by way of effortless spontaneity

At the time of death, in beings such as humans who possess the six elements, the knots within the central channel come undone on their own and the vital winds in the right and left channels stop moving. When the vital winds enter and then dissolve within the central channel, every conception of incidentally appearing objects ceases, and the primordial mind arises, free from all mentally elaborated extremes and in aspect like a completely empty sky. This is said to be the manifestation of the luminosity of death. Since the luminosity of death definitely cannot be experienced by ordinary individuals, from it they are pulled to the intermediate state of whichever of the six realms is appropriate and circle uncontrollably in saṃsāric existence.

2.6.2. The way of manifesting it through force of concentration

This is twofold: (1) a demonstration that the direct experience of the primordial mind requires the vital winds' entering, abiding, and dissolving within the central channel, and (2) the actual explanation of the way to cultivate the path of means for manifesting the primordial mind.

2.6.2.1. A demonstration that the direct experience of the primordial mind requires the vital winds' entering, abiding, and dissolving within the central channel

For the direct experience of the primordial mind, it is first necessary that the vital winds enter the central channel then dissolve there. The first summary of the "Elements" chapter [5] of the great commentary, *Stainless Light*, says:

> Thus the luminous nature of mind will not be seen
> even by pure methods for cultivating the concept of it.

> That being the case, you will see it by uniting
> the vital winds of the left and right channels.[1404]

This teaches that you should unite the vital winds of the left and right channels within the central channel; from their dissolution there, you will see the primordial mind. Also, the *Sacred Words of Mañjuśrī* says:

> The mind should be settled within the drop.
> When it is held there by its own power,
> the earth maṇḍala enters water.
> The water then enters fire,
> the fire then enters wind,
> and the wind then enters mind.
>
> When the mind enters just a little
> into the nondual gnosis, then,
> because you have entered Vajrasattva,
> the abiding marks—the five signs—
> will occur: appearances like a mirage,
> like smoke, like lamplight,
> like fireflies, and like a cloudless sky.[1405]

Also, Kukuripa says:

> By extreme mental exertion,
> you may see the shape of the drop,
> and when you have entered that,
> the five or eight signs will occur.
> Then you will abide in the luminosity,
> abiding there as long as you wish—
> a day, a month, a year—
> accomplishing with effortless spontaneity
> all deeds, such as working for the aims of sentient beings, and so forth.[1406]

1404. Pn*VP* 110a.

1405. Bj*MA* 12a.

1406. Kk*HS* 270b6.

The five signs are the four from mirage through fireflies with the fifth sign being the aspect of a completely empty sky, not subdivided into the trio of [white] appearance, [red] increase, and [black] near-attainment, [along with the empty sky itself.] The empty sky is the fifth sign indicated in the line from the *Sacred Words of Mañjuśrī* "the five signs will occur" and is the meaning of the line "and the wind then enters mind." The statement "eight signs will occur" includes [the first four signs, as well as] appearance, increase, and near-attainment, together with luminosity.[1407] Thus it is taught that for manifesting the primordial mind or the mind of luminosity, it is necessary that the vital winds, possessed of the eight signs, progressively enter and dissolve within the central channel.[1408] The *Precious Stairway* of Drogön Rinpoché [i.e., Phakmo Drupa] says:

> When you meditate with the channels,
> vital winds, and drops as the reference point
> and the vital winds and mind enter the central channel,
> you will see: smoke, mirage,
> fireflies, a blazing lamp, and sky.[1409]

The same text teaches similarly in the passage running from: "The marks of the path arise from the heart" to [6] "The flow of bliss, clarity, and nonconceptuality is unbroken."[1410] Also, the exalted Mila says:

> When breath no longer comes or goes, there is bliss;
> when movement has stopped, even if it returns, there is bliss.[1411]

1407. To be clear, in this version of the process (there are others), whether at death or during completion-stage meditation, (1) the absorption of the earth element into water is accompanied by a vision of a mirage, (2) the absorption of water into fire is accompanied by a vision of smoke, (3) the absorption of fire into air is accompanied by a vision of lamplight, (4) the absorption of air into mind (or space) is accompanied by a vision of fireflies, (5) the descent of the white drop from the crown cakra is accompanied by a vision of moonlight-like whiteness in an empty sky, (6) the ascent of the red drop from the navel cakra is accompanied by a vision of increasing sunlight-like redness in an empty sky, (7) the dissolution of the white and red drops into the indestructible drop at the heart cakra is accompanied by a vision of complete blackness in an empty sky, which is the "near-attainment" of (8) the final stage, luminosity, which is marked by a vision of a completely clear and empty sky. It is the controlled attainment of the latter that is equated by most Gelukpa writers with Mantra Vehicle mahāmudrā. For a presentation of the death-process in chart form, see, e.g., Tsering 2012, 100–101.

1408. On these matters, see Tsongkhapa 2013b, 309–13.

1409. Pg*RCTK* 96a–96b [171–72].

1410. Pg*RCTK* 96b–97a [172–73].

1411. SNL.

When the primordial mind manifests, saying "When breath no longer comes or goes, there is bliss" means that the vital winds enter the central channel, and saying "When movement has stopped, even if it returns, there is bliss" means that the vital winds must dissolve within the central channel.

Moreover, Mila says:

> In the state between sleep and dream,
> you see the luminous Dharma body of sleep.[1412]

This teaches that, at the time of sleep, when the coarse vital winds collect within the central channel, you need the pith instruction on collecting the vital winds within the central channel. If you do, then when the vital winds have been made to enter, abide, and dissolve within the central channel through meditation mixed together with sleep, you then will experience the basic Dharma body, the path luminosity, the primordial mind.

Moreover, Drogön Rinpoché, the glorious Phakmo Drupa, says in his *Precious Stairway*:

> Through the vital winds' penetration of the central channel,
> there arises the supreme concentration,
> the supreme and royal gnosis of isolated mind,
> blissful, clear, luminous, limpid, pure, and unmoving,
> free from grasping at subject or object,
> the abandonment of the eighty natural conceptions.[1413]

This teaches that from the penetration and dissolution of the vital winds within the central channel on the occasion of the arising of the gnosis of the isolated mind, there ensues the abandonment of the eighty natural conceptions. Likewise, since it is taught that the gnosis of the isolated mind and the yoga of single-pointedness from among the four yogas have the same meaning, the yoga of single-pointedness is established as the gnosis meditating on the abiding nature of the path luminosity, the primordial mind arising from the vital winds' dissolution within the central channel. If you wonder how it is taught that the isolated mind and the yoga of single-pointedness have the same meaning, those two having the same meaning is taught in Drogön Rinpoché's arrangement of the teachings of Gampopa Rinpoché, the *Precious Stairway:*

1412. SNL.

1413. Pg*RCTK* 60b [134].

> Rinpoché said: "The three death-time minds, single-pointedness from among the four yogas, the concentration achieved on the greater path of accumulation, and the isolated mind described by Ārya Nāgārjuna are designated by different names; nonetheless, they do not have different meanings."[1414]

Nevertheless, the isolated mind and the meditation on the abiding nature of luminosity that is the yoga of single-pointedness must be distinguished from the primordial mind of death. [7]

2.6.2.2. The actual explanation of the way to cultivate the path of means for manifesting the primordial mind

This is twofold: (1) how to meditate on the subitist path and (2) how to meditate on the gradualist path.

2.6.2.2.1. How to meditate on the subitist path

As it says in the *Epitome* (*Kā dpe*), as quoted in Gampopa's collected works:

> A person who has progressed in training
> is said to be a subitist;
> a person who is a novice
> is said to be a gradualist.[1415]

A person who relies on mahāmudrā meditation of the subitist variety is said to be a person who has trained in a previous life, or earlier in this life, in special instructions such as those on introducing the vital winds into the central channel, and who has experience in introducing the vital winds into the central channel. Also, as the *Precious Stairway* says:

> The subitist person
> is a person who has amassed the requisites to be collected,
> is a person who has trained in the tantras to be trained in,
> is a person who has tamed the mind as it is to be tamed,

1414. This prose passage does not occur in Pg*RCTK*, which is entirely in verse, nor have I been able to locate it elsewhere.

1415. Nr*AP* 271a. I have not identified the source for this quote within Gampopa's works.

> is a person who has produced the experience to be produced,
> is a supreme person.[1416]

Such a subitist is one who effects meditation on mahāmudrā as in the first example.[1417] And, as it says in the *Precious Lamp*, in the collected works of Drogön Rinpoché:

> A person who enters suddenly
> contemplates mahāmudrā right away.[1418]

The way of meditating is as follows. Subitist persons, who are experienced in introducing the vital winds into the central channel, settle themselves in single-pointed meditative equipoise on the nature of mind, and when, by that very meditation, they have made the vital winds enter, abide, and dissolve within the central channel, they directly experience the primordial mind. As the great Jé Tsongkhapa[1419] says:

> It is apparent that for one who is experienced in making the vital winds enter the central channel, the vital winds will gather in the central channel no matter the object of focus.[1420]

Accordingly, the subitist individual settles single-pointedly upon the intrinsic nature of mind and by that makes the vital winds enter, abide, and dissolve—all three—within the central channel. When the primordial mind with the nature of great bliss, the manifest primordial mind, settles into single-pointed meditation solely on the bliss-emptiness gnosis that contemplates emptiness, then single-pointedness, nonelaboration, single taste, and nonmeditation arise in succession, and the fruit is made manifest. Because of that, when the early Kagyüpas called mahāmudrā meditation the *white panacea*, they meant that when the primordial mind [8] arises in the nature of great bliss, through that single meditation on the abiding reality, attainment of the ultimate fruit will occur; this is the conclusion intended by the Indian tantric texts.

Also, as it says in the *Sacred Words of Mañjuśrī*:

1416. Pg*RCTK* 84b.

1417. Presumably, the definition from the *Epitome*, cited above.

1418. Pg*RCGM* 26a [361].

1419. For *btson kha pa*, read *btsong kha pa*; *btsong* is an alternate spelling of *tsong*.

1420. Ts*RNSG* 194b. This also is quoted by Paṇchen Chögyen and Thuken.

> The objectless gnosis, barren of attachment, is illumined in an instant; that gnosis is to be experienced for eight hours, or a day, or a month, or a year, or until the end of the eon.[1421]

This teaches that the primordial mind that has arisen in the nature of great bliss, when conjoined with the abiding nature, enjoys single-pointed placement for anywhere from eight hours to the end of an eon. Also, Nāropa's *Summary Illuminating the Five Stages* says:

> By gaining the ability to abide in luminosity,
> you will transcend saṃsāra:
> for a session or a day,
> for a month, a half a month, a year,
> or until the end of the eon,
> it will abide in every instant—
> refined gnosis occurring always.[1422]

Also, Kukuripa says:

> Thenceforth, the luminosity will abide.[1423]

He adds:

> It abides for as long as one desires:
> whether for a month or until the end of an eon,
> every deed devoted to the aims of sentient beings
> will be accomplished spontaneously, without effort.[1424]

Through passages such as these and others, it is taught that the primordial mind or luminous mind that has arisen in the nature of great bliss will—when settled single-pointedly upon the abiding nature—enjoy that placement as long as desired, even until the end of the eon.

Now such a subitist, through settling single-pointedly on the nature of mind, will make the vital winds enter, abide, and dissolve within the central

1421. SNL.

1422. Nr*PS* 277a.

1423. Kk*VS* 230b.

1424. Kk*VS* 230b–231a.

channel and will thereby manifest the primordial mind and arrive at single-pointed placement on reality—but when the primordial mind manifests, how does that primordial mind take on the nature of great bliss? The way that occurs is as follows. By settling single-pointedly on the nature of mind, that subitist, through the force of making the vital winds enter, abide, and dissolve within the central channel, ignites the secret inner fire at the navel. Through that, the bodhicitta[1425] element at the crown melts, and as it descends through the central channel, the four joys arise, and the primordial mind arises in the nature of great bliss. Further, that great bliss is made more and more intensive; as Saraha says in the *Dohā Treasury*:

> Eating and drinking and enjoying sex,
> always filling the cakras [9] more and more:
> through such a Dharma you'll reach the world's far shore;
> step on the heads of deluded worldlings and go on your way.[1426]

This passage teaches that, by way of eating foods, drinking beverages, and experiencing the joy of sex with a consort as a method to spread the bodhicitta element in the body, the yogī who manifests the primordial mind will perpetually, repeatedly, fill the cakras, such as the navel cakra, with bodhicitta drops. Through a Dharma such as that, where he contemplates the abiding nature through the great bliss based on that aforementioned process, he will accomplish the supreme state that reaches the far shore beyond saṃsāric worldliness. In that way, the yogī will step on the heads of deluded, saṃsāric worldlings and go on his way. As for bliss arising through filling up the cakras repeatedly by such acts as copulation and making the vital winds enter, abide, and dissolve within the central channel, the previous text continues:

> Where vital winds and mind do not move
> and sun and moon no longer enter,
> there, O ignoramuses, you should give your mind a breather.
> The archer has taught all these pith instructions and gone on his
> way.[1427]

1425. This is the same Sanskrit term as is used to refer to the "awakening mind," but here, in a distinctly tantric context, it denotes the white drop inherited from one's father at conception, which is situated at the crown cakra throughout one's life.

1426. Sa*PD*t 71b; cf. R. Jackson 2004, 66 (verse 24).

1427. Sa*PD*t 72a; cf. R. Jackson 2004, 66 (verse 25).

The *Dohā* also says:

> This entire triple world without exception:
> turn it the single color of great desire.[1428]

This teaches that the three realms, without exception, are great desire, which has the nature of the greatly blissful primordial mind; they must be seen solely as the play of great bliss.

Now when the primordial mind manifests, it suffices to settle single-pointedly on the nature of that primordial mind, so why is it necessary to contemplate emptiness? The primordial mind that has the nature of great bliss must single-pointedly contemplate the emptiness that is the abiding nature of all phenomena because, as also stated in the *Dohā Treasury*:

> Whoever enters emptiness bereft of compassion
> will not reach the supreme path,
> and if you cultivate compassion only,
> you'll remain here in saṃsāra and not obtain liberation.
> Whoever is able to conjoin the two
> won't abide in saṃsāra and won't abide in nirvāṇa.[1429]

The compassion taught here is the greatly blissful compassion of the uncommon unexcelled yoga [10] mantra. It is taught that one who solely contemplates an emptiness bereft of compassion will not attain the union of method and wisdom that is the highest path, while one who is greatly compassionate but solely contemplates the great bliss of the primordial mind will remain here in saṃsāra and will not obtain liberation. On the other hand, any yogī who is able to join both great bliss and emptiness into their inseparable intrinsic nature will attain the highest stage, where one does not abide in saṃsāra and does not abide in the lesser nirvāṇa.

To summarize briefly: When a subitist like that explained above settles single-pointedly on the nature of mind, the vital winds are made to enter, abide, and dissolve within the central channel. When the primordial mind arises in the nature of great bliss, then one progresses through the four yogas by way of the white panacea, which is just that union of great bliss and emptiness, of method and wisdom, effected solely by single-pointed placement on the emptiness that is the abiding nature of all phenomena—and will accomplish the supreme.

1428. Sa*PD*t 72a; cf. R. Jackson 2004, 67 (verse 26).

1429. Sa*PD*t 71b; cf. R. Jackson 2004, 61 (verse 15a–b).

Now, with respect to the early Kagyüpas' teaching mahāmudrā meditation as the white panacea, Sakya Paṇḍita asks in *Clear Ascertainment of the Three Vows*: "In your white panacea, is arousing the awakening mind necessary or unnecessary?"[1430] His refutation is just like the refutation of someone who, when told the two collections are sufficient for buddhahood, asks, "Isn't it also necessary to first be born from a mother?"

Well, how does the primordial mind that has arisen in the nature of great bliss become a union of method and wisdom through meditation on emptiness? In general, in any sūtra or mantra system, a path uniting method and wisdom will effect the achievement of unexcelled awakening. The union of method and wisdom of the Perfection Vehicle involves, on the method side, the perfections of generosity and so forth and, on the wisdom side, the perfection of wisdom. It is said that when one practices by way of encompassing method and wisdom simultaneously one practices the union of method and wisdom. However, when, on the training paths, one settles in meditative equipoise on the direct realization of emptiness, the methods of generosity and so forth are indirect; while when one trains directly in generosity and so forth, the wisdom directly realizing emptiness is indirect. So one unites method and wisdom [11] by practicing them each in turn.

In unexcelled mantra, method and wisdom become naturally inseparable at the time of meditative equipoise. The way in which that is so is as stated by Jé Tsongkhapa:

> It has been said that a bodhisattva who abides on the eighth level and is settled in single-pointed meditative equipoise on emptiness can be roused from cessation by the conquerors. Having been roused from that meditative equipoise by the tathāgatas, that eighth-level bodhisattva who is settled in single-pointed meditative equipoise on emptiness is told by the conquerors, "You do not possess our major and minor marks, our ten powers, and so forth, so you must amass a greatly extensive collection of merit, and you must not give up this way of forbearance."[1431] Then, when the discerning analyze the statement to the effect that the primordial mind that has arisen in the nature of great bliss should be placed

1430. Although *NGCS* (110n240) attributes this passage to Sp*DSRB*t 26a, I have not located it there, nor does it appear in David Jackson's careful cataloging of all of Sapaṇ's mentions of the white panacea (1994, 159–88).

1431. "Forbearance" (*kṣanti, bzod pa*) has the sense here of acceptance or understanding of the truth of emptiness, without falling into extremes of eternalism or nihilism.

> single-pointedly on emptiness until the end of the eon, they will be able to understand that when the primordial mind has arisen in the nature of great bliss, the meditative equipoise in which one is settled single-pointedly upon emptiness, is the single path that can substitute for the greatly extensive collection of merit of the Perfection Vehicle.[1432]

At the time when the mind of great bliss is in meditative equipoise on emptiness, the method that can substitute for the greatly extensive collection of merit is just that great bliss; the way in which it can substitute is as explained in the *Engaging in Bodhisattva Conduct*:

> All these limbs of practice
> were taught by the Sage for the sake of wisdom.[1433]

The bodhisattva's wisdom that directly realizes emptiness in the system of the Perfection Vehicle comes to have the special ability to abandon knowledge obscurations and so forth; one amasses limitless merit between sessions. Moreover, as merits are the substantial cause of the form body, the great bliss that has arisen in the nature of the greatly blissful primordial mind of the unexcelled mantra system has the purified special ability to abandon grasping at true existence along with the knowledge obscurations. This is the wisdom realizing emptiness in which one is, oneself, inseparable from the essence. When you have trained those very subtle vital winds to the point where you are, yourself, the youthful deity, you make the illusory body and so forth the cause of the form body. Then the bliss of the primordial mind that has come to have the nature of the great bliss and the great [12] bliss that is settled in meditative equipoise on emptiness are, respectively, a substitute for the greatly extensive collection of merit and a substitute for the wisdom settled single-pointedly on emptiness.

2.6.2.2.1. How to meditate on the gradualist path

> A person who is a novice
> is said to be a gradualist.[1434]

1432. SNL.

1433. Sd*BA* 30b (verse 9.1).

1434. Nr*AP* 271a.

Described thusly, gradualists, persons who are novices, are twofold: (1) persons ranging from those who have no experience of training on the path whatsoever to those who are in the process of training and (2) beginners who have entered the mantra path but have no experience of training on the completion stage and other aspects of the mantra path.

2.6.2.2.1.1. Persons ranging from those who have no experience of training on the path whatsoever to those who are in the process of training

Such a person is described by Drogön in such passages from his collected works as:

> The person who enters gradually
> repeatedly arouses the desire to avoid
> the desperate suffering of the lower realms
> in favor of the excellent abodes of gods and humans.[1435]

and:

> One engages gradually in amassing the two collections
> based on the recollection and aspiration that thinks,
> "When innumerable eons have passed,
> I will definitely obtain the fruit, the three buddha bodies."[1436]

A person wishing to manifest the three bodies through the Perfection Vehicle must first train the mind in the stages of the paths of the three types of individuals, then train in the method and wisdom of the Perfection Vehicle.

2.6.2.2.1.2. Beginners who have entered the mantra path but have no experience of training on the completion stage and other aspects of the mantra path

This is fivefold. As stated in the *Compendium of Vajra Gnosis Drawn from the Tantras*:

1435. SNL.

1436. SNL.

> Students are analyzed into five types of persons, namely: jewel, sandal, lotus, white lotus, and utpala.[1437]

From among the five types of persons—the jewel-like and so forth—the jewel-like person is one who in this life has engendered paths from the generation stage up to union and will awaken in a single body within a single life. The other four, the sandal-like and so forth, train gradually in the generation stage and so forth and will manifest the fruit within eight lives. The chief disciples who are wholly intent upon the unexcelled yoga tantras are the jewel-like persons. Why is that? It is because they will awaken in a single body within a single life through the stages of the path explained in the unexcelled yoga tantras. If that is the case, should they not be classified as subitist persons? They should be classified as gradualist [13] persons, because having manifested the primordial mind, when they contemplate the bliss-emptiness gnosis they must, as beginners, cultivate the inner fire and other completion-stage practices in which one concentrates on the channels, drops, and vital winds as methods for introducing the vital winds into the central channel. The greatest of the Kagyüpas, the exalted Mila, made inner fire the principal beginning practice. Dakpo Rinpoché [Gampopa] explained that he cultivated that inner fire in the presence of the exalted Mila, and the exalted Marpa says:

> Not including detailed teachings on the five stages,
> I know a hundred and eight great teachings;
> let there be rejoicing in the assembly of my fellow great meditators.[1438]

Meditation on the detailed teachings on the five stages is highly praised, and it is explained that jewel-like persons, those chief disciples who are completely devoted to the tantras, will awaken in just a single life through practicing gradually, beginning with the generation stage and going up through the completion stage. As explained above, gradualists—unlike subitists, who are experienced in making the vital winds enter, abide, and dissolve within the central channel—will have difficulty meditating on mahāmudrā. A scriptural passage drawn from the collected works of Drogön Rinpoché states:

1437. *VST* 186b. In the Dergé Kangyur text, several lines of text intervene before the five types of persons are listed.

1438. Th*MPNT* 101; cf. trans. Nālandā Translation Committee 1982, 105.

> The great medicine for the subitist
> is poison for the gradualist;
> the great medicine for the gradualist
> is poison for the subitist.[1439]

It is stated in the same collected works:

> A person whose practice is based upon gradually introducing the vital winds into that central channel should not initially perform signless meditation; a person whose practice is based upon the sudden [entrance, abiding, and dissolution of the vital winds within the central channel], should not train on any other topic.[1440]

This passage is drawn from the same text as the previous statement. By reason of that, a gradualist person, who has a little experience in meditating on the channels, drops, and so forth, may follow pith instructions for introducing the vital winds into the central channel by settling single-pointedly upon the nature of mind; but no matter how much they may meditate nonconceptually, it is impossible that the mahāmudrā path of the manifestation of the primordial mind will occur in their mindstream. Were that possible, one would manifest the primordial mind even through ordinary serenity meditation, because there would be not the slightest difference between the way of meditating on mahāmudrā and the way of practicing ordinary serenity, between the way someone focuses on some topic and the way of apprehending the nature of mind.

The way in which there would be no difference is this: The way of meditating for persons of the present time who desire mahāmudrā [14] but are inexperienced at introducing the vital winds into the central channel is to settle single-pointedly upon the essence of mind, because when they have placed awareness on that without any conceptuality at all, it is in every sense just like the way someone performs ordinary serenity meditation. The way in which it is similar is as Jowo Atiśa says in his *Lamp on the Path*:

> The mind is to be settled virtuously
> on any one suitable topic.[1441]

1439. Pg*RCGM* 20a [350].

1440. Pg*RCGM* 20a [350].

1441. At*BP* 240a (verse 40).

It is taught that any topic one makes the basis of serenity meditation—mind, form, and so forth—will suffice. With respect to making the nature of mind the topic, the *Stages of Meditation I* says:

> One does so because the nature of serenity is just single-pointedness of mind; this is the general definition of all serenity.[1442]

And, as the *Pith Instruction on the Perfection of Wisdom* says:

> Taking as one's topic that mind cognizing various appearances, one should abandon the expression of thought and cultivate serenity.[1443]

Taking as one's topic the nature of mind and then settling the mind single-pointedly upon that and placing it there without any conceptuality whatsoever is the common way of cultivating serenity. Through meditating thusly, the mind accomplishes the ninth stage of serenity, called "entering the stream of concentration" or "meditative equipoise."

As to when one fulfills the definition of serenity, the *Levels of the Śrāvakas* says:

> Because of its complete stability and familiarization, the mind engages its object spontaneously. It gains the path whereby it engages the object on its own and where manifest mental formations are absent. With just that degree of spontaneity, one will enter the stream of concentration in which one's mind does not stray. When matters are thus, one brings about concentration.[1444]

This states that when one has settled single-pointedly upon the nature of mind, then through long-term familiarization, one will engage the topic without effort, spontaneously, on one's own, and will remain engaged with it for a long time, without straying. It is a case of mistaken entailment to claim that at the conclusion of that the primordial mind will manifest, because if the primordial mind manifested through such meditation, that would mistakenly entail that non-Buddhist extremists would also contemplate the mahāmudrā that contemplates the abiding nature of the primordial mind, as this common way

1442. Km*BK* 31b.

1443. Rs*PU* 156b.

1444. As*YB* 8a.

of cultivating serenity is common to all, Buddhist and non-Buddhist, Great Vehicle and Small.

That being the case, [15]

> A person who has progressed in training
> is said to be a subitist;
> a person who is a novice
> is said to be a gradualist.[1445]

It is in accordance with this statement that one should know the way of fixing a person as subitist or gradualist; one should know the way in which those two types of persons practice the path by this:

> The great medicine for the subitist
> is poison for the gradualist;
> the great medicine for the gradualist
> is poison for the subitist.[1446]

Nowadays, persons among us who are inexperienced at introducing the vital winds into the central channel—whether jewel-like persons of sharp faculties or persons of dull faculties—first must train their mindstreams on the common path, then fully obtain the four empowerments. Not permitting the vows and pledges taken on at that time to deteriorate, these persons should grasp the generation stage and train well in the topics of the completion stage. Having undertaken to make the vital winds enter, abide, and dissolve within the central channel, and intending to contemplate the suchness of the primordial mind, consider this:

> In me, a man who has the blessings
> of Phakmo Drupa, there arises a happy thought:
> I will gain self-sufficiency in the awakening mind.
>
> As for the stallion of the awakening mind:
> if you do not race it along the course of altruism,
> the cheers of the crowd of gods and humans will not arise,
> so earnestly apply your mind to this preliminary practice.

1445. Nr*AP* 271a.

1446. Pg*RCGM* 20a [350].

As for seeing your own body as the royal divine body:
if you do not hold fast to your immutable throne,
clouds of ḍākinīs will not gather,
so earnestly apply yourself to seeing your body as the divine yidam.

As for the snow mountain of the guru's four bodies:
if the sun of respectful devotion does not rise,
the river of blessings will not flow,
so earnestly apply yourself to this mind of respectful devotion.

As for the sky of nonconceptual mind, the Dharma body:
if the cloud mass of deluded conceptions is not cleared away,
the planets and stars of the two knowledges will not shine,
so earnestly apply your mind to nonconceptuality.

As for the wish-fulfilling jewel of the two collections:
if it is not polished by your aspiration,
the results you need and desire will not arise,
so earnestly apply yourself to this final dedication.[1447]

In the above, the line "so earnestly apply your mind to this preliminary practice" teaches training the mind on the common path. The lines "As for seeing your own body as the royal divine body: / if you do not hold fast to your immutable throne," teaches the clarification of one's own body as a divine body, and it teaches the fulfilment of the generation stage, which is the stabilization of [16] divine pride in that visualization. Such lines as "As for the snow mountain of the guru's four bodies," teach in general the infinite attributes of the Mahāyāna, and in particular the arising of the attributes of the generation and completion stages in dependence on respectful devotion to the guru, and the necessity of appealing to the guru as a method by which those attributes arise. Such lines as "As for the sky of nonconceptual mind, the Dharma body," teach that one must first train one's mindstream by way of the common path and then, through single-pointed nonconceptual meditation like that mastered by such previous masters as Driging Jikten Gönpo, introduce the vital winds into the central channel and manifest the primordial mind. Through that, the cloud mass of conceptual delusions will dissolve into the sky of the Dharma body, which is single-pointed meditation on the abiding nature.

1447. Js*NDTG* 87.

3. Briefly summarizing and demonstrating the way of meditating on mahāmudrā and other topics

When the early Kagyüpas explained the way of meditating on mahāmudrā and other topics, they explained that there are three ways of meditating, for three [types of persons], whose respective faculties are dull, middling, and sharp.

Those with dull faculties, who are unable to cultivate the inner fire and other methods for introducing the vital winds into the central channel, must cultivate nonconceptual single-pointed placement on the essence of mind and attain single-pointed mental stability. When one casts a searchlight on the clear, knowing mind that is stabilized on the object thus attained—researching whether that exists outside the body or within it—and ascertains the lack of true existence that is the nonfinding of a unique essence of mind, then that single-pointed placement upon the intrinsic nature of a mind devoid of true existence is meditation on emptiness as a nonaffirming negation. This is as my guru, the splendid Chökyi Drakpa, taught the intention of Chöjé Nyernyi Rinpoché.

The way of meditating for those of middling faculties is that with respect to the channels, drops, and vital winds, they have the opportunity to contemplate the pith instructions on the methods for introducing into the central channel the vital winds that penetrate the vital points.

As for the way of meditating for those of sharp faculties: Jewel-like persons, who naturally have sharp faculties from the beginning, train gradually, from the generation stage up to final union. Those who have trained before as persons of sharp faculties—who will manifest the supreme achievement in this very life and who in previous lives learned to introduce the vital winds into the central channel—subitist persons like Drogön Rinpoché, Shang Rinpoché, and the conqueror Götsangpa—[17] will, just by single-pointed placement upon the nature of mind, once again make the vital winds enter, abide, and dissolve within the central channel and, through that, manifest the primordial mind that arises in the nature of great bliss. The path is effected by that bliss-emptiness gnosis that is placed single-pointedly upon the abiding nature. The way of manifesting the two buddha bodies through acting thusly is to be known in depth from previous explanations.

[Dedication]

By the white moonlight-like virtues
of this long-requested work of promulgation

that shows the essential profound meaning,
saying from afar, "This is the way
the early Kagyüpas cultivated mahāmudrā,"
may all darkness in the minds of beings be cleared,
and may all be set on the path of mahāmudrā.
Alas! The envious, who are commonly attached
to the commonplace and do not understand what is well explained,
slander the excellent explanations and the host of sages.
In times like these, we should resort to solitude.

[Colophon]

Khedrup Norsang Gyatso compiled this at the retreat of Rinchen Gang in response to the questions of the mighty yogī Kunkyang Chöjé, from the royal palace in Chongyé Taktsé, and of the Dharma king Dorjé Tsetenpa, and in response to a request by Jatang Maṇibhadra. Through this, may I be able to bring extensive benefit to many persons. This was printed at Ganden Phuntsok Ling for the purpose of[1448] widely spreading the clouds of Dharma. *Mangalaṃ*!

1448. Reading *phyir* for *phyar.*

8. Offering to the Guru[1449]

Paṇchen Losang Chökyi Gyaltsen

Note: The translation below includes both Paṇchen Chögyen's Offering to the Guru *and the ritual feast, or* tsok (tshogs)*, with which it often is practiced, which was substantially composed by Khedrup Sangyé Yeshé, and often incorporates as well the highly tantric* Song of the Spring Queen*, attributed to Tsongkhapa. Although modern Tibetan editions generally print* Offering to the Guru *in its entirety followed by the* tsok *in its entirety, I have interwoven them here so as to give the reader a sense of the way in which they typically are performed together on the 10th and 25th of each lunar month and other special occasions. Verse numbers are my own. Straightforward numbers indicate verses from* Offering to the Guru*; verse numbers preceded by a T indicate verses from the ritual feast. The italicized comments and instructions are not found in Paṇchen Chögyen's original text; they are, rather, passages from Yeshé Gyaltsen's great commentary, which are interpolated into most modern Tibetan editions of the text. In placing them in smaller type, I am simply reflecting the convention of the Tibetan editions. Bracketed italicized phrases are section headings supplied by me.*

[Prelude]

In the language of India: *Gurupūjasyakalpa*. In the language of Tibet: *Bla ma mchod pa'i cho ga* (*The Rite of Offering to the Guru*).

1449. Blo bzang chos kyi rgyal mtshan, *Zab lam bla ma mchod pa* [*The Profound Path Offering to the Guru*] (Oregon, WI: Deer Park Buddhist Center, 2012) (Bz*LMCP(1)*). Supplemental material from Blo bzang chos kyi rgyal mtshan, *Zab lam bla ma mchod pa bde stong dbyer med ma dang tshogs mchod bcas* [*The Profound Path Offering to the Guru, Inseparable Bliss and Emptiness, Together with Its Ritual Feast*] (India, 1974) (Bz*LMCP(2)*). Cf. trans. Kachen Yeshe Gyaltsen 2014, 393–426. See also Berzin et al. 1979, 8–59, and Dondrub 2001. For context and a summary, see above, chapter 9.

I bow to the feet of the incomparably kind holy gurus and go for refuge to them. I appeal to them: look after me with great benevolence in all times and circumstances.

He's the wish-fulfilling jewel who, when relied upon, grants us
the supreme for which we long, granting us in an instant
the three greatly blissful bodies, along with mundane yogic attainments.
Having bowed to the lotus feet of Vajradhara,
I will lay out a lovely garland, a beautiful necklace, picked
from the garden of pith instructions on sūtra and tantra,
the supreme sole method that accomplishes
the benefit and bliss of every fortunate disciple.

The basis of all excellence for those desiring liberation, the source of all good fortune, the root of all the countless supreme and common yogic attainments, the synopsis of the limitless pith instructions that are to be practiced by yogīs of the Supreme Vehicle is reliance on proper service to the spiritual friend who shows us the unmistaken path. The Blue Compendium *says:*

> *The summit, where all pith instructions are collected,*
> *is the indispensable spiritual friend.*
> *Through the spiritual friend arise faith and awakening mind;*
> *the spiritual friend is the treasure source of all good qualities.*[1450]

And the Omniscient Jé Tsongkhapa says:

> *Thus the root of auspicious circumstances*
> *for attaining as much good fortune as possible in this and future lives*
> *is earnest and zealous service, in thought*
> *and deed, to the holy spiritual friends who show the path.*
> *Seeing this, not giving them up even for the sake of our life,*
> *we should please them by offerings accomplished as they have advised.*
> *I, a yogī, have also practiced thus,*
> *and you who aspire to liberation, please do so as well.*[1451]

And also:

1450. The *Be'u bum sngon po* of the Kadam Geshé Potowa is considered a forerunner of the stages of the path literature.

1451. Ts*LRDD* 56a [308].

> *The root of all virtues conducive to mundane*
> *and transmundane abundance is the exalted, kindly guru.*[1452]

And, as stated in the Fifty Verses on the Guru:

> *Vajradhara himself has said,*
> *"Yogic attainments come from the exalted master."*
> *Knowing this, you should thoroughly*
> *please the guru in all ways.*[1453]

The Synthesis of Precious Virtues[1454] *says:*

> *Good disciples who are respectful to the guru*
> *should always serve their learned gurus.*
> *Why is that? The virtues of learning arise from them,*
> *and they teach the perfection of wisdom.*
> *Attaining buddha qualities depends on the virtuous spiritual friend.*[1455]

Also:

> *The Conqueror taught that the guru is in complete possession of the virtues.*[1456]

Thus the vajra master is superior even to all the buddhas as a field in which disciples can collect merit and gnosis and purify obscurations. The Saṃvarodaya Tantra *says:*

> *The self-originated Blessed One*
> *who is one with the superior deity—*
> *the vajra master surpasses them*
> *because he grants the pith instructions.*[1457]

1452. SNL.

1453. Ag*GP* 11b (verse 47); cf. trans. Dhargyey et al. 1976, 29, and Kachen Yeshe Gyaltsen 2014, 426.

1454. In Sanskrit, *Ratnaguṇasañcaya[gāthā]*. This is an alternate title for the *Condensed Perfection of Wisdom* (*PPG*t).

1455. *PPG*t 200a; cf. trans. in Conze 1973, 36. For the Sanskrit (verse 15.1), see *PPG*s 371.

1456. *PPG*t 200a (15.2); cf. trans. in Conze 1973, 36. For the Sanskrit (verse 15.2), see *PPG*s 371.

1457. SNL.

For that reason, Khedrup Sangyé Yeshé stated:

> *Cultivation of guru yoga, which is the key to fulfilment of the path, is the supreme method for taking the essential from our free and favored life; hence, it should be practiced as laid out here. So from within an especially virtuous mind, begin by going for refuge, arousing the awakening mind, and contemplating the four immeasurables. In the form of whichever superior deity you see yourself as, whether Guhyasamāja, Cakrasaṃvara, Vajrabhairava, or some other deity, imagine that you yourself emit from your yogic body rays of light that cleanse the cosmos and all its denizens of their impurities: the entire cosmos is solely a divine mansion and all its denizens gods and goddesses, naturally pure and all-encompassing.*[1458]

Accordingly, we begin by going for refuge and arousing the awakening mind as described in Khedrup Sangyé Yeshé's oral tradition.

[I. Going for Refuge]

[Refuge]

1.[1459] Within a state of great bliss, I myself am the guru-deity,
from whose radiant body a mass of light rays
goes forth to the ten directions, blessing the cosmos and its denizens
and transforming them into an especially excellent array
of qualities pure and all-encompassing.

2. From within the great mind of virtue, intensely pure,
I and old-mother sentient beings extending through space,
go for refuge to the guru and the Triple Gem
from now until the essence of awakening is attained.

3. *Namo gurubhyaḥ*
Namo buddhāya
Namo dharmāya
Namo saṅghāya (*3x*)

1458. SNL.

1459. Verses 1–6 are drawn verbatim from Sy*LMCP* 2a–b.

4. Having become the guru-deity for the sake
of all mother sentient beings, I myself
must establish all mother sentient beings
in the supreme state of a guru-deity. (*3x*)

[Arousing the special awakening mind]

5–6. For the sake of all mother sentient beings, I shall quickly, quickly, in this very life, manifest the state of the primordial buddha guru-deity. I must free mother sentient beings from suffering and establish them in the state of great bliss, buddhahood. Therefore, I will put into practice the profound path of guru-deity yoga. (*3x*)

[Inner offerings]

Bless the inner offerings and offering substances through any appropriate unexcelled-yoga-tantra rite or, in brief, recite:

7. *Oṃ āḥ hūṃ* (*3x*)

Think:
8. Their intrinsic nature is gnosis, their aspect is the inner offerings and the individual offering substances, their function is to produce the special bliss-emptiness gnosis in the domain of the six senses. Clouds of outer, inner, and secret offerings completely pervade the entirety of the earth, the atmosphere, and space, filling them with inconceivable presents made of the finest substances.

[II. Generating the Field of Merit]

The main practice is this: when you utter the verses, since they are easy to engage, practice them with an unwavering mind, contemplating their meaning.

9. In the vast space of inseparable bliss and emptiness, amid thick clouds of
Samantabhadra's offerings,
at the crest of a wish-fulfilling tree adorned with leaves, flowers, and fruits,
is a throne supported by lions and blazing with jewels, and on that a broad
lotus, the sun, and the moon.

10. There sits my triply kind root guru, who in essence is all the buddhas,
in aspect a saffron-robed monk with one face, two arms, and a bright, radiant smile.
His right hand is in the gesture of expounding Dharma; his left, in meditation pose, holds a begging bowl brimming with nectar.
He wears triple robes of saffron hue, and his head is adorned by a paṇḍita's golden hat.

Alternatively, you may skip the verse [including] "in essence is all the buddhas" and say:

11. At his heart is the pervasive lord Vajradhara, with one face and two arms, blue in color;
holding vajra and bell, he embraces Vajradhātvīśvarī. They delight in the play of connate bliss and emptiness;
they are adorned with jeweled ornaments of many kinds and draped in garments of divine silks.

Once you have arranged the verses to suit your inclination, regardless of which of the two you chose, continue the recitation thusly:

12. Adorned with the major and minor marks, blazing with thousands of light rays, surrounded by a five-colored rainbow,
he sits in the vajra posture. His aggregates are the five pure sugatas;
his four elements are the four consorts; his sense fields, channels, sinews, and joints are in fact bodhisattvas;
his hair pores are twenty-one thousand arhats; his limbs are the wrathful protectors;
his light rays are directional protectors and secret yakṣas; and worldly gods are but cushions for his feet.

13. Around him in an encircling sea sit ranks of actual and lineage gurus, yidams,
hosts of maṇḍala deities, buddhas, bodhisattvas, heroes, ḍākinīs, and guardians of the teaching.

14. The three doors of each are marked by three vajras. From the letter *hūṃ* at their hearts hooked light rays
draw forth gnosis beings from their natural abodes, and these become inseparably stabilized [within the members of the assembly].

[III. Invocation]

15. Sources of excellence and good fortune, root and lineage gurus
of the three times, yidams, the Triple Gem,
heroes and ḍākinīs, along with Dharma protectors:
by the power of your compassion, come here and firmly abide.

16. Though phenomena by nature are totally free of coming and going,
your acts born of wisdom and mercy issue forth everywhere
in accordance with the thoughts of various disciples.
I appeal to you, holy refuges and protectors: come here with your retinue.

17. *Oṃ guru buddha bodhisattva dharmapāla saparivara ehyahiḥ. Jaḥ hūṃ baṃ hoḥ.* Gnosis beings and pledge beings become nondual.

Seeing the guru and Vajradhara as inseparable in that way is the idea in many of the tantras. It is as stated in the Fifty Verses on the Guru*:*

> *The master and Vajradhara*
> *should not be considered different.*[1460]

With regard to meditation on the five aggregates and so forth as the five buddha families and so forth, it is as the Vajra Garland Tantra *and other texts teach:*

> *The bodies of the conquerors reside in sequence*
> *within the body of the vajra master.*[1461]

Visualize the field of assembly, summon and absorb the gnosis beings, and devoutly regard them as naturally embodying all three refuges. Then, as stated in the guardian Nāgārjuna's Five Stages:

> *Thoroughly forsaking all other offerings,*
> *undertake the perfect offering to the guru.*
> *By pleasing them, you will obtain*
> *the supreme gnosis of omniscience.*[1462]

1460. Ag*GP* 10b; cf. trans. Dhargyey et al. 1976, 18, and Kachen Yeshe Gyaltsen 2014, 430.

1461. *VMT* 94a.

1462. Ng*PKt* 53b.

[IV. The Sevenfold Worship Rite]

Once you have induced complete certainty in the teaching that offering to the guru is more important than offerings to all the buddhas and bodhisattvas, you should offer the sevenfold worship rite beginning with prostration.

[1. Prostration]

[Guru as enjoyment body]

18. Guru whose jewel-like body in an instant
compassionately grants blessings,
of the three bodies, the realm of great bliss—
to your lotus feet, O Vajradhara, I bow down.

[Guru as emanation body]

19. Gnosis of all the ubiquitous conquerors,
playing the role of a saffron-clad monk
but by supreme skillful means appearing as needed for disciples—
to your feet, O refuge and protector, I bow down.

[Guru as Dharma body]

20. Uprooter of all the flaws and their traces,
treasury of the jewel trove of infinite virtues,
sole source of all benefit and bliss—
to your feet, exalted guru, I bow down.

[Guru as emanation of the Triple Gem]

21. Teachers of gods and all beings, in actuality all buddhas,
source of the eighty-four thousand doctrines,
resplendent amid all the āryas' assemblies—
to the kindly gurus I bow down.

[Guru as all buddhas]

22. To the gurus residing in the three times
and the Three Supreme Jewels, all worthy of homage,

with faith and respect and a sea of songs of praise,
I emanate bodies numerous as atoms in the world—and bow down.

Having bowed down respectfully with the three doors, make offerings. Sealing the triple circle of offering (donor, recipient, and gift) into the quintessence of nonconceptual inseparable bliss and emptiness, you offer:

[2. Offering]

[Outer offerings]

23. To you, refuge and protector, exalted guru, together with your entourage,
I offer a sea of clouds of various offerings:

24. From vast vessels blazing with the light of jewels perfectly arrayed
gently descend four streams of purifying nectar.

25. Flowering trees, garlands perfectly arranged,
and beautiful flowers fill the earth and sky.

26. The sky is thick with blue summer clouds rising
from the azure smoke of the sweetest incense.

27. Joyous rays of light from sun, moon, gems, and masses of lamps
intensely blazing dispel the darkness of the three thousand worlds.

28. Great seas of scented waters perfumed by the fragrance
of camphor, sandal, and saffron swirl out to the horizon.

29. Delicious food and drink of a hundred flavors,
a feast for gods and humans, is heaped as high as Meru.

30. From a limitless variety of different instruments
rise melodies to fill the three-tiered world.

31. Bearing the splendor of form, sound, smell, taste, and touch,
goddesses of outer and inner desirable things pervade every direction.

[Short maṇḍala offering]

32. To you, O merit field surpassing and supreme, refuge and protector,
treasure of compassion, I offer with faithful mind
a billion times over: the four continents and Meru,
the seven precious emblems, the minor precious possessions and more,
excellent worlds with their denizens, arousing utter delight,
and a great treasury of enjoyments desired by humans and gods.

[Offering of practice]

33. For the delight of my exalted guru, I offer substances actually arrayed
and those envisioned, as a pleasure grove on the shore of a wish-fulfilling sea
strewn with thousand-petaled lotuses that captivate every heart—
these offering substances come from virtuous deeds in the worlds of saṃsāric existence and peace.
Arrayed everywhere are flowers of the mundane
and spiritual virtues of the three doors of myself and others,
emitting the myriad scents of Samantabhadra's offerings
and laden with the fruit of the three trainings, the two stages, and the five paths.

[Inner offering]

34. I offer a libation of Chinese tea the color of saffron,
pleasantly aromatic, conveying a hundred splendid flavors;
and the five hooks, the five lamps,[1463] and so forth—
these are purified, transformed, and increased into a sea of nectar.

[Secret offering]

35. I offer as well beautiful, magical consorts,
splendidly lovely and youthful, slender,
and skilled in the sixty-four arts of love—
a host of messengers, born in groves, mantra-born, or simultaneously born.

1463. These refer to the five meats (human, cow, horse, elephant, and dog) and the five nectars (semen, blood, urine, feces, and marrow) that are part of the "inner offering" in unexcelled-yoga-tantra practice.

[Suchness offering]

36. I offer you the supreme ultimate awakening mind,
the great blissful connate gnosis free from the obscurations,
the nature of every Dharma, the realm of nonelaboration,
inseparable, spontaneous, and transcending speech, thought, or expression.

[Offering of medicines and service]

37. I offer manifold doses of excellent medicines
to cure the disease that is the four-hundred-and-four defilements,
and to please you I offer myself as your servant;
I appeal to you: keep me your subject as long as space endures.

Having performed the outer, inner, secret, suchness, medicine, and service offerings, along with their visualizations, complete the previously noted limbs—confession and the others—thusly:

[3. Confession]

38. Whatever acts of vice and nonvirtue I have performed,
encouraged others to perform, or rejoiced in since beginningless time—
these I confess with a mind of regret in the presence of
the compassionate ones, and I vow not to repeat them.

[4. Rejoicing]

39. Although phenomena lack the signs of intrinsic nature,
we rejoice with the purest of thoughts
in the bliss and joy and any virtuous deeds that have arisen
in all common and ārya beings, dream-like though they are.

[5. Requesting]

40. I appeal: Let the myriad clouds of sublime knowledge and love
build up, and a rain of profound and extensive Dharma fall,
so as to create, sustain, and increase
a moonflower garden for the benefit and bliss of infinite beings.

[6. Entreating]

41. Although your vajra body is not subject to birth or death
and is the vessel of union, O mighty sovereign,
in accordance with our wishes, please
always remain until saṃsāric existence ends, and do not pass beyond sorrow.

[7. Dedication]

42. The collection of white virtuous deeds thus amassed
I dedicate, so that in all my lives I might be inseparable from
and cared for by the exalted guru who is triply kind,
and in the end attain the union of mighty Vajradhara.

In offering the seven limbs, if there is time after the confession verse, confess each transgression of the three vows and perform the general confession, the bodhisattva's confession of downfalls, and so forth. Thus, as stated in the Vajrapāṇi Empowerment Tantra*:*

> *Seize on your masters' virtues,*
> *and never seize on their faults.*
> *If you seize on their virtues, you'll obtain yogic attainments,*
> *while if you seize on their faults, you won't obtain those powers.*[1464]

Relying repeatedly on mindfulness and alertness, think, "I must not let my mind fall into thinking my guru has faults." Reflect well on the advice in the sūtras and tantras regarding the benefits of relying on the guru and the disadvantages of not thus relying. In particular, merely hearing the name of your root guru robs the lower realms of their terror, while remembering him or her clears away the sufferings of saṃsāra. Think that the guru is in nature the sum total of all Three Jewels, the abode of refuge that, if you appeal to him or her, will happily grant you all yogic attainments. Not resting your hopes on anyone else, rely on the guru with intense devotion, and recite as many Miktsemas *and other [prayers] as you can. Afterward, appeal to the guru thusly:*

[V. Appeals]

[The guru as upholder of Vinaya]

43. Saffron-clad lord who is a second Śākyamuni,

1464. *VPT* 63b.

you are the source of virtues, a great sea of morality
replete with the collected jewels of extensive learning—
to you, elder who upholds the Vinaya, I appeal.

[The guru as upholder of Mahāyāna]

44. You possess the ten virtues and so
are worthy to show the sugatas' path;
you are the Dharma-lord heir of all the conquerors—
to you, Supreme Vehicle spiritual friend, I appeal.

[The guru as upholder of Vajrayāna]

45. You control your three doors well, are great-minded, patient, and honest,
lack pretense or guile, know mantra and tantra,
possess the twin sets of ten principles,[1465] are expert in drawing and
exposition—
to you, foremost vajra holder, I appeal.

[Recalling the guru's kindness]

46. You show aright the excellent path of the tathāgatas
to the vicious, intractable beings of the degenerate age,
untamed even by the numberless buddhas who came—
to you, compassionate refuge and protector I appeal.

47. At a time when the sun of the Sage is in decline,
you perfectly enact the deeds of the conquerors
for the many beings without a refuge or protector—
to you, compassionate refuge and protector, I appeal.

1465. These are ten inner skills and ten outer skills possessed by a tantric guru, which are listed, among other places, in the last chapter of the *Vajra Heart Ornament* (*Vajrahṛdayālaṃkāra*) *Tantra*. The ten inner skills are those of (1) creating the protection circle, (2) drawing maṇḍalas and binding them to the body, (3) bestowing the vase and secret empowerments, (4) bestowing the wisdom-gnosis and fourth empowerments, (5) separating enemies from their protectors, (6) torma rituals, (7) various type of recitation, (8) wrathful actions, (9) consecration rituals, and (10) making offerings to the maṇḍala. The ten outer skills are those of (1) drawing outer maṇḍalas and contemplating inner maṇḍalas, (2) concentrations, (3) hand mudrās, (4) ritual dance, (5) sitting in vajra and other postures, (6) proclaiming mantras, (7) burnt offerings, (8) offering rituals, (9) ritual actions, and (10) summoning and dismissing the buddhas. See, e.g., Kachen Yeshe Gyaltsen 2014, 204–5, and Lessing and Wayman 1978, 272n4.

48. Even a single one of your pore hairs
is rightly praised as a merit field for us
greater than all the conquerors of the three times and the ten directions—
to you, compassionate refuge and protector, I appeal.

[The guru's outer qualities]

49. The wheels that adorn your three sugata bodies
guide beings in ordinary ways,
through a lovely magical lattice of skillful means—
to you, compassionate refuge and protector, I appeal.

[The guru's inner qualities]

50. Your aggregates, sense fields, elements, and limbs
are by nature the male and female buddhas, the bodhisattvas,
and the wrathful protectors of the five tathāgata-families—to you,
supreme guru who embodies the Triple Gem, I appeal.

[The guru's secret qualities]

51. You are the quintessence of ten million maṇḍala circles
arising from the play of all-knowing gnosis—
to you, pervasive lord of a hundred families, foremost of vajra holders,
guardian of primordial union, I appeal.

[The guru's suchness qualities]

52. You who are the play of unobscured connate joy,
the pervader of everything fixed and moving, the self of everything,
beginningless and endless, completely good—to you,
the actual ultimate awakening mind, I appeal.

Having expressed the outer, inner, secret, and suchness qualities of the guru, single-pointedly make a special appeal:

[Special appeal]

53. You are the guru, you are the yidam, you are the ḍākinīs and Dharma protectors;

from now until awakening I will seek no refuge other than you.
In this life, in the bardo, and in future lives, hold me with your hook of compassion,
free me from fearing saṃsāric existence or peace, grant me all yogic attainments, be my constant friend, and guard me from hindrances. (*3x*)

[Receiving the four empowerments]

54. By virtue of my having thusly appealed three times,
from my guru's body, speech, and mind, nectar and light rays,
—white, red, and dark blue—radiate singly and all together,
and dissolve into my three centers, singly and all together.
The four obstacles are purified, the four pure empowerments obtained,
and the four bodies obtained. A double of the guru
joyfully absorbs into me, and I am blessed.

If you are offering tormas and holding the ritual feast or other rituals, this is the place to do so.

[VI. Ritual Feast]

[Transforming the Offerings]

T1. *Oṃ āḥ hūṃ* (*3x*)
Inconceivable clouds of outer, inner, and secret offerings, sacred substances, and costly presents completely pervade the whole expanse of the earth, atmosphere, and space, filling it up. In intrinsic nature they are gnosis and in aspect the inner offering and the particular offering substances, so in the sphere of the six senses they produce a special gnosis of bliss and emptiness.

T2. *E ma ho.* In the grand play of gnosis,
all regions are vajra fields
and all habitations are vajra palaces;
a sea of clouds of Samantabhadra's offerings blazes forth.

T3. The beings who possess the splendor of longed-for
enjoyments are actually spiritual heroes and heroines;
not even the words "impurity" or "delusion" exist,
and there is only infinite purity.

T4. *Hūṃ*
Within the Dharma body where all elaboration is stilled,
on top of a blowing wind and a blazing fire,
on a tripod of three human heads,
Āḥ
inside a proper skull-cup,
Oṃ
each substance blazes forth.
Above them are placed *oṃ* and *āḥ* and *hūṃ*,
each blazing with brilliant color.

T5–6. The wind blows, the fire blazes, and the substances melt.
Great vapors are stirred by their boiling,
and from the three letters a mass of light rays
is emitted in the ten directions, inviting
the three vajras[1466] and their nectar,
which absorb, respectively, into the three letters,
and these dissolve into nectar and blend with the elixir,
purifying, transforming, and increasing them—*e ma ho*—
so they become a sea shining with the splendor of longed-for things.
Oṃ āḥ hūṃ (3x)

[Invocation]

T7. You root and lineage gurus who embody compassion,
hosts of yidams and deities, Three Jewels of refuge,
hosts of heroes, ḍākinīs, Dharma protectors, and guardians:
I invite you to come to this offering site.

T8. Amid this cloud sea of outer, inner, and secret offerings,
set your radiant feet firmly
on this beautiful throne made of jewels
and grant me, O siddha supreme, the yogic attainments I desire.

1466. Those of body (related to *oṃ*), speech (*āḥ*), and mind (*hūṃ*).

[The actual offering]

Next is the offering of the ritual feast: The vajra server collects the first portion, puts it into a vessel, then places it on top of the tripod and so forth. After making three prostrations, recite:

O great hero, please bless the first portion of the ritual feast.

The rest of the ritual feast should be practiced accordingly. With the master presiding, the awareness holders should recite in unison:

T9. *Ho*
This sea of uncontaminated ritual-feast offering
blessed by concentration, mantra, and mudrā
I offer for the pleasure of the hosts of root and lineage gurus.
Oṃ āḥ hūṃ
Content with enjoying this abundance of things desired—
e ma ho—please send down a great rain of blessings.

T10. *Ho*
This sea of uncontaminated ritual-feast offering
blessed by concentration, mantra, and mudrā
I offer for the pleasure of the hosts of yidams and deities.
Oṃ āḥ hūṃ
Content with enjoying this abundance of things desired—
E ma ho—please send down a great rain of yogic attainments.

T11. *Ho*
This sea of uncontaminated ritual-feast offering
blessed by concentration, mantra, and mudrā
I offer for the pleasure of the Three Jewels of refuge.
Oṃ āḥ hūṃ
Content with enjoying this abundance of things desired—
e ma ho—please send down a great rain of holy Dharma.

T12. *Ho*
This sea of uncontaminated ritual-feast offering
blessed by concentration, mantra, and mudrā
I offer for the pleasure of the hosts of ḍākinīs and Dharma protectors.
Oṃ āḥ hūṃ

Content with enjoying this abundance of things desired—
e ma ho—please send down a great rain of buddha deeds.

T13. *Ho*
This sea of uncontaminated ritual-feast offering
blessed by concentration, mantra, and mudrā
I offer for the pleasure of the hosts of motherly beings.
Oṃ āḥ hūṃ
Content with enjoying this abundance of things desired—
e ma ho—please quell the suffering arising from deceptive appearances.
(*T9–13 3x*)

[Offering the feast to the master]

T14. *E ma ho* The great ritual feast,
is the pathway of the tathāgatas,
the source of every yogic attainment—
knowing this, O great hero,
cast concepts from your mind
and always enjoy the ritual feast.
A la la ho.

[The master's reply]

After it has been offered to the master, the master says:

T15. *Oṃ*
I clearly see myself as the guru-deity,
the lord who is inseparable from the three vajras.
Āḥ
This uncontaminated nectar of gnosis
Hūṃ
I enjoy to satisfy the deities dwelling in my body,
without my moving from the awakening mind.
A ho mahā sukha.

[*Song of the Spring Queen*][1467]

If you like, sing the Song of the Spring Queen*:*

T16. *Hūṃ*
All you tathāgatas,
heroes and yoginīs,
ḍākas and ḍākinīs,
I appeal to all of you.
O Heruka who delights in great bliss,
come to the lady who is drunk with bliss
and, with enjoyment appropriate to the rite,
enter the union of connate bliss.
A la la la la ho a i āḥ a ra li hoḥ
O host of stainless ḍākinīs,
look on me with love, and perform all good deeds.

T17. *Hūṃ*
All you tathāgatas,
heroes and yoginīs,
ḍākas and ḍākinīs,
I appeal to all of you.
When the greatly blissful mind is deeply stirred
and the body sways fully in dance,
may the great bliss from play in the consort's lotus
be offered to the host of yoginīs.
A la la la la ho a i āḥ a ra li hoḥ
O host of stainless ḍākinīs,
look on me with love, and perform all good deeds.

T18. *Hūṃ*
All you tathāgatas,
heroes and yoginīs,
ḍākas and ḍākinīs,
I appeal to all of you.
O ladies dancing in your lovely, peaceful way,
and you, guardian of delight with your ḍākinī hosts,
come before me and bless me,

1467. This song, attributed to Tsongkhapa, is often sung during the distribution of offerings.

and grant me connate great bliss.
A la la la la ho a i āḥ a ra li hoḥ
O host of stainless ḍākinīs,
look on me with love, and perform all good deeds.

T19. *Hūṃ*
All you tathāgatas,
heroes and yoginīs,
ḍākas and ḍākinīs,
I appeal to all of you.
You possess the signs of greatly blissful liberation;
multiple austerities that leave great bliss behind
cannot lead to freedom in a single life—rather, great bliss
abides at the center of the lotus supreme.
A la la la la ho a i āḥ a ra li hoḥ
O host of stainless ḍākinīs,
look on me with love, and perform all good deeds.

T20. *Hūṃ*
All you tathāgatas,
heroes and yoginīs,
ḍākas and ḍākinīs,
I appeal to all of you.
Like a lotus rising amid the mud,
you, O yoginī, are born from attachment but are not sullied
by attachment; by the bliss conferred by your lotus
may I quickly be freed from the bonds of saṃsāric existence.
A la la la la ho a i āḥ a ra li hoḥ
O host of stainless ḍākinīs,
look on me with mercy, and perform all good deeds.

T21. *Hūṃ*
All you tathāgatas,
heroes and yoginīs,
ḍākas and ḍākinīs,
I appeal to all of you.
Just as a swarm of bees drinks up
nectar from the flowers that are its source,
may I be sated by tasting the captivating nectar

of the abundant lotus that bears six marks.[1468]
A la la la la ho a i āḥ a ra li hoḥ
O host of stainless ḍākinīs,
look on me with mercy, and perform all good deeds.

Then, the leftover tormas [or other offerings are collected].

T22. *Hūṃ*
Impure deceptive appearances are purified in the Dharma realm.
Āḥ
This great nectar made of gnosis
Oṃ
becomes a great sea of desirable things.
Oṃ āḥ hūṃ (3x)

T23. *Ho*
This sea of uncontaminated feast-leftovers
blessed by concentration, mantra, and mudrā
I offer for the pleasure of the hosts of oath-bound field-protectors.[1469]
Oṃ āḥ hūṃ
Content with enjoying this abundance of things desired
e ma ho—please accomplish yogic deeds in the proper way.

T24–25. *Ho*
May the remaining guests and their retinue
accept this sea of feast-leftovers.
May the precious teaching spread,
and may the teaching's upholders and its patrons, along with their
retinues,
and especially we yogīs,

1468. I have not been able to locate a list of the six marks of the lotus. A more general description of a mudrā, or consort, is found in the *Hevajra Tantra* (2:8.2–5, trans. Snellgrove 2010, 1:116): "She is neither too tall, nor too short, neither quite black nor quite white, but dark like a lotus-leaf. Her breath is sweet, and her sweat has a pleasant smell, like that of musk. Her pudenda give forth a scent from moment to moment like different types of lotuses or like sweet aloe wood. She is calm and resolute, pleasant in speech and altogether delightful, with beauteous hair and three wrinkles in the middle of her body." Cf. the description in Saraha's *Queen Dohās*, trans. R. Jackson 2012, 179.

1469. *Zhing skyong* may refer either to protectors of buddha fields or to the protectors of charnel grounds.

gain a sickness-free life, divine power,
[splendor, fame, good fortune,
and every enjoyment in profusion.

T26. Please bestow on me the yogic attainment of the activities
of pacification, increase, (subduing, and destruction);
please, O pledge-bound protectors, guard me
and grant me the achievement of every yogic attainment.

T27. Please quell all untimely death, all diseases,
demons, and interfering spirits;
please negate all nightmares,
evil signs, and evil deeds.

T28. May the world be happy and the harvests good;
may the crops increase and the Dharma increase;
may all joy and goodness come about
and our every desire be accomplished.][1470]

The foregoing was composed by Khedrup Sangyé Yeshé.

T29.[1471] Through the force of this expansive generosity,
may I become a self-arisen buddha for the sake of beings,
and through this generosity may I free the multitude of beings
not freed by previous conquerors.

[VII. The Stages of the Path to Awakening]

[Guru devotion as the root of the path]

55. By virtue of my offerings and respectful appeals
to the supreme field of merit, the holy and exalted guru,
I ask your blessing, O root of joy and goodness,
O protector, to be gladly cared for by you.

1470. The bracketed verses are elided in Bz*LMCP(1)* 30 and are drawn here from Bz*LMCP(2)* 58–59.

1471. This verse is not found in any of the Tibetan editions of the tsok text I have consulted but is found in all three English translations I have checked.

[Training in the path of the being of lower capacity]

56. Understanding how this free and favored life
is attained only once, hard to attain, and quickly destroyed,
I ask your blessing to take up its meaningful essence,
undistracted by the pointless activities of this life.

57. Afraid of the blazing fires of suffering in the lower realms,
with all my heart I go for refuge to the Triple Gem;
I ask your blessing to zealously strive
to abandon vice and establish a wealth of virtue.

[Training in the path of the being of middling capacity]

58. Fiercely tossed by the waves of defilement and karma,
tormented by the sea monsters of the three sufferings,
I ask your blessing to arouse a fierce desire for liberation
from the sea of saṃsāric existence, boundless and frightful.

59. Giving up the mind that sees this saṃsāra—
so like a prison—as a pleasure grove,
I ask your blessing to seize the āryas' jewel trove,
the three trainings, and uphold the banner of liberation.

[Training in the path of the being of greatest capacity: Arousing awakening mind]

[Generating compassion]

60. Thinking on how all these miserable beings
have been my mother, and nurtured me kindly again and again,
I ask your blessing to arouse genuine compassion,
like a mother's love toward her precious child.

[Equalizing oneself with others]

61. It is said that we do not wish for the slightest suffering,
and are never satisfied with pleasure,
so there is no difference between myself and others;
I ask your blessing to rejoice in the happiness of others.

[Contemplating the disadvantages of self-cherishing]

62. Seeing that the chronic disease of cherishing
myself is the cause giving rise to unwanted suffering,
I ask your blessing to destroy the great demon of self-grasping
by despising, rebuking, and expelling it.

[Contemplating the advantages of cherishing others]

63. Seeing that the mind that cherishes motherly beings
and would place them in bliss is the doorway to infinite virtues,
I ask your blessing to cherish these beings
more than my life, even if they rise up as foes.

[Exchanging oneself for others]

64. In short, childish beings work only for their own aims,
while the Sage works solely for the aims of others;
with a mind that understands the difference between the faults of the former and the virtues of the latter,
I ask your blessing to be able to equalize and exchange myself with others.

65. Cherishing oneself is the doorway to every problem,
while cherishing motherly being is the basis of every virtue;
I ask your blessing, therefore, to take as my essential practice
the yoga of exchanging self and other.

[Giving and Taking]

66. Thus, O exalted, compassionate guru,
I ask your blessing that every suffering, obstacle, or vice
of motherly beings ripen upon me right now,
none excepted, and that I give all my happiness and virtue
to others, so that every being may have bliss. (*3x*)

[Verses on mind training]

67. Even if the world and its denizens should be filled with the fruits of vice
and unwanted suffering fall down on me like rain,

I ask your blessing to see this as a cause for depleting the fruits
of my evil deeds and to take misfortune as the path.

68. In short, whatever good or evil appearances arise,
I ask your blessing to change them into a path that enhances
the two awakening minds through putting into practice the five powers[1472]—
the heart of every doctrine—and to cultivate only a blissful mind.

69. Whatever I encounter, I ask your blessing
to apply it directly to meditation by skillful means
possessed of the four applications,[1473] and to give great meaning to my free and favored life
by putting into practice the vows and advice on mind training.

70. So I may free beings from the great sea of saṃsāric existence
through love, compassion, and the highest aspiration,
conjoined with giving-and-taking imagined as fixed on the breath,
I ask your blessing to master the awakening mind itself.

[Taking the bodhisattva vows]

71. Binding my mindstream with the vows of the purified children of the conquerors,
the single path trodden by every conqueror in the three times,
I ask your blessing to make the most diligent effort
to put into practice the supreme vehicle's threefold ethics.

[Training in the path of the being of greatest capacity: Practicing the six perfections]

[Perfection of generosity]

72. I ask your blessing to complete the perfection of generosity

1472. Typically, these are faith, energy, mindfulness, concentration, and wisdom.

1473. There are a number of lists of four applications (*sbyor ba bzhi*), including, e.g., (1) collection of merit, (2) purification of negativity, (3) ritual recitation of scriptures, and (4) offering of tormas to spirits; or (1) complete application, (2) peak application, (3) serial application, and (4) momentary application. See Das 2009, 158–59.

through the instruction on enhancing the mind that gives without attachment,
that I may transform my body and wealth, and my virtues collected
in the three times, into the things desired by each sentient being.

[Perfection of ethics]

73. I ask your blessing to complete the perfection of ethics,
which entails not giving up, even for the sake of my life, the rules prescribed
by the prātimokṣa, bodhisattva, and secret-mantra vows;
engaging in virtuous practice; and achieving the aims of sentient beings.

[Perfection of patience]

74. Even if all the myriad beings in the three realms should be angry with me,
revile me, abuse, me, threaten me, or kill me,
I ask your blessing to complete the perfection of patience,
remaining undisturbed and responding to their harm by working for their welfare.

[Perfection of effort]

75. Even if, for the sake of each sentient being, I must dwell
inside the fire of the incessant hell for an ocean of eons,
I ask your blessing to complete the perfection of effort,
compassionately striving, undiscouraged, for supreme awakening.

[Perfection of contemplation]

76. Abandoning the faults of mental dullness, agitation, and distraction,
I ask your blessing to complete the perfection of contemplation,
through a concentration of single-pointed equipoise
on the abiding nature of all things, empty of true existence.

[Perfection of wisdom]

77. I ask your blessing to complete the perfection of wisdom
through the yoga of space-like equipoise on the ultimate
that is conjoined with the pliancy and great bliss induced
by the wisdom that discerns reality.

78. Realizing how outer and inner phenomena—like an illusion,
a dream, or the moon's reflection in a limpid pond—
appear but lack true existence,
I ask your blessing to perfect concentration on illusion.

79. I ask your blessing to realize the point of Nāgārjuna's thought:
that not an atom of saṃsāra or nirvāṇa intrinsically exists
yet the dependent arising of cause and effect never fails, and that these two
do not contradict but complement one another.

[Training in the path of secret mantra]

80. I ask then your blessing to cross the fathomless sea
of the tantras through the kindness of the helmsman,
Vajradhara, and to hold as more dear than my life
the pledges and vows that are the root of yogic attainments.

[Generation stage]

81. I ask your blessing to purify every stain of attachment
to ordinary appearances through the first-stage yoga
that changes life, death, and bardo into the three
conqueror-bodies, so that everything appears as the deity's body.

[Completion stage]

82. I ask your blessing to actualize in this very life
the paths of luminosity, illusory body, and union,
which arise from your setting your feet, O guardian,
on the eight-petaled heart-lotus in the central channel.

[Transference of consciousness]

83. If I have not completed the path at the time of death,
I ask your blessing to be led to the pure land
through special instructions on the forceful means to awakening,
the guru's transference, which perfectly applies the five powers.

[VIII. Prayer to Be Cared for by the Guru]

84. In short, O guardian, I ask your blessing
that in each and every birth I be cared for
unceasingly by you and that I become your chief disciple,
apprehending every secret of your body, speech, and mind.

85. Please, O guardian, confer on me the fortune
to be at the very front of your retinue
wherever you manifest awakening, and to accomplish, effortlessly and spontaneously,
everything needed and desired, whether temporary or ultimate.

86. Having appealed to you thusly, O guru supreme,
I appeal to you to come happily to the crown of my head
in order to bless me and to set your radiant
lotus feet again firmly at the center of my heart.

In that way, the guru, the superior deity, and your own mind become essentially inseparable. In all your everyday activities, see anything that arises as the nature of bliss and emptiness playing the roles of gods and goddesses. In perfecting the key points of the yoga of conjoining the generation and completion stages, of the stages of the path, and of Mahāyāna mind training, you should practice diligently, never far from those whose minds are trained. At the end, you should apply the seal of dedication prayer for your virtues, good deeds, and so forth. If you make a concise dedication, recite this:

[IX. Dedication of Merit]

87. Whatever bright virtue I have thus created
I dedicate as the cause for accomplishing all the deeds
and aspirations of all the tathāgatas of the three times and their children
and for upholding the holy Dharmas of scripture and realization.

88. Through the power of that merit, may I not be apart
from the four circles of the supreme vehicle[1474] in any of my lives,
and may I complete my journey on the path of renunciation,
the awakening mind, right view, and the two tantric stages.

1474. These are (1) abiding in a land conducive to practice, (2) relying on a holy being, (3) making prayers, and (4) collecting merit. See Das 2009, 114.

Dedicate and pray in this way. You should learn some of the key points of the pith instructions orally. If you are going to make this yoga a daily practice, you will be practicing the essence of all the sūtras and tantras, and it will be the basis of all good things in this life. I say:

The milk sea of holy pith instructions on sūtra and mantra
is churned by the mighty mountain king of discernment; through this,
the nectar jar of unprecedented excellent explanations
accomplishes the spiritual aims of the fortunate with well-written verses.

The collection of virtues that arises from striving in this way,
white like the moon—whoever obtains that,
may they dedicate it so that all beings may be held close
by the holy protectors who are the root of virtue and goodness.

[X. Expression of Auspiciousness]

T29. Through all my bright virtue in the realms of saṃsāric existence and peace,
may all be auspicious for me to be free, here and now,
from every misfortune and trouble, and to enjoy an excellent, splendid
heavenly trove of virtue and goodness, both temporary and ultimate.

T30. When the Dharma centers of the all-knowing Losang Drakpa
are filled full of assemblies of yogīs and monks
who strive for pure and single-pointed practice of the three trainings,
may all be auspicious for the Sage's teaching long to abide.

T31. Receiving the blessing of Losang Drakpa,
who appealed to the supreme guru-deity
from when he was young, may I accomplish the aims of others spontaneously,
and may all be auspicious for Lama Losang Thupwang Dojé Chang.

T32. May the abundance I seek swell like a lake during summer rains
and unceasingly flow through easy rebirths in faultless families,
and may all be auspicious for me to pass my days and nights
with Losang's holy Dharma, enjoying its excellence and splendor.

T33. Through all the virtue I and others have collected
and will collect from now until awakening,
may all be auspicious for your holy body of form
to remain in this land, as immutable as a vajra.

[Colophon to the main text][1475]

At the repeated urging of Dulzinpa Chökyi Drakpa and Losang Phuntsok, who said, "You must do so," this *Offering to the Guru* was compiled by the Śākya monk Losang Chökyi Gyaltsen. I reviewed the *Offering to the Guru* composed by the mahāsiddha Lingrepa; the *Offering to the Guru* composed by the great Pang Lotsāwa; the *Offering to the Guru* texts composed by many great Sakyapa spiritual teachers; the *Offering to the Guru* composed by the omniscient Gendun Gyatso; the *Offering to the Guru* composed by the great scholar-siddha, my precious master Sangyé Yeshé; and also many *Offering to the Guru* texts composed by greater and lesser lamas of the various traditions. Coming to understand their express meanings and collecting their best parts, while leaving aside certain sections so it was easy to understand, I wrote this according to the pith instructions of the holy masters of sūtra and tantra in the house called Lofty Banner at the great Dharma center of Tashi Lhunpo.

1475. This is omitted from Bz*LMCP*(1) but is found in Bz*LMCP*(2) 46–47.

9. The Crystal Mirror of Tenet Systems: Excerpts[1476]

Thuken Losang Chökyi Nyima

2. A partial explanation of the Kagyüpa presentation of view and meditation[1477]

2.1. The view

The view of Marpa, the wellspring of the Dakpo Kagyü, is the Prāsaṅgika Madhyamaka view. Marpa's principal gurus were Nāropa and the great Maitrīpa, and whenever Marpa explained any view, meditation, conduct, or tantra, he based it on those two; specifically, there is a statement in Marpa's own songs that Maitrīpa is the guru who severed his deluded exaggerations with regard to the view:

> I came to the banks of the Ganges River in the east.
> Through the kindness of Lord Maitrīpa,
> I realized the ground, the unborn reality.
> My mind was ablaze with emptiness;
> I saw the primordial nature, reality without elaboration;
> I met the three mother buddha bodies face to face.
> From then on, this man's elaborations were severed.[1478]

1476. Thu'u bkwan Blo bzang chos kyi nyi ma, *Grub mtha' shel gyi me long*. Tk*SGML* 99–102, 105, 108–13. Cf. trans. Thuken 2009, pp. 137–42, 145, and 149–56. Part 1 of the chapter is an account of the history and doctrines of the Kagyü. For a translation of the whole chapter, see Thuken 2009, 117–56; for context and summary, see above, chapter 13.

1477. For other works exploring this question, see, e.g., Broido 1980, Broido 1984, Broido 1985a, Broido 1985b, Broido 1988, Seyfort Ruegg 2010, Williams 1983, and, especially, Brunnhölzl 2004.

1478. Th*MPNT* 134; cf. trans. Nālandā Translation Committee 1982, 144–45. This passage also is quoted by Paṇchen Chögyen and Yeshé Gyaltsen.

When, through the kindness of Maitrīpa, he realized that mind is ultimately unarisen, he was ablaze with the so-called "original essence of mind," the real nature of mind, which is emptiness of true existence. When he meditated on that in connection with the profound path of the completion stage, there arose in general the three bodies and, in particular, the meeting of mother and son luminosities called the Dharma body; through that, all mental elaboration was severed—so it is said.

Lord Maitrīpa was not merely a Mādhyamika; he gave primacy to the system of Śrī Candrakīrti. According to Maitrīpa's most important text, the *Ten Verses on Thatness*:

> For those who wish to know suchness,
> it is neither aspected nor aspectless;
> Madhyamaka that is not adorned
> by the guru's speech is merely middling.[1479]

"Aspected" refers to the Sautrāntika view and "aspectless" refers to the Vaibhāśika view; both are Śrāvaka schools. Alternatively, "aspected" refers to true aspectarians and "aspectless" refers to false aspectarians, which are both Cittamātra; neither of them realizes the meaning of suchness. Not only that, but Maitrīpa also states that Madhyamaka that is not adorned by the guru's pith instruction is only a middling Madhyamaka.[1480] The instructions of the guru are solely the instructions of the glorious Candrakīrtipāda. It is explained thus in the commentary by Maitrīpa's direct disciple, the paṇḍita [100] Sahajavajra.[1481]

The great paṇḍita Nāropa also solely upheld the system of Candrakīrti. In a commentary on the later tantras, he himself states:

> In this commentary on the later tantras,
> I have relied on Candrakīrti's *Bright Lamp*
> to explain the pith instruction of Nāgārjuna.[1482]

He also states:

1479. Mt*TD* 113a.

1480. In line with Thuken's interpretation of the first two lines, "middling Madyhamaka" would be Svātantrika Madhyamaka. Although *madhyamaka* means "middle," there is no pun in the Tibetan, for which Madhyamaka is *dbu ma* and "middling" is *'bring po*.

1481. Jk*TT* 164a.

1482. Nr*GP* 234a.

I have relied on the successive pith instructions
of the masters Nāgārjuna and Āryadeva,
Nāgabodhi and Śākyamitra,
Candrakīrti, and others.[1483]

Because of those and other statements, and because his explanation of the view seems like that of Candrakīrti alone, [Nāropa was a Prāsaṅgika].[1484]

It is said that the songs of the exalted Mila, too, are mostly in accord with the Prāsaṅgika:

To accord with the thought
of inferior minds, the omniscient Buddha
stated, "Everything exists."
Where ultimate truth holds sway,
there is no buddhahood separate from obstructions;
there is no meditator, object of meditation,
levels to be traversed, or path to be realized;
there are no fruitional buddha bodies or gnosis,
and therefore there is no nirvāṇa—
everything is merely designated by names and words.
The three worlds, animate and inanimate,
from the beginning do not exist, so there is no arising.
There is no basis, there is no connate,
there is no action or ripening of action.
Therefore not even the name of saṃsāra exists.
The final reality appears like that.[1485]

This shows how all phenomena, from form through omniscience, are ultimately nonexistent. Also:

E ma! If there were no sentient beings,
whence would come the buddhas of the three times?
Since a result without a cause is impossible,
in the realm of phenomenal truth,

1483. Nr*GP* 234a.

1484. Thuken's claim rests on a conflation of the Mādhyamika philosopher Candrakīrti with the tantric commentator Candrakīrti, an identification modern scholars would be unlikely to accept.

1485. Th*MLGB* 347–48; cf. trans. Chang 1989, 1:325, and Tsangnyön Heruka 2016, 340–41. This and the following quotation from Mila also are cited by Paṇchen Chögyen, in *Lamp So Bright*.

everything in saṃsāra and nirvāṇa
exists—so said the Sage.[1486]

Thus, although they do not truly exist, saṃsāra and nirvāṇa, action and actor, cause and result all do exist conventionally. Also:

Sages who realize this
don't see consciousness, they see gnosis;
they don't see sentient beings, they see buddhas;
they don't see things, they see reality.[1487]

The gnosis of an ārya in meditative equipoise directly sees emptiness. It does not see what appears to a mistaken cognition; it sees what appears to an unmistaken gnosis. In the seeing in which that gnosis sees reality, no such thing as a sentient being exists; what does exist is reality, which has the name of *buddha* [101] or *Dharma body*. Thus it may be said that the view affirmed by Milarepa is very much in accord with Prāsaṅgika Madhyamaka.

Admittedly, Marpa had 108 gurus who were scholar-siddhas, and after he mastered countless instructions received from them and saw the mental capacity of some of his disciples, he also put forth instructions in accord with Cittamātra. Also, in some places in songs he sang, Mila introduces the four yogas and seems there to explain the view in those yogas in terms of Madhyamaka or Cittamātra, as is reasonable in a specific context. Thus authoritative holy beings of early times, like Marpa, Milarepa, and other masters who were skilled in guiding disciples, saw the intellectual capacity of those requesting instruction and taught view, meditation, and conduct in an appropriate manner. They were unlike contemporary teachers, who loosely expound all their ideas, such that we cannot be certain whether all the views they expound are consistently Madhyamaka.

2.2. Application of the term *mahāmudrā*

In the songs of Mila, "the fortress of mahāmudrā view"[1488] and other phrases that occur merely touch upon the word *mahāmudrā*. The one who made it

1486. Th*MLGB* 348; cf. trans. Chang 1989, 1:325, and Tsangnyön Heruka 2016, 341.

1487. Th*MLGB* 348; cf. trans. Chang 1989, 1:325, and Tsangnyön Heruka 2016, 341.

1488. Thuken has drawn this quotation from Paṇchen Chögyen's *Lamp So Bright*, and as mentioned above (note 1280), where Paṇchen Chögyen reads *rdzong* ("fortress") at the end of each line, the original has *bzang* ("good,"), which from the context (a discussion of six

most famous was Dakpo Lharjé. In his texts, the view is identified as twofold, the Perfection Vehicle system and the Mantra Vehicle system, and he applied the term "special instructions on mahāmudrā" to both. Drawing out from many sūtras the ways in which the emptiness of the Perfection Vehicle system is said to be mahāmudrā, he composed treatises proving that emptiness is mahāmudrā. Before Shang Tsalpa, *white panacea* was not a well-known term. Shang wrote a treatise dedicated mainly to the white panacea, and after that it became well known.

Thus, Marpa, Mila, Gampopa, and their disciples Phakmo Drupa, Drigung Jikten Sumgön of Kyura, Lingrepa, Düsum Khyenpa, Taklungpa, and others agreed in their assertions about the view. Their system appears to place importance on the appearance side—that is, dependent arising—and does not reject the analytical process of the wisdom that cognizes individual entities. Unfortunately, numerous students, both learned and unlearned, inserted many confused marginal notations into their collected works, which do not seem to be reliable. So says my omniscient [102] guru.[1489]

Now, in a song sung to Gampopa by the exalted Mila, it says:

> When you understand your own mind to be empty,
> don't be tethered to the one and the many:
> there's a risk of going into a nihilistic emptiness;
> rest within the unelaborated, Son.[1490]

How do we interpret this quote? It means that when we have achieved certainty that the mind lacks intrinsic existence and we rest in single-pointed meditative equipoise on that empty nature, free from the one and the many, we do not analyze. His statement "when you understand your own mind to be empty" shows where to cease analysis.[1491]

The mahāmudrā of the early Kagyüpas is divided into two: sūtra and mantra. I will first discuss the former. They assert that, having accomplished meditative equipoise, one meditates nonconceptually while settled single-pointedly on the nature of mind. The clear, aware mind that rests in meditative equipoise on that topic searches for the mind outside the body, inside the body, and so forth. After that, when one ascertains that mind does not truly exist

goodnesses) would appear to be the correct reading. Cf. trans. at Chang 1989, 2:364, and Tsangnyön Heruka 2016, 386.

1489. Ck*GTNZ* 21a.

1490. Th*MLGB* 595–96; cf. trans. Chang 1989, 2:494, and Tsangnyön Heruka 2016, 521.

1491. Literally, "to hold the line" (*mtshams 'dzin*).

because no single intrinsic nature is found in it, one settles single-pointedly on the intrinsic nature of mind as characterized by non-true existence and meditates on emptiness as an affirming negation.[1492]

Mantra-system mahāmudrā is asserted as the luminous mind of great bliss that arises through making the vital winds enter, abide, and dissolve within the central channel. That is the main subject-matter of the renowned Seven Attainment Texts and Saraha's Essential Trilogy; it is the quintessence of all the unexcelled yoga tantras. In meditation on that, it is necessary first to manifest the primordial mind. For that, it is necessary to make the vital winds enter, abide, and dissolve within the central channel. Establishing the intrinsic nature of the primordial mind, one settles single-pointedly upon it, and the vital winds then enter, abide, and dissolve within the central channel. By force of that, the inner fire at the secret navel center ignites, and based on that the four joys arise, induced by the melting [of the drop at the crown]. Then the primordial mind arises in the nature of great bliss. Settled single-pointedly in the bliss-emptiness gnosis—where that primordial mind and its object, emptiness, are inseparable—one successively traverses the four yogas and accomplishes the supreme. The mahāmudrā meditation that thus unites bliss and emptiness, method and wisdom, is termed the white panacea.[1493] . . . [103]

2.3. Later Kagyüpas: Seeking the mind[1494]

. . . [105] Most of the later Kagyüpas' written special instructions on seeking mind do not discuss the very subtle primordial mind. There is an explanation of what appears when the coarse mind thinks on its own, "I go," "I stay," and so forth—that is, the threefold way of seeking mind in which one examines how the mind arises, abides, and ceases. They intended or thought that—as befitted the mental capacity of students of their era—one would establish just the real state of the original abiding nature of the present mind and become familiar with it, and then it would be easy to shift over to the very subtle primordial

1492. This marks a major dividing line between Kagyüpas and Gelukpas. The latter insist that the emptiness on which one meditates is a nonaffirming negation (*med dgag*), while the Kagyü often insist that it is an affirming negation (*ma yin dgag*).

1493. There follows next (Th*MLGB* 103, trans. Thuken 2009, 142–43) a discussion, which I omit, of sharp- and dull-witted practitioners. The section on the sharp-witted is mostly drawn verbatim from Norsang Gyatso's *Bright Lamp Lamp of Mahāmudrā*; for a translation of the relevant portion of Norsang's text, see above, page 565.

1494. This section begins (Th*MLGB* 103–105, trans. Thuken 2009, 145) with a long passage, which I omit, taken verbatim from *Lamp So Bright* (Bz*YSGM* 127–29); for a translation of Paṇchen Chögyen's text, see above, pages 513–15.

mind. However, in some of their writings, there is a deliberate rejection of reasoning establishing an ultimate abiding nature of mind that is separate from its conventional abiding nature. This lack of training in textual systems deserves a reply. Therefore my omniscient lama states:

> If you reflect properly, then even if you meditate only on the syllogism establishing absence of the one and many, there is no lack of topics for meditation. Therefore those who boast that they see the very face of the Dharma body in their own minds would evidently be better off if they simply studied that reasoning and sat up straight.[1495]

There is still a great deal to be explained, but fearing excess verbiage, I have not written about it.[1496] . . . [106–8] . . .

3. Brief investigations

[3.1. Is there a Perfection Vehicle mahāmudrā?]

The peerless Dakpo Rinpoché wrote treatises in which he quoted many sūtras to prove that in the Perfection Vehicle emptiness is said to be mahāmudrā. Some say that such sūtra passages do not appear in the Kangyur; however, those sūtras do appear within the Kangyur that was translated into Chinese. Although the words are not exactly the same, phrases with the same meaning appear in some other sūtras translated into Tibetan, such as the *Sūtra on the Presence of the Present Buddha* (*Pratyutpannebuddhasaṃmukhāvasthitasamādhisūtra*) and others.[1497] So says my omniscient guru.

Jamyang Sapaṇ says in *Clear Ascertainment of the Three Vows:*

> Our mahāmudrā is
> the gnosis arising from empowerment.[1498]

1495. Ck*GTNZ* 115b.

1496. In Thuken's text, there follows next another section (2.4; Bz*YSGM* 105–8, trans. Thuken 2009, 146–49), entitled "Early Kagyü Arrangements of Mahāmudrā," that because it is drawn largely verbatim from *Lamp So Bright*, I omit; for a translation of Paṇchen Chögyen's text, see above, pages 499–503.

1497. See, e.g., *PSS* 98b, "What is the seal of the tathāgatas? It is . . . unobservable, emptiness, signless, wishless, without characteristics, nondual. . . ." Cf. trans. Harrison 1998, 103.

1498. Sp*DSRB*t 25b; cf. trans. Sakya Pandita 2001, 117.

Based on that passage, some say there is no term for mahāmudrā in the sūtra system, but I think that is unacceptable, for it has been explained by many paṇḍitas, siddhas, and scholars that superior, middling, and lesser Perfection Vehicle disciples who abide in serenity and insight with a stable mind meditate on the nonduality of method and wisdom—which is mahāmudrā. Jñānakīrti's *Distinguishing* [109] *Clearly the Entire Sum of the Buddha's Words* says:

> Those with the best sense faculties, who make special efforts in the Perfection Vehicle, meditate on serenity and insight, and because they have a proper realization arising from mahāmudrā right from the time they are ordinary individuals, they obtain the signs of irreversibility.[1499]

The same text also says:

> These practitoners initially meditate on serenity and insight because to do so is to engage in the preparatory meditation for nondual mahāmudrā.[1500]

Not only that, the term *mahāmudrā* is applied to emptiness. The *King of Concentrations Sūtra* says, "The intrinsic nature of all phenomena is mahāmudrā."[1501] This is shown by that and other passages.

Well, then, would all four authenticating seals of the Buddhist view be mahāmudrā? It is not like that: three of them—impermanence, suffering, and peace—seal only some objects, so they are not described as "great," while the lack of self of all phenomena seals all objects of knowledge, so it fulfills the meaning of "great."

3.2. Does the white panacea imply quietism?

Although the refutations in Jamgön Sapaṇ's *Clear Ascertainment of the Three Vows* are manifold, there are two main targets: (1) Shang Tsalpa's description of mahāmudrā as the white panacea, and (2) the way the Drigungpas describe

1499. Jk*TA* 40a.

1500. Jk*TA* 40a.

1501. *SRS*t 59a. In fact, this passage—often quoted in Tibetan writings on mahāmudrā—does *not* mention mahāmudrā (*phyag rgya che*); rather, it is best translated as "Whatever is the intrinsic seal of all phenomena . . ." (Tib. *chos rnams kun gyi rang bzhin phyag rgya gang*, Skt. *yā sarvadharmānaṃ svabhāvamudrā* [*SRS*s 112]).

the single intention. Echoing the statements of Sapaṇ, many from our own and other schools have said a great deal about those positions. It seems that they all make their refutations after having decided that the meaning of Shang Tsalpa's white panacea is not thinking anything at all, but if you honestly examine Shang Tsalpa's statements in detail, the position of not thinking anything at all clearly is not present, and it is evident that the refutations in *Clear Ascertainment of the Three Vows* are overstated.

3.3. Do Kagyü and Geluk have the same intention?

A student of the omniscient Jamyang Shepa, a logician named Losang Rinchen,[1502] at first was a Gelukpa. Later, he went to study grammar at Mindröl Ling. He converted to Nyingma and wrote *Harmonizing the Stages-of-the-Path Traditions*, a text full of careless statements arising from arrogance. It says there:

> In his *Proving that the Kagyü and Geluk Have a Single Intention,* Khedrup Norsang Gyatso insults *Clear Ascertainment of the Three Vows* and states that, after seeking the mind, it is meditation on emptiness as an affirming negation that ascertains the mind's lack of true existence and so forth. [110] If it is not impelled by the requirement for special skillful means, then Norsang's view accords with the Cittamātra way of meditating on emptiness as an affirming negation; and although that view was intended by both Chöjé Nyernyipa[1503] and Śrī Dharmakīrti, there remains in the white panacea the flaw that arousing the awakening mind may or may not be necessary. We hear nothing about the common paths, nor is there any mention of the generation stage and so forth, the stages of maturing one's mindstream through the completion stage, the vows and pledges to be taken on, and so forth. The white panacea called "the mahāmudrā of mental abiding" and the conqueror Tsongkhapa the Great's magnificent summation of how to practice the Sage's complete teaching—to try and prove that these have the same intention is ludicrous!

1502. Some works by Losang Rinchen are listed in a recently published catalogue of the holdings of Drepung Monastery in Tibet, but to my knowledge, they have not been studied or made available outside the monastery.

1503. I have been unable to identify this person, though it may refer either to Nyernyipa Rinpoché Chökyi Gyalpo (1340–1407), the eleventh abbot of Drigung, or the Densathil abbot Chöjé Nyernyi Rinpoché Sönam Gyaltsen Palsang (1386–1434), who was one of Gö Lotsāwa's teachers; on the latter, see Roerich 1976, 589–94.

In Norsang's *Bright Lamp of Mahāmudrā,* however, it says:

> When the early Kagyüpas called mahāmudrā meditation the *white panacea,* they meant that when the primordial mind arises in the nature of great bliss, through that single meditation on the abiding reality, attainment of the ultimate fruit will occur.[1504]

And:

> Now, with respect to the early Kagyüs' teaching mahāmudrā meditation as the white panacea, Sakya Paṇḍita asks in *Clear Ascertainment of the Three Vows*: "In your white panacea, is arousing the awakening mind necessary or unnecessary?"[1505] His refutation is just like the refutation of someone who, when told the two collections are sufficient for buddhahood, asks, "Isn't it also necessary to first be born from a mother?"[1506]

Although this is stated clearly, Losang Rinchen writes that "there remains in the white panacea the flaw that arousing the awakening mind may or may not be necessary." This denies the evidence.

Although Losang Rinchen derides the argument that the Kagyü and Geluk have the same intention, Norsang's *Bright Lamp of Mahāmudrā* only argues that the early Kagyü way of meditating on mahāmudrā is the way of meditating on the primordial mind intended by Saraha; there is no discussion anywhere in the work that argues that Kagyü and Geluk have the same intention. Later printers wrote the title as *The Bright Lamp of Mahāmudrā: Proving that the Kagyü and Geluk Have the Same Intention* [111] based on writing that had been added to the cover [of an earlier edition], so needless to say Losang Rinchen knew it thus. Even if Norsang did argue that Kagyü and Geluk have the same intention, an honest analysis reveals that there is not even the slightest inconsistency between Norsang's way of arguing and the assertions of Jé Lama. Therefore it is the discussion of someone drunk on partiality, who says whatever comes to mind, that ought to be derided.

1504. Nz*PCSG* 7–8, translated above in part 5, section 7.

1505. See note 1430 above.

1506. Nz*PCSG* 10.

3.4. Are the four yogas Cittamātrin?

As already articulated above, Maitrīpa upheld the Madhyamaka view, yet Losang Rinchen says, "It seems that Maitrīpa's view is explained in terms of practice by way of the four yogas of the False-Aspectarian Cittamātra of Śāntipa." Saying that Maitrīpa held a False-Aspectarian Cittamātra view is nonsensical. Therefore my omniscient guru says, "Some earlier and later logicians say that Maitrīpa was a proponent of Cittamātra because he was a student of Śāntipa. The statement that Maitrīpa was a proponent of Cittamātra is worth no more than than a toilet stone[1507] and should simply be discarded."[1508] [Losang Rinchen] also says:

> Since it is established that the Kagyüpas' view of the stages of the four yogas—single-pointedness, nonelaboration, single taste, and nonmeditation—is Śāntipa's way of meditating on the view, it seems that it is the Cittamātra view.

To think "as long as there are four yoga stages, it must be Cittamātra" without being at all familiar with early Kagyü literature is to jump carelessly to a conclusion. My omniscient guru states:

> Although the phrase "four yogas" is explained by master Śāntipa in terms of Cittamātra, it does not appear that the four yogas of the Kagyüpas can be ascertained as a Cittamātra system.[1509]

This is as already explained above.

3.5. Do the various types of mahāmudrā have the same intention?

The omniscient Paṇchen, Losang Chökyi Gyaltsen, states:

> The connate union, the amulet box,
> the fivefold, equal taste, the four letters,
> pacification, severance, the great perfection,
> and guidance in the Madhyamaka view: these and other teachings
> are called by many names individually,

1507. Literally, a "stone for wiping the bottom" (*'phongs phyis pa'i rdo*).

1508. Ck*GTNZ* 19b.

1509. Ck*GTNZ* 20b.

but when examined by a yogī who has mastered
definitive-meaning scriptures and reasoning and possesses
inner experience, they come down to a single intention.[1510]

Wishing to insult him, Losang Rinchen says: "Pacification, severance, the fivefold, the six cycles on equal taste, and so forth are not simply philosophical views; the Paṇchen's explanations are really sorcery." The Paṇchen also states:

The main practice of mahāmudrā [112]
has many modes of explanation,
but they are divisible into two: sūtra and mantra.
The latter is the great bliss-luminosity mind arising
from skill in the methods of penetrating the vital points
in the vajra body.
The mahāmudrā of Saraha and Nāgārjunapāda,
of Nāro and Maitrī,
is taught in the Seven Attainment Texts and the Essential Trilogy
and is the quintessence of the unexcelled tantras.[1511]

About this Losang Rinchen says: "Unless for the conversion of fools, this is difficult to accept." He also says, "The view of the great perfection accords with the *Sacred Words of Mañjuśrī* by the great master Jñānapāda,[1512] so there are many reasons for inquiring into the value of the Paṇchen's basis of examination." Such statements are senseless talk, nothing but biased chatter.

3.6. Did Tsongkhapa write *Queries from a Pure Heart*?

The great paṇḍita Jampa Lingpa[1513] and others explain that the text known as *Queries from a Pure Heart*[1514] is not the work of the great lord Jé, for in it there appear on occasion certain vulgar expressions, such as "useless as shit." Also, the phrasing is not like that in other works of Jé. In the colophon, another name, unknown to anyone, is written: "by one called Tended by Guru

1510. Bz*GBZL* 83–84 (verses 11–12); for context, see above, part 5, section 4.

1511. Bz*GBZL* 83 (verses 6–8); for context, see above, section 5, chapter 4

1512. Bj*MA,* which was cited above by Khedrup Norsang Gyatso.

1513. There are a number of distinguished figures named Paṇchen Jampa Lingpa in the history of Tibetan Buddhism; I have yet to ascertain which one Thuken is referring to.

1514. See above, pages 156–58.

Mañjughoṣa."[1515] Also, *Queries* was not included in the index to the collected works of the omniscient Jé compiled by his students and his students' students, so there seem to be grounds for doubt. Most in our own and other schools do consider it Jé's work.[1516] The questions were understood as criticism of the great Kagyüpa meditators, so Drukpa Pema Karpo[1517] and others wrote replies, and Shākya Chokden of Sakya, in his capacity as protector and defender of the Kagyüpas, wrote a reply mostly made up of insults.[1518] On our own side, it seems that after Dakpo Gomchen Ngawangpa (fifteenth century) wrote on the topic[1519] and, in particular, the omniscient First Paṇchen wrote his *Reply to Queries: Gentle Words of Explanation for the Noble-Minded* (Bz*ZPGB*), it was assumed that *Queries* was a work of Jé's. Thus it seems difficult to make a final decision one way or the other.

4. Conclusion

Nowadays, it seems that, from minor lamas in lesser monasteries on up, no one among the Kagyüpas produces even a single new rational critique. They do write scattered texts [113] on the three vows and, citing one or two critical verses by the Kagyüpas and Drigung Palzin, they write many texts refuting the Nyingmapas—they merely fatigue themselves, and it's essentially nothing but a waste of paper and ink.

Therefore, to those who desire their own welfare, the omniscient Paṇchen says:

> The life stories of ārya beings transcend the scope of ordinary beings, and negativity directed to the Dharma and holy beings is most unbearable, so I, Chökyi Gyaltsen, make this appeal: I ask

1515. Ts*LSRK* 104b [366].

1516. Indeed, as evidenced by the previous note, it did make its way into the standard edition of Tsongkhapa's collected works, where it is item 68 in the miscellanea (*gsung thor bu*) found in volume *kha*.

1517. In his *Storehouse of Mahāmudrā* (*Phyag chen gan mdzod*): Pk*PCGZ*.

1518. In his *Reply to the Queries from a Pure Heart: Ornamenting the Intention of the Pith Instruction* (*Dri ba lhag bsam rab skar gyi dris lan man ngag dgongs rgyan*); in his collected works, vol. *'a*. Thuken has a particularly negative view of Shākya Chokden; see, e.g., Thuken 2009, 210–11.

1519. In his *Garland of Yogic Attainments* (*Dngos grub kyi phreng ba mkhas rgyan*) and *Reply to Questions about the View and Meditation of "Queries from a Pure Heart"* (*Yang dri ba lhag bsam rab dkar gyi lta sgom gyi dris lan*), both of which are found in his collected works, vol. *kha*.

> that you reject the hateful power of sectarianism and fill yourself
> with the precious light by which everything is seen as pure.[1520]

His benevolent advice should be taken to heart.

5. Concluding verses

The medicinal elixir that tastes of freedom—combining
Maitrīpa's white panacea mahāmudrā,[1521]
Nārotapa's six deep and excellent Dharmas,
and the nectar of the Kadam mind-training instructions—
was dispensed as needed by the physician
Gampopa to those with gradualist or subitist inclinations.

Thenceforth, immortal Kagyüpa seers
filled every glacier, valley, and inhabited land.

Flying about on white cotton wings,
they are confused for a mass of vultures in the sky,
and the thick flock of the saffron-clad
is like all the earth saturated with ochre dust.

Indra, mightiest of gods, uses his thousand eyes
to view that wondrous congregation. Not only that:
oceans of conquerors in buddha fields everywhere
rise from the Dharma realm to see it—or so I think.

For those lacking the fortune to be freed
by seeing such past events,
I have given here an account to accomplish
something meaningful for those with ears to hear.

1520. Bz*YSGM* 152; for context, see above, part 5, section 5.

1521. The attribution of the white panacea to Maitrīpa is unusual and the provenance of this claim worthy of further study.

10. Poetic Expressions[1522]

Paṇchen Losang Chökyi Gyaltsen

1[1523]

Namo Guru Mañjughoṣāya!

Your body visibly blazes with meaningful brilliance,
your melodious speech sings forth in sixty voices,
your mind is a trove of knowledge and benevolence beyond saṃsāric existence and peace—
to the lotus feet of holy Vajradhara, I bow down.

The mind, shaken by the demon of delusive grasping at things,
imputes deluded exaggerations and clings to them;
through that our own and others' lineages are broken,
and we wander in saṃsāra, driven by action and defilement.

If I do not slay the enemy, self-grasping
with the sharp sword of realizing things as they are,
I will earn a fearful abode and won't interrupt the cycle
of repeated suffering in this sea of saṃsāric existence.[1524]

1522. Blo bzang chos kyi rgyal mtshan, *The Autobiography of the First Paṇchen Lama Blo-bzang-chos-kyi-rgral-mtshan* (Bz*AFPL*) and *Grub pa'i dbang phyug mid la la brtan pa'i bla ma'i rnal 'byor dang rnam thar du ma chud pa'i gsung mgur rnams* (Bz*MLNJ*). For context and summary, see above, chapter 9, pages 225–34. Summaries of each of the songs may be found there under the appropriate number.

1523. Bz*AFPL* 42b–43a [84–85].

1524. Cf. the translation of these two verses in Guenther 1976, 119.

When it's seen that the objects of this illusion machine,
the ignorant mind, are unarisen from the start,
conceptually elaborated subjects and outer objects dissolve into the Dharma realm,
like ice in the vastness of the sea.

The actual primordial abiding nature of all things,
their inseparable meaning, is free from all elaboration:
when you see for yourself such a realm,
whose nature cannot be shown by any example,
where even the signs of the holy Buddha, Dharma,
and Saṅgha cannot be imagined,
then where is the suffering of saṃsāric abodes
seen as soiled by the stains of ignorant mind?

Awareness enters into the luminous realm
and starkly sees the intrinsic nature of all phenomena;
even if you look again, you're beyond the realm of seeing:
it's like searching beyond the edge of unobstructed space.

All you beings in terror of saṃsāra,
take in the spectacle of basic truth, the empty expanse;
when you see it, even if everyone in the world
becomes your worst enemy, you've no need to fear.

Not imagining actions of virtue or vice or their fruits,
free as well from path, abandonment, antidote, refutation, or proof,
apart from the fruits accomplished by the striving mind:
in such a realm, think triumphant thoughts.

Looking beyond the phenomena of saṃsāra and nirvāṇa,
see just this fact: the Dharma
of cause and effect is unfailing and subtle,
like the rainbow path where immortals walk.

The middle path, united and free from extremes,
on which there is no alternation of appearance and emptiness,
the unelaborated real, primordially pure,
where action, cause, and effect do not fail:
a path such as this is attained through the guru's kindness;

be kind, O you second Conqueror, Jé,[1525]
and bless even unkind beings
to realize an aim such as this.

2[1526]

Namo Guru Mañjughoṣāya!

To the father who's like an untrue dream,
performing magical feats in every land
on the divine path where awareness and the Dharma realm are inseparable,
I, the illusory son, make heartfelt bows.

All the things we view are just illusions,
and when you look at reality, you see nothing.
The path that unites illusion and emptiness—
through the guru's kindness is this union attained.
A la la! Free from extremes of "is" or "isn't,"
I rest in equipoise in the realm beyond extremes.

When you look at reality, things are resplendent;
when you examine things, they slip into emptiness.
The non-alternation of appearance and emptiness—
through the guru's kindness is this union attained.
A la la! Beyond extremes of "is" or "isn't,"
I rest in equipoise in the realm beyond extremes.

Ultimately, cause and effect are shown to be unfailing;
discern the ultimate original face of conventions.
The natural inseparability of the two truths—
through the guru's kindness is this union attained.
A la la! Beyond extremes of "is" or "isn't,"
I rest in equipoise in the realm beyond extremes.

When you've cut to the ultimate realm,
not even the phrase "dependent arising" exists,

1525. Cf. the translation of the preceding two-and-a-half verses in Guenther 1976, 122–23.

1526. Bz*AFPL* 43b–44a [86–87].

yet emptiness and dependent arising are united—
through the guru's kindness is their noncontradiction known,
through the guru's kindness is this union attained.
A la la! Beyond extremes of "is" or "isn't,"
I rest in equipoise in the realm beyond extremes.

All phenomena of saṃsāra and nirvāṇa:
understand their truth by knowing they're untrue.
The natural inseparability of true and false—
through the guru's kindness is this union attained.
A la la! Beyond extremes of "is" or "isn't,"
I rest in equipoise in the realm beyond extremes.

Phenomena, which are only names, are empty of truth;
truly empty, all things appear as the play of cause and effect.
The path where emptiness and cause and effect are inseparable—
E ma ho! Through the guru's kindness is it attained.
A la la! Free from the abyss of eternalism and nihilism![1527]

3[1528]

Namo Guru Mañjughoṣāya!

I bow to the feet of the one who removes our fear
of saṃsāric foes, the mighty father guru Vajradhara,
the illusionist who makes even abstractions appear
as the connate great bliss of the ineffable realm.

The appearances experienced today,
arising as varied and wondrous pictures in the mind,
apparent contradictions that do not contradict—
I sing a song that exalts them in some small way.
Behold the intrinsic nature of any arising object
and know it is unstable,[1529] impotent, false, and hollow.

1527. Cf. the translation of the last verse in Guenther 1976, 123.

1528. Bz*AFPL* 44a–b [87–88].

1529. *Rang tshugs* ("stable, independent") does not make sense in this context; *ma tshugs* is preferable.

When you know that, the very face of truth is revealed:
the mind standing naked, draped in the finery of emptiness.

All the different phenomena distinguished as pure or not
are inseparably mixed in the ultimate realm;
the path is free from refutation or proof, but acts of virtue and vice
to be done and shunned occur to the minds of the wise.[1530]

The wise first view self-grasping as the enemy
and pierce its heart with the sharp swords of scripture and reason.
Now, in the vast mirror without reference point,
I view myself as well in a way that does not view.

Look at conventional things: they're without a basis or root;
look at the Dharma realm: anything can appear.
The vast path of the union of appearance and emptiness—
when you settle on a path such as this, all things are bound.

In the single taste where single and different are shunned,
even the one appears as the play of the many:
I assert the essential expression, this inexpressible meaning,
that no example can exemplify.

Though the basis—imagining saṃsāra's abandonment—
and the path—attainment of liberation—do not exist,
unable to bear the suffering of motherly beings,
may I quickly obtain the three buddha bodies supreme!

4[1531]

Namo Guru Mañjughoṣāya!

The Dharma realm where appearances are not blocked,
the mindstream where bliss and emptiness arise,

1530. Cf. the tranlation of the previous two verses in Guenther 1976, 119.

1531. Bz*AFPL* 44b–45a [88–89].

the single taste where they blend inseparably—
the bodhisattva mind passes into the vajra mind.

Thirsting sentient beings, my ancient mothers,
are bound by the noose of desirable things' allure
and enter the prison of unfreedom,
tortured by terrible feelings of pain.

When the sorcerer of self-grasping enters their hearts,
they cherish an independent self;
focused only on that, they're bedeviled by the many demons
of eternalism, nihilism, and other evil views.

Trembling with the fevers of attachment and anger,
they fall prey to the dysentery of evil deeds;
repeatedly blocked from a life with the things they desire,
they amass great suffering in repeated rebirths.

When you see things the way they appear, you dissolve in tears,
your heart weary, remorseful, and afraid;
when you see things the way they are, you dissolve into laughter,
your heart profoundly glad, your mind's mood blissful.[1532]

If a person's beholden to pleasure and pain
through impulses tainted by attachment and anger
toward a beautiful, barren woman,
what will discerning friends think?

Nobles who have the transmission reach the innermost mind,
having studied and pondered many texts of definitive meaning:
they're drenched with the pollen of essential deep meaning
and sprinkle dewdrops on the path of words.

1532. Cf. the translation of the last three verses in Guenther 1976, 119.

5[1533]

O triply kind noble guru Vajradhara,
master sitting at the center of my lotus heart,
please bless me to root out the enemy,
the eight mundane concerns and my clinging to shiny appearances.

If I live a long life, I'll practice the excellent path
of purity, but even if I die, I'll be blissful,
for I'll die when my actions and instincts are good.
A la la! To my mind life and death are the same,
and however life goes, it's delightful: it's a trove of delight.

If I get abundant support, I'll gather wealth
through offering and donation, but even if I'm poor, it's okay,
for I'm not painfully obsessed with things running out.
A la la! To my mind gain and loss are the same,
and however wealth goes, it's delightful: it's a trove of delight.

If I'm celebrated and praised by all and sundry,
my mind feels no bliss, and even if I'm despised, it's fine,
for words of praise are insubstantial illusions, beguiling deceptions.
A la la! To my mind praise and blame are the same,
and however fame goes, it's delightful: it's a trove of delight.

If my body and mind now are blissful, it's the kindness
of the Triple Gem, but even if I suffer, it's okay,
for my mind is brimming with renunciation and compassion.
A la la! To my mind pleasure and pain are the same,
and however happiness goes, it's delightful: it's a trove of delight.

Life and death, gain and loss, pleasure and pain,
praise and blame, and fame and shame:
whatever comes up is the guru's blessing.
A la la! Whatever I do, my mind is joyful,
and whatever my hopes or fears, it's delightful: it's a trove of delight.

1533. Bz*AFPL* 49b–50a [98–99].

Through this instruction that changes poison to nectar,
coming from Śrī Śāntideva,
Dīpaṃkāra, and the second Conqueror, Jé,
a la la! May all evil omens be taken as auspices,
and however bad conditions are, it's delightful: it's a trove of delight.

6[1534]

Namo Guru Mañjughoṣāya!

Father, who knows the whole extent of elaboration
yet eternally rests in the unelaborated realm,
Jé the second Conqueror, Losang Drak,
continue to protect us, your servants, with your compassion.

From the unreachable beginning until now,
a demon has dwelt in my heart;
taking as self the object that is not self,
I've been deceived by the lure of instant benefit.

The times I have burned in hell are beyond calculation,
but this very day, through the guru's kindness,
I know the enemy, the evil sorcerer of self-grasping,
and see the primordial essence: unelaborated mind.

The young groom of self-arisen awareness
meets the bride of objective luminosity in the Dharma realm;
awareness and its realm inseparable, the unity of wisdom and method—
it is excellent, this marriage without union or separation![1535]

From the outset nothing is established, so
objects are known for sure by understanding there is no self,
yet action, cause, and effect must be known as unfailing—
now, in the expanse of negation, I have no fear.

1534. Bz*AFPL* 50a–b [99–100].

1535. Cf. the translation of the last three verses in Guenther 1976, 119–20.

Every dependently arisen thing
I see as the illusory play of mere appearance;
seeing that, I destroy the bonds of reification
and am freed thereby from the extreme of eternalism.

I am the yogī in the sky of emptiness,
holding the seal of the falsity of any arising thing;
the bandit of grasping at true existence
flees into the primal realm without basis or arising.

Well, apart from the game of assigning names
to every phenomenon of saṃsāra or nirvāṇa,
there is nowhere a realm with intrinsic nature,
so I have no fear of either birth or death.

I once wandered compulsively, but now I've reached the abode
of healing and rest, the ambrosial essence, the emptiness of things.
I think this is the kindness of my exalted guru;
he's certainly most kind, my noble guru.

I, a son of Losang the second Conqueror,
amuse myself on the mahāmudrā path
and take up this song of the Dharma view.[1536]
All you friends who seek liberation should do the same.[1537]

7[1538]

Namo Guru!

To Jé, who is actually all the buddhas
of the three times, the triply kind fatherly guru,
the glorious, matchless Ikṣvākupāda,[1539]

1536. The phrase *chos lta* also may refer to viewing phenomena.

1537. Cf. the translation of the last three verses in Guenther 1976, 123.

1538. Bz*AFPL* 73b–74b [146–48].

1539. In Hindu mythology, this was the first king of solar dynasty, of which Śākyamuni is a member, and with which Tsongkhapa, as a second Buddha, here is associated.

the one who robs the enemy, saṃsāric existence, of its terror, I bow down.

Between snowy Tibet and southern Tibet,[1540]
on a slope where dwells a great teaching protectress,
beside a ravine in a fruited hidden valley
is a spot known as Auspicious Hut.

I'm taken with the seductive play of the emerald glow
of every mountain and stream.
Shapely flowers of various hues—
such as jewel and lotus, ruby and lapis,
gold that's refined, and conch-white and turquoise—
are like rainbows arrayed in every direction.

The mountains, so green, soar to heaven,
and by a turquoise lake grows a beautiful leafy grove,
where many and varied birds turn their voices to song.
Encircled by highland glaciers and surrounded by slate,
the waters—clothed with glistening crystal-white foam—
fall evenly, neither too much nor too little.

Above, clouds rise high in the blue;
sometimes, a fine light rain falls.
Here, the eighty-four thousand ills are destroyed,
and the ground in all directions is adorned by medicinal plants
of various tastes, colors, and potencies.
Sweet grass and bamboo, juniper and rhododendron,
send out continuous scents of sweet incense.

In that valley, an abode like the pleasure grove of gods,
I walk and sit, mindful and alert,
living the life of noble Śuddhodhana's son (the Buddha).
Today, in that medicinal forest in that mountainous valley,
I analyzed with a deluded mind and thought I saw
various wonderful images in my thoughts;
when I examine their meaning, their nature is unthinkable and empty.

1540. Paṇchen Chögyen presumably is describing a place in Tsang where central and west-central Tibet (Ü-Tsang) shades into the country's southern border regions.

The mind elixir of all the noble conquerors,
the essential meaning of the eighty-four thousand teachings,
the mother who gives birth in the three times to the bodhisattvas and the
four āryas[1541]—
the master who clearly shows this is cheerful:
his mind rejoices that objects are mere appearance and cannot be analyzed,
that the way things exist is like a lotus in the sky.

Not understanding this, saṃsāric sentient beings
again and again experience unbearable suffering
and are deluded by the demon of grasping at things,
but when my mothers, saṃsāric sentient beings of the three worlds,
understand such things, they will rejoice,
and when they attain a path such as this, they will be happy;
even if they're uncertain of his name,
Śuddhodhana's son is these people's defender.

The profound path taken from that self-same protector
is not found in the general transmission;
we must properly rely on the transmission-holding father guru,
the siddha who manifests this path.

The countless teaching-upholders of snowy Tibet
train in pure vision within their minds.
Suffused with tantric Dharma, they cannot be swamped by distorted views,
and they're blessed to understand that the teaching has no[1542] contradictions.

May the virtuous prayers of those who see and hear,
remember, and touch the truth[1543]—all deluded sentient beings
in general and especially spiritual friends
who are like objects in a dream—be fulfilled in every age.

Through the compassion of the infallible Triple Gem,
may I, this false, illusory monk,
consider myself content with the fruit, whatever the deed,
and even if I die, may I not have the slightest regret.

1541. Stream-enterers, once-returners, nonreturners, and arhats.

1542. Reading *med* for *mang*.

1543. Conjectural reading for *bdag*.

So, on this account, may all beings,
their mindstreams uncovered by stains of attachment and anger,
obtain the path whose essence is emptiness and compassion
and gain sight of the nature of all things.

8[1544]

Namo Guru Jé. To the Triple Gem
and the lord residing at my lotus heart
I appeal: confer on me this very instant
every supreme and common yogic attainment.

In general, buddhas rarely appear,
and a free and favored human life is especially hard to gain;
each of us must accomplish our aspirations
unattached to pleasure within this life.

Even the vigor of growing children's bodies
is a rainbow appearing in the midnight sky,
and since life is fragile as a bubble,
don't grasp at permanence now but apply yourself to Dharma.

Although Brahmā and Maheśvara and universal kings
live endowed with saṃsāric pleasures and possessions,
they may burn again in blazing Avīci fires,
so how secure are the mundane pleasures of now?

If in your heart you aspire to help yourself,
then it's best you rely constantly on the noble guru
who will guide you along the path and the three trainings,
which are a constant trove of virtue in all your lives.

This "glorious great bliss circle" was set down
at the urging of his spiritual son, Jinpa Gyatso,
by the crazed bee Chökyi Gyaltsen,
a do-nothing who wanders aimlessly.

1544. Bk*AFPL* 75a–b [149–50].

9[1545]

Namo Guru Mañjughoṣāya!

I bow to the feet of the triply kind guru
Vajradhara, the holy lord pervading every class of being.

This unwavering appeal
to the exalted qualified guru,
the means for becoming buddha in a single life,
sums up the essence of the profound path.

The unfailing dependent arising of cause and effect
is the real state of conventional appearances, like a moon in water,
and like the sharpness of a rabbit's horn
is the ultimate beyond elaboration.

The basis is a mind that understands the distinction between the two truths;
the method is esteeming the awakening mind;
the path is endowment with emptiness and compassion—
this is the ultimate essence of all the Dharmas.

The path arising from such meditation
is a sky treasury of unobstructed virtues;
the ultimate union, mahāmudrā,
is the fruit, the quintessence of the three buddha bodies.

Destroy the bonds of grasping at true existence!
[The nature of] everything in saṃsāra and nirvāṇa
is emptiness free from intrinsic existence—
realizing this is the supreme view.

Within the empty nature of saṃsāra and nirvāṇa,
aware of purity, we brandish the spear of insight
and meditate with single-pointed focus,
steady as the middle of a river.

1545. Bz*AFPL* 75b–76a [150–51].

In meditation on the ultimate, all elaboration is released;
in postmeditation, apply the three regards.[1546]
I follow the conduct of the Conqueror and his children,
conduct that is a great imperturbable wave.

I'm the yogī who meditates on such on a path.
E ma ho! The happy sun rises!
A la la! I raise up this song of joy!
Take this song as an offering, O Triple Gem!

10[1547]

Svāsti!

In distorted dreams as I slept last night,
various instinctive delusions arose.

At first, I was bound by the seal of true existence.
Later, aware of those delusions' defects,
my mind dissolved in the spacious Dharma realm itself,
like ice melting in the ocean.

In that azure realm I saw
various wonderful images, distinct
arrays of manifold things:
whatever their kind—rightly perceived or unreal—
they were like rainbows, or like the moon reflected in water.

Like that rainbow in the azure realm,
even words clearly arrayed deceive us, they lead to deluded exaggeration and understatement.[1548]
Because of that, I simply put labels away.

1546. The three regards (*'khyer so gsum*) involve regarding body as deity, speech as mantra, and mind as that of a buddha.

1547. Bz*AFPL* 79a–b [157–58].

1548. *Sgro skur* involves overstating or underestimating the ontological status of an object, asserting it to be either more real or less real than it actually is.

11[1549]

Namo Guru!

The sovereign of ten million maṇḍala wheels,
who plays a saffron-wearing monk in this final age,
performs the deeds of a buddha for all to see,
and by the eye of gnosis sees as far as one can.

The phenomena of saṃsāra and nirvāṇa are conventions;
don't cling to them as they appear but look at them as they are.
If you see the intrinsic nature of their appearance and existence,
you'll be free from extremes of eternalism and nihilism.

We are content to serve the exalted one who has the qualities
of the uncorrupted blessing transmission,
through which the solid wall of sūtras and tantras is built
and the inner sanctum of special instruction is locked.

If you have the fortune to desire liberation
and to raise your sights to the face of reality,
then entrust yourself to the renowned Jé,
who is not a master of conventional arid explanation
and does not speak the barbaric tongue of those with little learning;
extend your hard-earned training as far as you can![1550]

Amid appearances, cut the root of clinging;
within awareness, be free from the extremes of "is" and "is not."
The dependent arising of mere appearances does not fail,
and dependent arising shows the meaning of emptiness.

This yoga of maintaining both in union
is a practice that carries together
all three: view, meditation, and conduct.

1549. Bz*AFPL* 81a–b [161–62].

1550. Cf. the translation of the previous three verses in Guenther 1976, 123–24.

12[1551]

O triply kind Jé Vajradhara,
sovereign dwelling at the center of my lotus heart,
please confer on me right now
supreme and common yogic attainments, none excepted.

In the month of Vaiśākha in an auspicious year,
as I drowsily made my way one day
toward Ganden hill to offer incense,
images of manifold objects appeared distinctly to me.

My sense doors unstopped, I analyzed how they appear:
arising things are intrinsically empty,
and though there is no intrinsic nature, anything can arise,
so appearance and emptiness are not in conflict.

I think of their immeasurable union and rejoice,
maintaining the intrinsic nature of whatever arises, I see;
all of the eighty-four thousand divisions of Dharma
are said to come down to precisely this path.

Any appearance of good or bad that occurs
lacks even an atom to perceive
that's not just a name that's labeled by thought,
so what's the point of elaborate rejections and proofs?

For long eons I have burned in the blazing fires
of Avīci Hell, but I do not despair,
for I have burned in blazing fires in dreams, yet
where is the burner, the burned, the burning?

Because of that, Brahmā, Maheśvara, and others
do not cut the root of longing or attachment
toward all their abundance of mundane splendor,
which are but pleasures emanating from illusion.

1551. Bz*AFPL* 82a–b [163–64].

I ascertain such meaning through the guru's kindness;
I'm content to serve the widely renowned exalted father,
whose glorious and uncorrupted blessing transmission[1552]
is not a transmission of arid verbal explanation.

13[1553]

Ha ha! This unimpeded arising of mind's clear awareness,
the sight of nonarising—it's an astonishing sign!
In nonarising, whatever abides or ceases
is like the posturing of a barren woman's daughter.

The nature of mind is beyond the bounds of description.
In unceasing song, where is arising or appearance?
The Dharma realm is free from the snares of grasper and grasped,
so what is it that incites me to song today?

Guided in the view of "him" and "other," I meditate on mahāmudrā.
In this person that is "I" there is not even an atom of meditated,
meditating, or signs of meditation on this reality;
however much I practice meditation, it's delightful: it's a trove of delight.

It's easy for me to quickly die or also to live.
The mind, that supreme association of appearance, emptiness, and great
 bliss,
associates without a moment of separation and then departs.
However much I suffer, it's delightful: it's a trove of delight.

When conventional logicians, who see but externals,
hear this, they think it's a mass of contradictions;
when yogīs, who experience the actual meaning,
listen to such a song, they break out in smiles.

1552. Reading *brgyud* for *brgyur*.

1553. Bz*AFPL* 82b [164].

14[1554]

Namo mahāmudrāya!

Guru Jé, father unequaled in kindness,
please rest upon the anthers of my lotus heart.

The basis, a free and favored human life, is hard to attain,
and it's impermanent, quickly subject to death, so,
persistently and without laziness,
I now must make unwavering efforts to practice.

To the infallible guru Jé and the Triple Gem,
I go for refuge from the bottom of my heart.
For mother sentient beings of the three worlds,
I seek to arouse the mind induced by love and compassion.

From beginningless time until now,
I have wandered in saṃsāra by force of deluded mind.
Now, no longer chasing delusions,
I'm blessed by the primordial nature of all things.

The goal is unwavering vajra mind;
the path is what is known as mahāmudrā.
There, without indulging hope or fear, rejection or proof,
my mind gently relaxes into the Dharma realm.

My body is the body of a pure god, empty appearance;
my speech is vajra recitation, empty sound;
my mind is the nature of mahāmudrā, empty clarity—
at all times may I remain in unwavering equipoise.

Untinctured by the poison of signs or their traces,
I dedicate the glorious two collections to great awakening.

1554. Bz*AFPL* 83a [165].

15[1555]

Namo Guru Mañjughoṣāya!

O exalted fatherly guru, glorious wishing jewel
who is the source of all excellence—to your feet I bow
down.

The basis is discourse on the way the two truths abide,
the very nature of appearance and emptiness.
Isn't the yoga fulfilled by skillful means,
the practice of method and wisdom, called the path?
The unobscured inseparability of the deep and the vast
is union at the time of fruition—*e ma ho*!

The mind's original nature is unborn and stainless;
seeing this starkly is the king of all views.
Settling mindfully and alertly on that very object
is the key to prolonged meditation over time.
When the stake of internal self-grasping has been removed,
we move freely—that is supremacy of conduct.

The ground, path, and fruit of yoga,
and view, meditation, and conduct are thus—
if you want them, then feed on heavenly nectar
within the perfect vessel of your mind.
If you feed on this, it won't be long before the greatly blissful
three buddha bodies are right in your hand.

16[1556]

Namo Guru!

To all the circles of conquerors in their vast fields,
to the dancer who appears in various incarnations

1555. Bz*AFPL* 85b–86a [170–71].

1556. Bz*AFPL* 97a–b [193–94].

for the sake of leading beings of this tainted age,
to the feet of the fatherly guru, I bow down.

The basis, conventional phenomena of saṃsāra and nirvāṇa,
should be ascertained as they are in the Dharma realm,
where objects do not exist in distorted ways
but merely as appearances in our minds—that is the view.

We must take the life of the enemy, the sorcerer of self-grasping,
to whom we've been linked from beginningless time;
placing our minds single-pointedly on emptiness,
the nature of every thing—that is meditation.

Through the yoga that embraces the method,
awakening mind, while understanding it as illusion,
we put the three doors into practice without contradicting
the three glorious vows—that is supremacy of conduct.[1557]

The mind sealed by unerring mindfulness and alertness
expels[1558] the lying, foul arch-enemy, ego-grasping;
knowing well the way that all
arisen things exist—that is right view.

Through exceptionally subtle and detailed examination,
we know[1559] the original nature of all things
and purify awareness in the Dharma realm;
seeing this, the deep definitive meaning—that is meditation.

Seeing clearly that dependently arisen good and bad
are ultimately beyond elaborated extremes
and only nominal, like the rainbow path of the gods,
we unite method and wisdom—that is supremacy of conduct.

1557. That is, we place body, speech, and mind at the service of properly observing the prātimokṣa, bodhisattva, and tantric vows.

1558. Reading *btab* for *btib*.

1559. Reading *shes* for *shis*.

This summary of the key points of the glorious view, meditation, and
conduct,
as conceived by the noble conquerors of the three times,
was arranged by one named Chökyi Gyaltsen
as a necklace for faithful beings;
through its virtue, may every being
quickly obtain the stage of the three buddha bodies.

17[1560]

Namo Guru!

May the incomparably kind root guru
dwell inseparably in the lotus at my heart.

Our minds and other phenomena of saṃsāra and nirvāṇa
possess not even an atom of true existence;
realizing things as they are in reality, where
eternalism and nihilism are left behind—that is the royal view.

In that realm of profound realization, meaning, and nonelaboration,
the faults of dullness and excitement are cleared away well;
maintaining mindfulness[1561] and alertness so they flow
like the Ganges—that is supremacy of meditation.

When you're done with the nectar of equipoise,
then doing what you like on the pure path,
free from within from the three doors' vices,
the illusion-like yoga of postmeditation—that is supremacy of conduct.

This song on proper view, meditation, and conduct
is dedicated to all beings deceived by illusion—
may they win the battle against the four māras
with the wisdom sword of understanding the way things are.

1560. Bz*AFPL* 97b–98a [194–95].

1561. Reading *dran* for *dan*.

18[1562]

Namo Guru Mañjughoṣāya!

You who wear the mane of the Buddha's word, the sūtras and tantras,
emitting the lion's roar of the emptiness of things
and smashing the brain of the demon elephant of grasping at things—
to the feet of Jé Matibhadra I bow down.

I viewed sentient beings in their worlds as friends,[1563]
and when I thought of the way all those friends exist as real,
my mind became deeply drunk on the wine of grasping at things
and tired from collecting the chaff of denying cause and effect.
Seeing the truth, I experienced exuberant joy
within illusion's machine, and compassion arose.

Those whose minds are beguiled by the ghost of grasping at "I"
see appearances as utterly true and cling to them,
but when you view things through wisdom trained in scripture
and reason and the eye of detailed examination,
then the object of clinging, the fiend of self-grasping,
is seen like a lotus in the realm of space.

Through beginningless previous lives, in my heart
I've construed the "I" as if it really, truly existed,
but today, this old heap, inducing
so many regrets, has fled to the empty realm.[1564]

In the vast expanse of the spacious Dharma realm,
the wisdom that discriminates distinctive meanings
spins the spear of awareness with sharpened mind
and strikes and pierces the heart inside the breast
of the enemy within, self-grasping.

1562. Bz*MLNJ* 2b–3b [732–34].

1563. Reading *gnyen* for *gnyan*.

1564. Cf. the translation of the three previous verses in Guenther 1976, 120.

By virtue of that, all things, as many as there are,
dissolve in the naturally virtuous play of the Dharma realm,
free from other people's deluded exaggeration and understatement.

Mind, that she-fish that darts about,
lives deep in the sea of the Dharma realm that's free from extremes;
she enjoys the water play, delighting in every experience,
and has no concern for the waves of grasping at things.

The mind that's been frightened before by saṃsāric terrors
will not see at all the nirvāṇic goal
that's naturally different from saṃsāra,
even when it seeks liberation on the excellent path.

I am the yogī of unarisen sky:
no evil actions arise that I must reject,
and there is no virtuous path to perfect,
so I sleep within the inseparability of saṃsāra and nirvāṇa.

In the splendid, all-good Dharma realm,
not an atom of white or black karma is conceived,
nor can you fall onto the wrong path, the nihilistic extreme—
this is the point of ascertaining deep emptiness.

The āryas see the various appearances of saṃsāra
and nirvāṇa as unimpeded brilliance
and whatever appears as illusion's grand play,
so they're free from the abyss of eternal despair.

When I, the yogī of falsehood
and illusion, gazed upon all things,
they clearly revealed their actual duplicitousness
where they could not stand on their own.

I considered the key point of deep Dharma,
and when I heard the good news, deeply resounding,
"The foundation of saṃsāric existence has crumbled,"
I enjoyed blissful thoughts deep within.[1565]

1565. Cf. the translation of the last two verses in Guenther 1976, 123.

"The path whose nature is empty
dependent arising is the living path to liberation."
The Buddha's word, the sūtras and tantras, is established on the basis of valid cognition,
but whether I have little instruction or all, it's delightful: it's a trove of delight.

I touch the feet of Jé, the guru who has the meaning transmission,
the scholar-siddha who manifests
this supreme path seized from the Buddha.
May all the upholders of the words of the higher tantras dwell in bliss.

19[1566]

Namo Guru Mañjughoṣāya!

To one with the far-ranging eye, who knows as united
the middle path free from eternalism-and-nihilism
and the door to the dependent arising of various appearances,
to the great Mādhyamika, Sumati,
and the exalted one inseparable from him, Ensapa, I appeal:
please think lovingly of your devoted son,
and bless me to uproot
the enemy, grasping at self.

As if they're afflicted by tainted food
or defective vision or tumors,
beings grasp at self when there is no self
and choose pain in beginningless saṃsāra.

In the fertile field of bad karma,
the clever sow seeds of consciousness
and keep them moist with water from the river of craving.
Various sprouts of name and form
arise continually in this world of the six types of beings,
who are tormented forever and without respite

1566. Bz*MLNJ* 4b–5a [734–35].

by the painful hailstones of aging, death, and other afflictions:
fools purchase their own suffering.

When, drawn on by the path
of scripture and reasoning you see reality
face to face through discernment that realizes truthlessness,
when there is no saṃsāra or nirvāṇa,
then where could even the name of suffering occur?

In the spacious expanse of true emptiness,
the king, awareness and knowledge, soars high in the sky.

Any and all arising things are taken as the Dharma body,
and in postmeditation, whatever appearances arise
are seen to arise as empty from the start,
like a dream, the moon's image in water,
or substances charmed by magical spells.

Though dependent arising of cause and effect is unerring,
objects of knowledge have not an atom of real, true existence;
through display that is naturally empty,
the cause and effect of black and white deeds is manifest.

I do not see a single thing in saṃsāra
or nirvāṇa that exists as anything
but as a name that's merely labeled by thought.

Severing the root of self-grasping
with the sharp sword of wisdom,
meditating on nothing but the definitive meaning,
making no effort to squeeze out suffering,
I rest happily in the abiding nature.

When I'm aware of my nature, the friend I've known so long,
then all arising objects of the six sense collections
show themselves to be my own nature,
and the path arises as the play of labeling by thought.

When I maintain focus on the nature of whatever arises,
there is no cause for stopping true existence

and no cause for accomplishing truthlessness—
this is the unfixed yoga. O joy!

20[1567]

Namo Guru Mañjughoṣāya!

May Losang Drakpa—who saw as it is
the meaning of emptiness and dependent arising, the natural
essence of the Buddha's eighty-four thousand Dharmas—
remain forever an inseparable ornament at my crown.

Because things are empty of their own intrinsic nature,
they arise dependently, and because they arise dependently, they're empty;
this middle path, the union of appearance and emptiness—
e ma ho! May I gain it today through the guru's kindness.

Ha ha! Aware of my penchant for falsehood,
I have no cause for elsewhere attaining truth;
attaining the meaning of having no cause for attaining,
seeing the show where there is no cause for seeing—
e ma ho! I take up this song of expansive joy.

Pervading every knowable thing, as many as there are,
the primordial, abiding nature of every phenomenon
is free from every elaborated sign;
the varied elaborations of good and bad appear
like rainbows along their paths in the sky—
I see them as a grand illusion machine.

Ha ha! Aware of my penchant for falsehood,
I have no cause for elsewhere attaining truth;
attaining the meaning of having no cause for attaining,
seeing the show where there is no cause for seeing—
e ma ho! I take up this song of expansive joy.

1567. Bz*MLNJ* 4a–5b [735–38].

Birth, aging, sickness, death, and other afflictions are fearsome;
relief for those weary from wandering through saṃsāric existence
is found in maintaining carefree, childlike awareness
within suchness, reality.

Without further shifting between appearance and emptiness,
you know mere appearance itself as emptiness,
and mere emptiness itself dawns as appearance;
know that whatever dawns is wide-open Dharma body,
like a mighty ocean with its waves.

Ha ha! Aware of my penchant for falsehood,
I have no cause for elsewhere attaining truth;
attaining the meaning of having no cause for attaining,
seeing the show where there is no cause for seeing—
e ma ho! I take up this song of expansive joy.

Things that appear as truly existent and objects to which you cling:
when you examine those things using trustworthy reasons,
you see them as objects that cannot be shown,
unarisen, like a lotus in the sky.

Awareness and the visible realm inseparable,
the yoga of the space-like meditative equipoise,
where you settle gently without excitement or dullness—
that's what the conquerors in the three times meant.

Ha ha! Aware of my penchant for falsehood,
I have no cause for elsewhere attaining truth;
attaining the meaning of having no cause for attaining,
seeing the show where there is no cause for seeing—
e ma ho! I take up this song of expansive joy.

My ancient mothers who cling to utterly false
appearances as if they were true—when I see how they are,
I take to heart the mind of compassion and the understanding
that they have no intrinsic nature: the union of method and wisdom.
Practicing this postmeditation yoga of illusion
is the way of life of the transmission siddhas.

Ha ha! Aware of my penchant for falsehood,
I have no cause for elsewhere attaining truth;
attaining the meaning of having no cause for attaining,
seeing the show where there is no cause for seeing—
e ma ho! I take up this song of expansive joy.

The hearing transmission of that second Buddha,
Nāgarjunapāda, and old father Losang Drakpa:
this practice of the profound Madhyamaka path
is the single excellent path traversed
by the buddhas of the three times and their children.

Ha ha! Aware of my penchant for falsehood,
I have no cause for elsewhere attaining truth;
attaining the meaning of having no cause for attaining,
seeing the show where there is no cause for seeing—
e ma ho! I take up this song of expansive joy.

The mass of contradictory falsehoods
I have uttered and the yoga of truth have a common basis:
when you have the eye that sees that all is unseen,
that is the Dharma banner[1568] without a Dharma.

By virtue of this, may all beings beguiled by illusion
understand all things of saṃsāra and nirvāṇa as false;
obtaining the dream-like three buddha bodies,
may they teach the echo-like Dharma.

21[1569]

Namo Guru!

I go for refuge from the depths of my heart
to Jé, the guru who leads us along the path,

1568. Also a reference to the author's name: *chos kyi rgyal mtshan.*

1569. Bz*MLNJ* 11a–b [749–50].

and the infallible refuge, the Triple Gem,
and appeal to them with intense and powerful longing.

There are hindrances, vices, and obstacles to the arising
of higher path-realizations; the means of purification
is mainly to gather the collections and purify obscurations
by the sevenfold worship rite of pure aspiration.

Reject desire for the vulgar body, meditate on yourself as divine;
recite dhāraṇīs and mantras as empty speech:
the key to meditation is to rest the mind on a single point,
without straying away from its object.

In the practice of nonconceptual concentration of mind,
the principal enemies are two: excitement and dullness;
if your basic object is unclear or stagnant,
the hindrances of dullness and confusion arise, and you're gripped by great danger.

When you apprehend mind as merely clear
and aware, or meditate on the body as a divine body,
if the hindrances of instability or mental projection occur,
bear in mind that the objects are projected
by one of three foes—anger, attachment,
or delusion—and rely on the antidote.

If you're prone to project objects in different directions
through some manifest working of the three poisons,
turn your projection of any object, anywhere,
into the unwavering mind of excellent awareness.

If imagining mind as divine does not make you happy,
then completely reject thoughts born of the three poisons,
and at all times, without forgetting, be mindful
of the nature of mind—clear and aware.

22[1570]

Namo mahāmudrāya!

O incomparably kind father guru Jé,
please dwell as lord on the anthers of my lotus heart.

The basis, the free and favored human form, is hard to attain,
does not last long, and is easily destroyed,
so, killing complacency and idleness in my mindstream,
I should strive to practice without indolence.

I go for refuge, from the depths of my heart,
to the infallible refuges, the guru and the Triple Gem,
and arouse love, compassion, and the supreme awakening mind
for my mothers, saṃsāric sentient beings of the triple world.

My mind replete with respect and devotion tinged with tenderness,
I contemplate the profound path of guru yoga.

Through beginningless previous lives until now,
I have wandered in saṃsāra, compelled by deluded mind;
now that I'm aware of my penchant for delusion,
I see mind's own open face as emptiness.

The actual primordial nature of all things,
the vajra mind inseparable from truth,
this uncontrived and easy placement of mind—
is the practice of the mahāmudrā path.

Whatever good or bad appearances now arise
are nothing more than objects
depicted by my very own mind,
discarded in the realm beyond expression, the Dharma realm.

The body is a divine body of inseparable appearance and emptiness,
speech is the vajra recitation of empty sound,

1570. Bz*MLNJ* 12b–13a [752–53].

mind is the mahāmudrā of bliss and emptiness—
may I rest in unwavering equipoise upon these forever.

Unaffected by the poison of grasping after signs,
I dedicate to great awakening the splendid merit I've amassed.

Appendix A: The Geluk Mahāmudrā Uncommon Proximate Lineage

Figures in bold appear in the latest version of the *Mahāmudrā Lineage Prayer.* Figures in italics authored important texts on mahāmudrā. Those designated with a P are disciples of Paṇchen Chögyen, those with a Y disciples of Yeshé Gyaltsen.

1. Vajradhara

2. Mañjughoṣa

3. Tsongkhapa
(1357–1419)

First Dalai Lama Gendun Drup
(1391–1474)

Khedrup Norsang Gyatso
(1423–1513)

Second Dalai Lama Gendun Gyatso
(1475–1542)

Paṇchen Sönam Drakpa
(1478–1554)

Third Dalai Lama Sönam Gyatso
(1543–88)

Khöntön Paljor Lhundrup
(1561–1637)

4. Tokden Jampal Gyatso
(1356–1428)

5. Baso Chökyi Gyaltsen
(1402–73)

6. Dharmavajra (Chökyi Dorjé)
(b. 15th c.)

7. Gyalwa Ensapa
(1505–66)

8. Khedrup Sangyé Yeshé
(1525–91)

9. First Paṇchen Losang Chögyen
(1570–1662)

Khedrup Jé
(1385–1438)
↓

(Ü-TSANG-BASED)

Fifth Dalai Lama Losang Gyatso
(1617–82) P

10. Drupchen Gendun Gyaltsen
(1532–1607) P

(AMDO-BASED)

Shar Kalden Gyatso
(1607–77) P

23. Drungpa Tsöndru Gyaltsen
(1557–1650) P

11. Drupai Gyaltsen Dzinpa
(17th c.) P

12. Könchok Gyaltsen
(1612–87) P

13. Second Paṇchen Losang Yeshé
(1663–1737)

14. Losang Trinlé
(1642–1708/15)

15. Drupwang Losang Namgyal
(1670–1741)

16. *Kachen Yeshé Gyaltsen*
(1713–93)

17. Phurchok Ngawang Jampa
(1682–1762) Y

18. Third Paṇchen Palden Yeshé
(1738–81) Y

19. Khedrup Ngawang Dorjé
(1720–1803)

Gugé Losang Tenzin
(1748–1813) Y

20. *Ngulchu Dharmabhadra*
(1772–1851)

Keutsang Losang Jamyang
(b. 1791?)

21. Yangchen Drupai Dorjé
(1809–87)

22. Khedrup Tenzin Tsöndrü
(b. 19th c.)

24. Losang Dönyö Drupa
(17th c.)

25. Drupkangpa Gelek Gyatso
(1641–1713)

Jamyang Shepai Dorjé
(1648–1721)

26. Phurchok Ngawang Jampa
(1682–1762) Y

Changkya Rölpai Dorjé
(1717–86) Y

27. Kunkhyen Jikmé Wangpo
(1728–91)

Thuken Losang Chökyi Nyima
(1737–1802)

28. *Gungthang Tenpai Drönmé*
(1762–1823) Y

29. Jetsun Könchok Gyaltsen
(1764–1853)

Gyalrong Tsultrim Nyima
(18th–19th c.)

Akhu Sherab Gyatso
(1803–75)

30. Drupchen Ngödrup Rabten
(18th–19th c.)

31. Yongzin Gendun Gyatso
(1850–86)

32. Palden Tenpai Nyima
(19th–20th c.)

33. Phabongkha Rinpoché Dechen Nyingpo (1878–1941)

34. Trijang Rinpoché Losang Yeshé Tenzin Gyatso (1901–81)

35. Ling Rinpoché Thupten Lungtok Namgyal Trinlé (1903–83)

36. *Fourteenth Dalai Lama Tenzin Gyatso* (1935–)

Appendix B: The Geluk Mahāmudrā Uncommon Distant Lineage

This listing is according to the lineage identified by Kachen Yeshé Gyaltsen. Conjectural members have been added in square brackets in the chronological gap between Milarepa and Chenga Chökyi Gyalpo.

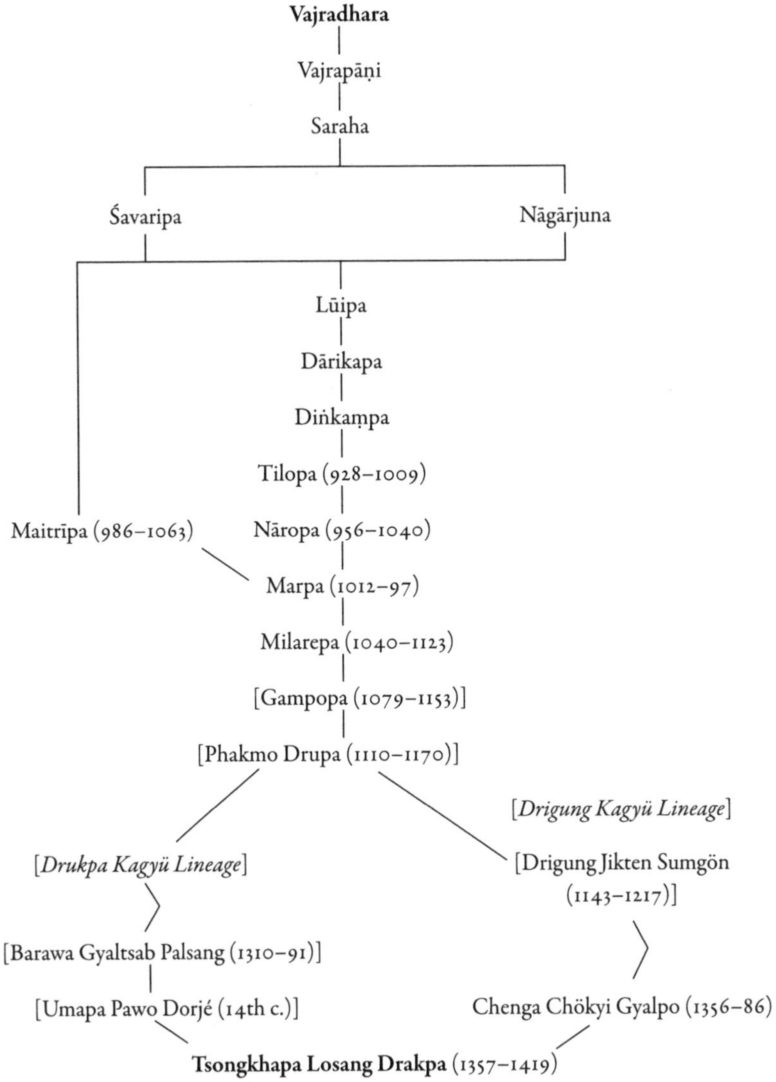

Appendix C: Keutsang Jamyang Mönlam's Outline of *Highway of the Conquerors*

The outline below appears in Keutsang's *Excellent and Completely Virtuous Path to Freedom*, which is discussed above on pp. 287–89. The page and line number for two editions is supplied alongside the relevant verses subsumed under each heading. The bracketed, unnumbered section titles are included to show the relation between Keutsang's text divisions and the major text divisions of Paṇchen Chögyen's *Lamp So Bright,* as translated above.

S Ke'u tshang Blo bzang 'jam dbyangs smon lam. *Dge ldan snyan brgyud kyi bka' srol phyag rgya chen po'i zin bris rnam grol kun tu dge ba'i lam bzang.* In: *Ke'u tshang Blo bzang 'jam dbyangs smon lam gyi gsung 'bum,* 2:7–149.

Z Ke'u tshang Blo bzang 'jam dbyangs smon lam. *Zab lam snyan brgyud phyag rgya chen po'i man ngag gi phyogs bsgrigs rgyal ba'i lam bzang gsal ba'i sgron me.* In *LZGM*, 90–259.

[Introduction]

1. Generating a method of entering into the treatise (S 12.2, Z 93.6; no root verses)
2. An explanation in harmony with the actual meaning of the treatise (S 14.4; Z 95.18; verses 1–46)
    1. Undertaking the composition (S 14.4, Z 96.2; verses 1–2)
        1. Expression of worship (S 14.4, Z 96.3; verse 1)
        2. Promise to compose (S 17.6, Z 99.18; verse 2)

[The Actual Instruction]

2. Explanation of the actual instruction (S 20.6, Z 103.10; verses 3–46)

[Preparation]

1. Preparation (S 20.6, Z 103.12; verses 3–5)
    1. Making effort in refuge and the awakening mind (S 20.6, Z 103.14; verse 3)

2. Preparatory accumulation and purification (S 31.4, Z 116.11; verse 4)
3. Making repeated requests (S 43.3, Z 130.9; verse 5)

[Various Modes of Explanation]

2. Main practice (S 52.2, Z 141.7; verses 6–38)
  1. Mode of division (S 52.3, Z 141.8; verse 6)
  2. Direct explanation of the divisions (S 52.4, Z 141.13; verses 7–38)
    1. Mahāmudrā of the mantra system (S 52.5, Z 141.15; verses 7–8)
    2. Mahāmudrā of the sūtra system (S 54.7, Z 144.13; verses 9–38)
      1. The way of indicating the subject, the mind (S 55.1. Z 144.15; verses 9–27)
        1. Resetting the thesis by way of correct reasons (S 55.2, Z 144.17; verses 9–10)
        2. Resolving doubts about multiple names [of traditions], and identifying the stages of meditation by rolling [the traditions] into one (S 56.1, Z 146.2; verses 11–13)

[Serenity]

3. The way of maintaining [stability] at the time of causal practice (S 60.4, Z 151.10; verses 14–23)
  1. Preparatory reliance on the collection of causes (S 60.5, Z 151.11; verses 14–15)
  2. The main practice of maintaining [stability on] the object (S 71.6; Z 164.18; verses 16–23)
    1. Identifying the object (S 71.6, Z 165.1; verse 16)
    2. Explaining the way to maintain [stability] (S 75.3, Z 169.3; verses 17–23)
      1. The way to maintain mindfulness in general (S 75.3, Z 169.4; verse 17)
      2. The way to maintain [stability] in particular (S 82.5, S 177.16; verses 18–23)
        1. The way to maintain [stability] via new mindfulness (S 75.3, Z 178.1; verse 18ab)
        2. The way to maintain [stability] via old mindfulness (S 83.4, Z 178.19; verse 18cd)
        3. The way to maintain [stability] via timely demarcation (S 84.6, Z 180.9; verses 19–20)
        4. The way to maintain [stability] via conventions known to others (S 86.3, Z 182.9; verse 21)

5. The way to maintain [stability] via the self-stopping of concepts (S 87.7, Z 184.4; verses 22–23)
4. The way [things] arise at the time of resultant accomplishment (S 89.6, Z 186.12; verses 24–27)
1. Identification (S 89.6, Z 186.13; verse 24)
2. Indication (S 92.5, Z 189.20; verses 25–27)
1. Wrong view (S 92.5, Z 190.1; verses 25–26)
2. Apprehending the unmistaken indication (S 93.6, Z 191.6; verse 27)

[INSIGHT]

2. The way of indicating the object, the Dharma realm (S 94.2, Z 191.18; verses 28–38)
1. Promise to explain (S 94.3, Z 192.1; verse 28)
2. The way to carry this out through practice (S 103.4, Z 203.6; verses 29–38)
1. Reliance on the collection [factors] for insight (S 104.4, Z 203.7; no verses)
2. The way to meditate on insight (S 104.1, Z 204.1; verses 29–38)
1. Identifying the subtle object of refutation (S 104.2, Z 204.2; verse 29)
2. The way of establishing, through meditation on lack of self, that [things] exist imputedly (S 113.5, Z 215.10; verses 30–38)
1. The way to meditate based on oneself (S 113.6, Z 215.12; verses 30–31b)
2. The way to apply that based on others (S 121.6, Z 225.12; verses 31b–32)
3. Alternatively, the way to view the mind (S 126.7, Z 231.16; verses 33–35)
4. In brief, the way to view whatever appears (S 132.6, Z 238.14; verses 36–38)

[FOLLOW-UP]

3. The after-stages (S 137.3, Z 244.5; verses 39–45)
1. The stage of dedication of the roots of virtue (S 137.4, Z 244.6; verse 39)

2. The stage of clearing away obstacles to improvement (S 138.1, Z 244.18; verses 40–44)
3. The stage of manifesting the excellent path (S 142.7, Z 250.17; verse 45)

[FINAL DEDICATION]

3. Dedication of the merit from having completed the work (S 145.3, Z 253.19; verse 46)

Final verses (S 147.3, Z 256.5)
Colophon (S 148.5, Z 257.17)

Bibliography

Indic Sources

AdCS: *Āryadeva. Catuḥśatakaśāstra. Bstan bcos bzhi brgya pa.* Dergé Tengyur (no. 3721). Dbu ma, *tsha* 1–18a.

AgGP: Aśvaghoṣa. *Gurupañcāśikā. Bla ma lnga bcu pa.* Dergé Tengyur (no. 3846). Rgyud, *tshu* 10a–12a.

AN: Aṅguttara-nikāya. Edited by R. Morris. 5 vols. Rpt. London: Luzac & Co. 1958.

ANS: Abhiniṣkramaṇasūtra. Mngon par byung ba'i mdo. Dergé Kangyur (no. 301). Mdo sde, *sa* 1b–125a.

ASPs: Aṣṭasāhasrikāprajñāpāramitā. Edited by P. L. Vaidya. Buddhist Sanskrit Texts Series 4. Darbhanga: Mithila Institute, 1960.

ASPt: *Aṣṭasāhasrikāprajñāpāramitā. Shes rab kyi pha rol tu phyin pa khri brgyad stong pa.* Lhasa Kangyur (no. 12). Khri brgyad, *ka* 1b–453a, *kha* 1b–449a, *ga* 1b–317a.

As*YB:* Asaṅga. **Yogācārabhūmi-viniścayasaṃgrahaṇī. Rnal 'byor spyod pa'i sa rnam par gtan la dbab pa bsdu ba.* Dergé Tengyur (no. 4038). Sems tsam, *zhi* 1b–289a, *zi* 1b–127a.

At*AV:* Atiśa. *Abhisamayavibhaṅga. Mngon par rtogs pa rnam par 'byed pa.* Dergé Tengyur (no. 1490). Rgyud, *zha* 186a–202b.

At*BK:* Atiśa. **Bodhipathakrama. Byang chub lam gyi rim pa.* In *Bka' gdams gsung 'bum phyogs bsgrigs glegs bam go chig*, edited by Dpal brtsegs bod yig dpe rnying zhib 'jug khang, 21–63. Ziling: Krung go'i bod rig pa dpe skrun khang, 2015.

At*BP:* Atiśa. *Bodhimārgapradīpapañjikā. Byang chub lam gyi sgron ma'i dka' 'grel.* Dergé Tengyur (no. 3948). Dbu ma, *khi* 241a–293a.

At*LC:* Atiśa. *Jo bo rjes dgon pa ba la gnang ba'i phyag chen.* In *Atiśa gsung 'bum*, 876–78. Beijing: Khrung go'i bod rig pa dpe skrung khang, 2006.

At*MS:* Atiśa. *Mahāyānapathasādhanavarṇasaṃgraha. Theg pa chen po'i lam gyi sgrub thabs yi ger bsdus pa.* Dergé Tengyur (no. 3954). Dbu ma, *khi* 299a–302b.

At*SA:* Atiśa. *Satyadvayāvatara. Bden gnyis la 'jug pa.* Dergé Tengyur (no. 3902). Dbu ma, *a* 72a–73a.

At*TG:* Atiśa. *Lta sgom chen mo.* In *Atiśa gsung 'bum*, 628–42. Beijing: Khrung go'i bod rig pa dpe skrung khang, 2006.

At*VG:* Atiśa. *Vajrāsanavajragīti. Rdo rje gdan gyi rdo rje glu.* Dergé Tengyur (no. 1494). Rgyud, *zha* 208a–209b.

At*VV:* Atiśa. *Vajrāsanavajragītivṛtti. Rdo rje gdan gyi rdo rje glu'i 'grel pa.* Dergé Tengyur (no. 1495). Rgyud, *zha* 209b–215a.

BAS: *Buddhāvataṃsakasūtra. Sangs rgyas phal po che mdo.* Lhasa Kangyur (no. 94). Phal chen, *ka–cha.*

Bj*MA*: Buddhaśrījñānapāda. *Dvikramatattvabhāvanānāmamukhāgama. Rim pa gnyis pa'i de kho na nyid bsgom pa zhes bya ba'i zhal gyi lung.* Dergé Tengyur (no. 1853). Rgyud, *di* 1b–17b.

BKT: *Buddhakapālatantra. Sangs rgyas thod pa'i rgyud.* Lhasa Kangyur (no. 400). Rgyud, *nga* 5b–43b.

Bv*MH*: Bhāvaviveka. [Bhāviveka.] *Madhyamakahṛdaya. Dbu ma'i snying po.* Dergé Tengyur (no. 3855). Dbu ma, *dza* 1b–40b.

Cg*ST*: Candragomin. *Deśanāstava. Bshags pa'i bstod pa.* Dergé Tengyur (no. 1159). Bstod tshogs, *ka* 204a–206b.

Ck*MA*: Candrakīrti. *Madhyamakāvatāra. Dbu ma la 'jug pa.* Dergé Tengyur (no. 3861). Dbu ma, *'a* 201b–219a.

Ck*VS*: Candrakīrti. *Vajravārāhītārāstotra. Rdo rje phag mo sgrol ma la bstod pa.* Dergé Tengyur (no. 1724). Rgyud, *sha* 91a–b.

DHP: *Dhammapada: A Practical Guide to Right Living.* Trans. Buddharakkhita Thera. Bangalore: Buddha Vacana Trust, 1966.

Dh*SS*: Ḍombī Heruka. *Sahajasiddhi.* In *Guhyādi-Aṣṭasiddhi-Saṃgraha* (*Gsang ba grub pa la sogs pa'i grub pa sde brgyad*), edited by Samdhong Rinpoche and Vrajallabha Dvivedi, 185–91. Rare Buddhist Text Series 1. Sārnāth: Central Institute of Higher Tibetan Studies, 1987. See also Shendge 1967.

Dk*PV*: Dharmakīrti. *Pramāṇavārttika. Tshad ma rnam 'grel.* Dergé Tengyur (no. 4210). Tshad ma, *ce* 94b–151a.

DZG: *Do ha mdzod brgyad ces bya ba phyag rgya chen po'i man ngag gsal bar ston pa'i gzhung.* Darjeeling: Kargyu Sungrab Nyamso Khang, 1978–85.

GPS: *Gaganagañjaparipṛcchā. Nam mkha'i mdzod pa zhus ba.* Lhasa Kangyur (no. 149). Mdo sde, *na* 319a–460b.

GST: Francesca Fremantle. "A Critical Study of the Guhyasamāja Tantra." Ph.D. dissertation. School of Oriental and African Studies, 1971.

HKS: *Hastikakayasūtra. Glang po'i rtsal ba'i mdo.* Lhasa Kangyur (no. 208). Mdo sde, *ma* 147a–169b.

HVT: David Snellgrove, ed. and trans. *The Hevajra Tantra: A Critical Study: Sanskrit Text, Tibetan Texts and English Rendering.* 2 vols. London: Oxford University Press, 1959. See also Farrow and Menon 1992.

Ib*JS*: Indrabhūti. *Jñānasiddhi.* In *Guhyādi-Aṣṭasiddhi-Saṃgraha* (*Gsang ba grub pa la sogs pa'i grub pa sde brgyad*), edited by Samdhong Rinpoche and Vrajallabha Dvivedi, 89–157. Rare Buddhist Text Series 1. Sārnāth: Central Institute of Higher Tibetan Studies, 1987. See also Mishra 1993.

JGT: *Jñānagarbhatantra. Ye shes snying po 'i rgyud.* Lhasa Kangyur, (no. 381). Rgyud sde, *ka* 472b–482a.

Jk*TA*: Jñānakīrti. *Tattvāvatārākhyasakalasugatavacastātparyavyākhyāprakaraṇa. De kho na nyid la 'jug pa zhes bya ba bde bar gshegs pa'i bka' ma lus pa mdor bsdus te bshad pa'i rab tu byed pa.* Dergé Tengyur (no. 3709). Rgyud, *tsu* 39a–76a.

Jk*TT*: Jñānakīrti. *Tattvadaśakaṭīkā. De kho na nyid bcu pa'i rgya cher 'grel pa.* Dergé Tengyur (no. 2254). Rgyud, *wi* 160b–177a.

KCT: *Kālacakratantrarājā. Rgyud kyi rgyal po dpal dus kyi 'khor lo.* Lhasa Kangyur (no. 373). Rgyud sde, *ka* 28b–186b.

Kk*HS:* Kukuripa. *Mahāmāyātantrānusāriṇīherukasādhanopāyika. Sgyu 'phrul chen mo'i rgyud kyi rjes su 'brang ba'i he ru ka'i sgrub pa'i thabs.* Dergé Tengyur (no. 1627). Rgyud, *ya* 228b1–230b2.

Kk*VS:* Kukuripa. *Vajrasattvasādhana. Rdo rje sems dpa'i sgrub thabs.* Dergé Tengyur (no. 1628). Rgyud, *ya* 286b–287a.

Km*BK:* Kamalaśīla. *Bhāvanākrama I. Bsgom pa'i rim pa.* Dergé Tengyur (no. 3915). Dbu ma, *ya* 22a–41b.

KPS: Kāśyapaparivarta. 'Od srung gi le'u. Lhasa Kangyur (no. 87). Dkon brtsegs, *cha* 211a–260b.

Lk*AS:* Lakṣmīṅkarā. *Advayasiddhi.* In *Guhyādi-Aṣṭasiddhi-Saṃgraha* (*Gsang ba grub pa la sogs pa'i grub pa sde brgyad*), edited by Samdhong Rinpoche and Vrajallabha Dvivedi, 161–64. Rare Buddhist Text Series 1. Sārnāth: Central Institute of Higher Tibetan Studies, 1987. Cf. Mishra 1993, 28–30.

Ma*MA:* Maitreya. *Mahāyānasūtrālaṃkāra. Theg pa chen po mdo sde'i rgyan.* Dergé Tengyur (no. 4020). Sems tsam, *phi* 1b–39a.

Ma*MV:* Maitreya. *Madhyāntavibhāga. Dbus dang mtha' rnam par 'byed pa.* Dergé Tengyur (no. 4021). Sems tsam, *phi* 43b–48b.

Mk*GA:* Mañjuśrīkīrti. *Sarvaguhyavidhigarbhālaṃkāra. Gsang ba thams cad kyi spyi'i cho ga'i snying po rgyan.* Dergé Tengyur (no. 2490). Rgyud, *zi* 232b–243b.

MMK: Mañjuśrīmūlakalpa. In *Mahāyānasūtrasaṃgraha*, part II, edited by P. L. Vaidya. Buddhist Sanskrit Texts Series 18. Darbhanga: Mithila Institute, 1964.

MMT: Mahāmudrātilakam. Phyag rgya chen po'i thig le. Lhasa Kangyur (no. 380). Rgyud sde, *ka* 433b–472b.

MNS: Alex Wayman, trans. and annot. *Chanting the Names of Mañjuśrī: The Mañjuśrī-Nāma-Saṃgīti, Sanskrit and Tibetan Texts.* Boston: Shambala, 1985. See also Davisdon 1981.

Mt*CA:* Maitrīpa. *Caturmudrānvaya. Phyag rgya bzhi rjes su bstan pa.* In Mathes 2015, 389–402; trans. 120–27.

Mt*DP:* Advayavajra [Maitrīpa]. *Dohākoṣapañjikā. De* [sic] *ha mdzod kyi dka' 'grel.* Dergé Tengyur (no. 2256). Rgyud, *wi* 180b–207a.

Mt*MD:* Maitrīpa. *Shes pa spro bsdu med par 'jog pa'i man ngag gsang ba dam pa.* [*Upadeśaparama*]. In Mathes 2015, 507–9; trans. 269–71.

Mt*MK:* Maitrīpa. *Mahāmudrākanakamālā. Phyag rgya chen po gser phreng.* In Mathes 2015, 511–42; trans. 273–311.

Mt*SN:* Maitrīpa. *Sekanirdeśa. Dbang bskur nges par bstan pa.* In Mathes 2015, 385–88 (stanzas 26–36); trans. 107–9. Cf. the complete edition and translation in Isaacson and Sferra, 2014.

Mt*SP:* Advayavajra [Maitrīpa]. *Saṃkṣiptasekaprakriyā. Dbang gi bya ba mdor bsdus pa.* Dergé Tengyur (no. 2244). Rgyud, *wi* 125b–134b.

Mt*TD:* Advayavajra [Maitrīpa]. *Tattvadaśaka. De kho na nyid bcu pa.* Dergé Tengyur (no. 2236). Rgyud, *wi* 112b–113a.

Mt*TV:* Maitrīpa. *Tattvaviṃśaka. De kho na nyid theg pa chen po nyi shu pa.* In Mathes 2015, 457–63; trans. 187–90. Cf. Shastri 1927, 52–53.

Ng*BV:* Nāgārjuna. *Bodhicittavivaraṇa. Byang chub sems gyi 'grel pa.* Dergé Tengyur (no. 1400). Rgyud, *ngi* 38a–42b.

Ng*MKs*: Nāgārjuna. *Madhyamakakārikā.* In Mark Siderits and Shōryū Katsura.

Nāgārjuna's Middle Way: Mūlamadhyamakakārikā. Boston: Wisdom Publications, 2013.

Ng*MK*t: Nāgārjuna. *Prajñānāmamūlamadhyamakakārikā. Dbu ma rtsa ba'i tshig le'ur byas pa shes rab ces bya ba*. Dergé Tengyur (no. 3824). Dbu ma, *tsa* 1b–19a.

Ng*PK:* [Nāgārjuna.] *Pañcakrama: Sanskrit and Tibetan Texts Critically Edited with Verse Index and Facsimile Edition of the Sanskrit Manuscript*. Edited by Katsumi Mimaki and Tōru Tomabechi. Biblioteca Codicum Asiaticorum 8. Tokyo: The Centre for East Asian Studies for Unesco, 1994.

Ng*PK*t: Nāgārjuna/Śākyamitra (II). *Pañcakrama. Rim pa lnga*. Dergé Tengyur (no. 1802). Rgyud, *ngi* 45a–57a.

Ng*PS:* Nāgārjuna/Rahulabhadra. *Prajñāpāramitāstotra. Shes rab kyi pha rol tu phyin ma'i bstod pa*. Dergé Tengyur (no. 1127). Bstod tshogs, *ka* 76a–b.

Ng*RA:* Nāgārjuna. *Ratnāvalī. Rin po che'i phreng ba*. Dergé Tengyur (no. 4158). Skyes rab/ Spring yig, *ge* 107a–126a.

Nr*AP:* Nāropa. *Ajñāsaṃyakpramāṇanāmaḍākinyupadeśa. Bka' yang dang pa'i tshad ma shes bya ba mkha' 'gro ma'i man ngag*. Dergé Tengyur (no. 2331). Rgyud, *shi* 271a–273a.

Nr*AS:* Nāropa. *Adhisidhisamā. Lta ba mdor bsdus pa*. In *Do ha mdzod brgyad ces bya ba phyag rgya chen po'i man ngag gsal bar ston pa'i gzhung*, 21a–24a. Darjeeling: Kargyu Sungrab Nyamso Khang, 1978–85.

Nr*GP:* Yaśobhadra/Nāropa. *Sarvaguhyapradīpaṭīkā. Gsang ba thams cad kyi sgron ma'i rgya cher 'grel pa*. Dergé Tengyur (no. 1787). Rgyud, *ha* 203b–234a.

Nr*KG:* Nāropa. *Karṇatantravajragāthā. Snyan brgyud rdo rje'i tshig rkang*. Dergé Tengyur (no. 2338). Rgyud, *zhi* 302b–304b.

Nr*MS:* Nāropa. *Mahāmudrāsaṅgamita. Phyag rgya chen po tshig bsdus pa*. In *Do ha mdzod brgyad ces bya ba phyag rgya chen po'i man ngag gsal bar ston pa'i gzhung*, 24a–26a. Darjeeling: Kargyu Sungrab Nyamso Khang, 1978–85.

Nr*PS:* Nāropa/Śrīman Naḍapāda. *Pañcakramasaṃgrahaprabhāva. Rim pa lnga bsdus pa gsal ba*. Dergé Tengyur (no. 2333). Rgyud, *zhi* 276a–278a.

Nr*ST:* Nāropa. *Sekoddeśaṭīkā*. Edited by Mario Carelli. Gaekwad's Oriental Series 90. Baroda: Oriental Institute, 1941.

PHS: "The Heart Sūtra: Sanskrit Text, Translation and Commentary." In *Buddhist Wisdom: The Diamond Sutra and the Heart Sutra*, translated by Edward Conze, 79–119. New York: Vintage, 2001 [1958].

Pn*VP:* Puṇḍarīka. *Vimalaprabhā. Dri ma med pa'i 'od*. Dergé Tengyur (no. 845). Dus 'khor, *shrī* 1b–469a.

*PPG*s: *Ratnaguṇasañcayagāthā*. In *Mahāyānasūtrasaṃgraha*, vol. 1, edited by P. L. Vaidya, 352–98. Buddhist Sanskit Texts Series 17. Darbhanga: Mithila Institute 1961.

*PPG*t: *Prajñāpāramitāsañcayagāthā. Shes rab kyi pha rol tu phyin pa sdud pa tshigs su bcad pa*. Lhasa Kangyur (no. 17). Sna tshogs, *ka* 189a–215a.

PPS: Pitāputrasamāgamanasūtra. Yab dang sras mjal ba'i mdo. Dergé Kangyur (no. 60). Dkon brtsegs, *nga* 1b–168a.

PSS: Pratyutpannebuddhasaṃmukhāvasthitasamādhisūtra. Da ltar gyi sangs rgyas mngon sum du bzhugs pa'i ting nge 'dzin gyi mdo. Lhasa Kangyur (no. 135). Mdo sde, *tha* 1b–106b.

Pv*GS*s: Padmavajra. *Guhyasiddhi*. In *Guhyādi-Aṣṭasiddhi-Saṃgraha* (*Gsang ba grub pa la sogs pa'i grub pa sde brgyad*), edited by Samdhong Rinpoche and Vrajallabha Dvivedi,

1–62. Rare Buddhist Text Series 1. Sārnāth: Central Institute of Higher Tibetan Studies, 1987.

Pv*GS*t: Padmavajra (a.k.a. Mahāusukha). *Sakalatantrasambhavasaṃcodanī-śrīguhyasiddhi. Rgyud ma lus pa'i don nges par skul bar byed pa, dpal gsang ba grub pa.* Dergé Tengyur (no. 2217). Rgyud, *wi* 1b–28b.

RGV: Ratnagotravibhāga-mahāyānottaratantraśāstra. In *The Uttaratantra of Maitreya, Containing Introduction, E. H. Johnston's Sanskrit Text and E. Obermiller's English Translation*, edited by H. S. Prasad, 69–187. Delhi: Sri Satguru Publications, 1991.

RPS: Rāṣṭrapālaparipṛcchā. Yul 'khor skyong gis zhus pa. Dergé Kangyur (no. 62). Dkon brtsegs, *nga* 227a–257a.

Rs*PU:* Ratnākaraśānti. *Prajñāpāramitopadeśa. Shes rab kyi pha rol tu phyin pa'i man ngag.* Dergé Tengyur (no. 4079). Sems tsam, *hi* 133b–162b.

Sa*BK:* Saraha. *Śrībuddhakapālatantrasya-pañjikājñānavatī. Dpal sangs rgyas thod pa'i rgyud kyi dka' 'grel ye shes ldan pa.* Dergé Tengyur (no. 1652). Rgyud, *ra* 104b–150a.

Sa*CK:* Saraha. *Cittakośājavajragīti. Thugs kyi mdzod skyes med rdo rje'i glu.* In Braitstein 2014, 204–8.

Sa*DD:* Saraha. *Dṛṣṭibhāvanācaryāphaladohāgīti. Lta bsgom spyod pa 'bras bu'i do ha'i glu.* Dergé Tengyur (no. 2345). Rgyud, *tshi* 3b–4b.

Sa*KD:* Saraha. *Dohākoṣanāmacaryāgīti. Do ha mdzod ces bya ba spyod pa'i glu.* Dergé Tengyur (no. 2263). Rgyud, *zhi* 26b–28b. See also Thrangu 2006, 141–51.

Sa*KK:* Saraha. *Kāyakoṣamṛtavajragīti. Sku mdzod 'chi med rdo rje'i glu.* In Braitstein 2014, 169–92.

Sa*PD*a: Saraha. *Dohākoṣagīti.* In R. Jackson 2004, 53–115.

Sa*PD*t: Saraha. *Dohākoṣagīti. Do ha mdzod kyi glu.* Dergé Tengyur (no. 2224). Rgyud, *wi* 70b–77a.

Sa*QD:* Saraha. *Dohākośopadeśagīti. Mi zad pa'i gter mdzod man ngag gi glu.* Dergé Tengyur (no. 2264). Rgyud, *zhi* 28b–33b.

Sa*VG:* Saraha. *Mahāmudropadeśavajraguhyagīti. Phyag rgya chen po'i man ngag rdo rje gsang ba'i glu.* Dergé Tengyur (no. 2440). Rgyud, *zi* 55b–62b.

Sa*VK:* Saraha. *Vākkoṣarucirasvaravajragīti. Sku'i mdzod 'jam dbyangs rdo rje'i glu.* In Braitstein 2014, 192–203.

SBS: Śrī-sarvabuddhasamāyoga-ḍākinījālasaṃbara-nāma-uttaratantra. Dpal sangs rgyas thams cad dang mnyam par sbyor ba mkha' 'gro ma sgyu ma bde ba'i mchog ces bya ba'i rgyud phyi ma. Lhasa Kangyur (no. 376). Rgyud sde, *ka* 246a–307a.

Sd*BA:* Śāntideva. *Bodhicaryāvatāra. Byang chub sems dpa'i spyod pa la 'jug pa.* Dergé Tengyur (no. 3861). Dbu ma, *la* 1b–40a.

*SDP*s: *Saddharmapuṇḍarīkasūtram.* Edited by P. L. Vaidya. Buddhist Sanskit Texts Series 6. Darbhanga: Mithila Institute 1960.

*SDP*t: *Saddharmapuṇḍarīkasūtra. Dam pa'i chos pad ma dkar po'i mdo.* Lhasa Kangyur (no. 116). Mdo sde, *ja* 1b–285b.

Sh*TT:* Sahajavajra. *Tattvadaśakaṭīkā. De kho na nyid bcu pa'i rgya cher 'grel pa.* Dergé Tengyur (no. 2254). Rgyud, *wi* 160b–177a.

SNS: Saṃdhinirmocanasūtra. Dgongs pa nges par 'grel pa'i mdo. Dergé Kangyur (no. 106). Mdo sde, *ca* 1b–55b.

SOT: The Samvarodaya Tantra: Selected Chapters. Edited and translated by Shinīchi Tsuda. Tokyo: The Hokuseido Press, 1974.

SPS: Sāgaramatiparipṛcchā. Blo gros rgya mtsho zhus pa. Lhasa Kangyur (no. 153). Mdo sde, *na* 1b–180a.

*SRS*s: *Samādhirāja Sūtram.* Edited by P. L. Vaidya. Buddhist Sanskit Texts Series 2. Darbhanga: Mithila Institute, 1961.

*SRS*t: *Samādhirājasūtra. Ting nge 'dzin gyi rgyal po'i mdo.* Dergé Kangyur (no. 127). Mdo sde, *da* 1a–170b.

SSS: Śrīmālādevīsiṃhanādasūtra. Lha mo dpal phreng gi seng ge'i sgra'i mdo. Lhasa Kangyur (no. 92). Dpal brtsegs, *cha* 418a–454a.

Sv*MU:* Śavaripa [or Saraha]. *Dohākoṣamahāmudropadeśa. Do ha mdzod ces bya ba phyag rgya chen po'i man ngag.* Dergé Tengyur (no. 2273). Rgyud, *zhi* 122a–124a.

Sv*SD:* Śavaripa. *Śūnyatādṛṣṭi. Stong pa nyid kyi lta ba.* Dergé Tengyur (no. 2273). Rgyud, *zi* 13a–b.

TJS: Tathāgatajñānamudrāsamādhisūtra. De bzhin gshegs pa'i ye shes kyi phyag rgya'i ting nge 'dzin gyi mdo. Dergé Kangyur (no. 131). Mdo sde, *da* 230b–253b.

Tp*AM:* Tilopa. *Acintyamahāmudrā. Rnal 'byor pa la gdams pa rang bzhin bsam gyis mi khyab pa.* Dergé Tengyur (no. 2305). Rgyud, *zhi* 245b–246b.

Tp*DK:* Tilopa. *Dohākoṣagīti.* In R. Jackson 2004, 129–41.

Tp*GM:* Tilopa. *Mahāmudropadeśa. Phyag rgya chen po'i man ngag.* Dergé Tengyur (no. 2303). Rgyud, *zhi* 242b–244a.

Tp*SO:* Tilopa. *Ṣaḍdharmopadeśa. Chos drug gi man ngag.* Dergé Tengyur (no. 1527). Rgyud, *zhi* 270a–271a.

Tp*VD:* Tilopa. *Śrīvajraḍākinīṣkāyadharma. Dpal rdo rje mkha' 'gro lus med pa'i chos.* Dergé Tengyur (no. 1527). Rgyud, *za* 84b–85b.

VAT: Mahāvairocanābhisambodhi. Snang mdzad chen po mngon par rdzogs par byang chub pa. Dergé Kangyur (no. 494). Rgyud, *tha* 151b–260a.

Vb*SK:* Vasubandhu. *Viṃśatikāvijñaptimātratāsiddhi.* In Fernando Tola and Carmen Dragonetti. *Being as Consciousness: Yogācāra Philosophy of Buddhism,* 122–33. Delhi: Motilal Banarsidass, 2004.

Vg*HP:* Vajragarbha. *Hevajrapiṇḍārthaṭīkā. Kye'i rdo rje bsdus pa'i don gyi rgya cher 'grel pa.* Dergé Tengyur (no. 1180b). Rgyud, *ka* 46b–126a.

VMT: Vajramālābhidhānatantra. Rdo rje phreng ba mngon par brjod pa'i rgyud. Lhasa Kangyur (no. 417). Rgyud sde, *ca* 1b–105b.

VPT: Vajrapāṇyabhiṣekamahātantra. Lag na rdo rje dbang bskur ba'i rgyud chen po. Lhasa Kangyur (no. 466). Rgyud, *ta* 1b–258a.

Vr*DK:* Virūpa. *Dohākoṣa. Do ha mdzod.* Dergé Tengyur (no. 2280). Rgyud, *zhi* 134a–136a.

VST: Vajrajñānasamuccayatantra. Ye shes rdo rje kun las btus pa'i rgyud. Lhasa Kangyur (no. 419). Rgyud sde, *ca* 181b–187b.

Vv*YS:* Vīryavajra. *Yoginīsaṃcaryānibandhapadārthaprakāśa. Rnal 'byor ma kun spyod kyi 'grel pa.* Dergé Tengyur (no. 1527). Rgyud, *na* 160a–176a.

Tibetan Sources

Ak*DTCG:* A khu Shes rab rgya mtsho. *Bla mchod phyag chen dang sbrags pa'i khrid kyi zin bris srid zhi gdung sel bdud rtsi'i chu rgyun.* In *A khu shes rab rgya mtsho'i gsung 'bum,* vol. *ga* 1–43a [3:355–440]. Lhasa: Zhol phar khang, 1998–99?.

Ak*LPZB:* A khu Shes rab rgya mtsho. *Bla mchod phyag chen dang sbrags pa'i khrid kyi zin* *bris*. In *A khu shes rab rgya mtsho'i gsung 'bum*, vol. *ga* 1–95a [3:185–354] Lhasa: Zhol phar khang, 1998–99?.

Bs*DMTK:* Ba so Chos kyi rgyal mtshan. *Dbu ma lta khrid chen mo*. In *Dbu ma'i lta khrid chen mo of Ba-so Chos-kyi-rgyal-mtshan: together with four other Lta-khrid and commentaries on Madhyamika, by Tshe-gliṅ Yoṅs-'dzin Ye-śes-rgyal-mtshan and the First Dalai Lama Dge-'dun-grub-pa*. New Delhi: Lha mkhar yongs 'dzin bstan pa rgyal mtshan, 1973.

Bt*TGKC:* Bu ston rin chen grub. *Bka' 'bum dkar chag*. In *Bu ston rin chen grub gyi bka' 'bum*, vol. *sa* 9–12. Delhi: International Academy of Indian Culture, 1971.

Bz*AFPL:* Blo bzang chos kyi rgyal mtshan. *The Autobiography of the First Paṇchen Lama Blo-bzang-chos-kyi-rgral-mtshan*. [*Chos smra ba'i dge slong blo bzang chos kyi rgyal mtshan gyi spyod tshul gsal bar ston pa nor bu'i phreng ba*]. Edited by Ngawang Gelek Demo, with an English introduction by E. Gene Smith. Gedan Sungrab Minyam Gyunphel Series 12. Delhi: Ngawang Gelek Demo, 1969. Also found in *Collected Works (gSuṅ 'bum) of Blo bzaṅ chos kyi rgyal mtshan, the First Paṇchen bLa ma of bKra śis lhun po* [Bkra shis lhun po edition], vol. *ka* 1–225 [1–450]. New Delhi: Mongolian Lama Gurudeva, 1973.

Bz*GBZL:* Blo bzang chos kyi rgyal mtshan. *Dge ldan bka' brgyud rin po che'i phyag chen rtsa ba rgyal ba'i gzhung lam*. In *Collected Works (gSuṅ 'bum) of Blo bzaṅ chos kyi rgyal mtshan, the First Paṇchen bLa ma of bKra śis lhun po* [Bkra shis lhun po edition], vol. *nga* 1–6 [81–89]. New Delhi: Mongolian Lama Gurudeva, 1973. Also found in *NGCS* 499–505. Also found in Pn*KYPS* 49–57. Also found in *LZGM* I–V.

Bz*LMCP(1):* Blo bzang chos kyi rgyal mtshan. *Zab lam bla ma mchod pa*. [*The Profound Path Offering to the Guru*.] Oregon, WI: Deer Park Buddhist Center, 2012. Also found in *NGCS* 303–16. Also found in *Collected Works (gSuṅ 'bum) of Blo bzaṅ chos kyi rgyal mtshan, the First Paṇchen Lama of Bkra śis lhun po* [Bkra shis lhun po edition], vol. *ka* 1–17 [777–830]. New Delhi: Mongolian Lama Gurudeva, 1973.

Bz*LMCP(2):* Blo bzang chos kyi rgyal mtshan. *Zab lam bla ma mchod pa bde stong dbyer med ma dang tshogs mchod bcas*. [*The Profound Path Offering to the Guru, Inseparable Bliss and Emptiness, Together with Its Ritual Feast*.] [India,] 1974.

Bz*LSLZ:* Blo bzang chos kyi rgyal mtshan. *Dge sbyor gyi gnad kyi dri ba snyan bskul lhag bsam rab dkar*. In *Collected Works (gSuṅ 'bum) of Blo bzaṅ chos kyi rgyal mtshan, the First Paṇchen bLa ma of bKra śis lhun po* [Bkra shis lhun po edition], vol. *nga* 1–11 [539–60]. New Delhi: Mongolian Lama Gurudeva, 1973.

Bz*MLNJ:* Blo bzang chos kyi rgyal mtshan. *Grub pa'i dbang phyug mid la la brtan pa'i bla ma'i rnal 'byor dang rnam thar du ma chud pa'i gsung mgur rnams*. In *Collected Works (gSuṅ 'bum) of Blo bzaṅ chos kyi rgyal mtshan, the First Paṇchen Lama of Bkra śis lhun po* [Bkra shis lhun po edition], vol. *ka* 1–18 [729–64]. New Delhi: Mongolian Lama Gurudeva, 1973.

Bz*PCSD:* Blo bzang chos kyi rgyal mtshan. *Phyag chen brgyud pa'i gsol 'debs*. In Bz*GBZL* 5a–6b [89–92]. Also found in *NGCS* 508–9.

Bz*TKBT:* Blo bzang chos kyi rgyal mtshan. *Dge ldan bka' brgyud rin po che'i zab lam brgyud pa'i rnam par thar pa mdor bsdud gter gyi kha byang lta bu*. In *Collected Works (gSuṅ 'bum) of Blo bzaṅ chos kyi rgyal mtshan, the First Paṇchen bLa ma of bKra śis lhun po* [Bkra shis lhun po edition], vol. *nga* 1–10 [565–84]. New Delhi: Mongolian Lama Gurudeva, 1973.

Bz*YSGM:* Blo bzang chos kyi rgyal mtshan. *Dge ldan bka' brgyud rin po che'i bka' srol phyag* *rgya chen po'i rtsa ba rgyas par bshad pa yang gsal sgron me.* In *Collected Works (gSuṅ 'bum) of Blo bzaṅ chos kyi rgyal mtshan, the First Paṇchen bLa ma of bKra śis lhun po* [Bkra shis lhun po edition], vol. *nga* 1–31 [93–154]. New Delhi: Mongolian Lama Gurudeva, 1973. Also found in *NGCS* 509–54 and in Pn*KYPS* 58–109.

Cg*PCGZ:* Karma pa Chos grags rgya mtsho, ed. *Nges don phyag rgya chen po'i rgya gzhung.* 6 vols. Xining: Mi rigs dpe skrun khang, 2009.

Ck*GTNZ:* Lcang skya Rol pa'i rdo rje. *Grub mtha' rnam gzhag pa'i thub bstan lhun po'i mdzes rgyan.* In *Lcaṅ-skya Rol-pa'i-rdo-rje gsuṅ 'bum,* vol. *cha* 1–330 [7–666]. Dharamsala: Library of Tibetan Works and Archives, 2002.

Ck*JSDL:* Lcang skya Rol pa'i rdo rje. *'Jam dbyangs bzhed pa'i sprul sku'i dris lan.* In *Lcang skya rol pa'i rdo rje gsung 'bum,* 5:101–12. Beijing: Khrung go bod brgyud mtho rim nang bstan slob gling nang bstan zhib 'jug khang, 1996.

Ck*LGDL:* Lcang skya Rol pa'i rdo rje. *Sgo mang gung ru rab 'byams pa blo gros kyi dris lan.* In *Lcang skya rol pa'i rdo rje gsung 'bum,* 5:113–58. Beijing: Khrung go bod brgyud mtho rim nang bstan slob gling nang bstan zhib 'jug khang, 1996.

Ck*TBSG:* Lcang skya Rol pa'i rdo rje. *Lta ba'i gsung mgur zab mo.* In *Lcang skya rol pa'i rdo rje gsung 'bum,* vol. *nga* 1–3 [4:389–94]. Dharamsala: Library of Tibetan Works and Archives, 2003.

Db*KPKS:* Dngul chu Dharmabhadra. *Zab lam phyag rgya chen po'i rtsa ba rgyal ba'i gzhung lam gyi steng nas zab 'khrid gnang skabs kyo zin bris 'khrul ba kun sel.* In *Collected Works (gsuṅ 'bum) of Dngul chu Dharmabhadra,* vol. *nya* [8] 1–28a [3–57]. New Delhi: Tibet House, 1981.

Dg*ZZBD:* Grags pa rgyal mtshan. *Zhen pa bzhi bral gyi gdams pa.* In *Rje btsun grags pa rgyal mtshan gyi gsung 'bum.* In *Sa skya pa'i bka' 'bum.* (*Collected Works of the Founding Sakya Masters*), vol. *ta* 297a–299b. Tokyo: Tōyō Bunko, 1968–69.

DKTD: Dung dkar Blo bzang 'phrin las. *Dung dkar tshig mdzod chen mo. Mkhas dbang dung dkar blo bzang 'prin las mchig gis mdzad pa'i bod rig pa'i tshig mdzod chen mo.* Xining: Grung go'i bod rig pa dpe skrun khang, 2002.

Dl*GDHG:* 'Dul nag pa Dpal ldan bzang po. *Dga' ldan lha brgya ma.* In *Srad brgyud lugs kyi bla ma'i rnal 'byor dga' ldan lha brga ma zhugs so.* Place, publisher, and date unknown. BDRC no. W1KG12431.

Dn*STSG:* Mdo sngags Chos kyi rgya mtsho. *Snyan dgon sprul sku gsung rab pa'i gsung rtsom gces bsgrigs.* Zi ling: Mtsho sngon mi rigs dpe skrun khang, 1996.

Es*LMSD:* Dben sa pa Blo bzang don grub. *Bla ma la gsol ba 'debs pa'i rim par phye ba dngos grub kun 'byung.* In *Collected Works by Geluk Master Paṇchen Lama 03 Lobzang Dondup (1505–1566) of Tashi Lhunpo,* vol. *ka* 1–171 [7–347]. Chengdu: Lho nub mi rigs par khang?, 200?.

Es*NGSG:* Dben sa pa blo bzang don grub [et al.]. *Dga' ldan snyan brgyud kyi skor gyi gsung 'ga'.* Edited by Pha sang dbang chen and Tshe ring g.yang 'tshoms. Lhasa: Bod ljongs mi dmangs dpe skrun khang, 2016.

Es*TKNP:* Dben sa pa Blo bzang don grub. *Lta khrid snying po dngos grub kun 'byung.* In *Collected Works by Geluk Master Paṇchen Lama 03 Lobzang Dondup (1505–1566) of Tashi Lhunpo,* vol. *ka* 1–25 [517–66]. Chengdu: Lho nub mi rigs par khang?, 200?.

Gg*NGBM:* Gu ge yongs 'dzin Blo bzang bstan 'dzin. *Dge ldan bka' brgyud rin po che bka' srol phyag rgya chen po'i rtsa 'grel rnams kyi 'grel bshad mchog mthun dngos grub kyi bang mdzod.* In *The Collected Works of Gu-ge yoṅs-'dzin Blo-bzaṅ-stan-'dzin alias Gdoṅ-grug-grub-pa'i-rdo-rje,* 5:1–227 [1–455]. New Delhi: Chophel Legdan, 1976.

Gp*CZDD:* Sgam po pa Bsod nams rin chen. *Chos bzhi mdor bsdus.* In *Collected Works (Gsuṅ 'bum) of Sgam po pa bsod nams rin chen*, reproduced from a ms. from the bKra-śis-chos-rdzoṅ Monastery in Miyud Lahul, 2:391–92. Delhi: Khasdub Gyatso Shashin, 1975.

Gp*PCBT:* Sgam po pa Bsod nams rin chen. *Snying po don gyi gdams pa phyag rgya chen po bum tig.* In *Collected Works (Gsuṅ 'bum) of Sgam po pa bsod nams rin chen*, reproduced from a ms. from the bKra-śis-chos-rdzoṅ Monastery in Miyud Lahul, 2:181–99. Delhi: Khasdub Gyatso Shashin, 1975.

Gp*PCTB:* Sgam po pa Bsod nams rin chen. *Chos rje dags po lha rje'i gsung phyag rgya chen po'i man ngag thog babs dang mgur 'bum rnams.* In *Collected Works (Gsuṅ 'bum) of Sgam po pa bsod nams rin chen*, reproduced from a ms. from the bKra-śis-chos-rdzoṅ Monastery in Miyud Lahul, 2:136–53. Delhi: Khasdub Gyatso Shashin, 1975.

Gr*LKPY:* Rgyal rong Tshul 'khrims nyi ma. *Phyag chen gyi 'khrid yig man ngag zhal shes dang bcas pa'i kha chems rlung la bskur ba'i 'phrin yig.* Qinghai: Sku 'bum byams pa gling, N.D. Also found under the title *Bla ma mchod pa'i 'khrid yig kha chems rlung bskur ba* in *NGCS* 317–498

Gt*DTTP:* Gung thang Dkon mchog bstan pa'i sgron me. *Dge ldan phyag rgya chen po'i khrid kyi zin bris zhal lung bdud rtsi'i thigs phreng.* In *LZGM* 39–88. Also in *The Collected Works of Guṅ-thaṅ Dkon-mchog-stan-pa'i sgron-me*, edited by Ngawang Gelek Demo, 3:563–619. Gedan Sungrab Minyam Gyunphel Series 35. New Delhi, 1972.

Gz*DTNP:* 'Gos lo tsā ba Gzhon nu dpal. *Deb ther sngon po smad cha.* Lhasa: Si khron mi rigs dpe skrun khang, 1984.

Jg*NTZD:* 'Jam dpal rgya mtsho. *Rje btsun tsong kha pa'i nam thar chen mo'i zur 'debs rnam thar legs bshad kun 'dus.* In *Tsong kha pa'i gsung 'bum* [Zhol edition], vol. *ka* 1–11 [147–68].

Jg*MDBT:* 'Jam dpal rgya mtsho. *Rje'i rnam thar shin tu gsang ba ngo mtshar rmad du byung ba'i gtam.* In *Tsong kha pa'i gsung 'bum* [Zhol edition], vol. *ka* 1–4 [215–20].

Js*GCTB:* 'Jig rten gsum mgon and Shes rab 'byung gnas. *Dpal 'bri gung pa'i dam chos dgongs pa gcig pa'i rtsa ba lhan thabs dang bcas pa'i gzhung chings khog dbub dang bcas pa.* In 'Jam-mgon Koṅ-sprul Blo-gros-mtha'-yas, *Gdams ṅag mdzod*, 6:357–96. Delhi: N. Lungtok and N. Gyaltsen, 1971.

Js*NDTG:* 'Jig rten gsum mgon. *Lnga ldan rtogs pa'i mgur.* In *Sgrub brgyud gong ma rnams kyi zhal gdams phyogs sgrig nor bu'i bang mdzod*, 87. Frederick, MD: Drikung Kagyu Meditation Center, [n.d.].

Jz*DDCG:* 'Jam dbyangs bzhad pa'i rdo rje. *Do ha mdzod kyi mchan 'grel.* In *The Collected Works of 'Jam-dbyangs-bśad-pa'i-rdo-rje*, 4:1–14 [639–65]. New Delhi: Ngawang Gelek Demo,1972–74.

Jz*ZJST:* 'Jam dbyangs bzhad pa'i rdo rje. *Bla ma mchod pa'i cho ga'i mchen 'grel gzung 'jug 'dren pa'i shing rta.* In *The Collected Works of 'Jam-dbyangs-bśad-pa'i-rdo-rje*, 3: 1–33 [24–67]. New Delhi: Ngawang Gelek Demo, 1972–74.

Kd*PCGD:* Skal ldan rgya mtsho. *Phyag chen brgyud 'debs.* In *Skal ldan rgya mtsho'i gsung 'bum*, vol. *kha* 1–3 [397–401]. Reb kong: Rong po dgon chen, 199-.

Kd*PCKY:* Skal ldan rgya mtsho. *Phyag chen gyi 'khrid yig.* In *Skal ldan rgya mtsho'i gsung 'bum*, vol. *kha* 1–9a [457–73]. Reb kong: Rong po dgon chen, 199-. Also found under the title *Dge ldan phyag rgya chen po'i nyams 'khrid* in *NGCS* 555–68.

Kd*PCNK:* Skal ldan rgya mtsho. *'Jam pa'i dbyangs skal ldan rgya mtsho'i gsung las dge ldan bka' brgyud phyag rgya chen po'i nyams khrid rje blo bzang bstan pa'i rgyal mtshan dpal *bzang po'i gsung gis bskul ba.* In *Skal ldan rgya mtsho'i gsung 'bum,* vol. *kha* 1–12a [431–54]. Reb kong: Rong po dgon chen, 199-.

Kd*SLDN:* Skal ldan rgya mtsho. *'Jam pa'i dbyangs skal ldan rgya mtsho'i gsung las dge ldan phyag chen zab khrid gdams ngag rgya mtsho nas btus pa.* In *Skal ldan rgya mtsho'i gsung 'bum,* vol. *kha* 1–14 [403–30]. Reb kong: Rong po dgon chen, 199-.

Kg*DPJN:* Mkhas grub rje Dge legs dpal bzang. *Rje btsun bla ma tsong kha pa chen po'i ngo mtshar rmad du byung ba'i rnam par thar pa dad pa'i 'jug ngogs.* In *Tsong kha pa'i gsung 'bum* [Zhol edition], vol. *ka* 1–72a [1–143].

Kg*RPCM:* Mkhas grub rje Dge legs dpal bzang. *Rje rin po che'i gsang ba'i rnam thar rgya mtsho lta bu las cha shas nyung di zhig yongs su 'jod pa'i gtam rin po che'i snye ma.* In *Tsong kha pa'i gsung 'bum* [Zhol edition], vol. *ka* 1–16 [167–201].

Kn*PCOZ:* Dwags po Paṇ chen Bkra shis rnam rgyal. *Nges don phyag rgya chen po'i sgom rim gsal bar byed pa'i legs bshad zla ba'i 'od zer. A Detailed Study of the Practices of Mahāmudrā Meditation.* Delhi: Karma chos 'phel, 1974.

Kp*NTSD:* Bkra shis dpal ldan. *Rje btsun bla ma blo bzang grags pa'i dpal gyi gsang ba'i rnam thar gsol 'debs.* In *Tsong kha pa'i gsung 'bum* [Zhol edition], vol. *ka* 1–4 [202–10].

Kt*GBLZ:* Ke'u tshang Blo bzang 'jam dbyangs smon lam. *Dge ldan snyan brgyud kyi bka' srol phyag rgya chen po'i zin bris rnam grol kun tu dge ba'i lam bzang.* In *Ke'u tshang blo bzang 'jam dbyangs smon lam gyi gsung 'bum,* 2:7–149. Dharamsala: Library of Tibetan Works and Archives, 1984. Also found in: *LZGM* 90–259.

Lc*CGZN:* Lce sgom pa [Shes rab rjo rje]. *Pha rin po che lce sgom zhal nas.* In *Bka' gdams kyis shes bu dam pa rnams kyi gzung bgros thor bu rnams,* 52. New Delhi: Geshe Paden Drakpa, 1983.

Lg*NTCG:* Blo gros rgyal mtshan. *Rje btsun 'jam dpal rgya mtsho'i rnam thar dad pa'i chu rgyan.* In *Rje spyan snga rin po che blo gros rgyal mtshan gyi bka' 'bum,* 2:1–13 [397–422]. Unsourced blockprint. BDRC no. W1KG2144.

Lr*GGRP:* Gling ras pa Padma rdo rje. *Rje grub thob chen po'i bka' 'bum las mgur gyi rim pa.* In *Gling chen ras pa padma rdo rje'i gsung 'bum,* 1:11–48. Delhi: Khams pa sgar gsung rab nyams gso khang, 1985.

LSGT: Lha sa'i dgon tho rin chen spungs rgyan. Edited by Bshes gnyen tshul khrims. Lhasa: Bod ljongs mi dmangs dpe skrun khang, 2001.

Lt*DNDZ:* 'Jam mgon kong sprul [I] Blo gros mtha' yas. *Gdams ngag mdzod: A Treasury of Instructions and Techniques for Spiritual Realization.* 12 vols. Delhi: N. Lungtok and N. Gyaltsan, 1971.

LZGM: Zab lam snyan brgyud phyag rgya chen po'i man ngag gi phyogs bsgrigs rgyal ba'i lam bzang gsal ba'i sgron me. Losel Literature Series 35. Distt. Karwar, Karnataka: Drepung Losel Ling Educational Society, 1999.

NGCS: Dpal dge ldan pa'i lugs kyi lam rim dang snyan brgyud kyi chos skor. [Edited by Thupten Jinpa.] Bod kyi gtsug lag gces btus 6. New Delhi: Bod kyi gtsug lag zhib dpyod khang (Institute of Tibetan Classics), 2005.

Ng*DPST:* Ngag dbang blo bzang rgya mtsho (Fifth Dalai Lama). *Khyab bdag rjo rje chang mkhan chen chos kyi rgyal po blo bzang chos kyi rgyal mtshan gyi gsang ba'i rnam thar dad pa'i shing rta.* In *Ngag dbang blo bzang rgya mtsho'i gsung 'bum,* vol. *nya* 1–9 [328–45]. Dharamsala: Rnam gsal sgron ma, 2007.

Nz*PCSG:* Mkhas grub Nor bzang rgya mtsho. *Bka' dge dgongs pa gcig bsgrub kyi phyag rgya chen po gsal ba'i sgron ma.* Library of Tibetan Works and Archives Accession no. 20379. [No bibliographic information available.]

Pb*NDSB:* Phur bu mchog Ngag dbang byams pa, *'Jam dpal dbyangs kyis rje bla ma la dngos su gnang ba'i gdams pa mdor bsdus kyi ṭikka gnad don gsal ba.* In *Phur bu lcog ngag dbang byams pa gsung 'bum,* 1:313–20. Beijing: Mi rigs dpe skrun khang, 2012.

Pg*LCKB:* Phag mo gru pa Rdo rje rgyal po. *Lhan cig skyes 'byor.* In *The Collected Works of Phag-mo gru-pa,* 4:272–98. Kathmandu: Khenpo Shedrub Tenzin and Lama Thinley Namgyal, 2003.

Pg*RCGD:* Phag mo gru pa Rdo rje rgyal po. *Rin chen rgyan 'dra.* In *The Collected Works of Phag-mo gru-pa,* 3:289–322. Kathmandu: Khenpo Shedrub Tenzin and Lama Thinley Namgyal, 2003.

Pg*RCGM:* Phag mo gru pa Rdo rje rgyal po. *Rin chen sgron me.* In *The Collected Works of Phag-mo gru-pa,* 3:323–406. Kathmandu: Khenpo Shedrub Tenzin and Lama Thinley Namgyal, 2003.

Pg*RCTK:* Phag mo gru pa Rdo rje rgyal po. *Rin po che'i them skas.* In *The Collected Works of Phag-mo gru-pa,* 3:13–198. Kathmandu: Khenpo Shedrub Tenzin and Lama Thinley Namgyal, 2003.

Ph*NGKY:* Khon ston Dpal 'byor lhun grub. *Snyan brgyud yid bzhin nor bu lta ba spyi khyab tu ngo sprod pa'i khrid yig.* In Pn*KYPS* 1–48. [Mistakenly attributed to Gnyal ston Dpal 'jor lhun grub.] Also found in *Sngags rdzogs dbu ma'i skor gyi dpe dkon thor bu'i rigs phyogs sgrigs.* Bla rung sgar: Ser ljongs bla ma rung lnga rig nang bstan slob grwa chen po, 2005.

Pk*PCGZ:* Padma dkar po. *Phyag rgya chen po'i man ngag gi bshad sbyar rgyal ba'i gan mdzod.* In *Collected Works (gsuṅ 'bum) of Kun-mkhyen Padma-dkar po,* 21:7–370. Darjeeling: Karegyud Sungrab Nyamso Khang, 1974.

Pn*KYPS:* Gnyal ston Dpal 'byor lhun grub sogs. *Phyag rgya chen po'i lta ba spyi khyab tu ngo sprod pa'i khrid yig phyogs sgrig.* Lhasa: Bod ljongs mi dmangs dpe khrungs khang, 2010.

Ps*DRGC:* [Pha] Dam pa sangs rgyas. *Zhal gdams ding ri brgyad bcu pa.* In *Gdams ngag mdzod,* 9:31–36. Delhi: N. Lungtok and N. Gyaltsan, 1971.

Ps*ZBDG:* [Pha] Dam pa sangs rgyas. *Dam chos sdug bsngal gyi zhi byed kyi snying por dril ba'i rdo rje'i mgur.* In *Gdams ngag mdzod,* 9:36–38. Delhi: N. Lungtok and N. Gyaltsan, 1971.

Sg*PCGD:* Paṇ chen Bsod nams grags pa. *Dam pa'i chos phyag rgya chen po la rgyan drug tu mdzad par byed pa'i rgyan drug.* In *Paṇ chen Bsod nams grags pa gsung 'bum,* 9:432–531. Lhasa: Bod ljongs mi dmangs dpe skrun khang, 2013.

Sp*DSRB*t*:* Sa skya paṇḍi ta Kun dga' rgyal mtshan. *Sdom pa gsum gyi rab tu dbye ba'i bstan bcos.* In *Sa skya pa'i bka' 'bum.* (*Collected Works of the Founding Sakya Masters*), vol. *na* 1a–48b. Tokyo: Tōyō Bunko, 1968–69.

Sp*DSRB*w*:* Sa skya paṇḍi ta Kun dga' rgyal mtshan. *Sdom pa gsum gyi rab tu dbye ba'i bstan bcos.* In Sakya Pandita 2001, 277–329.

Sp*KDZL:* Sakya paṇḍita Kun dga' rgyal mtshan. *Bka' gdams pa nam mkha' 'bum gyi zhus lan.* In *Sa skya pa'i bka' 'bum.* (*Collected Works of the Founding Sakya Masters*), vol. *na* 242a–44b [415–16]. Tokyo: Tōyō Bunko, 1968–69.

St*ZCSP:* Si tu Chos kyi 'byung gnas. *Sgrub brgyud karma kaṃ tshang brgyud pa rin po che'i rnam par thar pa rab byams nor bu zla ba chu shel gyi phreng ba.* Kun ming: Yun nan mi rigs dpe skrun khang, 1998.

Sy*ESKG:* Mkhas grub Sangs rgyas ye shes. *Dben sa bka' brgyud kyi bla ma'i rnal 'byor.* In *The Collected Works (gsuṅ-'bum) of Mkhas-grub saṅgs-rgyas-ye-śes,* vol. *pha* 1–12 [452–75]. New Delhi: Don 'grub rdo rje, 1973–76.

Sy*LMCP:* Mkhas grub Sangs rgyas ye shes. *Bla ma mchod pa'i cho ga dngos grub kun 'byung.* In *The Collected Works (gsuṅ-'bum) of Mkhas-grub saṅgs-rgyas-ye-śes*, vol. *nga* 1–30a [1:74–132]. New Delhi: Don 'grub rdo rje, 1973–76.

Sy*LMCT:* Mkhas grub Sangs rgyas ye shes. *Tshogs kyi 'khor lo'i mchod pa dngos grub kun 'byung.* In *Tshogs kyi 'khor lo'i mchod pa dngos grub kun 'byung dang / ja mchod bde chen kun bzang ma dang / bzlog pa'i man ngag zur bskor dang / dpal rdo rje nag po chen po phyag bzhi pa'i bskang ba bcas.* In *The Collected Works (gsuṅ-'bum) of Mkhas-grub saṅgs-rgyas-ye-śes*, vol. *'a* 1–4b [2: 149–56]. New Delhi: Don 'grub rdo rje, 1973–76.

Sy*SGDL:* Mkhas grub Sangs rgyas ye shes. *Gsung mgur chab shog dris lan sogs phyogs gcig tu bsdebs pa.* In *The Collected Works (gsuṅ-'bum) of Mkhas-grub saṅgs-rgyas-ye-śes*, vol. *ca* 1–71 [1: 135–276]. New Delhi: Don 'grub rdo rje, 1973–76.

Sy*TGNP:* Mkhas grub Sangs rgyas ye shes. *Lta sgom sbyong ba'i snying po gtan la dbab pa dang / bden gnyis lam gyi snying po'i bden gnyis rnam par bshad pa dngos grub kun 'byung bcas.* In *The Collected Works (gsuṅ-'bum) of Mkhas-grub saṅgs-rgyas-ye-śes*, vol. *ta* 1–12 [1:346–69]. New Delhi: Don 'grub rdo rje, 1973–76.

Th*MLGB:* Mi la ras pa. *Rje btsun mi la ras pa'i rnam thar rgyas par phye pa mgur 'bum.* [Edited by Gtsang smyon Heruka.] N.p.: Lobsang Tsultrim, 1971.

Th*MLNT:* Gtsang smyon Heruka. *Mi la ras pa'i rnam thar: Texte Tibétain de la Vie de Milarépa.* Edited by J. W. de Jong. Indo-Iranian Monographs 4. 'S-Gravenhage: Mouton, 1959.

Th*MPNT:* Gtsang smyon Heruka. *Sgrub bsgyur mar pa lo tsā ba'i rnam thar mthong ba don yod.* Chengdu: Si khron mi rigs dpe skrun khang, 1990.

Tk*SGML:* Thu'u bkwan Blo bzang chos kyi nyi ma. *Grub mtha' shel gyi me long.* Bod kyi gtsugs lag gces btus 25. Delhi: Bod kyi gtsug lag zhib dpyod khang (Institute of Tibetan Classics), 2007.

Ts*BSCG:* Tsong kha pa Blo bzang grags pa. *Ba so chos rje la gcig brgyud kyi tshul di gnang ba'i bla ma'i rnal 'byor.* In *Tsong kha pa'i gsung 'bum* [Zhol edition], vol. *kha* 1–3 [235–40]. New Delhi: Mongolian Lama Gurudeva, 1978–79.

Ts*BTMB:* Tsong kha pa Blo bzang grags pa. *Dpal 'khor lo bde mchog gi rim pa lnga pa'i bshad pa sbas pa'i don lta ba'i mig rnam par 'byed pa.* In *Tsong kha pa'i gsung 'bum* [Zhol edition], vol. *tha* 1–33 [110–207]. New Delhi: Mongolian Lama Gurudeva, 1978–79.

Ts*DTPB:* Tsong kha pa Blo bzang grags pa. *Zhu lan sman mchog rdud rtsi'i 'phreng ba.* In *Tsong kha pa'i gsung 'bum* [Zhol edition], vol. *ka* 1–13 [294–319]. New Delhi: Mongolian Lama Gurudeva, 1978–79.

Ts*GPRS:* Tsong kha pa Blo bzang grags pa. *Dbu ma dgongs pa rab gsal.* In *Tsong kha pa'i gsung 'bum* [Zhol edition], vol. *ma* 1–263a [3–535]. New Delhi: Mongolian Lama Gurudeva, 1978–79.

Ts*JBDD:* Tsong kha pa Blo bzang grags pa. *Rje btsun 'jam pa'i dbyangs kyis gsungs pa'i nyams len mdor bsdus.* In *Tsong kha pa'i gsung 'bum* [Zhol edition], vol. *kha* 50b–51a [298–99]. New Delhi: Mongolian Lama Gurudeva, 1978–79.

Ts*LLTD:* Tsong kha pa Blo bzang grags pa. *Nā ro'i chos drug dmigs skor lag tu lan tshul bsdus ba rjes gsung bzhin sems dpa' kun bzang pas bkod pa.* In *Tsong kha pa'i gsung 'bum* [Zhol edition], vol. *ta* 1–20 [125–63]. New Delhi: Mongolian Lama Gurudeva, 1978–79.

Ts*LRCM:* Tsong kha pa Blo bzang grags pa. *Skyes bu gsum gyi rnyams su blang ba'i rim pa thams cad tshang bar ston pa'i byang chub lam gyi rim pa byang chub lam rim che ba.* Ziling [Xining]: Mtsho sngon, 1985. [Also: Zhol edition, vol. *pa* 1–481].

Ts*LRDD:* Tsong kha pa Blo bzang grags pa. *Byang chub lam rim pa'i nyams len gyi rnam* *gzhag mdor bsdus*. In *Tsong kha pa'i gsung 'bum* [Zhol edition], vol. *kha* 55b–58a [307–13]. New Delhi: Mongolian Lama Gurudeva, 1978–79.

Ts*LSRK:* Tsong kha pa Blo bzang grags pa. *Dge sbyor gyi gnad kyi dri ba snyan bskul lhag bsam rab dkar*. In *Tsong kha pa'i gsung 'bum* [Zhol edition], vol. *pa* 1–441 [3–863]. New Delhi: Mongolian Lama Gurudeva, 1978–79.

Ts*LTNS:* Tsong kha pa Blo bzang grags pa. *Lam gyi gtso bo rnam gsum*. In *Tsong kha pa'i gsung 'bum* [Zhol edition], vol. *kha* 193b–194b [584–85]. New Delhi: Mongolian Lama Gurudeva, 1978–79.

Ts*NRCM:* Tsong kha pa Blo bzang grags pa. *Rgyal ba khyab bdag rdo rje 'chang chen po'i lam gyi rim pa gsang ba kun gyi gnad rnam par phye ba*. In *Tsong kha pa'i gsung 'bum* [Zhol edition], vol. *kha* 72b–85a [342–67]. New Delhi: Mongolian Lama Gurudeva, 1978–79.

Ts*PZSS:* Tsong kha pa Blo bzang grags pa. *Sgrub le'i phyag rgya bzhi zhib tu gsungs pa rgyal tshab chos rjes zin bris su bkod pa*. In *Tsong kha pa'i gsung 'bum* [Zhol edition], vol. *na* 1–11 [775–88]. New Delhi: Mongolian Lama Gurudeva, 1978–79.

Ts*RDSL:* Tsong kha pa Blo bzang grags pa. *De nyid la rje btsun red mda' ba'i gsung lan*. In *Tsong kha pa'i gsung 'bum* [Zhol edition], vol. *kha* 62a–68b [321–33]. New Delhi: Mongolian Lama Gurudeva, 1978–79.

Ts*RNSG:* Tsong kha pa Blo bzang grags pa. *Rgyud thams cad kyi rgyal po dpal gsang ba 'dus pa'i man ngag rim pa nga rab tu gsal ba'i sgron me*. In *Tsong kha pa'i gsung 'bum* [Zhol edition], vol. *ja* 1–312 [1–624]. New Delhi: Mongolian Lama Gurudeva, 1978–79.

Ts*SDPB:* Tsong kha pa Blo bzang grags pa. *Rje btsun 'jam pai' dbyangs kyi lam gyi gnad rje red mda' ba la shog dril du phul ba*. In *Tsong kha pa'i gsung 'bum* [Zhol edition], vol. *pha* 1–6 [671–82]. New Delhi: Mongolian Lama Gurudeva, 1978–79.

Ts*TKSY:* Tsong kha pa Blo bzang grags pa. *Rje rin po che blo bzang grags pa'i dpal gyi gsan yig*. In *Tsong kha pa'i gsung 'bum* [Zhol edition], vol. *ka* 1–27 [233–93]. New Delhi: Mongolian Lama Gurudeva, 1978–79.

Ts*YCSD:* Tsong kha pa Blo bzang grags pa. *Zab lam nā ro'i chos drug gi sgo nas 'krid pa'i rim pa yid ches gsum ldan*. In *Tsong kha pa'i gsung 'bum* [Zhol edition], vol. *ta* 1–60 [408–530].

Tt*GZNN:* Gung ru dge bshes Bstan pa bstan 'dzin. *Lta ba'i nyams mgur thun mongs ma yin pa a ma ngo shes kyi bsdus don gnad kyi drang thig dang de'i rnam bshad grub bzhi'i snying nor*. Mon-gho: 'Bras-gliṅ Rig-gźuṅ Gter mdzod 'phrul par khaṅ, 1985.

Yg*JLZL:* Ye shes rgyal mtshan. *Dga' ldan phyag rgya chen po'i man ngag gi gnad gsal bar ston pa 'jam dbyangs bla ma'i zhal lung*. In *Ye shes rgyal mtshan gsung 'bum*, vol. *pa* 1–8a [353–67]. Delhi: Bod kyi dpe deb khang, 2005.

Yg*LCKY:* Ye shes rgyal mtshan. *Bla ma mchod pa'i khrid yig gsang ba'i gdad rnam par phye ba snyan rgyud man ngag gi gter mdzod*. In *Ye shes rgyal mtshan gsung 'bum*, vol. *pa* 1–232 [1–463]. Delhi: Bod kyi dpe deb khang, 2005.

Yg*LRNT:* Ye shes rgyal mtshan. *Lam rim bla ma brgyud pa'i rnam thar*. Taipei: The Corporate Body of the Buddha Educational Foundation, 2007.

Yg*LZGM:* Ye shes rgyal mtshan. *Dga' ldan phyag rgya chen po'i khrid yig snyan brgyud lam bzang gsal ba'i sgron me*. In *Ye shes rgyal mtshan gsung 'bum*, vol. *tsa* 1–122 [201–443]. Delhi: Bod kyi dpe deb khang, 2005.

Yg*LZZL:* Ye shes rgyal mtshan. *Zab mo'i dbu ma'i lta khrid thun mong min pa blo bzang zhal lung*. In *Ye shes rgyal mtshan gsung 'bum*, vol. *ma* 1–17a [161–93]. Delhi: Bod kyi dpe deb khang, 2005.

YgNGNM: Ye shes rgyal mtshan. *Lha ma lha'i rnal 'byor gyi snying po dngos grub kyi snye ma.* In *Ye shes rgyal mtshan gsung 'bum*, vol. *ma* 1–7a [185–97]. Delhi: Bod kyi dpe deb khang, 2005.

YgPCMT: Ye shes rgyal mtshan. *Dga' ldan phyag rgya chen po'i smon tshig dngos grub kun 'byung.* In *Ye shes rgyal mtshan gsung 'bum*, vol. *tsa* 1–3a [445–49]. Delhi: Bod kyi dpe deb khang, 2005.

YgPCSD(1): Ye shes rgyal mtshan, with additional material by Pha bong kha. *Phyag chen brgyud pa'i gsol 'debs.* In Willis 1995, 107–10.

YgPCSD(2): Ye shes rgyal mtshan, with additional material by Pha bong kha. *Phyag chen brgyud pa'i gsol 'debs.* In Blo bzang chos kyi rgyal mtshan. *Dge ldan bka' brgyud rin po che'i phyag chen rtsa ba rgyal ba'i gzhung lam*, 5b–8a. Blockprint, n.p., n.d.

YgPGDM: Ye shes rgyal mtshan. *Dga' ldan phyag rgya chen po'i sngon 'gro bla ma'i rnal 'byor gyi bsdus don snyan brgyud mdzod brgya 'byed pa'i 'phrul gyi lde mig.* In *Ye shes rgyal mtshan gsung 'bum*, vol. *pa* 1–7 [267–80]. Delhi: Bod kyi dpe deb khang, 2005.

YgTBYC: Ye shes rgyal mtshan. *Lta ba'i gnad ston pa'i yig chung shin tu gsang ba dngos grub kun 'byung.* In *Ye shes rgyal mtshan gsung 'bum*, vol. *pa* 1–7a [339–51]. Delhi: Bod kyi dpe deb khang, 2005. Also in *NGCS* 569–76.

YgTKZM: Ye shes rgyal mtshan. *Dge ldan snyan brgyud kyi lta khrid zab mo dngos grub kun 'byung.* In Yg*LZGM* 2–37. Also found in *Ye shes rgyal mtshan gsung 'bum*, vol. *ma* 1–26 [27–77]. Delhi: Bod kyi dpe deb khang. Also found in *NGCS* 569–76.

YnPCTC: Yang dgon pa Rgyal mtshan dpal. *Phyag rgya chen po'i lhan cig skyes sbyor gyi thon chos.* In *Rgyal ba yang dgon pa rgyal mtshan gsung 'bum*, vol. *ka* 1–18a [209–41]. Thimphu: Kun bzang thob rgyas, 1976.

ZrLCTT: Zhang g.yu brag pa Brtson 'grus grags pa. [Zhang rin po che.] *Phyag rgya chen po'i lam mchog thar thug.* In *Gdams ngag mdzod.* 5:774–77. Delhi: N. Lungtok and N. Gyaltsan, 1971.

ZrPCNG: Zhang g.yu brag pa Brtson 'grus grags pa. [Zhang rin po che.] *Phyag rgya chen po sgom ma mo sngon 'gro dngos gzhi.* In *Gdams ngag mdzod*, 5:778–99. Delhi: N. Lungtok and N. Gyaltsan, 1971.

Secondary Sources

Abboud, Gerardo, trans. 2014. The Third Khamtrul Rinpoche, Ngawang Kunga Tenzin. *The Royal Seal of Mahamudra, volume 1: A Guidebook for the Realization of Coemergence.* Boston: Snow Lion Publications.

Abboud, Gerardo, Adam Kane, and Sean Price, trans. 2017. *The Supreme Siddhi of Mahamudra: Teachings, Poems, and Songs of the Drukpa Kagyu Lineage.* Boulder: Snow Lion Publications.

Abhayadatta. 1979. *Buddha's Lion's: The Lives of the Eighty-Four Siddhas.* Translated by James B. Robinson. Berkeley: Dharma Publishing.

Abhinavagupta. 1989. *A Trident of Wisdom: Translation of "Parātrīśikā Vivaraṇa."* Translated by Jaideva Singh. Albany: State University of New York Press.

Adams, Miranda. 2008a. "The Third Dalai Lama, Sonam Gyatso," Treasury of Lives. https://treasuryoflives.org/biographies/view/Third-Dalai-Lama-Sonam-Gyatso/12828. Accessed February 27, 2018.

———. 2008b. "The Third Paṇchen Lama, Wensapa Lobzang Dondrub." Treasury of Lives.

http://treasuryoflives.org/biographies/view/Wensapa-Lobzang-Dondrub/13026. Accessed September 1, 2017.

Apple, James B. 2009. *Stairway to Nirvāṇa: A Study of the Twenty Saṃghas Based on the Works of Tsong Kha Pa*. Albany: State University of New York Press.

———. 2017. "Atiśa's Teachings on Mahāmudrā." *Indian International Journal of Buddhist Studies* 18: 1–42.

———. 2019a. *Atiśa Dīpaṃkara: Illuminator of the Awakened Mind*. Lives of the Masters. Boulder: Shambhala Publications.

———. 2019b. *Jewels of the Middle Way: The Madhyamaka Legacy of Atiśa and His Tibetan Followers*. Studies in Indian and Tibetan Buddhism. Boston: Wisdom Publications.

Ary, Elijah S. 2015. *Authorized Lives: Biography and the Early Formation of Geluk Identity*. Boston: Wisdom Publications.

Avalon, Arthur. 1972 [1913]. *Tantra of the Great Liberation (Mahānirvāṇa Tantra)*. New York: Dover.

———. 1974 [1922]. *The Serpent Power: The Secrets of Tantric and Shaktic Yoga*. New York: Dover.

Barron, Richard (Chökyi Nyima), trans. 2003. *The Autobiography of Jamgön Kongtrul: A Gem of Many Colors*. Ithaca: Snow Lion Publications.

———, trans. 2013. Jamgön Kongtrul Lodrö Taye. *The Catalogue of "The Treasury of Precious Instructions."* New York: Tsadra Foundation.

Batchelor, Stephen. 2017. *After Buddhism: Rethinking Dharma for a Secular Age*. New Haven: Yale University Press.

Bell, Catherine. 2009. *Ritual: Perspectives and Dimensions*. Revised edition. New York: Oxford University Press.

Bentor, Yael. 1997. "The Practice of the Mantra Path According to Lce-sgom-pa." In *Religions of Tibet in Practice*, edited by Donald S. Lopez, Jr., 326–46. Princeton: Princeton University Press.

———. 2000. "Fourfold Meditation: Outer, Inner, Secret, and Suchness." In *Tibet, Past and Present: Tibetan Studies I. PIATS 2000: Tibetan Studies: Proceedings of the Ninth Seminar of the International Association for Tibetan Studies*, edited by Henk Blezer, 41–58. Leiden: E. J. Brill.

Berzin, Alexander, trans. 2001. The Fourth Paṇchen Lama. "Extensive Six-Session Yoga." Berzin Archives. https://studybuddhism.com/en/advanced-studies/prayers-rituals/tantric-practices/extensive-six-session-yoga. Accessed August 18, 2017.

Berzin, Alexander et al., trans. 1979. *The Guru Puja by the First Paṇchen Lama and The Hundreds of Deities of the Land of Joy by Dul-nag-pa Päl-dän*. Dharamsala: Library of Tibetan Works and Archives.

Beyer, Stephan V. 1974. *The Buddhist Experience: Sources and Interpretations*. Belmont, CA: Dickenson Publishing.

———. 1978. *The Cult of Tārā: Magic and Ritual in Tibet*. Berkeley: University of California Press.

Bharati, Agehananda. 1970. *The Tantric Tradition*. Garden City, NY: Doubleday.

Bhattacharya, B. 2000. *World of Tantra*. 2nd ed. Delhi: Munshiram Manoharlal.

"Blo bzang bstan 'dzin rgya mtsho." BDRC no. P308. http://www.tbrc.org/#!rid=P308. Accessed September 12, 2017.

"Blo bzang 'jam dbyangs smon lam." BDRC no. P4592. http://www.tbrc.org/#!rid=P4592. Accessed September 12, 2017.

Bod rgya tshig mdzod chen mo, 3 vols. Beijing: Mi rigs dpe skrun khang, 1984.

Bodhi, Bhikkhu, trans. 2012. *The Numerical Discourses of the Buddha: A Translation of the Aṅguttara Nikāya*. Boston: Wisdom Publications.

———. 2017. *The Suttanipāta: An Ancient Collection of the Buddha's Discourses Together with Its Commentaries*. Somerville, MA: Wisdom Publications.

Bolle, Kees W., ed. 1987. *Secrecy in Religions*. Leiden: Brill.

Braitstein, Lara. 2014. *The Adamantine Songs (Vajragīti) by Saraha*. New York: American Institute of Buddhist Studies.

Brauen, Martin, ed. 2005. *The Dalai Lamas: A Visual History*. Chicago: Serindia.

Broido, Michael M. 1980. "The Term *dngos-po'i gnas-lugs* as Used in Padma dkar-po's *gZhung 'grel*." In *Tibetan Studies in Honour of Hugh Richardson*, edited by Michael Aris and Aung San Suu Kyi, 59–66. Warminster, UK: Aris and Phillips.

———. 1984. "Padma dKar-po on Tantra as Ground, Path and Goal." *Journal of the Tibet Society* 4: 59–66.

———. 1985a. "Padma dKar-po on Integration as Ground, Path and Goal." *Journal of the Tibet Society* 5: 5–54.

———. 1985b. "Padma dKar-po on the Two *Satyas*." *Journal of the International Association of Buddhist Studies* 8.2: 7–59.

———. 1987. "Sa-skya Paṇḍita, the White Panacea and the Hva-shang Doctrine." *Journal of the International Association of Buddhist Studies* 10.2: 27–68.

———. 1988. "Veridical and Delusive Cognition: Tsong-kha-pa on the Two Satyas." *Journal of Indian Philosophy* 16: 29–63.

Brooks, Douglas Renfrew. 1990. *The Secret of the Three Cities: An Introduction to Hindu Śākta Tantrism*. Chicago: University of Chicago Press.

Brown, Daniel P. 2006. *Pointing Out the Great Way: The Stages of Meditation in the Mahamudra Tradition*. Boston: Wisdom Publications.

Brunnhölzl, Karl. 2004. *The Center of the Sunlit Sky: Madhyamaka in the Kagyü Tradition*. Ithaca: Snow Lion Publications.

———. 2007. *Straight from the Heart: Buddhist Pith Instructions*. Ithaca: Snow Lion Publications.

———. 2009. *Luminous Heart: The Third Karmapa on Consciousness, Wisdom, and Buddha Nature*. Ithaca: Snow Lion Publications.

———. 2014. *When the Clouds Part: The* Uttaratantra *and Its Meditative Tradition as a Bridge Between Sūtra and Tantra*. Boston and London: Snow Lion Publications.

Buddhist Canons Research Database. http://databases.aibs.columbia.edu/

Buddhist Digital Resource Center (BDRC). [Formerly: Tibetan Buddhist Resource Center.] https://www.tbrc.org/.

Burchardi, Anne. 2011. "The Role of *Rang rig* in the Pramāṇa-based *Gzhan stong* of the Seventh Karmapa." In *Mahāmudrā and the Bka' brgyud Tradition*, edited by Roger R. Jackson and Matthew T. Kapstein, 317–44. Andiast, Switzerland: International Institute for Tibetan and Buddhist Studies GmbH.

Cabezón, José Ignacio, trans. 1992. *A Dose of Emptiness: An Annotated Translation of the "sTong thun chen mo" of mKhas grub dGe legs dpal bzang*. Albany: State University of New York Press.

———. 1994. *Buddhism and Language: A Study of Indo-Tibetan Scholasticism*. Albany: State University of New York Press.

———. 1995. "On the *sGra pa Rin chen pa'i rtsod lan of Paṇ chen bLo bzang chos rgyan*." *Asiatische Studien/Études Asiatiques* 49.4: 643–69.

———. 2017. "Khedrub Norzang Gyatso." Treasury of Lives. https://treasuryoflives.org/biographies/view/Khedrub-Norzang-Gyatso/10168. Accessed September 3, 2017.

Cabezón, José Ignacio, and Geshe Lobsang Dargyay, trans. and annot. 2007. *Freedom from Extremes: Gorampa's "Distinguishing the Views" and the Polemics of Emptiness*. Boston: Wisdom Publications.

Chang, Garma C. C., trans. 1989 [1962]. *The Hundred Thousand Songs of Milarepa*. 2 vols. Boston: Shambhala Publications.

———, trans. 1986 [1963]. *The Six Yogas of Naropa and Teachings on Mahamudra*. Ithaca: Snow Lion Publications.

Changkya Rölpai Dorjé. 2019. *Beautiful Adornment of Mouth Meru: A Presentation of Classical Indian Philosophy*. Translated by Donald S. Lopez, Jr. Library of Tibetan Classics 24. Boston: Wisdom Publications.

Chattopadhyaya, Alaka. 1967. *Atīśa and Tibet: Life and Works of Dīpaṃkara Śrījñāna in Relation to the History and Religion of Tibet*. With Tibetan Sources, translated under Professor Lama Chimpa. Delhi: Motilal Banarsidass.

Chhosphel, Samten. 2010a. "Ngulchu Dharmabhadra." Treasury of Lives. http://www.treasuryoflives.org/biographies/view/Ngulchu-Dharmabhadra/4631. Accessed March 23, 2015.

———. 2010b. "Panchen Sonam Drakpa." Treasury of Lives. http://treasuryoflives.org/biographies/view/Panchen-Sonam-Drakpa/1637. Accessed September 3, 2017.

———. 2010c. "The Third Gungtang, Konchok Tenpai Dronme." Treasury of Lives. http://www.treasuryoflives.org/biographies/view/Third-Gungtang,-Konchok-Tenpai-Dronme/TBRC_P298. Accessed March 21, 2015.

———. 2011a. "The Fifty-Fourth Ganden Tripa, Ngawang Chokden." Treasury of Lives. http://www.treasuryoflives.org/biographies/view/Ngawang-Chokden/P412. Accessed April 17, 2015.

———. 2011b. "The First Jamyang Zhepa, Jamyang Zhepai Dorje." Treasury of Lives. http://www.treasuryoflives.org/biographies/view/Jamyang-Zhepai-Dorje/6646. Accessed April 13, 2015.

———. 2011c. "The Seventh Dalai Lama, Kelzang Gyatso." Treasury of Lives. http://treasuryoflives.org/biographies/view/Seventh-Dalai-Lama-Kelzang-Gyatso/3107. Accessed September 9, 2017.

———. 2013. "Paljor Lhundrub." Treasury of Lives. http://treasuryoflives.org/biographies/view/Paljor-Lhundrub/7294. Accessed June 18, 2015.

Chöden Rinpoché, H.E. 2013. *Hundreds of Deities of Tuṣita*. Translated and edited by Ian Coghlan and Voula Zarpani. Churchill, VIC, Australia: Awakening Vajra Publications.

———. 2020. *Mastering Meditation*. Translated by Tenzin Gaché. Boston: Wisdom Publications.

Choephel, David Karma, and Michele Martin, trans. 2012. *The First Karmapa: The Life and Teachings of Dusum Khyenpa*. Woodstock, NY: KTD Publications.

Cleary, Thomas, trans. 1993. *The Flower Ornament Scripture: A Translation of the Avataṃsaka Sūtra*. Boston: Shambhala Publications.

Collins, Steven. 1990. *Selfless Persons: Imagery and Thought in Theravāda Buddhism*. Cambridge: Cambridge University Press.

———. 2006. *Nirvāṇa and Other Buddhist Felicities.* Cambridge: Cambridge University Press.

Conze, Edward, trans. 1973. *The Perfection of Wisdom in Eight Thousand Lines and Its Verse Summary.* Bolinas, CA: Four Seasons Foundation, 1973.

———, trans. 1993. *Perfect Wisdom: The Short Prajñāpāramita Texts.* Devon, UK: Buddhist Publishing Group.

Cowherds, The, ed. 2010. *Moonshadows: Conventional Truth in Buddhist Philosophy.* New York: Oxford University Press.

Dakpo Tashi Namgyal [Takpo Tashi Namgyal]. 1986. *Mahāmudrā: The Quintessence of Mind and Meditation.* Translated by Lobsang P. Lhalungpa. Boston: Shambhala Publications.

———. 2001. *Clarifying the Natural State: A Principal Guidance Manual for Mahamudra.* Translated by Eric Pema Kunsang. Boudhanath, Hong Kong, and Esby: Rangjung Yeshe.

———. 2019. *Moonbeams of Mahāmudrā, with "Dispelling the Darkness of Ignorance" by Wangchuk Dorje, the Ninth Karmapa.* Translated by Elizabeth Callahan. Boulder: Snow Lion Publications.

Dalai Lama [XIV]. 1988. *The Union of Bliss and Emptiness: A Commentary on the Lama Choepa Guru Yoga Practice.* Translated by Thupten Jinpa. Ithaca: Snow Lion Publications.

———. 2006. *The Universe in a Single Atom: The Convergence of Science and Spirituality.* New York: Harmony Books.

———. 2017. *The Life of My Teacher: A Biography of Kyabjé Ling Rinpoché.* Translated by Gavin Kilty. Boston: Wisdom Publications.

Dalai Lama [XIV] and Alexander Berzin. 1997. *The Gelug/Kagyü Tradition of Mahamudra.* Ithaca: Snow Lion Publications.

Dalai Lama [XIV], Dzong-ka-pa, and Jeffrey Hopkins. 2005. *Yoga Tantra: Paths to Magical Feats.* Ithaca: Snow Lion Publications.

Dalai Lama [XIV], Khöntön Paljor Lhundrup, and José Ignacio Cabezón. 2011. *Meditation on the Nature of Mind.* Boston: Wisdom Publications.

Dalton, Jacob. 2004. "A Crisis of Doxography: How Tibetans Organized Tantra During the 8th–12th Centuries." *Journal of the International Association of Buddhist Studies* 28.1: 115–81.

———. 2019. "Mahāmudrā and Samayamudrā in the Dunhuang Documents and Beyond." In *Mahāmudrā in India and Tibet*, edited by Roger R. Jackson and Klaus-Dieter Mathes, 123–41. Leiden: Brill.

Das, Sanjib Kumar. 2009. *Basic Buddhist Terminology (Tibetan-Sanskrit-Hindi-English).* Sarnath: Kagyud Relief and Protection Committee.

Davenport, John T., trans. 2000. *Ordinary Wisdom: Sakya Pandita's Treasury of Good Advice.* Boston: Wisdom Publications.

Davidson, Ronald M. 1981. "The *Litany of the Names of Mañjuśrī*: Text and Translation of the *Mañjuśrīnāmasaṃgīti*." In *Tantric and Taoist Studies in Honor of R.A. Stein*, edited by Michel Strickmann, 1–69. Brussels: Institut Belge des Hautes Études Chinoises.

———. 1990. "An Introduction to the Standards of Scriptural Authenticity in Indian Buddhism." In *Chinese Buddhist Apocrypha*, edited by Robert Buswell, 291–325. Honolulu: University of Hawai'i Press, 1990.

———. 2002a. *Indian Esoteric Buddhism: A Social History of the Tantric Movement.* New York: Columbia University Press.

———. 2002b. "Reframing Sahaja: Genre, Representation, Ritual, and Lineage." *Journal of Indian Philosophy* 30: 45–83.

———. 2005. *Tibetan Renaissance: Tantric Buddhism in the Rebirth of Tibetan Culture.* New York: Columbia University Press.

de Rossi Filibeck, Elena 1990. "Sul commento alle parole 'dMigs brtse ma.'" In *Indo-Sino-Tibetica: Studi in onore di Luciano Petech*. Edited by Paolo Daffinà, 103–115. Roma: Bardi editore.

Dewar, Kevin, trans. 2008. *The Karmapa's Middle Way: "Feast for the Fortunate," A Commentary on Chandrakirti's "Madhyamakavatara."* Ithaca: Snow Lion Publications.

Dhargyey, Geshe Ngawang et al., trans. 1975. *The Great Seal of Voidness: The Root Text for the Ge-lug/Ka-gyu Tradition of Mahamudra*. Dharamsala: Library of Tibetan Works and Archives, 1975. [Revised in 2006 as "Commentary on 'Root Text for Mahamudra'—Geshe Ngawang Dhargyey": https://studybuddhism.com/en/advanced-studies/vajrayana/mahamudra-advanced/commentary-on-root-text-for-mahamudra-geshe-ngawang-dhargyey. Accessed December 10, 2017.]

———, trans. 1976. Aśvaghoṣa. *Fifty Verses of Guru-Devotion*. Revised ed. Dharamsala: Library of Tibetan Works and Archives.

Dilgo Khyentse and Padampa Sangye. 2006. *The Hundred Verses of Advice: Tibetan Buddhist Teachings on What Matters Most*. Translated by the Padmakara Translation Group. Boston and London: Shambhala.

DiValerio, David M. 2015. *The Holy Madmen of Tibet*. New York: Oxford University Press.

Döl-bo-ba Shay-rap-gyal-tsen. 2006. *Mountain Doctrine: Tibet's Fundamental Treatise on Other-Emptiness and the Buddha Matrix*. Translated by Jeffrey Hopkins. Ithaca: Snow Lion Publications.

"Don grub bzang po." BDRC no. P3303. http://tbrc.org/#!rid=P3303. Accessed July 11, 2014.

Dondrub, Gelong Thubten, trans. 2001. First Panchen Lama Losang Chökyi Gyältsän. *Lama Chöpa Puja, with practice additions from Lama Zopa Rinpoche*. Taos, NM: FPMT Education Services.

Dorje, Lama Sherab, trans. 1995. *Mahāmudrā Teachings of the Supreme Siddhas: The Eighth Situpa Tenpa'i Nyinchay on the Third Karmapa Rangjung Dorje's "Aspiration Prayer of Mahāmudrā of Definitive Meaning."* Ithaca: Snow Lion Publications.

Dowman, Keith, trans. 1994. *The Flight of the Garuda: Teachings of the Dzokchen Tradition of Tibetan Buddhism*. Boston: Wisdom Publications.

Draszczyk, Martina. 2015. "A Eulogy of Mind's Connate Qualities, Zhwa dmar Chos Grags ye shes on the Hidden Meaning of Luminosity." *Zentral-Asiatische Studien* 44: 99–119.

———. 2016. "Some Dwags po Mahāmudrā Responses to Sa skya Paṇḍita's Critique at 'Present-Day Mahāmudrā.'" *Journal of the International Association of Buddhist Studies* 39: 375–403.

———. 2019. "Mahāmudrā as Revelatory of the Key-Point of the Third *Dharmacakra* according to the *Sixty Verses of Mahāmudrā* by the Fourth Zhwa dmar pa, Chos grags ye shes." In *Mahāmudrā in India and Tibet*, edited by Roger R. Jackson and Klaus-Dieter Mathes, 204–36. Leiden: Brill.

Dreyfus, Georges B. J. 1998. "The Shuk-den Affair: History and Nature of a Quarrel." *Journal of the International Association of Buddhist Studies* 21.2: 221–70.

———. 2003. *The Sound of Two Hands Clapping: The Education of a Tibetan Buddhist Monk*. Berkeley: University of California Press.

Driver, Tom F. 2006. *Liberating Rites: Understanding the Transformative Power of Ritual.* Charleston, SC: BookSurge Publishing.

Ducher, Cécile. 2017. *Building a Tradition: The Lives of Mar-pa the Translator.* Collectanea Himalayica 5. Munich: Indus Verlag.

Dudjom Rinpoche. 1991. *The Nyingma School of Tibetan Buddhism.* Translated by Gyurme Dorje and Matthew Kapstein. Boston: Wisdom Publications.

Duff, Tony, trans. 2005. *The Bodyless* [sic] *Dakini Dharma: The Dakini Hearing Lineage of the Kagyus.* Kathmandu: Padma Karpo Translation Committee.

———. 2008a. *Dusum Khyenpa's Songs and Teachings: A Variety of Songs and Teachings from the First Karmapa's Collected Works.* Kathmandu: Padma Karpo Translation Committee.

———. 2008b. *Gampopa's Mahamudra: The Fivefold Mahamudra of the Kagyus.* Kathmandu: Padma Karpo Translation Committee.

———. 2010. *Maitripa's Writings on the View: The Main Indian Source of the Tibetan Views of Other Emptiness and Mahamudra.* Kathmandu: Padma Karpo Translation Committee.

Durkheim, Émile. 2008 [1917]. *The Elementary Forms of Religious Life.* Translated by Carol Cosman. New York: Oxford University Press.

Dviveda, Vrajavallabha. 1992. "'Having Become a God, He Should Sacrifice to the Gods.'" In *Ritual and Speculation in Early Tantrism: Studies in Honor of André Padoux*, edited by Teun Goudriaan, 121–38. Albany: State University of New York Press.

Dyczkowski, Mark S. G. 1987. *The Doctrine of Vibration: An Analysis of the Doctrines and Practices of Kashmir Shaivism.* Albany: State University of New York Press.

———. 1992a. *The Aphorisms of Shiva: The Śiva Sūtras with Bhaskāra's Commentary, the "Vārttika."* Albany: State University of New York Press.

———. 1992b. *The Stanzas on Vibration: The Spandakārikā with Four Commentaries.* Albany: State University of New York Press.

Edgerton, Franklin.1972 [1953]. *Buddhist Hybrid Sanskrit Grammar and Dictionary.* 2 vols. Delhi: Motilal Banarsidass.

Edou, Jérôme. 1996. *Machig Labdron and the Foundations of Chöd.* Ithaca: Snow Lion Publications.

Egan, Harvey G. 1978. "Christian Apophatic and Kataphatic Mysticisms." *Theological Studies* 39.3: 399–426.

Eliade, Mircea. 1970. *Yoga: Immortality and Freedom.* 2nd ed. Translated by Willard B. Trask. Bollingen Series 56. Princeton: Princeton University Press.

———. 1987 [1959]. *The Sacred and the Profane: The Nature of Religion.* Translated by Willard B. Trask. New York: Harcourt Brace Jovanovich.

Eliot, T. S. *Four Quartets.* http://www.coldbacon.com/poems/fq.html. Accessed October 30, 2017.

English, Elizabeth. 2002. *Vajrayoginī: Her Visualizations, Rituals, and Forms.* Boston: Wisdom Publications.

Evans-Wentz, W.Y., ed. 1958. *Tibetan Yoga and Secret Doctrines.* London, Oxford, and New York: Oxford University Press.

Farrow, G. W., and I. Menon, ed. and trans. 1992. *The Concealed Essence of the Hevajra Tantra, with the Commentary "Yogaratnamālā."* Delhi: Motilal Banarsidass.

Faure, Bernard. 1994. *The Rhetoric of Immediacy: A Cultural Critique of Chan/Zen Buddhism.* Princeton: Princeton University Press.

Forman, Robert K. C., ed. 1997. *The Problem of Pure Consciousness: Mysticism and Philosophy*. New York: Oxford University Press.

Fronsdal, Gil. 2016. *The Buddha Before Buddhism: Wisdom from the Early Teachings. A Translation of the "Aṭṭhagavagga" with Commentary*. Boulder: Shambhala.

Gamble, Ruth. 2013. *The View from Nowhere: The Travels of the Third Karmapa, Rang byung rdo rje, in Story and Song*. Ph.D. dissertation. Australian National University.

———. 2018. *Reincarnation in Tibetan Buddhism: The Third Karmapa and the Invention of a Tradition*. New York: Oxford University Press.

Gampopa. 1998. *The Jewel Ornament of Liberation: The Wish-Fulfilling Gem of the Noble Teachings*. Translated by Khenpo Könchog Gyaltsen. Edited by Ani K. Trinlay Chödron. Ithaca: Snow Lion Publications.

Gardner, Alexander. 2009a. "Baso Chokyi Gyaltsen." Treasury of Lives. http://treasuryoflives.org/biographies/view/Baso-Chokyi-Gyaltsen/6746. Accessed November 20, 2018.

———. 2009b. "The First Karmapa, Dusum Khyenpa." Treasury of Lives. http://treasuryoflives.org/biographies/view/First-Karmapa-Dusum-Khyenpa/2683. Accessed September 1, 2017.

———. 2009c. "The Fourth Panchen Lama, Lobzang Chokyi Gyaltsen." Treasury of Lives. http://treasuryoflives.org/biographies/view/Lobzang-Chokyi-Gyaltsen/9839. Accessed August 18, 2017.

———. 2011. "The Third Karmapa, Rangjung Dorje." Treasury of Lives. http://treasuryoflives.org/biographies/view/Third-Karmapa-Rangjung-Dorje/9201. Accessed August 14, 2017.

———. 2015 [2007]. "Chokyi Dorje." Treasury of Lives. http://treasuryoflives.org/biographies/view/Chokyi-Dorje/12883. Accessed September 1, 2017.

"Gelek Rimpoche." Jewel Heart. https://www.jewelheart.org/gelek-rimpoche/. Accessed September 16, 2017.

"Gelek Rimpoche." Wikipedia. https://en.wikipedia.org/wiki/Gelek_Rimpoche. Accessed September 16, 2017.

"Gelek Rinpoche." FPMT. https://fpmt.org/mandala/archives/older/mandala-issues-for-1999/may/gelek-rinpoche/. Accessed September 16, 2017.

Gelek Rinpoche. 2005. *Gom: A Course in Meditation*. [Ann Arbor:] Jewel Heart Buddhist Center.

———. 2006. *The Six Session Guru Yoga: An Essential Vajrayana Practice*. [Ann Arbor:] Jewel Heart Buddhist Center.

———. 2010. *Ganden Lha Gyema. The Hundreds of Deities of the Land of Joy*. Ann Arbor: Jewel Heart.

Gendun Drub, the First Dalai Lama. 1981. *Bridging the Sutras and Tantras, Including "Notes on Kalachakra."* Translated by Glenn H. Mullin. Ithaca: Gabriel/Snow Lion Publications.

Germano, David. 1994. "Architecture and Absence in the Secret Tantric History of the Great Perfection." *Journal of the International Association of Buddhist Studies* 17.2: 203–335.

"Geshe Kelsang Gyatso, Founder of the New Kadampa Tradition (NKT-IKBU)." *Info-Buddhism*. http://info-buddhism.com/geshe_kelsang_gyatso.html. Accessed June 13, 2015.

Giebel, Rolf, trans. 2001. *Two Esoteric Sūtras.* Moraga, CA: Numata Center for Buddhist Translation and Research.

Gnoli, Raniero, and Giacomella Orofino, intro. and trans. 1994. Nāropa. *Iniziazione Kālacakra.* Milano: Adelphi Edizioni.

Gold, Jonathan C. 2007. *The Dharma's Gatekeepers: Sakya Paṇḍita on Buddhist Scholarship in Tibet.* Albany: State University of New York Press.

Goldfield, Ari, Jules Levinson, Jim Scott, and Birgit Scott, trans. 2005. *The Moon of Wisdom: Chapter Six of Chandrakirti's "Entering the Middle Way," with Commentary from the Eighth Karmapa Mikyo Dorje's "Chariot of the Dagpo Kagyü Siddhas."* Ithaca: Snow Lion Publications.

Gonda, Jan. 1972. "Mudrā." *Studies in the History of Religions* 12: 21–31.

Goudriaan, Teun, ed. 1992. *Ritual and Speculation in Early Tantrism: Studies in Honor of André Padoux.* Albany: State University of New York Press.

Gray, David B. 2007. *The Cakrasamvara Tantra (The Discourse of Śrī Heruka): A Study and Annotated Translation.* New York: AIBS/CBS/THUS.

———. 2011. "Imprints of the 'Great Seal': On the Expanding Semantic Range of the Term *Mudrā* in Eighth through Eleventh Century Indian Buddhist Literature." *Journal of the International Association of Buddhist Studies* 34.1–2: 421–81.

———. 2016. "Tantra and Tantric Traditions of Hinduism and Buddhism." Oxford Research Encyclopedias. http://religion.oxfordre.com/view/10.1093/acrefore/9780199340378.001.0001/acrefore-9780199340378-e-59. Accessed January 25, 2017.

———, trans. and annot. 2017. Tsong Khapa Losang Drakpa. *Illumination of the Hidden Meaning (sbas don kun gsal). Part I: Maṇḍala, Mantra, and the Cult of the Yoginīs.* New York: AIBS/CBS/THUS.

———, trans. and annot. 2019. Tsong Khapa Losang Drakpa. *Illumination of the Hidden Meaning (sbas don kun gsal) Part II: Yogic Vows, Conduct, and Ritual Praxis.* New York and Somerville, MA: AIBS and Wisdom Publications.

Gregory, Peter, ed. 1987. *Sudden and Gradual: Approaches to Enlightenment in Chinese Thought.* Honolulu: University of Hawai'i Press.

Guenther, Herbert V. 1963. *The Life and Teaching of Nāropa.* London: Oxford University Press.

———. 1966. *Tibetan Buddhism without Mystification.* Leiden: E. J Brill.

———, trans. and annot. 1969. *The Royal Song of Saraha: A Study in the History of Buddhist Thought.* Seattle and London: University of Washington Press.

———. 1975. "Mahāmudrā: The Method of Self-Actualization." *Tibet Journal* 1.1: 5–23.

———. 1976. *Tibetan Treasures on the Middle Way.* Berkeley: Shambhala Publications.

———. 1977. *Tibetan Buddhism in Western Perspective: Collected Articles.* Emeryville, CA: Dharma Publishing.

———. 1993. *Ecstatic Spontaneity: Saraha's Three Cycles of Dohā.* Nanzan Studies in Asian Religions 4. Berkeley: Asian Humanities Press.

Guenther, Herbert V., and Leslie Kawamura, trans. 1975. *Mind in Buddhist Psychology: The "Necklace of Clear Understanding," by Ye-shes rGyal-mtshan.* Emeryville, CA: Dharma.

Gupta, Sanjukta, Dirk Jan Hoens, and Teun Goudriaan. 1979. *Hindu Tantrism.* Leiden: E. J. Brill.

Gyaltsen, Khenpo Könchog, trans. 1986a. *The Garland of Mahamudra Practices: A Translation of Kunga Rinchen's "Clarifying the Jewel Rosary of the Profound Fivefold Path."* Edited by Katherine Rogers. Ithaca: Snow Lion Publications.

———, trans. 1986b. *Prayer Flags: The Life and Spiritual Teachings of Jigten Sumgön*. Ithaca: Snow Lion Publications.

———. 1990. *The Great Kagyu Masters: The Golden Lineage Treasury*. Edited by Victoria Huckenpahler. Ithaca: Snow Lion Publications.

Gyatrul Rinpoche Sherpa, Trungram. 2004. *Gampopa, the Monk and the Yogi: His Life and Teachings*. Ph.D. dissertation. Harvard University.

Gyatso, Geshe Kelsang. 1982. *Clear Light of Bliss: Mahamudra in Vajrayana Buddhism*. London: Wisdom Publications.

———. 1991. *Guide to Dakini Land: A Commentary to the Highest Yoga Tantra Practice of Vajrayogini*. London: Tharpa Publications.

———. 1992a. *Clear Light of Bliss: Mahamudra in Vajrayana Buddhism*. 2nd ed. London: Tharpa Publications.

———. 1992b. *Great Treasury of Merit: A Commentary to the Practice of "Offering to the Spiritual Guide."* London: Tharpa Publications.

———. 2005. *Mahamudra Tantra: An Introduction to Meditation on Tantra*. Ulverston, U.K.: Tharpa Publications.

———. 2016. *The Oral Instructions of Mahamudra: The Very Essence of the Buddha's Teachings on Sutra and Tantra*. 2nd ed. Glen Spey, NY: Tharpa Publications.

Gyatso, Janet. 1985. "The Development of the *Gcod* Tradition." In *Soundings in Tibetan Civilization*, edited by Barbara Aziz and Matthew Kapstein, 320–41. New Delhi: Manohar.

Harding, Sarah. 2003. *Machik's Complete Explanation: Clarifying the Meaning of Chöd*. Ithaca: Snow Lion Publications.

———. 2010. *Niguma: Lady of Illusion*. Ithaca: Snow Lion Publications.

———. 2013. "Did Machik Lapdrön Really Teach Chöd?" Unpublished paper presented at 13th seminar of International Association for Tibetan Studies, Ulaanbaatar, Mongolia.

Harper, Katherine Anne, and Robert L. Brown, eds. 2002. *The Roots of Tantra*. Albany: State University of New York Press.

Harrison, Paul, trans. 1998. *Pratyutpanna Samādhi Sūtra, translated by Lokakṣema*. BDK English Tripṭaka 25-II. Berkeley: Numata Foundation.

Hartzell, James F. 2012. "The Buddhist Sanskrit Tantras: 'The *Samādhi* of the Plowed Row.'" *Pacific World* (3rd series) 14: 63–178.

Heller, Amy. 2005. "The Second Dalai Lama Gendun Gyatso." In *The Dalai Lamas: A Visual History*, edited by Martin Brauen, 42–51. Chicago: Serindia Publications.

Higgins, David. 2006. "On the Development of the Non-Mentation (*amanasikāra*) Doctrine in Indo-Tibetan Buddhism." *Journal of the International Association of Buddhist Studies* 29.2: 255–304.

———. 2015. "The Two Faces of Mahāmudrā: Padma dkar po on Yang dgon pa's *gnas lugs phyag chen* and *'khrul lugs phyag chen*." *Zentral Asiatische Studien* 44: 51–75.

Higgins, David, and Martina Draszczyk. 2016. *Mahāmudrā and the Middle Way: Post-Classical Kagyü Discourses on Mind, Emptiness, and Buddha Nature*. 2 vols. Vienna: Arbeitskreis für Tibetische und Buddhistische Studien Universität Wien.

Hookham, S. K. 1991. *The Buddha Within: Tathagatagarbha Doctrine According to the Shentong Interpretation of the Ratnagotravibhaga*. Albany: State University of New York Press.

Hopkins, Jeffrey. 1996. *Meditation on Emptiness*. Revised ed. Boston: Wisdom Publications.

———, trans. 2003. *Maps of the Profound: Jam-yang-shay-ba's "Great Exposition of Buddhist and Non-Buddhist Views of the Nature of Reality."* Ithaca: Snow Lion Publications.

———, trans. 2008. *Tsong-kha-pa's Final Exposition of Wisdom.* Ithaca: Snow Lion Publications.

———. 2011. *Tibetan-Sanskrit-English Dictionary.* Dyke, VA: UMA Institute for Tibetan Studies.

Huntington, Jr., C. W. 1983. "A 'Nonreferential' View of Language and Conceptual Thought in the Work of Tsoṅ-kha-pa." *Philosophy East and West* 33.4: 325–39.

Huxley, Aldous. 2009 [1945]. *The Perennial Philosophy.* New York: Harper Perennial.

Illich, Marina. 2006. *Selections from the Life of a Tibetan Buddhist Polymath: Chankya Rolpai Dorje (lcang skya rol pa'i rdo rje), 1717–1786.* Ph.D. dissertation, Columbia University.

Isaacson, Harunaga, and Francesco Sferra. 2014. *The Sekanirdeśa of Maitreyanātha (Advayavajra) with the Sekanirdeśapañjikā of Rāmapāla: Critical Edition of the Sanskrit and Tibetan Texts with English Translations and Reproductions of the MSS.* Napoli: Università degli Studi di Napoli "L'Orientale"; Hamburg: Asien-Afrika Institut, Universität Hamburg.

Jackson, David P. 1987. *The Entrance Gate for the Wise (Section III): Sa-skya Paṇḍita on Indian and Tibetan Traditions of Pramāṇa and Philosophical Debate.* 2 vols. Vienna: Arbeitskreis für Tibetische und Buddhistische Studien Universität Wien.

———. 1990. "Sa skya Paṇḍita the 'Polemicist': Ancient Debates and Modern Interpretations." *Journal of the International Association of Buddhist Studies* 13.2: 17–116.

———. 1994. *Enlightenment by a Single Means: Tibetan Controversies on the "Self-Sufficient White Remedy."* Beiträge zur Kultur- und Geistesgeschichte Asiens 12. Vienna: Verlag der Österreichischen Akademie der Wissenschaften.

———, trans. 2015. [Sakya Paṇḍita.] *Clarifying the Sage's Intent.* In Dölpa, Gampopa, and Sakya Paṇḍita. *Stages of the Buddha's Teachings: Three Key Texts,* 383–602. The Library of Tibetan Classics 10. Somerville, MA: Wisdom Publications.

Jackson, Roger R. 1982. "Sa skya Paṇḍita's Account of the bSam yas Debate: History as Polemic." *Journal of the International Association of Buddhist Studies* 5.1: 89–99.

———. 1992. "The Tibetan *Tshogs Zhing* (Field of Assembly): General Notes on Its Religious Function, Its Structure and Its Content," *Asian Philosophy* 2.2: 157–72.

———. 1993. *Is Enlightenment Possible? Dharmakīrti and rGyal tshab rje on Knowledge, Rebirth, No-Self, and Liberation.* Ithaca: Snow Lion Publications.

———. 1996. "No/Responsibility: Saraha, '*Siddha* Ethics' and the Transcendency Thesis." In *Felicitation Volume on the Occasion of the Sixtieth Birthday of H.H. the Dalai Lama,* edited by S. S. Bahulkar and N. Samten, 79–110. Sarnath: Central Institute of Higher Tibetan Studies.

———. 1997. "A Tibetan Fasting Ritual." In *Religions of Tibet in Practice,* edited by Donald S. Lopez, Jr., 271–92. Princeton Readings in Religion. Princeton: Princeton University Press.

———. 2001. "The dGe ldan–bKa' brgyud Tradition of Mahāmudrā: How Much Dge ldan? How Much Bka' brgyud?" In *Changing Minds: Contributions to the Study of Buddhism and Tibet in Honor of Jeffrey Hopkins,* edited by Guy Newland, 155–91. Ithaca: Snow Lion Publications.

———. 2004. *Tantric Treasures: Three Mystical Texts from Buddhist India.* New York: Oxford University Press.

———. 2008. "The Indian *Mahāmudrā* 'Canons': A Preliminary Sketch." *Indian International Journal of Buddhist Studies* 9: 151–84.

———. 2009. "Archer Among the Yellow Hats: Some Geluk Uses of Saraha." *Indian International Journal of Buddhist Studies* 10: 105–33.

———. 2012. "Saraha's *Queen Dohās*." In *Yoga in Practice*, edited by David Gordon White, 162–84. Princeton: Princeton University Press.

———. 2014. "Borrowed Texts, Fluid Genres, and Performative License: Reflections on a dGe lugs pa Offering Ritual." In *Tibetan Literary Genres, Texts, and Text Types: From Genre Classification to Transformation*, edited by Jim Rheingans, 89–109. Leiden and Boston: Brill.

———. 2015. "Did Tsongkhapa Teach Mahāmudrā?" *Zentral Asiatische Studien* 44: 79–97.

———. 2019. "Assimilating the Great Seal: The Dge lugs pa-ization of the *Dge ldan bka 'brgyud* Tradition of Mahāmudrā." In *Mahāmudrā in India and Tibet*, edited by Roger R. Jackson and Klaus-Dieter Mathes, 210–27. Leiden: Brill.

James, William. 1983 [1902]. *The Varieties of Religious Experience: A Study in Human Nature.* Baltimore: Penguin Classics.

Jamgon Kongtrul. 2003. *Timeless Rapture: Inspired Verse of the Shangpa Masters.* Translated by Ngawang Zangpo. Ithaca: Snow Lion Publications.

Jamgön Kongtrul. 2003–12. *The Treasury of Knowledge.* Translated by the Kalu Rinpoche Translation Committee. 10 vols. Ithaca: Snow Lion Publications.

Jampa, Gyumed Khensur Lobsang. 2013. *The Easy Path: Illuminating the First Panchen Lama's Secret Instructions.* Edited by Lorne Ladner. Boston: Wisdom Publications.

Jinpa, Thupten. 1999. "Tsongkhapa's Qualms about Early Tibetan Interpretations of Madhyamaka Philosophy." *The Tibet Journal* 24.2: 3–28.

——— 2002. *Self, Reality and Reason in Tibetan Philosophy: Tsongkhapa's Quest for the Middle Way.* London: RoutledgeCurzon.

———, trans. 2006. *Mind Training: The Great Collection.* Compiled by Shönu Gyalchok and Könchok Gyaltsen. Boston: Wisdom Publications.

———, trans. 2008. *The Book of Kadam: The Core Texts.* Attributed to Atiśa and Dromtönpa. Boston: Wisdom Publications.

———. 2019. *Tsongkhapa: A Buddha in the Land of Snows.* Boulder: Shambhala Publications.

———. n.d., trans. Panchen Lobsang Chögyen. *Root Stanzas on Mahamudra According to the Sacred Geden Lineage.* Unpublished ms.

Jinpa, Thupten, and Jaś Elsner, trans. 2000. *Songs of Spiritual Experience: Tibetan Buddhist Poems of Insight and Awakening.* Boston: Shambhala.

Jo.nang Tāranātha. 1983. *The Seven Instruction Lineages.* Translated and edited by David Templeman. Dharamsala: Library of Tibetan Works and Archives.

Kachen Yeshe Gyaltsen. 2014. *Manjushri's Innermost Secret: A Profound Commentary of Oral Instructions on the Practice of Lama Chöpa.* Translated by David Gonsalez. Seattle: Dechen Ling Press.

Kaiser, Jr., William C., and Moisés Silva. 2007. *Introduction to Biblical Hermeneutics: The Search for Meaning.* Revised ed. Grand Rapids, MI: Zondervan.

Kalzang Gyatso, The Seventh Dalai Lama. 1982. *Songs of Spiritual Change.* Translated by Glenn H. Mullin. Ithaca: Gabriel/Snow Lion Publications.

Kanakura Yensho et al. 1953. *A Catalogue of the Tōhoku University Collection of Tibetan Works on Buddhism.* Sendai, Japan: Seminary of Indology, Tōhoku University.

Kapstein, Matthew T. 1990. Review of *Mahamudra: The Quintessence of Mind and Meditation* (trans. Lobsang Lhalungpa). *Journal of the International Association of Buddhist Studies* 13.1: 101–14.

———. 2000. *The Tibetan Assimilation of Buddhism: Conversion, Contestation, and Memory*. Oxford and New York: Oxford University Press.

———. 2005. "The Seventh Dalai Lama Kalsang Gyatso." In *The Dalai Lamas: A Visual History*, edited by Martin Brauen, 103–15. Chicago: Serindia.

Karma Chagmé. 1998. *A Spacious Path to Freedom: Practical Instructions on the Union of Mahāmudrā and Atiyoga*. Translated by B. Alan Wallace. Commentary by Gyatrul Rinpoche. Ithaca: Snow Lion Publications.

Karmay, Samten G. 1988. *The Great Perfection: A Philosophical and Meditative Teaching of Tibetan Buddhism*. Leiden: E. J. Brill.

———, trans. 2014. *The Illusive Play: The Autobiography of the Fifth Dalai Lama*. Chicago: Serindia Publications.

Karthar Rinpoche, Khenpo. 2013. *Four-Session Guru Yoga by the Eighth Karmapa Mikyo Dorje*. Woodstock, NY: KTD Publications.

Kasawara, Kenjiu, and F. Max Muller. 1981 [1885]. *The Dharma-Saṃgraha: An Ancient Collection of Buddhist Technical Terms*. New Delhi: Cosmo Publications.

Katz, Steven T., ed. 1978. *Mysticism and Philosophical Analysis*. New York: Oxford University Press.

———, ed. 1984. *Mysticism and Religious Traditions*. New York: Oxford University Press.

———, ed. 1992. *Mysticism and Language*. New York: Oxford University Press.

Kay, David. 2004. *Tibetan and Zen Buddhism in Britain: Transplantation, Development and Adaptation*. London: Routledge.

"Keutsang Hermitage (Ke'u tshang ri khrod)." *Tibetan and Himalayan Library*. http://www.thlib.org/places/monasteries/sera/hermitages/pdf/sera_herm_keutsang.pdf. Accessed March 23, 2015.

Khedrup Norsang Gyatso. 2004. *Ornament of Stainless Light: An Exposition of the Kālacakra Tantra*. Translated by Gavin Kilty. Library of Tibetan Classics 14. Boston: Wisdom Publications.

Kilty, Gavin, trans. 2001. *The Splendor of an Autumn Moon: The Devotional Verse of Tsongkhapa*. Boston: Wisdom Publications.

———, trans. 2019. *Understanding the Case against Shukden: The History of a Contested Tibetan Practice*. Compiled by the Association of Geluk Masters, the Geluk International Foundation, and the Foundation for the Preservation of Geluk Monasticism. Boston: Wisdom Publications.

Kollmar-Paulenz, Karénina. 2005. "The Third Dalai Lama Sönam Gyatso and the Fourth Dalai Lama Yönten Gyatso." In *The Dalai Lamas: A Visual History*, edited by Martin Brauen, 52–63. Chicago: Serindia Publications.

Komarovski, Yaroslav. 2011. *Visions of Unity: The Golden Pandita Shakya Chokden's New Interpretation of Yogācāra and Madhyamaka*. Albany: State University of New York Press.

———. 2015. *Tibetan Buddhism and Mystical Experience*. New York: Oxford University Press.

Kragh, Ulrich. 1998. *Culture and Subculture: A Study of the Mahāmudrā Teachings of Sgam po pa*. M.A. research paper (special). Copenhagen University.

———. 2011. "Prolegomenon to the *Six Doctrines of Nā ro pa*: Authority and Tradition."

In *Mahāmudrā and the Bka' brgyud Tradition*, edited by Roger R. Jackson and Matthew T. Kapstein, 131–78. Andiast, Switzerland: International Institute for Tibetan and Buddhist Studies GmbH, 2011.

———. 2015. *Tibetan Yoga and Mysticism: A Textual Study of the Yogas of Nāropa and Mahāmudrā Meditation In the Medieval Tradition of Dags po*. Tokyo: The International Institute for Buddhist Studies.

Krug, Adam. 2019. "*The Seven Siddhi Texts* (*Grub pa sde bdun*): Remarks on the Corpus and Its Employment in Sa skya–Bka' brkyud Mahāmudrā Polemical Literature." In *Mahāmudrā in India and Tibet*, edited by Roger R. Jackson and Klaus-Dieter Mathes, 90–122. Leiden: Brill.

Kunga Rinpoche and Brian Cutillo, trans. 1995 [1978]. *Drinking the Mountain Stream: Songs of Tibet's Beloved Saint, Milarepa*. Boston: Wisdom Publications.

———, trans. 2008 [1984.] *The Flight of the Garuda: Three Texts from the Practice Lineage*. Kathmandu: Rangjung Yeshe Publications.

Kunsang, Lama, Lama Pemo, and Marie Aubèle. 2012. *History of the Karmapas: The Odyssey of the Tibetan Masters with the Black Crown*. Ithaca: Snow Lion Publications.

Kvaerne, Per. 1975. "On the Concept of Sahaja in Indian Buddhist Tantric Literature." *Temenos* 11: 88–135.

———. 1977. *An Anthology of Buddhist Tantric Songs: A Study of the Caryāgīti*. Oslo: Universitetsforlaget.

Kwon, Do-Kyun. 2002. *Sarva Tathāgata Tattva Saṃgraha: Compendium of All the Tathāgatas. A Study of Its Origin, Structure, and Teachings*. Ph.D. dissertation. University of London.

Lang, Karen. 1986. *Āryadeva's Catuḥśataka: On the Bodhisattva's Cultivation of Merit and Knowledge*. Indiste Studier 7. Copenhagen: Akademisk Forlag.

Larsson, Stefan. 2011. "What Do the Childhood and Early Life of Gtsang smyon Heruka Tell Us about His Bka' brgyud Affiliation?" In *Mahāmudrā and the Bka' brgyud Tradition*, edited by Roger R. Jackson and Matthew T. Kapstein, 425–52. Andiast, Switzerland: International Institute for Tibetan and Buddhist Studies GmbH, 2011.

———. 2012. *Crazy for Wisdom: The Making of a Mad Yogin in Fifteenth-Century Tibet*. Brill's Tibetan Studies Library. Leiden: Brill.

"The Last Upholder of the Gelug Mahamudra Tradition: Kelsang Gyatso." *Tibetan Buddhism: Struggling with Diffi-Cult Issues*. http://buddhism-controversy-blog.com/2014/08/03/the-last-upholder-of-the-gelug-mahamudra-tradition-geshe-kelsang-gyatso/. Accessed June 18, 2015.

Lesco, Phillip. 2009. "The *Sekoddeśaṭippaṇī:* A Brief Commentary." In *As Long as Space Endures: Essays on the Kālacakra Tantra in Honor of H. H. the Dalai Lama*, edited by Edwin A. Arnold, 51–92. Ithaca: Snow Lion Publications.

Lessing, F. D., and A. Wayman, trans. 1978. *Introduction to the Buddhist Tantric Systems. Translated from Mkhas grub rje's "Rgyud sde spyiḥi rnam par gźag pa rgyas par brjod," with Original Text and Annotation*. Delhi: Motilal Banarsidass.

Levering, Miriam, ed. 1989. *Rethinking Scripture: Essays from a Comparative Perspective*. Albany: State University of New York Press.

Lhalungpa, Lobsang P. trans. 1977. *The Life of Milarepa: A New Translation from the Tibetan*. New York: E. P. Dutton.

Li An-che. 1949. "The Bkaḥ-brgyud Sect of Lamaism." *Journal of the Royal Asiatic Society* 69: 51–59.

Lindtner, Christian. 1982. *Nagarjuniana: Studies in the Writings and Philosophy of Nāgārjuna*. Indiste Studier 4. Copenhagen: Akademisk Forlag.

Linrothe, Rob, ed. 2006. *Holy Madness: Portraits of Tantric Siddhas*. New York: Rubin Museum of Art; Chicago: Serindia Publications.

Loden, Geshe Acharya Thubten. 2009. *Great Treasury of Mahamudra*. Melbourne: Tushita Publications.

Lopez, Jr., Donald S., ed. 1992. *Buddhist Hermeneutics* Honolulu: University of Hawai'i Press.

———. 2006. *The Madman's Middle Way: Reflections on Reality of the Tibetan Monk Gendun Chopel*. Chicago: University of Chicago Press.

———. 2012. *The Scientific Buddha: His Short and Happy Life*. New Haven: Yale University Press.

———. 2019. *Seeing the Sacred in Samsara: An Illustrated Guide to the Eighty-Four Mahāsiddhas*. Boulder: Shambhala Publications.

Magee, William. 1999. *The Nature of Things: Emptiness and Essence in the Geluk World*. Ithaca: Snow Lion Publications.

Makidono, Tomoko. 2018. "*The Ornament of the Buddha-Nature*: Dge rtse Mahāpaṇḍita's Exposition of the Great Madhyamaka of Other-Emptiness." *Indian International Journal of Buddhist Studies* 19: 77–148.

Makransky, John J. 1997. *Buddhahood Embodied: Sources of Controversy in India and Tibet*. Albany: State University of New York Press.

Martin, Craig, and Russell T. McCutcheon, eds. 2012. *Religious Experience: A Reader.* Abingdon, UK: Routledge.

Martin, Dan. 1990. *Tibetan Histories: A Bibliography of Tibetan-Language Historical Works*. London: Serindia Publications.

———. 1992. "A Twefth-Century Tibetan Classic of Mahāmudrā: *The Path of Ultimate Profundity: The Great Seal Instructions of Zhang*." *Journal of the International Association of Buddhist Studies* 15.2: 243–319.

———. 2008. "Chegompa Sherab Dorje." Treasury of Lives. https://treasuryoflives.org/biographies/view/Chegompa-Sherab-Dorje/7373. Accessed July 29, 2018.

Mathes, Klaus-Dieter. 2004. "Tāranātha's 'Twenty-One Differences with Regard to the Profound Meaning': Comparing the Views of the Two gZhan-stoṅ Masters Dol po pa and Śākya mchog ldan." *Journal of the International Association of Buddhist Studies* 27.2: 285–328.

———. 2006. "Blending the Sūtras with the Tantras: The Influence of Maitrīpa and His Circle on the Formation of Sūtra Mahāmudrā in the Kagyu Schools." In *Tibetan Buddhist Literature and Praxis: Studies in Its Formative Period, 900–1400; Proceedings of the Tenth Seminar of the International Association of Tibetan Studies, Oxford, 2003*, edited by Ronald M. Davidson and Christian K. Wedemeyer, 201–27. Leiden: Brill.

———. 2007. "Can *Sūtra Mahāmudrā* Be Justified on the Basis of Maitrīpa's *Apratiṣṭhānavāda*?" In *Pramāṇakīrtiḥ: Papers Dedicated to Ernst Steinkellner on the Occasion of His 70th Birthday*, edited by Birgit Kellner et al., 545–66. Wiener Studien zur Tibetologie und Buddhismuskunde 70.2. Vienna: Arbeitskreis für Tibetische und Buddhistische Studien.

———. 2008. *A Direct Path to the Buddha Within: Gö Lotsāwa's Mahāmudrā Interpretation of the Ratnagotravibhāga*. Boston: Wisdom Publications.

———. 2015. *A Fine Blend of Mahāmudrā and Madhyamaka: Maitrīpa's Collection of Texts on Non-Conceptual Realization (Amanasikāra).* Vienna: Verlag der Österreichischen Akademie der Wissenschaften.

———. 2019. "Maitrīpa's *Amanasikāra*-Based Mahāmudrā in the Works of the Eighth Karmapa Mi bskyod rdo rje." In *Mahāmudrā in India and Tibet*, edited by Roger R. Jackson and Klaus-Dieter Mathes, 269–301. Leiden: Brill.

McRae, John R. 2004. *Seeing Through Zen: Encounter, Transformation, and Genealogy in Chinese Chan.* Berkeley: University of California Press.

Miller, W. Blythe. 2005. "The Vagrant Poet and the Reluctant Scholar: A Study of the Balance of Iconoclasm and Civility in the Biographical Accounts of the Two Founders of the 'Brug pa Bka' brgyud Lineages." *Journal of the International Association of Buddhist Studies* 28.2: 369–410.

Mishra, Ramprasad. 1993. *Advayasiddhi: The Tāntric View of Lakṣmīṅkarā.* New Delhi: Kant Publications.

Molk, David. 2008. *Lion of Siddhas: The Life and Teachings of Padampa Sangye.* Ithaca: Snow Lion Publications.

Monier-Williams, Monier. 1974 [1899]. *A Sanskrit-English Dictionary.* Delhi: Motilal Banarsidass.

Mookerjee, Ajit. 1983. *Kundalini: The Arousal of Inner Energy.* New York: Destiny Books.

Muktananda, Swami. 1978. *Play of Consciousness: A Spiritual Autobiography.* South Fallsburg, NY: SYDA Foundation.

Muller-Ortega, Paul. 1989. *The Triadic Heart of Śiva: Kaula Tantricism of Abhinavaguopta in the Non-Dual Shaivism of Kashmir.* Albany: State University of New York Press.

Mullin, Glenn H., trans. 1985. [Gendun Gyatso.] *Selected Works of the Dalai Lama II: Tantric Yogas of Sister Niguma.* Ithaca: Snow Lion Publications.

———, trans. 1994. [Gendun Gyatso.] *Mystical Verses of a Mad Dalai Lama.* Wheaton, IL: Quest Books.

———, intro., ed., and trans. 1996. *Tsongkhapa's Six Yogas of Naropa.* Ithaca: Snow Lion Publications.

———, intro. and trans. 1997. *Readings on the Six Yogas of Naropa.* Ithaca: Snow Lion Publications.

———. 2001. *The Fourteen Dalai Lamas: A Sacred Legacy of Reincarnation.* Santa Fe: Clear Light Publications.

Nāgārjuna, Ācārya. 1997. *The Precious Garland: An Epsitle to a King.* Translated by John Dunne and Sara McClintock. Boston: Wisdom Publications.

Nakamura Hajime. 1987. *Indian Buddhism: A Survey with Bibliographical Notes.* Delhi: Motilal Banarsidass.

Nālandā Translation Committee, under the direction of Chögyam Trungpa. 1980. *The Rain of Wisdom: The Vajra Songs of the Kagyü Gurus.* Boulder and London: Shambhala, 1980.

———. 1982. *The Life of Marpa the Translator.* Boulder: Prajñā Press.

Namgyal, Tsering. 2011. "The First Rongwo Drubchen, Shar Kalden Gyatso." Treasury of Lives. http://www.treasuryoflives.org/biographies/view/Shar-Kalden-Gyatso/9753. Accessed December 14, 2014.

———. 2012. "The Second Changkya, Ngawang Losang Choden." Treasury of Lives. http://www.treasuryoflives.org/biographies/view/Second-Changkya-Ngawang-Lobzang-Choden/3758. Accessed April 4, 2015.

Ñāṇamoli, Bhikkhu, and Bhikkhu Bodhi, trans. 1995. *The Middle-Length Discourses of the Buddha: A New Translation of the Majjhima Nikāya*. Boston: Wisdom Publications.

Napper, Elizabeth. 1989. *Dependent Arising and Emptiness*. Boston: Wisdom Publications.

Newman, John Ronald. 1987. *The Outer Wheel of Time: Vajrayāna Buddhist Cosmology in the Kālacakra Tantra*. Ph.D. dissertation. University of Wisconsin-Madison.

Ngulchu Dharmabhadra and the Vth Ling Rinpoche, Losang Lungtok Tenzin Trinley. 2012. *The Roar of Thunder: Yamantaka Practice and Commentary*. Translated by David Gonsalez. Ithaca: Snow Lion Publications.

Ngulchu Dharmabhadra and the First Panchen Lama, Losang Chökyi Gyaltsen. 2010. *Source of Supreme Bliss: Heruka Chakrasamvara Five Deity Practice and Commentary*. Translated by David Gonsalez. Ithaca: Snow Lion Publications.

———. 2014. *Blazing Inner Fire of Emptiness: An Experiential Commentary of the Practice of the Six Yogas of Nāropa*. Translated by David Gonsalez. Ithaca: Snow Lion Publications.

Nydahl, Ole. 1991. *Mahamudra: Boundless Joy and Freedom. A Commentary on the Wishing Prayer for the Attainment of the Ultimate Mahamudra Given by His Holiness Rangjung Dorje (The Third Karmapa, 1284–1339)*. Nevada City, CA: Blue Dolphin Publishing.

Panchen Lobsang Chökyi Gyaltsen. 2014. *The Panchen Lama's Debate Between Wisdom and the Reifying Habit*. Translated by Kenneth Liberman. Delhi: Motilal Banarsidass.

———. 2019. *The Essence of the Ocean of Attainments: The Creation Stage of the Guhyasamāja Tantra according to Paṇchen Losang Chökyi Gyaltsen*. Translated by Yael Bentor and Penpa Dorjee. Boston: Wisdom Publications.

Panchen Sonam Dragpa. 2006. *Overview of Buddhist Tantras, Captivating the Minds of the Fortunate Ones*. Translated by Martin J. Boord and Losang Norbu Tsonawa. Dharamsala: Library of Tibetan Works and Archives.

Patton, Laurie L., trans. 2008. *The Bhagavad Gita*. Baltimore: Penguin Classics.

Pearcey, Adam. 2013. "Dongak Chökyi Gyatso." Treasury of Lives. http://treasuryoflives.org/biographies/view/Dongak-Chokyi-Gyatso/7945. Accessed September 15, 2017.

———. 2014. "Japa Dongak Gyatso." Treasury of Lives. http://treasuryoflives.org/biographies/view/Japa-Dongak-Gyatso/12785. Accessed September 15, 2017.

Pettit, John W. 1999. *Mipham's Beacon of Certainty: The View of Dzogchen, the Great Perfection*. Boston: Wisdom Publications.

Phabongkha Rinpoché [Pabongka Rinpoche]. 1990–2001. *Liberation in Our Hands*. Translated by Sermey Khensur Lobang Tharchin, with Artemus B. Engle. 3 vols. Howell, NJ: Mahayana Sutra and Tantra Press.

——— [Pabongka Rinpoche]. 1991. *Liberation in the Palm of Your Hand: A Concise Discourse on the Path to Enlightenment*. Edited by Trijang Rinpoche. Translated by Michael Richards. Boston: Wisdom Publications.

——— [Phabongkha Dechen Nyingpo]. 2011. *The Extremely Secret Dakini of Naropa: Vajrayogini Practice and Commentary*. Translated by David Gonsalez. Ithaca: Snow Lion Publications.

Powers, John, trans. 1995. *Wisdom of Buddha: The Saṁdhinirmocana Sūtra*. Berkeley: Dharma Publishing.

Proudfoot, Wayne. 1987. *Religious Experience*. Berkeley: University of California Press.

Quintman, Andrew. 2014. *The Yogin and the Madman: Reading the Biographical Corpus of Tibet's Great Saint Milarepa*. New York: Columbia University Press.

Rabten, Geshé. 1983. *Echoes of Voidness.* Translated and edited by Stephen Batchelor. London: Wisdom Publications.

———. 1989. *Song of the Profound View.* Translated by Stephen Batchelor. London: Wisdom Publications.

Rangjung Yeshe Wiki Dharma Dictionary. http://rywiki.tsadra.org.

Rheingans, Jim. 2004. *Das Leben und Gesamtwerk des ersten Karma prhin las pa.* M.A. thesis. University of Hamburg.

———. 2008. *The Eighth Karmapa's Life and His Interpretation of the Great Seal.* Ph.D. dissertation. Bath Spa University.

———. 2011. "The Eighth Karma pa's Answer to Gling drung pa." In *Mahāmudrā and the Bka' brgyud Tradition,* edited by Roger R. Jackson and Matthew T. Kapstein, 345–86. Andiast, Switzerland: International Institute for Tibetan and Buddhist Studies GmbH.

Rhys Davids, T. W., and William Stede. 1994 [1921]. *Pali-English Dictionary.* New Delhi: Munshiram Manoharlal.

Ricard, Matthieu, trans. 1994. *The Life of Shabkar: The Autobiography of a Tibetan Yogin.* Albany: State University of New York Press.

———. 2007. "Zhabkar Tsokdruk Rangdrol." Treasury of Lives. http://www.treasuryoflives.org/biographies/view/Zhabkar-Tsokdruk-Rangdrol-/4611. Accessed April 11, 2015.

Richardson, Hugh. 1998 [1958–59.] "The Karma-pa Sect: A Historical Note." In *High Peaks, Pure Earth,* 357–78. London: Serindia Publications.

Rinchen, Geshe Sonam. 1994. *Yogic Deeds of Bodhisattvas: Gyal-tsap on Āryadeva's Four Hundred.* Translated by Ruth Sonam. Ithaca: Snow Lion Publications.

Ringu Tulku. 2006. *The Ri-me Philosophy of Jamgön Kongtrul the Great: A Study of the Buddhist Lineages of Tibet.* Boston: Shambhala Publications.

Roberts, Peter Alan. 2007. *The Biographies of Rechungpa: The Evolution of a Tibetan Historiography.* London: Routledge.

———, trans. 2011. *Mahāmudrā and Related Instructions: Core Teachings of the Kagyü Schools.* Library of Tibetan Classics 5. Boston: Wisdom Publications.

———, trans. 2014. *The Mind of Mahāmudrā.* Boston: Wisdom Publications.

Roerich, George N. [with Gendun Chöpel], trans. 1976 [1949]. *The Blue Annals.* Delhi: Motilal Banarsidass.

Roloff, Carla. 2009. *Red mda' ba, Buddhist Yogi-Scholar of the Fourteenth Century: The Forgotten Reviver of Madhyamaka Philosophy in Tibet.* Contributions to Tibetan Studies 7. Wiesbaden: Reichert.

Sakya Pandita Kunga Gyaltshen. 2002. *A Clear Differentiation of the Three Codes: Essential Distinctions among the Individual Liberation, Great Vehicle, and Tantric Systems.* Translated by Jared Douglas Rhoton. Albany: State University of New York Press.

Samuel, Geoffrey. 1993. *Civilized Shamans: Buddhism in Tibetan Societies.* Washington, DC: Smithsonian Institution.

———. 2008. *The Origins of Yoga and Tantra: Indic Religions to the Thirteenth Century.* Cambridge: Cambridge University Press.

Saunders, E. Dale. 1960. *Mudrā: A Study of Symbolic Gestures in Japanese Buddhist Sculpture.* Princeton: Princeton University Press.

Schaeffer, Kurtis R. 1995. *The Enlightened Heart of Buddhahood: A Study and Translation of the Third Karma pa Rang byung rdo rje's Work on Tathāgatagarbha*. M.A. thesis. Harvard University.

———. 2005a. *Dreaming the Great Brahmin: Tibetan Traditions of the Buddhist Poet-Saint Saraha*. New York: Oxford University Press.

———. 2005b. "The Fifth Dalai Lama Ngawang Lopsang Gyatso." In *The Dalai Lamas: A Visual History*, edited by Martin Brauen, 65–91. Chicago: Serindia Publications.

———. 2011. "The Printing Projects of Gtsang smyon Heruka and His Disciples." In *Mahāmudrā and the Bka' brgyud Tradition*, edited by Roger R. Jackson and Matthew T. Kapstein, 453–79. Andiast, Switzerland: International Institute for Tibetan and Buddhist Studies GmbH.

Schiller, Alexander. 2014. *Die "Vier Yoga"-Stufen der-Meditationstradition: Eine Anthologie aus den Gesammelten Schriften des Mönchsgelehrten und Yogin Phag mo gru pa rDo rje rgyal po (Kritischer Text und Übersetzung, eingeleitet und erläutert)*. Hamburg: Department of Indian and Tibetan Studies, Universität Hamburg.

Schleiermacher, Friedrich. 1996. *On Religion: Speeches to Its Cultured Despisers*. Translated by Richard Crouter. Cambridge: Cambridge University Press.

Schwieger, Peter. 2015. *The Dalai Lama and the Emperor of China: A Political History of the Tibetan System of Reincarnation*. New York: Columbia University Press.

Sells, Michael. 1994. *Mystical Languages of Unsaying*. Chicago: University of Chicago Press.

Sernesi, Marta. 2011. "The Aural Transmission of Saṃvara: An Introduction to Neglected Sources for the Study of the Early Bka' brgyud." In *Mahāmudrā and the Bka' brgyud Tradition*, edited by Roger R. Jackson and Matthew T. Kapstein, 179–209. Andiast, Switzerland: International Institute for Tibetan and Buddhist Studies GmbH.

Seyfort Ruegg, David. 1960. *The Life of Bu ston Rin po che, with the Tibetan Text of the Bu ston rNam thar*. Serie Orientale Roma 34. Rome: Istituto Italiano per il Medio ed Estremo Oriente.

———. 1989. *Buddha Nature, Mind and the Problem of Gradualism in a Comparative Perspective: On the Transmission and Reception of Buddhism in India and Tibet*. London: School of Oriental and African Studies, University of London.

———. 2010. "A Karma Bka' brgyud Work on the Lineages and Traditions of the Indo-Tibetan *dbu ma* (Madhyamaka)." In *The Buddhist Philosophy of the Middle: Essays on Indian and Tibetan Madhyamaka*, 323–56. Boston: Wisdom Publications.

Shabkar. 2004. *Food of Bodhisattvas: Buddhist Teachings on Abstaining from Meat*. Translated by the Padmakara Translation Group. Boston: Shambhala Publications.

Shakabpa, Tsepon W. D. 1984. *Tibet: A Political History*. New York: Potala Publications.

"Shangpa Kagyu." http://rywiki.tsadra.org/index.php/Shangpa_Lineages_Outline. Accessed July 11, 2014.

Shantideva. 2006. *The Way of the Bodhisattva*. Translated by the Padmakara Translation Group. Boston and London: Shambhala.

Sharf, Robert. 1998. "Experience." In *Critical Terms for Religious Studies*, edited by Mark C. Taylor, 94–116. Chicago: University of Chicago Press.

Sharpa Tulku Tenzin Trinley, trans. 2018. *The Magical Play of Illusion: The Autobiography of Trijang Rinpoché*. Boston: Wisdom Publications.

Shastri, Haraprasad, ed. 1927. *Advayavajrasaṃgraha*. Gaekwad's Oriental Seires 40. Baroda, Gujarat, India: Oriental Institute.

Shen Weirong. 2005. "The First Dalai Lama Gendun Drup." In *The Dalai Lamas: A Visual History*, edited by Martin Brauen, 32–41. Chicago: Serindia Publications.

Shendge, Malati J. 1967. "*Śrīsahajasiddhi.*" *Indo-Iranian Journal* 10: 126–49.
Sherburne, Richard, trans. 1983. Atiśa. *A Lamp for the Path and Commentary*. London: George Allen & Unwin.
Sherma, Rita, and Arvind Sharma, eds. 2008. *Hermeneutics and Hindu Thought: Toward a Fusion of Horizons.* New York: Springer.
Shizuka Haruki. 2015. "Expulsion of Maitri-pa from the Monastery and Atiśa's Participation." *Journal of Indian and Buddhist Studies* 63.3: 1315–21.
Singh, Jaideva, trans. 1991. *The Yoga of Delight, Wonder, and Astonishment: A Translation of the Vijñāna-Bhairva.* Albany: State University of New York Press.
Skorupski, Tadeusz, ed. and trans. 1983. *The Sarvadurgatipariśodhanatantra.* Delhi: Motilal Banarsidass.
Smith, E. Gene. 2001. *Among Tibetan Texts: History and Literature of the Tibetan Plateau.* Boston: Wisdom Publications.
Snellgrove, David L. 1987. *Indo-Tibetan Buddhism.* 2 vols. Boston: Shambhala Publications.
Snellgrove, David, and Hugh Richardson. 1967. *A Cultural History of Tibet.* New York: Frederick A. Praeger.
Sonam Gyatso, the Third Dalai Lama. 1982. *Essence of Refined Gold.* Translated by Glenn H. Mullin. Ithaca: Gabriel/Snow Lion Publications.
Sopa, Geshe Lhundub, and Jeffrey Hopkins, trans. 1989. *Cutting Through Appearances: Practice and Theory of Tibetan Buddhism.* Ithaca: Snow Lion Publications.
Sorenson, Michele. 2011. "The Second Karmapa, Karma Pakshi." Treasury of Lives. http://treasuryoflives.org/biographies/view/Second-Karmapa-Karma-Pakshi/2776. Accessed August 12, 2017.
Sparham, Gareth. 1992. *Ocean of Eloquence: Tsongkhapa's Commentary of the Yogācāra Doctrine of Mind.* Albany: State University of New York Press.
———. 2017. [2011.] "Tsongkhapa." *Stanford Encyclopedia of Philosophy.* http://plato.stanford.edu/entries/tsongkhapa. Accessed February 26, 2019.
Stace, W. T. 1960. *Mysticism and Philosophy.* London: Macmillan & Co.
Stearns, Cyrus. 2001. *Luminous Lives: The Story of the Early Masters of the Lam 'bras in Tibet.* Boston: Wisdom Publications.
———, trans. 2006. *Taking the Result as the Path: Core Teachings of the Sakya Lamdré Tradition.* Library of Tibetan Classics 4. Boston: Wisdom Publications.
Stewart, Jampa Mackenzie. 1995. *The Life of Gampopa: The Uncomparable Dharma Lord of Tibet.* Ithaca: Snow Lion Publications.
Sujata, Victoria. 2005. *Tibetan Songs of Realization: Echoes From A Seventeenth-Century Scholar and Siddha In Amdo.* Leiden: Brill.
———, trans. 2012. *Songs of Shabkar: The Path of a Tibetan Yogi Inspired by Nature.* Cazadero, CA: Dharma Publishing, 2012.
———. 2015. "*Nyams mgur* of Pha bong kha pa bDe chen snying po (1878–1941): An Analysis of his Poetic Techniques." In *Tibetan Literary Genres, Texts, and Text Types: From Genre Classification to Transformation*, edited by Jim Rheingans, 197–228. Leiden: Brill.
———. 2019. *Journey to Distant Groves: Profound Songs of the Tibetan Siddha Kälden Gyatso.* Kathmandu: Vajra Publications.
Suzuki, Daisetz T., trans. 1978 [1932]. *Laṅkāvatāra Sūtra.* Boulder: Prajñā Press.
Szántó, Péter-Dániel. 2012. "Selected Chapters from the Catuṣpīṭhatantra." Ph.D. dissertation. Balliol College, Oxford.

———. 2015. "Catuṣpīṭha." In *Brill's Encyclopedia of Buddhism*, 1:320–25. Leiden: Brill.

Tai Situ Rinpoche. 2001. *The Third Karmapa's Mahamudra Prayer.* Translated and edited by Rosemary Fuchs. Ithaca: Snow Lion.

Tarab Tulku. 2000. *A Brief History of Tibetan Academic Degrees.* Copenhagen: NIAS Press.

Tāranātha. 2007. *The Essence of Other-Emptiness.* Translated and annotated by Jeffrey Hopkins. Ithaca: Snow Lion Publications.

Tatz, Mark. 1987. "The Life of the Siddha-Philosopher Maitrīgupta." *Journal of the American Oriental Society* 107.4: 695–711.

———, trans. 2016. *The Skill in Means (Upāyakauśalya) Sūtra.* 2nd ed. Delhi: Motilal Banarsidass.

Taves, Ann. 2009. *Religious Experience Reconsidered: A Building Block Approach to the Study of Religion and Other Special Things.* Princeton: Princeton University Press.

Tāranātha, Jo.nang. 1983. *The Seven Instruction Lineages.* Translated and edited by David Templeman. Dharamsala: Library of Tibetan Works and Archives.

Thakchoe, Sonam. 2007. *The Two Truths Debate: Tsongkhapa and Gorampa on the Middle Way.* Boston: Wisdom Publications.

Thaye, Jampa. 1990. *A Garland of Gold: The Early Kagyu Masters of India and Tibet.* Bristol, UK: Ganesha Press.

THL Tibetan to English Translation Tool. http://www.thlib.org/reference/dictionaries/tibetan-dictionary/translate.php.

Thomas, Paul. Forthcoming. "The *Samādhirājasūtra* and 'Sūtra-Mahāmudrā': A Critical Edition and Translation of vv. 11–18 from Ch. 32 of the *Samādhirājasūtra.*" In *Mahāmudrā in India and Tibet*, edited by Roger R. Jackson and Klaus-Dieter Mathes. Leiden: Brill.

Thrangu Rinpoche, Khenchen. 1994. *King of Samadhi: Commentaries on the Samadhi Raja Sutra and the Song of Lodrö Thaye.* Translated by Erik Pema Kunsang. Hong Kong: Rangjung Yeshe Publications.

———. 1997. *Songs of Naropa: Commentaries on Songs of Realization.* Translated by Erik Pema Kunsang. Boudhnath: Rangjung Yeshe Publications.

———. 2006. *A Song for a King: Saraha on Mahamudra Meditation.* Edited by Michele Martin. Boston: Wisdom Publications.

———. 2018. *The Mahamudra Lineage Prayer: A Guide to Practice.* Boulder: Shambhala Publications.

Thuken Losang Chökyi Nyima. 2009. *The Crystal Mirror of Philosophical Systems: A Tibetan Study of Asian Religious Thought.* Translated by Geshe Lhundub Sopa et al. Edited by Roger R. Jackson. Library of Tibetan Classics 25. Boston: Wisdom Publications.

Thurman, Robert A. F., trans. 1976. *The Holy Teaching of Vimalakīrti: A Buddhist Scripture.* University Park, PA: Pennsylvania State University Press.

———, ed. 1982. *The Life and Teaching of Tsong Khapa.* Dharamsala: Library of Tibetan Works and Archives.

———. 1984. *Tsong Khapa's Speech of Gold in the "Essence of Eloquence": Reason and Enlightenment in the Central Philosophy of Tibet.* Princeton: Princeton University Press.

———, trans. 1995. *Essential Tibetan Buddhism.* San Francisco: HarperSanFrancisco.

———, trans. 2014. *The Universal Vehicle Discourse Literature (Mahāyānasūtrālaṁkāra): by Maitreyanātha/Āryāsaṅga, Together with Its Commentary (Bhāṣya) by Vasubandhu.* New York: AIBS/CBS/THUS.

Tola, Fernando, and Carmen Dragonetti. 1985. "Nāgārjuna's *Catustava*." *Journal of Indian Philosophy* 13: 1–54.

———. 2004. *Being as Consciousness: Yogācāra Philosophy of Buddhism.* Delhi: Motilal Banarsidass.

Townsend, Dominique. 2010. "The Third Changkya, Rolpai Dorje." Treasury of Lives. http://www.treasuryoflives.org/biographies/view/Chankya-Rolpai-Dorje/3141. Accessed April 4, 2015.

Tribe, Anthony. 2016. *Tantric Buddhist Practice in India: Vilāsavajra's Commentary on the Mañjuśrī-nāmasaṃgīti.* London: Routledge.

Tsangnyön Heruka. 2010. *The Life of Milarepa.* Translated by Andrew Quintman. New York: Penguin Books.

———. 2016. *The Hundred Thousand Songs of Milarepa.* Translated by Christopher Stagg. Boulder: Shambhala Publications.

Tsele Natsok Rangdröl. 1989. *Lamp of Mahamudra.* Translated by Erik Pema Kunsang. Boston: Shambhala.

Tsering, Geshe Tashi. 2012. *Tantra.* The Foundations of Buddhist Thought 6. Boston: Wisdom Publications.

"Tshul khrims nyi ma." BDRC. https://www.tbrc.org/#!rid=P1829. Accessed September 14, 2017.

Tsongkhapa [Tsong-ka-pa]. 1977. *The Tantra of Tibet: The Great Exposition of Secret Mantra.* Translated by Jeffrey Hopkins. The Wisdom of Tibet Series 3. London: George Allen & Unwin.

——— [Tsong-ka-pa]. 1981. *The Yoga of Tibet: The Great Exposition of Secret Mantra—2 and 3.* Translated by Jeffrey Hopkins. The Wisdom of Tibet Series 4. London: George Allen & Unwin.

——— [Tsongkapa]. 1988. *The Principal Teachings of Buddhism, with a Commentary by Phabongka Rinpoche.* Translated by Geshe Lobsang Tharchin, with Michael Roach. Howell, NJ: Mahayana Sutra and Tantra Press.

——— [Tsongkapa]. 1995. *Preparing for Tantra: The Mountain of Blessings, with a Commentary by Phabongka Rinpoche.* Translated by Geshe Lobsang Tharchin, with Michael Roach. Howell, NJ: Mahayana Sutra and Tantra Press.

——— [Tsong-ka-pa]. 2000–2002. *The Great Treatise on the Stages of the Path to Enlightenment.* 3 vols. Translated by the Lamrim Chenmo Translation Committee. Edited by Joshua W. Cutler. Ithaca: Snow Lion Publications.

———. 2005a. *Tantric Ethics: An Explanation of the Precepts for Buddhist Vajrayana Practice.* Translated by Gareth Sparham. Boston: Wisdom Publications.

——— [Dzong-ka-ba]. 2005b. *Yoga Tantra: Paths to Magical Feats.* Translated by Jeffrey Hopkins. Ithaca: Snow Lion Publications.

——— [rJe Tsong Khapa.] 2006. *Ocean of Reasoning: A Great Commentary on Nāgārjuna's "Mūlamadhyamakakārikā."* Translated by Geshe Ngawang Samten and Jay L. Garfield. Boston: Wisdom Publications.

——— [Tsong Khapa Losang Drakpa]. 2010. *Brilliant Illumination of the Lamp of the Five Stages (Rim lnga rab tu gsal ba'i sgron me): Practical Instruction in the King of Tantra, The Glorious Esoteric Community.* Translated by Robert A. F. Thurman. New York: AIBS/CBS/THUS.

——— [Tsong Khapa Losang Drakpa]. 2013a. *Great Treatise on the Stages of Mantra (sngags rim chen mo): Critical Elucidation of the Key Instructions in All the Secret Stages of the*

Path of the Victorious Universal Lord, Great Vajradhara, Chapters XI–XII: The Creation Stage. Translated by Thomas Freeman Yarnall. New York: AIBS/CBS/THUS.

———. 2013b. *A Lamp to Illuminate the Five Stages: Teachings on Guhyasamāja Tantra.* Translated by Gavin Kilty. Library of Tibetan Classics 15. Boston: Wisdom Publications.

Tulku Thondup. 1989. *Buddha Mind: An Anthology of Longchen Rabjam's Writings on Dzogpa Chenpo*. Ithaca: Snow Lion Publications.

van der Kuijp, Leonard W. J. 1983. *Contributions to the Development of Tibetan Buddhist Epistemology: Eleventh to Thirteenth Century*. Wiesbaden: F. Steiner.

van Schaik, Sam. 2004. *Approaching the Great Perfection: Simultaneous and Gradual Methods of Dzogchen Practice in the Longchen Nyingtig*. Boston: Wisdom Publications.

———. 2015. *Tibetan Zen: Discovering a Lost Tradition*. Boulder: Snow Lion Publications.

Vélez de Cea, Abraham. 2013. *The Buddha and Religious Diversity*. London: Routledge.

"Venerable Geshe Kelsang Gyatso." *Kadampa Buddhism.* http://kadampa.org/buddhism/venerable-geshe-kelsang-gyatso. Accessed June 13, 2015.

Von Denffer, Ahmad, 2009. *Ulum al Qur'an: An Introduction to the Sciences of the Qur'an.* Leicestershire, U.K.: The Islamic Foundation.

Wallace, B. Alan, ed. and trans. 1980. *The Life and Teaching Geshe Rabten: A Tibetan Lama's Search for Truth*. London: George Allen & Unwin.

———. 2003. *Choosing Reality: A Buddhist View of Physics and the Mind.* Ithaca: Snow Lion Publications.

———. 2013. *Meditations of a Buddhist Skeptic: A Manifesto for the Mind Sciences and Contemplative Practice*. New York: Columbia University Press.

———, trans. 2017. *Open Mind: View and Meditation in the Lineage of Lerab Lingpa*. Boston: Wisdom Publications.

Wallis, Glenn. 2002. *Mediating the Power of Buddhas.* Albany: State University of New York Press.

Walshe, Maurice, trans. 1995. *The Long Discourses of the Buddha: A Translation of the Dīgha Nikāya*. Boston: Wisdom Publications.

Wang Xiangyun. 1995. *Tibetan Buddhism at the Court of the Qing: The Life and Work of lCang-skya Rol-pa'i-rdo-rje (1717–86)*. Ph.D. dissertation. Harvard University.

Wangchuk Dorjé [Wang-ch'uk Dor-je, the Ninth Karmapa]. 1981. *The Mahamudra Eliminating the Darkness of Ignorance*. Translated by Alex Berzin. Dharamsala: Library of Tibetan Works and Archives.

——— [The Ninth Gyalwang Karmapa, Wangchuk Dorje]. 2001. *Mahāmudrā: The Ocean of Definitive Meaning*. Translated by Elizabeth Callahan. Seattle: Nitartha.

——— [The Ninth Karmapa, Wangchuk Dorje]. 2009. *Pointing Out the Dharmakaya*. Translated by Cortland Dahl. Hopkins, MN: Tergar International.

Wangyal, Geshe. 1995. *The Door of Liberation: Essential Teachings of the Tibetan Buddhist Tradition*. Boston: Wisdom Publications.

Watson, Burton, trans. 1994. *The Lotus Sutra*. New York: Columbia University Press.

Wayman, Alex, trans. 1985. *Chanting the Names of Mañjuśrī: The Mañjuśrī-nāma-saṃgīti, Sanskrit and Tibetan Texts*. Boston and London: Shambhala.

———. 1987. "Esoteric Buddhism." In *The Religious Traditions of Asia*, edited by Joseph M. Kitagawa and Mark D. Cummings, 241–56. New York: Macmillan.

Wayman, Alex, and Hideko Wayman, trans. 1974. *The Lion's Roar of Queen Śrīmālā*. New York: Columbia University Press.

Wedemeyer, Christian K. 2007. *Āryadeva's Lamp that Integrates the Practices (Caryāmelāpakapradīpa): The Gradual Path of Vajrayāna Buddhism According to the Esoteric Community Noble Tradition.* New York: AIBS/CBS/THUS.

———. 2013. *Making Sense of Tantric Buddhism: History, Semiology, and Transgression in the Indian Traditions.* New York: Columbia University Press.

Williams, Paul. 1983. "A Note on Some Aspects of Mi-bskyod rDo-rje's Critique of dGe lugs pa Madhyamaka." *Journal of Indian Philosophy* 11: 125–45.

Williams, Paul, with Anthony Tribe. 2000. *Buddhist Thought: A Complete Introduction to the Indian Tradition.* London: Routledge.

Willis, Janice D. 1995. *Enlightened Beings: Life Stories from the Ganden Oral Tradition.* Boston: Wisdom Publications.

Yamamoto, Carl. 2012. *Vision and Violence: Lama Zhang and the Politics of Charisma in Twelfth-Century Tibet.* Leiden: Brill.

Yeshe, Lama Thubten. *Mahamudra: How to Discover Our True Nature.* Somerville MA: Wisdom Publications, 2019.

Zasep Tulku Rinpoche. 2018. *Gelug Mahamudra: Eloquent Speech of Manjushri.* Nelson, BC: Wind Horse Press.

Zong Rinpoche, Kyabje. 2006. *Chöd in the Ganden Tradition: The Oral Instruction of Kyabje Zong Rinpoche.* Edited by David Molk. Ithaca and Boulder: Snow Lion Publications.

Index

A

Abhidharma, 2n2, 6, 389–90, 407, 428
Abhidharmakośa. See *Treasury of Higher Knowledge*
Abhisamayālaṃkāra. See *Ornament of Higher Realization*
Abhisamayavibhaṅga. See *Discerning the Higher Realization*
Achithu Nomenhan (*A chi thu no mon han*), 338
Acintyamahāmudrā. See *Inconceivable Mahāmudrā*
action tantra, 30–31, 33, 275n805
Adhisidhisamā. See *Summary of the View*
Advayasiddhi. See *Attainment of the Nondual*
Advayavajra. *See* Maitrīpa
Advice from the Wise (Losang Dongak Chökyi Gyatso), 310–12
Advice of Losang (Kachen Yeshé Gyaltsen), 270–71
Advice of Mañjughoṣa Lama (Kachen Yeshé Gyaltsen), 266, 268–70
Akhu Sherab Gyatso (*A khu Shes rab rgya mtsho*), 242, 291, 304–6, 334, 644
Altan Khan, 147, 194
Amanasikārādhāra. See *Upholding Nonmentation*
Amdo Geshé Jampal Rölpai Lodrö (*A mdo dge bshes 'Jam dpal rol pa'i blo gros*), 309
Amitābha Buddha, 33, 135, 361, 392
Anaṅgavajra, 190, 491
Anāvilatantrarāja. See *Royal Tantra on the Unpolluted*
Aṅguttara Nikāya, 24, 410n1128, 428
Annotations to the People Dohās (Jamyang Shepai Dorjé), 375–78
Answer That Teaches the View and Meditation of Mahāmudrā (Śavaripa), 443
Answers to the Questions of Gomang Gungru Rapjampa Lodrö (Changkya Rölpai Dorjé), 293
Answers to the Questions of the Jamyang Shepa Tulku (Changkya Rölpai Dorjé), 293
Answers to the Questions of the Kadampa Namkha Bum (Sakya Paṇḍita), 106, 535–36
anuyoga, 34, 81–82
Appeal to the Mahāmudrā Lineage (Shar Kalden Gyatso), 246–47
Appendix to the Great Biography of Jetsun Tsongkhapa (Tokden Jampal Gyatso), 134
Apple, James, 69–71
arhatship, 25, 389–94, 403, 417, 424–25
Arik Geshé Jampa Gelek Gyaltsen (*A rig dge bshes Byams pa dge legs rgyal mtshan*), 298–99
Arising of the Pledge Tantra. See *Saṃvarodaya Tantra*
Ariyapariyesanā Sutta. See *Discourse on the Noble Quest*
Āryadeva, 43, 205–6, 213, 446n1166, 477, 530, 532

Asaṅga, 56, 63, 110, 116, 211, 264, 269, 278, 353, 356, 396, 442, 506
Ascertaining the Four Seals (Nāgārjuna or Maitrīpa), 58. See also *Succession of the Four Seals*
Ātijñāna Sūtra. See *Death-Time Gnosis Sūtra*
Atiśa Dīpaṃkara Śrījñāna, 68–73, 181, 207–9, 300, 483, 487
  influence on Geluk of, 133, 135
  lineages including, 175, 217, 260, 302n877, 442
  promotion of Saraha by, 363
  relationship with Maitrīpa of, 56, 69, 416
atiyoga, 34, 81–82, 312
Attainment of Certainty about Wisdom and Means (Anaṅgavajra), 440, 491
Attainment of Gnosis (Indrabhūti), 42, 491
Attainment of the Connate (Ḍombī Heruka), 42, 51, 491
Attainment of the Nondual (Lakṣmīṅkarā), 42, 491
Attainment of the Principle of the Great Secret (Dārikapa), 491
Attainment of the Principle That Follows the Illumination of Entities (Yoginī Cintā), 491
Avadhūtipa. *See* Maitrīpa
Avalokiteśvara, 25, 136, 299, 540
Avataṃsaka Sūtra. See *Flower Ornament Sūtra*
awakening mind, conceptions of in mahāmudrā, 35, 97, 203–4, 221–25, 483–86, 557, 571, 605–6
Awakening of Vairocana Tantra, 483–84

B

Balpo Asu, 68, 87–88, 363
Barawa Gyaltsen Palsang (*'Ba' ra ba Rgyal mtshan dpal bzang*), 137, 149, 157, 162–63, 200, 283, 305, 334, 645
Barom Kagyü, 92
Baso Chökyi Gyaltsen (*Ba so Chos kyi rgyal mtshan*), 171–73, 175, 194–95, 246, 448, 458, 622
  transmissions through, 144, 146, 149, 159, 167, 195, 215–17, 246, 248–49, 302n877, 643
Berzin, Alexander, 334, 342
Bhagavad Gītā, 412
Bhāskara, 19–20
Bhavabaṭṭa, 43, 64
Bhāviveka, 366, 446n1167, 507
Biographies of the Lineage Lamas of the Stages of the Path (Kachen Yeshé Gyaltsen), 181n642
bliss-emptiness, gnosis of, 29, 36, 60, 66n199, 85, 151–52, 164, 168, 170, 183, 189–90, 220, 223, 272, 303, 328–30, 333–34, 350, 491, 553, 556, 560, 565, 581, 602, 641
Blue Annals (Gö Lotsāwa), 113, 363, 489
Blue Compendium (Potowa), 568
Bodhicaryāvatāra. See *Engaging in Bodhisattva Conduct*
Bodhipathapradīpa. See *Lamp on the Path to Awakening*
bodhisattva levels, 27, 97, 99, 127, 196, 214, 275, 534–35
Bodhisattvabhūmi. See *Levels of the Bodhisattva*
Body Treasury (Saraha), 45–46
Bön tradition, 76, 316
Book of Kadam, 72, 186
Book of Three Inspirations (Tsongkhapa), 151–52, 164, 323
Bright Lamp of Mahāmudrā (Khedrup Norsang Gyatso), 13, 182–83, 188, 198, 297, 344, 367–68, 543–66, 605–6
Bright Lamp of the Excellent Path (Kachen Yeshé Gyaltsen), 12–13, 176–77, 259–67, 273, 293, 343, 439–55
Broido, Michael, 91
buddha bodies, 26–30, 181, 322, 393
  association of mahāmudrā with, 47, 55, 57, 87–88, 125–27, 500–501
  Geluk versus Kagyü views of, 192
buddha families, 31–33, 361, 573
buddha mind, 33, 63, 110–11, 138, 336, 357–58, 399, 427–28

buddha nature
essentialism of, 153, 356–58
literature on, 8, 24–25, 56, 61, 141, 425
as mahāmudrā, 2, 10, 26–27, 63, 66, 88, 112–13, 125–26, 163, 355, 393–94
in *Sublime Continuum*, 59, 91, 110, 113, 116, 170, 189, 348, 384
synthetic interpretations of, 108–10, 183
Buddha Skull Tantra, 37
commentary to (Saraha), 44, 364–65, 378
Buddhakapālatantra. See *Buddha Skull Tantra*
Buddhapālita, 137–38, 366–67, 397, 446
buddhavacana, 382–83, 385
Butön Rinchen Drup (*Bu ston Rin chen grub*), 111–12, 135, 139, 283, 491

C

Cabezón, José, 166
Cakrasaṃvara Tantra, 2, 36–38, 42–43
commentaries and related works, 37, 43, 63, 69–70, 142, 151, 186, 202, 285
deity of, 142, 275n805, 302, 316, 570
lineages of, 87, 144, 366, 512
practices of, 52, 144–45, 171, 202, 272, 302
Candragomin, 211, 508
Candrakīrti
on emptiness, 138, 140, 209, 214, 249, 396–97
influence on Maitrīpa and Nāropa of, 598–99
Kadam role in promoting, 69
lineages including, 260, 294, 366, 441
and mahāmudrā, 323, 369–70, 406, 498
on mind and cosmos, 429, 526
as source for Nyingma theory and practice, 310
See also Prāsaṅgika Madhyamaka
canon, closed or open, 383
caryā tantra. *See* performance tantras
Caryāgītikoṣa. See *Treasury of Performance Songs*
Caryāmelapradīpa. See *Lamp That Integrates the Performance*
Caturmudrāniścaya. See *Ascertaining the Four Seals*
Caturmudrānvaya. See *Succession of the Four Seals*
Catuṣpīṭha Tantra. See *Four Seats Tantra*
Chan traditions, 80, 296, 382–84, 387–92, 394–95, 397, 400, 407, 411, 413, 418, 428
Changkya II Ngawang Losang Chöden (*Lcang skya Ngag dbang blo bzang chos ldan*), 146, 253, 291–92
Changkya III Rölpai Dorjé (*Lcang skya Rol pa'i rdo rje*), 162, 242, 258–59, 284, 291–96, 315, 321, 644
channels of subtle body, 21, 28–29, 35, 204n697, 330
associated with mahāmudrā, 5, 140, 151–52, 190, 209, 267, 297, 490, 494–95
in death process, 71, 494n1276, 548
in gradualist practice, 560–61
and primordial mind, 183, 369, 494, 548–56, 563–64, 602
Chanting the Names of Mañjuśrī, 31, 43
Chariot Leading to Union (Jamyang Shepai Dorjé), 253
Chariot of the Dakpo Kagyü Siddhas (Mikyö Dorjé), 120, 124–25
Chegom Sherab Dorjé (*Lce sgom Shes rab rdo rje*), 72–73, 191
Chenga Chökyi Gyalpo (*Spyan snga Chos kyi rgyal po*), 135–36, 149, 260, 444, 645
Chenga Drakpa Jangchup (*Spyan snga Grags pa byang chub*), 136, 149, 444
Chö. *See* severance practice
Chögyal Ngakyi Wangpo (*Chos rgyal ngag gi dbang po*), 299
Chögyam Trungpa, 4, 323–24, 421
Chökhor Gyal monastery, 185
Choklé Namgyal (*Phyogs las rnam rgyal*), 135
Chökyi Dorjé (*Chos kyi rdo rje*), 172–75, 215–16, 244, 448–50, 458, 470
transmissions through, 149, 165, 177, 185, 203, 217, 221, 246–49, 260, 302n877, 643

Chökyi Drakpa, Dulzinpa (*'Dul 'dzin Chos kyi grags pa*), 181, 184, 219, 565, 596
Chökyi Lama (*Chos kyi bla ma*). *See* Karmapa II Karma Pakshi
Chomden Raldri (*Lcom ldan ral gri*), 378
Choné Lama Lodrö Gyatso (*Co ne bla ma Blo gros rgya mtsho*), 242, 291, 306–8, 321
Chöpa Rinpoché Losang Tenpai Gyaltsen (*Chos pa rin po che Blo bzang bstan pa'i rgyal mtshan*), 245–49, 51
Chubar Khen Rinpoché Yönten Lhundrup (*mkhan rin po che Yon tan lhun grub*), 301
Cittakoṣa. See *Mind Treasury*
Cittamātra. *See* mind-only doctrine
Cleansing the Sage's Teaching (Khedrup Jé), 169
Clear Ascertainment of the Three Vows (Sakya Paṇḍita), 106–7, 193, 348, 416, 495–96, 557, 603, 605–6
Clear Light of Bliss (Geshé Kelsang Gyatso), 329–30
Clearing Away All Delusion (Ngulchu Dharmabhadra), 285–86
Cloud of Ambrosial Offerings (Losang Dongak Chökyi Gyatso), 310
Cluster of Yogic Attainments (Kachen Yeshé Gyaltsen), 273, 276–77
Collection of Guidebooks for Thoroughly Identifying the General View of Mahāmudrā (multiple authors), 338
Commentary Briefly Clarifying the Meaning of the Instruction Directly Given to Jé Lama by Mañjughoṣa (Phurbuchok), 259n783
Commentary on "Recognizing My Mother" (Achithu Nomenhan), 338
Commentary on the "Teaching on Empowerment" (Nāropa), 43, 54
Commentary on the "Ten Verses on Thatness" (Sahajavajra), 61, 64
Compendium of Sūtras (Nāgārjuna), 442
Compendium of the Realities of All the Tathāgatas, 32–33
Compendium of Vajra Gnosis Drawn from the Tantras, 559–60
Condensed Perfection of Wisdom, 525, 569
Condensed Sādhanas (Nāgārjuna), 442
Condensed Stages of the Path (Tsongkhapa) 134, 160–61, 568
connate union, 92, 95, 101, 108–9, 123–24, 135, 149
  Atiśa's teaching on, 71
  Gampopa's teaching on, 73, 90
  as gradual practice, 90n289, 389
  Paṇchen Chögyen's teaching on, 203, 209, 369, 471, 499–501, 607
Conquest of the Three Worlds Tantra, 33
Crystal Mirror of Tenet Systems (Thuken Losang Chökyi Nyima), 13, 242, 296, 344
  translated excerpts of, 597–610

D

Dakpo Jampal Lhundrup (*Dwags po 'Jam dpal lhun grub*), 315, 317
Dakpo Kagyü (*Dwags po bka' brgyud*), 84, 87, 92–93, 136, 185
  differences of from Geluk, 191–93
Dakpo Lharjé (*Dwags po lha rje*). *See* Gampopa Sönam Rinchen
Dakpo Tashi Namgyal (*Dwags po Bkra shis rnam rgyal*), 4, 71, 120–22, 346, 349–50, 353, 373
Dalai Lama I Gendun Drup (*Dge 'dun grub*), 147, 171, 179–81, 184–85, 643
Dalai Lama II Gendun Gyatso (*Dge 'dun rgya mtsho*), 147, 182, 184–87, 198, 200, 219, 416, 643
Dalai Lama III Sönam Gyatso (*Bsod nams rgya mtsho*), 147, 167, 188, 193–95, 643
Dalai Lama IV Yönten Gyatso (*Yon tan rgya mtsho*), 129, 147, 195, 201, 237
Dalai Lama V Ngawang Losang Gyatso (*Ngag dbang blo bzang rgya mtsho*), 129, 146–47, 165, 195–96, 201–2, 237, 316, 643
  on Geluk and Kagyü, 335, 342–45
  as recipient of mahāmudrā teachings, 241, 243–45

Dalai Lama VI Tsangyang Gyatso (*Tshangs dbyangs rgya mtsho*), 253–54
Dalai Lama VII Kalsang Gyatso (*Bskal bzang rgya mtsho*), 242, 254–56, 292, 313, 338
Dalai Lama VIII Jampal Gyatso (*'Jam dpal rgya mtsho*), 241–42, 257–58, 282, 292
Dalai Lama XIII Thubten Gyatso (*Thub bstan rgya mtsho*), 309, 316, 323
Dalai Lama XIV Tenzin Gyatso (*Bstan 'dzin rgya mtsho*), 5, 149, 163, 237, 242, 244, 303, 305, 314–16, 331–37, 341–43, 345, 467, 644
Dalai Lamas, 4, 11, 133, 147–48, 185, 194, 237, 243n731, 332
Dalton, Jacob, 33
Dārikapa, 260, 443, 491, 645
Daśabhūmika Sūtra. See *Sūtra on the Ten Levels*
death
  four phases of, 494
  luminosity of, 71, 183, 263, 545–46, 548, 550, 552
  as spiritual practice, 52, 224, 276, 501–2
Death-Time Gnosis Sūtra, 249
Denma Tsultrim Gyatso (*'Dan ma Tshul khrims rgya mtsho*), 245–46, 250
Densa Thil monastery, 95, 136, 149
dependent arising and emptiness, 2n2, 134, 138, 141, 155, 196, 206, 213–14, 227, 229–30, 233, 248–49, 269, 271, 293–94, 331, 355, 446, 477, 524, 530, 613–14, 625, 635–36
Descent to Laṅkā Sūtra, 61–62, 90n292, 189, 397
Desi Sangyé Gyatso (*Sde srid Sangs rgyas rgya mtsho*), 157, 253
Dewachen monastery, 135, 170
Dhammapada, 24, 428
Dharma Cycle on the Stages of the Path and the Hearing Transmission of the Glorious Gedenpa (multiple authors), 338
Dharma of the Bodiless Ḍākinī (Tilopa), 38, 490n1258
Dharmadharmatāvibhaṅga. See *Distinguishing Phenomena from Reality*
Dharmakīrti, 69, 73, 105, 138, 212, 425, 431, 446n1166, 518, 605
Dharmavajra. *See* Chökyi Dorjé
Diamond Song at the Diamond Seat (Atiśa), 70
Diṅkaṃpa, 260, 443, 645
Discerning the Higher Realization (Atiśa), 69–70
Discourse on the Noble Quest, 403
Discourse to Sigala, 413
Distinguishing Clearly the Entire Sum of the Buddha's Words (Jñānakīrti), 604
Distinguishing Phenomena from Reality (Maitreya), 90n292, 506
Distinguishing the Precious Lineage. See *Sublime Continuum*
Dohā Song on View, Meditation, Conduct, and Result (Saraha), 47
Dohā Treasury (Saraha). See *People Dohā Treasury*
Dohā Treasury (Tilopa), 6–7, 52
Dohā Treasury Instruction Song. See *Queen Dohā Treasury*
Dohā Tresaury of Mahāmudrā Instruction (Śavaripa or Saraha), 48–50, 48n129, 374n1082, 513
Dohā Treasury Song. See *People Dohā Treasury*
Dohākoṣa. See *Dohā Treasury* (Tilopa); *Treasury of Dohās*
Dohākoṣagīti. See *People Dohā Treasury*
Dohākoṣamahāmudropadeśa. See *Dohā Tresaury of Mahāmudrā Instruction*
Dohākoṣanāmacaryāgīti. See *King Dohā Treasury*
Dohākoṣopadeśagīti. See *Queen Dohā Treasury*
Dölpopa Sherab Gyaltsen (*Dol po pa Shes rab rgyal mtshan*), 110–11, 115, 118, 191
Ḍombī Heruka, 42–43, 51, 59, 72, 78, 491
Döndrup Rinchen (*Don grub rin chen*), 135, 444
Dorjé Denpa (*Rdo rje gdan pa*), 76

Dorjé Palwa of Kham (*Rdo rje dpal ba*), 172
Dorjé Shukden, worship of, 316–17, 328–29
Dose of Emptiness (Khedrup Jé), 168–69
Drakar Geshé Losang Tenzin Nyendrak (*Brag dkar dge bshes Blo bzang bstan 'dzin snyan grags*), 309
Drakpa Gyaltsen (*Grags pa rgyal mtshan*), 78, 208, 485
Drepung monastery, 133, 134n464, 143, 147, 185, 188, 252–53, 295
Drigung Kagyü, 92, 95–98, 106, 111, 536, 645. *See also* mahāmudrā: fivefold; Single Intention
Drigung monastery, 135
Drogön Rinpoché. *See* Phakmo Drupa Dorjé Gyalpo
Drogön Sangyé Rechen (*'Gro mgon Sangs rgyas ras chen*), 103
Drok José (*'Brog Jo sras*), 68
Drokmi Lotsāwa (*'Brog mi lo tsā ba*), 78, 83
Dromtönpa (*'Brom ston pa*), 69, 185–86, 363, 416, 487
Drop of Mahāmudrā Tantra, 37–38, 420, 489–90
Drukpa Kagyü, 84, 92–93, 98–100, 111, 122–23, 201, 645
  in Bhutan, 100, 201, 237, 313
  connection to Tsongkhapa, 137, 149, 157, 162
  criticism of by fifth Dalai Lama, 244–45
  madmen of, 114, 416
  Rechung hearing transmission in, 114
  three practices of, 210
Drungpa Tsöndrü Gyaltsen (*Drung pa Brtson grus rgyal mtshan*), 241, 246, 259n784, 454, 463, 643
Drupai Gyaltsen Dzinpa (*Sgrub pa'i rgyal mtshan 'dzin pa*), 241n729, 277, 454n1191, 460, 644
Drupai Wangchuk Losang Namgyal, 258–60, 278, 454–55, 461, 644
Dulkarwa Lodrö Bé (*'Dul dkar ba Blo gros sbas*), 175
Dulnakpa Palden Sangpo (*'Dul nag pa Dpal ldan bzang po*), 13, 144–45
Durkheim, Émile, 401

E

Echoes of Voidness (Geshé Rabten), 320–21
eight great guidances, 144, 210, 501
Eliade, Mircea, 401
Eliot, T. S., 432
Elucidation of the Intention of Madhyamaka (Tsongkhapa), 142, 520
emanation body, 9, 26–28, 39, 47, 55, 57, 126, 221, 574
empowerment, fourfold, 25–29, 34, 50, 58–59, 87, 107, 167–68, 267–68, 302, 348–49, 365, 490, 496, 579n1465
  as light rays, 248, 263, 275–76, 581
emptiness
  as basis for sectarian divisions, 336, 356–58
  and bliss. *See* bliss-emptiness, gnosis of
  and dependent arising. *See* dependent arising and emptiness
  intrinsic or extrinsic, 110–11, 118, 128, 138, 158, 164, 168, 191–92, 336–37, 356–58. *See also* shentong
  mahāmudrā as, 1, 6–7, 24–25, 63–64, 87, 128, 182, 187, 209, 265, 303, 325, 384, 399, 498
  positive or negative rhetoric of, 357, 396–99, 409–11, 427
  as single intention, 96–97
Engaging in Bodhisattva Conduct (Śāntideva), 119, 133n459, 328, 332, 503, 515, 517, 521–22, 527, 558
enjoyment body, 26–28, 39, 47, 55, 125–26, 221, 500, 574
Ensa Hearing Transmission, 145, 244, 252–54, 257–58, 296, 333. *See also* Ganden Hearing Transmission; Geden Hearing Transmission; Geden Oral Transmission
Ensa monastery, 175–77, 194, 199–201, 341
Ensapa Losang Döndrup (*Dben sa pa Blo bzang don grub*), 167n590, 173–78, 199, 235–36, 270–71, 449–52, 459, 463
  lineages including, 4n3, 149, 165, 169,

195, 203, 216–17, 246, 248–49, 260, 301n874, 302n877, 643
songs of, 478
Entrance into Thatness (Jñānakīrti), 62
Entry to the Middle Way (Candrakīrti), 120, 124–25, 133, 142, 200, 304, 320, 328, 516, 526, 534
Entryway to Faith (Khedrup Jé), 134, 217, 367
Epitome (*Kā dpe*), 249, 495–96, 552–53, 563
equal taste practice, 52, 92, 123, 203, 209–10, 369, 471, 499, 501, 607–8
esoteric teachings, promotion or restriction of, 386–88
Essence of Excellent Explanation (Tsongkhapa), 141, 250, 271, 300, 306, 319, 446, 449
Essence of Madhyamaka (Bhāviveka), 507
Essence of Refined Gold (Sönam Gyatso), 194–95
Essential Trilogy (Saraha), 8, 41, 44–45, 64, 118, 203, 268, 363–64
authorship of, 283, 491–92,
Paṇchen Chögyen on, 203, 209, 370, 440, 470, 489–92, 608
as root text for mantra mahāmudrā, 189–90, 470, 602
Excellent and Completely Virtuous Path to Freedom (Keutsang Losang Jamyang Mönlam), 286–89, 338, 647
Experiential Teaching on Mahāmudrā, An (Shar Kalden Gyatso), 162n580, 249–50
Exposition of Valid Cognition (Dharmakīrti), 133, 180, 200, 518, 545
explanatory tantras, 37, 39, 439
extensive activity, lineage of, 217, 260, 275n805, 442. *See also* profound view, lineage of
Extensive Exposition of the Arrangement of the Four Classes of Tantra (Khedrup Jé), 167–68
Eye-Opener of the Secret View (Tsongkhapa), 151

F

father tantras, 30n48, 34, 151, 350. See also *Guhyasamāja Tantra*
Faure, Bernard, 94
Feast for Scholars (Pawo Tsuklak Trengwa), 119
Feast for the Fortunate (Wangchuk Dorjé), 124–25
Fifty Verses on the Guru (Aśvaghoṣa), 569, 573
Five Maitreya Texts, 126, 269, 305, 396
five paths, 99, 127, 196, 214, 275, 534–35
Five Stages (Nāgārjuna), 43, 439, 442, 544–45, 573
five types of persons, 560
Flight of the Garuda (Shabkar Tsokdruk Rangdröl), 299
Flower Ornament Sūtra, 394, 400
Flowing River Ganges (Dalai Lama V), 244
Flowing River of Faith (Lodrö Gyaltsen), 170
Foundation for the Preservation of Mahayana Tradition, 322, 324, 327
Foundational Buddhism, 23n31, 381–83
absence of antinomianism in, 417
eighteen schools of, 499
exclusivism and inclusivism in, 424–25
as mahāmudrā, 24–25, 98, 386–87
on meditation, 90n292, 95, 403–4
on mind, 394, 428
philosophical views of, 389, 397, 400, 406–7
portrayal of Buddha in, 410, 413, 420, 424
ritual in, 413–14
four Dharmas of Dakpo, 208n704, 485
four difficult topics, 257n77, 537n1384
four joys, 29, 46, 151–52, 330, 555, 602
four noble truths, 26, 90, 389, 392, 403, 424
Four Praise Songs (Nāgārjuna), 410n1129
four seals, 32, 36, 38–39, 44, 58, 75, 97–98, 151, 168, 188, 208, 334, 488–89
four seals of Buddhist teaching, 24, 604
Four Seats Tantra, 52

four yogas, 90n292, 409, 556, 602
aligned with paths and levels, 534–35
criticism of, 193, 196
in Geluk teachings, 183, 191, 196, 214, 311
in Kadam teachings, 71
in Kagyü teachings, 90, 94, 96, 99–100, 117, 121–27, 129, 534, 551–52, 600
as mind only, 607
as Prāsaṅgika Madhyamaka, 298, 600
Fruit Cluster of Attainments (Tsongkhapa), 364

G

Gampopa Sönam Rinchen (*Gam po pa Bsod nams rin chen*), 87–88, 108, 190, 198, 209, 405–6
criticism of, 105–7, 344
disciples and their schools, 92–96, 101–2
four dharmas of, 208n704, 485
influence on Tibetan mahāmudrā of, 88, 91–92
lineages including, 84–85, 114, 645
merger of mind training and mahāmudrā by, 98, 305, 347–48, 485
on Perfection Vehicle as mahāmudrā, 3, 91–92, 116, 121, 189, 348, 386–88, 601, 603
practices taught by, 73, 89–90, 350, 389, 499–500, 560, 610
Gaṇḍavyūha Sūtra. See *Splendid Array Sūtra*
Ganden Hearing Transmission, 11, 13, 83, 145, 161, 165–78, 215, 220, 225, 236, 280, 301, 317, 324, 329–30, 333, 360
change of name from Geden, 257
Geluk and Kagyü elements in, 346–57
as syncretic, debate over, 341–45
two branches of, 241–42, 291, 317
See also Ensa Hearing Transmission; Geden Hearing Transmission; Geden Oral Transmission
Ganden Lhagyama. See *Hundred Deities of Tuṣita*
Ganden monastery, 133, 142, 216
Ganden Oral Transmission. *See* Geden Oral Transmission
Ganden Phodrang, 185, 243
Ganges Mahāmudrā. See *Mahāmudrā Song of Mother Ganges*
Garab Dorjé, 80
Garland of Nectar Drops (Gungthang Könchok Tenpai Drönmé), 282–83, 338
Garland of the Supremely Medicinal Nectar (Tsongkhapa), 155–56, 300
Garland of Views: A Pith Instruction (Padmasambhava), 502
Gayādhara, 78
Geden Hearing Transmission, 215, 252–53, 257. *See also* Ensa Hearing Transmission; Ganden Hearing Transmission; Geden Oral Transmission
Geden Oral Transmission, 13, 143, 145, 147–49, 165, 173, 188–89, 200, 203, 217–18, 249–50, 343, 470, 482. *See also* Ensa Hearing Transmission; Ganden Hearing Transmission; Geden Hearing Transmission
Gelek Gyatso, Drupkangpa (*Dge legs rgya mtsho*), 464, 644
Gelek Rinpoché (*Dge legs rin po che*), 314, 323–27, 337
Gelug/Kagyü Tradition of Mahamudra, The (Dalai Lama and Berzin), 334–35, 342
Geluk tradition
basic philosophical views of, 133–34, 138–39
conflict with Kagyü, 117, 128–30, 236–37, 243, 313
conservatism of, 133, 364, 379
curriculum of, 133–34, 147, 188, 253, 537n1284
diaspora scholarship of, 313–14, 337
distant mahāmudrā lineage of, 217, 260, 302, 367, 379, 442–44, 645
distinguished from Dakpo Kagyü, 191–93
emphasis on rational analysis by, 356–57, 406, 420
exclusivism in, 316–17, 335, 423–24

synthesis with Kagyü, 12, 163, 237, 244, 297–98, 335–36, 341–45, 605–6
uncommon proximate lineage of, 217, 253, 260, 262, 302n877, 440–41, 444–55, 643–44
Gendun Chöphel (*Dge 'dun chos 'phel*), 139
Gendun Drup. *See* Dalai Lama I Gendun Drup
Gendun Gyaltsen, Drupchen (*Grub chen Dge 'dun rgyal mtshan*), 200, 206n702, 241, 246, 249, 277, 459, 478, 537–38, 643
Gendun Gyatso. *See* Dalai Lama II Gendun Gyatso
General Presentation of the Classes of Tantra (Paṇchen Sönam Drakpa), 188
Germano, David, 80–81
Geshé Acharya Thubten Loden (*Dge bshes ācārya Thub bstan blo ldan*), 314, 321–23
Geshé Kelsang Gyatso (*Dge bshes Bskal bzang rgya mtsho*), 314, 327–31
Geshé Tamdrin Rabten (*Dge bshes Rta mgrin rab brten*), 314
Getsé Mahāpaṇḍita (*Dge rtse Mahāpaṇḍita*), 155n550, 163
Ghaṇṭapa, 144, 367
Gö Lotsāwa Shönu Pal (*'Gos lo tsā ba Gzhon nu dpal*), 3, 69, 87, 112–13, 115, 208, 349, 406, 489, 605n1503
Godan Khan, 105
Golden Garland of Mahāmudrā (Maitrīpa), 59–60, 443
Golden Rosary (Tsongkhapa), 141
Gom: A Course in Meditation (Gelek Rinpoché), 324
Gompa Tsultrim Nyingpo (*Sgom pa Tshul khrims snying po*), 93n302, 101
Gönlung Jampa Ling monastery, 253, 282, 291–92, 295–96
Gönpawa Wangchuk Gyaltsen (*Dgon pa ba Dbang phyug rgyal mtshan*), 71–72
Gonsalez, David, 342
Good Life, Good Death (Gelek Rinpoché), 324
Gorampa Sönam Sengé (*Go rams pa Bsod nams seng ge*), 139
Götsangpa Gönpo Dorjé (*Rgod tshang pa Mgon po rdo rje*), 3, 99–100, 107, 184, 334, 535
Gray, David, 37
Great Discourse on Mindfulness, 403
Great Exposition of Tenet Systems (Jamyang Shepai Dorjé), 292
Great Exposition of the Stages of Secret Mantra (Tsongkhapa), 120n425, 141, 150, 168, 364–65
Great Exposition of the Stages of the Path to Awakening (Tsongkhapa), 141, 153–56, 168, 172, 278, 301
Great Exposition of View and Meditation (Atiśa), 70
Great Guidance on the Madhyamaka View (Baso Chökyi Gyaltsen), 172
great perfection, 80–82, 155, 298–99, 431
cosmogonic notions in, 395
criticisms of, 106, 318, 344
identification with mahāmudrā and Madhyamaka, 76, 109, 163, 196–98, 203, 209–10, 242, 300–301, 309–11, 336, 347, 369, 373–75, 471, 502
Kagyü synthesis with mahāmudrā, 4, 82, 88, 92, 103, 109, 128–29, 295, 423
teaching of by fourteenth Dalai Lama, 332
Great Prayer Festival, 142, 185, 201
Great Treasury of Mahāmudrā (Geshé Acharya Thubten Loden), 322
Great Treasury of Merit (Kelsang Gyatso), 328–29
Gugé Losang Tenzin (*Gu ge Blo bzang bstan 'dzin*), 241, 279–81, 285–87, 343, 644
Guhyagarbha Tantra. See *Secret Essence Tantra*
Guhyasamāja Tantra, 35, 42, 52, 79, 81, 90n292, 323, 364, 378
combined with Cakrasaṃvara and Yamāntaka, 145, 171, 302
deity, 142, 275n805, 328, 570
five stages of, 29n46, 144, 300, 350

importance of for Tsongkhapa, 136n470, 139–41, 150–51, 350
mahāmudrā in, 113, 182–83, 208, 335, 345, 439, 489–90
related texts and commentaries, 38–39, 43, 151, 182, 186, 202, 300
transmissions of, 144–45, 152, 189–90, 252–53, 260, 444
See also *Lamp to Illuminate the Five Stages*
Guhyasiddhi. See *Secret Attainment*
Guidance in the View of the Prāsaṅgika System (Khedrup Jé), 146
Guidebook on Mahāmudrā (Shar Kalden Gyatso), 247–48, 338
Guidebook on "Offering to the Guru" (Kachen Yeshé Gyaltsen), 273–74
Guidebook on the "Hundred Deities of Tuṣita" (Dalai Lama VII), 338
Guṇaprabha, 133, 200, 446n1166
Gungru Geshé Tenpa Tenzin (*Gung ru dge bshes Bstan pa bstan 'dzin*), 295
Gungru[wa] Gyaltsen Sangpo (*Gung ru [ba] Rgyal mtshan bzang po*), 162–63, 250, 283, 293, 305–6, 334
Gungthang[sang] Könchok Tenpai Drönmé (*Gung thang [bzang] Dkon mchog bstan pa'i sgron me*), 162, 242, 279, 281–84, 288, 296, 304, 309, 464, 644
guru devotion, 97, 210, 273, 288, 360, 409–11, 588
Guru Yoga Given as a Unique Transmission to the Dharma Lord Baso (Tsongkhapa), 144
Guru Yoga of the Ensa Oral Transmission (Khedrup Sangyé Yeshé), 177
Gushri Khan, 129, 147, 201, 237, 243
Gyalrong Geshé Tsultrim Nyima (*Rgyal rong dge bshes Tshul khrims nyi ma*), 242, 291, 302–4, 344, 644
Gyalsé Losang Tenzin (*Rgyal sras blo bzang bstan 'dzin*), 245–48
Gyaltsab Jé Darma Rinchen (*Rgyal tshab rje Dar ma rin chen*), 142, 145, 151, 166, 310, 360, 645
Gyaltsen Dzinpa (*Rgyal mtshan 'dzin pa*), 246, 277n454, 454n1191, 460, 463n1203, 644. *See also* Drungpa Tsöndrü Gyaltsen
Gyütö and Gyümé, tantric colleges, 133, 144, 176, 188, 195, 252, 254, 315, 322

H

hand gestures, 1, 10, 18–19, 22–23, 31–34, 39, 64, 66, 150, 168, 387
Harmonizing the Stages-of-the-Path Traditions (Losang Rinchen), 605
Heart Sūtra, 6, 74, 133n459, 320, 328, 332, 421
Heshang Moheyan, 106, 128, 138–39, 153–54, 157, 169, 297, 311, 348–49, 389–91, 403
Hevajra Tantra, 42, 52, 544, 587n1468
associated with mahāmudrā, 8, 183
on buddhahood, 395
commentaries on, 43, 51, 120
deity, 25, 275n805
references to mahāmudrā in, 36–39, 58
in Sakya tradition, 78–79
studied by Tsongkhapa, 135, 150
Hidden Meaning of Luminosity (Chödrak Yeshé), 116
Highway of the Conquerors (Paṇchen Chögyen), 148, 176–77, 200, 202–6, 235–37, 301, 332
commentaries and related texts, 242, 247–50, 259, 268, 270, 273, 277, 279–87, 303–4, 324, 334
comparing Geluk and Kagyü elements of, 346–57
description of mantra mahāmudrā in, 370, 470
focus on sūtra mahāmudrā in, 203, 346–50, 369, 470–71
on Geden Oral Transmission, 173, 470
main contents of, 202–6
meaning of *kagyü* in, 335, 341–45
modern publications of, 338
relation of to *Offering to the Guru*, 225
as source of Geluk mahāmudrā, 4–5, 202
translation of, 469–78
on ultimate nature of mind, 327
Hīnayāna. *See* Foundational Buddhism

Hindu tantra, mahāmudrā in, 20–22, 39. *See also* Śaivism
Holy Pith Instruction on Settling Thought without Dispersion or Concentration (Maitrīpa), 57–58
Huayan tradition, 390, 397
Hundred Deities of Tuṣita (Dulnakpa), 13, 144–46, 304, 306, 317, 324–25, 333, 360, 413, 539–41
Hundred Thousand Songs of Milarepa (Tsangnyön Heruka), 114, 531–32, 599–601

I

Illuminating Lamp. See *Lamp to Illuminate the Five Stages*
Illuminating the Significance of the Yoginī's Pure Conduct (Vīryavajra), 63
Illumination of Great Bliss (Maitrīpa), 59
Inconceivable Mahāmudrā (Tilopa), 52–53
Indian Mahāmudrā Texts (Karmapa VII), 115
Indrabhūti, 42, 190, 367, 491
insight meditation
  early mahāmudrā teachings of, 62–63
  Geluk, 191, 250–51, 264–65, 267, 269, 278, 281, 289, 303–4
  Kagyü, 77, 88, 100, 108–9, 121–27, 351, 354–55
  Paṇchen Chögyen on, 5, 12, 204–5, 212–15, 351–52, 354–56, 372, 402
  relative ordering of, 123, 127, 155, 204, 210, 263, 285–86, 320, 350–52, 402–4
  Tsongkhapa on, 139, 153–55, 157–58, 161, 164
  See also serenity meditation
Instruction on Empowerment (Maitrīpa), 57
Instruction on Mahāmudrā. See *Mahāmudrā Song of Mother Ganges*
Instruction on the Six Dharmas (Tilopa), 52
Instructions for the Mahāmudrā Connate Union (Rangjung Dorjé), 108–9

J

Jackson, David, 106, 557n1430
Jain traditions, 18, 424
Jakchen Jampa Pal (*'Jag chen Byams pa dpal*), 136, 149
Jamchen Chöjé Shākya Yeshé (*Byams chen chos rje shākya ye shes*), 143
James, William, 390, 422
Jamgön Kongtrul Lodrö Thayé (*'Jam mgon kong sprul Blo gros mtha' yas*), 4, 76, 117, 129–30, 299, 317
Jamyang Chöjé Tashi Palden (*'Jam dbyangs chos rje Bkra shis dpal ldan*), 134, 139–40, 143, 159, 367
Jamyang Khyentsé (*'Jam dbyangs mkhyen brtse*), 299
Jamyang Shepa I Ngawang Tsöndrü (*'Jam dbyangs bzhad pa Ngag dbang brtson 'grus*), 145–46, 242, 252–54, 291–93, 306, 310, 344, 375–78, 605, 644
Jamyang Thupten Nyima (*'Jam dbyangs thub bstan nyi ma*), 304, 306
Jangchup Gyaltsen (*Byang chub rgyal mtshan*), 111
Jangtsé Chöjé Losang Tenzin (*Byang rtse chos rje Blo bzang bstan 'dzin*), 244n734, 315n905, 358, 360
Jé Rinpoché. *See* Tsongkhapa Losang Drakpa
Jewel Garland (Nāgārjuna), 205, 212–13, 248, 442, 475, 518, 521, 523, 525, 532
Jewel Garland of Thatness (Maitrīpa), 59
Jewel Garland of Yoga (Kṛṣṇācārya), 43
Jewel Heap collection, 189, 210, 250, 503, 527
Jewel Heart of the Four Tenet-Systems (Gungru Geshé Tenpa Tenzin), 295
Jewel Mound of Pith Instructions (Chegom Sherab Dorjé), 73
Jewel Storehouse Biography (Chimé Rabgyé), 162n579
Jeweled Mirror of Pure Appearances (Losang Dongak Chökyi Gyatso), 310
Jikmé Lingpa (*'Jigs med gling pa*), 311
Jikten Sumgön Rinchen Pal (*'Jig rten gsum mgon rin chen dpal*), 3, 95–97, 106, 136, 149, 182, 191, 210, 334, 367, 500–501, 535, 563–64, 601, 645
  on universality of mahāmudrā, 208, 349
Jinpa, Thupten, 146–47, 157, 338, 342

Jñānagarbha Tantra. See *Matrix of Gnosis Tantra*
Jñānakīrti, 62, 297, 386, 604
Jñānasiddhi. See *Attainment of Gnosis*
Jonang tradition, 4, 67, 78, 110–12, 124, 135, 138, 243, 283, 399. *See also* shentong

K

Kachen Yeshé Gyaltsen (*Dka' chen Ye shes rgyal mtshan*), 146, 161–62, 173–74, 236, 254–55, 284, 293, 329, 367, 461, 567, 644–45
  disciples of, 279–82, 287, 302
  as editor of lineage prayer, 215, 241n729, 246–47, 257, 277–78, 457n1197
  guru yoga works of, 272–78
  importance for Geluk mahāmudrā, 5, 12–13, 241, 360
  lack of interest in Kagyü mahāmudrā, 278, 343
  life and studies of, 257–59
  Madhyamaka works of, 270–72
  mahāmudrā works of, 259–70
  on sources for mahāmudrā, 439–40
Kadam tradition, 87–88, 98, 101, 119, 135, 191, 224n722, 275n806, 363–64, 478, 537n1384
  influence on Gampopa, 73
  and mahāmudrā, 4, 56, 67–73, 296, 305, 347, 485, 610
  relation to Gelug, 111, 133, 185–86, 188, 218, 379
  transmissions from, 217, 301
Kagyü tradition (*Bka' brgyud*)
  according to Thuken, 297–98
  centrality of mahāmudrā to, 92, 126–27
  conflict with Gelukpas, 117, 128–30, 236–37, 243
  criticized by Sakyapas, 79, 105–7, 344. *See also* Sakya Paṇḍita Kunga Gyaltsen: criticism of mahāmudra by
  criticized by Tsongkhapa, 153–58, 169
  Indian antecedents of, 52–56
  influence of Kadam tradition on, 73, 98, 101
  Madhyamaka tradition in, 120
  on path of means and path of liberation, 54, 66, 75, 85, 98, 126–27, 208
  place of meditation in, 359
  points of disagreement within, 128
  popularity of Saraha's songs in, 363, 373
  sūtra and mantra mahāmudrā in, 601–2
Kālacakra Tantra, 110, 135–36, 150–51, 172, 185, 218, 543–44
  on buddhahood, 395
  commentaries on, 43, 54, 62, 180, 182
  and mahāmudrā, 2, 36–37, 39, 183
  teaching of in diaspora, 332
  yogas of, 29, 144, 158
Kamalaśīla, 90n292, 133n459, 332, 390
Kambala, 43
Kangxi emperor, 254
Kāṇha. *See* Kṛṣṇācārya
Karma Chakmé (*Karma chags med*), 4, 82n257, 117, 129
Karma Kagyü (*Karma bka' brgyud*), 84, 92, 101–3, 108, 111, 119, 190, 313
Karma Trinlepa Choklé Namgyal (*Karma 'phrin las pa Phyogs las rnam rgyal*), 115, 117–18, 378
Karmapa I Düsum Khyenpa (*Dus gsum mkhyen pa*), 101–3, 601
Karmapa II Karma Pakshi (*Karma pa kshi*), 103, 105
Karmapa III Rangjung Dorjé (*Rang byung rdo rje*), 3, 82n257, 107–11, 118, 120, 129, 311, 350, 406, 416, 423
Karmapa IV Rölpai Dorjé (*Rol pa'i rdo rje*), 135
Karmapa VII Chödrak Gyatso (*Chos grags rgya mtsho*), 3, 8, 58n172, 112, 114–15, 117
Karmapa VIII Mikyö Dorjé (*Mi bskyod rdo rje*), 3, 119–20, 139
Karmapa IX Wangchuk Dorjé (*Dbang phyug rdo rje*), 4, 124–26, 128, 350, 353
Karmapas, political power of, 117, 129, 243
Karṇatantravajragāthā. See *Vajra Verses of the Hearing Transmission*
Karopa, 68
Katz, Steven, 426

Kāyakoṣa. See *Body Treasury*
Keutsang Losang Jamyang Mönlam (*Ke'u tshang Blo bzang 'jam dbyangs smon lam*), 14, 241, 279, 286–89, 329, 343, 512n1319, 644
Key Points of the Path: A Scroll Offered to Jetsun Rendawa (Tsongkhapa), 155
Key Points of the View (Kachen Yeshé Gyaltsen), 270–72
Khamtrul III Ngawang Kunga Tenzin (*Khams sprul Ngag dbang kun dga' bstan 'dzin*), 129
Khedrup Jé Gelek Palsang (*Mkhas grub rje Dge legs dpal bzang*)
  criticism of non-Geluk teachings by, 162–63, 283
  as first Paṇchen Lama, 4n3, 179
  lineages including, 143–46, 149, 159, 167, 171–72, 175, 177, 217, 302n877, 333
  on mahāmudrā, 167–70
  and Tsongkhapa, 134, 142, 149, 165–67, 310, 360
Khedrup Ngawang Dorjé (*Mkhas grub Ngag dbang rdo rje*), 284–85, 462
Khedrup Norsang Gyatso (*Mkhas grub Nor bzang rgya mtsho*), 13, 177, 181–86, 198, 212, 253, 297, 344, 367–69, 373, 520–21, 566, 605–6, 643
Khedrup Sangyé Yeshé (*Mkhas grub Sangs rgyas ye shes*), 167, 244, 260, 266, 284, 293, 459, 570, 588, 596
  instructions to Paṇchen Chögyen, 199–200, 205, 212–13, 235–36, 354, 474–76, 528
  lineages including, 149, 195, 216–17, 246, 248n748, 301n874, 302n877, 451–52, 479, 643
  studies and teachers of, 175–78
  on *tsok* ritual, 219–20, 222–23, 567
Khedrup Tenzin Tsöndrü (*Mkhas grub bstan 'dzin brtson 'grus*), 317, 463, 644
Khön Könchok Gyalpo (*Khon Dkon mchog rgyal po*), 78
Khöntön Paljor Lhundrup (*'Khon ston Dpal 'byor lhun grub*), 195–98, 201, 373–75, 378, 643
Khyabchok Palsang (*Skyabs mchog dpal bzang*), 174–75
Khyungpo Naljor (*Khyung po rnal 'byor*), 76–77, 500, 531
King Dohā Treasury (Saraha), 44, 68, 118, 283, 375. *See also* Essential Trilogy
King of Concentrations Sūtra, 170, 212–13, 269–71, 498, 516–17, 524–25
  as source for mahāmudrā, 24, 56, 61, 69, 91, 189, 209, 297, 498, 604
Könchok Gyaltsen, Dorjé Dzinpa (*Dkon mchog rgyal mtshan*), 277, 454, 460, 644
Könchok Jikmé Wangpo (*Dkon mchog 'jigs med dbang po*), 242, 281–82, 292, 295, 464, 644
Könchok Yarphel (*Dkon mchog yar 'phel*), 252–53
Kor Nirūpa (*Skor Ni rū pa*), 68, 363
Kragh, Ulrich, 91
kriyā tantra. *See* action tantra
Kṛṣṇācārya, 43, 51, 64, 150, 366–67
Kubilai Khan, 103, 194
Kukuripa, 549, 554
Kumbum monastery, 133, 194, 245, 296
Kuṇḍalinī, 20–21
Kunga Gyaltsen. *See* Sakya Paṇḍita Kunga Gyaltsen
Kyemé Dechen. *See* Balpo Asu
Kyirong Samten Ling monastery, 258

L

Labrang Tashi Khyil monastery, 133, 245, 253–54, 281–82, 304, 306
Lakṣmīṅkarā, 42, 73
Lajang Khan, 253
Lama Gurudeva, 337
Lama Losang Thupwang Dorjé Chang. *See* Tsongkhapa Losang Drakpa: visualization practices about
Lama Shang. *See* Shang Yudrak Tsöndrü Drakpa
Lama Thubten Yeshé (*Bla ma Thub bstan ye shes*), 315n905, 322, 324, 327
Lamp Dispelling Darkness (Khedrup Jé), 146, 169

Lamp Illuminating the Excellent Path of the Conqueror (multiple authors), 338
Lamp on the Path to Awakening (Atiśa), 68, 70, 141, 332, 561
Lamp So Bright (Paṇchen Chögyen), 148, 200, 202, 206–15, 235–37
  influence on later Geluk texts, 248–51, 287, 297, 305
  modern teaching and publication of, 332, 334, 338
  relation of to *Offering to the Guru*, 225
  as source of Geluk mahāmudrā, 4–5
  sources for, 346–47
  on sūtra and mantra mahāmudra, 346–50, 369, 489, 497
  translation of, 479–538
Lamp That Integrates the Performance (Āryadeva), 43
Lamp to Illuminate the Five Stages (Tsongkhapa), 151, 363–68, 492, 495, 553
Laṅkāvatāra Sūtra. See *Descent to Laṅkā Sūtra*
Larsson, Stefan, 114
Letter of Final Testament Cast to the Winds (Gyalrong Geshé Tsultrim Nyima), 302–4, 338
Letter of Guidance (Umapa Pawo Dorjé), 146
Levels of the Bodhisattva (Asaṅga), 269
Levels of the Śrāvakas (Asaṅga), 211, 562
Life of Marpa the Translator (Tsangnyön Heruka), 114, 443, 527, 560, 597
Life of Milarepa (Tsangnyön Heruka), 114
Light Rays from the Jewel of the Excellent Teaching (Dakpo Tashi Namgyal), 120
lightning strike practice, 89–90, 389
Like a Treasure Inventory (Paṇchen Chögyen), 11, 146n502, 148, 167, 176, 202, 216–18
Limitless Ocean Cycle (Karma Pakshi), 103
Ling Rinpoché (*Gling rin po che*), 242, 285, 315, 319, 323, 329, 466, 644
Lingrepa Pema Dorjé (*Gling ras pa Pad ma rdo rje*), 98–99, 212, 378, 513–14, 596, 601
Lithang monastery, 133, 194
Locanā, 39
Lodrö Gyaltsen (*Blo gros rgyal mtshan*), 170–71
Longchen Rabjampa (*Klong chen rab 'byams pa*), 80–81, 111, 197, 310
Longdöl Lama Ngawang Losang (*Klong rdol bla ma Ngag dbang blo bzang*), 306
Lorepa Wangchuk Tsöndrü (*Lo ras pa Dbang phyug brtson 'grus*), 84, 99–100
Losang Dongak Chökyi Gyatso (*Blo bzang mdo sngags chos kyi rgya mtsho*), 242, 309–12
Losang Dönyö Drupa. *See* Ensapa Losang Döndrup
Losang Rinchen (*Blo bzang rin chen*), 297–98, 344, 605–8
Losang Trinlé (*Blo bzang 'phrin las*), 277, 460, 644
Lotus Holder (anonymous), 62
Lotus Sūtra, 385, 418, 425, 478
Lūipa, 144, 150, 260, 366–67, 443, 446, 645

M

Maban Chöbar (*Rma ban chos 'bar*), 68
Machik Lapdrön (*Ma gcig lab sgron*), 75, 92, 210–11, 254, 502, 508
Madhyamaka
  apophatic or cataphatic, 112, 116, 384
  influence of Tsongkhapa on, 138–39
  Geluk approach to, 264–65, 355–56
  Great, 109–10, 126, 141, 196–97, 373n1080, 520
  as mahāmudrā, 24, 59, 61–63, 120, 126, 164, 198, 261, 270–72, 309–10, 347–48, 359–60
  of nonabiding, 59, 116, 118, 126
  Paṇchen Chögyen, on single intention of teachings, 203, 471, 499, 502, 608
  synthesis with great perfection. *See* great perfection
  synthesis with Yogācāra, 108, 311, 397
  See also Prāsaṅgika Madhyamaka; Svātantrika Madhyamaka

Madhyamakālaṃkāra. See *Ornament of the Middle Way*
Madhyamakaṣaṭaka. See *Six Verses on Madhyamaka*
Madhyamakāvatāra. See *Entry to the Middle Way*
Magic Key (Kachen Yeshé Gyaltsen), 273, 275–76
Mahābhārata, 17, 508n1311
Mahākāla, 48, 135
Mahāmāyā, 152
mahāmudrā
 after Tibetan diaspora, 313–14
 amulet box, 77, 135, 149, 203, 209–10, 369, 471, 499–500, 607
 anthologies of, 41, 115, 130, 338
 as consort, 1, 10, 19, 21–22, 32, 34–39, 43–44, 54, 64
 critique of, 105–7, 153, 157–58
 early occurrences of term in tantra, 30–33
 esoteric or nondual, 66–67, 74–77, 86–87, 93, 97, 115, 126–27
 essential, 91, 224, 348
 etymological explanations of, 38, 55, 89, 208–9, 489–90
 fivefold, 90, 92, 95–97, 119, 135, 149, 203, 209–10, 367, 471, 499–501
 of four letters, 129, 203, 209–10, 369, 471, 499, 501, 607
 graded practice of, 121, 125–27, 134
 and great perfection. *See* great perfection
 Hindu uses of term, 20–22
 in India, 5–10, 51–60
 ineffability of, 6–8, 419–20
 and Madhyamaka. *See* Madhyamaka: as mahāmudrā
 many referents of term, 1–2, 10, 22, 32–39, 43–45, 64, 66
 meditation, Geluk, 13, 157–58, 189–91, 196, 204–6, 210–15, 247–50, 263–70, 273–76, 305–6, 328–29, 350–55, 360–61, 471–77, 503
 meditation, Kagyü, 96, 98, 108–9, 123, 127, 129, 359–60
 nine-meaning, 92
 objective or subjective, 283, 304
 problems of studying, 5–10
 role of reason in, 405–6
 role of ritual in, 412–14
 in Saraha's songs, 377, 413
 scriptural authority of, 382–83
 six stages of training in, 331
 subsuming all Buddhist practices, 97–98
 sūtra or mantra, 5, 12, 164, 184, 190–91, 203, 208–10, 297, 311, 325, 335, 346–51, 386–88, 470, 489, 497
 synonyms for, 10, 30, 36, 42–43, 45–46, 51, 62, 66, 88, 93, 126
 threefold, 263
 transmission of to Tibet, 56, 65–68, 113
 See also four seals; Perfection Vehicle, mahāmudrā as
Mahāmudrā Eliminating the Darkness of Ignorance (Wangchuk Dorjé), 125–26, 346
Mahāmudrā Given by Atiśa to Gönpawa. See *Special Instructions on the Connate Union*
Mahāmudrā Instructions on the Lightning Strike (Gampopa), 88–89
Mahāmudrā Lineage Prayer (Paṇchen Chögyen), 148, 202, 215–16, 225, 267, 333, 338, 457–67, 643
 addenda to, 13, 215, 246, 257, 273, 277–78, 317, 329
Mahāmudrā of Symbols. *See* pacification practice
Mahāmudrā Song of Mother Ganges (Tilopa), 53, 108, 443, 514
Mahamudra Tantra (Kelsang Gyatso), 329–31
Mahāmudrāgaṅgāmā. See *Mahāmudrā Song of Mother Ganges*
Mahāmudrākanakamālā. See *Golden Garland of Mahāmudrā*
Mahāmudrāsaṅgamita. See *Verses on Mahāmudrā*
Mahāmudrātilaka. See *Drop of Mahāmudra Tantra*
Mahāmudropadeśa. See *Mahāmudrā Song of Mother Ganges*
Mahānirvāṇa Tantra, 19

Mahāsatipaṭṭhāna Sutta. See *Great Discourse on Mindfulness*
Mahāsukha. *See* Padmavajra
Mahāsukhaprakāśa. See *Illumination of Great Bliss*
Mahāyānasūtrālaṃkāra. See *Ornament of Mahāyāna Sūtras*
mahāyoga tantras, 30–31, 34–38, 41–43, 65–66, 80–82, 85, 419
Maitreya, 61, 113, 133, 150, 210, 217, 244, 260, 267, 539
  and Asaṅga, 56, 112, 116, 269, 353, 356, 396, 442. *See also* Five Maitreya Texts
  worship of, 142, 145
  Yogācāra teachings of, 63, 79, 110, 356
Maitrīpa, 2, 55–64, 213, 489–90, 610n1521
  connection to Atiśa, 56, 69, 416
  in Geluk lineages, 260, 311, 443, 645
  interpretation of *Sublime Continuum* by, 113
  on Madhyamaka, 59, 63, 116, 120, 191
  main teachings on mahāmudrā by, 57–61
  on nonmentation, 8, 56–60, 311
  as Prāsaṅgika Mādhyamika, 297–98, 597–98, 607
  as source for Perfection Vehicle mahāmudrā, 61–64, 91, 100, 348, 386
  teachers and disciples of, 8, 50, 56–62, 67–68, 73–74, 76–78, 83
  See also Twenty-Five Works on Nonmentation
Māmakī, 39
Mañjughoṣa
  in Geluk lineages, 149, 175, 217, 246, 260, 276, 302n877, 643
  visionary transmissions to Tsongkhapa, 4, 12, 137, 141, 143, 145, 149–50, 155, 159–60, 165, 172, 218, 220, 225, 260, 382, 435–37, 440, 444–46
  visions of by other Gelukpas, 137, 147, 174, 252, 367, 448
  visualized in guru yoga, 248–49, 262, 266
Mañjuśrī, 4, 31, 135, 208n705, 215, 292, 325, 457–58, 462. *See also* Mañjughoṣa
Mañjuśrīkīrti, 80
Mañjuśrīmūlakalpa. See *Root Tantra of Mañjuśrī*
Mañjuśrīnāmasaṅgīti. See *Chanting the Names of Mañjuśrī*
Mantra Ritual Section of the Supreme Primordial One, 34
Mantra Vehicle and Perfection Vehicle, relationship of, 347–48, 382–87, 557–58, 601–4
  for Geluk, 134–35, 140, 164, 168, 183, 209, 261–63, 276
  for Kagyü, 91–92, 95, 121, 126–28
  for Maitrīpa, 61–64
Marpa Chökyi Lodrö (*Mar pa Chos kyi blo gros*), 3, 136, 139, 149, 164, 198, 363, 490, 560
  in Geluk lineages, 152, 260, 302n877, 645
  on nature of mind, 213, 527
  as Prāsaṅgika Mādhyamika, 297, 597
  songs of, 85, 114, 250
  teachers and training of, 56, 67–68, 83–85, 600
  transmissions from Nāropa to, 56, 189, 443, 495
  visions of Saraha by, 382
Marpa Kagyü, 3–4, 59, 83–84
  creativity of later scholars in, 107, 111
  expansive understanding of mahāmudrā in, 79
  major transmissions of, 101
  relation to Shangpa Kagyü of, 76–78
  sources of, 51–56, 67
  synthesis of mahāmudrā and great perfection in, 82n257
Martsang Kagyü, 92
Marvelous Account (Tokden Jampal Gyatso), 134
Matrix of Gnosis Tantra, 39
Matrix of the Tathāgata Sūtra, 189
Māyājāla. See *Net of Illusion Tantra*
Mé tradition, 144, 146, 253
Middle-Length Stages of the Path (Tsongkhapa), 142

Miktsema (Rendawa), 136–37, 145, 262, 267, 361, 578
Mila Songs (Paṇchen Chögyen), 226
Milarepa Shepai Dorjé (*Mi la ras pa Shes pa'i rdo rje*), 3, 73–74, 85–88, 136n470, 152, 164, 330n954, 487, 502
  on awakening mind, 484–85
  in Geluk lineages, 149, 260, 443, 645
  guru yoga directed to, 226
  on mahāmudrā, 86–87
  as model for practice, 13, 85, 98, 114, 174, 181, 186, 200–201, 245–46, 251, 256, 299
  as Prāsaṅgika Mādhyamika, 187, 297, 599–600
  on six Dharmas of Nāropa, 443–44, 495–96
  songs of, 200, 208, 282, 301, 307, 322, 421
  use of inner-heat meditation by, 86–87, 99, 200, 495, 560
mind, primordial, 182–83, 263, 303, 336–37, 367–71, 492–96, 543–58, 564–65, 602, 606
  problems of gradualist approach to, 560–62
mind training, 69, 145, 275, 305, 590–91
Mind Treasury (Saraha), 45–46
mind-only doctrine, 63, 284, 297–98, 356, 425, 598, 600, 607. *See also* Yogācāra
Mipham Gyatso (*Mi pham rgya mtsho*), 139, 295, 299–300, 309
mixture and transference practice, 93, 122, 139
Mixture of Sūtras (Nāgārjuna), 442
Möngke Khan, 103, 105
Mönlam Chemo. *See* Great Prayer Festival
Moonbeams of Mahāmudrā (Dakpo Tashi Namgyal), 121, 346, 373
mother tantras, 2, 30n48, 34–37, 151, 168, 350. *See also* yoginī tantras
mountain Dharma, 4, 210, 501
Mountain Doctrine (Dölpopa), 110
mudrā, meaning and uses of term, 17–24
Mūlamadhyamakakārikā. See *Root Verses on the Middle Way*
mūlatantra. *See* root tantras
Munidatta, 64
mysticism, 6–7, 12, 381, 390–91, 398, 404–5, 421–26

N

Nāgārjuna, 2n2, 24, 43–44, 48, 407, 410, 439–40
  as apophatic philosopher, 112
  on emptiness, 63, 138, 140, 157–58, 209, 212–14, 248, 260–61, 263, 396–97, 400, 446, 475, 497–98
  lineages including, 217, 294, 260, 366, 441–42, 645
  as source for Kagyü and Nyingma views, 305, 310, 323, 369
  tantric teachings of, 43, 58n173, 64, 120, 139–40, 203, 260, 439, 470, 489–91
  visions of, 137, 150
  See also *Jewel Garland*
Nakpo Sherdé (*Nag po sher dad*), 68
Nālandā monastery, 61, 408
Naljorpa, 72
Namgyal College, 193–94
Namkha Gyaltsen (*Nam mkha' rgyal mtshan*), 135, 155, 300
Narendrakīrti, 43, 64
Nāropa, 2, 43, 103, 186, 203, 370, 408–9, 440, 470, 489–90
  Dharmas of. *See* six Dharmas of Nāropa
  disciples of, 56, 83–86, 443–44
  in Geluk lineages, 150, 152, 175, 217, 260, 311, 645
  interpretations of mahāmudrā by, 54–56, 64, 75, 420
  as Prāsaṅgika Mādhyamika, 297, 597–99
  transmissions from Tilopa to, 51–53, 189, 382, 408–9, 443
  visions of by Tsongkhapa, 139
Naturally Free Mahāmudrā (Nigumā), 77
Nectar Stream (Akhu Sherab Gyatso), 306
Net of Brahmā, 406
Net of Illusion Tantra, 34–35, 79–81, 195

New Kadam, 111, 133. *See also* Geluk tradition
New Kadampa Tradition (NKT), 327–28
New Translation schools, 67, 78–79, 81–82, 111–12, 374, 395
  classification of tantras in, 30–31, 34, 141, 309–10, 383
Ngaripa (*Mnga' ris pa*), 68
Ngawang Chokden (*Ngag dbang mchog ldan*), 254–55
Ngawang Gelek Demo. *See* Gelek Rinpoché
Ngödrup Rabten (*Dngos grub rab brtan*), 465, 644
Ngulchu Dharmabhadra (*Dngul chu Dharmabhadra*), 241, 279, 284–86, 289, 343, 462, 644
Nigumā, 68, 76–77, 136, 500. *See also* six Dharmas of Nigumā
nonmentation, 8, 41, 49–50, 56–60, 189–90, 210, 311, 501
nonsectarian movement, 82n257, 118, 129–30, 299–300, 309, 313, 317
Notes on a Teaching on Combining "Offering to the Guru" with Mahāmudrā (Akhu Sherab Gyatso), 304–5
Notes on Kālacakra (Gendun Drup), 180
Notes on Mahāmudrā (Pema Karpo), 123, 346
Nyernyi Rinpoché (*Nyer gnyis rin po che*), 184, 565, 605n1503
Nyingma tradition, 67, 76, 78–80, 88, 109–11, 128–30, 298–99, 310, 313, 383
  classification of tantras by, 34, 81
  Geluk associations with, 184, 195–98, 243, 332
  Geluk opposition to, 316–17, 336, 609
  influence of subitism within, 390
  mahāmudrā in, 4, 35, 81–82, 103, 423
  relation of Tsongkhapa to, 135, 155–56, 300
  treasure tradition of, 218, 296
  See also great perfection

O

Ocean of Definitive Meaning (Wangchuk Dorjé), 125–26, 346
Ocean of Kagyü Songs (Mikyö Dorjé), 119
Ocean of Reasoning (Tsongkhapa), 141
Ocean of Texts on Reasoning (Chödrak Gyatso), 115
Odantapuri monastery, 61
Offering to the Guru (Gendun Gyatso), 186, 596
Offering to the Guru (Lingrepa), 596
Offering to the Guru (Paṇchen Chögyen), 13, 146, 218–26, 301
  commentaries to, 253, 259, 273–76, 302–6, 328–29, 332–33
  importance of for Geluk liturgy, 202, 360
  mahāmudrā interpretation of by Yeshé Gyaltsen, 5, 257, 262–63, 273–76
  modern publications of, 338, 342
  preliminaries based on, 262–63, 280, 288, 302, 305, 325, 333, 413
  translation of, 567–96
  visualizations based on, 275, 283, 288, 317–18
Offering to the Guru (Pang Lotsāwa), 596
Ölkha, 159–60, 181–82, 185
Oral Teaching of the Precious Father Chegom (Chegom Sherab Dorjé), 72
Orgyenpa Rinchen Pal (*O rgyan pa Rin chen dpal*), 107
Ornament Beautifying the Meru of the Sage's Teaching (Changkya Rölpai Rojé), 292, 601, 603, 607
Ornament of Higher Realization (Maitreya), 133, 135, 141, 200, 304
Ornament of Mahāyāna Sūtras (Maitreya), 397, 503–4
Ornament of Stainless Light (Khedrup Norsang Gyatso), 182
Ornament of the Essence (Mañjuśrīkīrti), 486
Ornament of the Middle Way (Śāntarakṣita), 309
Outline of Mahāmudrā (Ngulchu Dharmabhadra), 286, 289

P

pacification practice, 4, 67, 73–78, 83, 101, 184, 203, 209–10, 288, 369, 471, 499, 501–2, 607
Padmasambhava, 73, 80, 197–98, 210, 218, 245, 300–301, 312, 317, 416, 502
Padmavajra, 42, 189, 209, 440, 490n1259
Padminī. See *Lotus Holder*
Palden Dorjé of Tölung (*Stod lung pa Dpal ldan rdo rje*), 172, 194
Palden Tenpai Nyima (*Dpal ldan Bstan pa'i nyi ma*), 317, 465, 644
Palmang Könchok Gyaltsen (*Dpal mang Dkon mchog rgyal mtshan*), 304, 465, 644
Pañcakrama. See *Five Stages*
Paṇchen Chögyen, 4n3, 11–13, 128, 156, 199–202, 459
  affinity of ideas with Kagyü teachings, 346–47, 352–56
  debates over intention of, 341–45
  disciples of, 242
  emphasis on sūtra mahāmudrā by, 5, 184, 203, 209, 325, 349–51, 369, 382, 384
  focus on mind by, 265–66
  and Hearing Transmission lineages, 145, 149, 165, 167, 169, 177, 200, 215–18, 246–47, 260, 277–78, 452–54
  as initiator of Geluk mahāmudrā system, 4–5, 177–78, 202, 219, 235–37, 278, 360–61
  mahāmudrā in songs of, 226–35, 259, 270–71, 321, 627–28, 640–41
  main mahāmudrā texts of, 4–5, 146–48, 202–26
  on meditation, 204–6, 210–14, 318, 351–55, 402
  possible influences on, 163, 186, 193, 198
  on Saraha's songs, 369–73
  on single intention of teachings, 203, 209–10, 237, 283, 288–89, 298, 325, 335–36, 344, 370–72, 423, 471, 607–8
  tutoring of fifth Dalai Lama by, 201–2, 241–45
  visions by, 199–200, 244
Paṇchen Lama I Losang Chökyi Gyaltsen. *See* Paṇchen Chögyen
Paṇchen Lama II Losang Yeshé (*Blo bzang ye shes*), 199, 241, 254, 258, 277, 292, 455, 460, 644
Paṇchen Lama III Palden Yeshé (*Dpal ldan ye shes*), 241, 258, 283, 287–88, 296, 299, 334–35, 344, 423, 462, 644
Paṇchen Lama IV Tenpai Nyima (*Bstan pa'i nyi ma*), 279–80
Paṇchen Lama VI Losang Thupten Chökyi Nyima (*Blo bzang thub bstan chos kyi nyi ma*), 309
Paṇchen Sönam Drakpa (*Paṇ chen Bsod nams grags pa*), 187–93, 198, 643
Pāṇḍaravāsinī, 39
Parphuwa Lodrö Sengé (*Par phu ba Blo gros seng ge*), 68, 72
path and fruit tradition, 50, 78–79, 83, 101, 117, 128, 170
Path to Bliss (Paṇchen Chögyen), 202, 301, 304
Patrul Rinpoché (*Dpal sprul rin po che*), 309
Pawo Tsuklak Trengwa (*Dpa' bo Gtsug lag phreng ba*), 3, 115, 118–19, 157
Pema Karpo (*Pad ma dkar po*), 3, 122–24, 139, 156, 349–50, 353, 416, 609
People Dohā Treasury (Saraha), 44–45, 118, 283, 491
  on mind, 45, 374, 376, 543–44, 546
  promotion of by Atiśa, 363
  quotations from, 376–77, 472–73, 491–95, 505–6, 508–9, 513, 544, 546, 555–56
  on sexual yoga, 555–56
  uses of by Geluk authors, 209, 253, 367–68, 370, 373–78
perennialism, 426
Perfection of Wisdom in Eight Thousand Lines, 189, 212, 250, 261, 450, 518, 527
Perfection of Wisdom sūtras
  on emptiness, 2n2, 6, 203, 209, 325, 356, 384, 396, 400, 421, 497

negative rhetoric of, 6, 394, 396–97, 400, 407, 410, 414
relation of Shiché and Chö to, 74–75, 369
as source for mahāmudrā, 8, 24, 43, 62–63, 91, 260–61, 305, 369, 384, 439, 471, 497
Perfection Vehicle, mahāmudrā as, 13, 24, 61–64, 91–92, 116, 121, 126–28, 164, 183, 189, 260–63, 276, 348, 386–87, 557–59, 601, 603–4
Performance Song Dohā Treasury. See *King Dohā Treasury*
performance tantras, 30–33, 275n805
Phabongkha Dechen Nyingpo (*Pha bong kha Bde chen snying po*), 236, 246, 315–18, 323, 328–29, 334, 361, 416, 466, 644
as editor of mahāmudrā lineage prayer, 13, 215, 241n729, 247, 277–78, 457n1197
Geluk exclusivism of, 316–17
on preliminaries, 325n930
revival of mahāmudrā by, 5, 242, 318–19
Phabongkha hermitage, 196, 253
Phadampa Sangyé (*Pha dam pa sangs rgyas*), 68, 73–75, 363, 476, 501–2, 528
on refuge and guru devotion, 207–8, 483, 487
studied by Gelukpas, 191, 198, 205, 213, 346
studied by Kagyüpas, 92, 101
See also pacification practice; severance practice
Phakmo Drupa Dorjé Gyalpo (*Phag mo gru pa Rdo rje rgyal po*), 95–98, 136, 149, 182, 191, 213, 283, 367, 488, 490, 528, 550–51, 601, 645
Phakpa Lodrö Gyaltsen (*'Phags pa Blo gros rgyal mtshan*), 105
Phurbuchok Ngawang Jampa (*Phur bu lcog Ngag dbang byams pa*), 242, 258, 299, 435n1154, 461, 464
Pith Instruction on the Perfection of Wisdom (Ratnākaraśānti), 562
Pledge Wheel. See *Cakrasaṃvara Tantra*
Poetic Expressions (Paṇchen Chögyen), 13, 611–41
Pomdrakpa Sönam Dorjé (*Spom brag pa Bsod nams rdo rje*), 103
postmeditative state, 121, 205–6, 248–49, 529–30
Potowa (*Po to ba*), 69, 568n1450
Praise for Dependent Arising (Tsongkhapa), 271, 300, 306, 446n1169, 449
Prajñāpāramitā (goddess), 37
Prajñāpāramitāhṛdaya. See *Heart Sūtra*
Prajñāpāramitāsañcayagāthā. See *Condensed Perfection of Wisdom*
Pramāṇavārttika. See *Exposition of Valid Cognition*
Prāsaṅgika Madhyamaka
identified with Kagyüpas, 198, 297–98, 323, 597–600
identified with Nyingmapas, 310–11
in Geluk philosophy, 134, 138, 153, 155, 191, 305–6, 359, 427–29
as mahāmudrā, 110, 126, 164, 186–87, 293, 423–24
modes of perception in, 519n1342
negative rhetoric of, 63, 112, 116, 372
Prātimokṣa discipline, 112, 190, 208, 489, 592, 630
Prayer of the Mahāmudrā of Definitive Meaning (Rangjung Dorjé), 108–9, 129
Precious Lamp (Phakmo Drupa), 553, 561, 563
Precious Stairway (Phakmo Drupa), 550–53
priest-patron relationship, 194
Profound Inner Meaning (Rangjung Dorjé), 108, 118
Profound Song on the View, A. See *Recognizing My Mother*
Profound Teaching on the View (Kachen Yeshé Gyaltsen), 266–68, 338
profound view, lineage of, 217, 262, 275n805. *See also* extensive activity, lineage of
Proudfoot, Wayne, 426
Proving That the Kagyü and Geluk Have a Single Intention. See *Bright Lamp of Mahāmudrā*
Puṇḍarīka, 39, 43, 64, 210
Puṇyākaragupta. *See* Dorjé Denpa

Pure Land traditions, 392, 411, 421
pure lands, 26, 28, 224, 400, 593
Purification of All the Lower Realms Tantra, 33

Q

Qianlong emperor, 291–92, 296
Queen Dohā Treasury (Saraha), 44, 118, 283, 587n1468
Queries from a Pure Heart (Tsongkhapa), 157–58, 161–62, 164, 169, 259, 288, 344, 416, 447, 512n1319
  authorship of, 153, 156–57, 298, 608–9
Questions of Gaganagañja Sūtra, 23
Questions of Rāṣṭrapāla Sūtra, 212, 515
Questions of Sāgaramati Sūtra, 23
Quotations from Kalden Gyatso's Ocean of Instructions (Shar Kalden Gyatso), 248–49

R

Radreng monastery, 185, 442
Raft to Cross the Ocean of Indian Buddhist Thought (Gendun Gyatso), 186–87
Rāhulagupta, 76
Ralung monastery (*Rwa lung*), 99
Rāmapāla, 59
Rāṣṭrapālaparipṛcchā. See *Questions of Rāṣṭrapāla Sūtra*
Ratnagotravibhāga. See *Sublime Continuum*
Ratnākaraśānti, 56, 90n292
Ratnakūṭa. See *Jewel Heap* collection
Ratnasambhava, 33, 361
Ratnāvalī. See *Jewel Garland*
Rechungpa Dorjé Drak (*Ras chung pa Rdo rje grags*), 68, 85, 87–88
  hearing transmission of, 92, 99, 114
Recognizing My Mother (Changkya Rölpai Dorjé), 293–95, 338
Recognizing the Dharmakāya (Wangchuk Dorjé), 125
Recognizing the Tathāgata Essence (Rangjung Dorjé), 108
Record of Teachings Received (Tsongkhapa), 134, 150, 152, 363n1038, 366
Rendawa Shönu Lodrö (*Red mda' ba Gzhon nu blo gros*), 136–37, 143, 145–46, 155–56, 159, 166, 262, 444
Reply to Queries from a Pure Heart (Shākya Chokden), 609n1518
Reply to Queries: Gentle Words of Explanation for the Noble-Minded (Paṇchen Chögyen), 609
Reply to Statements by Rendawa (Tsongkhapa), 155, 161–62, 447
Rikhu monastery, 180–81, 258
Rimé. *See* nonsectarian movement
Riwo Gephel monastery, 177, 252
ritual and contemplation, tension between, 412–15
Rongzom Chökyi Sangpo (*Rong zom Chos kyi bzang po*), 310
Root Song (Jikten Sumgön), 500–501, 563–64
Root Tantra of Mañjuśrī, 31
root tantras, 37, 43, 218
Root Verses on the Middle Way (Nāgārjuna), 133n459, 137–38, 141, 157n560, 332, 407n1126, 517
Royal Tantra on the Unpolluted, 115

S

Śabara. *See* Śavaripa
Sachen Kunga Nyingpo (*Sa chen Kun dga' snying po*), 78, 236n728
Sacred Words of Mañjuśrī (Jñānapāda), 549–50, 553–54, 608
Ṣaddharmopadeśa. See *Instruction on the Six Dharmas*
Sahajaṣaṭaka. See *Six Verses on the Connate*
Sahajasiddhi. See *Attainment of the Connate*
Sahajavajra, 61–62, 64, 164, 491, 598
Śaivism, 19–22, 34, 80n249
Śakta tantra, 19–21
Sakya Paṇḍita Kunga Gyaltsen (*Kun dga' rgyal mtshan*), 78, 214, 310, 334, 346
  criticism of mahāmudrā by, 94, 105–7, 154, 157, 348–49, 382, 389, 391, 394, 416
  on refuge and guru devotion, 207–9, 483, 487

responses to criticisms by, 116, 124, 126, 183, 189, 193, 196, 382, 387, 389, 391–92, 557, 604–6
restriction of mahāmudra to tantra by, 297, 382, 384, 387
Sakya traditions, 4, 11, 50, 67, 76, 78–79, 105, 111–12, 191, 283, 313, 316, 349, 396, 399. *See also* path and fruit tradition
Śākyamuni Buddha, 26, 100, 126, 268, 322, 619n1539
visualizations including, 173, 221, 449n1176
Samādhirājasūtra. See *King of Concentrations Sūtra*
Saṃdhinirmocana Sūtra. See *Unraveling the Intention Sūtra*
saṃsāra and nirvāṇa, inseparability of, 26, 44, 89, 118, 213–14, 334, 400, 612, 623, 625, 630–31, 633
Samuel, Geoffrey, 359
Saṃvarodaya Tantra, 37, 569
Samyé debate, 106, 389–90, 404
Sangphu monastery, 195
Śāntarakṣita, 309
Śāntideva, 59, 73, 205, 207, 210, 212–13, 228, 270, 303n878, 475, 483, 618
Śāntipa, 483, 607
Saraha, 2, 5, 8–9, 44–48, 64, 73, 115, 126, 344, 390, 392, 395, 420–22, 440, 470
as author of *Dohā Treasuries*, 283, 491
influence on Karma Kagyü, 92, 363
lineages including, 100, 120, 260, 311, 346, 442–43, 645
on mind, 182, 211–12, 264, 268–69, 353, 508, 513–14, 543–44, 606
Nyingma study of, 82
path of means teachings of, 75
radical views of, 400, 405–6, 409, 412, 416, 555
studies of songs in Tibet, 68–69, 72, 87, 108, 118, 253, 363–79
visions of, 85, 139, 150, 382, 446
Sarvabuddhasamāyoga. See *Union of All the Buddhas Tantra*
Sarvadurgatipariśodhana. See *Purification of All the Lower Realms*
Sarvatathāgatatattvasaṃgraha. See *Compendium of the Realities of All the Tathāgatas*
Śavaripa, 2, 59, 120, 353, 372n1077, 374n1082, 490–91
life and teachings of, 44, 48–50, 73
lineages including, 48, 100, 260, 442–43, 645
as model for practice, 171, 200, 448, 453
visions of, 50, 56
Schleiermacher, Friedrich, 411
scriptural hermeneutics, 384–86
Sé tradition, 144, 146, 252–53, 333, 360
Secret Assembly. See *Guhyasamāja Tantra*
Secret Attainment (Padmavajra), 42, 209, 440, 490
Secret Biography (Khedrup Jé), 134
Secret Essence Tantra, 35, 80–81
Secret Life Prayer (Tashi Palden), 134, 139–40, 367
Secret Mantra Vehicle, basic characteristics of, 25–30
Sekanirdeśa. See *Instruction on Empowerment*
Sekoddeśaṭīkā. See *Commentary on the "Teaching on Empowerment"*
Sera monastery, 133, 143
serenity meditation
early mahāmudrā teachings of, 62–63
Geluk, 183, 191–92, 261–64, 267–69, 278, 281, 289, 303
Kagyü, 77, 88, 100, 108–9, 121–27, 352–54
Paṇchen Chögyen on, 5, 12, 204–5, 210–12, 234, 352–55, 371–72, 402
relative ordering of, 123, 127, 155, 204, 210, 263, 285–86, 320, 350–51, 402–4, 503
sixfold methods for, 325–26, 509–10
Tsongkhapa on, 139, 153–55, 157–58, 160–61, 164
uses of Saraha for describing, 371–75, 379
Serlingpa, 442, 483
Seven Attainment Texts, 8, 41–43, 189–90, 203, 209, 260, 268, 370, 440, 470, 489–91, 602, 608

seven-point mind training, 275n806
sevenfold worship rite, 27, 221–22, 574–78, 639
Seventy Verses on Emptiness (Nāgārjuna), 186
severance practice, 67, 75–76, 92, 137, 272, 471, 499, 502–3, 607–8
in Geluk tradition, 145n501, 147, 170–71, 175, 203, 209–10, 254, 259, 369
lineage of, 137n473
sexual yoga, 1–2, 21–22, 28–29, 35–39, 66, 85, 143, 168, 180, 311, 366, 387, 417, 555
Shabkar Tsokdruk Rangdröl (*Zhabs dkar Tshogs drug rang grol*), 218, 298–301, 309
Shākya Chokden (*Shākya mchog ldan*), 107n367, 110, 112, 117, 139, 156, 609
Shalu monastery, 296
Shamarpa IV Chödrak Yeshé (*Chos grags ye shes*), 112, 115–18
Shang Yudrak Tsöndrü Drakpa (*Zhang g.yu brag Brtson grus grags pa*), 93–94, 99, 102, 416, 601, 604–6
author of white panacea teaching, 94, 105–6, 344, 348, 382, 601
on four yogas, 191, 214, 535
on mind, 212, 513–15
as proponent of subitist realization, 3, 94, 389, 405
Shangpa Kagyü, 4, 67, 76–78, 112, 149, 184–85, 191, 209–10, 500. *See also* Tsalpa Kagyü
Shar Kalden Gyatso (*Shar Skal ldan rgya mtsho*), 146, 215, 242, 245–52, 277–78, 298, 467n1211, 643
Sharf, Robert, 390, 426
shentong, 110–11, 115, 117, 120, 138, 158, 191, 336–37, 356, 372, 399–401
Sherab Sangpo (*Shes rab bzang po*), 181, 202
Sherab Sengé (*Shes rab seng ge*), 144, 146, 180, 249
Shiché. *See* pacification practice
Shuksep Kagyü, 92
Sigālaka Sutta. See *Discourse to Sigala*
Single Intention (*dgongs gcig*), 3, 92, 96–98
criticism of, 106–7, 193, 348, 382, 604–5
Situ Paṇchen Chökyi Jungné (*Si tu paṇ chen Chos kyi 'byung gnas*), 4, 117, 129, 170
Śiva, 19–20, 419
Śiva Sūtra, 19
Six About Equal Taste (Tsangpa Gyaré), 99
Six Collections of Madhyamaka Reasoning (Nāgārjuna), 439–40
six Dharmas of Nāropa, 29n46, 52–54, 501, 610
as basis for mantra mahāmudrā, 126–27, 348–49
Geluk studies of, 135–36, 149, 151–52, 170, 175, 186, 191, 202, 209–10, 259, 285, 300–301, 322–23, 367
importance of for Barom Kagyü, 92
inner heat meditation of, 200, 330, 350, 489, 495–96, 560, 565
Kagyü studies of, 76–77, 83–87, 108–9, 116, 120
and transference practice, 122–23
transmissions of, 101, 144, 443
six Dharmas of Nigumā, 136, 149, 186, 210, 500
Six Ornaments, 446n1166
Six Ornaments Beautifying Mahāmudrā (Paṇchen Sönam Drakpa), 188–93, 198
Six Verses on Madhyamaka (Maitrīpa), 59
Six Verses on the Connate (Maitrīpa), 59
six yogas of Kālacakra, 29, 158
Six-Session Guru Yoga (Paṇchen Chögyen), 202, 325, 361
Six-Session Guru Yoga (Phabongkha Dechen Nyingpo), 317, 361
Sixty Verses on Mahāmudrā (Chödrak Yeshé), 116
Smith, E. Gene, 114, 122, 337
Sönam Choklang (*Bsod nams phyogs glang*), 4n3, 169
Sönam Gyaltsen (*Bsod nams rgyal mtshan*), 135

Sönam Gyatso. *See* Dalai Lama III Sönam Gyatso
Song of Secret Vajra Instruction on Mahāmudrā (Saraha), 374
Song of the Profound View (Geshé Rabten), 320–21
Song of the Spring Queen (Tsongkhapa), 220n718, 223, 567, 585–87
Source of All Attainments (Kachen Yeshé Gyaltsen). See *Profound Teaching on the View*
Source of All Yogic Attainments (Ensapa Losang Döndrup), 167n590, 175
Source of All Yogic Attainments (Kachen Yeshé Gyaltsen), 273–75
Special Instructions on the Connate Union (Atiśa), 71
Speech Treasury (Saraha), 45–46
Splendid Array Sūtra, 270
Śrāvakabhūmi. See *Levels of the Śrāvakas*
Stages of Meditation (Kamalaśīla), 90n292, 133n459, 332, 561
Stages of the Path to Awakening (Atiśa), 70–71
Stainless Drop of Mahāmudrā. *See* pacification practice
Stainless Light (Puṇḍarīka), 39, 43, 210, 502–3, 544, 548–49
storehouse consciousness, 141, 427
Storehouse of Attainments Concordant with the Supreme (Gugé Losang Tenzin), 280
Storehouse of Mahāmudrā (Pema Karpo), 124, 609
Sublime Continuum (Maitreya), 56, 59, 69, 91, 110, 113, 116, 133n459, 170, 188–89, 249, 348, 384, 397
Succession of the Four Seals (Maitrīpa or Nāgārjuna), 58. See also *Ascertaining the Four Seals*
sudden and gradual approaches, 73, 88, 93, 96, 117, 182–83, 209, 214, 283, 297, 349–50, 368, 389–92, 552–53
Sujata, Victoria, 246, 251
Sukhasiddhī, 76–77
Summary Illuminating the Five Stages (Nāropa), 554
Summary of the View (Nāropa), 55–56
Sumpa Khenpo Yeshé Paljor (*Sum pa mkhan po Ye shes dpal 'byor*), 295
Śūnyatādṛṣṭi. See *View of Emptiness*
Śūnyatāsaptatī. See *Seventy Verses on Emptiness*
Surmang tradition, 87n278
Sūtra on Skillful Means, 418
Sūtra on the Elephant's Exertion, 523
Sūtra on the Presence of the Present Buddha, 603
Sūtra on the Ten Levels, 535
Sūtra That Gathers Intentions, 80
Sutta Nipāta, 407
Svātantrika Madhyamaka, 110, 141, 187, 191, 214, 297, 358n1029, 397, 533
Synopsis of the Spiritual Practice Taught by the Exalted Mañjughoṣa (Tsongkhapa), 12, 159–60, 258n783, 435–37

T

Takdrak Rinpoché (*Stag brag rin po che*), 315
Taking the Practice in Hand (Tsongkhapa), 152
Taklung Kagyü, 92, 106, 170, 536, 601
tantra
  classifications of, 30–31, 34, 141, 383
  definition of, 18
  Śaiva influence on, 19, 34
  transgressive behavior in, 18, 29, 34, 41, 56, 415–19
Tantra of the All-Creating Sovereign, 80
Taphukpa Losang Damchö Gyaltsen (*Rta phug pa Blo bzang dam chos rgyal mtshan*), 241n729, 454, 463n1203
Tārā, 25, 39, 324
Tara Box, The (Gelek Rinpoché), 324
Tāranātha, 69
Tashi Lhunpo monastery, 4, 133, 147–48, 171, 179–80, 202, 537n1384, 538, 596
Tashi Palden. *See* Jamyang Chöjé Tashi Palden
tathāgatagarbha, 2, 189. *See also* buddha nature
Tathāgatagarbha Sūtra. See *Matrix of the Tathāgata Sūtra*

Tattvadaśaka. See *Ten Verses on Thatness*
Tattvadaśakaṭīkā. See *Commentary on the "Ten Verses on Thatness"*
Tattvaratnāvalī. See *Jewel Garland of Thatness*
Tattvāvatāra. See *Entrance into Thatness*
Tattvaviṃśaka. See *Twenty Verses on Thatness*
Teaching of Vimalakīrti Sūtra, 394, 400, 418
Teaching on the View, A (Ensapa Losang Döndrup), 175
ten bodhisattva levels, 97, 99, 127, 196, 214, 275, 534–35
Ten Verses on Thatness (Maitrīpa), 57, 59, 64, 443, 491, 598
Tertön Sogyal Lerab Lingpa (*Gter ston bsod rgyal Las rab gling pa*), 309
Thangsakpa Ngödrup Gyatso (*Thang sag pa Dngos grub rgya mtsho*), 146, 253
Thangtong Gyalpo (*Thang stong rgyal po*), 112, 416
Thirty-five Confession Buddhas, 136
Thösam Ling monastery, 245
three poisons, 26, 510, 639
three principal aspects of the path, 161, 262, 270
Three Principal Aspects of the Path (Tsongkhapa), 300, 533–34
three turnings of wheel of Dharma, 113n391, 116, 128, 141, 163, 189, 192, 322, 356, 384–86
Thubten Zopa Rinpoché (*Thub bstan bzod pa rin po che*), 13, 215, 246, 324, 457n1197
Thuken II Ngawang Chökyi Gyatso (*Thu'u bkwan Ngag dbang chos kyi rgya mtsho*), 292, 295–96
Thuken III Losang Chökyi Nyima (*Thu'u bkwan Blo bzang chos kyi nyi ma*), 13, 74, 163, 182, 242, 282, 292, 295–98, 306, 644
  ecumenicism of, 237, 298, 336, 344–45, 423–24, 605–8
  on great perfection, 81, 603–4
  on Kagyü mahāmudrā, 297–98, 344, 597–603
Tiantai tradition, 385, 390, 397
Tibetan Renaissance, 1, 11, 64–68, 77, 79–82, 92, 106–7, 111, 119
Tilopa, 2, 514
  life and teachings of, 51–53
  lineages including, 48, 152, 217, 260, 443, 645
  on mind, 212
  on reality, 6–7
  songs of, 395, 409, 412, 420
  transmissions from, 51–53, 189, 382, 408–9, 443
  visions of, 139
Tipupa, 87
Tokden Jampal Gyatso (*Rtogs ldan 'Jam dpal rgya mtsho*), 4, 170–71, 260, 446–48, 458
  biography of Tsongkhapa by, 134, 149
  lineages including, 145–47, 149, 165, 167, 195, 215, 217, 302n877, 305, 439n1157, 643
Trailokyavijaya. See *Conquest of the Three Worlds Tantra*
treasure literature, 80, 99, 218, 254, 296, 298
Treasury of Dohās (Virūpa), 50–51
Treasury of Higher Knowledge (Vasubandhu), 133, 200, 389–90
Treasury of Knowledge (Kongtrul Lodrö Thayé), 130
Treasury of Performance Songs (multiple authors), 64
Treasury of Special Instructions (Kongtrul Lodrö Thayé), 130
Trijang III Losang Yeshé Tenzin Gyatso (*Khri byang Blo bzang ye shes bstan 'dzin rgya mtsho*), 13, 215, 242, 315, 318–19, 321, 323, 327–29, 334, 466, 644
Trophu Kagyü, 92, 112
Trove Containing Myriad Treasures of Profound Mahāmudrā (Mikyö Dorjé), 120
Tsalpa Kagyü, 84, 92–94, 190, 297. *See also* Shangpa Kagyü
Tsangnyön Heruka (*Gtsang smyon He ru ka*), 3, 112–14

Tsangpa Gyaré Yeshé Dorjé (*Gtsang pa rgya ras Ye shes rdo rje*), 99–100, 501
Tsechok Samten Ling monastery, 258
Tselé Natsok Rangdröl (*Rtse le sna tshogs rang grol*), 129
Tsongkhapa Losang Drakpa (*Tsong kha pa Blo bzang grags pa*), 4, 111, 134–38, 179–80
  biographies of, 134, 149, 162n579
  criticism of Kagyü views by, 153–58, 169, 259, 288, 298, 344–45, 416
  emphasis on Guhyasamāja by, 350
  esoteric teachings of, 143–46
  hidden transmission by, 305–6
  influence on Shabkar, 300–301
  mahāmudrā studies and teachings by, 135–36, 149–52, 156–64, 446–47
  major works of, 141–42
  as practitioner of great perfection, 155n550
  on Saraha's songs, 363–67
  in Shangpa lineage, 136n468
  transmissions through, 643–45. *See also* Ganden Hearing Transmission
  visions experienced by, 4, 139–41, 367, 382. *See also* Mañjughoṣa
  visualization practices about, 173, 220–21, 261–62, 266–68, 273–76, 280–81, 302, 317–18, 331, 360, 449
Tsurphu monastery, 102, 108, 115, 170
Twenty Verses (Vasubandhu), 24n40
Twenty Verses on Thatness (Maitrīpa), 57
Twenty-Five Works on Nonmentation (Maitrīpa), 8, 41, 56–60, 189–90

U

Ultimate Supreme Path of Mahāmudrā (Lama Shang), 93–94
Umapa Pawo Dorjé (*Dbu ma pa Dpa' bo rdo rje*), 136–37, 146–47, 149, 157, 162–63, 283, 293, 305, 645
Uncommon Pith Instruction Offered to Rendawa (Tsongkhapa), 143
Union of All the Buddhas Tantra, 36
Union of Bliss and Emptiness (Dalai Lama XIV), 333–34
Unique Khedrup Jé Transmission, 143–44, 144n495, 172, 333
Unraveling the Intention Sūtra, 113n391, 384–85, 397
Upholding Nonmentation (Maitrīpa), 59
Uttaratantra. See *Sublime Continuum*

V

Vairocana (Buddha), 32, 361
Vairocana (Indian teacher), 80
Vairocana posture, 204, 210, 247, 250, 261, 266
Vairocanābhisambodhi Tantra. See *Awakening of Vairocana Tantra*
Vairocanarakṣita, 68
Vaiśravaṇa, 135
Vajra Garland Tantra, 38, 196, 573
Vajra Heart Ornament Tantra, 579n1465
Vajra Lines of the Amulet Mahāmudrā (Nigumā), 77
Vajra Peak Tantra, 33, 366
Vajra Tent Tantra, 151, 189
Vajra Verses (Virūpa), 50, 236n728
Vajra Verses of the Hearing Transmission (Nāropa), 53–55
Vajrabhairava, 144, 570. *See also* Yamāntaka
Vajradhara, 51, 143, 173, 268, 323, 593
  lineages including, 175, 189, 215, 217, 246, 248n748, 249, 302n877, 442, 493, 643, 645
  mantra of, 268
  visualization of, 221–22, 266–67, 361, 449n1176, 572–74
Vajrakīlaya Tantra, 78–79
Vajramālā. See *Vajra Garland Tantra*
Vajrapāda. See *Vajra Verses*
Vajrapāṇi (bodhisattva), 135, 144, 445, 540
Vajrapāṇi (disciple of Maitrīpa), 8, 56, 59, 67–68, 87, 113, 363
Vajrapāṇi Empowerment Tantra, 578
Vajrapañjara Tantra. See *Vajra Tent Tantra*
Vajrāsanavajragīti. See *Diamond Song at the Diamond Seat*
Vajrasattva, 38, 250, 275, 361, 549

meditation and recitation, 203, 208, 247, 262, 275, 281, 322, 455, 484, 486, 499
Vajraśekhara. See *Vajra Peak Tantra*
Vajrayoginī, 2, 48, 77, 172, 272, 316, 324, 328
Vākkoṣa. See *Speech Treasury*
Vasubandhu, 24n40, 200, 260, 389, 442, 446n1166
Verses on Mahāmudrā (Nāropa), 55
Vidyākokila, 366, 441
View of Emptiness (Śavaripa), 48
Vikramaśīla monastery, 56, 61, 69, 416
Vimalamitra, 80–81, 198, 312, 390
Vimalaprabhā (Puṇḍarīka). See *Stainless Light*
Vinaya Sūtra (Guṇaprabha), 133, 200, 304
Virūpa, 2, 48, 50–51, 59, 75, 78–79, 236
Vīryavajra, 43, 63–64
visionary encounters, authority of, 382–84
vital winds, 548–58, 561–65, 602

W

Way to Condense the Empowerments (Maitrīpa), 57
Wedemeyer, Christian, 416
Wheel of Time. See *Kālacakra Tantra*
white panacea (*dkar po gcig thub*), 90, 92, 94, 101, 124, 389, 601
  criticism of, 105–7, 183, 193, 297, 344, 349, 382, 604–6
  as subitist practice, 389, 391, 553, 557
Wish-Fulfilling Gem of the Hearing Transmission (Khöntön Paljor Lhundrup), 196–98, 338, 373–75

X

Xanadu, 108

Y

Yalpa Kagyü, 92
Yamāntaka, 135–36, 142, 144–45, 171–72, 186, 266, 275n805, 285, 302, 316, 323
Yangchen Drupai Dorjé (*Dbyangs can grub pa'i rdo rje*), 285, 462, 644
Yangönpa Gyaltsen Pal (*Yang dgon pa Rgyal mtshan dpal*), 84, 100, 137, 211, 346, 509
Yasang Kagyü, 92
Yogācāra, 24, 112, 113n391, 141, 306, 311, 356, 407, 431
  emptiness in, 27, 63–64, 168
  as mahāmudrā, 61, 63
  positive rhetoric of, 384, 397
  synthesis with Madhyamaka, 108–10, 126, 311, 397
  theory of consciousness in, 141, 427–28
  three natures doctrine of, 63
  Tsongkhapa's views on, 287
Yogaratnāvalī. See *Jewel Garland of Yoga*
Yoginī Cintā, 491
yoginī tantras
  in India, 41–44, 47, 52, 54
  in Tibet, 65–67, 78, 81, 85, 87, 101, 139, 168, 180, 350
  mahāmudrā in, 34–40
  See also mother tantras
Yongzin Gendun Gyatso (*Yongs 'dzin Dge 'dun rgya mtsho*), 465, 644
Yuan dynasty, 105, 108

Z

Zen. *See* Chan traditions

About the Author

Roger R. Jackson is John W. Nason Professor of Asian Studies and Religion, Emeritus, at Carleton College, where for nearly three decades he taught the religions of South Asia and Tibet. He has also taught at the University of Michigan, Fairfield University, McGill University, and Maitripa College. He has a BA from Wesleyan University and an MA and PhD from the University of Wisconsin, where he studied under Geshe Lhundub Sopa. He maintains a scholarly interest in Indian and Tibetan Buddhist systems of philosophy, meditation, and ritual; Buddhist and other types of religious poetry; the study of mysticism; and the contours of modern Buddhist thought. His books include *The Wheel of Time: Kalachakra in Context* (with Geshe Sopa and John Newman, 1985), *Is Enlightenment Possible?* (1993), *Tibetan Literature* (with José Cabezón, 1996), *Buddhist Theology* (with John Makransky, 1999), *Tantric Treasures* (2004), *The Crystal Mirror of Philosophical Systems* (with Geshe Sopa et al., 2009), and *Mahāmudrā and the Bka' brgyud Tradition* (with Matthew Kapstein, 2011). He has published dozens of articles, book chapters, and reviews and has presented regularly at national and international scholarly conferences. He was editor-in-chief of *The Journal of the International Association of Buddhist Studies* from 1985 to 1993 and served as coeditor of the *Indian International Journal of Buddhist Studies* from 2006 to 2018.

Studies in Indian and Tibetan Buddhism
Titles Previously Published

Among Tibetan Texts
History and Literature of the Himalayan Plateau
E. Gene Smith

Approaching the Great Perfection
Simultaneous and Gradual Methods of Dzogchen Practice in the Longchen Nyingtig
Sam van Schaik

Authorized Lives
Biography and the Early Formation of Geluk Identity
Elijah S. Ary

The Buddha's Single Intention
Drigung Kyobpa Jikten Sumgön's Vajra Statements of the Early Kagyü Tradition
Jan-Ulrich Sobisch

Buddhism Between Tibet and China
Edited by Matthew T. Kapstein

The Buddhist Philosophy of the Middle
Essays on Indian and Tibetan Madhyamaka
David Seyfort Ruegg

Buddhist Teaching in India
Johannes Bronkhorst

A Direct Path to the Buddha Within
Gö Lotsāwa's Mahāmudrā Interpretation of the Ratnagotravibhāga
Klaus-Dieter Mathes

The Essence of the Ocean of Attainments
The Creation Stage of the Guhyasamāja Tantra according to Panchen Losang Chökyi Gyaltsen
Yael Bentor and Penpa Dorjee

Foundations of Dharmakīrti's Philosophy
John D. Dunne

Freedom from Extremes
Gorampa's "Distinguishing the Views" and the Polemics of Emptiness
José Ignacio Cabezón and Geshe Lobsang Dargyay

Himalayan Passages
Tibetan and Newar Studies in Honor of Hubert Decleer
Benjamin Bogin and Andrew Quintman

How Do Mādhyamikas Think?
And Other Essays on the Buddhist Philosophy of the Middle
Tom J. F. Tillemans

Jewels of the Middle Way
The Madhyamaka Legacy of Atiśa and His Early Tibetan Followers
James B. Apple

Luminous Lives
The Story of the Early Masters of the Lam 'bras Tradition in Tibet
Cyrus Stearns

Mipham's Beacon of Certainty
Illuminating the View of Dzogchen, the Great Perfection
John Whitney Pettit

Omniscience and the Rhetoric of Reason
Śāntarakṣita and Kamalaśīla on Rationality, Argumentation, and Religious Authority
Sara L. McClintock

Reasons and Lives in Buddhist Traditions
Tibetan and Buddhist Studies in Honor of Matthew Kapstein
Edited by Dan Arnold, Cécile Ducher, and Pierre-Julien Harter

Reason's Traces
Identity and Interpretation in Indian and Tibetan Buddhist Thought
Matthew T. Kapstein

Remembering the Lotus-Born
Padmasambhava in the History of Tibet's Golden Age
Daniel A. Hirshberg

Resurrecting Candrakīrti
Disputes in the Tibetan Creation of Prāsaṅgika
Kevin A. Vose

Scripture, Logic, Language
Essays on Dharmakīrti and His Tibetan Successors
Tom J. F. Tillemans

Sexuality in Classical South Asian Buddhism
José I. Cabezón

The Svātantrika-Prāsaṅgika Distinction
What Difference Does a Difference Make?
Edited by Georges Dreyfus and Sara McClintock

Vajrayoginī
Her Visualizations, Rituals, and Forms
Elizabeth English

About Wisdom Publications

Wisdom Publications is the leading publisher of classic and contemporary Buddhist books and practical works on mindfulness. To learn more about us or to explore our other books, please visit our website at wisdomexperience.org or contact us at the address below.

Wisdom Publications
199 Elm Street
Somerville, MA 02144 USA

We are a 501(c)(3) organization, and donations in support of our mission are tax deductible.

Wisdom Publications is affiliated with the Foundation for the Preservation of the Mahayana Tradition (FPMT).